★ ★ ★ ★ ★ ★ ★

SCRIBNER'S
HISTORICAL
SERIES
Under the Editorship
of
Arthur Cecil Bining

★ ★ ★ ★ ★ ★ ★

EUROPE AND TWO WORLD WARS

BY

ARTHUR JAMES MAY

UNIVERSITY OF ROCHESTER

CHARLES SCRIBNER'S SONS

New York   Chicago   Boston   Atlanta   San Francisco   Dallas

TO

MY MOTHER

PREFACE

THIS book surveys the main developments in the life of Europe from the eve of World War I through the first year after World War II. It is not, however, restricted to Europe, but necessarily concerns itself with the United States, Asia, and Africa at points where they impinged vitally upon the Old World. As never before the history of Europe merged into global history.

It is the author's conviction that acquaintance with elements of social and cultural history is essential for an understanding of Europe in the epoch between World Wars. Accordingly, chapters are devoted to social trends, to the advancement of science, and to religious and cultural tendencies and achievements.

This volume is designed particularly for Americans, whose countrymen, twice within living memory, have fought in wars originating in Europe and whose future is inextricably bound up with the Old World. Not so very long ago, as time runs, it was the duty of the historian to educate prospective diplomatists and potential statesmen. Nowadays in the democratic United States instruction must reach that ever growing body of men and women who concern themselves actively with public affairs.

The author is cognizant of the peculiar pitfalls in writing the history of his own time. No account of the recent and the contemporary can pretend to be definitive. In spite of efforts to ensure accuracy and balance, fresh evidence and a longer perspective are bound to compel some revision in present judgments and emphases.

The selective bibliography at the end of the book reveals the author's obligation to many students of recent and contemporary history. It remains to acknowledge special debts. Professor Arthur C. Bining, as editor of Scribner's Historical Series, has been most generous with advice at every stage in the progress of the book, and meticulous in the editorial task. Professor Kent Forster of Pennsylvania State College read the whole manuscript and made recommendations for its improvement. Colleagues at the University of Rochester have been fruitful in suggestions and help: in particular, Professors Neil C. Arvin (French), Roth Clausing (Economics), and Dexter Perkins (American History) have critically read sections of the manuscript. Most of the book has profited from use in preliminary form by students in the University of Rochester. The maps were prepared by Mr. Robert Tschirky.

An expression of gratitude is due, finally, to Misses Marjorie Gilles, and Marguerite Lyons of the University of Rochester staff, to Mrs. Otto Kline and Miss Anne Hale, and to my wife, Hilda Jones May, for assistance in preparing the manuscript for publication.

A. J. M.

The University of Rochester

Rochester, New York

CONTENTS

WORLD WAR I

PAGE

I. Europe in Cross Section: 1914   3
II. World War I: First Phase   33
III. The Road to Allied Victory   63
IV. Peacemaking, 1919-1920   86

THE NATIONS BETWEEN WARS

V. Soviet Russia   117
VI. Europe's Middle East—Austria to Finland   151
VII. Fascist Italy   180
VIII. The Near East   198
IX. Republican France   219
X. Spain and the Smaller States of Western Europe   239
XI. Great Britain   254
XII. The British Commonwealth and Empire   279
XIII. Germany: Democratic and Hitlerian   296

THE HIGHER LIVING

XIV. Society and Science   333
XV. Religion and Religious Organizations   357
XVI. Literature and the Fine Arts   376

INTERNATIONAL AFFAIRS

XVII. Groping Toward Stability (1919-1928)   411
XVIII. The Great Depression and German Resurgence (1929-1935)   447
XIX. The Road to War   474
XX. The Last Phase   497

WORLD WAR II

		PAGE
XXI.	World War II: Ascendancy of the Axis	521
XXII.	Enter the Giants	545
XXIII.	The Swing of the Pendulum	566
XXIV.	The Allied Triumph	594
XXV.	In Search of Peace	627
	Bibliography	655
	Index	681

MAPS

	PAGE
Europe and North Africa in 1914	21
The Western Front, 1914-1918	41
The Eastern Front World War I	55
Africa in 1919	97
War Losses of the Hapsburg Monarchy	103
Europe and North Africa in 1919 after Paris Peace Settlements	113
Linguistic Minorities in Czechoslovakia	161
Minorities in Central Europe	179
The Near and Middle East after Lausanne Settlement 1923	213
Eastern Asia in 1919	419
Manchurian Arena	461
Mussolini's Realm, 1936	477
Expansion of Nazi Germany 1935-1939	501
Europe in 1939	515
World War II, Western Europe	529
World War II, Eastern Europe	553
Japanese Conquests as of Mid-1942	569
The Russian Battleground	573
Campaigns in North Africa and Italy, 1942-1943	577
Allied Convergence on Germany, April, 1945	609
The Pacific Scene, 1945	615
The United Nations: Its Organization and Functions [diagram]	636-637
Europe and North Africa in 1946	649

*

WORLD WAR I

*

CHAPTER I

Europe in Cross Section: 1914

The Pre-eminence of Europe

THOUGH the second smallest continent, Europe in 1914 held first place in power and influence as it had for centuries past. It was the political center of gravity of the entire globe. Through the expansionist movement, beginning with the Crusades, all the world had been drawn into the European orbit. The Americas in a very real sense were an offshoot of European civilization; the colored populations of Africa, Asia, and the islands of the seven seas had been affected in greater or lesser degree by institutions and ideas emanating from the "Old World." And commercially the globe by 1914 had become one world, each continent more or less knit up with the others.

In no other area of comparable size anywhere on the globe was there such a profusion of languages, nationalities, cultural patterns, creedal diversities, or such a variety of social, economic, and political institutions as in Europe. Europe's energetic and aggressive population, which had grown prodigiously in the preceding century, accounted in part for her pre-eminence in world affairs. Geography, food, and philosophy encouraged an assertive, expansionist spirit.

Surrounded on three sides by water and penetrated by the Baltic and Mediterranean Seas, Europe had an incomparably long and broken coastline and excellent harbors which were an invitation to seafaring and commerce. Except in eastern Russia no part of the continent was more than five hundred miles from the sea, and few points were more than seventy miles from sea or major river. Inland communication was facilitated by splendid waterways which man had supplemented by a superb railway network, save in eastern Europe.

The large population of Europe was maintained by the natural wealth of the continent, its machine industry, and trade with the rest of the world, which radiated principally from the industrialized central and western areas. Most of Europe had sufficient rainfall for intensive agriculture; nowhere were there desert areas, and much of the soil was moderately rich, though it could only be kept in fertility by increasing resort to chemical fertilizers. The best farmlands were in the United Kingdom, France, the Low Countries, and in a wedge reaching from western Germany to the Carpathian Mountains. Parts of Scandinavia, the Danube valley, and southern Russia had naturally alluvial soil, but in eastern Germany and in large areas of Russia the land was poor and the rainfall inadequate. Southern European areas were mountainous and had a Mediterranean type of climate which dictated the production of somewhat specialized crops.

Except in the northern region grain and foodstuffs were grown extensively all over Europe. Wheat which requires a relatively warm climate and a dry harvest season thrived best in France, Hungary, the Ukraine, and southern Europe, while rye, the staple cereal of eastern Europe, could be raised profitably in thin soil and cool climate. Oats and corn were generally grown farther south and rice production was limited to warm areas easy to irrigate, such as northern Italy. Beet sugar was a specialty of France, Germany, and Bohemia; the olive and the vine of the Mediterranean countries.

Some of the European countries had a larger area given over to timber-producing trees than others. In Great Britain, for instance, forests covered only a twentieth part of the land in contrast with a quarter of Germany and a still higher percentage in the east and south of Europe. Fast-growing softwoods which flourished where nothing else could be economically raised were in much greater demand than hardwood.

Europe's industrial structure rested solidly on her mineral resources, increasingly supplemented by importations from outside. Iron ore was mined in Lorraine and Silesia, in Sweden, England, and the Donetz basin of Russia. Coalfields lay in or near the favorable agricultural belt for the most part: England and Wales, northern France, the Ruhr valley, Saxony, Silesia, and Bohemia; coal in Russia was being worked in the Donetz area, around Tula in the center, and in the Urals, especially the eastern slope. Outside of Russia the coal reserves of Europe were probably little more than a quarter as large as those of the United States.

Waterpower, while potentially large, was in the main remote from the established centers of industry; and, by 1914, only beginnings had been made in the exploitation of this alternative to coal. The mining of petroleum was largely confined to Rumania and to either side of the Caucasus Mountains. In other minerals Europe was poorly endowed, possessing only small quantities of copper, zinc, and nickel, and little silver or gold.

On the whole, Europe's wealth in 1914 resided less in the quantity and quality of its natural resources than in their proximity, in splendid transport, and in the temperate climate, stimulating to energy and initiative. Areas of intense summer heat and bitter cold in winter were found only to the east of the Vistula River, away from moderating oceanic influences.

Population density was, of course, greatest in the regions of developed industry and trade, and there general standards of living were highest. It is probable that the average real income per capita in the agrarian eastern and southern districts of Europe was not much more than a third that of the industrialized center and west.

In any full analysis of the sources of Europe's pre-eminence among the continents consideration must be given to such items as the accumulated legacy from the past, the wisdom of men of genius and their disciples, the stability of governments, standards of education and public health, the moral implications of religion, and scientific and mechanical achievements.

Economic Foundations

Europe on the eve of World War I was the beneficiary of the unexampled material progress which distinguished the preceding century from all other periods of history. Never before had industry experienced such growth; never before had trade and commerce expanded so rapidly; never before had the mechanism of finance undergone such intricate proliferation; never before had the productivity of the soil risen in such a phenomenal manner. By virtue of all this, standards of comfort—food, clothing, housing, recreation—surpassed anything society had hitherto known, though the improvement was greater in countries where manufacturing was mature than where agriculture predominated.

Owing to the relative newness of machine production and the consequences thereof, there is a tendency to exaggerate the importance of industrialism in the common life of Europe. Actually more families relied upon the soil for their livelihood than upon the mill and factory. Land tenure varied considerably. Over considerable parts of central and eastern Europe—Spain and even England as well—large landed properties, in a few instances exceeding 250,000 acres, belonged to ruling dynasties, the Church, and noble families. Latifundia—great landed estates—were particularly large in the Junker provinces of Germany, in the Austrian provinces of Bohemia and Galicia, in Hungary, and imperial Russia.

All over the continent peasant farmsteads, commonly made up of

a number of scattered strips of land, yielding a comfortable existence
and also producing for the market, were found. That type of tenure
predominated in France and Belgium, northern Italy, western and
southern Germany, and in substantial areas of Austria and Hungary.
Less well-off were the essentially subsistence farm owners of the
Balkan states, of sections of the Hapsburg monarchy, and of Russia.
Many a peasant family owned only a dwarf holding and was obliged
to piece out its income by work on large estates, handicraft industry
in the home, lumbering, and the like. In Russia much of the cultivated
land belonged to village communities, though under governmental
auspices some of these communities were being slowly converted into
private proprietorships.

In eastern and middle-eastern Europe there were multitudes of
rustics with no land of their own. They lived by laboring in their
native country or migrated in gangs to neighboring countries to furnish cheap labor during harvests. Throughout peasant Europe, cooperative societies had been organized to raise or at least hold steady
living standards. At first cooperatives were designed to supply the
peasant with credit on reasonable terms and to release him from the
clutches of the local usurer, but they subsequently spread to the
purchase and sale of goods and so eliminated the middleman. These
societies no doubt did more for the general welfare of the peasantry
(some townworkers joined in) than protective tariffs.

Like agriculture, European industry was carried on in large, me-
dium-sized, and small undertakings. In the main, large-scale factories
and mines were located in Great Britain and Germany but there were
a few big establishments in Austria, Italy, and Russia. Cartels, business organizations to fix prices, quantity of output, and kindred matters, held a prominent place in the industrial life of Germany and
Austria, concentrating economic power in a relatively small number
of hands. And in many different fields, international cartels were
operating in 1914.

To the west, where the institution of private capitalism as it had
evolved through generations of experience, and where concepts of
individual enterprise were deep rooted, industrial establishments were
privately owned. And that was very largely true too in central and
eastern Europe, though in Russia where machine production and capitalism were adolescent, the paternalism of the state in economic affairs was more conspicuous than anywhere else. A primitive form of
"planned economy" had in fact started to emerge in Russia.

In many places on the continent village workshops, gild manufacturing, and handicrafts persisted. Cottage industries in immature manufacturing areas such as Bohemia, the Balkans, and Russia were important suppliers of household utensils, clothing, and sundry specialties, though that type of production had steadily fallen in competition with factory-made goods.

On the continent, more so than in Great Britain, finance and banking were intimately knit with industry through interlocking directorates. In each country a few huge financial institutions with branches in cities and large towns, dominated the lending of capital both for domestic purposes and in external investment. Britain was, of course, the world's chief banker, with France, Germany, and Holland following in that order.

Means of communication in western and central Europe had been transformed after the middle of the 19th century with the advent of the locomotive. All the continent was tied together with bonds of steel, but the railway facilities in eastern Europe were decidedly inadequate. Russia had, however, recently completed a gigantic single track line across Siberia, while German capital and engineers were building a road—the Bagdad railway—through Asia Minor and Mesopotamia with the Persian Gulf as the projected terminus. For the greater part, railways on the continent were owned and operated by governments; in the more backward regions the slow-moving cart and barge still carried a large share of the goods traffic.

Novel means of transportation, the automobile and the motorcycle, were growing in popularity. But British and French concerns which had turned out the finest motorcars were already being eclipsed by the mass-production techniques of Detroit in the United States. As yet the automobile had scarcely started to change the urban topography of Europe. Still very much of an innovation, the sportsman's fancy, was the airplane. In July, 1914, an American flier, W. L. Brock, startled the world by a flight from London to Paris and back in seven hours, thirteen minutes and six seconds, but only two of the six who started in the race were able to negotiate the round trip. Less hazardous for travel, apparently, was the airship and by 1914 German Zeppelins had established regular services.

Sea-transportation in the great competing liners of the Cunard and Hamburg-America companies had attained a speed and comfort scarcely imaginable a century before. There was the big Cunard *Aquitania* of 47,000 tons on which to cross the Atlantic or the Hamburg-American liner *Imperator* of 54,000 tons which made her first western voyage in May of 1914. Tramp steamers shuttling from port

to port hauled a large volume of goods, and even small seafaring
nations like Norway and Greece had large investments in vessels of
that kind.

Commerce, in spite of the high tariff barriers of most of the
countries of the continent, had drawn the nations into economic inter-
dependence. Ukrainian wheat, for example, was exchanged for machinery made in Germany or British textiles, while coal mined in the
Ruhr paid for the silk goods and other specialties of Italy. Exchange
between highly industrialized Britain and Germany exceeded that
with the preponderantly agricultural nations.

Trade between Europe and the rest of the world had risen to
unprecedented dimensions. In the half century before 1914 the larger
nations of Europe (except the Hapsburg monarchy) and some of the
smaller ones had engaged in imperial expansion, which took the form
of outright ownership of colonies or the establishment of spheres of
influence, zones of interest, and financial protectorates. The primary
dynamic of that scramble for position and possession in the backward
areas of the globe—Africa, Asia, the islands of the Pacific, and Latin
America—was no doubt the quest for raw materials to feed the white
man and his machines or for places in which to sell manufactured
goods advantageously. Then, too, there was the passion for the investment of capital and the motivating power of surplus initiative,
exhibited on the playing fields of Eton or in the technical institutes
of Leipzig.

But the economic motive for overseas expansion did not stand
alone. Empire was a stimulus to national pride. Empire provided
places of strategic value or areas in which to recruit troops. Empire
offered (in theory at least) employment and settlement opportunities
to reduce the pressure of population in the more congested areas of
Europe. Empire meant regions in which a nation might give play to
aggressive altruism, carry on the civilizing and Christianizing
process, and bear, in a phrase, its fair share of the "White Man's
Burden."

The Social Fabric

The social structure of Europe reflected the heritage of the past
and the economic status of the population. Top place in the society
of central and eastern Europe was occupied by the titled aristocracy as
had been true since the age when knighthood was in flower. And
quite commonly the higher dignitaries of the churches were drawn
from the nobility, or, failing that, shared the social outlook of that
historically-privileged caste. The influence of the wealthy aristocracy

was most potent in Russia, the Hapsburg monarchy, Spain, and Germany.

Deriving their income principally from landed estates the upper aristocratic class was an anachronism in an era of rising industrialism and upthrusting bourgeoisie. Yet the Russian grandee, the Bohemian magnate, the Junker landlord tenaciously clung to his ancient privileges and now and again family fortunes were enhanced by the marriage of a noble to a wealthy American heiress. Not as a rule much given to serious education, the upper nobility, like their counterparts of 18th century France, frittered away the time in gay social frolics, gaming, and hunting. Pleased with the best of all possible worlds, seldom did the wealthy nobleman reflect upon the spirit of the age or act to mitigate its discontents.

Something of the luxury of the better-off aristocrats is conveyed by the report of a Britisher who in 1907 spent a week in a Russian province as guest of a Polish nobleman, Count Joseph Potocki. "There were over a hundred English hunters in the stables," he wrote. "One went down there in the evening and selected the two one would ride the next day. There were three studs—one of pure Russian, one of Arab, and one of English thoroughbreds . . . There were two packs of hounds . . ." and nearby there was "a vast enclosed territory of forest many square miles in extent, . . . containing every animal, except beasts of prey, which could live in Europe."

On leaving, the guests were drawn fifty miles or so in sleighs to the nearest railway station. "The first sleigh had two horses and was empty, but on each side of the driver was a flaming torch to show the road. The next was a *troika,* that is to say, with three horses . . . carrying passengers, then next again only torches, and so on through the cavalcade of about thirty-eight sleighs. Altogether it needed ninety-five horses and . . . halfway we changed them for another ninety-five, and it was all done in about five minutes." [1]

Deferred to by their social inferiors, the upper nobility of central and eastern Europe possessed authority over the workers on their estates not radically different from that which prevailed in the heyday of feudalism. They were steeped in a narrow class outlook and imbued with born-to-rule convictions. When members of this caste participated in affairs of state (aside from having seats in the upper chambers of legislatures), they preferred assignments in the more glamorous branches of the fighting services or in the diplomatic corps.

Not all noble families, it is true, lived a life of luxurious gaiety

[1] Neville Henderson, *Water under the Bridges* (London, 1945), pp. 35-36.

and irresponsibility. Many continental aristocrats, possibly a majority indeed, kept aloof from their titled fellows, dwelling in rural obscurity and constantly plagued by financial worries. And England's nobility, whose importance did not approach that of the upper aristocracy east of the Rhine, tended to be more in harmony with the times, partly, no doubt, because of frequent intermarriage with rich middle class families and the ennoblement of commoners who had achieved distinction in their vocations. Many a Magyar squirearch, too, not to be sure of the highest social echelon, fulfilled his responsibilities as conscientiously as the English gentry.

In proportion as machine production and business flourished, the European middle class or bourgeoise had prospered. Measured by income this social category contained many gradations ranging from the manufacturing and financial plutocracy to well-to-do artisans—"the labor aristocracy." In between were the professional folk, the bulk of the clergy included, small and middling shopkeepers and industrialists, the rentier, with investments in government or private bonds, public officials in their several ranks, and prosperous peasants. These men of property, comfortably situated, had a greater feeling of security than less fortunate members of the community.

Great Britain, France, and some of the smaller countries were managed essentially by the bourgeoisie. All over Europe this class was rising in significance and gaining greater importance in state affairs. South of the Pyrenees and east of the Rhine the bourgeoisie cut less of a figure than in western Europe, but they carried more weight in Germany and Austria than in Hungary or Russia. Optimistic devotees of the idea of progress, energetic, the bourgeoisie universally and confidently believed that the future belonged to them.

Townsmen at work in factory or forge were hardly less differentiated in income than other social groupings. Skilled artisans had better homes, better diet, better terms of employment than their semi-skilled or unskilled fellows. Many of the latter lived under substandard physical conditions, not a few of them in eastern Europe having streamed into the cities from the countryside without immediately sloughing off their rural outlook and habits.

For the purpose of defending the interests of their class, industrial workers had formed trade unions as instruments of collective strength to bargain for standards of health and subsistence. They had also affiliated with political parties of their own, some of which were secular in character, while others operated under religious auspices. In Great Britain by 1914 trade unions embraced large numbers of unskilled workers as well as the better paid, but on the continent labor organization was mainly, though not exclusively, confined to the skilled. It was from the industrial wage workers that the rank and file and part of the leadership of the Socialist movements, described later, were recruited. In 1914 strikes and other manifestations of unrest among urban workers was a common phenomenon, being especially serious that year in Russia.

City workers profited more from social welfare programs than the peasantry. So far as economic standing was concerned workers on the soil were not less differentiated than the toilers in the factories; well-to-do peasants diverged in outlook from the very small land holder or the landless rustic of eastern and southern Europe. Prosperous small proprietors of France and Germany tended to be contented with their lot; they were conservative, unsympathetic to city-bred innovations, hard-working, penurious, and deeply attached to their church. To them farming was a way of life as well as a means of raising food.

. In contrast large numbers of poverty-stricken and ignorant countryfolk in the east and south of Europe were brothers to the ox, wandering about in search of employment, pursued by hunger and exposure, squeezing the "grapes of wrath" as best they could. Squalor approaching Oriental levels made such men susceptible to the appeal of social radicalism or to the lure of the New World. From eastern and southern Europe originated the bulk of the 14,000,000 emigrants to the United States between 1900 and 1917; because of the lack of schooling these newcomers were mostly illiterate and by act of Congress in 1917 a literacy test for admission was established, the forerunner of more restrictive immigration measures later on.

By 1914 many accepted European social customs of a century earlier were branded as cruelties and some had been eradicated or at least mitigated. Treatment of the insane was more humane; punishment for crime less harsh, with methods more enlightened in western and central Europe than to the east and south. The status of women had been raised in the industrialized states, but in agricultural nations wives were often pieces of furniture or perhaps more accurately, part of the farming equipment. A vigorous temperance agitation was making itself felt in Britain and the Scandinavian countries, while in Russia in 1914 drastic legislation was enacted to curb the national vice of drunkenness.

Another oddity of a few generations before, the public school and general instruction, was firmly established in most of Europe by 1914 and the proportion of literates was rising even in backward Russia, the Balkans, Spain, and Italy. Universities, with those of Germany admittedly foremost, were flourishing as never before in their seven hundred year history and professors of distinction took an active hand in guiding or seeking to guide the course of public affairs.

Intellectual Patterns

From one angle of vision the transcendent fact in the Europe of 1914 was the cumulative achievement of science which had effected swift changes in everyday living and had subtly wrought a profound revolution in thought. The mental atmosphere of the time was saturated with the implications of scientific findings; so marked indeed was the ascendancy of science that its practitioners were tempted to pronounce with seeming authority on subjects remote from their own.

The dominant intellectual novelty was the optimistic idea of progress—the next generation would inescapably be wiser and better than this. The evolutionary hypothesis won acceptance not because it could be proved true but because the alternative of special creation imposed too great a strain on the faith of many men. Yet it would be easy to overestimate the extent and depth of the "intellectual revolution"; new ideas, springing from scientific revelations about the nature of the universe, about the world of workaday affairs, and life itself, were largely restricted to the educated middle-class and by no means were they accepted by all members of that group.

By many European thinkers "progress" had come to be regarded as inevitable as the growth of a tree. Had not the highly respected Darwin asserted that "man in the distant future will be a far more perfect creature than he now is . . . after long continued slow progress?" The faith was admirably expressed by another English savant, Herbert Spencer: "Progress is not an accident but a necessity. What we call evil and immorality must disappear. It is certain that man must become perfect."

That sunny optimism was echoed by the learned English historian, J. B. Bury, who was assuring his readers in 1913 that "the struggle of reason against authority has ended in what appears now to be a decisive and permanent victory for liberty. In the most civilized and progressive countries freedom of discussion is recognized as a fundamental principle. . . ." He specifically excluded Russia and Spain from the company of the enlightened, for though Russia had scientists of high merit free inquiry was fettered there by a notorious censorship.

Having thus delivered himself on freedom, Bury proceeded to express doubt, asking, "Can we be certain that there may not come a great set-back? . . . The possibility cannot be denied, but there are

some considerations which render it improbable (apart from a catastrophic sweeping away of European culture) . . ." And, he went
on, "If a revolutionary social movement prevailed, led by men inspired by faith in formulas (like the men of the French Revolution)
and resolved to impose their creed, experience shows that coercion
would almost inevitably be resorted to. . . ." Writing thus, Bury
was vastly more prophetic than he may have imagined.[2]

Bury's creed placed him in the ranks of the liberals. Yet liberalism
is a coat of many colors. At the outset of the twentieth century liberalism embraced such concepts as private ownership of the means
of production (which is capitalism), freedom of international trade,
self-determination of nations, fluidity of social classes, careers open to
talents, civil and religious liberties; in short, the minimum of state
control over the affairs of the individual. But the acceptance of that
faith was confined to western Europe and to knots of intellectuals in
other parts of the continent.

Much more prevalent were the ideas and practices of conservatism
which harked back to the 18th century and earlier. They laid the
accent on the traditional and the static, on constraint and control,
involving restrictions on press, speech, and assembly, religious orthodoxy, conventionalism in thought, a caste structure of the social
order, and authority reposing in the hands of a ruling élite. Whereas
liberalism as itemized previously flourished most vigorously in industrialized countries, conservatism held sway in agricultural Europe.

Competing with them, the challenger of historic capitalism, was the
philosophy of collectivism which had been gathering momentum since
about 1870, and which because of its newness requires fuller exposition. Like liberalism, like conservatism, the collectivist pattern was
not clear-cut but contained many variants growing out of diverse soils.
The common denominators of collectivist philosophies were the conviction that the common fellow had not gained a fair share of the
fruits of modern economy, hostility to the prevailing economic regime
grounded upon laissez faire and the normal stimuli of private enterprise and imagination, and an imperious determination to lift the
curse of poverty from all mankind.

One version of collectivism was formulated by a nineteenth century
German thinker and economist, Karl Marx, in his *Communist Manifesto* and more elaborately in fat volumes on *Capitalistic Production*,
which were completed by his life-long friend and collaborator, Friedrich Engels. A man of vast reading, Marx was crammed with strong

[2] J. B. Bury, *A History of Freedom of Thought* (New York, 1913), pp. 247-251.

opinions and was doctrinaire. To distinguish his body of principles from other unorthodox social philosophies of the age—which he repudiated as "unrealistic," "Utopian"—Marx called his massive structure "Communism." It was based upon historical interpretation and imaginative speculation.

In Marx's scheme of things the dynamic force in human affairs, past, present, and future, was the economic; all else was subordinate to or a reflection of material conditions and institutions. Religion, for instance, was only a cunningly compounded opiate serviceable in keeping the affections of the lowly and the exploited riveted on the world beyond and in making them submissive and gullible. Churches were mere tools manipulated by capitalists and landowners. Materialistic Marxism, denying purposive human strivings, affirmed that men were pawns of inexorable forces and fate; circumstances could be relied upon to bring forth leadership as needed.

Marx further affirmed that history in its fundamentals was a harmonious rhythm of the possessing social class battling against non-possessors. In the era of capitalistic industrialism and finance, owners and controllers of productive property (the bourgeoisie) were aligned against the toilers with hand and brain (the proletariat). These latter created all wealth, but part of their product—surplus value in Marxian language—accrued to the owners of factories, mines, banks, railways, and the like. That arrangement Marx condemned as unfair and immoral. When conditions were ripe, when the grinding poverty of the many was no longer endurable, the propertyless, by a revolutionary seizure of power, would abolish private ownership root and branch and transfer productive facilities to the state, which would operate them for the equal advantage of all.

It was Marx's conviction that the scheme of society he envisaged was bound to come in accord with unswerving historical law. In the meantime the propertyless of all nations should prepare to establish the new world of new men and to that end they should repudiate national ties in the deeper consciousness of class solidarity. Love of country, instead of being a noble emotion welling up within man, was regarded as a tricky fraud devised by the ruling class in order to perpetuate itself. Workers of the world should unite in the common struggle to strike off the chains of the possessing few which bound them.

These explosive Marxist doctrines excited furious dialectical controversies in European intellectual and working class circles. Men argued and felt about Marxism as Puritans of the 17th century argued and felt about religion. With the passing of time devotees of Marxism split into two main factions. For the one, orthodox and revolutionary, the coming revolution was a great reality and the millenium no cynical phrase but an order of society they themselves would build once capitalism was overthrown. Uncompromising in zeal the straitlaced Marxist was confident that international Socialism would conquer, save the world, and usher in an epoch of unapproached felicity and fraternity. Nowhere numerically large in 1914, the adherents of this pattern of Marxism underwent a disillusioning experience as World War I came on and Socialists of all countries except Russia loyally rallied round their respective national flags.

The other major school of Marxists was referred to as evolutionary or gradualist or democratic. While paying lip-service to the ultimate goals of the faith, its members inwardly revolted against the prophetic comprehensiveness of Marx, revised his original theories in the light of the changing environment, and preferred to create a Socialist commonwealth by peaceful constitutional processes. They favored legislation that promised to benefit the propertyless worker directly and immediately, and advocated that productive facilities should be taken over by government, sector by sector, until society was fully organized on Socialist principles.

To that end, gradualist Marxians organized political parties, entered into politics and sought to win a majority of the electorate to their aims. And in 1914 they had more deputies in the German Reichstag than any other party. They scored sensational gains in the French national elections of 1914, and had large and disciplined followings in Austria, Italy, and Sweden.[3] These parties were united in a loose international federation, the Second International, which held frequent congresses to discuss Socialist policy and to declaim against militarism, imperialism, and war. Yet for the party leadership in the main the pull of national affections transcended the orthodox Marxian teaching of the international fraternity of toilers.

Socialism, or better, collectivism, was not a monopoly of the disparate disciples of Marx alone; it was a creed that admitted of varied meanings and applications. Without adopting the Marxian formulas certain reform-minded men, moved by vague inward feelings of unrest, sought ways to prevent poverty within the framework of the regime of private capitalism. To their way of thinking it was the duty of the state to cooperate in securing an adequate standard of subsistence for workers and in guaranteeing that standard against the normal hazards of life. Wherefore they pressed for social welfare

[3] Of the thirteen Marxian Socialists in the Russian Duma of 1914, six belonged to the revolutionary Bolshevik wing.

laws, wage worker insurance measures—to provide assistance in time
of accident, sickness, and old age—and public ownership of railways
and public utilities. In legislation of that character imperial Germany
was pathfinder and pace-setter and other countries copied her more
or less faithfully.

In religious circles, too, active movements were seeking the social
betterment of the weary and heavy laden, demonstrating faith by
works. Roman Catholic groups, inspired by the social teachings of
Pope Leo XIII, who was hailed as the workingman's Pope, inveighed
against the misuse, not the existence of private property; through
political parties they fostered peasants' and workers' banks and social
welfare reforms. The Austrian party of Christian Socialists governed
the great metropolis of Vienna and introduced innovations in municipal Socialism. Without organizing formal parties many Protestant
churchmen were concerned to "Christianize the social order" and to
work for "the establishment of the Kingdom of God on earth."

Still another—and less widespread—challenger of existing institutions was the social philosophy of Anarchism. While Anarchism subscribed to the Marxian indictment of the inequalities and tyranny of
wealth, it differed sharply from Socialism because it would extinguish
the state utterly and allow men absolute and unfettered liberty. Persons, it was asserted, were innately good (or by public pressure
could be made so) and would dwell in contentment and harmony if
the compulsive shackles of government, private property, organized
religion, and received social conventions were stricken off. Once that
was done men would cooperate for mutual advantage in a wholly
voluntary society; each kind of work would be carried on by autonomous bodies freely formed of those who chose to join them and
cooperating by free arrangement with groups in other types of employment.

One school of Anarchism, exemplified by the Russian novelist and
mystic, Count Leo Tolstoi, advocated reaching the declared objectives
by pacific, non-violent means, and appealed to contemplative rather
than activist spirits. But there was also a militant sect of Anarchism,
founded by the most feared revolutionary of his time, Michael Bakunin, a Russian, too, which frankly preached "direct action," sabotage
of productive properties, incitement of workers to strike and revolt
leading to a general insurrection and the overthrow of the prevailing
society.

In the name of their faith violent Anarchists boldly assassinated
prominent political personages in the quaint belief that the governing
class, out of fear, would yield to the way of Anarchism. An active

force in the Russia of 1914 and in the nations of Latin Europe (with its largest following in Spain), revolutionary Anarchism and terroristic techniques had also touched the emotions of romantic nationalists among the subject peoples of eastern Europe and the Balkans.

The Political Framework

"Who talks of Europe is wrong," Prince Bismarck once observed, thus tersely expressing his conviction that the continent was not to be thought of in terms of solidarity. The bond of a universal religion which once had united most of Europe was shattered during the Reformation, and in spite of many things that were shared by the nations in common, no secular basis for unity had appeared.

Those national states which by reason of their economic resources, manpower, geographical extent, and war potential enjoyed the highest respect were referred to as Great Powers: Great Britain, Germany, Russia, France, Austria-Hungary, and Italy. The last three claimed a place at the top out of historical tradition or by courtesy rather than because of their inherent strength.

Spain and Sweden, once real counters in European affairs, but now of less importance, were able to hold aloof from the turmoil of high politics because of their location on the edges of the continent. In the very maelstrom, however, were the small states of Belgium, the Netherlands, Switzerland, and the Balkan powerlets of Rumania, Bulgaria, Serbia, Montenegro, Albania (barely set up), Greece, and Turkey; and on the fringes Portugal, Denmark, and Norway.[4]

For some of the European states, pride, power, and prestige were enhanced by the ownership of colonial empires. Britain stood first in this regard, followed in order by Russia, France, Holland, Germany, Belgium, Portugal, Italy, Spain, and Denmark.

Compared with the situation half a century earlier the noteworthy shifts in the power status of the European nations were the spectacular advance of Germany, the enlarged prestige of Russia, French recovery from the disastrous military defeat by Germany in 1870, the modest increase of Italian power, the relative decline of Britain and the Hapsburg monarchy, and the absolute falling off of Turkey, whose counterpart was the emergence of independent Balkan nations.

So far as governmental forms were concerned distinctions may be drawn in the character of both the executive and legislative organs of the European states. Without exception by 1914 they had constitutions defining, among other things, the scope and authority of the

[4] There were also the tiny entities of Liechtenstein, Luxembourg, Monaco, and Andorra, discoverable only on a large-scale map.

several branches of government. The monarchical version of the executive prevailed most widely, being found in all the countries except France, Portugal, and Switzerland, which were republics with elected chiefs of state. Of the outlook for republicanism in Europe the foremost authority on the subject, writing in 1910, concluded: "There can be little question that since 1870 the cause of Republicanism has made no substantial progress in Europe. France is still the only great European republic and the political history of France under her new regime has not been such as to invite imitation. The position of the monarchies . . . has been considerably, indeed progressively improved. . . . The republican movement has done its work. Its ideals have been appropriated and used." He asserted that there was "a very general belief that the cause of European peace is assisted by the social and family ties which subsist between monarchs." [5]

But the form of the government meant far less than the authority of the executive and the relative strength of law-making bodies in the governing process. Whatever the name of the titular executive, the real executive organ universally was the ministry or cabinet. In Great Britain, France, Italy, Sweden, and some of the smaller countries, a ministry retained office only so long as it commanded a majority in the popularly elected legislature. In Germany, in the Hapsburg monarchy, and in Russia, ministries depended for their tenure upon the favor of the crown. There the philosophy of the divine right of kings to rule, the idea that a monarch was father to his people, still dominated the stage.

Democratic political concepts—a hallmark of the 19th century—which seemed predestined to sweep all humanity in their train, had by 1914 touched the nations of Europe in varying degrees. Universal manhood suffrage for legislatures had been adopted everywhere except in the Kingdom of Hungary. Yet only in the Scandinavian North had women been admitted to the franchise on conditions of equality.[6] The British and French governments and less clearly the Italian were directly responsive to the public will as expressed through parliaments, more so in domestic than in foreign affairs. Of the Reichstag of Germany it has been aptly remarked that it could "bark but not

[5] H. A. L. Fisher, *The Republican Tradition in Europe* (New York, 1911), pp. 320, 337, 356.

[6] Militant British suffragettes in 1914 were waging a violent campaign for the vote. Bills to enfranchise women were before the German and other legislatures; Socialist parties were strongly in favor of general women's rights and of women suffrage.

bite," for it was a forum in which deputies could air opinions rather than an effective instrument for determining public policies. And the same estimate held true for the Austrian Reichsrat and the Russian Duma. Into these latter countries the shadow of political democracy had penetrated, but the substance was not present. True, representative assemblies in these states occasionally asserted themselves but if deputies spoke out too critically or balked at doing the bidding of the ministry the assemblies might be dissolved by the executive.

Moreover, whatever constitutions might prescribe, to the east of the Rhine and south of the Pyrenees the essential liberties of the democratic ideology were circumscribed. The repressive hand of authority interfered, for instance, with freedom of teaching and learning, with freedom of association and expression. Yet press censorship was not ironclad. Even in Russia, the revolutionary Marxist daily, *Pravda,* was permitted to circulate, though its editors were frequently fined.

Standards of administration for the day-to-day discharge of public services tended to run parallel in western Europe. Each country, however, had administrative features peculiar to itself. Throughout Europe, German methods of public administration, stemming from the severely austere ways of Prussia, were extensively imitated.

Regardless of international importance each European state jealously guarded its national sovereignty and acted in foreign relationships in accordance with its own concept of national interest. Each nation itself decided the armaments it required; each maintained a caste of professional military and naval officers, who busily mapped out plans for war upon potential enemies and who were eager to have the largest defense forces they could get. As a class they deserved the reproach once uttered by Britain's Lord Salisbury that "if they were allowed full scope, they would insist on the importance of garrisoning the moon in order to protect us from Mars." The professional military group carried greatest weight in Russia, Austria, and Germany, rather less in France, and in Great Britain the military chiefs were on tap, not on top.

Each European state had its particular set of prides and prejudices, its own pattern of individuality, its own special hopes—and fears—for the future. And each state had its own version of nationalism. Like many another word ending in "ism," nationalism was a term of protean ambiguity, but it covered the most powerful political and psychological phenomena of the age. It displayed itself in a variety of ways. Nationalism was thought of as an attitude of mind and emotion which placed loyalty to one's nationality above every other loyalty; it inspired an intense desire to see one's own people and nation great and respected; it kindled blazing pride in one's national language, history and traditions, "race" and cultural attainments; it assumed that one's government in dealings with other nations could do no wrong. With insolence and bragadoccio nationalism imputed inferiority to other nationalities while extolling the superiority of one's native or adopted folk.

Nationalism differed from patriotism, for the latter, while implying genuine devotion to one's own country and recognizing a duty to it, acknowledged that other nations had their meritorious points. Patriotism was not averse to healthy criticism of one's government in its international relations. Nationalism in its most provocative form was called chauvinism. Chauvinist and nationalist alike invested his state or nationality with attributes transcending mere reason and paid them the sort of adulation once reserved for religion and Deity.

While nationalism flourished throughout the length and breadth of Europe and affected all social classes it was undoubtedly most blatant in 1914 in those countries which recently had achieved nationhood or which had "unredeemed brethren" in adjoining states. And nationalism seems to have been most potent among the bourgeoisie. State school, popular press, and conscript army were prime agencies for the cultivation of the national mind, the quickening of national emotions, and the diffusion of false prides and dangerous prejudices.

Minorities

Every major country of Europe, except France and Italy, was troubled in 1914 by the presence and agitation of restless minority populations in various stages of national consciousness. For Great Britain the sore-spot was Ireland. There the generation-old clamor for home-rule gave rise in 1914 to apprehension that the island would be immersed in civil war, with the northern, mainly Protestant, counties fighting the rest of Ireland. Angry and stormy debates in the British Parliament at the time testified to the gravity of the tension in "John Bull's other island."

If by 1914 German administration had gone far to appease the inhabitants of Alsace-Lorraine, wrested away from France in 1871, there was still a large and vocal Francophile party and other Alsatian elements demanded fuller and more effective home-rule than was granted in a constitution of 1911. On the northwestern fringe of Germany a small Danish-feeling minority chafed under alien rule and sporadic attempts to blend them in the German national community.

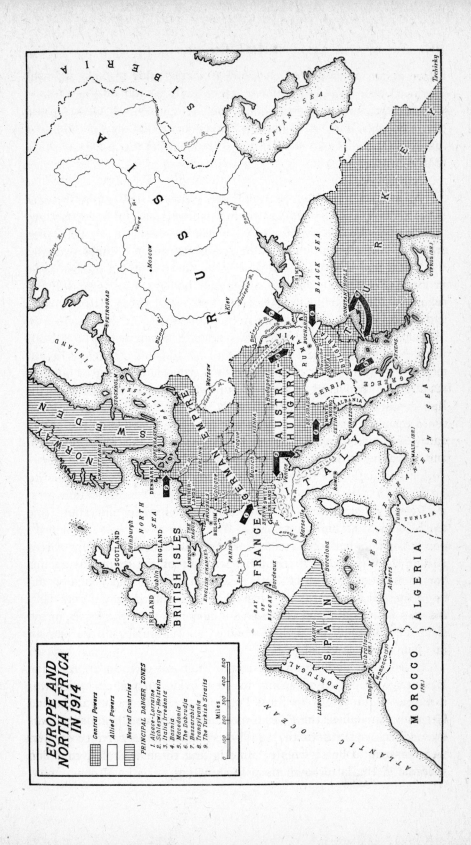

EUROPE AND
NORTH AFRICA
IN 1914

Central Powers
Allied Powers
Neutral Countries

PRINCIPAL DANGER ZONES
1. Alsace-Lorraine
2. Schleswig-Holstein
3. Italia Irredenta
4. Bosnia
5. Macedonia
6. The Dobrudja
7. Bessarabia
8. Transylvania
9. The Turkish Straits

Miles
0   100   200   300   400   500

More obstreperous and much larger was the Polish Catholic minority
in the eastern German provinces, whose political and religious leaders
strenuously combatted Prussianization and encouraged hopes against
the day when Poland would again take her place in the family of
nations. Of the fifteen seats in the German Reichstag assigned to the
Polish-peopled districts, fourteen were consistently occupied by men
of Polish speech.

Minorities in the European portion of the Russian empire included
some 25,000,000 Ukrainians, few of whom seem to have had any
feeling of distinctive national spirit. There were about 8,000,000 Poles,
many of whose vocal spirits were Polish nationalists; Finns exceeded
3,000,000 and were strongly separatist; there were an almost equal
number of Lithuanians, and substantial bodies of Letts and Esths,
whose middle-class spokesmen cried for release from Russian rule;
and a sprinkling of Rumanian-feeling folk dwelt in the province of
Bessarabia. Last but by no means least, there were over 5,000,000
Jews in Russia, though whether they should be classed as a nationality or rather as a cultural-religious group is a matter of opinion.
At any rate, badgered as were Jews nowhere else in the world in the
half century before 1914, the Jewish community of Russia supplied
more than a proportionate share of the active enemies of the autocracy. Men and women dedicated themselves to the replacement of
the prevailing order by a regime in which discrimination and persecution on "national" or religious grounds would be absent. Minority
groupings had been subjected for years to severe Russification pressures; and all save possibly the Ukrainians longed for liberation from
tsarist oppression and abuse.

As Britain had one Ireland, so the Hapsburg monarchy was a
congeries of Irelands. In the Austrian half of the monarchy, which
was dominated by men of German speech, a small noisy faction desired that German-speaking areas should be joined to imperial Germany. Czech politicians clamored for home-rule for the Czech provinces, and, to manifest their discontent, they brought the Parliament
at Vienna to a standstill in 1914 (as had repeatedly happened before)
which led to its dissolution just before the onset of the war. Austrian
Poles enjoyed virtual autonomy in the province of Galicia which was
a haven of refuge for militant Polish nationalists from Russia and
Germany. In Galicia the Poles lorded over a restive Ukrainian minority. Italian speakers to the south were divided between those who
were content to be citizens of Austria and those who desired union
with Italy, the latter perhaps predominating.

Of Hungary, Austria's partner in the Hapsburg monarchy, the dominant nationality was the Magyar and for years Magyars had been striving to uproot national sentiments among their non-Magyar fellows. Leaders of the large Rumanian minority in the eastern provinces were mainly impassioned champions of union with the Kingdom of Rumania. Among Slovaks an earnest band of intellectuals complained hotly against Magyar rule, but efficient processes of Magyarization pointed to the denationalization of the Slovaks in the not-distant future.

Both Austria and Hungary contained large Yugoslav minorities: Slovenes, Serbs, and Croats, the last having a semblance of autonomy. And Bosnia-Herzegovina, also under Hapsburg rule, was likewise inhabited by Yugoslavs. Among politically articulate Hapsburg Yugoslavs two main attitudes prevailed in 1914: the first was sympathetic to the existing regime, while the other, and no doubt the larger, was working for the merger of the Yugoslav districts with the neighboring Kingdom of Serbia. As a means of reconciling the Yugoslavs of the monarchy to the status quo certain Austrian policymakers had prepared plans for the creation of an autonomous Yugoslav state which would be essentially the equal of Austria and Hungary in the Hapsburg realm. But Magyar politicians, fearing for their own power, were intransigently opposed to any far-reaching proposals for the reformation of the ancient monarchy.

National minorities were scattered indiscriminately about the Balkan peninsula and kept, or helped to keep, the Balkan cauldron boiling. On the eve of World War I, just after wars in the Balkans had brought drastic revisions in the map of southeastern Europe, there were Bulgars and Albanians in Serbia; Bulgars in Rumania; Bulgars, Turks, and Albanians in Greece; Bulgars and Greeks in European Turkey, while in the Asiatic part of the Ottoman Empire there were more Greeks, Arabs, and Armenians. Small wonder that the Balkans were spoken of as the most dangerous of the danger-zones of Europe! [7]

Internationalism

Even as nationalism had attained an unprecedented peak in 1914 so internationalism had reached levels hitherto unknown. Reigning houses, high society, and high finance, making little of national lines, were interlocked by marriage and business ties. Never had there been

[7] Spain and Belgium had minorities which desired at least more freedom for the exercise of their language and culture.

so many international institutions, associations, societies, commissions, bureaus, congresses, expositions, and publications, touching almost every phase of human interest and endeavor from professional study of history through Socialism to sports. At England's Epsom Derby in May of 1914 the winner was Durban II, owned by an American, H. B. Duryea, and trained in France. A little later the horse ran a poor third at the Grand Prix de Paris—on the very day that the shots of an assassin in an obscure Balkan town blew up the European powder keg.

On the political plane there was the Hague Court of Arbitration, set up in 1907, whose judges, men of the highest eminence in the legal profession, were entitled to settle disputes which quarreling governments might submit to them. That body conducted its deliberations in a splendid palace at the Hague built with funds furnished by the American steelmaster, Andrew Carnegie. The literature of pacifism, condemning recourse to arms to settle international disputes and stressing religious and philosophical themes or the economic folly or the social stupidity of war, had persuaded many a European that warfare was the darkest of sins, not to be countenanced however noble the objectives.

The Swedish inventor of dynamite, Alfred Nobel, after amassing a huge fortune from his international munitions concern, had established, paradoxically, his well-known peace prizes to reward those who were active in the prevention of war. Among the recipients before 1914 were President Theodore Roosevelt and the German Emperor William II. Interest in the peace movement was quickened by the death, on June 21, 1914, of the pacifist, Baroness Bertha von Suttner, daughter of an Austrian military man, and author of the novel, *Die Waffen Nieder*, (*Lay Down Your Arms*). Translated into many languages, the book had done something 'to foster indifference to the glamour and glories of war.

So vocal had the pacifist spirit grown in Italy in 1914 that the government laid a ban on anti-militarist meetings. The Carnegie Peace Foundation issued a bulky report on the atrocities in the Balkan struggles of 1912 and 1913, and ventured the hope that the document might "have some weight with civilized nations as one more argument against war." President Wilson speaking at Annapolis proclaimed that "the new things in the world are the things that are divorced from force." To him, as to many another, it appeared that a progressive age of reason lay just ahead. If the beast in man had not been exorcised it seemed at least to have been tamed.

Alignments and Alarms

The Europe of 1914 was divided into two clearly defined heavily-armed diplomatic partnerships, each intent upon preserving the precarious equilibrium of force and avoiding a devastating clash of arms. But in reality in the supreme diplomatic crisis of that year the international partnerships instead of serving to keep the peace converted a local war into a general conflict. On one side was the Central Powers group—or the Triple Alliance—embracing Germany, Austria-Hungary, Italy, and Rumania, the last two lukewarm in their loyalty; Turkey was a silent partner in this alignment, and Bulgaria was strongly inclined toward it. Balancing that bloc was an array of power spoken of as the Triple Entente: France, Russia, and Great Britain. Portugal was in alliance with Britain while Serbia was on terms of closest intimacy with Russia; Japan, allied to Great Britain, may also be reckoned in the Entente camp.

The Central Powers group had come into being late in the 19th century and rested upon two principal treaties. A pact, signed originally in 1879, bound Germany and Austria-Hungary to fight shoulder to shoulder if either were attacked by Russia. A second secret treaty, quite independent of the first, allied Germany, Austria-Hungary, and Italy against France and Russia, in effect. That agreement which was periodically renewed and added to in a manner desired by Italy, led the three signatories to work together diplomatically until the opening of the 20th century when Italy took a line independent of her allies. Rumania was attached to the Triplice by a treaty directed against imperial Russia.

The initial important documentary link in the Entente chain was forged in 1893 when France and Russia negotiated a secret defensive alliance, promising to fight Germany, if either was attacked by Germany. A decade later Great Britain, which had kept aloof from diplomatic commitments to other nations, entered into a military alliance with Japan (1902)—pointed directly against Russian expansion in the Far East—and arranged a friendly understanding (1904) with France, the Entente Cordiale. By that arrangement specific Anglo-French colonial disputes were liquidated, mutual confidence was established, and the way was smoothed for general diplomatic cooperation. Friendship was later cemented by plans for military and naval coordination in the event of war with Germany.

Presently Great Britain concluded (1907) an entente with Russia which tempered hostility and mounting discord over the territories lying between Britain's India and the sprawling empire of the Tsar in southern Asia. That accommodation, though never amplified by any military bargain, made it easier for the statesmen of these two widely divergent countries to work together in the international arena, and paved the way to cooperation in war seven years later.

The Franco-Russian alliance plus the British ententes with France and Russia equalled the Triple Entente, though no formal treaty bound the three states together. So far as Britain was concerned the ties were rather tenuous and elastic and she hesitated to commit herself to much more than general friendship. Yet the very existence of the Entente, standing against the Triplice, in itself accentuated international tension, and made it probable that if individual members of the rival combinations became embroiled in war the other members would be drawn in. To ensure the solidarity and prestige of the bloc to which it belonged, each country considered it essential to back its friends in political quarrels that arose, even though it had no direct interest in the controversy.

Between 1905 and 1914 these two partnerships crossed diplomatic swords in repeated tests of strength, any one of which might have precipitated a general war and each of which aggravated ill-feeling and resentment among the nations. German statesmen loudly trumpeted that British diplomacy was forging an iron ring of hostile powers around the Fatherland, and apprehension was accentuated by signs of the untrustworthiness of Italy to the Triplice.

Principally with the object of disrupting the Anglo-French alignment, partly for imperialistic gain, Germany in 1905 kicked up a fuss over Morocco on the northwestern shoulder of Africa. With the acquiescence of Britain, Spain, and Italy, France was making preparations to take over Morocco, or most of it. Germany's Kaiser spoke about Morocco in such a provocative tone as to create a general war scare.

To stave off a conflict diplomatists of the powers met in conference at Algeciras, Spain in 1906. At that meeting Britain, Russia, and even Italy seconded the French pretensions while only Austria-Hungary backed Germany.[8] Though the French were unable to obtain all they desired, the Germans not only failed to upset the new balance of power implicit in the Anglo-French entente, but by their rough blusterings they actually tightened the bonds of interest between the Channel neighbors.

---

[8] Credit or part of it for summoning the conference belonged to President Theodore Roosevelt. The American representative at Algeciras generally voted with France.

The next major duel arose out of the Balkans over the status of Bosnia-Herzegovina which Austria-Hungary, administrator of the region for thirty years, blandly annexed in 1908. It happened that the region was inhabited mainly by Yugoslavs, national brethren of the Serbs, and the Serbian government, which coveted the district for itself, raised a heaven-rending protest in which Russia joined.

Whereas France and Germany had been the leading protagonists in the Moroccan imbroglio, Russia and Austria were the principals in the Bosnian crisis and in each case the diplomatic partners of the contestants were implicated. Germany made it plain that it would support its Austrian ally "in shining armor" if the occasion required. Russia and her western associates were unwilling to appeal to force, so they reluctantly acquiesced in the Austrian annexation of Bosnia. And Serbia, left in the lurch, promised to pursue a policy of the "good neighbor" in future relations with Austria—a promise she neglected to fulfill. For the Entente the Bosnian test resulted in a humiliating diplomatic defeat.

Two years later Morocco was a second time the theatre of a grave international wrangle. For the announced purpose of putting down nativist disorders in Morocco, France marched troops into the interior of the kingdom. It was inferred in Germany that the French move would be only the veriest prelude to French control, something the Berlin policymakers were determined should not come to pass unless suitable colonial compensation were made to Germany. Accordingly a small German warship laden with marines was rushed to the Moroccan port of Agadir.

Once more dark clouds of war hung low over Europe. Once more as in the earlier Moroccan quarrel the British government stood firmly by France, warning Germany that if hostilities broke out, Britain would fight. Eventually a peaceful accommodation was worked out which allowed France to assert a protectorate over the greater part of Morocco, and gave Germany a large slice of the French Congo as compensation.

From Morocco the center of danger shifted again to the Near East. Italy in 1911 declared war upon Turkey and, as fruits of victory, appropriated African Tripoli and established herself in the Dodecanese archipelago off the coast of Asia Minor. That conflict not only produced serious strains within the Triple Alliance, since both belligerents belonged to that diplomatic camp, but encouraged the Christian nations of the Balkans to fall upon weakened Turkey and despoil her.

Under Russian guidance and patronage, Bulgaria, Serbia, Greece, and Montenegro had organized a united front and in 1912-1913, they fought and thoroughly whipped Turkey. But then the victors fell out over the division of the booty, especially over Macedonia, and fought a second Balkan war. In that struggle Serbia, Montenegro, and Greece were lined up against Bulgaria; and before the savage conflict was over Rumania and resurgent Turkey attacked hapless, ambitious Bulgaria. Bulgaria was decisively conquered and overrun.

By reason of these two Balkan wars Serbia, Greece, and Rumania made handsome territorial gains, taking land which nationalistically-minded Bulgars contended belonged of right to their kingdom. Turkey in Europe was reduced to a small zone including Constantinople. Aside from heightening animosities and jingoism among the Balkan nations, the wars of 1912-1913 intensified ill-will between Austria and Russia, troubled European chancelleries generally, and inspired a veritable mania of armament expansion.

While the fighting was on, Austria vetoed Serbian claims to the northern part of the Turkish province of Albania fronting on the Adriatic Sea, while Russia supported the pretensions of her Serb protégé. Once more Austria and Russia stood face to face, and, as they had done during the Bosnian crisis, both mobilized part of their military services. It appeared to be only a question of time until these two ramshackle empires of eastern Europe clashed. But, as matters turned out, British and German diplomacy intervened and patched up a settlement; Serbia, however, failed to acquire Adriatic coastlands and, despite territorial aggrandizement elsewhere, Serb hatred of Austria surpassed anything previously known. By giving way on the Albanian issue Russia had sustained another grievous blow to her international standing.

From 1905 to 1913, then, a clash of arms which might have involved all the members of the competing European diplomatic partnerships was on several occasions only narrowly averted. Wherefore many a European adopted the fatalistic belief that a general war was bound to come. Wherever he turned he heard talk of the impending conflict.

The International Anarchy

This sketch of the European scene of 1914 may fittingly be concluded with a description of the deeper forces and tendencies which had combined to produce the diplomatic alignments, to churn up burning international animosities, and in the end to make a general war possible.

At the head of the list may be placed the prevalent concepts of national self-interest and the rampant nationalism which had been quickened by the international stresses and strains of the preceding decade. Energetic and assertive Germany, intoxicated by national achievements in industry, commerce, and science and by the national capacity for war, felt she ought to have a larger share in world affairs. Responsible public men, beginning with the erratic and indiscreet Emperor William II, spoke grandiloquently about world power, hinted at world domination, and there was no little disquieting and mischievous chatter about Pan-Germanism. Moreover, it was firmly believed by fearful Germans that a sinister, encircling league of enemies was bent upon denying their great and proud nation her rightful place in the international scheme of things. Only by force or the threat of force, many Germans believed, could the legitimate ambitions of the nation be achieved.

The rapid upsurge of Germany as the strongest nation of Europe had provoked genuine apprehension in Great Britain, which had been the world leader since the humiliation of Napoleon at Waterloo and would not tamely be dislodged from that proud eminence. For the island kingdom it was an axiom to resist the mightiest constellation of power in Europe. In British thought "a just equilibrium" among the nations on the continent was (and had long been) an immutable requisite of British survival and the safety of the globe-girdling realm. It was that reasoning which substantially dictated the course of British diplomacy in the early twentieth century; it was that reasoning that led Britain to conceive of a strong France as a national interest and to reconcile differences with Russia.

French nationalists longed to regain for their country the lofty role in European affairs that France had played before the defeat by Germany in 1870. Symbol of the national humiliation and loss of prestige were the provinces of Alsace and Lorraine, which many Frenchmen, though perhaps not most, declined to recognize as eternally lost. At no time was there any official inclination in Germany to retrocede Alsace-Lorraine peacefully, for in the German view their country had the stronger claims to the provinces. Frenchmen bitterly resented, too, the bullying tactics which the hereditary enemy across the Rhine had applied in the Moroccan controversies and were minded to fight rather than submit to another diplomatic humiliation.

Imperial Russia, smarting under successive diplomatic defeats administered by Austria and Germany, was desirous of restoring her prestige in general and in the Balkans in particular. For Serbia, Russia cherished a warm fraternal affection and highly-placed Muscovite authorities deliberately emboldened Serb nationalists in their soaring territorial ambitions. That brotherly sentiment for Serbia symbolized the mutual bonds linking Russia with the smaller Slav nationalities; and the broad community of Slav feeling fostered active Russian enmity toward Germany and the Hapsburg monarchy with their Slavic-speaking minorities. Beyond that, the idea of fulfilling an "historic national mission" by raising the flag of the tsars over the ancient capital of Constantine the Great and of gaining mastery over the thoroughfare to the warm waters of the Mediterranean haunted the minds of Russian policymakers. They thought this long cherished goal could only be reached by war.

The directors of the Hapsburg monarchy on their part were resolved on preventing Russian hegemony in the Balkans, on strengthening the influence of their own country in that area, and on thwarting the further growth of Serbia, which menaced the very continuance of the monarchy as a Great Power. For Italy the supreme national ambition was to win possession of districts in the Hapsburg realm where Italian speech predominated; and subordinate to that was the desire to broaden the national position in the Balkans.

It was in the vexed Balkan peninsula that national aspirations and mutual jealousies had generated the most provocative and bellicose chauvinism. Not one of the Balkan nations was satisfied with the status quo; each of them coveted territory under another flag or flags. And elsewhere in Europe unrest among "nations rightly struggling to be free" was a fecund source of international disquietude.

Imperial and economic rivalries contributed their quota to the international anarchy. Sharp competition over colonies and overseas rights roused mutual antipathies and envenomed hatreds growing out of divergent interests inside Europe. Germany and Italy, newcomers in the lush game of empire and relatively "have not" imperialisms, pressed vigorously for a place in the colonial sun commensurate with their rank in the European hierarchy. In so doing they antagonized the countries which had carved out impressively wide colonial dominions. Colonial underdog that it was, Germany was rough and provocative in the methods employed to extend her overseas holdings. The remark of the French savant, Leroy Beaulieu, that colonies might not be signs of strength today, but that they held the strength of the future, epigrammatically hit off one dynamic of German imperialism.

An important manifestation of German imperialism was the loudly heralded Bagdad railway, which, while intended to open up the economic potentialities of Asiatic Turkey to the mutual gain of both countries, implied designs upon Egypt and India. That undertaking excited uneasiness and distrust in Russia as well as in Britain. To the Russians the Bagdad line signified the growth of German power in

Turkey and pointed to German dominance over Constantinople and the Straits.

It is often asserted that it was commercial envy, rivalry over markets, competition of merchant marines, and the export of capital which turned British diplomacy against Germany. That indeed was the stock interpretation of British foreign policy in German circles. But the thesis, while not without some substance, contains more surface plausibility than the facts in the case appear to warrant. American merchants were not less serious competitors of British exporters than were Germans, yet Britain was on a friendlier basis with the United States in the years before 1914 than at almost any time since the Americans won their independence.

What probably did more than anything else to embitter the European atmosphere and undermine international confidence were the growing military services, at once a cause and a result of the prevailing tension. Armaments were the ultimate support of diplomacy, ready if need be to coerce an opponent, destroy his will to resist, and compel his surrender. The only assurance of safety that a nation had was the knowledge that it could not be attacked with impunity.

Military forces were prodigiously and competitively enlarged after 1895, and trials of strength between the rival diplomatic partnerships in the decade before 1914 were followed by greater outlays for preparedness. Each nation believed that its own armaments were for purely defensive purposes, but potential foes thought otherwise. It all depended on the angle from which a glistening cannon was looked at— the stern of a gun meant one thing, the mouth something else. Ever and again the press of the several nations, under official "inspiration" or otherwise, stimulated armament expansion by playing up real or alleged dangers to national security; and spokesmen of munitions companies indulged in similar activity.

Military chiefs, publicists, and others boastfully warned the world what their national war-machines would do once the signal to attack was given. Inescapably sword-rattling in one country caused resentment and mistrust abroad. Apart from provoking primitive fears in potentially enemy countries, the spirited race in armaments nourished the beliefs that war had moral and therapeutic value and that war was inevitable. In that tense atmosphere militarism thrived—passionate delight in armed combat, admiration verging on worship of the warrior, willingness to fight and bleed and die in an impersonal national cause.

A really novel feature in the armament competition was the emergence of Germany as a first-class seapower. Possessed of the

world's most respected army, Germany in 1898 started to create a
mighty navy. By 1914 the German fleet ranked second only to the
British in Europe. As the directors of German policy saw it, a powerful
High Seas Fleet would be a mark of national greatness, a weapon to
protect the growing overseas interests, and serviceable as an instrument of political pressure in time of diplomatic crisis.

Germany's naval program seriously embittered relations with Great
Britain, ruler of the waves since Elizabethan days and dependent
upon sea-borne commerce for its livelihood. It was not unnatural for
Britishers to believe that the growing German fleet was intended to
wrest Neptune's trident from Britain's grasp and to reduce the island
kingdom perhaps to another Holland among the nations. Determined
not to be surpassed on the ocean Britain steadily voted appropriations
to keep the fighting strength of her navy well ahead of the exuberant
continental rival. Several times the government of Great Britain proposed fleet limitation by consent but met with no response. Naval
competition was the largest direct cause of the deadly Anglo-German
antagonism. Yet, from 1912 to 1914, the tension between these two
most powerful nations tended to lessen, which caused certain continental statesmen to wonder whether Britain was seeking to grope
her way back to her 19th century role as the international balancer
par excellence.

Reporting on the European atmosphere in the spring of 1914,
Colonel E. M. House, special agent of President Wilson, correctly
declared, "Everybody's nerves are tense. It only needs a spark to set
the whole thing off." No doubt had House conducted a similar survey
at any time in the preceding decade his estimate would have been
much the same. In reality the international scene was if anything more
tranquil in 1914 than it had been for some time. "If we take a general
survey of the world," concluded the distinguished German historian,
Erich Marcks, early in that year, "we shall perceive that the clouds
have grown less menacing."

CHAPTER II

World War I: First Phase

The Sarajevo Crime

GREAT wars do not spring up overnight. They gather momentum over fairly long periods of time. Great wars evolve. As has been explained, a huge pile of highly combustible materials had accumulated in twentieth century Europe. Yet recurrent international fires had been quenched by one contrivance or another before they got out of hand. In July, 1914, it was otherwise.

The event that led to the European conflagration took place on Sunday, June 28, 1914, at Sarajevo, Bosnia, hitherto an obscure provincial capital. There the Archduke Francis Ferdinand, heir of the Hapsburg crowns, and his wife were assassinated by a youthful Yugoslav nationalist, Gavrilo Princip. Without that crime it is not unreasonable to suppose that Europe would have escaped a general war in 1914. The murderer, who eventually was installed in the Yugoslav pantheon of heroes, was animated by burning hatred of Austria and the Hapsburg "oppressor" and by an ardent passion to do something to facilitate the political unification of the Yugoslavs.[1]

To reconstruct the Sarajevo murders and their seamy antecedents in all their fullness is impossible because of gaps in the testimony and conflicting evidence on several important points. Yet certain items are reasonably well established. Francis Ferdinand, who was detested by Yugoslav extremists as the personification of Austrian arrogance and enmity, had gone to Sarajevo to be officially honored after having witnessed troop maneuvers in Bosnia. Killer Princip and his chief accomplices had shortly before returned to Sarajevo from Serbia bringing with them the tools to commit the crime—tools supplied them by members of Serbian secret societies dedicated to the holy cause of Greater Serbia, and by others who had assisted them on their journey to Sarajevo.

[1] For an intimate and lucid portrayal of the Sarajevo tragedy and the events which culminated in the European war, consult B. E. Schmitt, "July 1914: Thirty Years After," *Journal of Modern History*, XVI (1944), pp. 169-204.

It seems probable that the Serbian ministry of the day knew of the specific conspiracy to murder the Archduke well in advance of the deed but neglected to acquaint the government in Vienna with that knowledge. On the fateful day police measures to protect the Austrian celebrities in an unfriendly community were less thorough than they might have been. Yet it was the chance stoppage of the motorcar in which the archducal pair was riding which afforded Princip a perfect opportunity to discharge his bullets at the Hapsburg scion and his lady, and they died very quickly. "The older one gets," said Frederick the Great, "the more convinced one becomes that His Majesty King Chance does three quarters of the business of this miserable universe."

For a dozen years Austria (which is substituted in the following narrative for Austria-Hungary) and Serbia had been snarling and scrapping. Tempers in both countries were at white heat. Austria was intent upon fencing Serbia in, and, above all, upon safeguarding its own territorial integrity, while Serbia was driven on by an impetuous desire to possess Austrian areas inhabited by men of Yugoslav speech. Austria seized upon the Sarajevo assassination as a welcome basis for a definitive showdown with the troublesome and ambitious little neighbor across the Danube.

What Austrian diplomatists could not immediately prove concerning the complicity of Serbia and Serb officials in the Sarajevo tragedy, they assumed. Evidence later uncovered sustained their hypotheses at many points, though not at all. The Austrian bill of indictment drawn up against Serbia not long after the murders contained large gaps, and, except in Austrian and German circles, the case against Serbia failed to convince any reasonable person that recourse to armed punishment was warrantable.

Indignation and horror over the Sarajevo outrage spread widely across Europe, becoming most intense, naturally, in Austria. The British Prime Minister, Asquith, described the murder as "one of those incredible crimes which almost makes us despair of the progress of mankind." Yet the authorities in Vienna, headed by the Foreign Minister, Count Leopold von Berchtold, hesitated to move promptly against Serbia. It seemed necessary, first of all, to make sure of support by the German ally and to Berlin was despatched a statement of the case against Serbia and an incomplete outline of Austrian intentions. Without hesitation German policymakers assured the men in Vienna of unqualified backing, handed their sole trustworthy ally a blank cheque, which the Austrians proceeded to fill in—and cash.

Not until July 23 did Austria present Serbia with its list of demands and insist that complete acquiescence must be forthcoming within forty-eight hours. Specifically, Austria called upon the Serbian government to apologize for the part Serb nationals had in preparing the Sarajevo plot, and to give solid assurances that agitation against the monarchy would no longer be tolerated. Serbia was also asked to permit Austrian representatives to assist in suppressing anti-Austrian propaganda, in tracking down Serb accomplices in the murder, and to allow them to take part in their trial and punishment. In all it was an ultimatum such as no self-respecting nation could accept, and in Vienna that was precisely the calculation.

Actions of the Powers

Publication of the Austrian demand ushered in a hectic twelve-day period in the history of European diplomacy, which closed with most of the continent in battle array. Events marched so swiftly that the diplomatists, had they been supermen, could scarcely have kept track of all the bewildering developments; and historical investigators working with meticulous care have not been able to unravel the tangled skein completely. By a judicious selection of incontestable facts—not to mention inferences reasonable and otherwise—it would be possible to lay the blame for the climactic catastrophe upon the doorstep of any one of the major chancelleries (except the Italian). The deeper truth would seem to be that every government that was heavily involved in the crisis must be assigned some measure of responsibility. On the degree of blame which each party must bear historical specialists of the highest competence have debated ever since World War I commenced, and there is small reason to suppose that this acrimonious "war of words" has run its course.

Diplomatists and military hierarchs in each capital maneuvered for position seeking to escape responsibility for war, striving to pin blame upon their opposite numbers in other countries. None of the principal principals was disposed to yield in such manner as to impair the solidarity of the diplomatic partnership to which it was attached. Directors of foreign policy in all capitals resembled heroes of a Balaclava where everybody blundered.

A recommendation from Entente foreign offices that Serbia be granted more time to consider its reply to the Austrian ultimatum was summarily vetoed in Vienna. When the Serbian answer was published, it was seen to be conciliatory in tone, submissive on several points, though it flatly declined to permit Austrian officials to search for alleged conspirators. Shrewdly the Serbs recommended that if the reply should prove unsatisfactory to Austria, the dispute be turned over to the Hague Court or to an international conference for review and settlement.

But the Austrians, determined upon military chastisement of Serbia, severed diplomatic relations and on July 28 delivered a declaration of war to the southern kingdom. Next morning shells rained down on Belgrade. Could the conflict be confined to the Balkans or would it engulf Europe entire? That was the supreme question.

Imperial Russia in the meantime had let it be known that she would protect the kindred Slav state by force of arms if necessary. Repetition of earlier diplomatic humiliations would not be tolerated and military measures preparatory to war were ordered. France, though her interests were not directly at stake in the Austro-Serb quarrel, assured the Russians that she would faithfully fulfill alliance commitments.

Russia's course, together with growing skepticism on British aloofness from war—the British fleet had been posted at battle stations—caused German policymakers to strike out on a new line. To that point in the crisis Germany had loyally—and with reckless unwisdom—stood by Austria. In so doing Germany had encouraged the men in Vienna to plunge ahead and had excited deep animosity and suspicion in the Russian chancellery. Now Germany moved to rein in her ally, proposing that Austrian arms should merely occupy Belgrade and its environs, and remain there while Serbia executed the pledges given in the reply to the ultimatum. That overture, unhappily, received no immediate response.

While clouds of war had been rapidly gathering in central Europe, the British cabinet (Sir Edward Grey, Foreign Minister) advanced several plans to keep the peace. Grey recommended first, that Austrian and Russian diplomatists should try to work out an accommodation; subsequently, he advocated combined diplomatic action of France, Italy, Germany, and Britain to effect a pacific settlement. But neither of the rival partnerships warmed up to these proposals. In the meantime French (and Russian) appeals to Britain for reaffirmation of solidarity with the Dual Alliance, elicited only non-committal answers from London. And German requests for the conditions upon which Britain would remain neutral were similarly dealt with.

After vacillating in a manner that bred suspicion, Russia, on July 30, ordered the mobilization of some 3,600,000 soldiers. These Russian forces would be pointed not alone against Austria but against Germany too. By that fateful mobilization act Imperial Russia went far in converting a Balkan struggle into a broad European war. Military plans and schedules, the products of years of painstaking study by strate-

gists and impossible of quick modification, thenceforth crowded aside
the efforts of diplomacy to preserve the peace. The calling of tsarist
troops to the colors, like the parallel action of Germany a little later,
signified the ascendancy of the military chiefs in matters of high
policy and in both instances the consequences were calamitous.

Russian mobilization intensified alarm in Berlin. On the valid
assumption that in a general war Germany would be confronted by
French armies on the west and Russian on the east, military experts
had devised plans for a speedy decision by a swift overwhelming assault upon France. To force the strong fortress system along the
French frontier would consume precious time, so German strategy
called for the circumvention of that obstacle by a thrust across the
level terrain of Luxembourg and Belgium. Once France was crushed,
the military might of Germany would attend to the slow-moving Russian "steamroller."

Germany summoned Russia to revoke the general mobilization
order without delay. And at the same time the Germans inquired in
Paris whether France would stand aside in the event of a German-
Russian war.

From St. Petersburg there was no response. The French said that
national policy would be in harmony with national interests. Whereat
Germany declared war on Russia—August 1—and two days later
issued a like declaration against France. When Belgium manfully
refused free passage to German troops, soldiers were hurled into the
country whose perpetual neutrality was guaranteed by an old treaty of
which Germany was a co-signer.

While these vast and cataclysmic events were occurring, Italy,
third member of the Triplice, had announced her intention of staying
on the sidelines. Italy asserted that treaty commitments obligated her
to fight only in a defensive war and that this struggle did not belong
in that category. Rumania likewise chose the way of neutrality.

Great Britain, third partner in the Entente, after much squirming
and agonizing of spirit, lined up with Russia and France. On the question of war or peace Britain was a house divided; inside the cabinet
itself a majority seems for days to have been averse to participation.
Wherefore Grey's inability to assert categorically what Britain would
do; wherefore his equivocal responses to both French and German
requests for light on Britain's intentions. But after the German declaration of war upon Russia, Grey promised France that the British navy
would keep Germany from attacking French coasts and French shipping. Loud was the clamor for immediate intervention on the part of
Britishers who were anxious to remove the standing challenge of the

German High Seas fleet, and to forestall German mastery over Europe. On the other side, a group of British scholars declared that a war with Germany would be "a sin against civilization."

For many an ordinary Britisher the decisive reason for intervention was the pressure of German arms into Belgium, trampling upon a solemn international engagement and a small unoffending nation. When Germany declined to withdraw from Belgian soil, Britain declared war. Because of the global dimensions of the British realm, the struggle became forthwith a world war.

Within a month formal declarations of war on all sides rounded out the portrait of conflict. Rather curiously Austria refrained from declaring itself at war with Russia until insistently pressed to do so by Germany. Montenegro entered the lists against Austria, as presently did Great Britain and France. The Entente powers soon arranged a conventional alliance to supersede the pre-war diplomatic understandings, pledging themselves neither to seek nor make peace with the Central Powers without previous agreement. The press of the world thenceforward designated the Entente group as the "Allies."

Before the close of 1914 each belligerent camp was joined by an important satellite; the Allies by Japan, the Central Powers by Turkey. Britain's Oriental ally dispatched an ultimatum to Germany on August 15 "recommending" the prompt withdrawal of German naval units from Far Eastern seas and the surrender to Japan of German rights in the Chinese province of Shantung, "with a view to the eventual restoration of the same to China." When the Berlin government disdained to respond Nippon announced a state of war with Germany and proceeded to execute its conception of "manifest destiny" in the East. Japan acceded to the Allied treaty of alliance in October, 1915.

The Turkish alignment with the Central Powers followed a more complicated pattern. Just after Germany declared war upon Russia, hereditary enemy of the Ottoman and deeply covetous of Constantinople and the Turkish Straits, the Turks signed an old-fashioned secret military alliance with Berlin. Seemingly the treaty contained no promises of territorial reward to Turkey though the Turks evidently anticipated acquiring something on the conclusion of a victorious war. Undercover, Turkish diplomatists carried on bargaining with Allied foreign offices ostensibly to secure promises of gain for remaining neutral, but really to win time to prepare to fight.

The arrival of two hunted German men-of-war in Constantinople stimulated Turkish war fervor, and, when vessels flying the Ottoman flag shelled coastal towns in southern Russia, the Allies with one accord declared themselves at war with the Turks. For the Central

Powers, the participation of Turkey was a resounding diplomatic success and had large strategic advantage. For the Allies it meant the closure of the Straits to shipping to Russia, but it also smoothed the way for the furtherance of the tsardom's pretensions to Ottoman territory with Constantinople as the main prize. Britain annexed Cyprus and proclaimed herself the protector of Egypt without any strings attached.

The United States, in the meanwhile, on August 4 had proclaimed its neutrality, hoping to keep clear of all European entanglements.

War in the West: 1914

Popular enthusiasm over the coming of war, on the part of a generation which had little personal experience in armed combat, was almost universal. Press, priest, and politician dinned into men's ears the notion that "our country" was the innocent victim of a malevolent and predatory attack by the enemy. Men of every land, believing their country and their homes in peril, believing in the righteousness of their national cause or swept along in the billowing flood of national fervor, quit their everyday routine, and loyally responded to the summons to the colors.

Citizens of St. Petersburg staged impromptu patriotic demonstrations such as "Holy Russia" had seldom witnessed, serenading the Serbian, French, and British legations with juvenile boisterousness, and sacking the German embassy. Stolid, hearty mooshiks, called from the harvest field, marched singing to their mobilization depots. Masses of German civilians and soldiers chanting fierce Teutonic warrior hymns paraded down Berlin's famous Unter den Linden from the Brandenburg Gate to the imperial Schloss, there to hear stirring patriotic exhortations from the Kaiser in shining armor. Parisians, too, sang their battle anthems and congregated before the statue in the Place de la Concorde symbolizing the Alsatian city of Strasbourg and listened to the mayor of the district plead eloquently for revenge for 1870.

Everywhere light-hearted maidens garlanded marching legions with flowers, threw them kisses, or an occasional bottle of wine. Cheering burghers reminded youth that to die for one's country was a fine and noble ideal, that it was after all the other fellow who would not return to his family, that the whole glamorous business would be over by Christmas. The machinery of mobilization, long planned, moved like clockwork. It was imagined that the war would be of short duration in the manner of wars of the 19th century, and anyone who, like the British General Kitchener, intimated that the struggle might last two or even three years was howled down as a black-hearted pessimist.

Into the west of Europe seven highly-trained German armies moved, the most formidable military machine of history. Two armies were posted to contain the expected French thrust into Alsace-Lorraine, the other five swept into Belgium, pulverizing the fortifications of Liége en route. Belgian forces, after putting up a sturdy resistance, which disarranged the delicate German timetable, pulled back into fortified Antwerp thence to sally forth in sorties against the enemy until the city was reduced by bombardment. Like a tide—fast, gray, irresistible—the onrushing Germans struck into northern France, driving civilians by the hundreds of thousands before them with such possessions as they could carry.

It looked as though the German design of capturing Paris within six weeks would be achieved. French plans for a headlong smash across Alsace-Lorraine on the way to Berlin swiftly collapsed in sorry confusion. In order to escape envelopment or annihilation French troops steadily fell back before the German hosts. The British professional army of 160,000 which had promptly taken its place beside the French poilus, according to pre-arranged plan, shared in the general retreat to the Marne river. The Germans hammered their way as far as Meaux, a mere seventeen miles from Paris, from which the French government and half the civilian population fled.

Then occurred "the miracle of the Marne." So swiftly had the Germans advanced that the troops were exhausted, and the service of supply failed to keep pace. The right wing of the invading force, General von Kluck commanding, which had been entrusted with the assignment of encircling Paris, was weakened by the transfer of troops to the eastern end of the battlefront and by the diversion of divisions to East Prussia, where the soldiers of the tsar had marched more expeditiously than the German High Command had calculated. Before reaching Paris, von Kluck turned eastward, exposing his flank to counterattack. That opportunity the Allies grasped. Troops rushed from Paris in taxicabs, stabbed at the German line; the main body of the French armies under General Foch struck the enemy at the center. The British army gave a good account of its quality; the enemy fell back in precipitate withdrawal. Paris was spared and the grandiose German dream of a lethal knockout blow went glimmering.[2]

[2] When a battle or a war is lost, there are any number of explanations, as the rival memoirs of participating commanders bear witness. And, as the Battle of the Marne well illustrates, seldom is a battle won without the honor being claimed for one of several generals. Credit for the victory on the Marne in September, 1914, has been given to Joffre, the slow-moving French commander-in-chief; to Galliéni who rallied the taxicab army; to Manoury on the Ourcq; to Foch in the center; and to others. Actually they were all pieces in the collaboration for success; they all helped.

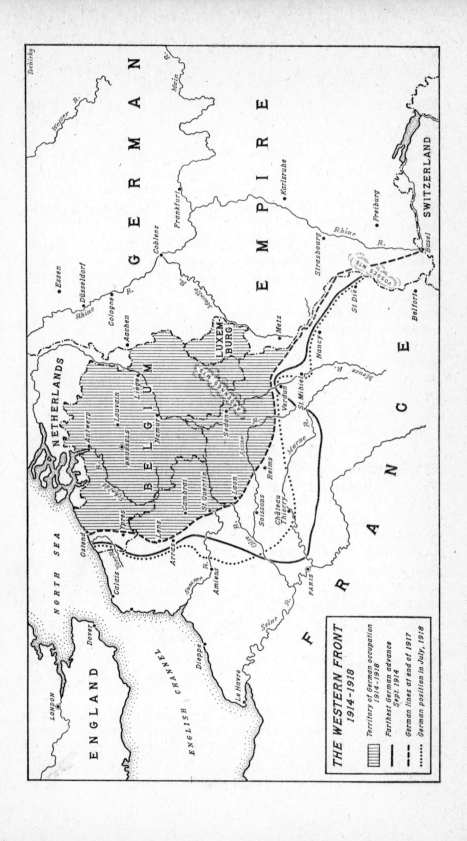

THE WESTERN FRONT
1914-1918

||| Territory of German occupation
1914-1918

——— Farthest German advance
Sept. 1914

– – – German lines at end of 1917

········ German position in July, 1918

Along the line of the Aisne river, a splendid natural rampart, the Germans dug themselves in, and the deadly machine-gun frustrated the Allied hope of forcing them back into Belgium. So, too, the German attempt to capture the French Channel ports, through which men and supplies were poured in from Britain, came to grief. From the Channel to the Swiss frontier two unbroken series of trenches were thrown up, barricaded with barbed-wire, and defended by rifle, machine gun, and artillery. The war of movement in the West was over, and little change in the battle line was to be effected for more than three dreary years.

Save for large-scale thrusts undertaken by both sides from time to time, fighting in the West meant forays out of one set of trenches toward or into those of the enemy, often only thirty yards away, rifle with bayonet attached and grenade in hand—that and repelling rival warriors trying to pierce the opposing trenches. The natural advantages in that kind of warfare were wholly on the side of the defenders. Fighting men learned to crouch in trenches and crawl on hands and feet in skirmish lines. Supporting the infantry and blasting the way for infantry assaults were thundering artillery. Planes overhead served chiefly as the eyes of the ground forces and were seldom employed on bombing missions.

Though not unknown before World War I, trench fighting amidst muck, mire, and vermin robbed combat of the romance with which military historians and novelists had invested it. Soldiers did not, with Walter Scott, experience "the stern joy which warriors feel in foemen worthy of their steel." War was hazardous, ugly, dirty, monotonous business for those who actually fought, regardless of the language they spoke. Still there was adventure, excitement, opportunity for personal valor and the men displayed remarkable endurance, patience, and no little good humor trying "to pack up their troubles in their old kit bags." The discomforts and agonies of the combatants contrasted with the patriotic fervor of civilians at home.

As masters of almost all of Belgium and northern France the Germans exploited the labor power, the valuable factories, and mineral resources of those areas. Fact and fable concerning the German mistreatment of the gallant and restive Belgians roused the pity and the anger of the outside world.

Since it was evident that the war would not soon be over, Britain proceeded to raise a large volunteer army. Placards appealed to youth that "King and Country Need You." By Christmas a million were undergoing training. In the Dominions, too, and among colonials, soldiers were recruited for the most gigantic of wars.

The Eastern Theater: 1914

Owing to the vastness of the area and the open terrain, eastern Europe offered a theater for larger operations than France. The armies of Russia, which had been the beneficiary of French military science and matériel and of the laying of strategic railways to the west, advanced faster than had been expected, moved out of Poland into East Prussia and into the Austrian province of Galicia. For several weeks the abounding faith of the western Allies in the juggernaut of the Tsar was amply rewarded.

Moving into East Prussia en route to Königsberg the dreaded Cossacks swept the countryside bare, driving panic-stricken peasants before them. Some of the refugees carried to Berlin tales of barbarity matching the horror stories of the Belgians. While the Allies exulted, German spirits drooped. At that juncture, as so often in the next four years, the Central Powers benefited from the advantages that operations on interior lines brought them, and profited from the superb German railway network. Soldiers were shunted east from the French front, and an old general of unexciting career, von Hindenburg, was summoned from retirement and put in nominal command of the armies in the East. Associated with him was a Bavarian staff officer, Ludendorff, whose daring in the attack on Liége had brought him into the limelight.

Before the end of August the Germans fought and defeated the Russians in the Battle of Tannenberg, the one really decisive struggle in the first phase of the war, for it meant that Germany would not be overrun by Russia. The soil of the Fatherland was cleared of the invader, and Hindenburg was hailed as the national savior. Though the triumph should largely be credited to the genius of a young officer, Colonel Hoffmann, Tannenberg made the reputation of Hindenburg and Ludendorff. It started them along the path that would eventually land them in supreme command of Germany's military energies and carry Hindenburg into the presidency of the German Republic. One day the mortal remains of the legend-encrusted hero would be interred on the edge of the Tannenberg battle-ground. Losses of Russian manpower and war matériel were huge, and optimistic Allied imaginings about the Russian "steam-roller" were dissipated. On the other side, German efforts to capture Warsaw fell short of their goal, though Lodz, the Polish textile capital, was taken.

Farther south the tide of battle had gone more favorably for the Allies. The multi-nationality armies of Austria made a slight advance into the southern sector of Russian Poland, only to be driven out and compelled to retreat in great confusion. Russians then marched across most of Galicia, taking small but strategically significant oil-fields on the way, and capturing half of the opposing Austrian troops, many of whom, especially dissident Czechs, preferred desertion to service under the Hapsburg flag. Only German victories to the north saved Austria from still more damaging humiliation. Thenceforth Germans largely planned Austrian campaigns and directed the disposition of Hapsburg armies. See-saw fighting yielded place to a primitive form of entrenchment reaching from the Baltic to Rumania, the longest battle-front of history.

Defeated in Galicia, Austria suffered another reverse in warfare with Serbia. The pre-war plan of administering swift and severe military punishment to the troublesome southern kingdom ended disastrously, in the tradition of Austrian arms of the 19th century. At some points, in fact, tough-fibered Serb soldiers crossed into Hapsburg territory and it was no light task to expel them. Balkan neutrals, who might have been influenced to join the Central Powers had Serbia been quickly crushed, continued to hang back.

Sea Warfare in 1914

Both sides having failed to score overmastering victories on land, seapower became an extremely important factor. This really meant the British fleet, for the vaunted German navy was reluctant to seek a resolute decision. Both Admiralties expected the other to take the offensive promptly, but they were disappointed. True, the British made an assault upon the German bases sheltered by the Heligoland fortress and German battle cruisers thrice made sallies against the east coast of England. But those episodes involved few warships and none of them implied departure from the fundamental policy of cautious conservatism.

In China, at Kiaochau, German forces in command of Admiral von Spee took to the sea just before Japan declared war. They sailed into the southern Pacific, destroyed a British squadron off Chile, and, in turn, were themselves sent to the bottom near the Falkland Islands.

In the meantime the British fleet cleared the Mediterranean of enemy surface craft and effectively closed the routes from the North Sea to the Atlantic to German shipping. The Allied blockade was aimed at starving out the Central Powers by denying them the importation of much needed war supplies. Within a week after fighting started, all but one enemy merchantmen were immured in neutral harbors or taken captive. Small German warships which roamed the seas destroying commerce carriers were eliminated before the end of 1914, with a solitary exception.

Allied command of the waves was then complete, making it feasible to move men and supplies freely and facilitating the conquest of Germany's colonies. Except for German East Africa, the Allies occupied the overseas holdings with little trouble. Japan established itself in the German position in Chinese Shantung and the Pacific island possessions above the equator, while Britishers occupied the islands to the south of that line.

But Allied mastery did not penetrate beneath the waves. Holding their battle-fleet in leash the Germans relied upon mines and the submarine to overcome British sea supremacy. In September, 1914, a U-boat torpedoed three old British cruisers, the biggest single bag of warships of the entire war. Submarine activity got on British nerves and caused the authorities to shift the stations on which the Grand Fleet was based to the west of Scotland. Early in 1915 the Germans applied the submarine weapon against vessels engaged in commerce.

The Dardanelles Fiasco

After Turkey entered the war Allied strategists set about devising means of unbolting the Straits and of capturing Constantinople, well-defended by nature and man. Russia, whose industry was unequal to a prolonged struggle, desperately needed munitions and guns from the West, which, so long as the Straits were barred, could only be secured in driblets by way of Archangel or across the Siberian vastness. Besides, if the passageway to the Black Sea were opened, the West might procure bread-grains from Russia and have the use of merchant shipping cooped up in the Black Sea.

If Turkey, moreover, were knocked out of the war, wavering Balkan neutrals might plump for the Allied cause. Mastery over Constantinople and the Straits, too, stood high on the agenda of Russian war objectives. In March, 1915, Britain and France formally agreed that Russia should have them at the end of the war, together with a strip of Turkish territory in Asia Minor. Imperial Russian policy-makers exulted over the prospect of achieving, in the language of one of them, "the immemorial and sacred dream of the Russian people."

All in all the gains which a successful attack upon Turkey would bring were quite alluring. The virtues of immediate operations were vigorously argued by Winston Churchill, first sea-lord of the Admiralty, while British and French army leaders contended that the war could only be won in France and frowned upon the diversion of military resources against Turkey. They, however, were overborne. First, an exclusively naval expedition was ordered to smash through the Dardanelles, but the attack was broken off because of the hazards of mines, just when the Turkish resistance (as was later learned) had almost run out.

The task was then assigned to an Allied military contingent composed mostly of eager raw troops from Australia and New Zealand—the Anzacs, for short—with modest naval support. Greek military assistance was proffered but vetoed by Russia, which was itself unable to despatch a cooperating army as promised. Against superhuman odds Allied troops were landed on the Gallipoli peninsula in April. Wasting fighting ensued, leaving the invaders with only precarious toeholds. After a small offensive, made in August at heavy cost, the Allied commanders reluctantly decided to admit failure. At the end of the year the remaining soldiers were disembarked to the Greek port of Salonika.

The Dardanelles enterprise, which entailed some 150,000 British casualties, was a tragic fiasco, costly for Allied prestige and depressing to morale. Probably if greater resolution and better cooperation had been displayed in the initial assault the goal would have been achieved. If the door to Russia had been opened, admitting war supplies from the West, it is possible that the Revolutions of 1917 would not have occurred.

Italy Enters

In the midst of the Dardanelles adventure, while stagnation persisted in France, and the Germans were driving the Russians eastward with sledgehammer blows, Allied spirits were lifted by news that Italy had forsaken her old Triplice friends and had entered the Entente partnership. It was a striking Allied coup, hailed as assuring the speedier termination of the conflict and an act that might induce Rumania to join the Allies.

The Italian decision for war was made after months of tortuous, realistic diplomacy, whose guiding purpose was, in the words of the war-time Premier, Salandra, "the completion of Italian unity, the extension of Italy to the boundaries consecrated by nature and tradition." Translated, that meant possession of Hapsburg territory inhabited by men of Italian speech and adjacent areas that were considered desirable either for security or for national prestige.

Three schools of opinion emerged in the confused debate in Italy on war or peace. The least weighty group subscribed to the maintenance of neutrality without reservation. Much stronger was a group that would hold to neutrality and negotiate with the Central Powers for the cession of *Italia Irredenta* (Unredeemed Italy). It was urged that at least part of the territorial aspirations could be realized without the shedding of blood and the balance would be gained upon the dissolution of the Hapsburg monarchy, which could not be long postponed. Prominent advocate of that line of diplomatic strategy was Giovanni Giolitti, the most influential figure on the Italian political stage and the manipulator of a majority of the deputies in the Parliament.

To the third, the frank interventionist school, belonged the Salandra ministry and miscellaneous political fragments, among them the faction of Socialists which followed the lead of a young and radical journalist, Benito Mussolini. Once a militant internationalist and fiercely critical of militarism, he had come forward as an arch-interventionist in the columns of his Socialist newspaper.

Meantime the Italian ministry was having the exciting experience of being wooed by two suitors, both ardent: the Central Powers, with Germans acting as spokesmen, and the Allies. Negotiations on the Italian side were cold, calm, calculating in the best traditions of Old World diplomacy. Baron Sonnino, more financier than diplomatist, albeit a canny and hard bargainer, directed the transactions for Italy.

Without giving Vienna much say in the matter the Germans sought to purchase continued Italian neutrality with promises of Austrian soil, in itself a sign of Austrian subordination to Germany. Austria, in fact, agreed to cede the southern end of the Tyrol, but balked at handing over Trieste, the "lung" of the monarchy, which the Italians demanded.

On their part the Allies could barter away the whole Hapsburg realm and be none the loser. Allied agents were somewhat disconcerted by Italian pretensions to Dalmatia, peopled largely by Yugoslavs and coveted by Serbia. But they gave way in order to have Italian military cooperation. The final Allied-Italian bargain was embalmed in the famous Treaty of London of April 26, 1915; for concrete rewards, Italy would fight the Central Powers and make peace in company with the Allies. The latter bound themselves to support Italy with naval forces and funds and promised indemnities from the enemy when the war was over. In the matter of territory Italy would obtain the Tyrol up to the peak of the Brenner Pass, Trieste, the Istrian peninsula, and the northern stretch of Dalmatia, together with fringing islands. Somewhat elastic articles promised Italy colonial expansion in Africa and a sphere of interest in Asiatic Turkey.

Presently Italy formally announced withdrawal from the Triplice. Furious excitement gripped the Italian public mind as interventionist battled non-interventionist. Giolitti adamantly stood his ground. But when enflamed militant mobs fell upon non-interventionist deputies, Giolitti fled from Rome. The Chamber then voted Salandra a free hand, and on May 23, 1915, a declaration of war was delivered to Austria, though not until August, 1916, did Italy make war upon Germany. It was a divided nation that entered the titanic struggle. Some Italians were quite unreconciled to the war verdict, while the interventionists themselves held markedly divergent ideas as to the objectives for which war was being waged.

Geographical conditions limited Italian military operations mainly to the comparatively level terrain of the Isonzo area, pointing toward the prized city of Trieste. Battle after battle was fought, with heavier casualties for Italy than Austria and precious little territorial gain for either belligerent—that and rugged mountain fighting, artillery duels from mountain peak to mountain peak. In the spring of 1916 Austria launched a campaign out of the Tyrol, planned on a vast scale, and pushed the foe back by sheer weight of metal. Then a renewed thrust of the Russians into Galicia obliged Austria to concentrate her strength in that theatre and break off the Italian operations. Whereupon the Italians assumed the offensive and made meager advances, only to be stopped by German gunners and commanders rushed in to stiffen the Hapsburg troops.

Conquest of Poland: 1915

The Polish province of Galicia changed hands several times during World War I. In 1914 the Russians, as has been recounted, expelled the Austrian armies from most of the district, but in 1915, due in substantial measure to German leadership and troops, Galicia was reconquered. A surprise attack in May, 1915, accompanied by an immense concentration of artillery, caused the poorly-weaponed Muscovites to crumple up and abandon almost all of the province.

That Galician campaign was a part—and not the major part—of the German attempt to knock Russia completely out of the struggle in 1915. As early as February, amidst frightful weather conditions, German armies, striking into Poland from the north, sent the enemy reeling. A small-scale repetition of Tannenberg—the battle in Masuria— was added to the string of German victories, but the Russian armies were not entrapped and fresh battalions were thrown onto the fighting line. Pressing then from the west the Germans relentlessly hammered

their way into Warsaw, focal point of converging railways, which capitulated in August, just a year after the start of the fighting. Polish
refugees by the hundreds of thousands choked the lines of Russian
retreat or were shoved to their death in marshlands along the highways by desperate soldiers.

By the coming of winter the hard-beset Muscovites had fallen back
of the dreary Pripet Marshes after one of the most terrible routs on
record. Well over a million Slavs had been killed or wounded in the
ruinous fighting in Poland, and almost as many had been taken prisoner—losses approached 2,300,000—and indispensable stocks of military equipment had fallen to the enemy. Russian zest for the war,
Russian national patriotism, never so robust in the empire of peasants
as in the countries to the west, dwindled sharply. In fact, the regime of
Nicholas II never recovered from the ghastly consequences of the
debacle in Poland. Yet by drawing troops of the Central Powers away
from other fronts the Russians had materially benefited the cause of
the Allies.

Conquest of Russian Poland precipitated a debate in Berlin and in
the Hapsburg capitals on the administration of the region. Germans
wanted it kept under their military rule, while Austria proposed that it
be merged with Galicia and form a third state in the Hapsburg realm.
But that plan was anathema to Magyar oligarchs and to Germans as
well, who were sure that a reunited Poland would seek to acquire the
Polish districts of Prussia. The Germans carried the day but at the
cost of alienating Polish patriots who up to that point had fought
loyally for the Central Powers.

The Near Eastern "Side-Show"

Impressed by the course of the war against Russia, Bulgaria
aligned itself with the German coalition, the last of the states to do
so. Bulgaria's intervention was in harmony with the national peasant
saying, "We will choose for our aunt the one who will give us the
largest cake." The Bulgarian ruling caste, headed by foxy Tsar Ferdinand, nursed memories of grievous defeats in 1913 and of land to be
redeemed. Most desired were irredentist claims on Serbia and feeling
against Russia, the long-time friend and liberator of Bulgaria, ran high
because of the Tsar's failure to restrain Serbian avarice in 1913.

Yet Russian agents offered Bulgaria "cake" in the shape of a piece
of Turkey and besought Serbia to appease Bulgarian ambitions—but
in vain. To promises of territorial gains and material support the

Central Powers added cash, judiciously distributed among Bulgar
leaders in exchange for leading their country into war. A formal treaty
was signed in September, 1915, assuring Bulgaria of a large area of
Serbia after victory was won. Anti-war and pro-Entente spokesmen
were imprisoned or otherwise silenced as Bulgaria, her armies somewhat recovered from the disasters of 1913, launched out in new war on
the hereditary foe, Serbia. Bulgar leaders were confident that in allying their country with Germany they were backing a sure winner.

Bulgaria's intervention sounded the death-knell for Serbia. While
Bulgar troops punched in from the east, two large German and Austrian armies, with the able German, August Mackensen, in command,
marched down from the north. Such massive superiority overbore the
Serbs, who, fighting hard and scorching the earth as they went, retreated southward and into Albania. Greece, which by treaty was
bound to rally to the assistance of Serbia, proved faithless to her bond.
And the decimated remnant of the gallant Serb army together with
the government took sanctuary in the island of Corfu, there to await
an opportune time to re-enter the struggle. Conquest of Montenegro
followed the conquest of Serbia. After that, the Central Powers could
boast that they held uninterrupted mastery from the North Sea to
the Tigris River.

To the Tigris River, for at that point, a small British army was
posted. Not long after Turkey entered the struggle, an Anglo-Indian
force was landed at the head of the Persian Gulf for the twin purpose
of safeguarding vital oil supplies from Persia (Iran) and of buttress-
ing British prestige throughout the Near East. That army slogged its
way into Mesopotamia, moving to within easy reach of fabled Bagdad.
Stiffened Turkish resistance along the Tigris, however, obliged the
invader to pull back to Kut-el-Amara to await re-enforcements. But
after a grueling siege the small British army at Kut capitulated to the
Turk in April, 1916.

Somewhat offsetting that humiliating reversal for Allied arms in
the Near East were the gains won by Russia at the expense of the
Turk. Early in the fighting tsarist forces had penetrated into north-
eastern Turkey, and had subsequently invested the "Armenian" stronghold of Erzerum. That city was captured in February, 1916, and the
Russians pushed on to the Black Sea port of Trebizond and into
provinces inhabited by Armenians. Aware that Armenian nationalists
were ready to cooperate with the invader in order to liberate themselves from the Ottoman yoke, the Turkish authorities ordained a
wholesale and revolting massacre of the defenseless population. Scores

of thousands perished or became homeless wanderers, as that pitiless chapter in the long record of man's inhumanity to man was written.[3]

Farther south Allied agents, British chiefly, caused trouble for Turkey by stirring Arab chieftains to rebel. Though Moslems in religion Arab leaders had declined to respond to a proclamation of the Turkish sultan for a "jihad" or holy war against the Christian foe; rather they saw—or some of them did—an opportunity to free themselves of Turkish overlordship and create some kind of an independent Arab state. Nascent nationalism, lust for booty, and British cash brought certain of the chieftains to the Allied side. Vague promises of political independence for a substantial Arab empire were made to Hussein, the Sherif of Mecca, who roused his Bedouin warriors to insurrections against the Turk.

With a bit of precision the extent of the prospective Arab kingdom was defined in an inter-Allied secret treaty of May, 1916—the Sykes-Picot Pact—parceling out the Ottoman estate in Asia. It was agreed that after hostilities had ceased, Britain would have most of Mesopotamia; France, Syria and Lebanon; Russia, Armenia and Kurdistan. The fourth major ally, Italy, was overlooked. Palestine would be assigned a special international status, and the remaining districts of Arab residence would constitute an Arab state, half under British, half under French tutelage.

Rumania Joins the Allies

After hemming and hawing, and assiduously bargaining with both sets of belligerents for two years Rumania, at length, in August, 1916, placed her sword at the disposal of the Allies. That decision was a direct by-product of a sensational Russian offensive—and the last— into battered Galicia. In a measure the Russian thrust, which was initiated in the mid-summer of 1916, was made in response to urgent pleas from the western Allies for operations that would compel the Germans and Austrians to shift troops to the east and so relieve pressure in the Verdun and Italian theaters.

At the start the Russians, under the command of General Brusilov, crowded into Galicia with surprising momentum, corralling 350,000 Austrian prisoners and deserters, and conquering some 10,000 square miles in a month. The rosy vision of an irresistible tsarist

---

[3] The incredible suffering of the Armenian Christians has been dramatized in Franz Werfel, *The Forty Days of Musa Dagh* (New York, 1934).

steam-roller danced once more before western eyes. But those fond expectations swiftly evaporated; for with re-enforcements from France and Italy the Central Powers counterattacked in great force, causing heavy Russian losses, though not on the grandiose scale of 1915.

For the last time the Russians had sacrificed themselves in the common cause of Allied victory and by then the reserve capital of Russian national patriotism had been about used up. The objective of lessening German and Austrian pressure on other fronts had been achieved, and, as another consequence of the Brusilov offensive, Falkenhayn, director-in-chief of the German war-machine since his supersession of Moltke after the reversal on the Marne, was dismissed in favor of the Hindenburg-Ludendorff team.

Beyond that, as has been remarked, Rumania chose the Galician offensive to announce her affiliation with the Allies. Though secretly allied to the Triplice, Rumania had declared its neutrality, like Italy, with the onset of war; and, like Italy again, Rumania's support was courted by both belligerent groups and her political leaders were divided over the course to pursue. Realistically they decided to seek the highest possible price for the invaluable oil resources and the grain of their nation. German agents first tried to obtain Rumanian cooperation by dangling Bessarabia and other parcels of coveted Russian territory before Rumanian eyes. Subsequently, the Germans tried to repeat the process attempted with Italy in 1915, of buying off Rumania with promises of Hapsburg territory, mainly the Hungarian province of Transylvania which contained a Rumanian majority. But the Magyar ruling oligarchy imposed a veto on any territorial concession.

By promising Rumania all of the Hapsburg monarchy that the kingdom desired, the Allies purchased her intervention on their side. According to a secret treaty of August, 1916, Rumania would go to war with the Hapsburg monarchy and would not make a separate peace. As compensation the Allies gave the kingdom territorial pledges that were "scandalously immoderate," as one British admirer of Rumania judges the contract. Rumania would obtain not alone Transylvania but also the Banat of Temesvar and the Austrian province of the Bukovina—much more than Rumania could rightfully claim on grounds of nationality. Assurances of Allied military assistance were also made.

At the end of August, in spite of the inferior character of her fighting services, and fully aware of the nature of contemporary warfare, Rumania went to war against Austria-Hungary. Germany and her Balkan satellites at once took up arms against Rumania. For a brief, intoxicating moment, Rumanian soldiers occupied sections of promised Transylvania.

Then disaster followed disaster. Austro-German armies, well-equipped and skillfully directed, cleared the foe from Transylvania and stormed through the passes of the Carpathians, while a Bulgarian force marched into Rumania from the south. Less than four months after the fighting started, Bucharest, the Rumanian capital, had fallen to the invaders. Crippled Rumanian armies beat their way to the north where for a year they conducted a courageous but futile resistance. Almost all of the kingdom's resources—of which the oil fields were of major significance—passed to the Central Powers; and the Russian battlefront was lengthened by about 300 miles.

Greece and Portugal Abandon Neutrality

Greece, the only Balkan nation not yet at war, teamed up with the Allies in the summer of 1917. From the beginning of the European conflict Greece was the scene of a bitter tug-of-war between the pro-German King Constantine and the pro-ally Cretan politician, Eleutherios Venizelos, and their respective followers. Venizelos' repeated efforts to get Greece into the war on the Allied side were successfully thwarted by the king, though he did secure permission for Allied forces, evacuated from the Dardanelles area, to establish themselves in the port of Salonika. That city and its environs passed under untrammeled Allied control, and in time half a million troops were collected there—the biggest camp of Allied war prisoners, the Germans jibed, and with reason—until the closing stage of the great conflict. Greek protestations that the Allies were violating the sovereignty of the little kingdom were brushed aside with casuistry.

At Salonika Venizelos proclaimed a provisional revolutionary government and organized a revolutionary army, with the blessing of Britain and France. Then in the early summer of 1917 King Constantine was sent on his travels and Greece formally declared war on the Central Powers. Greece came in without benefit of a secret treaty, but verbal assurances of golden rewards were given to Venizelos.

Portugal, in the meantime, had joined the swelling Allied throng. Attached to Britain by bonds of sentiment, interest, and by ancient treaty, the Portuguese government reacted hostilely to raids of German colonials into her African colonies. On urgings from Britain Portugal seized German merchantmen tied up in the country's harbors, to which Germany retorted in March, 1916, with a war declaration. Soldiers of Portugal fought on the battlefields of France and in African theaters.

The Persistent Neutrals

Spain to the end of the war contrived to hold to a policy of friendship with all belligerents without too great intimacy with any of them. On ideological grounds there was no little pro-Ally sentiment in Spain which might have attained interventionist dimensions if the British, for example, had been willing to hand over the citadel of Gibraltar, but of that there was not the slightest sign. Sympathizers with the Central Powers were numerous, but Allied supremacy on the sea, if nothing else, prohibited any Spanish assistance to Germany. Serving as an arsenal for the Allies, Spain prospered materially. It performed much useful humanitarian service, and often acted as a kind of diplomatic errand boy between the warring coalitions.

Holland and the Scandinavian countries, too, escaped involvement in World War I. Surrounded as it was by belligerents, Holland managed to keep out of the struggle because it behaved as a neutral was expected to behave. Neither coalition felt it desirable to implicate her in the war, though hostilities were threatened at least three times by Germany. Dutch shipping was ravaged by U-boats and domestic well-being was greatly disturbed by the Allied blockade, by German economic controls, by the presence of about a million Belgian refugees, and the necessity of keeping the national army on a war footing.

Wartime conditions in Denmark closely paralleled those in Holland, except that Danish economy profited moderately from sales to belligerents. The heart of Denmark was with the Allies, for one reason because Danes hoped that German defeat would make possible the recovery of the province of Schleswig, which Prussia had filched away in the 1860's.

Neither belligerent group seriously tried to enlist the active participation of Norway or Sweden. Norwegian shipping suffered heavy losses through submarine action, almost half the tonnage being destroyed, and more than 2,000 Norwegian sailors perished. But Norway remained neutral or, to speak more accurately, became a "nonbelligerent ally" of the Allies who hired her merchant navy. Unemployed Norwegian shipwrights found their way to the United States, where they applied their skills to the construction of ships.

Sweden, too, remained neutral though traditional distrust of Russia, and suspicions that the tsardom had hostile designs upon the country's integrity predisposed many Swedes to open sympathy with Germany. Trade between Sweden and Germany boomed; and Britain's rigorous blockade created ill-feeling against her. Individual Swedes

THE EASTERN FRONT
WORLD WAR I

Germany, Austria-Hungary
and their Allies

Countries at war with
Teutonic Allies

German position in 1918

Miles
0   100   200   300

busied themselves in a variety of Red Cross and kindred relief activities serving all belligerents with even-handed impartiality.

Campaigns in France: 1915-1916

Prodigious though the scale of military operations was in Europe's east, and impressive though the triumphs of German and Hapsburg arms were, the ultimate verdict would be delivered in France where the fighting had resolved itself into siege and countersiege on a magnitude unparalleled in history. Here and there the line of battle bent, now this way, now that, without however breaking.

British armies in March, 1915, opened up an offensive at Neuve Chapelle with a terrific hurricane of steel, but supplies of munitions were insufficient to keep the attack going and only slight gains of territory were made. Presently the Germans attacked with chlorine gas, a novel weapon, which surprised the enemy, but the Germans failed to follow through, apparently because they had little faith in the efficacy of gas. Though gas warfare was not explicitly banned by international convention the inhumanity of the weapon sent a thrill of horror across the Allied world and the United States; here was a fresh manifestation of German barbarism and brutality. The Allies retaliated in kind and in the long run gas warfare hurt the Germans far more than the Allies; it is significant that gas was not used in World War II, though whether out of fear of retaliation or because of tactical limitations and the thoroughness of enemy preparations to meet such an attack is an open question. Before long, the French brought forth an equally repulsive weapon, the flame-thrower, which burned men to death by liquid fire.

Several other Allied attempts to break the deadlock in France were undertaken in 1915 without accomplishing anything noteworthy. It was clear that more shells and guns were urgently needed, and to that end British munitions factories were speeded up and large orders were placed with manufacturing firms in the United States. The Germans, on their part, improved their defensive position in France, preferring to concentrate their fire-power in 1915 on the massive onslaught into Russian Poland.

On February 21, 1916, the bloodiest chapter in the history of war began in France and it lasted more than nine months. That was the epic Battle of Verdun on the Meuse. Verdun, the main pillar of the Allied defense line, was the very gateway into France. To capture it the German High Command assembled the flower of its armies. Having learned in the eastern campaigns of the effectiveness of artillery, the Germans started the attack on Verdun with the heaviest bombardment of big projectiles known to history.

A triple girdle of ramparts encircled Verdun. Strongest of them was Douaumont, which William II described as "the cornerstone of the most powerful fortress of our principal enemy." The Germans captured it in the first week of the battle. But that success was not the end; it was merely the beginning. French re-enforcements were rushed in by motor truck and for weeks the struggle swayed back and forth.

On July 1 the British opened a large scale counter-offensive on the Somme causing the Germans to reduce the suffocating pressure on Verdun. But the fighting at Verdun raged on into October when the French, after laying down a mighty barrage, retook Douaumont. Inspired by the battle cry, "Ils ne passeront pas," popularized by General Pétain, the French poilus by their unfaltering endurance and grim heroism, in week upon week of desperate fighting, had saved their country—and shattered the popular illusion that Frenchmen were a race of nimby-nambies.

The Germans did not pass, but from the territorial standpoint the Verdun operations achieved little, for trench lines at the end of the fighting had returned almost to their former positions. French casualties at Verdun passed the 450,000 mark, while the German losses ranged even higher. After Verdun the British bore the main brunt of the Allied fighting on French soil.

Almost equally destructive of life and not much more productive territorially speaking was the British-German Battle of the Somme. General Haig, the British commander-in-chief, relied mainly on the "New Army" which had been raised by voluntary enlistment; universal conscription was not made law in Britain until the spring of 1916. A prolonged intense artillery barrage preceded British infantry assaults, which netted only small gains. Then the Germans counter-attacked and the rival armies slugged it out doggedly for four months with sickening casualties in British ranks—the "Blood Bath," the Germans called it.

It was on the Somme that the "land-dreadnaught" or "tank," a British weapon, made its debut. Though not particularly successful at first, the potentialities of the tank were immediately apparent and mass production of the new weapon was authorized. When the cannon on the Somme were silenced, British arms had conquered a strip of soil thirty miles long and seven miles deep, at a cost of 410,000 casualties!

In spite of prodigal expenditures of men and matériel, battlelines in France at the end of 1916 almost paralleled those at the beginning of the previous year.

Sea Warfare, 1915-1916

On the blue sea the Allies were supreme and drew the noose of the blockade ever tighter round the Central Powers. It was the British intention, as Sir Edward Grey wrote, to secure "the maximum of blockade that could be enforced without a rupture with the United States." In pursuing that policy British seapower repeatedly did violence to the American contention that the property of neutrals was exempt from capture at sea. Indeed, Anglo-American relations were on occasion strained almost to the point of snapping. But the challenge of German submarine warfare to American lives, as distinguished from the British seizure of property, for which compensation was assured, stirred up much more violent antagonism in the United States.

To war upon the Allies at sea and to counteract the British blockade, the Germans counted heavily on mine and submarine, especially on the submarine, "the weapon of opportunity," as it was called by the experts, a novel and "untried naval toy." Early in February, 1915, the German government announced that U-boats would torpedo vessels entering the ports of Great Britain, and thereby stirred up a hornet's nest. According to international custom a warship was obligated to visit and search a merchantman and to remove the crew before destroying it, but no rules had been devised for the submarine, whose size made it ordinarily impracticable to take care of the crew of a merchant vessel. Moreover, if a U-boat warned an intended victim of an attack, it might invite destruction by gun-fire or ramming.

At the outset of the submarine warfare German commanders observed the traditional procedure of sending boarding parties onto enemy ships, but British defensive measures on the main sea-lanes proved so deadly that the U-boats resorted to sniping cargo carriers with dread torpedoes. Yet more frequently than not, to the end of 1916, submarine commanders warned their prey of an attack, permitting people on board to take to life boats.

Britain replied to the German submarine order of February, 1915, by extending the list of articles, spoken of as contraband, that might not be shipped to central Europe without danger of capture and expropriation. And the United States, most powerful of neutrals, and extremely sensitive to any infringement of freedom on the seas, protested angrily over the February proclamation, condemning it as a violation of international law. The United States declared that it would hold the imperial German government to "strict accountability" if American ships were attacked and would do whatever seemed necessary to protect American lives and property on the high seas, presumably whether on a belligerent or a neutral vessel. From the position thus taken the United States never really budged throughout the ensuing controversy with the Berlin government over the submarine weapon. Indeed, retreat from that attitude once it was assumed would have been very difficult.

On its part Germany disclaimed any intention to torpedo American ships deliberately but warned that accidents might happen. At the same time Germany registered a bitter complaint over the sale of American-made war materials to her enemies. It was, however, established convention for a belligerent to buy war supplies in a neutral country and the United States declined to debate the matter.

With only about twenty five submarines in commission in February, 1915, the German destruction of shipping was not large in the beginning—some ninety vessels in the first eleven weeks. Yet among the ships attacked was an American tanker, the *Gulflight,* and three Americans were drowned. In the early afternoon of May 7, 1915, a torpedo from the submarine U-20 streaked through the water a dozen miles off the southern coast of Ireland and struck the British liner, *Lusitania,* squarely amidships on the starboard side. Within eighteen minutes the great ship settled by the head after listing far to starboard, and then plunged to the bottom. With her 1,198 persons, including 128 Americans, several of them prominent, were carried to watery graves.

The *Lusitania* tragedy had momentous repercussions in the United States. For, in addition to the inhumanity of it all, the American doctrine of the immutable rights of its nationals on the seas had been wantonly defied in a shocking manner. Indignation against Germany surged across the nation and, for the first time, the possibility of war with Germany was seriously debated in public. By sinking the *Lusitania,* the German U-boat commander immensely and permanently increased American hostility toward his country. Yet the decision of the United States to become a belligerent was not taken until twenty three months later.

The government of the United States chose to seek redress for the loss of American lives on the *Lusitania* and the infringement of neutral rights on the sea through diplomatic channels. For weeks exchanges were carried on with the Berlin authorities, who tried to justify the *Lusitania* attack on the ground that she was transporting munitions, as she was. Nonetheless the United States insisted that unrestricted submarine warfare must be abandoned under pain of war.

Eventually, though not until other guerilla attacks at sea had taken several more American lives, Germany promised not to fire on unarmed liners without warning and without providing for people aboard. That decision had been reached only after furious controversy between German civilian and naval leaders. Admiral von Tirpitz, who believed that unfettered use of the U-boat would bring quick victory, resigned as head of the Admiralty in protest. It appeared that the United States had won its case. For eighteen months the undersea craft performed only limited operations. But the Germans had not assented to the American thesis that unrestricted U-boat warfare was unlawful.

Britain strove to combat the U-boat by arming merchant vessels, by fighting it with units of the fleet and, up to a point, by convoying ships. Construction of commerce carriers was also accelerated.

The closest approach to a naval battle in World War I took place off Jutland on May 31, 1916, when the British and German fleets met accidentally. Fought in a haze, the battle lasted only six hours. While engaged in one of its periodic sweeps down the North Sea the vanguard of the British Grand Fleet sighted German warcraft and opened fire at 16,000 yards. The German force bested its opponent and followed in hot pursuit when the British ships turned north to join the main body of the Grand Fleet. As the immensely stronger Grand Fleet steamed up, the Germans pulled back. Britain's commander-in-chief, Jellicoe, cautiously kept his ships out of areas where he suspected there were enemy submarines and mines. The Germans adopted hit-and-run tactics.

After inflicting more damage than it had suffered, the German navy found itself cut off from its bases, but under cover of darkness the ships slipped into home ports. Both sides claimed victory. With accuracy the British statesman, Lloyd George, summed up the Jutland battle as "a muddled and drawn Trafalgar, where both fleets sailed at full speed from each other's range and each claimed victory as soon as they reached the port of safety." German tactics and gunnery were superb and losses in men and tonnage were only half the British. On the other hand, British superiority in seapower was still very great and the British fleet still ruled the surface of the seas. Bickering and recrimination over the British conduct at Jutland raged for years.

After Jutland, surface operations at sea were merely of a spasmodic character. Very soon the decision was taken in Germany to seek victory by the unrestricted application of the submarine weapon.

Peace Gestures

Until 1916, at least, the opinion prevailed in belligerent countries that the only way to peace was through total military victory. From almost the beginning of the fighting Pope Benedict XV had initiated moves to bring about the return of peace by diplomatic action. And twice the American Colonel House, as special emissary of President Wilson, toured the principal belligerent capitals seeking to arrange conditions under which peace might be restored by diplomacy. But neither of these missions yielded productive results.

Toward the end of 1916, however, the general European situation appeared to be favorable for gestures looking toward peace without victory. More than two years of wasting and expensive fighting, and growing privations, had generated considerable war-weariness. Everywhere the effervescent enthusiasm that had characterized the first months of the struggle had disappeared. Something akin to gloom pervaded the Allied world because of the "Blood Baths" at Verdun and on the Somme, the indecisiveness of Jutland, the stalemate on the Italian front, multiplying evidences of an impending explosion in Russia, and the virtual elimination of Rumania from the struggle.

Though popular morale in Germany was still high, there were gnawing doubts as to ultimate victory, especially in view of the failure at Verdun. Food prospects were dim, and a left-wing Socialist faction was stirring up agitation for a compromise peace. More perilous by far were the situation and the prospects in the Hapsburg monarchy. Restlessness among minority populations, injurious to the war effort, was rising and desperate food shortages in the Austrian half of the realm, together with heavy casualties, had seriously impaired the will to fight. Moreover, in November, 1916, the patriarchal Francis Joseph having died at long last, a new Emperor-King, Charles, had assumed the Hapsburg crowns and he was known to be peace-minded, if not indeed a pacifist.

It was against that background that the German government, shortly before Christmas of 1916, published a call for a negotiated peace—the first gesture of the sort made by a belligerent country. The Central Powers, the note affirmed, had no desire to annihilate their foes, preferred rather a parley to consider how to end the war. But no mention was made of the terms upon which the Central Powers would stop fighting. An arrogant tone suffused the document and the enemy was warned of the dire fate which would follow if the fighting was continued. The Allied governments ridiculed the German overture as transparently insincere and uncompromisingly rejected it, which elicited from William II an assertion to the effect that arms would compel the enemy to sue for peace.

President Wilson, meantime, had come to the conclusion that he should try his hand at preparing the way for cessation of hostilities. His thought was shaped partly by considerations of national self-interest, above all, by the belief that the United States might be implicated in the war unless it were stopped, and partly by the dictates of humanity. The President requested the belligerents to state explicitly the terms on which they would be willing to cease fighting, as a basis for discussion, and he added that once peace was restored the United States would cooperate in maintaining peace.

Without immediately stating any exact conditions of peace the German government expressed a willingness to enter into a discussion with the other belligerents. The Allies, indignant that the President should ask what they were fighting for, disclaimed any desire to dismember Germany, but laid down territorial conditions that could not have been realized short of complete military victory. Both replies viewed favorably, although vaguely, Wilson's suggestion for a union of the nations for lasting peace and justice after the war.

Nothing of consequence, in short, resulted from the President's initiative. But, undaunted, he proceeded to deliver one of his more memorable orations, setting forth his own ideas on the conditions of peace and stressing his conviction that a settlement made after crushing military defeat by either side would not long endure. "Victory," said the President prophetically, "would mean peace forced upon the loser. . . . It would be accepted in humiliation, under duress, at an intolerable sacrifice, and would leave a sting, a resentment, a bitter memory upon which terms of peace would rest, not permanently, but only as upon quicksand. Only a peace between equals can last."

Wilson was thinking in terms of a settlement resting upon democratic principles, "freedom of the seas," limitation of armaments, and an international league for security. Hardly had the echoes of the President's utterance died away before Germany revealed that submarine warfare without pity would be revived. With that announcement, notions of peace without victory were put aside.

CHAPTER III

The Road to Allied Victory

The United States and the War

WHEN war broke over Europe in the summer of 1914, the common reaction in the United States was one of shocked incredulity. Poorly informed on the international anarchy of the Old World—and little interested in it—men and women in a country where hatred of war was deeply embedded looked upon the European struggle as the acme of unreason and folly, an anachronism hard in truth to comprehend.

At the moment American public interest was concentrated on such domestic questions as combatting depression in business, anti-trust legislation, proposals to restrict the use of alcoholic beverages, or to extend the voting right to women. In the press of the nation a lively controversy was raging as to whether a third-rate French print, *September Morn*, portraying a maiden, nude and shivering on the water's edge, should be applauded as artistic or banned as obscene. On the international horizon the big issues from the standpoint of the United States were not the gathering of war clouds in Europe but an acute contretemps with Mexico, a dispute with Japan growing out of discriminatory land laws in California, the gala opening of he Panama Canal, and the expansion of American seapower.

With the onset of the European conflict, President Wilson proclaimed the neutrality of the United States, an act that was entirely in keeping with the established principle of holding aloof from the political controversies of the Old World. The President wishfully summoned his countrymen to observe neutrality in mind and spirit. But in this "nation of nations" that was not to be. News on the war, coming very largely through Allied channels, stirred up ardent responses in governing circles and in the public at large.

Kinship of language, community of political ideals and democratic traditions, bonds of literature and religion and culture, and economic ties rallied warm personal feelings in the United States for

Britain. Prince Bismarck, it is said, once remarked that the community of language between Britain and the United States would be a cardinal factor in world politics of the 20th century. Hallowed memories of the indispensable French aid given to the American colonists struggling for independence, and the broad identity of French and American ideologies, made France the most popular of the Allied belligerents in the United States.

Besides, the heroic resistance of Belgium to the German invader and the physical outrages visited upon the population by the Germans elicited widespread sympathy and relief for that plucky little country. Only Imperial Russia among the original Allies had few well-wishers in the United States. Italy's intervention roused an instinctive response among the sons of that nation who had taken up residence in the New World.

Over against the groups in the United States that were sympathetic to the Allied cause, eager to have that side win through, were men of German or Austro-Hungarian ancestry who faithfully sympathized with their homelands. And they were buttressed by chance intellectuals, fond of Teutonic ways or scholarship, by men who resented British imperialism whether of the 18th or the 20th century, by friends of Ireland who despised Britain, and by Pole and Jew who detested the Imperial Russian regime of abuse and persecution.

Anti-Allied sentiment, weaker from the beginning than pro-Allied feeling, declined as the war marched on, as the martial deeds of the Germans, such as the use of poison gas and the torpedoing of the *Lusitania,* and machinations and sabotage of agents of the Central Powers in the United States, were extensively publicized.

Firmly opposed to any acts which savored of intervention in the war were men in the American Republic who were convinced that the national interest would best be served by adherence to the time-honored policy of keeping clear of controversies in Europe. For some minds the struggle seemed no more than a war on a pattern familiar to Europe, while "left-wingers" and agrarian reformers declaimed against involvement in "a clash of rival imperialisms," in "a capitalists' war."

Protesting voices spoke out against what they regarded as departures from wisdom and safety in allowing the shipment of munitions to belligerents and permitting nationals of the United States to travel into war-zones on Allied vessels. Also aligned with the forces of non-intervention were numerically negligible groups who, out of religious or philosophical convictions, were irreconcilably against the use of physical force to settle international disputes.

Both sets of European belligerents displayed singular ingenuity, not to say subtlety, in shaping or trying to shape American prejudices and convictions in a manner favorable to their cause. For linguistic reasons as well as because of the broad affinity in political and moral outlook, the British appeals carried greater weight, being vivified by stories of German atrocities, some real, some fabricated. After the destruction of the *Lusitania* spokesmen for Germany, aware of the futility of trying to prove the reasonableness of the war objects of the Teutonic Powers, concentrated on spreading the merits of peace and the horrors which would result from American involvement in the broils of Europe.

The export trade of the United States, which was violently dislocated by the coming of the war, rapidly recovered and before long had attained unprecedented, boom dimensions. Sales to the warring nations not only put an end to the business slump, but brought buoyant prosperity to factory, forge, and farm. Quite in harmony with established international custom the government laid no restraints on commerce with the belligerents and vigilantly and vigorously defended the rights of the United States on the bosom of the Atlantic. It must, however, be said that a double standard of neutral conduct was pursued. Much stricter adherence to the conventions of the sea was demanded of Germany than of Britain.

Munitions for the Allied armies made up the largest item of exports and goods shipped to April, 1917, had a value of approximately $7,000,000,000. For those supplies, the Allies paid principally with commodities or gold, with shipping services or the repatriation of American securities owned by foreign investors—the balance, in excess of $2,000,000,000, was covered by loans floated for the Allied governments in the United States. As the tremendous struggle progressed a kind of tacit economic alliance linked the United States to the Allies. Early in 1917 grave doubts were expressed in British official and financial circles as to whether funds to sustain the vital trade with the United States could much longer be found. In point of fact, Britain, the paymaster of France, Italy, and Russia, was nearing the bottom of the barrel.

Commerce between the United States and Germany and her allies was limited, for the British fleet barred the way to central Europe. German wartime borrowings in America were only fractional.

Germany and the nations allied to her endeavored to interrupt the flow of supplies from the United States to the Allies in two ways: by promoting strikes among workmen producing Allied war-goods, and by incitement to sabotage in factories, on railways, and at harbors. Such activities had little effect upon production or shipment and accentuated hostility in the United States toward the Central Governments.

But the chief weapon employed against Allied commerce was, of course, the submarine. As has been recounted in the preceding chapter, the United States adopted a firm policy on the U-boat in the first year of the conflict and after much patient and tortuous diplomacy induced the Germans to impose drastic limitations on submarine operations. If Germany had faithfully held to that pledge, it may be doubted whether the United States would have been drawn into the war.

There was yet another current that operated—and with growing persuasiveness—upon the American mind: the fear that victory for the Teutonic Powers would enthrone the philosophy of force and expediency in international affairs and degrade the democratic ideology. With the equilibrium of power in Europe radically unbalanced the Central Governments, Germany pre-eminently, would become a standing peril to the security and peace of mind of the Americas. A glance at the far-ranging extent of Teutonic Europe at the end of 1916 accentuated such dreads.

Might not another year of war witness the defeat of France while the German High Seas fleet and the submarine arm humbled Britain on the sea? Might not the Americas stand next on the German agenda of conquest? Suspicious German maneuverings in the Carribean area at the turn of the century and imperialistic literature bearing the imprint of Pan-Germanism and pointed lustfully at Latin America, helped frame an affirmative answer to that question. Therefore it would be only elementary wisdom, some Americans reasoned, to fight shoulder to shoulder with the Allies, fight to "save our own hides," rather than wait until the odds were definitely more favorable for Germany.

Widespread sympathy for the embattled Allies, growing dread of the consequences that German victory would have for the institutions and the security of the United States, the idea that the United States had a bounden duty to do something to eliminate war as the agency for settling international disputes, the companion notion that the United States was obligated to reorder the Old World along the lines of New World democracy, the reinforcing impact of Allied advertising activities, the subversive doings of agents of the Central Powers, and commercial and financial intimacy with Britain and France—all these factors created a climate of opinion in the United States which made war with Germany possible. The German resumption of unrestricted submarine warfare, with its explicit challenge to the interests and the honor of the United States, made conflict certain.

Germany Forces the Issue

The fateful decision to resume uninhibited application of the U-boat weapon was not come to lightly by the German policymakers. On the contrary, it was reached after no little travail of mind and realistic weighing of alternatives. The military and naval chiefs, who had previously yielded to the logic of civilian chiefs in limiting submarine activity, argued that full use of the U-boat would humble Britain in short order and end hostilities quickly.

To the civilian contention that indiscriminate sinkings would surely draw the United States into the war, the directors of the German fighting services—Ludendorff at their head—retorted that with the submarines then available (more than 100) the struggle would be over before the admittedly massive resources of the transatlantic giant could be effectively applied. In fact, an elaborate memorandum, compiled by the German Admiralty "proved" that Britain could be forced to her knees by August, 1917.

Not without grave misgivings, the German civilian authorities bowed to the will of the military professionals. It was decided on January 9, 1917, that, beginning on February 1, shipping to Britain and France would be torpedoed without reservation. The momentous resolve was communicated to the United States. Simultaneously the United States was informed that a single American ship might go to Britain each week provided it was clearly marked for identification, and steamed within a prescribed sea-lane!

Without hesitation President Wilson severed diplomatic relations with Germany. But he waited for the commission of "actual overt acts" before calling upon the Congress to declare hostilities.

By presidential order, meanwhile, merchant vessels of the United States were outfitted with weapons to protect themselves against U-boats and the notorious Zimmermann note was released to the public. In that document, of whose authenticity there is not the slightest doubt, the German foreign office instructed its representative in Mexico to inveigle that country into attacking the United States, in case the United States fought Germany. Before Mexican eyes, the minister was to dangle the prospect of territorial rewards at the expense of the United States. German diplomacy, it was further revealed, would seek to pry Japan loose from the Allied partnership and get Nippon to turn its guns upon America. By lending credence to the hypothesis that Germany had sinister designs upon the integrity of the United States, the Zimmermann note resembled oil deliberately tossed upon the blazing American war mentality.

Then, too, word reached the United States that Russian revolutionaries had overthrown the tsarist autocracy and proclaimed a democratic republic. The thesis was thus fortified that the nations arrayed against the Teutonic Powers, Japan alone excepted, had governments responsive to the popular will, like that of the United States.

After evidence was at hand proving that additional Americans had fallen victim to German submarine action, President Wilson recommended to the Congress a declaration of war upon the imperial German government. "God helping her," said the President in a paraphrase of Martin Luther's ringing sentence, "She (the United States) can do no other." From beginning to end—from April, 1915, to April, 1917—209 citizens of the United States were drowned by U-boat warfare, twenty-eight of them on ships flying the Stars and Stripes. Those losses were not a tenth part of the Norwegian drownings, for example, but it was one thing for German submarine commanders to treat Norway, small and weak, with impunity and quite another to deal with the proud and powerful United States in similar fashion. On a ratio of eight to one members of both houses of the Congress, on April 6, voted the resolution for war.

Declaration of hostilities upon the Hapsburg monarchy was withheld until December, 1917, and the United States never offically went to war with the Teutonic satellites, Bulgaria and Turkey. Instead of identifying itself contractually with the Allies, the United States chose to regard itself as an "Associated Power."

The United States at War

More than a century had elapsed since the United States had fought a major European nation. Yet the enthusiasm which the titanic conflict evoked surpassed in volume and intensity anything in the national record. Though the United States took up arms fully aware of what contemporary war entailed, zest for victory and confidence in the quick ending of hostilities recalled the patriotic fervor which had surged across the nations of Europe in the summer of 1914.

A mood of high exaltation and militant patriotism gripped the Republic. Like Crusaders of old many an American conceived his country as the predestined liberator of Europe, charged with a high moral duty to smash German militarism and set the Old World aright forever. Wilsonian idealism thought of the war as a supreme adventure to make "the world safe for democracy"—a phrase open to more than one interpretation—and to write finis to the waging of war. It was the self-same motive spoken of by Shakespeare in *Richard III*:

> To reap the harvest of perpetual peace
> By this one bloody trial of sharp war.

Dissenting voices, never numerous, were silenced by social pressures or by the strong arm of government.

The contribution of the United States to the ultimate Allied triumph over the Central Powers followed three main lines: economic, psychological, and military. Some months before intervention, preliminary steps had been taken to convert the huge economic machine of the United States to purposes of war; and after fighting started industry, agriculture and all the material resources of the nation were harnessed to the chariot of victory. Step by step the American economy was brought under the direction of the government and the results in most types of production dazzled Americans only less than Europeans in the know.

For the prosecution of the war, goods and services were consumed in large quantities by the United States itself and at the same time supplies to the embattled Allies were furnished in huge amounts. Since Britain's financial resources were practically exhausted and she could no longer provide credits to the continental Allies, the United States Treasury stepped into the breach, making loans to the Allies which by the day of the Armistice approached $10,000,000,000.

While the entry of the United States, brimming with confidence and commanding the abundant resources of a young continent, buoyed up flagging spirits in the Allied nations, it had a depressing effect upon the Central Powers. That a great nation untainted with any responsibility for the coming of the war, a nation which cherished no predatory designs, a nation which pitched its participation upon lofty moral and philosophical planes, had entered the struggle—all that could not fail to operate in a demoralizing manner upon German and Hapsburg hearts and minds. The official German interpretation, that the United States had entered the war in the illusory hope of recovering the millions that American finance had loaned to the Allies, availed little in counteracting the impression which American intervention produced.

On the other side, the inexhaustible might of the United States strengthened the faith of Allied peoples in the righteousness of the cause in hand and inspired fresh confidence in eventual victory. Immediate evidence of the significance of American intervention in the shape of food, munitions and the like was presently reinforced by the appear-

ance of soldiers of the United States, few in number at first, though
enough for tonic purposes, and steadily swelling into an invincible host.

On the impression which the marching Yankees made upon the
Allies, one British eyewitness has testified: "I heard an excited excla-
mation from a group of Sisters behind me. 'Look! Look! Here are the
Americans.' I pressed forward with the others to watch the United
States physically entering the war, so god-like, so magnificent, so splendidly unimpaired in comparison with the tired, nerve-wracked men of
the British Army. So these were our deliverers at last. There seemed
to be hundreds of them, and in the fearless swagger of their proud
strength they looked a formidable bulwark . . . ." [1]

It had been assumed at home that the role of the United States
would be confined to economic and financial aid to the Allies and possibly naval support—a few cruisers perhaps to clear shipping lanes of
deadly U-boats. When the idea of raising troops for military service in
Europe was broached, an urbane Senator blurted out: "Good Lord,
you aren't going to send soldiers there are you?" Yet by Armistice
Day some 2,000,000 American fighting men had been transported to
Europe.

In response to requests from Allied leaders for a few American
troops to enhearten popular morale, 15,000 regulars reached Paris in
time to participate in a parade on the Fourth of July, 1917. General
John J. Pershing, who had gone to Europe with a staff of experts, requested the government for a million men by July, 1918, and double
that many eventually. The enactment of a conscription law provided
the necessary troops, 4,800,000 of them in all; training camps rose
out of the American earth as though by magic; "a bridge of ships" to
Europe was designed and partly completed; factories buzzed in the
manufacture of supplies and equipment. America had in truth gone
all-out for victory.

Naval resources, too, were whole-heartedly flung into the conflict.
By May, 1917, a flotilla of American destroyers had reached Europe
to cooperate in the hunt for submarines, and a division of battleships
was over there by December. The United States navy sowed a cordon
of mines from the Orkney Islands across to Norway in order to prevent the passage of U-boats, and restraints upon neutral rights on
the seas against which the United States as a neutral had hotly protested were swept aside. At the end of the war more than 300 American
warships and 75,000 officers and sailors were on duty in European
waters.

---

[1] Vera Brittain, *Testament of Youth* (New York, 1933), pp. 420-421.

The entry of the United States into the great struggle induced other neutral nations to take similar action. Brazil and half a dozen of the smaller Latin American countries declared war, while others cut off diplomatic relations with the Central Powers. China's decision to become a belligerent was also affected by the course taken by the United States.

Struggles in France and Italy: 1917

Until almost the end of 1917 the Allied military record was studded with discouraging reverses. The French commander-in-chief, General Robert Nivelle, had come to the conclusion that a succession of well-coordinated blows would break the prolonged deadlock on the Western Front. But before the first attack could be launched the German forces were cleverly pulled back some thirty miles to a shorter line spoken of as the Hindenburg Line. Starting off with a heavy bombardment, the Allies carried the battle furiously for three weeks against the enemy, only to be repulsed at the end.

Among war-weary French poilus, demonstrations of disaffection cycled into mutiny in the ranks, of which apparently the Germans learned nothing. Moreover, upsets in the French ministry recurred into November, 1917, when the irrepressible and tenacious Clemenceau undertook the premiership. General Henri Pétain, whose prestige rested upon his spirited defense of Verdun, replaced the discredited Nivelle, and restored discipline and confidence among the French soldiery. Pétain decided against further offensive operations until American troops were landed in France in force.

British forces under Haig, however, opened a large-scale push into Belgium, with the immediate aim of expelling the Germans from submarine lairs along the coast. Seldom in the war was fighting more bitter, but the Germans doggedly held their positions. Toward the end of November, near Cambrai, the British, for the first time, sent tanks into action. On a surprise assault, tanks in clusters of three, smashed enemy trenches, clearing the way for the infantry to advance; the ground gained was impressively large and casualties slight, but the inadequacy of reinforcements imposed limitations on the exploitation of the tank arm. Germany neither had nor could create efficient defenses against the tank, whose terrorizing effect upon troop morale was at least as important as the physical damage that was wrought.

Offsetting the British success at Cambrai was a heavy reversal suffered by the armies of Italy. Months of grinding warfare, amid great natural obstacles, and with only modest gains, had eaten into the martial ardor of the soldiers of Victor Emmanuel. Then, in front of Caporetto, in October, 1917, German and Hapsburg forces unleashed a massive attack, driving the Italians back to the Piave river, a mere fifteen miles from Venice.

French and British support was rushed in from the western front and assisted in checking the enemy torrent. By that time Italy had lost about half a million soldiers—deserters mostly—and over a quarter of a million, along with large quantities of war-matériel, had been captured. From the crippling blow at Caporetto, Italy never fully recovered, though morale among the soldiers improved during the winter. Warned by the Italian setback of the need for greater coordination to win the war, an Allied Supreme War Council was formed with a joint military board having command, up to a point, of the general reserve of troops.

Russia Withdraws

On the eastern theatre the supreme event of 1917 was the complete withdrawal of Russia from the war. Signs that the Russian nation was cracking had not gone unmarked in other countries since the catastrophic military setbacks of 1915 in Poland. Acute deficiencies in military and administrative leadership, shortages of war supplies and foodstuffs, and loss of faith in Russia's national destiny presaged the revolutionary upheavals of 1917.

As is explained in another context (Chap. V), an uprising in March, 1917, brought about the overthrow of the tsarist government and the establishment of a weak, more or less democratic-republican order. After a futile attempt to infuse new vigor into the prosecution of the war, which revealed the utter bankruptcy of national morale, the Russian provisional regime was superseded by the radical Bolsheviks in November. Right away the new rulers of Russia called for complete cessation of hostilities and when that proposal was spurned, they turned to arranging a separate peace with the Teutonic Powers. Negotiations dragged on into March, 1918, when a formal treaty was concluded at Brest-Litovsk.

It was a harsh document cutting away the western provinces of pre-war Russia and the broad Ukraine. From these areas the Central Powers expected to obtain food and other supplies which would counteract the shortages imposed by the Allied blockade. Similar hopes of assistance from the granaries of Rumania were roused when that country finally capitulated in May, 1918, and signed a treaty granting the Central Powers unfettered control of the economic resources.

Russia's withdrawal from the fighting had other significant consequences. Not only were peoples of Central Europe encouraged to support one more herculean offensive in France, but German troops released from the Russian front were available to fight in that effort. And, partly for the purpose of creating another battleline in the east against the Teutonic Powers, contingents of Allied soldiers were landed in northern Russia and in Siberia. Throughout the Allied nations, finally, the idea gained ground that unless the fighting were brought to a speedy conclusion all of Europe, nearly exhausted after forty months of war, would succumb to Bolshevik preachments on world revolution.

Allied pessimism over the dubious course of military events in 1917 and the defection of Russia was only slightly tempered by triumphs at the expense of tottering Turkey. British soldiers early in the year captured Bagdad in Mesopotamia, and just before Christmas another British army marched into Jerusalem, thus placing the Holy City in Christian possession for the first time since the Crusades.

That moral fillip was achieved by British arms with the cooperation of Arab guerilla warriors who had been rallied to the Allied banner by Colonel T. E. Lawrence, perhaps the most glamorous personality that World War I cast up. A gentle, youthful archaeologist who was searching for Hittite relics in the valley of the Euphrates when the war started, Lawrence turned diplomatist and strategist, leading Bedouin tribesmen, of whom he had a profound understanding, in a "revolt in the desert." Turkish troop trains were joyfully dynamited, and Arab raid after Arab raid was conducted against the fringes of the Turkish army. It was Lawrence's belief—and promise—that after the war a large independent Arab state would be set up with Allied concurrence.

Peace Gestures and War Aims

Bound up with the entry of the United States into the war, the deadlock in France, popular war-weariness, the revolutionary drama in Russia, and the dread that the foundations of conventional society were on the verge of cracking, were several moves to stop the conflict. These were made through diplomatic negotiation and official avowals by Allied spokesmen of the objectives for which the fighting was being pressed on.

First of all came a peace gesture early in 1917 from Vienna. Emperor-King Charles, freshly come to the Hapsburg thrones, despatched his brother-in-law, Prince Sixtus, on a secret diplomatic errand to Paris and London. In a vague sort of way the young Hapsburg ruler seems to have realized that only a speedy cessation of hostilities could possibly save his decaying realm from ruin. For a quick compromise

peace, the Hapsburg agent agreed, among other things, that Alsace-
Lorraine should be restored to France, but he balked at meeting the
Italian territorial aspirations in full. Allied statesmen lavishly entertained Prince Sixtus, listened attentively—and stopped there. Publication of the Austrian peace overture by Clemenceau in 1918 not only
infuriated Germany but cost the Hapsburg dynasty the allegiance of
many of its German and Magyar subjects.

Inside Germany sentiment favorable to a negotiated settlement
appeared to be growing in 1917. Unrest among workmen, evidences
of sedition among sailors, and frank recognition of Austro-Hungarian
decadence inspired the German Reichstag to adopt peace resolutions
in July. These proposals, voted by 212 to 126, bore an interesting re-
semblance to Wilson's peace without victory utterance, in that they
implied that Germany desired neither territorial nor economic advantages. Welcomed rapturously in Allied capitals as a plain sign of the
drooping martial spirit in Germany, the Reichstag Resolutions so
greatly angered the German military masters, Hindenburg and Ludendorff, that they drove Chancellor Bethmann-Hollweg from office for
permitting the discussion.

Shortly, Pope Benedict XV offered a program for a negotiated
peace which would restore the territorial status quo of 1914, while
leaving disputed territorial questions to be settled by arbitration. No
belligerent would be asked to pay indemnities and in the future, plans
would be worked out for general reduction of armaments and the
adjustment of international quarrels by pacific means. The most
cordial response to that papal overture came from Hapsburg circles
and from philosophical pacifists. Elsewhere the Pope's peace plan was
denounced as a snare and a delusion, and individual leaders in both
belligerent camps excoriated Benedict XV as working in the interest of
the other side.

In France and Britain voices were raised on behalf of the restoration of peace by diplomacy. French defeatist sentiments on the home
front, the counterpart of the mutinous disturbances in the army, were
most vigorously preached by Joseph Caillaux, sometime premier, and
cautiously echoed by another ex-Premier, Aristide Briand. But their
pens and tongues were silenced by Clemenceau after his accession to
the headship of France. Caillaux and other like-minded men were
summarily clapped into prison as traitors. A sensational appeal for
peace negotiations issued by Lord Lansdowne, one of the most respected leaders of the British Conservative Party, enlisted little enthusiasm in the island kingdom. Popular yearnings in Italy for the

ending of hostilities, which penetrated into the armed forces, contributed to the military disaster at Caporetto.

These and other manifestations of a desire for peace, together with popular ferment caused by Bolshevik publication of secret treaties arranged by the Allies in the course of the war, induced the British Prime Minister and the American President to set forth Allied war aims with something like definiteness. These utterances were intended, too, to steel the Allied nations to prosecute the war to victory.

Asserting that he spoke for the whole British realm, David Lloyd George reaffirmed, on January 5, 1918, that Britain had no intention of destroying the German empire, though he believed that a democratic reformation there would hasten the dawn of peace. Yet by implication at least he insisted that France must recover Alsace-Lorraine, and that the German colonies should be disposed of at an international conference. Moreover, the Central Powers would have to make restitution to the Allied countries which they had overrun and pay reparations for the drowning of British seamen. An independent Poland Lloyd George described as an "urgent necessity" for the stability of Europe.

Autonomy would have to be granted to the nationalities of the Hapsburg monarchy and the Austrian areas of Italian speech would have to be ceded to Italy. As for the Ottoman Empire, said Lloyd George, it might retain its foothold in Europe, though the Straits zone would be internationalized, and non-Turkish peoples of Asia were entitled to a "recognition of their separate national conditions." Without particular enthusiasm the British premier expressed himself in favor of an international organization as "an alternative to war as a means of settling international disputes."

Three days after Lloyd George had spoken, President Wilson delivered his historic Fourteen Points address on war aims. On the territorial side Wilson called for the restoration of Belgium, the return of Alsace-Lorraine to France, the readjustment of the frontiers of Italy along clearly recognizable lines of nationality, autonomy for the peoples of Austria-Hungary, and an outlet on the Adriatic for Serbia. Poland should be resurrected and should embrace areas that were indisputedly Polish in nationality and should have "free and secure access" to the Baltic Sea; Russia should be allowed to develop on its own, aided by the Allies; and national minorities in the Ottoman Empire should be permitted "autonomous development." German colonies should be disposed of on "absolutely impartial" terms.

Beyond these items, the President's agenda for enduring peace specified the lowering of tariffs, reparations from the Teutonic nations to rebuild the regions which their armies had invaded, and the abrogation of restrictions upon the use of the seas by merchantmen in wartime. As positive aids for keeping the peace, Wilson recommended that diplomatic negotiations and treaty-making should be carried on in the open, not secretly, that armaments be cut to the lowest point consistent with domestic safety, and that the nations mutually guarantee the political independence and territorial integrity of one another.

That Fourteen Points program, which was elaborated and clarified in later addresses, set the basis for the eventual armistice negotiations between Germany and the United States and the Allies. As an instrument for lessening the will-to-win in Teutonic Europe and for hardening morale in the Allied nations, the Wilsonian utterances were of no small importance, though the President's expressed objectives were not integrally endorsed by Allied statesmen and diplomatists.

Battling the U-boat

By the time these Allied pronouncements on the objectives of the war had been delivered, the U-boat menace had been effectively scotched. An all-out campaign against Allied commerce was launched in February, 1917, with remarkable dash and enterprise. More than five times as many submarines were then available as two years earlier and their destructiveness in the first three months of unrestricted operations threatened to match the calculations of the German Admiralty. In April alone, one out of every four ships leaving the British Isles was torpedoed and the losses reached nearly 900,000 tons. Small wonder that British naval men doubted whether their country could stagger on much longer.

But countermeasures presently turned the tide. Of them by far the most important was the provision of destroyer and cruiser escorts for merchant ships in convoy. Earlier such protection had been furnished only for troop carriers. The British Admiralty on order of Lloyd George buried their objections to general convoys and worked out an immense service of protection which went far to check the ravages of the furtive undersea craft. Convoys moved in precise formation surrounded by the armed vessels of the escort. Each merchantman had to keep strictly to its assigned position and no running lights could be used at night, which made navigation extremely hazardous, especially when long zigzags were executed.

In carrying out the convoy program the British navy had the cooperation of American naval units and also of a few Japanese destroyers which operated in the Mediterranean. The convoy system was defensive in that it compelled the enemy to keep his periscope down and offensive, too, because depth bombs forced the U-boat to the surface where the escort could strike with its guns. Enthusiasts have made an appealing case for the proposition that it was the convoy system which "really won the war."

Novel instruments to detect the presence of submarines, lavish use of depth bombs—never weapons of precision—and the extensions of mine barrages, all took their toll of the U-boats. Allied submarines fought German submarines in a manner that had a Jules Verne flavor about it. Heavy losses spread demoralization among U-boat crews, which special favors were not wholly able to counteract.

In mid-summer of 1917, Allied ship casualties started to decline and fell off steadily until the war was over. By then, the submarine was no longer the invincible weapon that some experts had assumed it to be. Yet from first to last more than 11,000,000 tons of shipping were sent to the ocean floor—over half of it British—and as much more had been damaged to a greater or lesser extent. It is not surprising that Britishers were mortally fearful of the submarine and after the war they took the lead in seeking to abolish it.

By the end of the war 178 German submarines had gone down, 121 were still in service, and some 200 were in various stages of construction. Prodigious though the German efforts were, unrestricted guerilla war at sea had deceived the fond expectations of its sponsors, who had invoked it at the fatal price of aligning the United States against their country.

The Air Arm

Except perhaps for the submarine, the most striking technological advance of the war was in aeronautics. Although aircraft had been employed by the Italians in the War of 1911-1912 with Turkey, experts regarded planes chiefly as instruments of reconnaissance or as useful for patrol purposes. In the beginning of World War I airmen were equipped only with small arms.

But in 1915 the Germans brought out a machine that was specially designed for fighting, the Fokker, which ruled the skies for a year, only to be outclassed by Allied aircraft. Thereafter superiority in the sky oscillated back and forth until the war was over. Combats between individual "knights of the air," in which the wastage of flyers was appalling, were superseded in 1916 by battles between rival squadrons.

To a limited extent the air weapon was applied against enemy

communications and military installations, the tempo and efficiency
rising considerably in the final stage of the war. Steady improvements
were also made in aerial photography, in the cooperation of planes
with artillery and infantry, and in showering propaganda literature
upon the enemy. Almost from the beginning the Germans employed
giant dirigible Zeppelins to unload bombs on English seaports, and
later they turned to spectacular raids on London. But these craft were
vulnerable targets and weather hazards restricted their efficiency.

More formidable in warring upon urban communities was the airplane. The first daylight raid—June, 1917—on London caused panic
in sections of the metropolis. Britain immediately organized the Royal
Air Force which in 1918 effectively retaliated upon cities of western
Germany. To protect London a pattern of barrage fire was evolved,
balloon aprons constructed, and height finders and range locaters
devised. In all, over 100 air raids were made upon Britain, taking more
than 1,400 lives and wounding nearly thrice as many. Yet the property
damage was slight, the interruptions to normal life scarcely noticeable,
and instead of embarrassing the prosecution of the war, enemy attacks
from the sky simply intensified civilian hatred of Germany which was
reflected at the Paris Peace Conference.

At sea German Zeppelins were serviceable in patrol and reconnaissance work, but the Germans manufactured no seaplanes. British
ingenuity, on the other hand, developed the aircraft carrier to which
planes could return as well as take off. From 1917 on, planes were used
increasingly as scouts in the convoy service, and they even destroyed
a few enemy vessels.

Despite the progress in aeronautics, the opinion prevailed among
experts at the end of the war (as at the start) that the principal
function of aircraft was observation. True, in 1918, the Allies possessed huge air armadas for fighting, half again as large perhaps as the
German forces, and still bigger and faster planes were being readied
for 1919, but the potentialities of aircraft as bombers or even as support for ground forces were understood by only a few military men.
In a single day of World War II, British planes dropped more tonnage
in bombs than in the entire four years of World War I!

Germany's Final Bid

The year 1918 was one of climaxes unequalled to that time in
modern history. Kaleidoscopic changes and breath-taking events
crowded so furiously upon one another that it was difficult to grasp
their import. Frustrated in the U-boat adventure the Germans re-

solved upon a last gamble on land—a herculean campaign (or series of them) to capture Paris and retrieve the failure of the first months of the war.

The Bolshevik capitulation had released many German divisions for fighting in France. Whereas a year before the ratio of German to Allied soldiers in the West was two to three the balance had now shifted to four to three. Ludendorff was resolved upon knocking out the Allies before large masses of Americans could reach the battle-fronts. From March 21 to July 15 four ferocious German onslaughts were delivered, the heaviest in history, but all in vain.

After a bombardment of unmatched volume and violence the Germans in March, 1918, struck the British in Picardy, a dense fog shielding the attackers. It was intended to separate the British armies from the French and roll them back on the Channel ports—the Nazi achievement of 1940. But on the earlier occasion, though the British line was bent in for forty miles, it could not be broken. Never had British arms sustained so severe a setback and only the deficiencies of German supply seem to have prevented a disastrous break-through. Now, belatedly, the Allied armies were placed under the supreme direction of one commander—the French general, Marshal Ferdinand Foch.

A second formidable German lunge, started in April, pushed the British perilously near to the seacoast with costly losses on both sides. Another breathing-spell and then, at the end of May, the Germans focused upon the French in Champagne, hurling them back to the Marne river and to within forty two miles of Paris—no question of the skillful manipulation of the German resources, nor of the hardihood and verve of the soldiers in this tremendous contest of metal, muscle, and will. All over the Allied world men trembled lest the strategic objectives of the enemy should be attained.

But the reserve contingents of Ludendorff had been consumed with abandon and the successive German penetrations into the Allied front left exposed flanks which were an invitation to counter-thrusts. Moreover, in response to anxious appeals of Allied statesmen, soldiers of the United States were being rushed across the Atlantic, in British vessels largely, at a rate that surprised friend and disappointed utterly the calculations of the foe. Between the opening of the German drive in March and the signing of the Armistice in November, 1,700,000 Yanks were transported. Not that they were ready for fighting at once, but after a brief spell of special training abroad they were brigaded with seasoned Allied veterans in the battle lines.

Ludendorff's sledge-hammer descended for the last time on July 15 in the vicinity of Rheims. Once more the French staggered back, pulling across the river Marne, but there with American support they stood firm. The offensive might of Germany had spent itself without gaining a decision.

The Allied Counterstroke

Three days later Generalissimo Foch inaugurated a masterly counterattack, in what the French call the "Battle of Liberation." Blows would be delivered thick and fast on exposed points of the enemy flank, and each thrust would be broken off as soon as the original momentum had been exhausted. Swarms of Allied tanks accompanied by foot-soldiers quickly snatched the initiative from the enemy. Seven divisions of United States Regulars had a prominent part in the early stage of this "Second Battle of the Marne." Gloomy apprehensions in Allied hearts were rapidly dispelled.

On August 8 British armies in the Amiens pocket fought a resounding tank victory, which Ludendorff later confessed was "the black day of the German army in the history of this war." At points the enemy withdrawal verged closely on a rout. That August disaster appears to have convinced the German commanders that the game was about over. Mile by mile the Germans were thrust back, digging in once more on the supposedly impregnable Hindenburg line of fortifications. United States divisions, now organized as an independent army, pinched off the salient of St. Mihiel. German battle casualties since the opening of the March onslaught approached the 2,000,000 mark.

Cheered by the results since mid-July, Foch decided to seek a quick conclusion to hostilities by a monster converging movement on the enemy. Britishers would strike on the left or western flank, Americans would hammer their way through the Meuse-Argonne region. Those plans in part were effectuated, the British smashing across the vaunted Hindenburg fortifications, though the advance was not fast enough to produce a general German collapse.

As for the American assault, it was initiated on September 26 and lasted until November 11, forty seven days and nights of the most desperate fighting in American history. Fully 1,200,000 troops were engaged in this Meuse-Argonne campaign, and the killed and wounded were half of all the American casualties in the war. The Briey iron mines were taken and the Americans were pressing toward the Rhine when the Armistice was proclaimed. It was the splendid martial quali-

ties of "doughboy" and artilleryman that were primarily responsible
for the victorious American advance; while quite inaccurate, aerial
bombing of enemy ammunition dumps and concentration centers
helped the cause along.

As the German armies reeled back, morale sagged and letters from
home recounting tales of starvation and dread of the oncoming winter
impaired the flickering will to win. And so did evil tidings of what was
happening to Germany's allies.

The Central Powers Cave In

Bulgaria was the first enemy state to capitulate as it had been the
last to enter the Central Powers coalition. Allied armies, long immobil-
ized at Salonika, unleashed a slashing drive northward which caused
the Bulgarian front to disintegrate. On September 29 the Bulgarian
government signed an armistice as King Ferdinand fled for his life.
Thus an avenue was opened for a quick march into the Hapsburg monarchy, and the Turkish capital, Constantinople, could likewise be
easily threatened from the west.

On other sectors Turkish resistance crumbled fast. While one British army pushed through Mesopotamia, another defeated the Turks
in northern Palestine, a decisive encounter, not inappropriately, taking
place at Megiddo—the ancient battlefield of Armageddon. Arab caval-
rymen, moreover, galloped into Syrian Damascus and hoisted their
national flag. When Turkey surrendered on October 30, an Allied
fleet steamed into Constantinople, three years after the Dardanelles
fiasco.

It was then the turn of the Hapsburgs. The elimination of Russia
from the war and the promise of grain and other foodstuffs from the
Ukrainian bread-basket had momentarily raised spirits in the ancient
Danubian monarchy. At the end of May, 1918, the fighting in Italy
had been resumed and the Hapsburg flag had been carried beyond the
Piave, but there the offensive stalled and before long precipitate
retreat had commenced.

Gathering chaos in Austro-Hungarian economy, desertion of soldiers, the diffusion of Bolshevik doctrines by prisoners freed from
Russian camps, and mounting enthusiasm for independence among
national minorities heralded the impending dissolution of the venerable
monarchy. In a last desperate gamble to preserve the ramshackle
realm, Emperor-King Charles promised to create a federal union of
Hapsburg peoples. But the bid came too late. The armies had quit
fighting. Wherefore an armistice was negotiated with Italy on Novem-

ber 3, but before it became operative the soldiers of Victor Emmanuel won a token victory at Vittorio Veneto, taking prisoners and equipment wholesale. Meekly Charles abdicated the thrones of his fathers. Europe's oldest dynasty lay in ruin.

Germany itself in the meantime had approached the Allies for a truce, Ludendorff and Hindenburg alike having concluded that hostilities must be brought to an end. Neither of them had the slightest desire to fight suicidal battles on the soil of the Fatherland, something the Nazis in their fanaticism forgot in 1944-1945. Ludendorff himself evaluated the situation something like this: his own military reserves were gravely depleted while fresh American reinforcements were rapidly strengthening Allied power and millions more were being trained for combat across the Atlantic; Allied tank resources were an obstacle Germany could not overcome; Germany's allies must soon succumb and gloom and disaffection inside the exhausted German nation were deep and growing progressively deeper.

The High Command instructed the German political heads to get busy on the making of an armistice. So, for the first time since July, 1914, the timetable passed from army to civilian control. And the deterioration on the hungry German home front proceeded at an accelerated pace.

As is described in the next chapter, the Berlin government, on October 3, started to parley on the conditions under which the Germans would lay down their arms. A little later, as the advance of the Allied troops slackened, a spasm of hopefulness seized Ludendorff; he executed a somersault and recommended further resistance. But mutiny in the German fleet and the crumbling German nation nullified any chance of carrying on the war in a serious manner.

On November 11, 1918, the New York *Times* blazoned in banner headlines: "Armistice Signed, End of the War! Berlin Seized by Revolutionists; New Chancellor Begs for Order; Ousted Kaiser Flees to Holland."

And on all the battlefronts the guns were quiet.

The Shared Triumph

Debate over the sources of the Allied victory and the comparative importance of the contribution made by each Allied country was only less acrid and less learned after the war than the scholarly war of words over the outbreak of the conflict. Persuasive cases were made out for the proposition that any one of several factors was uniquely decisive; and patriotic pride tended to befuddle, not to clarify, the causes of the Allied triumph. Unquestionably the actuality is that while special pleadings contain kernels of truth, it was the combination of nations and resources which added up to victory.

The triumph of each Ally was in reality the triumph of the Grand Alliance. Britishers pointed with pride to the role of the Grand Fleet, to British financial and industrial power, to British fighting men in the French theatre and in the scattered side-shows. But while Britain was girding for full participation in the struggle, the French army had stemmed the onslaught of the enemy in 1914, checked him again at Verdun, and shared importantly in the decisive campaigns of 1918.

To the French patriot who was inclined to take credit for the victory for his own country, the proper retort was penned by the French novelist, Drieu La Rochelle, who wrote, "France held her head too high in this war, but her bloodless body would have been unable to sustain the weight had not the strength of twenty nations been added to her limbs. We French cannot claim to have been the sole possessors of this mistress—Victory." The same line of argument was valid for other partners in the Allied coalition.

For the United States there was glory in the moral tonic which its intervention and the Wilsonian vision of a warless society gave the jaded Allies. Then, too, there was pride in the material assistance that it rendered, in the reinforcing role of American seapower, and in the valor of the fighting men in the closing year of the agonizing conflict.

The part of Russia in the ultimate victory, somewhat obscured by the withdrawal in 1917, must not be minimized. The stubborn bravery of the Muscovite armies, incompetently commanded and inadequately equipped though they were, saved the Allies from possible defeat at several points in the first two years of the war; and propaganda, issuing from Russia, both Pan-Slav and Bolshevik, had corroding effects upon morale in Central Europe. Italy, too, pinned down large enemy forces, launched repeated campaigns across as formidable terrain as is to be found in Europe, and delivered the *coup de grâce* to the demoralized Hapsburg services. And the smaller Allies, among whom Belgium and Serbia merited special commendation, contributed their mite to the eventual outcome.

Nor was the victory by any means achieved solely on the battle-fronts or on the seas. To an unparalleled extent World War I was fought in shipyard, on farm, in factory, and in laboratory. It was in literal truth total war, waged and won by production and consuming the energies, the brawn, and the brains of civilian and uniformed citizen alike.

The Harvest of War

Although many attempts have been made to compute the human costs of World War I, none of them pretends to be much more than a rough approximation. Imperfect records, the unwillingness of governments to publish some statistics, and divergent definitions of "wounded," for instance, preclude exact calculations. It appears, however, that deaths in the armed services were between 10,000,000 and 13,000,-000, and the wounded exceeded 22,000,000. The American casualty toll was about 126,000 dead and rather more than 200,000 wounded.

Incalculable are the civilian casualties resulting directly from the war, though they seem to have been heavier than for the armed forces. And, at least aggravated by the war, was a devastating influenza pandemic, which originated in the United States early in 1918 and swiftly spread round the globe. That malady, one of the three most terrible scourges of infection in recorded history, carried off something like 21,000,000 human beings.

On the financial side, too, the costs, direct and indirect of World War I, are not susceptible to satisfactory computation and estimates contain a large admixture of guesswork. One careful investigator, just after the war, suggested a total figure of $337,000,000,000.[2]

To study the consequences of the war for the social and economic fabric of the nations, the Carnegie Endowment for International Peace enlisted a host of distinguished experts in many countries. Their investigations, completed in 1937, and published as the *Social and Economic History of the World War,* ran into 152 stately, fact-filled, and informing volumes. It is a monumental quarry of data on the ramified meaning of the war for men and nations.

On any balance sheet of the war must be posted such immeasurable items as the gains in technology and science, notably medical science, which accompanied the conflict. Yet among scientists themselves the predominant opinion appeared to be that on an overall and long-range view, World War I retarded more than it promoted the advancement of science. Many an ingenious war-time improvisation to meet needs normally satisfied by imports and certain instruments of war, like the airplane and tank, found uses in peace-time economy.

So long ago as 1887, it was boldly prophesied that "a war of unexpected duration and violence" was coming, which would "scrape

[2] E. L. Bogart, *Direct and Indirect Coats of the Great World War* (New York, 1919), pp. 267, 299.

Europe as bare as a swarm of locusts." The sequel would be "irremediable disorganization of our artificial system of commerce, industry, and credit, ending in general bankruptcy . . . crowns rolling by the dozens on the pavements and no one found to pick them up; general exhaustion, and conditions out of which the workingclass will finally achieve victory."

That remarkable forecast, expressed by Friedrich Engels, the ally of Karl Marx, was dug out of a forgotten brochure and printed in 1918 by Nicholas Lenin, foremost of Bolshevik revolutionaries.

CHAPTER IV

Peacemaking, 1919-1920

Atmosphere

OF all the arts diplomacy is the most exacting, and peacemaking is no doubt the most difficult work of diplomacy. Now that victory had been won could the peacemakers fashion an order of society that would be at once constructive and durable?

Wherever one turned in Europe the outlook was dark and foreboding. Ancient states had been shattered beyond repair and out of their death throes new nations were struggling to be born; an exciting game of territorial grab had started at a dozen points and that spirit was infectious. Desperate refugees were beating their way to their homelands and millions of soldiers and prisoners of war were eager to be discharged so they might resume normal pursuits. The masses of the population in the defeated countries and in revolutionary Russia were on the edge of starvation—some of them over it; in Italy and in France prospects were bright only by comparison.

Statesmen would have not only to liquidate the war, they would also have to govern much of the continent and provide it with sustenance lest uncontrollable anarchy should break loose. And never out of mind was the disturbing spectacle of Russia where a vast upheaval was ushering in a new regime and whence Communist spokesmen ceaselessly appealed for world revolution. Risings of "Reds" at several points in Europe proper warned the peacemakers to hasten on with their complex tasks.

The statesmen of 1919 did not have a clean slate on which to write the terms of peace and the charter for an international organization to keep the peace. Rather the victors were bound by commitments, by secret treaties negotiated in the heat of conflict, and by specific understandings with Germany before the Armistice went into force. Those agreements figured largely in the ultimate content of the peace treaties.

Beyond that, the peacemakers could not reach decisions without taking into account the probable (or expressed) reaction of press and parliament in their respective countries. The Allied public mind, vindictive after the horrors and anguish of the war, enflamed by emotion-searing propaganda, and embittered by the harsh treaties the Germans had dictated to Russia and Rumania, clamored for vengeance for the past and solid guarantees of security for the future. Nationalism sometimes impelled the peacemakers to accept terms which prudence and far-sightedness would have ruled out.

Peace conferences previously had been confined to European nations, but in 1919-1920, of the thirty seven countries represented, only fourteen of them were of the Old World. The presence of the United Sattes more than anything else distinguished the Paris Conference from its predecessors.

Armistice

The Central Powers had collapsed more swiftly than Allied leaders had anticipated. In consequence, statesmen, preoccupied with the task of winning the war, had not prepared any concerted program for world settlement. The victors, it has been said, were "magnificently unprepared for the littleness" of peace. But after the German government, on the insistent demand of Field Marshal Ludendorff, who saw inescapable defeat facing him, appealed to President Wilson for an armistice, telegraphic exchanges defined the conditions of German surrender. In the end the Germans agreed to cease firing on the basis of the Wilsonian principles for peace as set down in his Fourteen Points speech and subsequent addresses, and on military terms which were hammered out by the Allied commanders.

Upon the completion of his negotiations with the Germans, Wilson presented the product of his labors to the Allied policymakers. After some haggling and interpretative explanations on the purport of the Fourteen Points—and an American threat to make a separate peace, if the Wilsonian conditions were not endorsed—the Allied statesmen consented to the American program, with two important qualifications. First, the matter of the freedom of the seas, in which Great Britain was keenly concerned, would be discussed at the peace conference; in point of fact that issue, which was directly responsible for the entry of the United States into the war, was put aside permanently. The other Allied interpretation defined the reparations to be exacted of Germany as sufficient to cover the "damages done to civilians and their property on land on sea, and in the air."

On the military side, the armistice clauses as drawn up by the military experts, required the evacuation of German troops from Russia, Austria, Hungary, the Balkans, and from west of the Rhine river. Allied armies would occupy the Rhineland territory and also the chief bridgeheads beyond the Rhine. The Germans, furthermore, would surrender specified quantities of war matériel, all submarines, and the bulk of the German battle fleet would be interned in neutral or Allied ports; the naval blockade of Germany was to continue. All in all the military and naval conditions would render Germany impotent to renew the fighting and foreshadowed part of the peace settlement.

Well aware of the broad outlines of the ultimate treaty which acceptance of the armistice terms implied, representatives of Germany signed the document which officially ended hostilities. True, the Fourteen Points lacked exactness on certain territorial problems, and the Allied reservation on reparations was an elastic formula, but the Germans in signing the armistice knew a good deal of what submission really entailed; they knew, for instance, that Alsace-Lorraine would revert to France, and that German territory inhabited by Poles would pass to Poland.

Peacemakers: The Big Three

A mere two months after the signing of the German Armistice, and before the bitter passions generated in the gruelling war had been given time to cool, representatives of the victor nations met to draw up definitive treaties with the enemy. Only Russia of the nations that had fought against Germany was absent. If well-established diplomatic etiquette had been followed, delegates of the conquered countries would have been invited to participate in the negotiations. That bit of international custom was brushed aside mainly because of fear that if Germans were present they would exploit discord among the Allies. Only after settlements had been drafted would enemy spokesmen be requested to make observations.

On the proposal of the French government the conference convened in Paris, the very center, not alone of the most intense hatred of Germany, but of a most intemperate, cynical, and unprincipled press.

At Paris, in the making of the peace, three statesmen towered head and shoulders above the others: President Wilson, the British Prime Minister, David Lloyd George, and Georges Clemenceau, Premier of France. These were not seraphic supermen, but men with the mingled virtues and frailties of men, the strengths and limitations of men. Vehement controversies have raged over them all and their handiwork, as is the common fate of the conspicuous public servant.

President Wilson cherished nobly optimistic ideals in international affairs and expressed them with engaging and compelling eloquence.

Not untypical of his conception of the world settlement is this piece of war-time rhetoric: "The cause being just and holy, the settlement must be of like quality. A supreme moment of history has come. The eyes of the people have been opened and they see. The hand of God is upon the nations. He will show them favor, I devoutly believe, only if they rise to the clear heights of His own justice and mercy."

"The eyes of the people"—that phraseology furnishes a clue to one of the deepest convictions held by the President: Whence came wars and rumors of wars? From the greedy ambitions of a wicked governing minority, Wilson was sure. Hardly less certain was he that European statesmen were wily practitioners of the black and sinister art of diplomacy, bent solely on advancing national self-interest. The war-time secret treaties of the Allies, of which the President had almost complete knowledge before he set off for Paris, symbolized the evil forces which he felt he must combat and vanquish.

If only the "plain people" were given active direction of affairs of state, the world would undergo "a cleansing process" of regeneration. Wilson believed that ordinary folk were reasonable and desired a peace of reconciliation which would prove more compulsive than a peace based upon force. The rapturous ovations given the President by war-weary European masses on the eve of the Paris Conference deepened the feeling that he uniquely embodied the aspirations and the wishes of the common folk. Before the Conference was over the popular response to some of Wilson's gestures challenged his fundamental faith without, however, disillusioning him.

Tall, spare, formidable, deliberate in thought, Wilson looked and acted the scholar in politics that he was. Less than nine years before his appearance in Paris, he had quit the presidency of Princeton University after a distinguished career in college and university teaching and administration. But neither that academic experience, nor early legal training, nor his governorship of New Jersey, had taught him precision of mind.

At the Congressional elections in 1918, in which he had appealed to the voters to choose representatives belonging to his own, the Democratic, party, Wilson suffered a political setback, for Republican majorities were returned. That lessened his prestige among knowing Europeans, who were aware that the President did not command the sovereign majority at home. Wilson blundered again when he declined to appoint a Senator or an influential Republican to the commission to write the peace. On crudely partisan grounds some rock-ribbed Republicans would certainly assail any treaty as a Democratic party document.

It is also arguable that it was mistaken judgment for the President to have attended the Paris parley. True, his presence may have compelled desirable decisions which might otherwise not have been taken, or prevented undesirable decisions, but Wilson was not at his best in the rough and tumble of face-to-face debate, and during his absence abroad unsympathetic critics had an opportunity to weaken further his popularity and prestige on the home front.

Be that as it may, the Wilsonian design for the new and better world order rested on two major premises: the self-determination of peoples, and an international organization for security and enduring peace. The first harmonized fully with democratic concepts and implied that frontiers in Europe should be drawn in accordance with the nationality of the populations involved as the way to lasting pacification. Unhappily national groupings were so intermixed in parts of Europe that it was humanly impossible to implement the Wilsonian maxim fully. The President's acquaintance, as he candidly acknowledged, with vexed nationality tangles and broad European perspectives left much to be desired. Unhappily, too, in the mouths of Adolf Hitler and his henchmen the explosive potentialities of self-determination would one day be disastrously exploited.

The idea of a world league of states to keep the peace and to smooth out faults in the treaty settlements themselves was central in Wilson's scheme of thought. Of secondary significance were the reduction and limitation of armaments and the principle that the indemnities demanded of the enemy should not be of a punitive character.

At Paris Wilson was confronted by the stark, tough actualities of European high politics. On several vital issues he contrived to bend his colleagues to his will and so gave to the peace a quality of mercy it might not otherwise have had. At other points he equivocated on his declared plans primarily in order to secure the acceptance of his project for a league of nations.

Britain's foremost spokesman at the conference was David Lloyd George, who owed his selection as Prime Minister to his personality and demonstrated ability—and to nothing else. The "Wizard of Wales" resembled in some respects a veteran American politician. He knew how to win friends and influence people. Behind him he had a long and contentious career in the Commons. When he spoke at Paris he did so with the confidence that command of the strongest navy, army, and airforce in the world afforded him.

An avowed pragmatist in public affairs, adroit, resilient, a good listener, Lloyd George was inclined to approach problems in an intuitive rather than a logical manner. He managed on more occasions than one to find a middle way that was acceptable to Wilson and Clemenceau.

Lloyd George had little experience in international politics, but he was a genius at picking the brains of men who possessed the knowledge that he himself lacked. He was blessed with a broad and cheerful sense of tolerance. For him British world interests outweighed universal ones. He adopted, for example, a lukewarm attitude on the League of Nations, took a dubious and disastrous stand on reparations, but in general he subscribed to moderate treatment of the enemy in order that war wounds might quickly heal and German economy might speedily recover. His whole course of action could not fail to be shaped by the facts that the once-dreaded German navy had been interned and that German warplanes were no longer a menace to the security of the island kingdom.

Just before the conference convened Lloyd George had won a smashing victory in a parliamentary election, and so had assurance of support at home which Wilson lacked. But he had promised to hang the Kaiser and to make Germany pay to the last penny. At Paris he found himself the prisoner of those rash election slogans; the more chauvinistic British newspapers and M. P's. stridently clamored for literal fulfillment of campaign promises.

And Lloyd George had another heavy millstone round his neck. This was the secret war-time treaties which the British cabinet had negotiated either to purchase the intervention of a foreign power or to induce an ally to make a larger contribution to the war effort. Britain's Prime Minister felt legally and morally obligated to see that those commitments were honored in the peace treaties.

Honorary chairman of the Paris Conference and manipulator of his hand-picked French delegation was Georges Clemenceau. He was the "old tiger," to friend and foe alike, though to one acute observer he "looked more like a walrus than a tiger, a poor old walrus in a traveling circus." Like Lloyd George the Frenchman had crowded to the top in politics the hard way, through the hurly-burly of the Chamber of Deputies. At a critical stage in the war, in 1917, he had fought his way into the premiership, and on the conclusion of hostilities he was toasted as the "father of victory." Shortly before the assembling of the conference the Chamber of Deputies had expressed by a thumping majority of more than four to one its confidence in Clemenceau to secure the kind of peace that France demanded.

Clemenceau was old, short, plump, an adept at coining sardonic bon mots, a born polemicist whose approach to problems of peacemaking was coldly stoical—realistic as he liked to think. "He came to the conference," writes a thoughtful biographer, "not as a knight of humanity riding forth to redress all wrong, but as a lawyer comes to a courtroom with a specific brief. His client was France; his assignment, to protect essential French interests . . ." [1] Compared with France and her future all else was trivial in Clemenceau's sight.

In the peace negotiations Clemenceau faithfully reflected the dominant moods of the French nation. Had he neglected to do so he would swiftly have been hurled from power and replaced by another more attuned to the popular will. More moderate than the angry and fearful French extremists, Clemenceau actually lost caste by his performance at the conference and thus was robbed of the presidency of the Third Republic.

After the making of the German Armistice Clemenceau disclosed a desire for the perpetuation of the victorious Grand Alliance though he had little hope and less faith in the League as an instrument to preserve the peace. But the Wilsonian principle of self-determination he applauded as an ingenious formula whereby enemy countries could be reduced and France's young Slavic friends in eastern and central Europe could be made strong.

Clemenceau's thinking on the peace (and his course at the conference) was ruled by a double and overmastering conviction: fear of another war with Germany, a country more powerful than France, which twice within the Premier's memory had overrun and devastated French soil. The hereditary enemy, Clemenceau believed, was simply incorrigible, beyond regeneration, understanding superior physical force and nothing else. Gestures of conciliation he rejected with scorn and contumely, for they would not only prove futile; they would be positively dangerous in the light of Germany's black and untrustworthy record—hence Clemenceau's stubborn insistence upon solid guarantees to assure the safety of the Third Republic in the world of tomorrow.

He also feared the economic collapse of his beloved France, burdened as it was with a prodigious debt and faced with the expensive task of rebuilding war-ravaged provinces—hence his insistence upon full financial compensation by the enemy. And coloring his whole outlook was the resolution to do unto Germany what Bismarck had done unto France in 1871. He felt compelled to reassert the greatness of France.

Clemenceau did not by any means have his way on every contentious issue affecting French interests that arose at Paris. He fought

[1] Geoffrey Bruun, *Clemenceau* (Cambridge, Mass., 1943), p. 198.

hard and tenaciously, but he yielded when he saw that he could get no more. Yet he more nearly realized his purposes than either of his chief colleagues.

Lesser Ones

The other victor nations sent distinguished sons to Paris to advance their national claims and to speak up for their national ambitions. For Italy there was Prime Minister Orlando, a genial but disillusioned scholar who was constantly plagued by political convulsions at home. He was reluctant to involve himself in questions not directly of concern to Italy. Where application of the doctrine of self-determination fortified Italian aspirations, Orlando and his fellows appealed to it; but where the principle was disadvantageous they pursued other lines of argument.

Japan's principal delegate was Marquis Saionji, elder statesman of Nippon, who as a youth had studied in Paris and counted Clemenceau among his French acquaintances. The objectives of Japan were limited. They were: the recognition of the racial equality of nationalities; the formal transfer of former German islands in the Pacific above the equator; and the securing of ex-German rights and interests in the Chinese province of Shantung.

Smaller countries dispatched their choicest diplomatists and most persuasive tongues to the Paris conclave—men intoxicated with the champagne of victory, intent on satisfying their own national claims rather than obtaining a general and enduring peace. They were bent on getting the maximum territory for their respective countries, on putting old wrongs to rights, and on redressing new grievances. Picturesque figures from Arab and other Asiatic lands imparted splashes of color and a flavor of Oriental drama to the gathering.

Accompanying each delegation was an appropriate array of technical specialists in political, economic, and military affairs.

While the decisive work of the conference was carried on behind closed doors, there were agents of uninvited nations and of minorities —pressure groups, too—who felt their future in jeopardy. They circulated propaganda for their causes or aired their opinions on every ill to which humanity is heir.

And Paris entertained shoals of newsmen, avid for fact, fertile in imagination, and resentful over their exclusion from the official doings except plenary sessions. A host of eager sightseers, likewise, attended the grand sweepstakes. All in all it was a race such as society seldom before had seen.

Machinery

When the Allied statesmen came together on January 12, 1919, no arrangements had been made on conference procedure. Should the treaty with Germany be written first or treaties with all the enemies simultaneously? Would the conference be preliminary, to draft an agenda for a definite congress, or would it make final treaties? Would the League of Nations form part of the treaties or be the subject of a separate covenant? What part should the delegates of the less than Great Powers have? These questions were answered by time or by quick decisions. The impracticable Wilsonian point calling for open diplomatic deliberations was promptly jettisoned in favor of secret negotiation.

As a sort of executive board of the Conference, an Inter-Allied Council of Ten was created, made up of the heads of the delegations of the five largest states and their foreign ministers—the successor to the Supreme Allied War Council. That body dominated the treaty-making until mid-March, assigned commissions to their several tasks, and listened to the opinions of spokesmen on controversial matters. The order of business was prepared largely by French diplomatic experts and meetings were usually held in the stately French Foreign Office.

At the middle of March treaty discussions entered upon a new phase. Vital questions of armaments, of territory, and reparations were thenceforward debated by the Big Three with Orlando often in attendance. Those sessions, which took place in Wilson's study, were so informal and so secret that part of the time not even a secretary was present to record what was said. Violent cleavages frequently brought the negotiations to the verge of a general brawl, and more than once the utter breakdown of the conference threatened. Asked on one occasion how the Big Three were getting along, Clemenceau growled, "Splendidly. We disagreed about everything."

Much of the actual content of the eventual treaties was prepared by commissions and committees, of which there were seventeen principal ones and over two score others. These bodies which contained politicians, experts, and men who had hurriedly studied up on special problems during the war, examined the problems of the peace with exemplary fullness of detail. Committees worked more or less on their own with a minimum of supervision or coordination by the Council of Ten. Sometimes conclusions were reached only after painful debate, and then were transmitted to a higher level—from mid-March on, to the big Three—for acceptance, rejection, or modification.

Last of all, the finished reports were offered to the conference as a whole. Only six times was the general conference assembled and, except for the session devoted to the League Covenant, the meetings were nothing more than perfunctory formalities, called to assent to what had already been decided upon.

Germany Accepts

Toward the end of April the treaty with Germany was sufficiently complete to warrant summoning German delegates to Paris. Handed the draft document the Germans forthwith protested that the proposed settlement violated the Wilsonian platform for peace, which, with amendments, had been the basis on which Germany had ceased fighting.

In an elaborate set of "Observations" on the treaty, running into a book of 443 pages, the Germans attacked the document with unmeasured vehemence and tactlessness. These criticisms in an embellished form were echoed inside Germany and were to be reiterated by Germans and by Allied critics of the treaty for the next twenty years.

The Germans denied the validity of a clause which was interpreted to impute moral guilt for the coming of the war to their country. They indignantly insisted that articles relating to Alsace-Lorraine, the Saar Basin, the Polish boundary, and forbidding the union of Austria with Germany contradicted the principle of self-determination. They protested the loss of African colonies. They protested that the financial terms would condemn their nation to eternal slavery. They resented the exclusion of Germany from the projected League of Nations. In a word, in the eyes of the Germans the treaty was a death warrant for their nation; it was a peace of violence, not of justice.

To the German "Observations" the peacemakers replied brusquely point by point. One major modification prescribing a plebiscite in Upper Silesia was admitted and several minor ones. Other than that, the Germans were bluntly ordered to sign on the dotted line.

For days there was grave anxiety in Allied circles as to whether the Germans would accept. Allied troops on the Rhine made ready to march deeper into Germany—the Yankees were prepared to advance into the region whence Hessian mercenaries had been brought to crush the American Revolution—and plans were put in train to revive the blockade on foodstuffs and industrial raw materials.

Faced by those prospects and on other considerations, the newly-created German National Assembly after tense and stormy scenes consented to ratify the treaty. Formal signature took place on June 28, 1919, five years to a day after a young Serbian zealot had assassinated an Austrian Archduke and his wife in the obscure Balkan town of Sarajevo. The ceremony was staged in the grand chateau of Louis XIV at Versailles—exactly the place in which Bismarck forty eight years earlier had proudly proclaimed the birth of the German Empire.

But on this occasion France was in the ascendant, Germany the humiliated one. "Nine and forty years," exulted old Clemenceau, "have I waited for this. The treaty is something fixed and final which settles the affairs of Europe forever." For one who prided himself on his arch realism that remark was either jest or unwisdom.

Once the treaty with Germany was autographed, President Wilson and other top-ranking policymakers save, of course, Clemenceau, withdrew from Paris. They left to subordinates and technicians the tasks of putting the finishing touches on the treaties with Germany's late allies—treaties which were patterned on the Versailles model.

The Versailles Treaty: Territorial

By the territorial provisions of the Treaty of Versailles, Germany in Europe was reduced about ten per cent in area and population. In the ceded regions, pre-war Germany had mined almost three quarters of its iron ore and a quarter of its coal. They also contained valuable industrial establishments and good farmlands. The end result was to fence Germany in much as France had been hemmed in after 1815.

Alsace-Lorraine was retroceded to France in line with the Wilsonian program, though whether the population in majority preferred French to German status is susceptible to more than one guess. It was the intention of French diplomacy to separate the left bank of the Rhine from Germany permanently and to make it an autonomous buffer state. Of all the controverted matters at Paris this French Rhineland plan provoked the most prolonged and passionate debate. From the time of the French Revolution onward it had been standard French doctrine that the Rhine was the natural frontier of France and needful for national security. To detach the left bank Clemenceau fought with might and main, but when that objective was uncompromisingly vetoed by outraged American idealism and British interest in continental stability, the Frenchman retreated. Wilson and Lloyd George, however, signed treaties of guarantee committing their countries to go to the aid of France in case of an unprovoked German attack.

That second best alternative Clemenceau accepted over the impassioned protest of Marshal Foch and other military chieftains. (As matters turned out Clemenceau got nothing, for the treaties of guar-

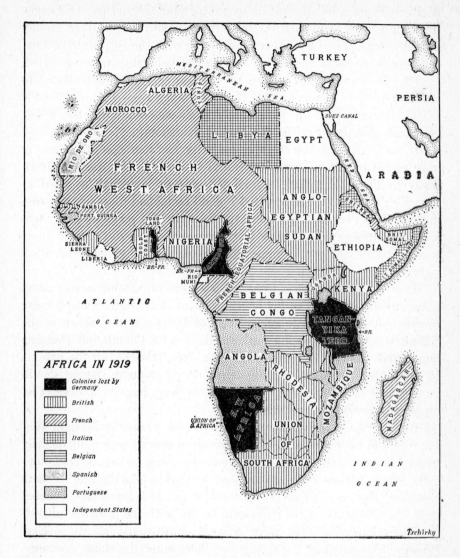

AFRICA IN 1919

- ■ Colonies lost by Germany
- British
- French
- Italian
- Belgian
- Spanish
- Portuguese
- Independent States

Trchirky

antee were never ratified). As a further concession to France clauses were written into the treaty prohibiting armaments or fortifications in the Rhine district up to some thirty miles east of that river; and Allied troops would occupy the left bank and bridgeheads beyond for a minimum of fifteen years at German expense.

French pretensions to sovereignty over the Saar Valley, valuable for coal resources and mills, were balked by Wilson, since the population was overwhelmingly German. As a compromise the French might have the coal of the Saar in reparation for destruction of mines in northern France, but the region would be administered by the League for fifteen years, and then the inhabitants would decide their destiny in a plebiscite. The German customs union with the tiny state of Luxembourg was terminated and its permanent neutrality was reasserted.

Farther north, small parcels of German soil were surrendered to Belgium, subject to plebiscites. Territory taken from Denmark in the 1860's was disposed of in a similar manner, the northern section eventually voting to rejoin the Danish Kingdom.

If, with the passing of time, majority German opinion seems to have reconciled itself to the territorial cessions in the west, it steadfastly declined to regard as final the eastern boundary as fixed at Versailles (or later). Resurrected Poland reclaimed most of the province of West Prussia and Posen. In the main, the population in these areas was indisputably Polish in speech and sentiment, though there was a substantial German minority. Poland was also given plebiscitary rights in Upper Silesia.

The Wilsonian peace program had promised the new Poland access to the Baltic. The implementation of that pledge caused acute controversy at Paris. The ancient city of Danzig at the mouth of the Vistula was the only feasible outlet to the sea for Poland, but Danzig's population was almost entirely German. Nevertheless, all the experts on the Polish boundary commission at Paris thought Danzig should be assigned to Poland—and small bits of East Prussia as well. Clemenceau strongly backed that plan.

But Lloyd George adamantly resisted and eventually brought Wilson round to his point of view. As a result, a special regime for Danzig under League auspices was worked out, assigning to Poland communications and harbor rights in the free city. Through Danzig, Poland obtained the promised access to the sea, but the Danzigers retained their liberties in a state of their own. In line with the principle of self-determination plebiscites were ordered in disputed areas of East Prussia. That province itself, to which Poles entered a claim, remained with Germany, but between it and the Reich proper there lay a tongue of Polish land to which the Germans succeeded in pinning the label of "Polish Corridor." That district and Danzig were to be the direct sources of World War II.

High up on the Baltic, the port of Memel and the countryside surrounding were detached from Germany with a view to possible inclusion in Lithuania. It was also stipulated in the Versailles Treaty that the German Republic of Austria might not unite with Germany—a decision that almost certainly was at variance with the wishes of the

Austrians at the time, but to have permitted union would have made Germany potentially stronger than in 1914.[2]

Outside of Europe Germany was deprived of all colonial holdings and of special trading privileges in China, Morocco, Siam, and elsewhere. The former German-African empire was divided between the British realm, France, and Belgium, while the island possessions in the Pacific passed to the British realm and Japan.[3] None of these colonies was annexed, but, on the insistence of Wilson, they were defined as mandates with the holding country as guardian under League oversight, not as technical owner.

One of the thorniest problems at Paris was the disposition of the extensive rights which Germany had in the populous Chinese province of Shantung. Chinese delegates claimed the reversion of these rights to their country and Wilson warmly supported them. But Japan put in a counter-claim and demanded its validation on the grounds that soldiers of the Mikado had occupied Shantung during the war; that a Chinese government had assented to the substitution of Japan for Germany in conventions of a dubious character; and that Britain and France had secretly bound themselves in wartime treaties to back the Japanese pretensions.

Those considerations and the desire to have Japan in the League persuaded Wilson to consent to Nipponese predominance in Shantung, though with extreme reluctance, and after an explicit Japanese promise to pull out at some future time. Because of the Shantung decision China declined to sign the Versailles Treaty, and the flare-up against Wilson for "surrendering" to Japan helped to encompass the defeat of the Treaty in the United States.

Military Provisions

The military clauses of the Versailles Treaty, which had no parallel in history, were aimed at giving the Grand Alliance a lasting strategic advantage over Germany. At the behest of Wilson a preamble was drawn up which imposed a moral obligation on the victors to reduce their armaments. It was an imprecise statement which turned out to be a fecund source of international dissension in the twenties and thirties.

---

[2] German rivers and ports which were used by ships of other nations were placed under international authority and the defenses of the Kiel Canal were razed.

[3] Japan secured the Marianas, the Marshalls, and the Carolines, whose conquest was to prove so costly for the United States in the Great Pacific War.

The German army might not exceed 100,000—a police force merely—and could only be raised by voluntary enlistment for a long term; the organization of the army was prescribed in minute detail. Such weapons as big guns, tanks, armored vehicles, and planes were absolutely prohibited. Besides, as has been noted, German territory to the west of the Rhine and for about thirty miles to the east was completely demilitarized, presumably forever. As for the navy it was severely restricted in size and equipment, and submarines were proscribed.

If the French had had their way at Paris, an Inter-Allied inspectorate would have been stationed in Germany indefinitely to see that the military restrictions were not transgressed. In opposition to that proposal Lloyd George and Wilson spoke with an identical voice. So it was agreed that an Inter-Allied Control Commission would stay in Germany simply long enough to make sure that armaments were scaled down to the levels prescribed in the Treaty.[4]

Only if the military limitations written into the treaty were enforced would the rest of the Versailles Treaty be likely to stand for an indeterminate period. For, in spite of the territorial transfers, Germany was still the most populous country of Europe, except for Russia, and the most industrially mature and energetic of them all.

Reparations

For exacting financial retribution from Germany there was ample precedent in principle. After the German victory in 1871, for example, France was obliged to pay about a billion dollars. President Wilson, who candidly acknowledged that he was not much interested in economic matters, had declared against any damages in the nature of punishment. But in the pre-Armistice agreement it had been decided that Germany was liable for all damages done to the civilian population of the Allies and their property.

To clothe that formula with reality provoked argument and produced sophistry at Paris. Popular fancy in Britain and France, as reflected in press and parliament, imagined that Germany was not only able to pay the full costs of the war but would be summoned to do so.

Estimates that were offered by professional experts as to what Germany might be capable of paying ranged from a modest $10,000,-

---

[4] There was an article in the Treaty requiring Germany to answer any inquiry that the League Council might make concerning armaments, but the actual value of that safeguard was nil.

000,000 into a realm where only astronomers could feel intelligent. The American official opinion that Germany should be informed at once how much she should pay, as a spur to fulfillment, was overborne by Anglo-French insistence that the bill should not be rendered until popular expectations had had time to tone down, studies had been made of Germany's capacity to pay, and the bill had been carefully prepared.

It was agreed at Paris that reparations should cover not only the cost of repairing districts ravaged in the war but also pensions and separation allowances granted by Allied governments to war veterans or their families. Lloyd George pushed vigorously to have that second item put on the list of damages, for without it Britain would receive precious little reparations. British Tories gingered up the Prime Minister with a telegram calling for blood (such as he had promised in the parliamentary electioneering).

Wilson's first impulse was to resist the inclusion of pensions in the reparations bill, but the South African Premier, Jan Christian Smuts, prettily explained to him that pensions were legal and logical inasmuch as Allied soldiers were simply civilians temporarily in uniform. That may have convinced Wilson. At any rate he consented, and about two thirds of the reparations as ultimately fixed were for pensions.

So the Versailles Treaty prescribed what Germany should pay *for* without fixing the gross amount. As a first installment Germany should pay about $5,000,000,000 by May of 1921, at which time an Inter-Allied Reparations Commission would have the complete bill ready. Credit would be given for all German merchant ships over 1,600 tons and for railway rolling stock that had been appropriated. For a dozen years and more, reparations, which in fact were laced in with the war debts which the Allies owed to one another and to the United States, were to plague the economics and politics of the entire globe.

Other Items

As the preface to the reparations chapter in the Versailles Treaty and indeed as the technical justification for damages, Germany was obliged to accept responsibility for bringing on the war. But Germans and many outsiders interpreted that clause as placing moral and ethical guilt for the war upon Germany.[5] To pay the financial cost of defeat

[5] Nothing on "war guilt" was contained in the Armistice nor in the Wilsonian Fourteen Points; in fact, in 1916 the President had denied the exclusive responsibility of any single belligerent.

was one thing, but to be told that it was not so much the price of defeat but the wages of sin fostered a violent state of emotion in Germany. Out of this some day the demagoguery of National Socialism would cleverly build political capital.

An article was inserted in the Treaty calling for the trial of the Kaiser and other war criminals for their share in causing hostilities or for their immoralities and cruelties in the prosecution of the fighting. Germany was also ordered to hand over literary and artistic treasures to Belgium to replace damaged or stolen articles. And the Treaty contained some diverting historical curiosa, such as a provision for the delivery to Great Britain of the sacred skull of the Sultan Mkwawa of East Africa. Since the skull could not be accurately identified, the Germans shipped three skulls to London and asked the British to take their pick.

Austria (St. Germain)

In the closing stage of World War I the ancient Hapsburg monarchy had split asunder and the victors signed separate armistices with Austria and Hungary. Those documents provided for unconditional surrender, so that there was no contractual obligation to apply the Wilsonian formulae. Uprisings of hitherto subject nationalities, declarations of independence, and "jumping of claims" went far to determine the territorial settlements before the Paris Conference convened.

By the Treaty of St. Germain Austria was reduced to a diminutive land-locked republic of fewer than 7,000,000 of whom almost a third lived in the capital of Vienna. Flags of Czechoslovakia, of Poland, of Rumania, of Yugoslavia, of Italy fluttered over sections of the pre-war Austria, and it was forbidden Austria to merge with the German Reich. Armed forces were limited to 30,000; conscription was banned; and heavy financial reparations were demanded.

Four main controversies over former Austrian territory presented difficult problems for the peacemakers: the boundary between Italy and Yugoslavia, the boundary between Italy and Austria, the boundary between Czechoslovakia and Germany, and the status of eastern Galicia.

Sharp disputes involving Italy were the most serious, and for believers in democratic perfectionism quite disillusioning. Under the secret Treaty of London of 1915 (p. 46) with which the Allies had purchased Italian intervention, Italy had been promised the Austrian

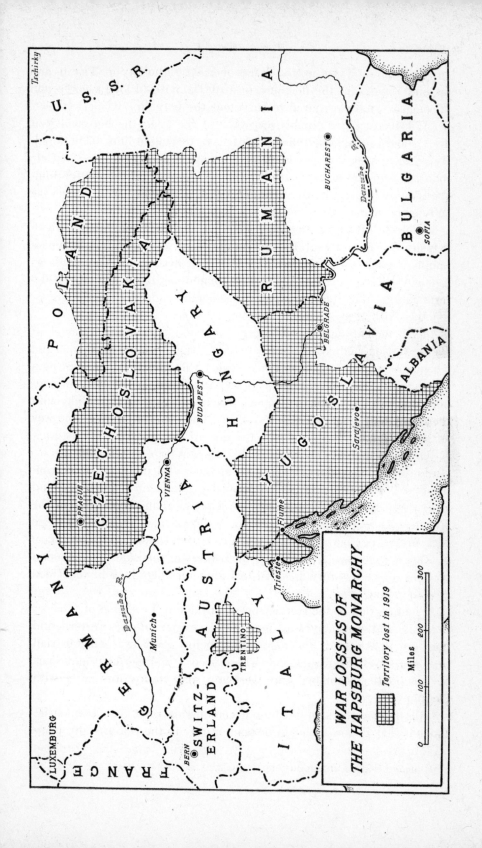

WAR LOSSES OF
THE HAPSBURG MONARCHY

Territory lost in 1919

Miles

0   100   200   300

province of the Tyrol up to the Brenner Pass, the city of Trieste and its hinterland, and the northern part of Dalmatia. Lloyd George and Clemenceau were prepared to carry out the bargain.

Wilson dissented. In his program for the peace he had said that Italy should be enlarged along "clearly recognizable lines of nationality." Yet in a part of the Tyrol lived almost a quarter million of Germans, and in the other districts which Italy claimed there were hundreds of thousands of Slavs of Yugoslav nationality who were very self-determined.

Adding to the complications was an Italian demand brought forth at Paris for the city of Fiume,[6] at the head of the Adriatic, whose population was mixed Italian and Slav, and desired by Yugoslavia as a good outlet to the sea. While Slav champions harped upon self-determination, the Italians stressed economic and strategic interests, together with Italy's part in winning the war.

That violent conflict of appetite created a dramatic quarrel at Paris. Wilson belligerently rejected the Italian claim to Fiume and when he could not bend Orlando to his will, the President issued a moving and unorthodox appeal to the "plain people" of Italy to support him. But the "plain people" proved disappointing, siding with their own policymakers against Wilson. The disposition of Fiume was left unresolved.

On other points Orlando had his way. Wilson sanctioned the inclusion of the German-peopled area of the Tyrol in Italy (on reasoning that is still unclear), which seemed to many an indefensible and a depraved betrayal of American principle. Italian pretensions in the Trieste zone were likewise approved. Italy was also awarded strategic isles in the northern Adriatic and given the Dalmatian coastal city of Zara. Yugoslav patriots and their foreign partisans looked upon sections of the territory assigned to Italy as irredentas to be redeemed at some future date.

The question of the frontier between the novel creation of Czechoslovakia and Germany was much less vexing. In the western and northern districts of Bohemia, which before 1918 was an Austrian province, dwelt over 3,000,000 whose speech was German, and some of the politically-minded expressed a strong desire for union with Germany.

All the members of the peace commission on Czech boundaries thought that Bohemia should belong entirely to the Czech state, justi-

---

[6] Fiume belonged to Hungary, not Austria.

fying that infringement of self-determination on the score of economic necessity and by the fact that the mountains encircling Bohemia formed an indispensable strategic rampart against Germany. That logic was written into the treaty with Austria. Over the future of eastern Galicia there was a clash of opinion (and arms) between Poles and Ukrainians. No decision on that area was reached at Paris.

Hungary (Trianon)

From the standpoint of self-determination Hungary fared least well of the enemy nations. Hungary was reduced to a third of its prewar dimensions, large districts being ceded to Czechoslovakia, to Rumania, to Yugoslavia, and even a few acres to Austria. For the most part the populations in the areas that were lost were non-Magyar in nationality, but intermingled with them were authentic Magyars, perhaps 3,000,000 altogether. Hungary's army might not exceed 35,-000, and Hungary was committed to pay substantial sums in reparations.

That small monarchy without a monarch vied with Germany for the dubious distinction of Europe's most discontented nation.

Bulgaria (Neuilly)

Balkan Bulgaria having put her money on the wrong horse by backing Germany in the war was penalized by losing her entire frontage on the Aegean Sea, and by ceding four parcels of land in the west to Yugoslavia. Neither of those arrangements seemed wholly wise or desirable to the American delegates at the conference; but they were outvoted. Bulgaria had to pay reparations and was permitted only a small army.

Turkey (Sèvres)

Immediately after Turkey became a belligerent in 1914, Allied diplomatists started to work out secret bargains for the long-heralded dismemberment of the Ottoman Empire. By the time of the Paris Conference these secret treaties, which contained some extremely tricky and irreconcilable promises, were no longer wholly relevant. A pledge to Russia, for example, gratifying her age-old yearning to be master of Constantinople and the Straits, was cancelled by the Bolshevik Revolution.

At Paris, in the Treaty of Sèvres, Constantinople was retained by

Turkey as was most of Anatolia. Other Ottoman territories were distributed with a generous hand. Armenia was defined as a national home for the Armenians, though most of the area gravitated into the Soviet Union. Greece was given handsome tracts in Europe and in Asia Minor. But in fact the fragile Sèvres Treaty never went into force. It was quickly converted into a scrap of paper by militant Turkish nationalism (p. 211).

Minorities Treaties

The modern history of all areas of mixed tongue or nationality in Europe, Switzerland alone excepted, is a story of unrest, oppression, hatreds, and brutalities. In the "new Europe" as blocked out in 1919-1920 substantial minorities perforce lived under alien rule. The idea of mitigating minority discontents by exchange of populations had little popularity at Paris. True, the crude number of minority peoples was radically scaled down by the new territorial arrangements, but there was one striking difference: the principal minorities of the new Europe had belonged to dominant majorities before 1914, and were afflicted with a *Herrenvolk* complex. Discontent, in other words, was redistributed. If the mathematics of the minority situation had improved, the psychology had become worse, and history—the glutton—profited.

Over 3,000,000 German-speaking people, for instance, were inhabitants of Czechoslovakia, hundreds of thousands of Poland, and so on. Similarly, Magyars were subjects of countries that were beneficiaries of Hungary's dismemberment. Other national minorities and religious minorities, notably the Jews, were scattered indiscriminately about central and eastern Europe. The healing salve of time, economic well-being, and the operation of democratic principles might be relied upon to soften asperities, but that would be a tedious and prolonged process.

Meanwhile the peacemakers endeavored to assure fundamental political and personal rights to minorities and to give them some protection against unfair discrimination by special treaties, under the supervision of the League of Nations. Five states—Poland, Czechoslovakia, Yugoslavia, Rumania, and Greece—solemnly bound themselves "to protect the interests of inhabitants who differ from the majority of the population in race, language or religion." Minorities might freely submit grievances to the League. The logic underlying those arrangements harmonized well with the conception of the rights of minorities which prevailed in English-speaking countries.

Unhappily the minority agreements were not faithfully executed and exerted only a limited restraining influence on the majorities. The League lacked authority to compel respect for its word. Too much, no doubt, was expected of dull human nature too quickly. Tolerance of the dissenter, of the different, grows slowly as the history of Europe amply testifies.

Beyond that, it was asserted by nations which had signed the minority treaties that these rights imperilled national integrity, since they encouraged treasonable and secessionist agitation. On that ground and because of the feeling that it ought to be looked upon as a Great Power, Poland arbitrarily cancelled its minority treaty in 1934. Much as before 1914, minorities living under an alien flag filled the air with lamentations, and their cries were taken up and inflated by zealots in the national homeland. That was a contributory cause of the coming of war in 1939.

The League of Nations

The Covenant of the League formed the first section of the treaties signed by Germany and her former allies. In some sense the Covenant embodied the hopes and plans of a long line of men of good will who had dreamed of a warless world. For President Wilson the making of the Covenant was the paramount business of the Paris Conference. The charter would be a beacon light for future humanity; and he had himself chosen as chairman of the League Constitutional Commission.

Wilson's success in getting the Covenant drafted at once and woven into the peace treaties is accounted his largest victory at Paris. He accomplished this against the wish of European policymakers who, out of apathy or for reasons of political strategy, preferred to postpone consideration of a world organization for peace. It was Wilson's assumption that by tying the Covenant tightly to the treaties and the treaties tightly to the Covenant, he would assure the ratification of the entire fabric by the United States Senate. Never, he thought, would the Senate have the audacity to reject "the whole vital structure." In so thinking Wilson erred tragically.

In the preparation of the Covenant several specific stages may be singled out. Before going abroad Wilson had worked out his own ideas as to what the constitution should contain. A battery of British legal specialists, headed by Lord Phillimore, had drawn up a draft constitution, much of which was incorporated in the ultimate instrument.

At Paris the League of Nations Commission, Wilson presiding, discussed the merits and defects of these two plans and debated suggestions offered by spokesmen of other countries. The French, for instance, strongly urged that the League should be equipped with international military services, capable of enforcing decisions. That recommendation, however, savored too much of an international state to attract universal concurrence. From the Japanese delegation came a proposal to recognize the inherent equality of races, something that was extremely dear to the proud, sensitive Japanese heart. When the proposal was put to a vote eleven of the seventeen commissioners voted favorably, but since the vote was not unanimous Chairman Wilson ruled that the clause was rejected. Many a Japanese newspaper pilloried the decision as demonstrating anew the white world's belief in Nipponese inferiority.

In ten sessions lasting in all only thirty hours the League Commission hammered out the first draft of the constitution. Then changes were inserted in the light of discussion, official and unofficial, in the United States. And, by a unanimous vote, the final draft was approved in a plenary session of the conference.

The Essence of the Covenant

Central in the entire League project was the idea that in the future the security of each nation would be the joint responsibility of all nations. Provision was made for the rectification of faults and weaknesses in the treaty settlements and for the consideration of international conditions dangerous for peace; international social, labor, and intellectual interests would be furthered. Upon the League would devolve certain administrative responsibilities such as general supervision of mandated territories and of the treaties promising rights to minorities.

But the transcendant purpose of the League was to prevent a recurrence of the civilized barbarities of very modern war. It was obvious that quarrels between nations would arise in the future and the Covenant contemplated settling them on an international basis. Each member committed itself to submit disputes to League authority for peaceful adjustment, by means of conciliation, arbitration or judicial decision. In no case should a state fight until a verdict had been rendered under League auspices; that article rested on the hypothesis that if hostilities were delayed and a search for a pacific solution were made, war might be avoided.

If any state took up arms in violation of its obligations, all the other states might apply economic pressure against the Covenant breaker, and as a last resort military force might also be exerted. But there was no compulsion for a state to act automatically against a disturber of the peace and so no really effective guarantee of security resulted.[7]

Most important of the organs of the League was the Council made up of permanent representatives of the five Great Powers and others elected periodically to represent the middle-sized and small states. The Council would meet quarterly at least and unanimity was required on any matter of consequence. Each member had the veto power. The Assembly on which all members were equally represented would come together once a year to promote international cooperation along broad lines; it may be thought of as an embryonic world legislature. The Secretariat, or international civil service, located at League headquarters in Geneva, would look after the continuing business and the administrative assignments of the League. A judicial body was provided for which eventually took the name of the Permanent Court of International Justice.

Any self-governing state was eligible to membership in the League and any nation might withdraw after giving two years notice. Amendments to the constitution required the concurrence of the Great Powers and of a majority of all members.

Such were the salient features of an institution which the more ardent exponents believed would rid the globe of the scourge of international war. Less sanguine minds looked upon the League as a brave and worthy beginning toward cooperation among the nations, while others were positively hostile to the whole undertaking as a

---

[7] The salient articles of the Covenant which fixed the nature of the League as an institution for international security read as follows:

Article 10. The members of the League undertake to respect and preserve as against external aggression the territorial integrity and existing political independence of all members of the League. In case of any such aggression the Council shall *advise* upon the means by which this obligation shall be fulfilled. (The imprecision in this article will readily be perceived.)

Article 12. The members of the League agree that if there should arise between them any dispute likely to lead to a rupture, they will submit the matter either to arbitration or to inquiry by the Council, and they agree in no case to resort to war until three months after the award by the arbitrators or the report by the Council.

Article 16. Should any member of the League resort to war in disregard of its covenants . . . it shall *ipso facto* be deemed to have committed an act of war against all other Members of the League, which hereby undertakes immediately to subject it to the severance of all trade or financial relations . . . It shall be the duty of the Council in such case to recommend to the several Governments concerned what effective military, naval or air force the members of the League shall severally contribute to the armed forces to be used to protect the covenants of the League. (This article was of British authorship as Article 10 was the product of Wilson's thought.)

snare and a dangerous delusion. Outside of these groups the enterprise was regarded with stolid indifference.

Critique of the Paris Peace

Hardly an article in the treaties of Paris has escaped adverse and acrimonious censure. Some foes assailed the treaties, especially the Versailles document, from first item to last, holding that they represented the marriage of ignorance to iniquity and were calculated to produce not the warless world of ancient aspiration, but rather to invite another holocaust. Not unnaturally that line of interpretation was popular in beaten Germany. Men there of varied political faith harped upon the "injustice" of the Versailles Treaty, a theme that in time was melodramatically exploited by Hitler and his fire-eating National Socialists.[8]

Critics reviled the territorial arrangements as deviating in places from the principle of self-determination, which was true. Weighty considerations of strategy and economics which fixed certain boundaries embittered democratic perfectionists in the victor nations and nationals of the mutilated countries alike. To some, the mandate system seemed nothing short of vicious compromise, while others thought of it as an advance in the direction of freedom for colonial populations.

Idealist and professional economist alike poured vitriolic scorn on the reparations articles. The standard reply was that nothing better could be agreed upon. French sentiment generally resented the failure to secure control up to the Rhine; but elsewhere it was contended that the military clauses were too drastic. The doctrine that "war and peace are both affairs of power" was anathema to critics of that sort.

Taking into account the tropical climate of opinion in which the treaties were written, the piece-meal manner in which settlements were worked out, the cleavage in outlook of the major peacemakers, and the inherent limitations and foibles of human nature, the broad conclusion must be that the Paris treaties, for all their regrettable features, were about as satisfactory as mortals could devise at that time.

If the Versailles Treaty was effectively carried out, Germany at least would not be capable of fighting on the grand scale again. Acknowledged flaws and deficiencies in the treaties might be tempered through the instrumentality of the League as memories of the horrors and destruction of the war years receded. In the language of General

---

[8] In satisfaction of Ph.D. requirements in German universities, 287 theses on the Treaty of Versailles were written by the end of 1932. They were mainly concerned with the legal aspects of the document.

Smuts, explaining why he was ready to sign the Versailles Treaty, "The real work of making peace will begin after the treaty is signed."

The United States Spurns Versailles

Before the treaties could have validity so far as the United States was concerned, they had to be approved by two thirds of the Senate. After a heated and historic and prolonged debate carried on in official chambers and unofficially, the Senate refused to concur in the Versailles Treaty. Peace with Germany was subsequently arranged in a separate instrument.

To the defeat of the Treaty many influences and forces contributed, and no one of them alone can reasonably be singled out as wholly responsible for the end result.[9] Wilson had led the United States into the war, albeit reluctantly, to protect national interests, to uphold national honor, and to vindicate American values. For a large body of Americans, who had favored intervention, the values implicit in the complex democratic way of life, United States style, transcended the starker concerns of physical security.

The Versailles terms deviated so considerably from the war-time idealism that many an American was disillusioned and frustrated. Few critics of the Treaty were more vehement in condemnation than the whole-souled American advocates of more than earthly policies in international affairs. To them it seemed that Britain and France had profited too generously from the settlements and that Germany was the victim of vindictive hatred, calculated to prepare the way for another appeal to arms.

Many an American, moreover, was never really convinced of the thesis that the country had gone to war because Germany and her allies were a direct threat to national security. Some Americans frankly ridiculed that idea. In any case, with Germany completely beaten and disarmed, the old confidence that the United States could repel all danger of war at her own shore-lines forged to the front. Many Americans relaxed into a mood of repose and optimism, choosing to attend to individual and national affairs, little concerned about the world scene. As the crusading idealism of the war era slumped, mistrust of Europe and Europe's ways mounted. New vigor was infused into the old dichotomies of a virtuous America and a wicked Europe, of a peace-loving New World versus a selfish, ungrateful, belligerent Old World.

[9] For a brilliant and penetrating analysis of after-war states of mind in the United States, "the retreat from reality," see Hamilton F. Armstrong, "Last Time," *Foreign Affairs*, XXIII (1945), pp. 349-377.

Spokesmen of special interest groups in the United States, further-more, condemned particular sins of commission or omission in the treaty settlements. For Americans having sympathies with Germany, the Versailles document seemed outrageously harsh and unjust. Friends of Italy and Greece were antagonized by the treatment accorded the extremist demands of those countries. Sinophiles and Japanophobes resented the Shantung compromise. Friends of Ireland denounced the neglect of the Irish claims for political independence.

But the heaviest barrage of criticism was levelled at the League Covenant and its alleged menace to unfettered American sovereignty. It seemed to many that this scheme of collective security promised to cost more than it was worth. For the hypothetical security which the United States would gain the country would be permanently embroiled in the blood-feuds and insoluble quarrels of Europe and Asia, it was said.

Out of the welter of argument and emotionalism four main varie-ties of opinion concerning treaty ratification emerged in the Senate. One faction favored acceptance of the Versailles Treaty as it stood. At the opposite end a smaller contingent—the Irreconcilables—de-manded rejection of the Treaty. That group formed not alone the spearhead of the attack on the Treaty but the nucleus round which all opponents gathered. Between those two extremes stood Senators ready to vote for ratification if safeguarding revisions were made in the Covenant, some holding out for far-reaching reservations, others for less drastic ones.

Wilson's inability to conciliate moderate revisionists, his unwilling-ness to make compromises in detail, his stubborn determination to break the will of the "Irreconcilables," had their part in preventing ratification of the Treaty. Rehearsal of the litany of virtues which the Covenant possessed failed to carry the necessary conviction.

With sublime confidence on the outcome Wilson summoned the electorate to think of the presidential election of 1920 as "a solemn referendum" on American membership in the League. But the over-whelming defeat of the Democratic Party at the polls could be (and was) interpreted as popular repudiation of the League. Yet the con-fusion and profusion of the domestic issues in the campaign and am-biguous utterances of Republican Party leaders concerning member-ship in the League largely nullified the 1920 election as a plebiscite on participation in the world organization for peace and security.

In a notable cartoon, "Home from Home," London *Punch* portrayed Wilson steaming across to Europe, and saying, "Time I was getting back to a hemisphere where I am really appreciated." Certainly the

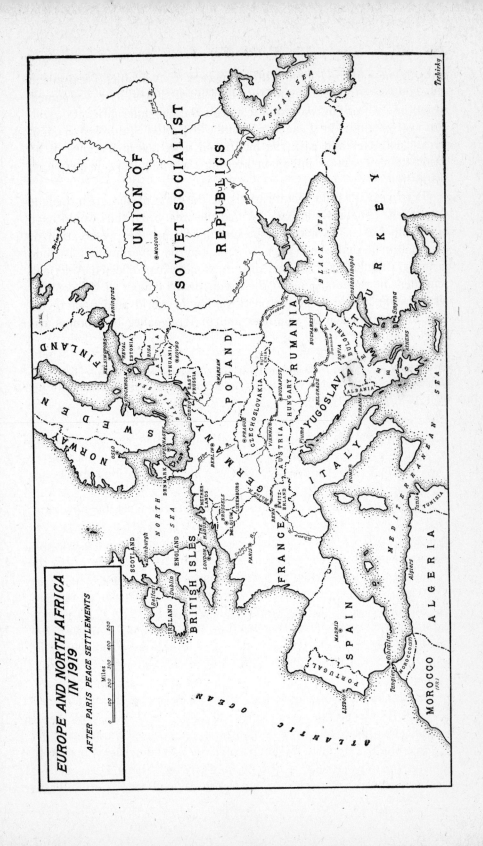

EUROPE AND NORTH AFRICA
IN 1919

AFTER PARIS PEACE SETTLEMENTS

Miles
0 100 200 300 400 500

unwillingness of the United States to accept the Versailles Treaty dealt a heavy blow to the League, for the United States, it was assumed, would be the very bulwark and leader of the new international organization. Certainly the League without the United States lost its universal character and gave the institution more the appearance of an association of victors intent on keeping the vanquished in perpetual subjection.

Perhaps with mild modifications at the time of the great League debate, the Senate would have ratified the treaty and thus would have made the League a more potent instrument for the preservation of peace. But of that one cannot be sure, for the government's attitude in any particular international dispute would have reflected American sentiment at the moment and the predominant temper of the country was unsympathetic to active participation in world affairs—a reversion to the tradition of aloofness and of repugnance to "foreign entanglements."[10]

[10] The Senate never took up the Treaty of Guarantee which Wilson made with Clemenceau, and the British cabinet felt no inclination to ratify the special treaty that Lloyd George had signed.

*

THE NATIONS
BETWEEN WARS

*

CHAPTER V

Soviet Russia

Russia in Two World Wars

IN World War I Russia went down in total defeat before the armies of Germany and her allies. In World War II Russian troops, though they reeled before the massive onslaught of the German war machine, regained their breath, and then delivered sledge-hammer counter blows which carried them all the way to Berlin. Just before the final withdrawal from the first struggle Russia was immersed in revolutionary convulsions. After the Second World War, Russia alone among the European belligerents showed no visible signs of far-reaching change in domestic affairs.

Part of the profound difference in the Russian record in the two struggles and their sequel is to be found in the vast transformation that came over the eastern colossus in the epoch between World Wars. Yet it would be false to assume that Soviet Russia is an entirely new creation. It is sometimes asserted that the Soviet Union and its way of life appeared out of the blue heaven or erupted from the red hell, but both of these judgments do violence to historical fact.

Downfall of the Tsardom

For many months after Russia took up arms in 1914 the soldiery displayed the stolid courage, the sturdy endurance, and the unconscious heroism that had enabled their great-grandfathers to expel the troops of Napoleon from the soil of Muscovy. But Imperial Russia for all its size and human resources lacked the industrial facilities so indispensable in 20th century warfare. Nor could the western Allies send goods in sufficient quantities to meet desperate shortages. Morale in camp and home-front ebbed as the slaughter of soldiers reached gigantic dimensions. Incompetence and treachery were patent in high places, the bureaucratic machine faltered, means of transport broke down, and the essentials of bare existence were hard to obtain in the cities.

117

Out of those conditions, out of popular discontent from the deeper past, and out of a thin thread of ideological radicalism, issued two revolutions in 1917, one in March, the other, in November. The first, centering in the capital city of Petrograd, was precipitated by food riots and carried along by the military garrison which cast in its lot with the insurgents. Without much trouble the discredited Romanov dynasty was swept away and a provisional Republic, dedicated to liberal and democratic principles, was proclaimed.

Authority was assumed by a ministry of freedom-loving nobles and middle-class men who were members of the Duma or parliament. A volcanic little-known lawyer, Alexander Kerensky, professed to speak for the working classes. This provisional government promised fundamental civil freedoms, fair treatment for minority peoples, the arrangement of elections for a constitutional assembly, and the prosecution of the war against Germany and Austria. This "new Russia" was hailed with transports of delight in western Europe. It was "a fit partner for a League of Honor" in President Wilson's elegant language.

But the tenure of power of the provisional government lasted only eight months. Misinterpreting the dominant mood of the nation the new regime endeavored to infuse fresh energy into the war effort and procrastinated in making economic changes of a thorough-going sort. It failed to satisfy the deep longings of the Russian masses and it witnessed the steady disintegration of discipline in the armed forces.

The Bolshevik (November) Revolution

In rivalry with the provisional Republic, orators and pamphleteers of the revolutionary organization known as the Bolsheviki promised "peace, land, and bread" if Russia were entrusted to their care. Bolshevik is the Russian word for majority and in the present context refers to the band of Russian revolutionaries of the Marxist school of thought who, at a conference in 1903, parted company with a smaller faction over matters of tactics and doctrine. Bolshevik Marxists believed in the overturn of the existing Russian society by revolutionary violence and the establishment of a collectivist commonwealth, the movement being engineered by a hardened, strictly disciplined corps of professional revolutionaries.

Some of the early Bolsheviki joined the cause less out of any burning altruistic desire to improve the lot of mankind in conformity with Marxian principles than because they thirsted for revenge against tsarist oppressors. After participating in an abortive rising against the monarchy in 1905, some of the Bolshevik leaders fled abroad, but others strong in the faith, such as Joseph Stalin, carried on active propaganda inside Russia and even elected a few deputies to the Duma.

Acknowledged chief of the Bolsheviki and their guiding genius was Nicholas Lenin, who was spirited to Russia from his Swiss exile in April of 1917 by the German High Command, which intended to exploit him as a military weapon. Lenin did not fail them. He immediately took command of Bolshevik activities and turned them into revolutionary channels. At his elbow was another veteran revolutionary, Leon Trotsky, who had hurried to his homeland from a place of refuge in New York City.

At the back of these and other leaders were some 80,000 resolute, disciplined, class-conscious workers in the major cities of Russia. Bent on converting "the imperialist war into a civil war," and overthrowing the provisional regime, the Bolsheviki wormed their way into local Soviets or councils of workers and soldiers which had burgeoned forth in city, town, and the armed services. Presently a loose national federation (or congress) of Soviets was organized under the leadership of the Soviet in Petrograd. "All power to the Soviets!" cried Lenin and his henchmen and they meant it.

With the provisional government, never strong, degenerating into complete futility, with soldiers trekking home in multitudes, and peasants joyously pouncing upon the property of the privileged, the Bolsheviki in July of 1917 staged a small-bore rising against the new Republic. It failed. An ambitious tsarist general, Kornilov, attempted to set up a military dictatorship by a coup d'état. That failed. Then on November 7 (October by the old Russian calendar) the military revolutionary committee of the Petrograd Soviet, on orders from Lenin, seized authority and the next day handed power over to the All-Russian Congress of Soviets. The successful uprising in Petrograd was followed by parallel Bolshevik insurrections in other leading cities. These were events that shook the world.

Kerensky, who had forged to top place in the provisional regime, fled the country, and with him vanished the only democracy that Russia had ever known. For the Bolsheviki set up an iron dictatorship more complete than the tsarist despotism: a dictatorship, managed by a Council of People's Commissars and headed by Lenin, with Trotsky as director of foreign relations (later of military affairs) and veteran Bolsheviki in other top administrative posts. The Bolsheviki not only reverted to the Russian custom of autocratic government, but recreated the imperial bureaucracy and secret police. The last, under the title of the Cheka, was a potent instrument in establishing Bolshevik rule over the country.

In an atmosphere of disorder and general confusion the Constituent Assembly promised by the provisional government was elected. Most of the deputies belonged to the Socialist Revolutionary Party, which held that Russia should develop a unique form of rural communism, dissolve big landed properties, and build up small local industries in keeping with old national tradition. Constantly in conflict with other radical movements, the Socialist Revolutionaries were weakly led and no match for the Bolsheviki to which the left-wing of the party gravitated. After a single session the Constituent Assembly was dispersed by armed Red forces in favor of the Congress of Soviets. The Bolshevik minority had triumphed. They signalized their victory by suppressing other parties and taking the name of the Russian Communist Party.

In the meantime the Bolsheviki had taken steps to create a collectivist society and to arrange peace with Germany and her allies. Private property of all descriptions used in production was proclaimed state property and the profit motive was abolished practically at one stroke; foreign and domestic debts were cancelled; foreign properties were confiscated. All that was in conformity with the Marxian principle of ending the "exploitation of man by man" through the transfer of the instruments of production to the state, which would then operate them for the community.

Class distinctions were ended; equality of sexes and nationalities was proclaimed; blatant attacks were made upon conventions of sex, family responsibility, and religious institutions. Moscow replaced Petrograd as the national capital and the new masters of Russia seated themselves in the ancient fortress called the Kremlin, thereafter a synonym for the Communist government. The red banner of Communism, on which hammer and sickle were superimposed, was adopted as the emblem of the Bolshevik order.

Soon after the seizure of power, Bolshevik agents ransacked tsarist diplomatic archives and published secret literature which revealed the machinations of capitalist diplomacy. Then Russia's wartime allies were summoned to make peace on the basis of no annexations and no indemnities. When that proposal was ignored by the Allies, the Bolsheviki entered into separate negotiations with the Central Powers which resulted in the notorious Treaty of Brest-Litovsk (March, 1918). That document, while it cut from Russia large slices of territory, including the huge and economically-vital Ukraine, formally closed World War I so far as the Bolsheviki were concerned.

To colleagues who demurred at acceptance of the harsh treaty, Lenin snapped back, "He is no Socialist who does not realize that victory over the bourgeoisie may require loss of territory and who would not sacrifice even his fatherland for the triumph of the social revolution." The favorite Allied thesis that the Bolsheviki were nothing other than gullible and traitorous tools of the German General Staff seemed to be confirmed by the total withdrawal of Russia from the fighting. Foreign hatred blended with fear bred the grossest mistrust and dislike of the Bolsheviki.

Under the November, 1918, armistice Germany cancelled the Brest-Litovsk Treaty and the larger part of the territory that had been taken away was subsequently reclaimed by the "newest Russia."

Bolshevism and the World

According to the oracular Marx a universal world revolution was inevitable. Lenin and his fellows confidently expected that the rest of Europe, shattered by war, would soon be ablaze with the fire of Communism. They cared less indeed about the revolution in Russia than a collectivist upheaval in a highly-industrialized country such as Germany. Holding fast to the Marxian dictum that "the workers of the world should unite," they abhorred the very notions of nationalism and fatherland. It was their belief that out of the general holocaust a collectivist world would arise, and for the first time in history mankind would be genuinely happy.

As an instrument to promote universal revolution and the destruction of capitalism, the Bolsheviki founded the Comintern or Third International early in 1919. Though Communist delegates from other lands had places in the Comintern, the Russian Communist Party by reason of its prestige and power dominated the organization. And agents of Moscow scurried about Europe wherever the prospects of revolt seemed promising. Several "Red" risings occurred in sections of Germany and symptoms of "Red" fever appeared in Italy and countries of eastern Europe, but nowhere was revolution on the Russian model successful. Uniformly the radical revolutionary cause was defeated by the unwillingness of industrial workers or peasants to engage in armed violence, by the weakness of class solidarity when pitted against the sentiment of nationalism, and by the resistance of social elements which preferred the existing order of society.

In Asia Bolshevik missionaries joined forces with anti-imperialistic nationalists without, however, winning any permanent successes. Nevertheless, Bolshevik intermeddling in the Orient haunted foreign governments and the belief prevailed widely, rousing mingled fear and anger, that the Comintern was adroitly plotting to destroy all governments by violence.

Bolshevism failed to overcome the world and equally the world failed to overcome Bolshevism. Within Russia there were irreconcilable foes of the Revolution, armed and resolute. Against these enemies the Bolsheviks turned all their resources. In the horrible civil war that began in 1918 the "Whites," the adversaries of the "Reds," who were marshalled by men of the pre-war ruling caste, benefited somewhat from Allied military intervention. Britain, France, the United States, and Japan each dispatched fighting forces to Russia, and Polish armies (p. 414) penetrated deep into the Ukraine.

According to the Allies the intervention was undertaken in order to re-establish a fighting front against the Central Powers in the east, to protect military stores that had been shipped to Russia, and to facilitate the evacuation of Czechoslovak soldiers who had been released from Russian military prisons. But in the Bolshevik interpretation the real aims of the Allies were the overthrow of Bolshevism and the elimination of the menace of world revolution.

After many months of hard and terrible fighting the Bolsheviki overwhelmed their "White" enemies and thus assured the victory of the Revolution. To the Bolshevik side rallied Russians who believed that a "White" victory would bring back the dispossessed landlords or whose patriotism was enflamed by the presence of foreign troops on the national soil. Physical excesses committed by "White" forces seemed to many Russians worse than "Red" brutalities. Poorly equipped though the Red armies were, they had the advantage of a central position, controlling the cities of Moscow and Petrograd, and what they lacked in weapons they made up in enthusiasm, in discipline, and in propaganda.

To the soldier the Bolsheviki promised, "You will own the land and be able to help yourself to anything you like. But first you must obey and fight." The "Whites" held out no such "red apple." The White armies were wanting in coordination and riven by embittering jealousies and quarreling of commanders. No compelling persuasive personality emerged on the White side to fuse the disparate elements into a unified striking force. When war-weary Allied governments withdrew their forces the White "counter revolution" sagged lower and lower and then ingloriously collapsed.

By the end of 1920 the Reds were almost everywhere victorious. Opponents of the Bolshevik regime in the hundreds of thousands were either liquidated, or compelled to flee abroad, or to adjust themselves as best they could to the new life, passively accepting their fate. Civil wars are seldom tame affairs, and the one in Russia was no exception. Brutalities, atrocities, and massacres taught many foreigners to hate and execrate everything connected with the Revolution. For them Bolshevik Russia was a land of pillage, murder, and licentiousness—a barbarous land which should be treated as a pariah.

For others who were impressed by the altruistic aspirations and visions of the Revolution, it seemed that the Bolsheviki had emancipated Russia from an intolerable tyranny and had laid the foundations for a society from which the ills and follies of the past would be eradicated—a land of rich promise, provided it was given a chance to prove itself. Men of the Left had written and talked of the coming revolution for almost a century and here it was. Here was the pioneer land of the New Age! Here was the Kingdom of Heaven for those who felt that Paradise was lost! Here a purified humanity seemed to be starting anew from scratch! Bolshevik inhumanities, repression of freedom, the iron dictatorship, while hateful and detestable, were unavoidable and justifiable means to desirable ends and would in time pass away, foreign sympathizers with the Revolution felt.

One by one foreign governments pulled their armies out of Russia, Japan last of all in 1922. Foreign intervention left bitter memories which nourished official and popular Russian suspicions of capitalist nations. The Kremlin was forever haunted by the belief that Russia lived in a world of "capitalist encirclement," bent on her destruction. Even so, overtures looking to the return of Russia to the community of nations had their reward. Germany in 1922 resumed commercial and diplomatic relations and by 1924 all major countries except the United States had extended formal recognition to the Moscow regime.

Nicholas Lenin

Lenin, as dictatorial head of the Bolshevik state, guided the destinies of Russia until his death, aged fifty-four, in 1924. In the thinking and emotions of the outer world, this man and Revolutionary Russia were identical. Contemporaries were prone to paint him in colors of pure white or jet black, but fuller knowledge and the perspective of time compel the use of gray pigments. Lenin was neither a flawless demigod, endowed with unerring wisdom, nor a bloodthirsty maniac. Among his conspicuous personal traits were an inexhaustible passion for learning, unconcern for ordinary physical comforts, remarkable gifts as an organizer, a stubborn will, and unwavering confidence in the rightness of his ideas.

Son of a minor Russian nobleman and well-educated, Lenin, early in life, adopted the doctrines of Karl Marx as his own, revising them here and there to fit the peculiar environment of Russia. To that faith, to the belief that its application would usher in a happier and brighter era for mankind he clung with the tenacity of religious devotion. As a professional revolutionary Lenin was very largely responsible for the objectives, the strategy, and the tactics of the Bolshevik Party. He abhorred, for example, isolated deeds of violence against tsarist functionaries, holding that mass action only, properly channeled by a disciplined organization of resolute revolutionaries, and unleashed just when the time was ripe, could encompass the downfall of the established regime and ensure the victory of Marxism.

A strong believer in rigid party organization as indispensable for success, Lenin was probably at his best in winning colleagues in the inner circle of the Bolshevik Party to accept his thinking on immediate courses of action. His knowledge and understanding of Russia were broad and deep. He combined in rare proportions talent as a pamphleteer with practical ability for getting things accomplished in the face of formidable obstacles. It has indeed been persuasively argued that without Lenin the Bolshevik Revolution would never have come to pass.[1]

After the November Revolution Lenin held unflinchingly to the course which he felt was required by his version of Marxism. No considerations, whether of conventional ethics or of the sanctity of human life, were allowed to deflect him from the goal he had set. Seldom did Lenin wear his heart upon his sleeve. It can scarcely be denied that Lenin was the outstanding political figure to emerge from the tumult of World War I. Inside Russia he was exalted as the most distinguished and selfless character ever to parade across the stage of history. His embalmed body, placed in a red-black mausoleum, just beyond the frowning brick walls of Moscow's Kremlin, became the object of pious, popular veneration.[2]

The Soviet Land and Peoples

At the close of the exhausting civil war the Russia of Lenin had almost the same frontiers as the tsardom except on the west.[3] It was Europe's largest and most populous country. All in all the Soviet Union sprawled across more than a seventh part of the earth's surface, though the Siberian vastness was only sparsely peopled and its natural wealth largely a secret for the future to unlock. Size and distances afforded Russia security such as no other European country enjoyed;

[1] See Sidney Hook, *The Hero in History* (New York, 1943), Chap. X.

[2] To honor Lenin Petrograd in 1924 was renamed Leningrad.

[3] Finland, Estonia, Latvia, and Lithuania were set free, a large portion of land was ceded to Poland, and Rumania took possession of Bessarabia.

in World War I Field Marshal Hindenburg decided against marching upon Moscow because "Russia is so vast she would swallow the largest army." He had learned wisdom as Hitler did not from the catastrophic tragedy of Napoleon's invasion of Russia.

Topographically Russia falls into several belts which run with remarkable regularity from west to east. To the far north is the tundra zone on which little more than scrub growth thrives, and the sub-soil is permanently frozen. Archangel and Murmansk, the only substantial communities in this area, serve as commercial windows to the west by way of the Arctic Ocean. Then follows a zone of forests of some 800 miles in depth, mostly soft woods; swamps, marshland, and long cold winters impose limitations upon agriculture in this zone; near Moscow the soil resembles rock for five months out of the year.

A third and narrower district contains broad forests of hardwood but is principally an agricultural steppe. Below that comes the famous Black earth region of the Ukraine, trending off into the foothills of the Caucasus mountains. Almost treeless, this region has magnificent soil whose productivity is somewhat handicapped by dryness. To the south begin the semi-arid steppes, much of which are covered with scrubby grass. They merge with a still drier area to the north of the Caspian Sea and east of the Volga. Historically this section of Russia was called "the famine belt."

Natural wealth in timber resources is enormous, forming a third of the world's supply. In certain sections of European Russia, wood-cutting was considerable but elsewhere, especially in Siberia, there are inexhaustible tracts of virgin forest.

In the matter of mineral wealth the Russian state is well-stocked with iron ore and coal. Extensive prospecting for metals in the epoch between World Wars revealed hitherto unknown stores, but fully authentic information on these physical resources was a closely guarded secret inside Russia. Coal and iron ore are mined in the southern Ukraine (the only major exploitation before the Revolution), in the Caucasus, the Urals, and in several Siberian fields.

No European country approaches the USSR in the output of oil and it is believed to possess ten per cent of the oil reserves of the world. Principal fields lie on either side of the Caucasus—the larger to the south in the vicinity of Baku. Newer oil lands north of the Caspian Sea and in the Ural districts may actually be richer than those in the Caucasus sector.

In the Ukraine and the Caucasus areas, manganese is mined extensively. There are important deposits of platinum, gold, and asbestos, and large discoveries of copper, lead, zinc, potash, silver, and bauxite have been reported. Russia, in short, has large undeveloped potentialities for industrial growth and expansion.

If nature has dealt bountifully with Russia in subterranean wealth, it has been less considerate in climate. Russia has a northerly location —the Black Sea lying in about the same latitude as the Great Lakes of North America. Over the greater part the climate is continental, with long, rigorous winters and short, hot summers. But so extensive is Russia that wide varieties of climate prevail, from arctic to subtropical. Prolonged cold and months of snow over wide areas of the country, followed by the extreme heat of summer, explain for some scholars much in her life that otherwise would be inexplicable.

A geographical feature of Russia that has had constant bearing upon foreign policies is the extent of the coastline that is serviceable. The Arctic littoral, while extensive, has only slight commercial importance and the frontage on the Baltic is narrow and ice-bound for several weeks of the year, as are certain ports on the Black Sea. Whoever controls the Straits leading out of the Black Sea commands maritime and naval shipping there. Vladivostok and other harbors in the Soviet Far East are remote from the main centers of Russian activity.

Riverways have historically been of sovereign importance in the life of the Russians. But the principal rivers of European Russia are clogged with ice for part of the year. The largest in Siberia are frozen over most of the year and empty into the unfriendly Arctic Ocean. Canals, several of them built or improved after the Bolshevik Revolution, link up rivers and seas in European Russia.

Within this geographical framework a little more than 170,000,000 persons lived in 1939, an increase of some 28,000,000 over 1918. In 1939 the heterogeneous peoples of the Soviet Union spoke more than 150 tongues, and books were printed in more than 100 languages. But three groups accounted for over eighty per cent of the languages spoken. The Great Russians, living in a belt from the Baltic to the Pacific and found in all sections of the Union, numbered more than 100,000,000; the Little Russians, or Ukrainians, some 32,000,000, and the White Russians, facing Poland, about 6,000,000.[4]

That left about 30,000,000 for all the other groupings, some of them extremely small. Uniformly Great Russian was the second tongue, the *lingua franca* of the realm. Several of the Soviet nationalities, no-

---

[4] The White Russians (the origin of the name is unknown) as a linguistic group should not be confused with the "White" Russians who fought against the Bolshevik Revolution.

tably the Ukrainians, the White Russians, and the Armenians, had kinsmen across the border. The areas which they inhabited were regarded as Russian irredentas.

For generations tsarist officials had tried to "russify" the non-Great Russian elements of the empire, suppressing languages, folk-customs, and religions. Many non-Great Russians lived in territories which were lost after World War I and the Soviet regime did not revive the russification program. Rather, equality of peoples was prescribed in the Soviet Constitution and the use of local tongues was encouraged in schools, law courts, literature, and public administration. Literatures, in fact, were created in forty languages that did not even have alphabets in 1917. On the other hand, symptoms of anything resembling political nationalism were punished severely, as in the case of the Ukrainians, hundreds of thousands of whom perished or were deported to Siberia. In the interest of Soviet ideological and national unity, the purge was ruthlessly and freely applied to non-conformists.

The Communist Government

That the Bolshevik Revolution by no means represented a clean break with the Russian past is attested in one way by the institutions and practices of Soviet government. For the autocracy of the tsars was substituted "a dictatorship of the proletariat", which in reality meant the rule of an inner ring of the Bolshevik elect, themselves subject to the will of one man: Lenin first, Stalin subsequently.

Nominally, under a Soviet Constitution promulgated in 1923 and in force for thirteen years, the mass of Russian adults participated in public business, through an integrated system of Soviets or councils rising from the local Soviet in hamlet, town or factory through regional Soviets to the All-Union Congress of Soviets. Voting rights were accorded to all citizens over eighteen except members of families which had been identified with the tsarist regime. So arranged was the electoral law that the urban population carried greater weight than the rural elements numerically much larger; and voting was done by a show of hands.

On paper the All-Union Congress of Soviets had very broad powers in determining national policies, though in practice its principal responsibility was to choose the personnel of a Central Executive Committee. When that latter body was not in session, decisions were made by a Council of People's Commissars of seventeen or more members, corresponding to the ministry or cabinet of a western country. Officially the new state was known as the Union of Soviet Socialist Republics (USSR) comprising the Russian Soviet Federated Soviet Republic which covered about nine tenths of the country, and the allied republics of the Ukraine, White Russia, and Transcaucasia. Subsequently other constituent republics were added so that in 1936 there were eleven in all. Equality of nationalities was proclaimed as a fundamental principle of the USSR.

The Communist Party

Such was the shadow of the Communist government, but the substance thereof was tightly held by the Communist Party. The secretary-general of the party was in reality the supreme leader. Not a political party as understood in the west, the Communist Party was composed of pre-1917 Bolsheviks and such other citizens as satisfied rigorous requirements for membership. Admission to the party, which carried with it a good deal of prestige and might bring material advantages, followed a term of probation. From time to time party lists were scrupulously combed and individuals believed to be less than complete in their devotion to party and state were summarily dropped, if no more drastic fate befell them. Lenin was wont to refer to some party folk as radishes—red on the outside but white within—who had to be uprooted and allowed to dry.

As of 1935 the Communist Party, which was organized in local, regional, and national units, embraced rather less than three per cent of the Soviet population, predominantly industrial workers, with peasants and professional folk trailing well to the rear. Almost everyone who exercised power in the Soviet Union belonged to the Communist Party: political leaders, army and police officials, directors of the vast economic machine, and their subordinates in factory, farm, and mine. And besides them the party contained many "ordinary" citizens. In every factory and mine, on every farm there was a Communist "cell" which watched over operations and which was tied in with other organs of the party.[5]

Decisions on major party policies as well as control over the Soviet political organization rested with the handful of nine men who comprised the political bureau (Politburo) or executive body of the central committee of the Communist Party, the final policymaking authority.

Ancillary agencies of government contributed to the Bolshevik triumph in the civil war and then helped to consolidate the ascendancy of the party in the state. Important here was the secret police —known successively as the Cheka, the Gay Pay O (O.G.P.U.) and the N.K.V.D.—which was active all across the Union in fer-

---

[5] During the war with Nazi Germany 3,000,000 new members were admitted to the party, the test being demonstrated political, vocational, or military ability.

reting out dissenters and subjecting them to summary trial and swift punishment. This arm of government perpetuated the profound popular fear of authority which the tsarist Okhrana had done so much to create. In cases where the death penalty was not exacted, culprits were confined to concentration camps or more commonly sentenced to forced labor under harsh conditions on projects for the general welfare. This kind of punishment, which was a source of criticism of the Soviet Union in foreign parts, supplied mobile labor for many of the spectacular achievements of the Communist regime.

Censorship was even more thorough than under the tsarist government. Newspaper, press, and radio had to hew to the line of party and state orthodoxy, once a given course of action had been decided upon; theirs was the duty to proclaim to the citizenry day by day what the Kremlin desired to be known. Principal newspapers were *Pravda,* mouthpiece of the Communist Party, and *Izvestia,* the official organ of the Soviet government.

Ever at the call of government were the armed forces growing in efficiency and equipment as the years passed. In carrying out foreign policies the Communist state counted on the assistance of Communist parties in other countries who were linked together in the Comintern or Third International with headquarters in Moscow. Foreign Communists the globe over were pledged to work for the defense of the Socialist Commonwealth, to influence public policies in their own nations in conformity with the desires of the Soviet Union. The link with Moscow and the commitment to Russian interests was responsible to a considerable degree for the resentment and fear of national Communist parties and of the USSR itself that prevailed in other countries. So intimate were the bonds between the Soviet government and the international Communist organization that only an adept in casuistry could feel sure where the one ended and the other began.

A dramatic (and vital) chapter in the domestic history of the Soviet Union was the fierce struggle for power between Stalin and Trotsky, Lenin's first lieutenants, which came to the fore on the death of Lenin in 1924. While personal jealousies and ambitions were not absent from the controversy, differences over fundamental policies of state resulted in a head-on collision. Trotsky and his followers—Trotskyites—argued that the USSR should concentrate on fostering revolution in other countries, since collectivism could never be achieved in a single land, least of all in industrially primitive Russia; and they protested against the resurgence of economic individualism in the Soviet countryside.

Rejecting the international approach, Stalin and his clique believed that a collectivist society in Russia alone was both desirable and attainable. Successful collectivism in the Soviet Union, they held, would surely invite imitation outside the frontiers of Russia. As secretary-general of the Communist Party, Stalin commanded power which was denied his brilliant rival. Quarreling culminated in 1927 with the banishment of Trotsky, first to Siberia and eventually to foreign exile; in 1940 he was assassinated in Mexico. Abroad, Trotsky resumed his unrelenting vendetta against Stalin, branding him an arch-conservative and the betrayer of the authentic collectivist cause. Some of his sympathizers within the Union were removed by violence. The Revolution devoured some of its makers.

Joseph Stalin

As for the triumphant Stalin, he moved from strength to strength until his prestige in the world of affairs eclipsed that of any Russian on record. In 1945 he was accurately described as "the single most powerful man in the world." Son of a shoemaker in the province of Georgia, short, swarthy, reticent, Stalin was the product of his own qualities and the peculiar conditions of Russia and the world of his age.

Intended for the priesthood by a pious mother, Stalin—or Joseph Dzhugashvili to give him his original name—chose instead the way of the Marxian agitator. He fell under the magnetic spell of Lenin, teamed up with him, and resorted to unlawful acts to secure funds for the Bolshevik cause in the day of the tsars. As agitator and lawbreaker this "man of steel" was several times arrested and shipped to Siberia. The career of conspiracy and abusive treatment by tsarist police left their mark upon his personality, hardened him in his hatred of things as they were.

After the November Revolution Lenin assigned Stalin to the relatively unimportant office of Commissar of Nationalities in the Bolshevik ministry. In the civil wars he showed unusual intuitive qualities as a military tactician. In 1922 he was given the key position of secretary-general in the Communist Party and he held a seat in the powerful political bureau.

Inscrutable, a keen judge of character, elastic, formidable, Comrade Stalin had a firm grasp on the obvious. His authority after the elimination of Trotsky may be likened to that of the "boss" in an American municipality. In time he resembled an uncrowned tsar, only more potent than Peter the Great or his successors ever were. So complete in fact was Stalin's mastery that President Franklin D. Roosevelt was led to remark in 1940: "The Soviet Union, as everybody knows that has the courage to face the fact, is a dictatorship as absolute as any other dictatorship in the world."

A man who could climb to top-place in a country of oceanic dimensions, who could guide that nation through the most stupendous industrialization on record, and then lead it to military victory over the mighty Nazi-German war machine was surely not the mediocrity painted by Trotsky and like-minded schismatics.

Stalin's Constitution

In 1936 a new constitution was drawn up for the Soviet Union which was spoken of as Stalin's Constitution. Published at a time when representative and democratic institutions were on the decline in much of the rest of Europe, the document seemed to herald Russian adoption of western political ways and manners. In the Constitution the USSR was described as a Socialist country of workers and peasants, the political units of which were the traditional Soviets. To the Soviets all central and local authority belonged, constitutionally speaking. The Union consisted of eleven constituent republics, each with a governmental structure akin to that of the Union itself and, according to the Constitution, each was free to secede at any time from the Union.

Part of the older machinery of the USSR was discarded. Instead of the All-Union Congress, for instance, the parliamentary function was assigned to a Supreme Council made up of two chambers having equal legislative power: deputies in one chamber, the Council of the Union, would be chosen directly by electors from single-member constituencies, while the Council of Nationalities would be composed of representatives chosen in the constituent republics. Voting for deputies would be done in secret, not by show of hands as before, and classes of citizens which had previously been denied the franchise were allowed to vote.

It would be inaccurate to dismiss Soviet elections as the merest facade, as sometimes has been done. True, voters had no alternative than to approve policies of the government but those policies—or some of them—were first discussed at every level of a complicated set of representative bodies, with the decisive word reserved to the Communist political bureau (Politburo). True, too, only one person might "stand" in each constituency, yet he was chosen from candidates often nominated after a process of debate which allowed voters some choice. An election itself formally registered the outcome of that process.

It was, furthermore, prescribed in the Constitution of 1936 that the fundamental civil and religious liberties of western tradition would, with some reservations, be granted the Russians.

But as under the older form of government, supreme executive and administrative power belonged to the Council of Peoples Commissars, similar in a way to the Cabinet of the United States. That body was declared to be responsible to the elected parliament and was authorized to legislate by decree in time of emergency. Stalin himself assumed the chairmanship of the Council just before the onset of war with Germany in 1941.

And Stalin's Constitution ranged beyond political institutions. It was asserted that private property in the form of personal belongings, the usufruct of small peasant plots, and individual savings would be respected along with the right of inheritance. The principle of "greater reward for greater services" was formally recognized in the fundamental law of the land. Citizens were obligated to work, to discipline themselves, to abide by the precepts of Socialist human intercourse, and to perform military service. No mention was made in the Constitution of the hitherto standard Soviet doctrine that the world was irreconcilably split between collectivist and capitalist systems.

But the Communist Party was in no wise shorn of its traditional supremacy. No other party was tolerated and the Constitution specifically declared that the party should "form the directing nucleus of all organizations of the toilers," which was tantamount to safeguarding its monopoly in public affairs.

Hardly had the Constitution been published before the world reverberated with tales of fresh and fierce feuds inside Communist Party ranks and wholesale arrests. Charges of counter-revolutionary activity, treasonable plotting with secret agents of Nazi Germany and Japan, murder or contemplated murder, were levelled against some of the most prominent Communists, not a few of them "old Bolsheviks," allies of Lenin and Stalin before and after the November Revolution. Government officials, party leaders, and members of the international Communist revolutionary organization were implicated.

All of that formed the background for the notorious Moscow treason trials and the Great Purge of 1937-1938. Confessions by suspects bordered on the incredible. It is impossible to determine in what measure the accused were actually guilty of the indictments brought against them or to what extent the action of the government was animated by personal antipathies or to unorthodoxies in doctrine.

On the results of the Moscow trials the evidence is clear enough.

Thousands of malcontents were killed, imprisoned, or banished. Whatever conspiratorial trafficking there may have been with foreign governments was scotched. Opposition to the Soviet ruling class, whether incipient or merely potential, was removed by ruthless surgery, and that was a lesson taken to heart in all levels of Soviet society.

Stalin emerged from the bloody and revolting business stronger than he had ever been, without any possible alternative to his leadership on the horizon. Many a foreigner concluded that the wholesale liquidation of Communists holding responsible offices in government, diplomacy, and the fighting services had seriously weakened the foundations of the Socialist Commonwealth. Whatever access of popularity the Constitution of 1936 had gained for the Kremlin in the western democracies was nullified by the Great Purge. The Soviet government ruled by fiat certain that none of its acts would be questioned and blind to the benefits which accrue to a nation from frank discussion and confession of faults and shortcomings.

Main Trends in Soviet Economy

It is a favorite thesis of the Communists that economics dominates everything. It was their objective—and their achievement—to eliminate individual ownership of productive property in favor of state ownership and operation. On the morrow of the November Revolution a series of Bolshevik edicts, noted above, proclaimed that factories, mines, farmlands, banks, and the like belonged to the state. Workers were expected to toil for the common good rather than for their own immediate and personal advantage.

It is possible to over-exaggerate the revolutionary character of the economic changes that were made in the Soviet Union. Before the November Revolution the Imperial Russian state had assumed a greater part in the national economy than was the case in countries where the capitalist or individualist system was deeply rooted. And Russian industrialism, though it had grown substantially in the 20th century, was still in the embryonic stage and more than eight out of ten of the population were still peasants. Therefore Russia could withstand the violent convulsions of 1914 to 1921 more readily than nations having a highly complex industrial economy. As for the rustics, most of them were accustomed to communal ways of labor and life such as had prevailed in Russia for centuries and that peasant psychology did not vanish with the Revolution.

In its broad outlines Soviet economic history falls into three stages: the era of war communism lasting to 1921; an interlude in

which strategic compromise was made with collectivist principles;
and, after 1928, the epoch of total planning in all branches of economic
activity, rapid industrialization and the collectivization of agriculture.

War Communism

The first phase of Bolshevik rule was marked by economic chaos
verging on anarchy. To the disorderly conditions left by World War I
was added the even greater devastation and turmoil attendant upon
the November Revolution and the subsequent warfare inside Russia.
Workers seized factories and chose committees to undertake the tasks
of management, but inexperience and lack of discipline on the part
of the men brought the wheels of industry to a halt. In vain the
Kremlin sought to revive production by appointing trusted managers
to direct individual factories. Money wages were superseded by a
ticket system with which to obtain necessities of life. Unemployment,
beggary in the cities, hordes of homeless waifs, and mass exodus
from cities, tragically testified to the breakdown of the experiment in
extreme collectivism. Peasants in the meantime had expropriated the
land of the old privileged classes and were reluctant to yield up their
surpluses to feed the cities.

In a desperate maneuver to stave off complete disaster the Bolsheviki requisitioned the grain stocks of the peasants. When they balked
and declined to plant more than was necessary for the bare requirements of their families, the government resorted to coercion. The
peasantry replied with risings and riots. Famine—the worst experienced in thirty years—accompanied by typhus spread over large
areas of Russia in 1921-1922, carrying off perhaps as many as 5,000,-
000. The death toll would have been even higher had not foreign
relief agencies shipped in food and medical supplies. An ominous
mutiny of sailors in the Red Navy in the Baltic warned the Bolshevik
leaders that the very continuance of their regime was imperilled.

The New Economic Policy

Realist that he was, Lenin decided that considerable modifications
in the collectivist program were imperative, and in 1921 a new orientation in economic affairs was adopted. Thereby the peasant millions
were permitted to sell the products of their farmsteads in the open
market, paying fixed taxes in commodities and later on in money.
As one consequence the spirit of economic individualism reasserted
itself in rural Russia. Moreover, concessions were awarded to adventuresome foreign companies to work certain Soviet mineral resources
and even to operate a few factories; and the government obtained

short-term loans abroad. In both retail and wholesale trading, private enterprise was restored, and a new variety of currency, the *chervonetz*, was printed.

Such a monetary unit seemed indispensable to record costs and indicate prices in those undertakings over which the state retained full authority, for the new economic course by no means allocated all productive facilities to independent initiative. Rather, the larger factories and mills, the banks and most of the mines, all the means of transportation and communication, and foreign commerce remained in the orbit of the Soviet government.

During the epoch of the New Economic Policy the USSR was more thoroughly subjected to the rule of the Communist Party and material conditions improved in a remarkable manner. By 1928, in fact, some branches of industry and agriculture approached or even surpassed the output of 1913. The inherent toughness and submissiveness of the Russian stock, the freer opportunities granted the cultivators, the splendid natural wealth of the realm combined with the energy and resourcefulness of government and party folk and modest financial and technical help from abroad accounted fundamentally for the surprising upsurge in Soviet production. It was intended by the Soviet high command that the partial restoration of capitalism should be merely a temporary expedient, a distasteful strategic retreat, and that indeed it proved to be.

Planned Industrial Progress

From the Kremlin it was announced in 1928 that the USSR would embark on a definite schedule of economic and social advancement, based upon a prearranged plan, and making use of the vast and varied national resources. That was the first of three Five Year Plans, intended to "overtake and surpass" the West. In 1941 still another plan was in the making, though World War II forced its deferment to 1946. By means of state planning the Soviet leadership aimed at making Russia economically self-sufficient, at enlarging the wealth produced, and avoiding the periodic recurrence of depression and the attendant evils of capitalist society. The theory and practice of state-planned economy form one of the distinctive and gigantic phenomena of Soviet totalitarianism.

While the process of Soviet planning is full of complexities the major features are susceptible to brief exposition. Goals to be reached in the various types of production were set by government and party. To the Council of Commissars was attached a State Planning Commission (Gosplan), founded in 1921, which was responsible for working

out the details of the blueprint in consultation with regional boards of
review. After that, each productive unit—trust, mill, farm—was privileged to discuss the part in the program that had been assigned to it,
without much chance however of securing a downward revision. Actually, in each Five Year Plan, schedules were altered by the Gosplan
before they had been finished because of new decisions on national
needs or the failure of branches of production to attain the output
that had been estimated.

Each factory or other unit of production was instructed how much
to pay out for rawstuffs, in wages, and how much to charge for its
products. Industries in a given branch of production were often
grouped together in one or more trusts, which participated in drawing
up schedules for production and controlled raw materials and output.
If a profit was earned, part passed to the state, the rest being retained
by the trust for expansion or for worker welfare and education. But
considerations of profit or loss appear to have counted little in reaching decisions as to what should be manufactured and in what quantity.

Planned economy necessitated an immense administrative staff,
both in the central offices and in the local districts. Revisions in the
Soviet administrative organization were often made, but a large bureaucracy (as compared with workers engaged directly in production)
persisted.

High-speed industrialization wrought a veritable revolution in
Russian economy after 1928. Even the most sober foreign estimate
puts the increase of industrial workers at between 10,000,000 and
15,000,000. So rapid in fact was the movement of workers from
village to city that the rural population declined. By 1939 probably
one of three citizens of the USSR was an urban dweller. New towns
rose phoenix-like around new industrial giants and many an old community grew rapidly in response to the Soviet dynamic. By 1939 there
were eighty one cities of over 100,000 inhabitants as against fifteen
such cities forty years before.

Factory managers complained of shortages of employees. In the
decade of the thirties, billions were poured into Soviet steel mills,
tractor, precision instrument, and other machinery works, hydroelectric plants, chemical and rubber and armament factories. Airports
and warehouses were laid out, hitherto unknown or improperly exploited mineral resources were developed; old highways were improved
and new ones constructed to carry the vastly increased traffic by
truck and motorcar.

Substantial extensions were made to the Russian railway network.
New lines connected the cities of the northwest with expanding in-

dustrial and mining communities in the Ukraine and in the Urals. The
long road across Siberia to the Pacific was double-tracked and a branch
line wormed its way down to Russian Turkestan, while another road,
running north of Lake Baikal to an outlet close to the Pacific, was
authorized and work on it pushed. In all, the railway trackage inherited from Imperial Russia was enlarged by half and rolling stock
was considerably improved. Furthermore, new canals were dug; one
joining the White Sea and the Baltic had immediate commercial
importance. In 1935 the famous Moscow subway was put into operation.

Appraisal of the results of Soviet industrialization in terms of
volume of production is not easily made because published statistics
cannot always be relied on and questions are raised concerning the
quality of the goods produced. But in any case, it is evident that the
overall increase in output was enormous as a few figures believed to
be reasonably accurate suggest.

Manufacture of railway equipment was more than three times
greater in 1937 than in 1928. Plants were then turning out a hundred-
fold more tractors than in 1928, and Russia led the world in the output
of agricultural machinery. While in 1928 there were some 22,000
trucks and automobiles, ten years later there were 200,000, Soviet
automotive production standing second only to that of the United
States.

At the outbreak of war with Germany in 1941 the USSR was
manufacturing almost as much iron and steel as German mills, some
22,000,000 tons, an increase of more than 500 per cent over 1913.
The output of chemical goods had shot up fifteen times. Production
of industrial rawstuffs, although three to five times greater than in
1913, seems not to have kept pace with the growth of machinofacture.
In particular copper production and coal-mining fell below the
planned levels, but shortages of coal were more or less covered by a
twenty-fold rise in electric power. Lenin himself had set great store on
electrification as the stimulus to economic progress. He would have
rejoiced over the immense Dnepropetrovsk hydroelectric facility,
built under the eye of American engineers, and symbolizing the taste
of both Russia and the United States for bigness.

Throughout the period of Five Year Plans the accent in Soviet industry was on the output of producers' goods—machines to facilitate
later production of commodities for consumers—and on matériel of
war. Only to a small extent did the new age of technology yield articles that would immediately satisfy the almost limitless demand of
the Soviet millions for goods of all kinds. Consumers suffered from

shortages of such ordinary commodities as clothes, shoes, and household utensils. Although construction of dwelling places was pressed with vigor, housing lagged behind the general economic advance, so that urban congestion, long an unsavory feature of the Russian city, reached a point where lodgings were likened to coffins.

As personal incentives to greater efficiency in work, a graduated scale of wages was introduced and awards of honor, to which economic advantages were attached, were conferred upon workers and managers who scored outstanding records. Much respected were the "Stakhonovites," "speed king" piece-workers, who set the pace for their fellows in mine and mill. Their income far exceeded that of the average worker, which Stalin reported in 1939 as 287 roubles a month, or the equivalent of the cost of a pair of good shoes or a mediocre suit of clothes.

Aside from money income Russian industrial workers benefited from social welfare services in time of sickness, accident, and old age and were granted vacations with pay. Rent for living quarters was fixed in keeping with income and the size of one's family. Workers, moreover, could eat inexpensive meals at their place of employment in line with the Soviet policy of making the factory or mine the center of most of the worker's life. In or around the factory the worker got most of his recreation and education, and the factory administration operated summer camps for his young children. Soviet trade unions were more serviceable in speeding up output than as agencies for promoting the welfare of the workers. Management was in no wise required to bargain with the employed and the right to strike or even to change jobs was denied.

To administer and direct the productive units an army of managers and technical experts was trained in special schools. By 1932, 165,000 engineers were on the job, the greater part of them young workers or sons of workers. During the Great Purge of 1937-1938 many specialists and managers were removed; their successors appear to have been more efficient and were given almost unlimited authority to deal with unsatisfactory workmen. Managerial personnel was more highly remunerated than the workers and cases were reported of factory managers who were paid ten times as much as the most skilled operatives. Wide though differences in income were, they were less so than in capitalistic economies and when rationing was in vogue (as, for example, between 1926 and 1934) disparities in real income were still narrower. With few exceptions, all earnings were work-incomes.

Supplementing native executives and engineers were specialists in management, production, engineering or one of the other technical professions brought in from outside. These foreign experts carried with them and applied western—not least American—managerial "know-how" and methods of mass production and distribution.

Revolution in the Countryside

Intertwined with the planned industrial advance and indeed its very buttress was the drastic transformation that was effected in the Soviet countryside. Until 1928 the predominant trend in landholding was toward individual proprietorships on the model of France. In that year some 25,000,000 separate holdings existed, many of them made up of scattered strips. Certain of the peasantry were relatively well-off—kulaks or fists, they were called—and for that reason were despised by their less fortunate fellows and detested by Communist doctrinaires in the Soviet leadership.

As part of the first Five Year Plan a concerted campaign was undertaken to put an end to individual ownership of land by consolidating small holdings into large farms. In that way official Soviet doctrine would be served and collectivization, it was urged, coupled with mechanization of agriculture, would result in greater efficiency in production and larger output to sustain the mounting urban population. Displaced peasants too would furnish manpower for industry.

Once adopted as state policy, collectivism was pushed with ferocious zeal. By 1938 virtually all the land formerly on individual tenure was merged in cooperative farms (*kolkhoz*), of which there were about 240,000. That change-over, which was in fact more radically revolutionary for the peasantry than the events of 1917, was undertaken before agricultural implements for collective farming were available. It was attended by violent resistance on the part of many peasants, especially in the Ukraine. Instead of handing their farm animals over to the collective community, well-to-do peasants (*kulaks*) in many cases slaughtered them. So extensive were the killings that even at the end of the 1930's Soviet meat and milk production had not recovered.

To combat resistance and to prevent the peasantry from reverting to individual holdings, punitive expeditions were despatched to areas of disaffection, causing virtual civil war. Death or deportation was the fate of hundreds of thousands of recalcitrants. Adding to the national woes, in what has been aptly called "Russia's Iron Age," famine swept the country in 1932-1933, though starvation was not quite on the gigantic scale of 1921-1922.

Nonetheless collectivization was carried through. It took years, however, for Soviet factories to turn out the machinery for the mechanization of farming and only then did the *kolkhoz* system become really stable. Machine-tractor stations, which serviced one or more collective farms, were set up, and huge combine-harvesters were supplied to grain-growing Ukraine. It was reported in 1938 that three quarters of the cultivated land of the USSR was plowed by tractors and that half the sowing and reaping and practically all the threshing were performed by machinery.

Apart from the machines themselves, rural Russia became heavily dependent upon oil to drive farm equipment. An increase in crop output resulted from mechanization. Production was further raised by the opening up of hitherto uncultivated areas and the planting of settlers on them.

Land, buildings, and equipment on a collective farm belonged by law to the peasant community in perpetuity. Managers and agricultural experts were sent in by the state. They reached decisions with the advice of a village committee and peasants performed tasks assigned to them. The products a collective was to raise and the prices at which they were to be sold were fixed by state planning agencies.

Out of the income, taxes were taken, compensation for the use of state-owned machinery, and sums for local welfare purposes. What remained was divided among the villagers in keeping with individual contribution to the collective output. In many collectives, peasants were allotted small plots of ground on which they were free to grow what they chose and they also had the right to have a few animals and dispose of them as they saw fit.

Aside from the collective farms there were huge state farms. In 1930 about 5,000 of them existed, the largest ranging over 500,000 acres. These properties were operated like factories with trained managers, up-to-the-minute equipment, and the workers paid in wages. Seemingly the vast Soviet state farms were less successful as producing units than had been calculated. At any event, in the late thirties, many of them were split up, used for experimental purposes, or converted into collectives. By 1939 the Soviet agricultural revolution had almost completely eliminated the individual peasant proprietor. Something like four per cent of the total harvest in that year was raised on individual properties; twelve per cent on state farms; and eighty four per cent on the collective farms.

Other Aspects of Soviet Economy

So profoundly does Soviet economy diverge from the ways of free enterprise that several other aspects deserve short comment. The principal source of government income was the "turn-over tax," akin to a sales tax, a levy imposed upon goods at each stage in production until they reached the consumer. On some articles the tax represented more than sixty per cent of the sales price. Other sources of public revenue were income and personal taxes, receipts from the sale of government bonds, fees for the use of agricultural machinery, and a share of profits, if any, made by industrial establishments. Out of these funds the state met the customary running expenses of a government, and financed the building of new factories, railways, and the like. Soviet Russia, in contrast to Imperial Russia, avoided long-term borrowing from western bankers.

Foreign trade was rigidly monopolized by the state and, like other branches of the economy, was planned in minute detail. Imports were regulated primarily with an eye to building up industry; exports paid for imported goods, salaries of foreign technicians, and the like. Russia, which before 1914 had been a major exporter of grains, cut only a small figure in world trade under the Soviets. In the thirties, Russian foreign business, in fact, was smaller than that of Switzerland.

Private traders who had thrived under the new economic policy inaugurated in 1921 were extinguished after 1928. Collective farmers might sell milk, eggs, and garden vegetables of their own in the markets found in every town. Here and there a peasant rented out a horse and cart, but that relic of the old days was rapidly disappearing by 1939. The only other lawful private enterprises were handicraft industries: tailoring, shoe-making, cabinet-making. Although the tools belonged to the artisan, the materials had to be supplied by the customer, and the craftsman was subject to drastic special taxation.

The right of inheritance was explicitly recognized in Stalin's Constitution, but not a great deal could be accumulated to hand on to heirs. Savings could be invested only in state bonds or placed in banks at an interest of three and one half to four per cent. No citizen could draw income from rent, royalties, or the possession of property.

Stalinism

By the middle thirties the USSR had recovered from the blighting consequences of World War I, revolution, and civil wars. Machine-production was surging upward and collectivization and machinery were transforming the countryside. A new generation, moreover, had grown to maturity in the Bolshevik environment and new ideas as well as the constantly changing physical surroundings had made an immeasurable impact upon a population that had historically been noted for lethargy and stagnation.

Concurrently and subtly, deviations from Leninist principles were apparent on many sides of the home front. Leninism gradually yielded pride of place to Stalinism. For instance, instead of economic equality there was differentiation in income both in city and country. A new class of party folk, bureaucrats, and managers had emerged as the counterpart in a sense of the middle class of capitalist society. There was much talk, too, of the Russian Fatherland, a term utterly hateful to Lenin and other makers of the November Revolution. The older spirit of Russian national patriotism was silently crowding aside the international ideology of militant Bolshevism.

Characteristic of the nationalist trend was the official praise heaped upon strong-willed Russian tsars and pre-revolutionary military heroes. In 1937, for example, celebrations marked the anniversary of Napoleon's invasion and retreat. General Suvorov, who won his fame in 18th century wars against the Turks and revolutionary France, a commander memorable for self-effacing zeal, iron resolution, and recklessness with the lives of his troops, was extolled as history's only general who never lost a battle. In literature, as well, worthies of the Russian past such as the poet Pushkin, were restored to public favor. And the new accent on the distinctive in Russian life colored the books that were prepared for use in the schools.

When decrees were issued tightening up Soviet divorce laws, prohibiting abortion, encouraging strong home ties and wholesome parenthood, and in other ways ordering a return to conventional standards of personal morality, it was possible to believe that the Soviet Union was not only swinging to nationalism but was going "puritan" as well. The Constitution of 1936 formed the capstone of Stalinism in domestic affairs.

Simultaneously, Russia had resumed her place in the family of nations. Another sign of the times was a modification in the tactics of the Third International. The victory of Hitlerism in Germany in 1933, which had come to pass in part because of implacable divisions in the opposition, argued the advisability of a new course for Communist parties in foreign nations. Instead of battling against middle-of-the-way political groupings, as in Weimar Germany, would the Communists not fare better by allying with them against the common foe of "fascist" authoritarianism? To that question the delegates to the

Seventh Congress of the Third International, held at Moscow in 1935, gave an affirmative answer. Accordingly, the policy of the Popular Front, as in France (p. 233), was inaugurated, though too late as the event was to prove. Fear and abhorrence of Communism and world revolution in foreign countries—in business, religious, and diplomatic circles—while less pronounced than at the time of the Bolshevik Revolution, had by no means disappeared. That dread of Communism created an insuperable obstacle to whole-hearted diplomatic cooperation on the part of other countries with the Soviet Union.

Religion Under the Soviets

Not less sweeping than the economic changes that came over Soviet Russia—arguably more so—were the altered outlook and attitude on life's purpose. The Soviet regime fostered a set of values conceived strictly in terms of worldly satisfactions and enjoyment. That was in direct contrast to the dominant European tradition which held moral and spiritual values to be paramount.

Against organized conventional religion Bolshevism struck ruthlessly and relentlessly. In the thought of Lenin and his disciples religion was nothing other than emotional opium which deadened believers to earthly realities in the expectation of a future life of eternal bliss. As dogmatic atheists and convinced materialists they despised all religions. They hated the official Russian Orthodox Church, which was so tightly fettered to the old regime as to be an instrument of tsarist domination, which battened upon the credulity of the humble, and which waged vigorous war upon the findings of science. Russian Christianity had never undergone a quickening experience like that which had affected the western Church during the Reformation. Now, instead of the paradise portrayed by religion, the Communists promised to build a heavenly kingdom on earth.

In the first period of the Revolution, financial and other ties between State and Church were severed, and the landed properties of the Church, which were nearly as extensive as those of the imperial family, were declared forfeit. To carry on charitable activities, or evangelical missions, or to teach religion to youths under eighteen was made an offense against the state. Thousands of religious structures were pulled down, converted to secular purposes, or allowed to go to wrack and ruin. Subsequently some of the places of worship became anti-religious museums. Many a Russian clergyman who resisted the drive against religion or who identified himself with the foes of the Communists during the civil wars was slain or imprisoned.

As a competitor to the historic Orthodox Church the Kremlin sponsored a "Living Church" which seems to have attracted little popular support. An untiring crusade against traditional religion was waged by the militant League of the Godless, which by word and pen strove to win converts to atheism.

It was the Communist conviction that if Russians had an innate need for the satisfactions of religion they should find them in the Communist ideology and party. As a creed or cult Communism roused in its followers a passionate fervor, a sense of dedication, transcending the bounds of mere social and political doctrine. It was emotional, optimistic, and secular; it was equipped with a body of dogmatic principles and a wealth of ceremonialism.

Devout Communist ideologues flaunted Red flags, chorused Red hymns, addressed one another as *tovarich* (comrade), replaced icons in hut and apartment dwellings with portraits of Marx, Lenin, and Stalin, and worshipped at the shrine of Lenin in Moscow's Red Square. To this, add the intense passion for missionary work and it becomes apparent that Communism possessed many of the attributes of the religious faiths with which it competed.

Any estimate of the consequences of Communist treatment of organized religion must give prominence to the sharp decline in the influence of religious societies, a decline that was as patent psychologically as physically. In Russian towns and cities more than in the rural areas, among youth more than among oldsters, materialism and atheism supplanted Christianity, Judaism, and Mohammedanism. Yet for the faithful who survived the ordeal, persecution appears to have had democratizing and invigorating effects. But in the outer world the repression and abuse of religion raised up enemies against the Bolshevik regime in its entirety.

In the mid-thirties there were symptoms of a softening attitude on the part of the state toward religion—another facet of Stalinism. Indeed the Constitution of 1936 speaks of "freedom of religious worship" for all citizens, without however recognizing freedom of religious instruction. Anti-religious propaganda, on the other hand, was freely tolerated and in 1937-1938 the drive against the clergy was renewed. But as the war with Nazi Germany approached, the campaign against religion slackened and then ceased.[6]

The new policy of leniency toward religion was calculated to appease Russian churchmen and to rally the religiously inclined in

[6] According to Soviet figures, in 1941 there were a tenth as many Orthodox churches as in 1900 and a sixth as many secular clergy; monastic orders were by then completely broken up.

patriotic service to the Soviet state. Besides, among Orthodox Christians in the Balkans and elements in western or Moslem countries which resented the anti-religious course, sympathetic treatment of church interests would surely find favor. It would counteract, too, the oft-reiterated Hitlerian assertion that Nazi Germany was the defender of religion against the peril of Communism.

During the war with Germany the Orthodox Church served once more as a pillar of the Russian state, more fully state-controlled in fact than in the tsardom. To administer the affairs of Orthodoxy and other religious communions special councils of public officials and church leaders were created. The office of Orthodox Patriarch which had been discarded by Peter the Great was revived and its occupant was permitted to publish an official newspaper. Bans on private religious education were relaxed, training schools for priests were opened, and agencies of atheism were curbed.

Russian churchmen welcomed these concessions and lent their energies to the prosecution of the war effort. On the twenty-fifth anniversary of the November Revolution, in 1942, the chief dignitary of the Orthodox Church lauded Marshal Stalin as "the divinely anointed leader of our military and cultural forces." Prominent clergymen of other faiths echoed that sentiment.

If freedom of conscience had not been fully restored, if the ideological conflict of Communism and Christianity still remained, religion nonetheless had secured liberties which a decade earlier had seemed to lie beyond the possible. Out of it all might emerge a new Russian synthesis between religion and government.

Soviet Education

The Soviet Union took just pride in providing for popular education and in the spread of literacy. Early in the 20th century, before the Revolution, literacy was rising in Russia and perhaps half the recruits mustered into military service in 1914 could read and write. But older folk, women, and smaller national groupings of Russia whose cultural level resembled that of colonial populations were still unlettered. All that was drastically changed in the interval between World Wars.[7]

[7] Soviet official sources published the following data on education: As of 1937, 38,000,000 pupils were in school as against 8,000,000 in 1913; attendance on secondary schools rose from 635,000 to 11,000,000. There were 700 institutions of higher learning in 1936 as compared with ninety one in 1914. In the first twenty five years of Soviet history nine billions of books and pamphlets were published in 100 languages.

Soviet interest in schools was dictated in part by the desire to inculcate the collectivist ideology in the oncoming generation and to uproot the heritage from the imperial past. Attendance was obligatory from eight years of age, (seven after 1943), and the leaving age was higher in towns than in the villages. Coeducation prevailed until 1943 when separate schools for boys and girls became the vogue in urban areas. Special attention was paid to instruction of a practical and technical character.

It was through the social studies that the Communist outlook was most fully taught. History and life's purpose were interpreted along materialistic lines. Individualism and capitalist economy were portrayed not only as antiquated but wicked, the root of all evil in society. The ideal of equality, service to the state and to the collective community were inculcated. The notion that conventional religion was a narcotic was reinforced by class excursions to anti-religious museums. Boys from twelve to fifteen years of age received elementary military training in school (or factory) and then were ready for the conscript army.

It was through the Soviet schools too that distorted ideas about foreign lands and peoples were deliberately implanted in the mind of the young. Interpretations in history manuals faithfully conformed to the Communist and materialistic outlook. The treatment of the United States, to illustrate, strummed upon the iniquities of Negro slavery, the misery of the masses in a capitalistic economy, the struggle of the under-privileged against the possessing classes; it ignored the freedoms and liberties in America and the comparatively high standards of comfort that generally prevailed.

At holiday seasons and after school days were over the collectivist ideology was imparted through the Young Pioneers organization—similar in form to Boy Scouts and Girl Scouts. Subsequently this was carried on in the Young Communist League (*Komsomol*), membership in which was eventually made a prerequisite for admission to the Communist Party.

In the thirties, as an aspect of Stalinism, Russian national patriotism was stressed in education. Efforts were made to stimulate and maintain an active sense of pride in Russia's achievements past, present, and prospective. The older indiscipline in the school was reduced. Teachers were given greater authority in the classroom and regular examinations were introduced. Whereas attendance on secondary schools had been free, fees now were charged. From primary school through the highest institutions of learning the Soviet educational system was rigidly controlled by central authority. Learners were conditioned to accept economic planning and to place the interests of the state above individual concerns.

The Red Fighting Forces

After the November Revolution the armies of the old Russia completely disintegrated, some of the units entering the service of the Bolsheviks. Early in 1918 a decree from the Kremlin called for the organization of a "Socialist army, built up from below on the principles of the election of officers, a mutual comradely discipline and respect." But with Trotsky as Commissar of War troops were actually raised by conscription, the election of officers was abandoned, discipline was tightened, and political commissars—whole-souled Communist Party men—were attached to military formations for the triple purpose of keeping an eye on officers, whipping up martial enthusiasm among the troops, and of conducting propaganda among the civilian population. This peculiar institution of the Red army was not abolished until October, 1942.

The hastily improvised Bolshevik army not only carried war and revolution deep into Poland but smashed the opposing "White" armies. It aided fundamentally in consolidating Bolshevik power. At the time, the Red army was equipped only with obsolete weapons, and probably not more than one out of five of the soldiers had a rifle. After the victory over the "Whites" the bulk of the Soviet army was organized on a sort of militia system, with brief formal training followed by short annual "refresher courses." Soviet top-commanders believed strongly in "lightning war." They preached the virtues of, and necessity for, mechanized and armored equipment.

Officer training was patterned on western models. There were periods of study alternating with service in the field. The most promising men completed their military education in the famous Frunze Academy which can be compared to the Army War College of the United States. Many high-ranking officers in all branches of the fighting service were removed in the purges of the late thirties. Their places were taken by young men so that the officers corps of the Russian army in World War II was probably the youngest and as well the most audacious in the world. Gradually the familiar comraderie of the original revolutionary army disappeared and orthodox notions of discipline and obedience of men to officers were restored.

In the successive Soviet plans for industrialization, particular pains were taken to provide for the production of military equipment. The doctrine of "guns before butter" ruled in the Soviet Union and the quality of war matériel was undoubtedly better than that of other goods. Military mechanization began as early as 1930 and in time huge reserves of tanks and planes were accumulated. Russian designers created superior weapons for defense against aerial attack and anti-tank guns. Many armament plants were built deep in the interior of the Union, particularly in the Ural district, beyond the range of potential enemy bombers. In the air forces and the mechanized branches of the army a high proportion of Communist Party men and probationers were enrolled.

As more and more up-to-date equipment became available the Soviet militia system was abandoned in favor of a large standing army. It was officially stated in 1935 that the existing forces of 600,000 would be raised to 1,300,000 the following year. In 1939 the active army was variously estimated at from 1,900,000 to 3,000,-000 and that year a fourth part of the state appropriations went for military purposes. If fully mobilized, it was then believed that the Soviet Union could put 15,000,000 men on the field, and that army combined the advantages of the latest weapons with the primitive gusto of a preponderantly peasant nation.

For centuries, especially when the homeland was invaded, the Russian soldier had displayed unusual capacity for endurance and privation and stoical valor. Those qualities were cultivated by the "new patriotism" and by Communist indoctrination to the effect that the Soviet Union was a workers' paradise surrounded by jealous and predatory enemies. Soldiers enjoyed better living conditions than civilians and were taught trades to be pursued when the term of service was over. Sports in military camps fostered the national cult of athletics. Army morale touched heights never before known in Russian history.

By 1939 the Soviet army was probably the most powerful military force in existence. Its intervention at full strength at the beginning of World War II might conceivably have brought the struggle to an early conclusion. Yet military experts of western countries seem to have held the Red fighting machine in low esteem. Its stock fell even lower when purges removed so many trained commanders and a war against little Finland in 1939-1940 seemed to tax the Soviet military resources to the utmost. (Chap. XXI).

As of 1939

Although foreign judges, whose studies on the Soviet Union merited and carried weight, expressed doubts on the stability of the USSR, the foundations of the Soviet state by 1939 were firmly and solidly laid. Acrimonious debate, learned and popular, raged in western circles concerning what and how much had actually been accomplished since 1917.

It was plain that the totalitarian autocracy, upheld by the Communist Party, which reached into every nook of the far-flung realm, showed no sign of withering away as original Bolsheviks had prophesied. The effigy of dictator Stalin—commonly flanked by one of Lenin and other worthies of the Revolution—was met with everywhere. His praises were on every tongue. Revived traditions of the Russian nation had obscured international visions, for the Soviet Union was following after Peter the Great more than Marx and Lenin.

That prodigious progress had been achieved in mass education could not be questioned. The abuse or repression of national and religious minorities, so conspicuous a trait of Imperial Russia, had well-nigh vanished. That is not to say, however, that liberty prevailed. Rather, believers in freedom, whether intellectual, religious, or economic, had been bludgeoned into conformity or silence. On every hand, individual interests were subordinated to those of the state. For generations Russians, of course, had been accustomed to look upon the individual as merely an atom in a huge social body.

In matters of Soviet family life and parenthood, far-reaching changes had been effected since the first stage of the Revolution. Women had been released from the traditional subjection to husband or parent and were lawfully the equal of men.

The institution of privately-owned income-producing property had been destroyed by 1939 beyond possibility of restitution. In its stead a version of state capitalism—with the accent on planned production—had been established. Its methods, such as the drive of personal incentive, had certain similarities with private capitalism. The moral concept that it was wrong to live by the work of others had taken deep root.

If standards of material comfort had not generally been raised—and on that point the testimony was extremely divergent—if the ideal of economic equality had been by-passed, at least economic leveling had been achieved in considerable measure. Facilities for improving living standards had been created and the belief that better times were in the offing had laid hold of millions of Soviet hearts. Less importance was attached to income and style of living in the USSR than to official position and public recognition. As never before in Russia's long history, careers were open to those possessing talents.

To the assertion that the Soviet workman or peasant was less well-off than his counterpart in the west, the proper retort was that that had "always" been true. Yet shrewd and pervasive propaganda had persuaded masses of Soviet citizens that their conditions were really better than those in other countries. It had indeed fostered an attitude of superiority toward "backward" foreign nations which had not benefited from a liberating revolution.

Materialism and this-worldliness as ethical values were clearly in the ascendant as of 1939. Yet organized religion, which on the surface appeared to be dying, seems rather to have been merely slumbering.

On the larger problem as to whether the Soviet way of life had brought greater happiness to the Russians, the answers were as varied as the temperament and the general outlook of students of the Bolshevik experiment. It required the perspective of a century before the deeper implications of the great French Revolution had been brought into focus. Scarcely less time would be needed before the dust had settled on the confusion and violence of the more far-reaching Russian Revolution and before its world-meaning was fully manifest.

Whatever else might be true of the Communist regime, it was certain that no other government in history had ever undertaken such ambitious tasks or carried through changes on so gigantic a scale. The Soviet Russia of 1939 differed profoundly from the Tsarist Russia of 1914. But the new Russia was neither a complete break with the national heritage, nor was it a mere continuation of the past with new trimmings.

CHAPTER VI

Europe's Middle East: Austria to Finland

The Area in General

THE downfall of the ancient Hapsburg monarchy must be accounted one of the largest political consequences of World War I. For all its faults and shortcomings that imperial state had given economic cohesion to the valley of the Danube and in spite of nationalistic commotion, growing with the years, a semblance of political unity. Whether the Hapsburg monarchy either could or should have been preserved has been variously argued; the fact is, it was not.

Whether instead of the Hapsburg complex, a Danubian confederation of free and equal nations could have been contrived—or should have been—was a subject that attracted speculation and an occasional "Danubian" conference in the inter-war years. A better life for all would no doubt have been furthered by regional cooperation in practical matters. But the fact is that no union of that sort ever got very far in the realm of practical politics.

The history of the states which entered into the Hapsburg heritage, some of them the beneficiaries, too, of the overthrow of the old Russia by the Bolsheviks—the history of Europe's "Middle East"—is the record of the internal development of these countries, and their role as pawns in the game of high diplomacy. In the end all were engulfed in one manner or another by the Nazi tidal wave, only to escape when the counter-wave of Soviet Russia swept over them.

Very largely agricultural communities, very largely in a state of agrarian backwardness, these countries experienced economic improvement in the era between wars. But they were in general harassed as the Balkan nations were harassed by the overplus of people living off the soil. Cooperative societies for economic ends flourished in sections of Europe's Middle East but over wide areas the uneducated peasantry were unwilling to combine for the common good. Industrialism opened up new avenues of employment for the few. The quality of machine-economy in Czechoslovakia and Austria was in no way behind that of the most advanced states of the west. But in other parts of Europe's Middle East industrialism had by 1939 scarcely started.

The Austrian Republic

By defeat in war Austria was cut down to a region of wholly German speech no greater than Maine. A republic and a president replaced the empire and the hereditary Hapsburg sovereign. In contrast to her pre-war partner, Hungary, Austria contained a large and well-organized urban working class, and soil that was far less fertile, cultivated in the main by peasant owners. She also had the huge city of Vienna to support.

At once Austria's glory and despair, the Danubian metropolis of Vienna had grown up as the capital of the Hapsburg realm of over 50,000,000. Then suddenly it discovered itself the capital of a mere 6,700,000. Vienna has been described as "an enormous head on a stunted body, a hydrocephalous monstrosity." Unsurpassed as a home of culture and learning, and a major financial, manufacturing, and commercial center, Vienna was shut out of pre-war markets by tariffs. If it were to live at all it had to be content with lower standards of material comfort than had prevailed before 1914.[1]

After the armistice had been signed Austrian political parties resumed their activities. Two of them had enduring importance: the Social Democrats and the Christian Socialists. The first, whose growth under the leadership of a band of able organizers had been rapid in the 20th century, professed the ideology of Karl Marx but would attain its objectives by peaceful democratic processes. Vienna was the stronghold of Austrian Social Democracy and other large cities and towns had efficient Socialist organizations. Revolutionary Marxism attracted only a meager following in Austria. Despite proportional representation no Communist was ever elected to the Austrian parliament, nor even to the city council of highly-industrialized Vienna.

Just as Social Democracy spoke the mind of the bulk of the urban dwellers, so Christian Socialism represented the outlook and the concerns of most of the peasants, the little tradesmen, and the clericals. Sponsor of "municipal socialism" before the war, this party was by no means averse to social welfare reforms within the bounds set by Catholic principles. It was as a rule the staunch champion of Austrian

---

[1] At the Paris Conference it was suggested that Vienna might be chosen as the seat of the League. Her wealth of empty palaces and palatial residences would have furnished splendid and immediate accommodation, and the Viennese would have profited economically. But inasmuch as a time might come when Austria would unite with Germany, the ancient Kulturstadt was ruled out.

independence and a vocal faction anticipated the day when the legitimate Hapsburg monarch would return to reign over them.

Numerically small in the early years of the Austrian Republic was a Pan-German party. Even in imperial Hapsburg days this faction had advocated the union of the German-speaking areas with Germany. What Pan-Germanism lacked in popularity it made up for in the intensity of its propaganda. Until the emergence of National Socialism as a potent force in Germany the Pan-Germans of Austria counted for little practically. Thereafter their progress was marked, and when Germany annexed Austria in 1938, they became supreme.

As has been intimated, Austria was organized as a republic with an extremely democratic constitution providing for universal adult suffrage, proportional representation, and ministerial responsibility to parliament. It was a federal union so that the Vienna municipality enjoyed a wide degree of local independence. Dr. Michael Hainisch, an obscure republican, was chosen as the first President, through the combined votes of Christian Socialists and Pan-Germans. On his retirement in 1928 a Christian Socialist, Dr. Wilhelm Miklas, was made President, holding on until the extinction of the Republic.

In the first period of republican history the Social Democrats commanded the parliament, but in 1922 the Christian Socialists gained top place and retained it to the end. From the beginning, parliamentary affairs, reflecting the sorry material plight of the little country, were turbulent. Only financial hypodermics administered from time to time by the western nations enabled Austria to stagger along at all. Unemployment in the cities ran high. The currency fluctuated violently until, in concert with the inflationary debauch of 1923 in Germany, Austrian money lost all value and the national treasury went bankrupt. At that juncture the League of Nations came to the rescue and through foreign loans and astute financial administration put the currency back on its feet.

The general upswing in material conditions which took place in the late twenties brought a distinct improvement in Austria and the country appeared to be a going concern, capable of preserving its independent position. But the Great Depression sounded the knell of Austrian democracy. The evils of stagnation in foreign trade and urban employment reappeared in a magnified form.

In the meantime, the Social Democrats had transformed the city of Vienna into a model of municipal socialism. Vienna's thorough program of public welfare began with the unborn child and ended with a municipally-operated funeral establishment. Certain industrial enterprises were partly owned by the municipality. Schools, playgrounds, hospitals, and public utilities all responded to the dynamic zeal of Social Democracy. But the most publicized achievement of the administration was a huge housing scheme to relieve the congestion which had existed in Vienna since the onset of industrialism. More than 80,000 dwelling units were erected, large apartment blocks principally, conforming to the latest thought on safety and comfort. The largest of them, the massive Karl Marx Hof, sheltered 1,400 families and was equipped with kindergartens, communal laundries, and dining rooms.

To finance these undertakings the Socialist government enacted tax legislation which bore heavily upon the well-to-do and brought about a considerable levelling in real incomes. Municipal officials from all over the world made pilgrimages to Vienna to study the welfare institutions and administrative techniques for which the Socialists were responsible. Only Paris, among European cities, surpassed Vienna as a magnet for tourists.

Though master of Vienna the Social Democrats lacked the voting strength to control the federal government, which was managed by the Christian Socialists. Sharp, ideological quarrels between the two parties were accentuated by the business paralysis and destitution in the cities which accompanied the Great Depression. So bad, in fact, did conditions become that government posters implored the Viennese to feed their starving fellows. In 1932 the Christian Socialist head of the Austrian ministry, Chancellor Engelbert Dollfuss, established a semi-dictatorship. It was only a step to a frontal assault upon the Socialists.

On urgings from Mussolini, his friend and counsellor, Dollfuss, in February, 1934, ordered troops into Vienna to suppress the Socialist administration. Though short on weapons the Socialist wage workers heroically defended themselves. Heavy artillery was turned upon apartment blocks which the embattled residents had converted into fortresses. Hundreds perished in Vienna and other industrial communities and Social Democracy was crushed. Many leaders escaped abroad, but the less fortunate were hurled into concentration camps. The Socialist trade unions were broken up. Dollfuss and his Christian Socialists had triumphed but in so doing they had fatally embittered a large proportion of the urban working class, the strongest bulwark against the Nazi menace.

Unwittingly, the cannonading of Vienna played squarely into the hands of the militant Nazis and other Austrian elements who held that salvation lay in union with Germany—Anschluss, as it was called. Such a merger was, of course, prohibited by the peace treaties, for in the language of a French diplomatist, "We could not reward Germany for having lost the war." The popularity of the Anschluss idea was a barometer of Austrian economic conditions. Just after the war, sentiment appears strongly to have favored union, but that faith ebbed in the late twenties only to revive again with the Great Depression. A project of 1931, to link Austria with Germany in a customs union which might very well have been the prelude to political unity, came to grief (Chap. XVIII).

After the Nazis gained power in Germany a decided shift of opinion took place in Austria. For many a Socialist, for many a Catholic, for the large Jewish minority in Vienna, the Hitlerian regime was anathema and they had no desire to be subjected to it. The same was true of the Austrian group which had consistently stood for independence.

On the other side, the Austrian Nazis intensified the agitation for union. In their minds were the boastings of the Austrian-born Hitler: "Fate decided," he cried, "that Braunau on the Inn should be my birthplace. The little town lies on the frontier between the two German states, the reunion of which we younger men at any rate regard as our life's work, to be accomplished by every means in our power." In the Austrian pro-Anschluss camp were aligned the confirmed Pan-Germans, certain Catholics who applauded the anti-Communist feature of the Nazi ideology, fatuous admirers of Hitler—the Austrian lad who had "made good"—some peasants and manual workers who believed that union with Germany would bring economic advantages, and high-spirited youths in university circles.

Hitlerian decrees which made it very difficult for Reich holiday-makers to cross the frontier into Austria worsened the economic situation and from Germany a large volume of provocative propaganda intended to undermine the Dollfuss dictatorship flowed into the little Republic. Suspicious of Hitlerian designs, foreign governments issued a solemn warning that Austria's integrity and independence must be preserved. Mussolini stood forth as the special guardian of the Republic with which he had intimate diplomatic ties.

Before the echoes of the Dollfuss destruction of Viennese Socialism had died away the capital was the scene of another affray. Armed Austrian Nazis penetrated to the executive offices of the government in July, 1934, and mortally wounded Chancellor Dollfuss. It was the intention of the conspirators to seize the government buildings preliminary to ʌ general insurrection and then to unite with Germany. In what measure Nazi authorities in Berlin were implicated in this crude plot it is difficult as yet to say. In any case the rebels were quickly overpowered by loyalist forces. Frightened by the prospect of a greater Germany on his northern frontier, Mussolini mobilized several divisions along the Brenner Pass and threatened to send them across if German soldiers intervened to assist the Austrian Nazis.

Thenceforth the maintenance of independence eclipsed all other concerns of Austrian politics. Upon the death of Dollfuss supreme responsibility passed to his first lieutenant, Dr. Kurt von Schuschnigg, an earnest champion of Austrian freedom but devoid of the personal attributes of a successful dictator. Neither the faith nor the form of democracy impressed Schuschnigg, for he remarked that he was interested "not in the most votes but in the best votes." Evidently he thought that the restoration of the monarchy was highly desirable, but he understood that such a radical change would not receive international sanction.

Backed by the patriotic Fatherland Front, the only lawful political party in the Republic, Schuschnigg extended the authoritarian character of the dictatorship, and in April of 1936 he revived compulsory military service in defiance of the peace treaty. But measures to revitalize the national economy and efforts, wise and otherwise, to keep Austria a free country proved sterile. Austria was incorporated in Nazi Germany in the spring of 1938.

Kingless Hungary

By the peace signed at the Trianon Palace in 1920 the thousand-year-old Kingdom of Hungary lost two thirds of its pre-war territory and population. Rumania got slices of territory, and so did Yugoslavia and Czechoslovakia; even Austria, Hungary's old partner, was awarded a strip. In the main the transfers of territory could be squared with the principle of self-determination, taking language as the essential test of nationality. But in the ceded areas lived some 3,000,000 who spoke the Hungarian tongue, or more exactly the Magyar, for Magyar is the name of a nationality, while Hungarian refers to a state.

Inside truncated Hungary the population—nearly 9,000,000— was Magyar in sentiment except for half a million Germans, farmers and tradesmen, whose ancestors had been imported centuries ago as "scientific" agriculturalists or to develop commerce and business. Among this German minority an active pro-Nazi movement developed in the thirties. As for Hungarians of the Jewish tradition, about half a million, they frequently were more Magyar in spirit than the Magyars. But some Jews participated in a Communist regime of 1919, and others were resented as recent immigrants or because of their professional and financial success. Anti-Jewish feeling was a constant force in the life of Hungary, manifesting itself openly in discriminatory laws and in physical outrages against Jewry. The "numerous clausus," limiting the number of Jewish students in Hungarian universities, antedated anything of the sort in Germany.

Late in the 9th century the Magyars had ridden into the heart of the Danube valley, coming from somewhere in Asia and carrying with them a strange Oriental tongue which to this day is their distinguishing trait. These marauding Asiatics made themselves masters of a large area in central Europe, conquering less bellicose Slavic-speaking stocks, and as conquerors, the Magyars remained. Despite vicissitudes of political fortune the Magyar ruling class preserved the superiority complex of the conqueror toward conquered peoples into the 20th century.

Immediately after the armistice in 1918, a moderately Socialist republic was set up, soon to be followed by a short-lived Communist dictatorship more or less on the Russian model. Then came another brief Socialist interlude, and finally the conservatives gained the upper hand by military force and remained in power to 1944. The stormy post-war years, marred by terrorism, atrocities and bloodshed, indulged in alike by radical and conservative, left scars never effaced.

After their victory the conservatives formally revived the monarchy and named Admiral Nicolas Horthy of the Hapsburg navy as regent for life. So Hungary became a kingdom without a king, presided over by an admiral without a fleet. Twice in 1921 the legitimate claimant to the throne, Charles I, the last ruler of the Hapsburg monarchy, dropped into Hungary and demanded that royal prerogatives be given him, but pressure from the countries which had profited by the dissolution of Hungary—the Little Entente—forced him to withdraw. Throughout the epoch between the wars an active monarchical coterie worked for the restoration of the crown, but the odds against them were overpowering. Though the Hungarian government was parliamentary in form, it was generally authoritarian in spirit and performance. In the last analysis the will of Regent Horthy was the law. Ministerial responsibility and political parties existed, but suffrage was restricted and at election times arbitrary and brutal methods of influencing voters were invoked. Until 1937 balloting was done by word of mouth in rural Hungary.

Much of Hungary is a marvellously fertile plain, one of Europe's most productive agricultural regions. Big estates owned by the colorfully anachronistic aristocracy dominated the Hungarian countryside and because of the resistance of the politically powerful landlords not much was accomplished in the way of breaking up the great latifundia. Thousands of Hungarian peasants owned only dwarf farms insufficient to support a family, and perhaps a quarter of the rustics was entirely landless, victims of chronic underemployment and remunerated very poorly even when they found work.

Notoriously inequitable tax legislation discriminated against the small holder to the advantage of the grandees. Though Hungary as a whole did not suffer from overpopulation, being unique among the agrarian states of eastern Europe in that respect, there were districts in which the population was too dense for comfort. In rural Hungary a semi-feudal atmosphere prevailed, not unlike that in the Junker provinces of Germany.

Industry was little developed. Though Hungary was deprived of valuable mineral resources and forests by the peace settlement she retained rich bauxite deposits and enough coal for her limited domestic needs. The only large city, the capital, Budapest, noted as a milling center, was sometimes called the Minneapolis of Europe.

In international affairs the supreme concern of Hungary in the interval between world wars was the recovery of provinces that had been taken away by the peace settlement. Agitation for treaty revision through the agency of the League of Nations ran through all ranks of Hungarian society and was pushed by all political groupings except a left-wing faction whose hatred of the kingdom's social structure made it immune to irredentist clamor. Unofficial voices in Britain and America echoed the revisionist contentions heard inside Hungary.

To all overtures for changes in the status quo the beneficiaries of Hungary's dismemberment turned a deaf ear, though they consented in 1938 to the expansion of the armed forces beyond the narrow bounds set in the Treaty of Trianon. Diplomatically, Hungary aligned herself with Mussolini who advocated revision, and later teamed up with Hitlerian Germany, the market for the great bulk of Hungary's agricultural exports. That course paid dividends—tinsel dividends. When in 1938 Germany appropriated a part of Czechoslovakia, Hungary was assigned two parcels of that Republic, and after Hitler devoured another section of the Czech state, Hungary snatched a second share.

Thus the Magyar irredentist claims upon Czechoslovakia were fully satisfied, but pretensions to territory under the Rumanian and Yugoslav flags were still unappeased. With the object of rectifying those "injustices" Hungary moved close to the Axis coalition and fought shoulder to shoulder with it in World War II.

Czechoslovakia

Of all the political creations born of World War I, that of Czecho-slovakia, which was an heir of the crazy-quilt Hapsburg monarchy, was most fully attuned to democratic principles and practices. During most of its twenty-year existence Czechoslovakia knew freedom, sta-bility, and prosperity unapproached elsewhere in Europe's Middle East. Not only did Czechoslovakia stand well among Slavic-speaking countries, it was also the key-land of central Europe. And the de-struction of the Czech Republic by Hitlerian Germany in 1938-1939 forms a large milestone on the way to World War II.

More than most countries Czechoslovakia was favored with a line of broadminded, progressive, and creative statesmen who helped no-tably to found and then to guide the nation. Highest honors belong to Thomas G. Masaryk, who is venerated as the George Washing-ton of his country. From humble surroundings at birth, Masaryk forged his way upward, winning acclaim as an erudite scholar and dynamic university teacher as well as an editor and astute politician. It was his role as an encourager of Czechoslovak national consciousness and subsequently as a builder of the democratic state that made Masaryk the hero of heroes of the twentieth century Czech. He bril-liantly epitomized the teacher turned statesman.

Shortly after the fighting started in 1914, Masaryk betook himself to foreign capitals, Washington included, in search of practical sup-port for an independent Czech nation. In that errand he was abun-dantly successful and at Philadelphia a Czechoslovak declaration of independence was published to the world. Long since Masaryk had adopted the democratic faith as his political philosophy and that assured him a sympathetic hearing in western countries. As soon as Czechoslovakia was proclaimed a free land, Masaryk was chosen President and installed in the ancient castle of the Bohemian kings on a high eminence looking down on the teeming city of Prague.

For his newly-created country Masaryk set a high mission. As he himself put it, "Our purpose is to make of Prague the mecca of democracy. We have the task to liberate central Europe. From here must radiate the only gospel acceptable to freemen. It is a great and noble task, but I am confident my people will prove equal to it—with God's help." This scholarly old gentleman, President of Czechoslo-vakia from 1918 to 1935, lived by that creed and in its spirit worked tirelessly to preserve his young nation as an island of progress and freedom in the sea of dictatorship which covered central Europe in the thirties. Masaryk's courage, when the odds against him seemed almost insuperable, matched his calmness and his unfailing courtesy.

On Masaryk's retirement from the presidency, his mantle fell upon Dr. Edward Beneš, his disciple and lifelong collaborator, sometime a university lecturer, too, who served as Foreign Minister without interruption while Masaryk was chief executive. A hard-headed realist, more the nationalist than his master, Beneš gained a unique reputation for diplomatic competence among the statesmen of Europe's smaller countries. At the side of these two talented public men worked a host of lesser figures, some Slovaks, more Czechs, fashioning the Czechoslovak nationhood.

Almost all the territory of the Czechoslovakian Republic belonged to the Hapsburg monarchy before 1914.[2] The larger part of the state was the ancient Kingdom of Bohemia which had been a political entity for hundreds of years before its absorption into the Austrian realm. For the rest, the regions of Slovakia and Ruthenia, formerly parts of the Hungarian kingdom, were backward in economy and enlightenment as compared with the Bohemian area. All told, Czechoslovakia covered an area slightly greater than Illinois. At its creation it had a population of 13,000,000, which increased 1,500,000 in the next two decades. Having much the shape of a banana, a conspicuous feature of the Republic's geography was the long, exposed frontiers.

In a memorable phrase the British statesman, Lloyd George, once characterized the old Austro-Hungarian monarchy as a ramshackle realm. The same description was broadly applicable to the Republic of Czechoslovakia. For though Czechs made up the largest national grouping in the state, there were about 3,000,000 German-speaking folk, large Magyar and Ukrainian (or Ruthenian) minorities, and a handful of Poles. And among the Slovaks, stolid, conservative peasants in the main, deeply attached to their Roman Catholic faith, political convictions were divided. "Cousins" though they were of the Czechs, the historical evolution of the Slovaks had been different and while one political faction favored a tightly-integrated Czechoslovakia, a second and somewhat smaller element, led by politically-minded Catholic priests, desired at least home-rule for the districts of Slovak population. As testimony to the multi-linguistic composition of Czechoslovakia the printed matter on banknotes appeared in six tongues: Czech, Slovak, German, Magyar, Polish, and Ukrainian.

Families of these several groupings, more especially the Czechs and the German, were scattered about the Republic, though the Germans largely lived along the western and northern rim in an area fa-

---

[2] A very tiny parcel of land was obtained from Germany. It is a popular illusion that much of the Czech Republic was German soil prior to the war.

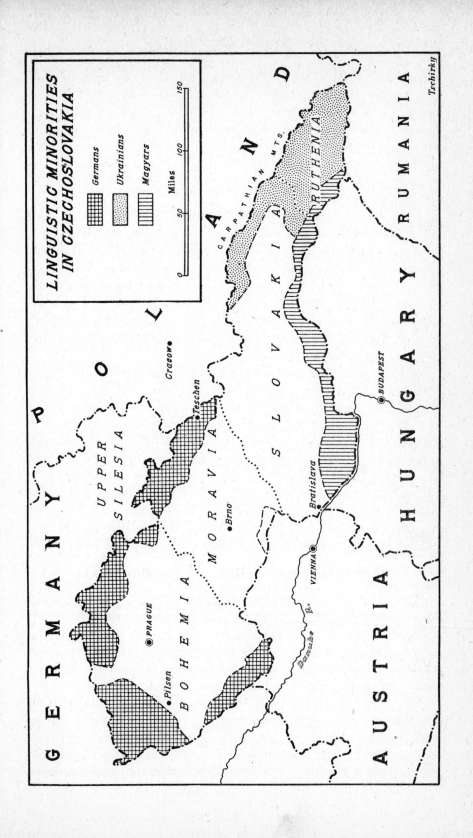

LINGUISTIC MINORITIES
IN CZECHOSLOVAKIA

Germans

Ukrainians

Magyars

Miles

0   50   100   150

GERMANY

POLAND

UPPER SILESIA

BOHEMIA

MORAVIA

SLOVAKIA

RUTHENIA

CARPATHIAN MTS.

Cracow

Teschen

Brno

Pilsen

PRAGUE

VIENNA

Danube R.

Bratislava

BUDAPEST

AUSTRIA

HUNGARY

RUMANIA

Tschirky

miliarly spoken of as the Sudetenland. Thus came the name of Sudetens for this German minority whose ancestors had settled there as
long ago as the 12th century. For generations Germans and Czechs
of Bohemia had been involved in an unending feud, which was greatly
intensified in the late 19th century in response to a remarkable
renaissance that awakened the Czechs to a new consciousness of
nationality. In some respects the case of the Sudeten area paralleled
that of Ulster in Ireland.

Ever since the foundation of the German Empire in 1871, a small
but militant party in the Sudetenland had agitated for the union of
the region with Germany. Following the collapse of the Hapsburg
monarchy in 1918, an independent Sudeten government was set up,
but was suppressed by Czech arms. Sudeten clamor for union with the
Austrian Republic, which was intense in the first years of Czechoslovakia history, tended to die away in the late twenties. This was chiefly
because economic conditions improved and Czech authorities treated
Sudeten susceptibilities tenderly.

In conformity with the treaty of minority rights which the Prague
government had signed, political, linguistic, and press freedoms were
enjoyed by the minorities of Czechoslovakia. Differences were tolerated
to a commendable degree in this model democracy in the heart of
Europe. Indeed, only Estonia and Finland surpassed Czechoslovakia
in the generosity and wisdom displayed in the treatment of minorities.
In response, some Sudetens loyally cooperated with the Republic,
while others—and many Magyars, too—thought it intolerable that they
should be politically subordinate to the Czechs, whom they despised
as culturally and socially inferior. Among the Sudeten and Magyar
middle classes the *Herrenvolk* complex was strong and ineradicable.

Constitution and Politics of Czechoslovakia

To prepare the fundamental law of the Republic, Czechs who had
been deputies in the last Imperial Austrian parliament worked with
a selected group of representative Slovaks. For an interval of more
than a year the country was administered under a provisional constitution. Germans and Magyars participated in local governmental
affairs, but had no hand in framing the national charter.

Proclaimed in February, 1920, the permanent Czechoslovak Constitution was a singularly enlightened document, democratic and for-
ward-looking, which drew generously upon the experience of France
and the United States in matters of government. The Constitution
provided for a President, elected by the parliament, whose authority

exceeded that of his French counterpart. He had, for instance, restricted powers of veto over legislation without, however, approaching the power vested in the American President. The real executive was the Ministry which depended for its tenure upon majority support in the lower branch of the legislature.

It was the intention of the founding fathers to have the Upper House or Senate a "conservative" body. Accordingly, the right to vote for Senators was restricted to all citizens over twenty six, and candidates had to be at least forty five. For the Chamber of Deputies, on the other hand, one might vote at the age of twenty one. A clause establishing proportional representation assured every substantial bloc of opinion representation in the Legislature.

Czechoslovakia's parliamentary system was crippled by the multiplicity of parties and a confusing chorus of voices. As in France parliamentary groups represented a wide assortment of interests, economic, social, and religious. In the Czech Republic the parliamentary situation was gravely complicated by the existence of political groupings based upon national or linguistic attachments. In consequence every ministry was a coalition body, drawing its support from several strata of opinion. Alone among the parties of Czechoslovakia the Communists contrived consistently to surmount "national" considerations.

At the outset the Prague administration followed decidedly Czech policies as necessary for the consolidation of the infant state. After that, there was a short period in which moderately Socialistic views dominated. Subsequently for about a decade, the farming interests of the Republic, to which part of the time the forces of clericalism were allied, guided the destinies of the nation. In the critical era which opened in 1935, with the sensational success of the Sudeten German Party, described later, the conservative, anti-Communistic Agrarian Party and its outlook held sway.

Social and Economic Progress

The Prague government pointed proudly to the social and economic record that was written. By making public schooling compulsory, the state raised the proportion of literates, notably in the historically retarded southern and eastern areas. The program of technical education compared favorably with that of Germany. Much attention was also paid to the physical fitness of youth and to mass sports as a pleasant means to that end. Comprehensive schemes of social insurance, public health and hygiene services, public-financed housing and road-building projects kept Czechoslovakia abreast of the socializing trends of the age. Heavy taxation, both direct and indirect, produced the revenues to pay for these undertakings.

Individual ingenuity, joined to state legislation, operated to keep Czechoslovakia well-balanced economically and almost self-sufficient in foodstuffs. Soon after the founding of the state, laws were passed to distribute the large landed properties among the toiling peasants, many of whom had only small farms or none at all. A thousand individuals, it was estimated, owned over a quarter of the acreage, and most of the big landowners were either German or Magyar in speech and outlook.

By law, the state expropriated land in excess of a certain minimum, paying modest compensation except in the case of crown and noble estates. These properties in turn were parcelled out among workers on the soil; altogether some 5,000,000 acres of ground, arable and forest, were distributed. Thereby the material lot of hundreds of thousands of rural families was bettered and their fidelity to the Czechoslovak state was cemented. Increased diversification of crops and model cooperative organizations, practically free of state interference, likewise helped to elevate or hold steady the living standards of the countryside. Save for certain limited sections, Czechoslovakia did not suffer seriously from rural over-population.

It was the maturity and diversity of the industrial establishment, built up from the late 19th century onward, that distinguished Czechoslovakia from the other small states of central Europe, Austria alone excepted. Coal and iron were available in good quantity and fair quality, and the country produced other industrial rawstuffs in commercial quantities. The Bohemian half of the Republic was crisscrossed by a splendid network of railways and canals, which were linked up with means of communication in adjoining countries. By treaty Czechoslovakia possessed transportation rights on the Elbe and the Danube rivers and commercial facilities at Hamburg, Trieste, and other seaports.

Given anything like stable world economic conditions the export business of Czechoslovakia flourished. But foreign trade slumped catastrophically during the Great Depression and unemployment soared close to the million mark. On the other hand, after 1933, an upswing began, being encouraged by currency devaluations. Sales of goods to western countries rose prodigiously, which exempted Czechoslovakia from dependence upon Hitlerian Germany for its economic welfare. The success of Czechoslovakia in meeting foreign debts made the country unique among the small states of central and eastern Europe.

While manufacturing was carried on in many parts of Czechoslovakia, the most efficient plants and equipment, and the most skillful artisans, were located principally, though by no means exclusively, in the areas of German speech. Textile production topped the list, but the chemical, paper, sugar, and mining industries were highly developed. The vast Skoda iron and steel works—and smaller concerns —had a world reputation for machinery and armaments. The fabulous Bata shoe company, patterned upon American mass-production technology, disposed of its inexpensive footwear not alone in the home market but throughout eastern Europe—and even in Chicago. Among the specialties of Czechoslovakian industry were Pilsener beer— known and imitated the globe over, Bohemian glass, chinaware and pottery, and smoked meats of which Prague ham is a choice delicacy. Cottage industries wove lace and hammered out toys, musical instruments, and gadgets.

Separatist Agitations

It was the tragedy of the Republic of Masaryk that in spite of her devotion to the principle and practice of democratic freedom she could not wholly convert the larger minority groupings to the Czechoslovak way of life. Even among the Slovaks there was a vocal dissident element, which would not be appeased by minor concessions, and whose spokesmen cried to heaven about "oppression" and "exploitation." Restlessness among articulate Ukrainians and Magyars varied in intensity, but did not disappear, and was frequently the subject of investigation by the League of Nations.

These discontents were vexing, but dissatisfaction and irredentist sentiments among the Sudeten Germans was perilous to the very integrity of the Republic, for Germany, unlike Hungary, could bite as well as bark. It has been remarked previously that the attachment of Sudetens to the Prague regime improved in the late twenties, and a faction of "Activist" Sudetens representing the majority cooperated with the Czechs to the extent of taking cabinet portfolios.

But grievances arising out of the land redistribution measures, discrimination in the award of public contracts and in the appointment of officials, and controversies over educational institutions kept bitterness alive in some Sudeten hearts. The tide of nationalism which swept over Europe with the Great Depression powerfully affected the political outlook of the German minority. Unemployment in the highly industrialized Bohemian area much exceeded that in the balance of the Republic. Sudeten chiefs charged that the Prague government neglected to provide adequate relief for impoverished citizens of German speech, and, indeed, in a manner familiar to democratic countries, held the government blameworthy for all the economic woes.

The victory of Hitlerism in Germany quickened the irredentist ferment among wide sections of the Sudetens. Swiftly, Germany took on the guise of a powerful nation in which the wheels of industry hummed, in which employment was excellent, in which the peasants prospered. Union with that country promised to satisfy Sudeten national and economic longings. True, the Sudetens shared richly in the Czechoslovak revival of the late thirties, but by that time the desire to become citizens of Germany was held as a conviction by hosts of German speakers. Hitler bombastically proclaimed himself the champion and savior of German minorities wherever they were located. A flood of propaganda in the form of leaflets, films, and radio broadcasts engulfed the Sudetenland, portraying the grandeur and the prosperity of the "new Germany" and harping upon the "racial affinity" of the Sudetens with their kinsmen across the border.

In the meantime, certain Sudetens had organized a staunchly national political party which inscribed the word "autonomy" on its banners. They demanded that the Wilsonian shibboleth of self-determination should be applied in the Czech Republic, carrying on a lively and provocative campaign to that end. At the polls in May, 1935, this Sudeten German party attracted the votes of rather more than three out of five of the German electors. That triumph enheartened the leadership, headed by Konrad Henlein, some time a gymnastic instructor, who, though posing as a Czechoslovak loyalist, cherished the notion that he was the Sudeten Moses destined to lead his fellows into the promised land of Hitlerian Germany.

Though the Prague government offered concessions to the Sudetens which would remove the specific causes of resentment—and after each set of proposals the Henleinists asked for more—it rejected the claim for autonomy. In the Sudetenland, autonomy would almost certainly have been the merest preface to secession and, if granted, would encourage the separatist agitation among Magyar and other minorities. President Beneš and his colleagues would have none of it.

Against the day when its integrity might be challenged, Czechoslovakia had made as much preparation as possible. From the beginning of its free existence the Prague government was a warm partisan of the League as a bulwark of the status quo. It had solid alliances with Rumania and Yugoslavia, pointed specifically against the return of the Hapsburg to the throne of Austria or Hungary. Best of all, from 1924 on, Czechoslovakia had a military alliance with France. Armed assistance in time of need had also been pledged by Soviet Russia, contingent, however, upon French fulfillment of commitments to Czechoslovakia. Moreover, the military strength of the Czech Republic, both in armies and armament industry, was considerable.

How the Republic of Masaryk was destroyed, how the last democratic stronghold east of the Rhine succumbed to the swastika, is a melancholy story which is reviewed in its appropriate setting (p. 499).

Poland

For many minds the establishment of a free Poland after World War I represented the triumph of justice. For generations Poland had been nothing more than a geographical expression and a political aspiration, its people subject to the rule of Prussia, Russia, and Austria. But in the dark night of Polish subjection, romantic memories of an illustrious past and the national language and culture were kept alive by noble, by intellectual, by schoolmaster, by priest. Roman Catholic churches in every center of Polish population were custodians of the unquenchable belief that Poland would live again. Toward the end of the 19th century Poles by the thousand forsook their European homes for larger opportunities in the New World,[3] adding thus an interesting and valuable strain to the richly mingled blood of the American nation—and in time doing extremely well by college football teams. Some Polish immigrants and their descendants retained an active and natural sympathy for their homeland and contributed counsel and cash or exerted political pressure on behalf of the national interests of their countrymen.

By singular good fortune all three of the states which had profited by Poland's dismemberment went down to defeat in World War I. From Prussia, from Austria, from Russia, the new Poland inherited territory which made up a state thrice the size of New York. It contained about 28,000,000 inhabitants, sixth in population among the nations of Europe.[4] Many Polish political leaders were imbued, when not obsessed, with the conviction that their nation was the chosen folk of Europe's middle east, the champion of liberty, the bulwark of western culture against what they were prone to call Muscovite barbarism. Yet only about two out of three living within the borders of the Republic spoke Polish as their mother tongue. A large and

---

[3] The United States census of 1940 reported a shade under two and a half millions claiming Polish as their mother tongue.

[4] How Poland's frontiers were fixed is explained on p. 98.

aggressive German minority and even bigger communities of Ukrainians and Jews, not to mention groups of Lithuanians and White Russians, gave Poland a polyglot complexion and were the source of
discord.

An Adventure in Democracy

To hammer a durable Polish state out of the heritage of the
three defunct monarchies was a large assignment. The country had
been ravaged by warfare to an extent unequalled in Europe—millions
of acres of arable soil blasted; millions of acres of woodland devastated; ruined farmsteads by the thousands; machinery and cattle
carted away or destroyed; railways disrupted; populations destitute.
The new Poland, in a word, was in an incredibly desperate condition.

Against that somber background a Constitution was drafted and
put into operation in 1921. That document faithfully reflected the
democratic currents in the ascendant after the war and borrowed lavishly from the French governmental system. The head of the state,
the President, for instance, was assigned precious little authority, which
was a mistake in a country beset with so many perplexities; nor was
the Upper House of the legislature given much effective power. Real
authority rested in the popularly-chosen *Seym*, which was modelled on
the French Chamber of Deputies; to it the Cabinet was responsible.

Poland's try at thorough-going democracy proved a fiasco, as it
was almost bound to be. The Poles had no traditions of self-government. Too many politicians were mercurial in temperament and
touched by sectional or class jealousies. Strong personalities of moderate views—politicians who understood that compromise is the
essence of democratic statecraft—were lamentably scarce. And public
questions of all sorts were extremely complex. The record of Polish
democracy sustained the thesis that effective parliamentary government is not the product of spontaneous combustion but rather of
lengthy evolution.

It was in November, 1922, that the first national election under
the Constitution was conducted. Fifteen parties returned deputies to
the *Seym*. A wide variety of opinions on public affairs was represented
and minority groupings won a fifth of the seats. At the top of the
agenda was the selection of a President. An obvious choice would have
been Marshal Josef Pilsudski, titular head of the state since 1918,
and the supreme hero of Poland reborn.

Pilsudski was no Masaryk. Of mixed Polish-Lithuanian ancestry,
he had grown up as a subject of the Russian tsar. A warm partisan
of the idea of a free Poland from boyhood, he adopted as his economic

philosophy a national brand of Socialism. For conspiracies against Imperial Russia and for his radicalism as a Socialist editor, Pilsudski was repeatedly imprisoned or banished to Siberia. Subsequently he took up residence in Austrian Poland where he established military organizations against the day when the Poles might strike for a state of their own.

In World War I Pilsudski's legionnaires fought against hated Russia, as allies of Austria and Germany, but by his insistence upon political rights for Poland he antagonized the German authorities, who consigned him to prison. Released just before the Armistice of 1918, Pilsudski hurried to Warsaw, proclaimed Poland's independence, set up a temporary administration, and whipped a national army into shape. The success of that army in repulsing a Russian invasion in 1920 heightened Pilsudski's already great prestige.

As a military man, accustomed to command and to be obeyed, the cast of the Marshal's mind was unsympathetic to self-government. He did not hanker for the office of Poland's President, which was so plainly decorative, much preferring to administer the armed forces. So the dignity of chief executive was conferred upon one of his obscure followers.

Endless wrangling in the *Seym* stultified the conduct of state business. The currency was recklessly inflated, causing wild fluctuations in prices and uncertainty in trade. Ministries were weak, Cabinet crises recurrent. Ominously the discords in government resembled the conditions that had preceded the break-up of Poland in the 18th century.

Dictatorship

Much disgusted with the trends and feuds in politics, Pilsudski, who had temporarily withdrawn from the public stage, gathered soldiers around him and in May of 1926 marched into Warsaw and took matters into his own strong hands. After the coup d'etat, Pilsudski's power rested on the army, whose direction he again assumed. Like Cromwell of England he had no wish to be rid of parliament but wished rather to curtail its authority. Like the 17th century English dictator he insisted that executive power in time of emergency must reside in a single person.

Revisions that were made in the Constitution strengthened the authority of the President. The civil administration was tightened. Pilsudski's henchmen, not all of whom by any means cherished the Marshal's high standards of public morality, divided up the loaves and fishes of patronage. Although political parties hostile to Pilsudski's ways were permitted to carry on, and the opposition press was allowed considerable latitude, the will of the Marshal was for most practical purposes the law of Poland until his death in 1935. Outspoken critics of the thinly-disguised dictatorship were arbitrarily imprisoned or otherwise silenced.

Friends of the Marshal drew up a new Constitution and jammed it through parliament after opposition deputies had withdrawn from the *Seym* or been arrested. That Constitution of 1935 set up an "authoritarian democracy" which had some of the earmarks of a totalitarian state, and invested the President with exceptionally broad authority.

When Pilsudski died in 1935, a set of his military subordinates— the Colonels—took charge of Poland's affairs and tried to build up a successor to the Marshal in the person of General Edward Rydz-Smgly. By making the authoritarian regime more severe, the Colonels invited more vehement protestations than ever from opponents. With the weights in the international balance trembling in 1938—as though Europe were a ball on the gambler's wheel—it behooved Polish politicians to smother their differences and to accent the things that united them, lest the sorry history of the nation in the 18th century be duplicated.

A semblance of unity greater than at any time since the war with Soviet Russia was actually achieved. With it grew sublime confidence in the national capacity for war. But as the terrible events of the German invasion of September, 1939, demonstrated, Poland, in spite of the desperate resistance of the nation, was utterly unequal to a war against tanks and Stukas.

The National Economy of Poland

Poland was overwhelmingly an agricultural nation having only two cities of western stature: the capital, Warsaw, and Lodz, Poland's Manchester. Over large sections of the Republic the soil was comparatively fertile, though west and east it was inferior by nature; and forests covered a fifth of the country. The largest mineral resource of Poland was coal; there was some low-grade iron, zinc and lead, a trifling supply of copper, and to the southeast, small oilfields. It was not nature's intention that Poland should become highly industrialized.

For Polish history a crucial fact was the swift growth in population, jumping from 28,000,000 to 35,000,000 between wars. In the existing state of economic development Poland was heavily overpopulated and the struggle for existence harsh and relentless. From that circumstance arose in part a demand for colonies into which the surplus might be sent.

At the very outset of its independent existence the Polish government wrestled with the large problem of landlordship. Here, as commonly in eastern Europe, patriarchal noble and church owned huge properties over against a mass of the landless and small holders. In 1920, at the time of the Russian invasion, the Warsaw government successfully bid for the loyalty of the rural masses by promising to partition the big estates.

Only in part was that pledge fulfilled. In the face of formidable opposition from the landlords, the *Seym* passed two acts (1921, 1925) dividing large properties among peasants. But in both instances, the owners were allowed relatively high compensation which angered the poorer recipients, and the legislation was not rigorously executed. Well-to-do farmers were the chief beneficiaries of the land reforms. Peasant leaders expected that Pilsudski after the coup of 1926 would speed up the parcellation program but actually the pace was slower than before. In all some 6,000,000 acres—about a tenth part of the arable—were transferred to medium and small holdings. To exert pressure on the government in behalf of the rustics a United Peasants' Party was organized in 1930 out of previously competing factions, but the results of its activity were negligible, and its foremost leaders were harried from the land.

Unappeased land hunger was a standing danger and challenge to the Polish Republic. It was estimated that two rural families out of three lacked sufficient land to eke out a decent existence. Even in time of world prosperity poverty was writ large on wide areas of the Polish countryside, due not alone to the inequitable distribution of land but also to inefficiency in cultivation and to the density of population; in periods of depression appalling destitution gripped the peasantry. If they borrowed funds they were likely to discover themselves chained to the village usurer. Cooperative societies for rural welfare were not extensively developed.

Because of the scarcity of private capital for industrial purposes the Polish government assumed an ever larger role in this branch of the national economy. The state owned and operated railways, shipping lines, banks, mines, and partly or wholly owned some fifty industrial concerns; and the sale of alcohol, salt, matches, and tobacco was monopolized by the state. Under state auspices a gigantic plan of industrialization was launched in 1936 for the "central industrial region." Its features were the expansion of power facilities, the construction of steel and munitions works, automobile and cellulose factories. As of 1939 the state was employing more workers than private industry, which was mostly foreign-financed.

Perhaps the outstanding economic innovation of Poland reborn was the building of the port and city of Gydnia on the Baltic, only a few miles from venerable Danzig. A mere fishing village in 1924, Gydnia in the thirties grew into the busiest harbor on the Baltic and had a population of 110,000. French capital and engineers participated in the creation of this "miracle community" and in the construction of railways leading to it.

Minority Groupings

Cutting across every aspect of Poland's public life and invading private affairs as well were intricate and unsettled minority problems. One out of three dwellers under the Polish flag spoke another tongue than Polish. What proportion of these folk felt themselves to be Poles in nationality lies beyond objective analysis. Owing to the profusion of tongues and religions Poland was obliged in 1919 to sign an international treaty promising safeguards for minorities, but in 1934, holding the treaty to be an intolerable infringement on national sovereignty, the Warsaw government denounced it. Guarantees of minority rights incorporated in the Constitutions of 1921 and 1935 were not fully carried out.

Largest of the minorities was the Ukrainian, numbering about 5,000,000, most of them living in the area that before 1918 was part of Austria; the rest, in former Russian Poland. Divided along religious lines between the Uniate, Orthodox, and Roman Catholic Churches, the Ukrainians also held divergent political views, some pro-Russian, some pro-Polish, some dreaming of an independent Ukrainian state. Polish treatment of this minority oscillated between efforts at conciliation and measures of forcible assimilation, attended by stern repression of advocates of autonomy or separatism. The feud was envenomed by the circumstance that many Ukrainian peasants toiled for Polish landlords at pitiful wages. Yet the Ukrainians, for all the restraints laid upon them, had their own press, deputies in the *Seym,* cooperative societies, and cultural associations. It would seem that they had greater freedom for national expression than their kinsmen in the Soviet Union.

From pre-war Russian Poland, the Polish Republic inherited groups of White Russians and Lithuanians. The former, more than a million, were mostly illiterate peasants with little sense of national

consciousness. Among them there was a marked tendency to assimilate with the Poles, though the largest political party appears to
have favored some kind of merger with the White Russians of the
Soviet Union. Because of agitation to that end, they were repressed
by Polish authorities. Charges of Polish persecution of the Lithuanian national fragment were endemic and factually well-grounded.

Next to Ukrainians, Jews formed the biggest minority element of
Poland. There were more than 3,000,000, scattered widely across the
Republic, though they were preponderantly town and city dwellers.
Warsaw, for instance, was one quarter Jewish and in certain towns the
percentage was over eighty. Assuredly the Jews in great majority
were a religious minority but what were they in political or national
sympathies? Some of them were warmly attached to the Polish nationality, while a much larger bloc were political Zionists devoted
with varying degrees of ardor to the language, the literature, the historical traditions of Jewry and the political aspirations of Zionism.
Most of the immigrants to Palestine hailed from Poland and other
Polish Jews lived by the faith that one day they too would be able to
move thither.

From the past, anti-Jewish feelings were bequeathed to the new
Poland. Animosities were intensified by the hardships which accompanied the Great Depression and by the anti-Jewish propaganda and
policies of Nazi Germany. Rights guaranteed Jews under international engagements and special agreements inside Poland were never
entirely enforced. Resentment against Jewry found open expression
in discriminations of various kinds—limitations on Jewish attendance
at educational institutions and boycotts on Jewish traders, artisans,
and professional folk. Not infrequently Jews were victims of vandalism, hooliganism, and physical violence. An organized Polish campaign demanded the emigration of poor Jews who were potential
parents.

Polish political authorities understood that anti-Jewish activities
damaged the reputation of their country abroad. Toward the very
end of the thirties, therefore, as the international sky darkened, the
police were ordered to protect Jewish rights and property in letter
and in spirit. Unhappy as was the lot of Jewry under the Polish Republic, an infinitely worse fate befell them after the German conquest
of Poland in 1939 when hundreds of thousands were slaughtered by
sadistic Nazi fanatics.

From the viewpoint of international politics the German minority
of Poland had the highest significance. Located largely on the western

side of the Republic, and numbering around 900,000, the Germans belonged in the main to the Lutheran Church and were economically better off than other citizens of Poland. Cursed with a *Herrenvolk* complex, the Germans looked to the German Reich for comfort and aid and not in vain. Irredentist longings were immensely heightened after the triumph of National Socialism across the border.

Hundreds of specific disputes envenomed relations between the German minority and Polish officials. Endless controversies arose over schools, land distribution, appointments to public office, and the other familiar grievances of aggressive minority populations. Hitlerian exuberance among Polish Germans invited police intervention of which exaggerated reports were circulated abroad, intensifying hatred among Germans everywhere. It was directly in the name of "liberating" the Germans of Poland that the Third Reich went to war in 1939.

The Danzig Free State

Hitler's other avowed objective in unsheathing the sword was to recover the Danzig Free State, which had been detached from Germany by the Treaty of Versailles. Danzig occupied the mouth of the Vistula, Poland's great waterway, and before the development of Gydnia, was the only port through which Poland had direct access to the outside world. Placed under the general supervision of the League of Nations Danzig was permitted a government of its own to deal with matters of a local nature, but the community was included in the Polish customs system and Poles were permitted to use the harbor and railway facilities.

Yet Danzig's population was almost wholly German and quarrels over customs, port regulations, schooling privileges, and such minor questions as the color of mailboxes provoked constant tension. Every dispute was surcharged with nationalistic electricity. The Danzig experiment yielded nothing but sustained antagonism, except during a short period when a Socialist majority controlled the government.

A High Commissioner representing the League in Danzig endeavored to adjust disputes. If he failed, the issue was tossed into the lap of the League Council; but the League could do little more than pour tranquillizing oil on the troubled Danzig waters from time to time. The building of the rival port at Gydnia inescapably embittered relationships. Poles explained that their expanding foreign trade required greater shipping facilities than Danzig afforded, but Danzigers complained angrily, though unconvincingly, that their very livelihood was being eaten away by smart, up-to-date Gydnia.

Resentment among Danzigers was matched by irredentist agitation in the German Reich to recover the city. The record of this enclave of German nationalism in the Polish state, which in time was poisoned by the Nazi virus, provides a rather gloomy precedent for the internationalization of a port. The Nazi drive to regain Danzig and the German-peopled districts of western Poland is explained, together with other aspects of Poland's foreign relations, in another place (Chap. XX).

The Baltic Republics

Along the eastern Baltic four sovereign states—Finland, Estonia, Latvia, and Lithuania—took their places on the map after World War I. All had previously belonged to Imperial Russia, and, though the beginnings of the independence movements antedate 1914, it was the war, the revolutions in Russia, and strife with Bolshevik Russia that brought them freedom. Each of these countries was a distinct individuality, with a separate language and literature, some sense of kinship, and the belief that it constituted a unique cultural society.

Governmental institutions in all the Baltic Republics were based upon the democratic ideology, with universal secret suffrage, ministerial responsibility to the legislature, civil freedoms, and proper safeguards for the well-being of minorities. Because of the system of proportional representation that prevailed, ministries were invariably coalition groups and characteristically unstable. Only Finland managed to hold fast to popular self-government throughout the era between wars.

None of the Baltic Republics was large; the area of the whole was smaller than Texas, the population a trifle more than 11,000,000. Yet any one of these little, peace-loving, agricultural states was bigger than the small countries of northwestern Europe, and their foreign trade in 1938 exceeded that of Soviet Russia. Lying athwart the crossroads of international politics, unenviably sandwiched between Germany and Russia, the independence of the Baltic Republics depended directly upon the broad course of European politics. From time to time, Baltic statesmen conferred on plans for a confederation, but the Finns, aware of Soviet hostility to such a union, never lent the idea positive support. A loose political alignment of the other three was realized in 1934, and Estonia and Latvia formed a virtual customs union, into which it was hoped Lithuania would be drawn.[5]

---

[5] Polish diplomatists discussed a general federation with Baltic leaders but got nowhere.

Finland

Finland stands apart from the other Baltic Republics by reason of its success in preserving democratic institutions and in paying its obligations to foreign lenders. The prime natural wealth of Finland was the "green gold" of the abundant forests; timber and products of wood were the leading exports. The discovery of deposits of nickel, the largest stock in Europe, enhanced Finland's importance. The greater part of the population lived on the land—dour, hard-working peasants. Not a few of their relatives moved to the United States, many taking up and profitably cultivating farms in Maine which Yankees had found unprofitable; there they established rural cooperative societies such as had netted advantages in their homeland.

Economic equality prevailed in Finland to a remarkable degree. The capital city, Helsinki, the size of Rochester, New York, was world famous for its architectural experimentation. Popular education was considered a first responsibility by the Finnish government and was reinforced by peasant cultural organizations, so that illiteracy was reduced almost to the vanishing point. Finnish devotion to athletics is attested by the proud record of the country at the Olympic games; the fleet long-distance runner, Paavo Nurmi, made Finland known in the department of sports. The majestic strains of Sibelius' *Finlandia* were cherished by music lovers the world over.

Before Finland passed under Russian sovereignty in 1809, it had been attached to Sweden. That connection was reflected in the predominance of the Lutheran religion in Finland and in the existence of a small but influential Swedish-speaking population. A dispute with Sweden over the status of the strategically-significant Åaland Islands was satisfactorily resolved with the assistance of the League of Nations (Chap. XVII). After the demarcation of boundaries with the Soviet Union, Finnish patriotism regarded an area beyond Lake Ladoga as an irredentist region, peopled by Carelians, national kinsmen. In the name of national security Moscow, in turn, advanced pretensions to Finnish territory that lay a mere twenty three miles away from Leningrad.

Differences in economic and political outlook and memories of past struggles also disturbed good relations between Finland and Russia. These rival claims and ideological divergencies helped pave the way for two bitter Russo-Finnish wars between 1939 and 1945. Toward Germany, whether Weimar or Nazi, the Finnish government observed a benevolent attitude, seeing in Germany a potential asset in case of serious trouble with the Soviet Union, and finding there a market, second only in value to Great Britain, for exports.

Estonia and Latvia

Though separate entities, Estonia and Latvia exhibit striking parallelisms in their historical evolution. Never independent before 1918, these states, once they were released from Russian domination, launched out on a free existence with democratic governments.

Among the first acts of the new regimes was the liquidation of the landlord class and the transfer of their holdings to the peasantry. For the greater part the landlords were German Balts, baronial families descended from medieval Teutonic Knights who had pushed into the eastern Baltic to convert the natives from heathenism. In the towns well-to-do traders prided themselves on their German origins. From these Balts Imperial Russia had recruited court officials and some of them who emigrated to Germany attained high prominence in the Nazi Party.

Until the onset of the Great Depression, Estonia and Latvia prospered, finding outlets in Germany and Britain for their agricultural wares which formerly had been marketed in Russia. Their respective capitals, Tallinn and Riga, flourished as commercial and shipping centers, and the latter attained importance in manufacturing. Superior schooling facilities brought illiteracy to a low point, and the Estonian university at Tartu, once spoken of as "the Oxford of the East," and the corresponding Lettish institution at Riga specialized in the preservation and advancement of national cultures. State subsidies were furnished for the theatre and the fine arts.

Without experience in the processes of self-government and badly hurt by the world slump in trade, Estonia and Latvia became executive dictatorships in 1934 and remained substantially unchanged to 1939.[6]

Lithuania

Late in the Middle Age the frontiers of Lithuania swept from the Baltic to the Black Sea. Uniting subsequently with Poland, Lithuania eventually passed under the rule of Russia by reason of the partitioning of Poland in the 18th century. Nationalistic stirrings late in the

---

[6] Latvia's dictator, Karlis Ulmanis, previously President, was a graduate of the University of Nebraska.

19th century presaged the rebirth of Lithuanian freedom in 1920, though only for a state a tenth the size of medieval Lithuania.[7]

Lithuania's experimentation with republican democracy left much to be desired. In 1926 an autocratic regime took over. For ten years Parliament was not convoked and when it was reinstated, deputies had to be chosen from an official state party. Broadly regarded, the domestic history of Lithuania repeated that of other of the Baltic states. Unpopular Polish landlords were deprived of their estates for the benefit of the peasants. But economic and educational progress failed to keep pace with that of Latvia. Of all the Baltic republics, Lithuania was the most backward.

It was international tangles as well as the Roman Catholic faith of the population which differentiated Lithuania from her southern Baltic neighbors. With Poland a bitter feud raged over the Vilna district, cradle of Lithuanian culture and the ancient capital of the country, but claimed by the Poles on debatable grounds of nationality. Occupation of the Vilna area by Polish forces so infuriated the Lithuanian government that until 1938 it kept its frontiers sealed to Polish communication.

Even more grievous was a controversy with Germany over the Memelland, an ethnic mélange, over which the Lithuanian flag was hoisted in 1923 (p. 416). For Lithuania, the seaport in the district, Memel—or Klaipéda to the Lithuanian—was an indispensable window on the Baltic. Endless wrangling between Lithuania and the German element in the community persisted until 1939 when Nazi German forces marched in and the Memelland was rejoined to the German realm.

That act which could be interpreted in Soviet Russia—and in fact was—as a warning of a Nazi thrust to the east, of which *Mein Kampf* spoke so eloquently, invited counteraction on the part of the Soviet Union. That came shortly after the start of World War II with Russian military occupation and later, the annexation of Lithuania, Latvia, and Estonia. When in 1941 Germany and Russia fought one another, the Nazis took possession of these small countries, only to be driven out by the Red Army in 1945. Then, as before 1918, the Baltic peoples were again subjected to Russia.

[7] Some 800,000 Lithuanians lived overseas, principally in the United States. Certain of them took a lively interest in the land of their birth and sent it cash and advice.

MINORITIES IN CENTRAL EUROPE

Miles
0   100   200   300   400   500

Tschirky

CHAPTER VII

Fascist Italy

Defeat by Victory

NEVER a Great Power except by diplomatic courtesy, Italy emerged from the war with national morale at a low ebb. Her record on the battlefield had not been particularly impressive. Her territorial gains in the peace settlement, though they brought under the royal flag all districts of Italian speech, were smaller than had been popularly anticipated. But on the other hand, Austria, the ancient national foe, had been shattered beyond hope of repair; and Italy would share in the reparations to be paid by Germany and her allies. Allied diplomatists had fobbed off the kingdom with meagre colonial tracts, leading Mussolini to declare that Italy got nothing from "the rich, colonial dinner" that was devoured at Versailles.

When the peacemakers vetoed Italy's bid for the Adriatic port of Fiume (p. 103), the Italian nationalist, d'Annunzio, fell upon the community with a band of storm-troopers and remained in charge for fifteen months, until expelled by the Italian government. His administration exhibited many features which Mussolini later copied and applied in Italy itself.

Italy's war losses in men were severe and her economy, at no time really stable, had suffered deep dislocations. Therefore it was possible to believe that Italy had won the war but lost the peace. Just after the consolidation of the kingdom in 1870, D'Azeglio, a prominent politician, exclaimed, "We have made Italy, now we must make Italians." What he meant was that the legacy of particularist sentiments in the several Italian states, which generation after generation had barred the path to nationhood, would have to be replaced by an authentic national spirit. No little progress to that end had been achieved by 1919, but the process was as yet incomplete. It was widely held that the spectacle of the Italian troops deserting at Caporetto in 1917 proved the immaturity of the national spirit; though on the Piave in the closing cycle of the war, the soldiers had exhibited gallant qualities.

A rapidly rising population, poverty in mineral resources, indifferent agriculture in wide stretches of the kingdom, burdensome taxation to sustain an energetic colonialism and to finance a military establishment befitting an ambitious "Great Power"—these diverse circumstances had kept Italy from going forward equally with her neighbors. Parliamentary institutions, largely modelled on those of Great Britain, had done none too well in a country whose constitutional evolution and economic environment were dissimilar from Britain's, a country in which illiteracy was heavy, the press without conspicuous vigor, and concepts of liberalism imperfectly understood.

Popular participation in public affairs was limited before 1912 to a narrow élite and not much enlarged after that. Italian politicians displayed greater talent for parliamentary juggling than for forthright and effective statesmanship. Of local self-government there was precious little. No moneys could be appropriated by the humblest village in the Apennines nor the largest cities of the North without the sanction of officials in Rome. Whenever an adroit politician got control of the bureaucratic machinery, he was the essential master of the realm. Frequently the Prime Minister also held the portfolio of Home Secretary which gave him jurisdiction over the prefects—the keymen in the ninety provinces—and therewith patronage and an instrument to manipulate elections. Too many of Italy's democratic roots lay on the surface. The kingdom was not a democracy in the American or British or Swiss connotation of the term.

Old Forces and New

Political restlessness together with social and economic misery troubled Italy as, of course, the other countries after the war. The demobilization of the armed forces, the reconversion of industry to peace-time production, the rehabilitation of the transportation facilities, and mass undernourishment in the final stage of the war gave rise to similar tensions universally. But other countries had a larger capital of national faith to draw upon than Italy. Revolutionary sentiments which were stimulated by the Bolshevik Revolution in Russia found considerable acceptance among the Italian workless and the hungry in industrial communities and in the countryside. Currents that were abroad in the kingdom came into focus in an election for the Chamber of Deputies in November of 1919.

Old parties, right wing and middle-of-the-way groupings, won 265 out of 535 places, seats being distributed in proportion to the popular vote. But the largest of the parties was the Socialist with 156 deputies, a huge increase, which reflected the unhealthy social and economic conditions of the time. Although unwilling to take office in a coalition ministry the bulk of the Socialists preferred to reach the standard Socialist objectives by peaceful methods. A small left-wing faction, however, frankly preached imitation of the Bolsheviki—"a dictatorship of the proletariat," forceful dispossession of property owners, and the like. Moderate Socialism for all its electoral strength was hampered by the scarcity of effective dynamic leaders.

New on the Italian political stage was a Catholic party, the Christian Democrats, founded in 1919 by an energetic, forthright, democratically-minded Sicilian priest, Don Luigi Sturzo, who was derided by critics as "the long arm of the Holy See." The social program of the party called among other things for the dissolution of large estates, but the party was dedicated to the prevention of a revolutionary overturn such as had taken place in Russia. At the election of 1919 ninety nine disciples of Sturzo were elected by peasant voters of the north, by Catholic trade unionists, who were only slightly less numerous than the members of the Confederation of Labor which was allied to Socialism, and small tradesmen.

Of the novel political forces in Italy the largest significance attaches to the Fascist movement, founded at Milan in 1919 by Benito Mussolini. Taking its name from the *fasces* of ancient Rome, a bundle of rods bound tightly round an axe, symbolizing strength and authority and unity, the Fascist movement was strictly organized on a military pattern.

As a badge of distinction Fascists wore black shirts and saluted one another with raised right arm, as had d'Annunzio's insurgents in Fiume. Fascismo's ideas were fluidly opportunistic. At first great emphasis was put upon radical economic changes which promised to benefit industrial worker and peasant, and the substitution of a republic for the monarchy. Fascism would discipline youth, improve the police, repress leftward internationalism, exalt the army, and reinvigorate patriotism. From beginning to end the Fascist accent was on national glory and national greatness.

That, despite the fact that the Fascist chief, addressed as il Duce, had himself once been an impassioned internationalist. Mussolini, born in the village of Predappio in the Romagna, and arbitrary ruler of Italy from 1925 to 1943, belonged like Hitler to the class of common men. He was the son of a revolutionary village smith and a school teacher. Once a stone-mason, once a schoolmaster, once an agitator for international Socialism, once a doctrinaire pacifist, Mussolini experienced a radical change of heart just before Italy's entrance into World War I.

Wounded in the fighting, Mussolini returned to journalism, establishing a personal journal, *Popolo d'Italia,* in Milan, and proving that the pen was mightier than the sword. At war's end Mussolini's love of peace seems to have revived. He printed the League Covenant in his paper under the headline: "Now begins the new history of the peoples." But that mood swiftly evaporated and he stood forth as a flaming chauvinist, a shameless advocate of the use of violence to subvert parliamentary government and to purge those citizens who dared to disagree with him.

To dismiss Mussolini contemptuously as a "sawdust Caesar" as one hostile analyst does is less than accurate. In his understanding of human nature, his misunderstanding of foreign nations, his strong will, his arrogance and dogmatism, his enormous capacity for work, and his vaulting, restless ambition he resembled Napoleon, himself an Italian or leastwise a Corsican. To live dangerously was Mussolini's glory. Faith in his personal "star" served as religion for this intensely superstitious man. "Of my life I will make a masterpiece," he boasted —and he did.

Mussolini developed considerable talent for appealing to masses of men, always in public the swaggering, strutting poseur. A theatrical, emotion-stirring orator, who radiated self-confidence, he thought of humanity as so much putty to be kneaded to his will. "There must be music and banners," he declared in one of his typical utterances "to kindle enthusiasm. The mob is as loose and dispersed as a shoal of fish until they're well disciplined and led. . . . The tendency of our modern folks to believe is quite past belief."

From its cradle in Milan the Fascist movement spread widely, gathering unto itself societies of a like temper that had been formed here and there in the peninsula. Followers were enlisted among war-veterans who were disillusioned by the puny fruits of victory, among discontented youths who were attracted by the prospect of adventure, jobs, and the promise of power, and among propertied folk, haunted by the specter of revolution, or grown weary of the fumbling parliamentary system. Knowing something of the horrors in revolutionary Russia, many an Italian who was well-off feared a Communist reign of terror—wholesale looting, violence, and bloodshed. By men of wealth in city and country, funds were provided to finance the Fascist cause.

As adherents joined up, squads of tough black-shirts were formed to reinforce the persuasion of the Word. It was these armed forces, il Duce's private army in reality, which gave grim meaning to Fascist blustering and boasting of the shape of things to come. Growth of the movement came rather slowly. Not a single Fascist candidate was returned to the Deputies at the balloting in 1919.

How Fascism Rode into Power

Nothing more vividly attested the decadence of Italian democracy than the return to the premiership in mid-1920 of Giovanni Giolitti, almost an octogenarian, who by ability and trickery had driven the parliamentary machine with a strong pair of hands from 1900 to 1915. Because he persisted to the last in opposing Italian intervention in World War I, Giolitti had been forced into retirement and was branded a traitor to the motherland. His political comeback in 1920 implied that for Italy the war had been a costly blunder and that the conventional parliamentary tactics of drift and manipulation would be restored to favor.

Outside the Chamber harsh conditions of life and labor provoked social disorders, strikes, and sporadic riots which might have culminated in civil war. Land-hungry rustics expropriated some estates; in industrial communities there was a mania for strikes and lockouts. Ridicule of patriotism and mocking insult of discharged war veterans were favorite outdoor diversions.

Lawlessness reached its summit in the summer of 1920 when wage workers in northern Italy occupied plants in which they were employed. In Milan alone 280 establishments were seized. Giolitti's ministry refused to move against this challenge to property rights, holding that, if left alone, the radical flame would flicker out of its own accord. That was a sound judgment.

It was easy to occupy factories but to operate them was quite another story. After a few days or weeks at most, workers gave up possession of seized properties. Reports on the misadventures of Communism in Russia chilled the radical ardor of some Italian extremists. But, on the other side, radicals who had thought of the factory occupations as the preliminary to large-scale revolution now separated themselves from Socialism, and organized a Communist Party, which affiliated with the Third International of Moscow.

True to form Giolitti enlisted the cooperation of the Fascists, still a minor though a growing party, to advance his own fortunes and to combat what was left of leftism. To his traditional electioneering techniques Giolitti joined black-shirted plug-uglies who intimidated their leftward enemies without interference by government. That attitude of neutrality further discredited the tottering parliamentary regime.

Giolitti was disappointed in his expectation of securing a majority of the deputies at a general election in May, 1921. Moderate Socialists still commanded the largest bloc. The Christian Democrats gained and about fifteen Communists were elected. So were Mussolini and thirty-four other Fascists. In all, the electors had chosen thirty non-Communists for every Communist.

The oldest and strongest apology for Mussolini's *coup de main* in October of 1922 was that he helped to keep Italy from sliding down the Bolshevik road. But the cold facts of the election of 1921 refute that claim as indeed do words from il Duce's own pen, written in June of 1921. "The Italy of 1921," he wrote, "is fundamentally different from that of 1919. To say that the Bolshevik danger still exists in Italy represents an attempt to substitute fear for reality, out of motives of self-interest."

True, social ferment persisted but less seriously than in 1920 and by 1922 the worst poisons of the war heritage seemed to have been ejected. A general strike engineered by "Reds" in August of 1922 quickly fizzled out. Profitable tourist business, improvement in the state budget, the willingness of foreign bankers to offer loans to Italy, were positive symptoms of economic convalescence.

Not the menace of Bolshevism but the instability of ministries afforded Fascism the opportunity to ride into power. Blackshirts, now more than 300,000 strong, seized control of administration in many northern cities—Milan for one—and provinces. Then in October, 1922, they demanded that the national government should be entrusted to them and staged a dramatic parade into Rome. Il Duce led his men by following them into the Eternal City—traveling in a prosaic sleeping car.

· Fearful of civil war and not unmindful of his father's death by an assassin's bullet, King Victor Emmanuel III instructed the thirty-nine year old Mussolini to form a ministry. The Chamber voted the new Cabinet unlimited authority for one year. Thus opened one of most astonishing chapters in very modern history which was to end only when the Fascist regime crumbled in May, 1945. As a climax, the mutilated body of Mussolini, slaughtered by his own countrymen, was left hanging head downwards, the corpse of his favorite mistress alongside, in a public square in Milan.

It was felt in 1922 by many foreign observers that Fascism was merely a temporary phenomenon, and that it would quickly lose its dynamic and be relegated to the dustbin of history, or that the responsibilities of office would teach reasonableness to the Fascists. Instead, the October coup in Rome marked the beginning of the successful challenge by dictatorship to representative government. Not the least of Mussolini's titles to memory is that his achievement inspired or encouraged similar campaigns in other countries by other men, of whom Hitler is only the most important from a world viewpoint. Fascism was in a word the prototype of all that the Nazis did by way of personal indignity and cruelty in their hideous political career.

At the time it thrust itself into office Fascism had no solidly formulated ideology; rather "at most the Fascists were united in a conspiracy of ardent negations." They were against individualism, against democracy, against laissez faire, against socialism, against pacifism. As it evolved, Fascism subordinated individual rights to the welfare or assumed welfare of the state, contended that the state was everything, that the individual must believe, obey, work, and fight as instructed. It was the essence of Fascism that an élite should govern, for the many were dumb, utterly incapable of deciding what was best for themselves or the nation.

Upon democratic ways and institutions, Mussolini loosed torrents of coarse vulgarity. "Demo-plutocracies," Fascism's architect thought, belonged to an earlier, less heroic epoch of time. In the "new age" through whose portals he had stepped, human affairs in all their diversity would be regulated by omniscient, totalitarian authority. "Everything in the State, nothing outside the State, nothing against the State," epigrammatically summed up Mussolini's political theory and practice. "Fascism," Mussolini grandiloquently declared, "is certain to become the standard type of civilization of our century for Europe—the forerunner of an European renaissance."

According to Fascist doctrine Italy had failed to obtain its rightful place in the European and colonial sun because of the feebleness of the national spirit and of the fighting services. Therefore a more virile nationalism must be infused in the population and the armed forces would need to be enlarged and improved. That accomplished, Italy would be capable of achieving desirable national ends by rattling the sword or withdrawing the blade from the scabbard. "One cannot deprive a nation of liberty unless one gives her glory," Mussolini said.

Fascism as Government

Voted plenary power by the Chamber of Deputies, Mussolini constructed a coalition ministry, including some of his own followers, and others from political parties of the Right and Center, the Christian Democrats among them. Under a new electoral law passed by the Chamber the party which secured the largest popular vote in a general election would in the future be entitled to seat two thirds of the deputies. As the prelude to a new election the Fascists established a monopoly over facilities of electioneering and applied ruthless terrorism against adversaries. The result of the balloting—held in April, 1924— was a sweeping victory for Mussolini and mastery of the Chamber, though the opposition vote in Lombardy was impressively large.

Among the opponents of Fascist techniques of influencing voters and its whole career of violence, none was more fearless than Giacomo Matteotti, a leading moderate Socialist.[1] For his courageous criticisms Matteotti was pounced upon by Fascist thugs and brutally murdered. The extent of il Duce's personal complicity in this crime has not yet been established. But the deed shocked the kingdom from end to end and provoked sharp reverberations abroad. If the anti-Fascist deputies had merged in a united front, Mussolini might then and there have been unhorsed, as he himself feared. Some members of the Ministry were dismissed, but the known culprits in the Matteotti crime were let off with light prison sentences.

Anti-Fascist deputies contented themselves by withdrawing from Parliament, which eased the way for Fascismo to run berserk. Quitters were formally expelled from the Chamber and draconian measures were applied against dissenters, against anyone indeed who did not conform to Fascist orthodoxy. Cruel violence to human personality was a hallmark of the dictatorship. Hundreds were done to death, thousands of anti-Fascists were thrown into concentration camps, while others escaped the axe of Fascism by fleeing to foreign countries, there to wage relentless verbal warfare against the Fascist tyranny. Even abroad opponents were not safe from the long hand of Fascismo or the lure of the "rolling lire" and more than one émigré was murdered by agents of Mussolini.

In the meantime, a Fascist dictatorship was proclaimed in January, 1925, Mussolini becoming responsible only to King Victor Emmanuel III, an innocuous nonentity upon whom il Duce was to bestow a tinsel crown of emperor. The Cabinet presently became very nearly identical with Mussolini himself. At the same time he was Commander-in-Chief of the Fascist militia and the leader of the rigidly disciplined Fascist Party. These latter roles provided him his effective authority. The dictum "I am the State," ascribed to Louis XIV, fairly described the dictator's authority. True, the national legislature was perpetuated but its functions were either perfunctory or unimportant. In place of the popularly-elected Chamber, which was wholly suppressed in 1938, a Chamber of Fasci and Council of *Corporazione* was set up. Members were either individuals high in the Fascist hierarchy or in the *corpora-*

---

[1] Matteotti's book, *Un Anno di Dominazione Fascista*, contains a long catalogue of misdeeds and crimes committed in the name of Fascism.

zione, organizations of the economic and professional interests of the nation.

By application of force and terrorism, to recapitulate, the small original Fascist company had firmly established its grip upon the Italian state. Insignificant from the standpoint of practical politics until the national election of May, 1921, the movement then returned thirty five deputies and later in the year the Fascist Party was formally organized. During 1922, Mussolini asserted allegiance to the monarchical form of government, which attracted fresh strength to his movement, spurred on his henchmen to drive unsympathetic public servants from local offices, and in October the decisive Fascist coup d'état was boldly carried through. Forthwith Parliament on a vote of three to one granted Mussolini freedom of action and the process of transforming the Italian bureaucracy into a wholly Fascist caste was accelerated. Next came the revision in the parliamentary electoral law and the thumping triumph of the Fascist Party at the polls in April, 1924. In January, 1925, the Fascist dictatorship was given constitutional sanction and the work of emasculating Parliament reached its finished form in 1938.

Long since, the institutions of local government had been shorn of what little freedom they possessed; long since, the Fascist Party had been proclaimed the only lawful political grouping in the kingdom. Before being admitted to the party, a candidate had to take a blood oath of loyalty to il Duce and the Fascist cause even unto death. As of 1930 slightly over a million members belonged and a decade later four times as many. Wholesale purges from time to time, as in the Communist Party of Russia, eliminated the fainthearted. This thoroughly-disciplined machine, pledged to a "continuous, ceaseless fight" was the bulwark of the Fascist dictatorship. From party ranks came public officials of all descriptions, the militia and the sinister secret police, who by spying and violence did much to stifle all open opposition. The rank and file of the party had to be kept reasonably satisfied and one of the ways of doing that was to make advancement dependent on loyalty and service.

Party affairs were coordinated by the Fascist Grand Council, made up of prominent original Fascists, top military men, and heads of government departments. The Secretary-General of this Council filled a similar office in the Fascist Party. Not only was the Grand Council the supreme deliberative body of the party, it was also an organ of the state, tendering advice on legislative and constitutional matters, and it was assigned the responsibility of picking a new dictator should Mussolini pass from the scene. It was the members of this Council, previously Mussolini's puppets, who mutinied in July, 1943, and swept their chief from power.

Piece by piece civil liberties were cancelled and machinery for manufacturing blind obedience was forged. Italy was put into prison. Press, movies, and radio were subjected to strict censorship and institutions of learning, from lowest to highest, were converted into active instruments of Fascist indoctrination. They missed no chance to discredit democratic ways and institutions. The school-leaving age was eventually raised to fourteen years and compulsory attendance was strictly enforced. By 1940 general literacy had been achieved, except among oldsters in the southern provinces.

Fascism cracked down on terroristic brotherhoods such as the Camorra and the Sicilian Maffia, whose brigandage had for generations made life and property unsafe. And as part of the program of regimentation, organizations at various age levels were created to inculcate the Fascist faith and hope, so that when young men entered the conscript army they were imbued with the Fascist outlook, already disciplined for rigorous military training.

Quite in line with the ideal of full national unity, il Duce negotiated settlements with the Vatican (Chap. XV). These accords softened the traditional antagonism between State and Church.

Minorities

Within the borders of the Italian Kingdom lived two small but internationally significant minorities: Yugoslav and Austrian-German. Late in the thirties Fascismo conjured up a "Jewish problem." The Yugoslav group, dwelling in the northeast, on land taken over in 1918 from the Hapsburg monarchy, approached half a million, part of them in a compact settlement, others scattered, many residing in and around the port city of Trieste. Even before the advent of Fascism to power the Italian government had started the compulsory merger of these Slavs into the Italian national community, and Mussolini intensified the denationalization campaign imposing restrictions on Yugoslav schools, churches, and language.

Many of the victims chose to move away and their places were promptly filled by Italian settlers. Fascismo's treatment of Yugoslavs inescapably invited reprisals against tiny colonies of Italians in Yugoslavia. In Dalmatia, particularly, anti-Italian riots and vandalism flared up from time to time. These episodes did not fail to embitter diplomatic relations between Italy and Yugoslavia. Slav patriots looked forward to the day when the revolving wheel of European politics would enable them to gratify their irredentist claims upon Italy.

Another story was written for about a quarter million Germans in the strategically valuable South Tyrol. They, too, before 1918 had been citizens of Austria. They, too, were subjected to an assimilationist program pressed, if anything, with greater vigor than in Yugoslav communities. The first results were identical: embitterment of the harassed Tyrolese, perfervid protestation in Austrian and German circles. But official attitudes on both sides changed radically after 1936 when Italy and Hitlerian Germany teamed up in the Axis partnership. Arrangements were then made for the emigration of German "feelers" from the southern Tyrol. Apparently two thirds of them actually departed, being compensated for their properties by the Italian government.

The official Italian census of 1931 reported 47,875 professing Jews or an eighth of one per cent of the inhabitants. Many of these Jews had attained distinction in high Fascist circles and a Jewess even composed a panegyrical biography of Mussolini, her long-time friend. By a process of quiet assimilation the tiny Jewish minority had been pretty thoroughly submerged in the Italian nationality.

But in 1937 press attacks against Jewry began, seeking to divert mass emotions from social discontent, or in open imitation of Hitlerian mythology not excluding pæans to "racial purity," a doctrine alien to Italian tradition. Action followed words. Foreign-born Jews, who had fled into Italy to escape the whiplash of the Nazis, were ordered to depart and restrictions were laid upon native-born Jews. Although the persecution was less brutal and less thorough than in Germany, it was made more hideous after Italy became a belligerent in 1940.

Fascism as Economics

One mark of the Fascist regime was the corporative state. Fascism parted company with the theories and practices of laissez faire, holding that the state had a duty to share decisively in such matters as competition, wages, conditions of employment, prices, profits, and the coordination of different types of production. Equally, Fascism repudiated the Marxian doctrines of complete state ownership and operation of productive facilities. As with other economic systems, Fascism professed that its program was intended to alleviate "the sufferings and the sorrows of the humble."

While permitting private initiative and imagination in agriculture, in smaller industries, and in internal trade, the Fascist state insisted upon active collaboration of management and men in the common interest. Wherever private initiative faltered and in types of production in which "the political interests of the state are involved"—such as foreign trade, defense plants, and banks—the dictatorship assumed effective control. In the mature form that the system reached after 1935, Fascismo very largely dominated economic affairs, Mussolini and party chiefs having the final word. So radically had state intervention transformed competitive capitalism that the term was no longer applicable; Fascist economy had in reality moved extremely close to the collectivism of the Soviets.

Instead of trade unions and employers associations to safeguard their respective economic interests, Fascismo fashioned an elaborate mechanism under the aegis of the state. That regime had two salient institutions: the *sindacato* in which Italians were brought together on the basis of their occupations; and the *corporazione,* knitting together all productive agencies to regulate production in the national interest.

It was prescribed by laws of 1926-1927 that in all types of economic activity, occupational unions, called *sindacato,* should be formed. There were *sindacato* for employers and employees in each kind of occupation, except the learned professions and the fine arts in which employers and employee were not differentiated. Hundreds of these *sindacato* were set up in municipalities, in provinces, and there was an overall national body.

The main function of the *sindacato* was the negotiation of agreements on wages, hours, holidays, and working conditions for a particular occupation in a given administrative area. In the making of contracts representatives of management bargained with spokesmen of the workers, and all decisions were binding throughout the occupation in question. If agreement could not be reached the matter in dispute was referred to courts of arbitration whose verdict was final. Under no circumstances might employers legally shut workers out of employment nor might workers go out on strike. Such was the law, but violations were not unknown.

For purposes of planning and regulating production an intricate pattern of *corporazione* was created. At the top of the pyramid was a national Council of *Corporazione,* whose chief executive was the state Minister of *Corporazione,* a post that Mussolini at first reserved for himself.

Subordinate to it were twenty two vocational groupings or *corporazione;* for instance, in textiles, grain, mining, or domestic communication. Each had a council made up of delegates of management and workers as well as state officials and technical experts. As in the *sindacato* only men whose loyalty to the Fascist order was beyond suspicion were appointed to the councils. Seldom were "natural leaders" of the workers chosen; seldom did spokesmen of the workers carry equal weight with the management. The dice of Fascismo were loaded in favor of employers and the State.

Each *corporazione* advised the government on matters of production, distribution, prices and wages, the establishment of new industries, and the training of apprentices. Under certain circumstances they might settle industrial disputes and, after 1938, as has been mentioned, the *corporazione* were tied in with the national legislature.

Fascismo's corporate machinery was heralded as the means of promoting "unity of classes" for the common good—or rather for the advancement of the totalitarian despotism. It professed to eliminate strife between producing classes by reconciling their divergent interests and by abolishing the uncontrolled competitive capitalism of nineteenth century tradition.

The Economic Record

Most Italians relied upon mother earth for their livelihood.[2] Outside of the Po valley, which is one of the world's garden regions, much of the soil of Italy is of inferior quality and one acre out of three is either mountainous or sterile. About a fifth of the wheat, which, as spaghetti, macaroni, or otherwise disguised, is the staple of the Italian national diet, had ordinarily to be imported.

No fully reliable statistics on land tenure in Italy are available, but the broad outlines are clear. About a million landowners rented out their properties, preferring to live in the cities. Peasants tilling their own acres exceeded 2,500,000; another 1,500,000 country-dwellers were without land or owned only very small farms and pieced out their incomes by day labor for others. In this section of the population which ordinarily had work for only half the year, sub-standard conditions of housing and food were as prevalent as among their city counterparts who were engaged in manufacturing and transportation. Large estates were found in the extreme south, in Sicily, in the vicinity of Rome, in a corner of Tuscany, and parts of Lombardy. Plans for the distribution of large holdings in Sicily among the peasants were published in 1939.

Improvement of the lot of the large rustic population was an avowed object of Fascism. To make the country self-sufficient in bread grains an energetic "Battle of Grain" was launched, which yielded an impressive increase in output. Domestic requirements were met in 1937 and surpassed in the bumper harvest of 1938. But it must be

[2] As of 1936, about 8,750,000 men and women were engaged in agriculture, and 3,800,000 in industrial employment.

said that wheat yield in Europe generally advanced in the inter-war years and that the emphasis on wheat production in Italy entailed a falling off in other crops and in cattle-raising. For all its coercive powers the Fascist state could not compel some of the peasants to adopt newer methods of cultivation.

Fascismo boasted much of the achievement in reclaiming the pestilential Pontine marshes below Rome, on which three thousand peasant families were settled. That expensive project, and less advertised ones, had high propaganda value at home and abroad. So did the success of the dictatorship in getting trains to run on time and in tidying up the country. In places reforestation protected mountain sides from erosion.

On the industrial front much was done in the exploitation of hydro-electrical resources to furnish power for factories and transportation. Industry, which was concentrated in the north, turned out textiles, machinery, motor cars, and armaments principally. Shipbuilding was encouraged by lavish state subsidies and in the name of national prestige the luxury liners, *Conte di Savoia* and *Rex* were built, whereas the real commercial needs of the country required plebian tramp steamers. As of 1939 the Italian merchant marine exceeded 3,250,000 tons.

Deficient in almost all the rawstuffs and fuel consumed by machine industry, Italy had to purchase them from foreign countries, exporting in exchange the specialized products of her native skill and climate. Coal, for example, had to be brought in at the rate of about a million tons a year, chiefly from the German Ruhr mines by way of Rotterdam, but a substantial part was obtained from Wales. Foreign trade was kept in balance by "invisible" items, notably remittances of emigrants, expenditures of tourists and resident foreigners, all of which declined under the dictatorship, and shipping services.

In the first phase of Fascist rule, state participation in economic affairs went little beyond what had previously existed. By tax concessions and easy bank credit some encouragement was given to industry and factory output increased. The budget was balanced in 1926 and the lire was pegged at nineteen to the dollar, which was too high in relation to foreign currencies, but gratifying to national self-esteem. As a result business activity slackened and in time the slender gold reserves were drained away. Settlements on the war debts owed to the United States and Great Britain were negotiated in which Italy's obligations were deeply slashed.

With the onslaught of the Great Depression, unemployment shot up, passing the 1,100,000 mark, somewhat higher proportionately than in countries such as Sweden whose economic structure was broadly comparable. Government stepped in with various expedients: monopolistic control over foreign trade, higher tariffs, subsidies to industry, and public works programs. Miles of highways and a relatively small number of houses were built.

The trend toward autarchy was given a push during the Ethiopian war (p. 474) when League members drastically cut their commercial transactions with Italy. Thereafter the lire was sharply devaluated, duties were lowered, and money wages generally increased. As World War II approached, state control over economic life was tightened and presently became virtually complete.

Under Fascismo the normal work-week was set at forty hours; it was made unlawful to employ children under fourteen or youths and women at dangerous or unhealthy jobs. Workers were paid a modest "social wage" in the form of recreational and cultural facilities operated by the state. Insurance schemes were broadened and state agencies combatted cancer, tuberculosis, and malaria; even so, only about one per cent of the national budget was expended for social welfare services.

On the other hand, appropriations for armaments and for officialdom—including the Fascist police—devoured a large part of the state income. It appears that Italian outlays for military purposes rose faster in proportion to the national income than those of any other country. To meet the imperative demands of the state, indirect forms of taxation were steadily raised, and forced loans and capital levies were made.

Not only was the Italian bureaucracy vastly increased, not only did the national debt soar into the astronomical, but earnings and living standards declined, preliminary studies reveal. But how far the economic ills were attributable to Fascist doctrine and how far to other circumstances such as the poverty in natural resources, the Great Depression, the Ethiopian war, and the huge outlays for armaments and colonies, can only be conjectured.

Despite the hard struggle for existence in Italy, Fascismo ordained many measures to discourage celibacy, to raise the birth-rate, already high, to make emigration difficult, and to attract Italians who had moved abroad—especially those living in France—back to their native soil. "To count for something in the world," Mussolini exclaimed in 1927, "Italy must have a population of not less than 60,000,000 by 1950." But pro-natalist legislation netted no significant returns. Seldom is parenthood undertaken purely out of patriotic motives. The downward trend in the birth-rate which antedated Fascism went unchecked.

Italy's Empire

Italy's colonial dominions looked more impressive on the map than as real estate. Before the conquest of Ethiopia (Chap. XIX) the overseas possessions were Libya on the Mediterranean, the Dodecanese Islands in the Aegean, and Eritrea and Italian Somaliland in northeast Africa. None of the colonies contained mineral wealth of commercial importance; none had much land that was suitable for agriculture; none attracted many Italian settlers.[3]

Colonial expansion and development stood high on the agenda of Fascist objectives. One of Mussolini's favorite propaganda posters depicted a magnificent specimen of young Italian manhood, bound hand and foot but struggling to break loose from his chains which were labelled: Gibraltar, Tunisia, Malta, Suez, Dardanelles. Il Duce was fond of rehearsing the grandeur and greatness of imperial Rome. He reminded his countrymen that Rome once dominated the world by the wisdom of her rule and the might of arms. He stated that "nothing forbids us to believe that what was destiny yesterday may again become our tomorrow." Parroting his chief, a Fascist propaganda merchant thundered, "Look at the Mediterranean, Mare Nostro, where Italians have ever been victorious. This sea has always been ours and will be ours once more." Colonies as places for the expanding Italian peasantry to emigrate was a popular text for imperialistic sermons.

For the development of the colonies Fascismo poured out cash with great liberality. Prestige, not prospect of reasonable economic return, dictated that policy. Libya, far the largest of the colonies, triple the size of Italy itself, had fewer than a million inhabitants of whom Italians never exceeded ten per cent. Under a line of aggressive Fascist governors, Libyan port towns were embellished with stately architecture, schools, public buildings, homes. Bengazi blossomed out as a bustling little community, an airline center, its harbor alive with ships shuttling to and fro across the Mediterranean—a much-advertised feature of the Fascist empire. Although the Libyan soil is good for farming only on the narrow Mediterranean fringe, funds were plunged into costly irrigation works, but vastly more capital was required if the Libyan desert were to be made to blossom. It was expensive, too, to extend the area of effective Italian occupation by conquering restless tribesmen.

[3] Pantelleria, a small island outpost in the Mediterranean, was attractive to dreamers and mystics, and tolerable for those content to raise olives and grapes on a few ungrateful acres. Its value was strategic, lying between Sicily and Africa, while Libya furnished a base for pressure on Egypt, and Eritrea, a route into Ethiopia.

Such commerce as was carried on by the colonies—and it was extremely modest—was very largely handled by Italian firms. For the advancement of the natives a few primary schools and training institutes were founded. Prestige and perhaps strategic advantage apart, the Fascist empire instead of mitigating added to the onerous burdens of the Italian population.

Italy, 1939

For all its shortcomings, its sins of omission and commission as weighed in the democratic scales, Fascismo in 1939 could point to the greater respect which Italy enjoyed in world politics, higher no doubt than at any time since unification. Fascist bombast, arrogance, and fanatical jingoism had replaced the older Italian feeling of national inferiority. Regional sympathies too had softened, though they were not entirely submerged in the consciousness of the Italian nation.

What part of the Italian population had by 1939 ranged itself squarely on the line of the Fascist order, whether out of conviction or coercion? Nobody knows, nor ever will know. But that many Italians had not been converted was amply demonstrated after Allied armies invaded the peninsula in 1943. An interesting and suggestive guess on the varieties of political opinion has been offered by an arch-enemy of Mussolini, Professor Gaetano Salvemini, sometime professor of history at Florence, who was harried from his homeland and who found asylum at Harvard.

Salvemini wrote: "I think I am not far away from the mark if I say that one tenth of the Italians were actively Fascist, one tenth were actively anti-Fascist, two tenths were silent but never gave their consent, three tenths never took any interest in what was happening, and three tenths wavered from time to time from hot-headed band-wagonism or hysterical enthusiasm to bewilderment, discontent, and ire when fiascoes set in."

With the passage of time, Fascism had come to cover a multitude of ideas and attitudes and the term *fascist* was employed with confusing looseness, as an epithet of condemnation, innocent of precise meaning. Fascist, indeed, was applied all the way from an individual hostile to Soviet Communism to an acrid opponent of the Roosevelt Administration in the United States. In the language of the Supreme Court of the United States Fascism is "one of those undefined slogans that are part of the give-and-take in our economic and political controversy."

Strictly speaking, Fascism referred to the scheme of national organization evolved under Mussolini in Italy or any broadly similar pattern. Therein total authority was allocated to a dictatorial leader, who exercised power without restraint by any representative organ of government. Fascism repudiated the historic freedoms of the individual and silenced critics by terroristic devices; it established unfettered state control over all aspects of national activity; it exalted bombastic and provocative nationalism. Any regime exhibiting these traits might properly be called fascist and any believer in such a scheme of things, a fascist.

CHAPTER VIII

The Near East

The Near East in General

ALTHOUGH the term Near East has an elastic quality about it, it may be thought of as coterminous with the Ottoman Empire of the early 19th century: the Balkan peninsula with its profusion of nationalities, the Asiatic region of Turkish habitation, and the lands of Arab speech to the south. The gradual disintegration of Ottoman power, which reached culmination in World War I, permitted a galaxy of separate states to take its place on the map. But the legacy of generations of Turkish domination was by no means sloughed off, neither in government, nor in economics, nor in mentality.

The Balkans have an earned reputation for political instability, violence, explosive eruptions. Yet in the thirties, signs of rapprochement among the contentious powerlets gave reason for hope that a loose political federation would in time be fashioned. In fact, a Balkan Entente was created in 1934. Bulgaria and Albania to be sure held aloof, but sincere efforts were made to encourage a common Balkan outlook through periodical gatherings of politicians, economists, and professional men. In itself that trend challenged Solomon's ancient dictum that there was no new thing under the sun.

On the other hand, the intensity of the individual Balkan nationalisms, controversies over minorities and boundaries and national rights attested that the heirs of the Sultans had not overcome the pugnacity and the romanticism of their youth. For the perennial ferment in the Balkans and the rest of the Near East, the activity of agents of Great Powers having interests and ambitions there was responsible in considerable measure. On the governmental side the Near Eastern countries after varying experience with democratic forms were transformed into dictatorships. The low moral sense of Balkan politicians often made government the instrument of bribery, jobbery, and tyranny; and the Turkish heritage of conspiracies and assassinations was not rooted out. What western political morality thought of as criminal was an idiosyncrasy by Balkan standards.

All the Near Eastern countries were preponderantly agricultural societies and largely self-sufficient. In the Balkan states land was fairly evenly distributed, thanks to redistribution programs in places between the wars, but the population was too dense to live decently on the limited arable soil. Emigration offered no substantial relief and only a fraction of the growing Balkan population could find employment in town and city.

Average standards of living were appallingly low. Impoverished peasants were wedded to a one-crop tradition and bowed down by rural conventionalism, usurious money lenders, and vicious taxation and tariff policies which were designed to benefit infant industry. A diet mainly of cereals and a high incidence of infant mortality were obvious evidences of rural poverty in the Near East. Peasant political parties, though strong in numbers, were unable to exert effective political power in proportion to their followings, for they were short on educated leaders with clear-cut policies.

Here and there innovations sponsored by Balkan governments or promoted by American philanthropy brought better techniques of cultivation, more diversified farming and improved home welfare and public health. And peasant cooperative societies attained ever larger significance, though not infrequently they were manipulated by state officials for political purposes. Machine production progressed moderately, notably in the thirties. The middle class in the towns and cities grew correspondingly, but in no country was that element large. Yet bourgeois influence upon government was extensive, sustained, and class-centered.

To pay for imported manufactures the Balkan countries depended on the sale of agricultural surpluses abroad. But the Balkan peasantry failed to keep abreast of the improved farming methods of overseas competitors. With the collapse of agricultural prices in the Great Depression and the tariff protectionist policies of western Europe, the Balkan peasantry found itself in a desperate plight. Nazi Germany thrust itself into the breach, negotiated special commercial arrangements with the Balkan countries, and appeared to many in the guise of a savior.

Facilities for elementary education in the Near East were generally extended and literacy rates rose. Institutions of higher learning sent forth youths with classical or professional training in the main, and all too few with preparation for engineering and scientific agriculture. Many an unhappy, ambitious Near Eastern intellectual found an outlet for his energies and talents in unorthodox economic and political causes or in fanning the flames of petty nationalisms. Educational institutions largely manned and financed by Americans, such as the splendid American University in Cairo, made a valuable contribution to the civic and social growth of their students and through them of a widening circle of their fellows.

Albania

Even before Albania won its independence in 1913 from Turkey, the covetous eyes of Italian expansionists were fastened upon the region. The destruction of Austria in World War I removed all serious competition for paramount influence in the mountainous little country, which might serve Italy as a gateway into the Balkans. Yugoslavia and Greece both advanced claims to parts of Albania on grounds of nationality, while Albanian minorities residing in both those countries set up counter-claims.

Italian soldiers moved into Albania during World War I and Italian diplomacy solicited international sanction for "protective" control over the country. But the Albanians, led by a tribal chieftain, Ahmed Bey Zogu, forced the Italians from the mainland and the government in Rome made no effort to reassert its claims.[1] Chosen President in 1925, Zogu proclaimed himself King of Albania three years later.

In the meantime suspicions that Greece and Yugoslavia had designs on his country induced Zogu to enter into a pact of friendship with Fascist Italy and subsequently to sign a defensive alliance, much to the displeasure of Yugoslavia which promptly aligned itself with France. Italian agents took an active hand in the political, military, and economic life of Albania. Up-to-date roads were laid down, small oil fields were more thoroughly exploited, conventional Moslem customs such as polygamy and veils were discarded, and the city of Durazzo took on something of a western complexion. But Albanian agriculture continued to be primitive, unprogressive, and of the self-sufficient type. In the mountainous interior, ancient family feuds were little checked. Excellent forests yielded a surplus of timber for export.

Try though he did, King Zogu could not loosen the octopus-like hold which Fascist Italy had on his country. Albania was earmarked for Italian conquest and the job was done in the spring of 1939 (p. 507).

[1] The tiny island of Saseno off southern Albania was ceded to Italy in 1920.

Yugoslavia

Italian aggressiveness naturally caused alarm in Yugoslavia, whose patriots declined to renounce irredentist pretensions to Trieste, Fiume, and their environs which had passed to Italy after World War I. With each of its other five neighbors Yugoslavia had more or less grave boundary disputes.

Never before 1918 had there been a Yugoslav state, though the dream of creating such an entity had long inspired patriot and seer. The idea was of the utmost importance in bringing on World War I. In its final form the Kingdom of Yugoslavia covered an area twice as broad as New York State and had a population of fully 12,000,000.

Core of Yugoslavia was the pre-war Kingdom of Serbia, whose dynasty and governmental apparatus were transferred to the new creation. Serbia's King, Alexander, became monarch of Yugoslavia. To the old Serbia was added, after World War I, former Austrian and Hungarian territories—notably Croatia—and small bits of Bulgaria. Under duress the tiny principality of Montenegro was fused with Yugoslavia. Serbian nationalists thought of the new state as a Greater Serbia, but as a concession to the political sensibilities of the Croatian and Slovenian populations, it was officially styled the Kingdom of the Serbs, Croats, and Slovenes.

From the beginning, Serbian ambitions clashed with Croat and Slovene interests. Although the spoken language of all three was the same,[2] they differed in historical, religious, and broadly cultural traditions. Whereas the Serbs belonged largely to the Orthodox Church and had for long centuries been under the thrall of the Turk, the Croats and Slovenes were predominantly Roman Catholic in faith. They were more literate, more progressive in a western sense, and historically they had been linked with Hungary and Austria, respectively.

These almost intractable cleavages were accentuated by political and constitutional strife. In keeping with the desires of the dominant and more numerous Serbs, the government of Yugoslavia was of a highly centralized, unitary character. The Croats, who as citizens of Hungary before World War I had limited rights of home-rule and a Parliament of their own, never ceased to clamor for the federalization of the kingdom and autonomous rights for Croatia. In these demands the Croats as a rule had the backing of Slovene politicians. It was contended by Croat and Slovene that Yugoslav policies were slanted to benefit the Serbs. Tax laws, it was charged, favored the Serbs as did legislation parcelling out some large estates. Plaints of a

[2] The Slovene tongue has dialectical differences with Serbo-Croat.

similar nature were made by an unreconciled Montenegrin minority.

Sharp controversies on these questions along with problems incidental to the establishment and administration of the new kingdom
kept Yugoslav politics in turmoil and made for chronic ministerial
instability. Matters came to a head in 1928 when, after an angry
debate in Parliament, a Serb deputy whipped out his revolver and
fired into the Croat benches killing two deputies and mortally wounding Stefan Radich, the fiery leader of the Croat peasants. The Croats
and Slovenes withdrew from Parliament. Dr. Vlasko Machek carried
on the martyred Radich's campaign for Croatian home-rule.

Avowedly to put an end to Croatian particularism King Alexander proclaimed a royal dictatorship in 1929 and formally altered
the name of the kingdom to Yugoslavia. Not only was the Constitution suspended, but political parties were broken up and Croat malcontents were sternly repressed. Before the Parliament was revived it
was retailored and as such responded obediently to the wishes of the
crown.

While on a visit to France in 1934 King Alexander was slain by a
Macedonian fanatic who had been aided by Hungarian and Italian enemies of Yugoslavia. Thus was sustained the evil tradition
that every Serb ruler since emancipation from the Turks was either
murdered or obliged to abdicate the throne. In the name of the royal
heir, boy-king Peter, a regency with his uncle, Prince Paul, at the
head assumed the direction of national affairs.

Alexander's assassination brought a pause in political contentions
within Yugoslavia. Gathering war clouds over Europe persuaded politicians of all colors that the safety of the country imperatively demanded that the feud between Serb and Croat be settled. Minor concessions to the Croats, amnesty to imprisoned Croat chiefs, and relaxation of the dictatorship led to an agreement of August, 1939,
which gratified the moderate wings of Croatian and Serbian sentiment.
To the Croatian area was given an assembly with jurisdiction over a
wide range of purely local affairs, and Croats consented to serve in the
national Ministry.

In the meantime, Yugoslavia's foreign policy, under the supreme
direction of Regent Paul, had undergone drastic change. As one of
the Little Entente nations, and formally allied to France after 1927,
Yugoslavia belonged to the French diplomatic bloc. But in the late
thirties as French international prestige dwindled and the power of
Nazi Germany soared, Yugoslavia's orientation was bent Axis-ward,
not, to be sure, without protest from haters of Germany. Rapprochement with Italy was signalized in 1937 by a treaty of friend-

ship to run for five years, and trade agreements with Germany openly attested Yugoslavia's new diplomatic course.

German traders penetrated deeply into Yugoslavia's foreign commerce, handling in the end approximately half of all exports and imports. Agricultural surpluses, raised on the small peasant farms which were typical of the country, were profitably marketed in Germany.

Yugoslav farms tended not only to be small but as a rule they were worked with primitive tools and by antiquated methods, with living standards highest in the northeast. Since the population of Yugoslavia jumped from a little more than 12,000,000 in 1921 to over 16,-000,000 in 1941, the struggle for existence in the countryside grew progressively more acute. Yugoslav industry was very unevenly developed, being concentrated in the northwest. The opening up of the considerable and diversified mineral resources of the kingdom was retarded by the scarcity of capital and the inadequacy of means of transportation. State subsidies created a splendid little merchant marine. Propaganda in foreign countries to attract tourists to the lovely Yugoslav Riviera and to the scenic grandeurs of the interior netted some results.

Rumania

Rumania backed the winning horse in World War I and the payoff was impressively handsome. From the Hapsburg monarchy Rumania acquired a wide expanse of land which included Transylvania, the very cradle of Rumanian nationality. From Russia she took the coveted province of Bessarabia over the protests of Moscow. Altogether the kingdom was more than doubled in size and the population exceeded 16,000,000, the largest of the Balkan countries. Rumania contained much excellent soil in the Danubian valley, forests were rich in timber, and the oil resources of the kingdom, which were largely developed by foreign capital, were the most extensive in Europe outside the Soviet Union. Command of the mouths of the Danube and good harbors on the Black Sea enhanced Rumania's commercial and strategic importance.

To appease the restless peasantry and to counteract the revolutionary influence of Bolshevik Russia the Rumanian government adopted land acts which deprived most of the big landlords of their properties and distributed them among small holders and the landless. First and last, fully 1,500,000 peasant families obtained parcels of land; about ninety per cent of the arable soil of the kingdom belonged to peasant proprietors and no Communist movement of consequence appeared in the Rumanian countryside despite the woefully degraded character of rural existence.

Thanks to state subsidies and foreign capital Rumanian commerce and industry grew modestly between World Wars. A small but energetic middle class boldly challenged the virtual monopoly in politics which the large landlords had traditionally exercised.

As of 1939 the population of Greater Rumania approached 20,-000,000; about seventy per cent were Rumanian in nationality, but there were also a million Magyars and half as many German-speaking folk in the kingdom. Bessarabia was a veritable babel of tongues and nationalities. Rumanians formed a clear majority in the province, but there were large Russian and Ukrainian minorities. And scattered all over the kingdom were Jews, exceeding 900,000. It was the conviction of Rumanian officials that heat would have to be applied in order to fuse the diverse peoples in this melting pot, and they had few scruples against doing just that. Assimilationist pressures inescapably aggravated tensions inside the kingdom and roused fierce criticism from outside.

Greater Rumania preserved the parliamentary monarchy that had existed for forty years. The king, Ferdinand, reigned but the uncrowned monarch after the war was Jon Bratianu, who manipulated the government in accordance with his personal desires. Although an electoral act of 1923 established universal manhood suffrage and promised minorities political rights, democracy in Rumania was a sham. It was absurd indeed to speak of democracy in a country where the Ministry "managed" elections, where the civil service was notoriously corrupt, where the peasantry and minority groupings lived in constant terror of the gendarme or mob violence.

Key-figure in Rumanian politics after the death of Bratianu in 1927, was colorful Prince Carol, who, having once renounced the throne, took the crown in 1930 as Carol II. With the decline of Bratianu's illiberal National Liberals, the National Peasant Party led by Transylvania-born Dr. Julius Maniu crowded to the front. In contrast to the Liberals this party espoused progressive social reform, conciliatory treatment of minorities, and tried to attract foreign capital for industrial development.

Early in the thirties the All-for-Fatherland Party—known, too, as the Iron Guardists—whose ideology closely resembled that of the German Nazis, attained practical importance. Directed by militant and romantic Rumanian chauvinists this fanatical brood desired a totalitarian dictatorship and did not hesitate to terrorize minority groups or to assassinate public men whose principles or practices they disliked. By promises of more land the Iron Guardists enlisted hosts of peasants under their banner.

Mounting economic perplexities, political confusion, and the darkening international scene caused King Carol, who frankly admired the techniques of Mussolini, to establish a royal dictatorship in 1938. Thenceforth the monarch and his court advisers, who confidently relied upon the army, dictated public policies. Old political parties were compelled to sink their identity in the king's party, the Front of National Rebirth. In the course of a vigorous drive against the Iron Guards, hundreds were killed, though the movement itself was merely driven underground.

Three of Rumania's neighbors, Soviet Russia, Hungary, and Bulgaria, cherished irredentist claims upon the kingdom. For purposes of security Rumania negotiated alliances with France, which was spoken of as the national shield and buckler, and with Poland, and she belonged to the Little Entente (p. 416) and the Balkan Entente (p. 470).

As the shadows of impending conflict spread across Europe in the late thirties, Rumania became an arena of intense rivalry between Nazi Germany and the Anglo-French coalition. Step-by-step Rumanian economy was harnessed to the Nazi chariot in spite of British and French efforts to prevent it. In the spring of 1939 the western powers guaranteed to protect Rumania should its independence be challenged, but it was impossible to give the guarantee anything more than paper significance.

Bulgaria

Bulgaria, the heartland of the Balkans, has been labelled the Black Sheep of the peninsula. Others have chosen to call the Bulgarians the "Prussians of the Balkans," an epithet warranted by the turbulent course of the nation's history since full liberation from Turkish overlordship was secured in 1908. Bulgaria has furnished more than her share of librettos for operas comic—and tragic.

As delimited in the Treaty of Neuilly of 1919, Bulgaria was about as large as Kentucky and had just over 6,000,000 inhabitants. The population was wholly Bulgar in nationality except for some half million Turks (or at least Moslems) who were given full religious and cultural freedom. Mountains and other natural obstacles covered three fifths of the country, but the Orient Express Railway and branch lines provided relatively good transportation facilities.

Bulgar literally means "man with a plow." Four out of five of the Bulgars were typical peasants, working their own small farms, frugal, obstinate, suspicious of all outsiders as well as black-coated state officials. On the average, twice as many Bulgars were engaged per unit of land as Frenchmen, yet the productivity of the agricultural worker was two to three times as great in France as in Bulgaria. About ten per cent of the Bulgars earned their living in industry which was almost wholly confined to small textile, food and tobacco-processing establishments. After 1936 the organization of Bulgarian industry was patterned intimately on the Italian corporative system. It was Bulgaria's boast that hers was the most literate population in the Balkans.

Bulgaria was a parliamentary monarchy whose ruler, King Ferdinand, as penalty for leading his adopted country into World War I on the German side, was forced to renounce the throne. His son, Boris III, reigned in his stead,[3] and the parliamentary regime was perpetuated. Far stronger, however, than the new king was the domineering postwar Prime Minister, Alexander S. Stambulisky, rough-hewn, demagogic, and skillful organizer of the peasantry. Though governing with an iron hand and along lines that infuriated middle-class townsmen, whom he despised, Stambulisky sponsored legislation that benefited the peasantry, such as measures dissolving the landed estates of Crown and Church.

His chief monument was a labor service law obligating young men —and for a time young women too—to work in labor battalions. That substitute for military conscription, which was banned by the peace treaty, furnished Bulgaria with inexpensive manpower for public works projects, for workshops and farms, and for other social undertakings. The essential idea was subsequently imitated in Nazi Germany and in the volunteer Civilian Conservation Corps of the United States.

And Stambulisky's thinking was not bounded by Bulgaria. He advocated, for example, the formation of a Balkan Union, starting with the merger of Bulgaria and Yugoslavia; and he dreamed of a "Green International," embracing the peasant nations of eastern Europe, banded together to protect private peasant property in land and generally to promote rural interests. It would be a counterweight to collectivist international movements pledged to improve the lot of the urban wage workers.

Neither of these projects amounted to much. The first was vetoed by Serb politicians of Yugoslavia and antagonized ambitious Bul-

---

[3] Boris' number and subsequently that of his son and successor, Simeon II, was derived from their medieval namesakes and was a sign that the notion of "Big Bulgaria" was still very much alive.

garian irredentists. A "Green International," however, came into being and sections enrolling several million peasants were founded in six countries with headquarters in Prague. More conservative than Stambulisky desired, the movement achieved little of note and the universal depression of the 1930's doomed the enterprise in its infancy.

Both in home and foreign affairs the Stambulisky regime raised up a pack of enemies, nationalistically-minded city dwellers in particular, who organized a coup d'état in 1923, in which many followers of the Premier were killed and he himself was barbarously murdered.

For eleven years Bulgaria was governed by a succession of ministries which tended to foster urban interests and to neglect the welfare of the rural masses. Political feuds took the form of street battles and in a single year more than two hundred political assassinations, not to speak of countless executions, were reported. Throughout this period ministries bowed to the will and whim of the notorious International Macedonian Revolutionary Organization, whose bloodless chiefs conspired by day and night to bring under the Bulgarian flag the "Macedonian areas" of Greece and Yugoslavia. Full-scale war with Greece was only narrowly averted by the effective intervention of the League of Nations (p. 433). Communism, which was probably a stronger force in Bulgaria than anywhere else in southeastern Europe, was officially banned after an abortive rising. When men who were Communist in faith, though not in name, swept the polls at the municipal elections of 1932 in Sofia, they were denied the right to take office.

In the spring of 1934 a clique of Bulgar politicians and professional soldiers, disgusted with the turbulence in Parliament and the economic unrest, executed another coup and abolished almost every semblance of political democracy. Without any positive program, though strong enough to suppress the Macedonian revolutionaries, the rebels presently allowed King Boris to rule as well as reign. Under his guidance something akin to stability was restored. In 1937 Parliament was restored, though without the traditional prerogatives.

Outside of the Bulgarian boundaries, in Greece, in Yugoslavia, in Rumania, there lived about 2,000,000 Bulgars who provoked much dissension. With Greece, Bulgaria had a special and vexatious bone of contention. It was prescribed in the Neuilly Treaty that Bulgaria should have an outlet on the Aegean Sea but all attempts to implement that pledge came to naught.[4] Proposals for a Balkan Union were

[4] Whereas the Greeks were prepared to grant Bulgaria a zone at Dedeagach, Sofia adamantly insisted upon an outlet at Kavalla and control over a corridor of land leading to that port.

spurned by Bulgaria because adjoining states would not appease her irredentist claims. Yet in 1938 Bulgaria entered into a non-aggression pact with her neighbors, who, as a reward, agreed to the cancellation of the military restrictions imposed by the Treaty of Neuilly.

For Russia, the big Slav brother, and the principal liberator of the nation from Turkey, Bulgaria cherished a deep sentimental attachment which nothing could wholly shake. But Germany, too, had friends and sympathizers in Bulgaria, especially in military, financial, and university circles. Late in the thirties the Nazi economic octopus wrapped itself round this little nation of peasants. Economic power reinforced German diplomatic prestige at the court of King Boris. With Italy relations were excellent, being consolidated in 1930 by the marriage of the ruler to a princess of the House of Savoy. Bulgaria belonged to the camp of the Axis. There she remained during World War II.

Greece

By reason of her achievements in classical antiquity Greece holds a peculiar place in the affections of cultivated men the world over. Her language, which is a renovated version of the ancient tongue, her noble architectural monuments, and the revival of the Olympic games, linked modern Greece with old Greece, as did the excessive political partisanship and political unruliness. Like the Serbs, the Greeks took their politics passionately, very passionately. Greece had a higher proportion of inhabitants engaged in non-agricultural pursuits than the other Balkan countries and unlike them changed her governmental form in the inter-war period from limited monarchy to republic and then back again to monarchy.

After the final peace settlement with Turkey (p. 413) Greater Greece comprised an area equal to New York State, with a population of over 7,000,000, more than 1,250,000 of whom were repatriated from Turkey. To provide for these newcomers until they could look after themselves, the government had to borrow and more foodstuffs had to be imported. The immigrants brought new light industries with them, which tended to make sections of the Greek countryside factory-conscious as they had never been before.

Athens, home of less than 700,000, and cosmopolitan Salonika—the pearl of the Aegean—a third as big, depended on textile industry, trade, and shipping for their well-being. At its peak the Greek merchant marine reached nearly 2,000,000 tons. The rest of the Greeks made their living from the soil of the coastal plains and interior valleys. Farms were small and backward; peasant proprietorships were the vogue. Currants and tobacco were major items of export.[5]

Beyond the frontiers of "Greater Greece" there were two compact bodies of Greek-speaking folk—in the Italian Dodecanese archipelago, and in British-owned Cyprus which has not been in the possession of Greece since the time of the Persian conqueror, Darius. These areas Greek patriotism coveted but the more extravagant aspirations of "the Great Greek Idea" were buried with the exchange of populations with Turkey. The pre-war parliamentary democracy and the royal dynasty were preserved, but the king, Constantine, was compelled to abdicate, on the score that he was responsible for a disastrous campaign against Turkey in 1920-1922. By virtue of a plebiscite Greece was converted into a republic and remained so until 1935.

In the interval, Greek politics was more tumultous and stormy than that of any other Balkan country. The nation was in an almost perpetual ferment: army men against civilians; royalists against republicans; town against country; business and shipping interests against an emergent Communism. But something akin to order prevailed from 1928 to 1932, when Eleutherios Venizelos occupied the Premier's office. That rebellious and tough-minded statesman, the Olympian personality of 20th century Greece, suffered extraordinary vicissitudes of political fortune. Extolled by admirers as the father of his country, Venizelos was reviled by equally ardent enemies as the foe of all that was sound and desirable in Greek life.

Venizelos, who on eight occasions served as Prime Minister, gained an international reputation for diplomatic skill and political sagacity. In the course of his long and chequered career he had shaped Greek foreign policy before and during the wars that were fought from 1912 to 1920. He was a friend of Britain, an impassioned nationalist, a republican, and something of a democrat in the motherland of democracy.

The downfall of Venizelos' Ministry in 1932 was followed by renewed political and economic turmoil. Someone has counted no fewer than twenty coups and revolutions against established authority in Greece in the inter-war years. In 1935 Venizelos, alarmed by the growth of royalist opinion and in league with demoted or discharged military leaders, raised the standard of rebellion against a ministry which was scheming to restore the monarch. But the insurgent forces were swiftly routed and Venizelos fled abroad, dying an exile in Paris,

[5] Before 1914 Greece sent thousands of her sons and daughters to the United States, but after the war emigration was reduced to a trickle.

and bequeathing to his countrymen a tradition of fierce political individualism and consuming patriotism.

Forthwith King George II, who had been dismissed a dozen years before, was proclaimed monarch, a decision that was confirmed in a "managed" plebiscite in which almost everyone voted royalist. But in a few months Greece marched down the familiar path of dictatorship.

At the general election of 1936 royalists and their republican opponents were returned in about equal numbers, leaving a Communist minority holding the balance of power. That faction, whose following came from the wage workers in the big cities and from repatriated Greeks, had separated itself from the small Socialist party in 1929 and was affiliated with the Third International in Moscow.

When the Greek ministry decreed compulsory arbitration of labor disputes industrial workers threatened to go out on a general strike. Whereupon the Prime Minister, General Yanni Metaxas, a professional soldier with strong royalist convictions, set himself up as dictator and held the country in an iron grip until his death in 1941. Professing to believe that Greece was menaced by a revolution such as was then convulsing Spain, Metaxas suppressed the Parliament, dissolved trade unions, and suspended ordinary civil liberties. Greece, in short, joined the police-states.

But social welfare was promoted by improvements in roads and railways, the extension of irrigation facilities, and industrial worker legislation fixing minimum wages, an eight hour work day and so forth. National fighting services were strengthened, frontiers were fortified, and politics banned from the barracks. Communists, because of the hostility of the dictatorship, were compelled to work undercover, to emerge once more as redoubtable guerilla fighters after Greece was overrun by the Axis in World War II (p. 541).

In its foreign relations Greece effected a remarkable rapprochement with the proverbial national enemy, Turkey. The Balkan pact of 1934 consolidated Greek friendship with the Balkan states other than Bulgaria. As the result of commercial dealings, Nazi Germany gained no little influence at Athens, but Britain continued to be, as it had long been, the foremost friend and financier of Greece.

Memories of Mussolini's bombardment of Corfu (p. 433), coupled with Italian possession of the Dodecanese islands and seizure of Albania in the spring of 1939, kept these Mediterranean neighbors hostile. When Italy threatened the independence of Greece in 1939, Britain and France stepped in and guaranteed the territorial integrity of the country, precisely as they did in the case of Rumania. Upon the outbreak of World War II Greece remained neutral in spite of much provocation from Italy. Her refusal to yield to Italian demands and to render unneutral assistance to the Axis eventually brought the Axis war-machine clanking across the historic hills and valleys of the kingdom.

The New Turkey

Foreign diplomatists were wont to label the doddering empire of the Ottoman Turks as "Europe's sick man." That realm perished in wars from 1912 to 1918. On its ruins was built a new Turkey which not only defeated Greek ambitions in Asia Minor but carried through one of the most far-reaching domestic transformations of the inter-war years. From being a backward Oriental state, the prey of preda-tory foreign nations, Turkey emerged as a "modern" country, capable of standing on its own feet, and facing westward. And other peoples of western Asia were inclined to walk in the footprints of the Turk.

Warfare had cost Turkey all Asiatic territory not occupied by Turkish-feeling folk.[6] In Europe a district no bigger than Maryland, which included the historic but faded metropolis of Constantinople, renamed Istanbul, was salvaged from the once far-ranging Ottoman Empire. In all, the new Turkey covered an area six times as large as New York State but contained only about 17,000,000 inhabitants. It occupied a superb strategic position on the Mediterranean and Black Seas, guarded the vital Straits joining those two seas, and formed a gateway from Europe to the Middle East and India.

Asiatic Turkey is a plateau with a slightly hollowed central zone. High, forbidding mountains and much arid land provide admirable natural defenses but are useless for the pursuits of peace. From Turk-ish mines a quarter of the world's supply of chrome ore was quarried and there are modest stocks of coal, zinc, and other mineral resources. Despite the promotion and progress of industrialism, Turkey re-mained overwhelmingly a country of plodding peasants.

Once boundaries had been delimited after World War I, Turkey settled down to the twin tasks of reconstruction and of Europeaniza-tion. The new era was fully personified in Mustapha Kemal, organizer of final victory over the Greeks and thereafter the dictator of his country. He belonged to the brotherhood of "Young Turks," a pro-gressive nationalist set which was bent upon infusing new energy into the old Turkish state and bringing it abreast of the more ad-

[6] A large and restless minority of Kurds, who had kinsmen in neighboring Iran (Persia) and Iraq, troubled Turkish politics, but they tended in time to merge their identity in the Turkish nationality.

vanced nations of Europe. As signs of the new day Kemal abolished
the Ottoman Sultanate, proclaimed a Republic, and moved the capital
from Constantinople to Ankara, deep in Anatolia—away from foreign
intrigue and interference.

Chosen President of the Republic in 1923, Kemal was four times
re-elected, and although the forms of representative democracy were
introduced, only one political party was permitted. Public criticism of
public policies was discouraged when not ruthlessly suppressed, and
the Turkish press reflected the wishes of the head of the state. Power
belonged to a small Turkish oligarchy which was as indifferent as
the masses to the implications of such western words as liberty,
republic, and constitution. Agencies of government strove to inculcate
warm loyalty to the nation, to teach that, "We are we and unlike
anybody else," and to build up intense pride of "race."

Kemal's revolutionary course brought forth many another innovation, all inspired by western or Bolshevik Russian ways. It was
hoped, among other things, to make Turkey industrially independent.
Borrowing the Soviet principle of planned economic progress, the
Turks created textile, glass, sugar, and cement industries; railways
and highways were extended and improved. Part of the new industry
was state controlled, part state owned and operated. Kemal even
ordered that a charming beer garden should be laid out on European
lines and he did not neglect to build a brewery nearby. Capital for
these undertakings came principally from state revenues, the rest in
the form of loans from Soviet Russia or European financiers. Among
the ruling Turkish oligarchy there was much admiration for Soviet
Russia, first of states to recognize the Kemalist regime, and thereafter
the source of technical assistance as well as financial and diplomatic
aid.

Agriculture, which furnished a living for two out of three Turks,
felt the driving impulse of the Nationalist regime. Through a four-
year plan the output of cotton and tobacco was substantially increased
and irrigation facilities were much enlarged. Murmurings of the Anatolian peasantry against these changes, though lively, were less pronounced than the outcry provoked by Kemalist social and religious
reforms. The wearing of the conventional fez and veil was banned,
polygamy was prohibited, women were given the same suffrage rights
as men (1934), and seventeen women were elected to the national Parliament. All this meant the passing of the Oriental mentality in
Turkey.

Similar in import was the substitution of Latin characters in the
Turkish language for the Arabic alphabet. The whole nation was

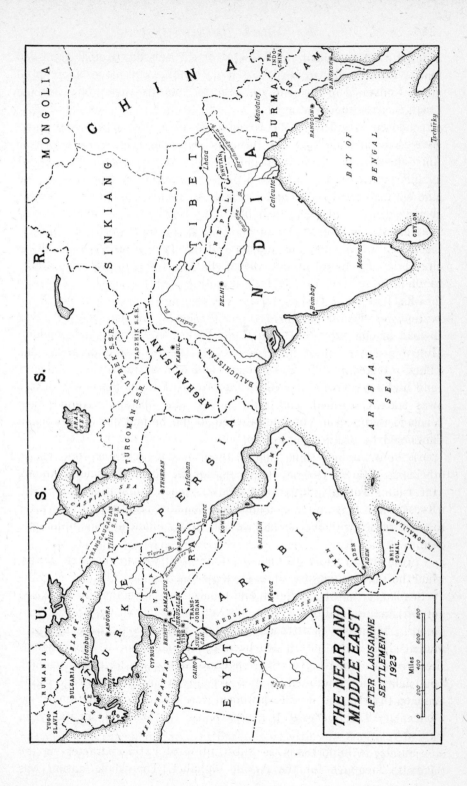

THE NEAR AND MIDDLE EAST

AFTER LAUSANNE SETTLEMENT 1923

Miles
0   200   400   600   800

ordered to go to school; in a single generation half the Turkish population was taught to read and write, whereas illiteracy had been almost universal in the era of the Sultans. At the apex of the educational pyramid was the ancient University of Istanbul to which was attached an Institute of Turkology where future national leaders were to be trained. Schools and colleges which were conducted by Americans or other foreigners, and in which West and East intimately mingled, were strictly supervised by the state and obliged to conform in their teaching to nationalist orthodoxy under pain of suppression or the expulsion of erring teachers.

Kemal's benevolent and secularizing despotism drastically altered the ties between Mohammedanism and the Turkish government. The office of Caliph or spiritual leader of the Moslem faith, formerly filled by the head of the Turkish state, was discarded. No longer was Islam the official creed of Turkey. New law codes were adopted, patterned on western models and uninfluenced by the teachings of the sacred Koran. Instead of the Moslem Friday, Sunday was made the day of rest. Mohammedan religious foundations were deprived of their extensive landed properties.

Republican Turkey, in short, was radically made over and voices of protestants were silenced in the manner customary in dictatorships. When Kemal died in 1938, his first mate, Ismet Inönü, steered along the course that had been charted.

If there was one thing that distinguished Kemalist Turkey from other authoritarian regimes it was the almost complete absence of an aggressive spirit in international affairs. Mistrust of European diplomacy, born of long and melancholy experience, caused the new Turkey to treat warily with the Great Powers. An exception was made in the case of Soviet Russia. That country posed as friend and benefactor and professed to have abandoned tsarist ambitions in the Near East which had brought on eleven recognized Russo-Turkish wars.

Suspicion that Italy harbored designs on Turkish territory was not without foundation. After a new settlement at the Straits, negotiated at Montreux in 1936 (p. 483), the Ankara government leaned toward Great Britain with which an ambiguous treaty of mutual assistance was signed in 1939. At that very moment, the friendship of "the sick man," now recovered, was being sought by Hitlerian Germany, cash in hand.

Kemal's effective pursuit of the policy of the good neighbor in Balkan relations was fitly symbolized in a stamp portraying a large olive tree growing in the Near East with a root extending to each of the Balkan countries and to Turkey. As a mark of the unprecedented good feeling toward Greece a Turkish minister laid a wreath on the cenotaph of the unknown warrior in Athens.

The Free Arab States [7]

It would be possible to write large chapters of Egypt's history in terms of water: the Nile, in whose narrow alluvial valley western man probably first rose from savagery to civilized ways of living, and which nowadays is the only settled section of the sprawling kingdom, the rest being desert; the Mediterranean, which lends strategic and commercial importance to the country; the Suez Canal and the Red Sea which afford a short route to Asia and the Pacific; and the rivers of the Sudan which feed the Nile and irrigate rich cotton plantations.

For long years Egypt, as part of the Ottoman realm, had been the theatre of competing imperialisms, but Great Britain outdistanced all her rivals. When Turkey took up arms on the German side in 1914, the British government established a formal protectorate over the ancient land of the Pharoahs and its 16,000,000 of people. Britain's authority was fully confirmed by Turkey in the Lausanne Treaty of 1923. But in the meantime, in 1922, the protectorate had been cancelled and the native claimant to the throne was recognized as king. Egypt thereafter was technically an independent sovereignty, though only technically.

A characteristic nationalist agitation had emerged under the banner of "Egypt for the Egyptians." Drawing its leadership from the small mercantile and intellectual class, the independence cause gathered force in consequence of British requisitions of men and materials during World War I and of the glowing Allied rhetoric about self-determination and the rights of small nations. Egypt seethed with nationalism after the war but was controlled by British officialdom which, even at its best, was nonetheless bureaucratic. The question at issue was whether resurgent Egypt should remain under foreign tutelage or develop genuine self-government.

In the van of the freedom movement was the Wafd or home-rule party, founded in 1924 by the firebrand Zaghlul Pasha, Egypt's foremost politician until his death in 1927. Nationalist orators and university students demanded the withdrawal of British officials and cried aloud against the penetration of their Moslem land by western and Christian ideas. As for the masses of the Egyptian population, the poverty-stricken, disease-ridden, largely illiterate, child-rich fel-

[7] For the history of the Arab lands held as mandates by Britain and France see pp. 435-439.

lahin or peasantry, they were so busy keeping body and soul together that they showed only tepid interest in matters beyond their daily round. While many were owners of tiny farms, the bulk of the fellahin toiled on estates in the Nile valley for patriarchally-minded masters. Apart from food, cotton was the chief production of Egypt.

The domestic history of Egypt was studded with nationalist demonstrations, assassinations, constitutional experiments, and bitter feuds between crafty native politicos. British repression alternated with moderate concessions to Egyptian claims.

After more than one false start British and Egyptian representatives hammered out a Treaty of Alliance and Friendship in 1936 which, while safeguarding essential British interests, assured Egypt of a more independent status. It was prescribed in the treaty that British soldiers in fixed numbers might be posted for defense purposes in the Suez Canal Zone,[8] and that British naval stations might be maintained at Alexandria and Port Said. British experts, moreover, would assist in building up the Egyptian army and would share with Egyptians in the administration of the huge Sudan area.[9]

Ambassadors would be exchanged, Egypt might apply for admission to the League of Nations, and British diplomacy would urge foreign governments to cancel their special, long-standing legal rights in the kingdom. These arrangements were appropriately implemented in due course to the gratification of all Egyptian factions except a small and extremely nationalistic group.

For most purposes the settlement of 1936 authorized the Egyptians to work out their own salvation. Thanks to a comparatively progressive constitution patterned on western precedents, the politically-minded

[8] In case of war or threat of war the limitations on the number of troops would be waived.

[9] The article in the treaty touching on the Sudan reaffirmed in a sense a bargain that had been struck years before. The Sudan region contained over 4,500,000 inhabitants, largely Moslems, who in outlook and interest belong to the Arab world rather than to Africa. Once a free people the Sudanese had been finally overpowered by Anglo-Egyptian forces in 1898 and thereafter had been jointly administered by Britishers and Egyptians, with far the larger responsibilities exercised by the British. Progress was made in the political education of the Sudanese and in the growing of cotton; one interesting cooperative cotton-raising experiment covered 5,000,000 acres. Among the small educated class Sudanese nationalism appeared, which Egyptian politicians spoke of as a spurious fanaticism fostered by selfish British interests. In the Egyptian view the Sudan was simply a province of Egypt. But the treaty of 1936 shelved the crucial question of Sudanese sovereignty for twenty years and perpetuated the joint Anglo-Egyptian administration. Sudanese chiefs put in claims for recognition as a nation with a right to eventual independence.

took an active part in deciding public policies, though the king, Faruq I, after 1936 was far more than a decorative figurehead.

Part of Egyptian political energies which had been concentrated on winning independence could now be turned to national defence and social betterment or to the furtherance of the Pan-Arab cause. The reality of Egypt's freedom was exhibited in World War II when the kingdom declared its neutrality. Even so the authorities cooperated militarily with Great Britain, and whenever necessary, British diplomacy applied effective pressure at the royal palace, which infuriated Egyptian Nationalists. As the war progressed Egyptian expansionists brought forth claims to a part of Italian Libya and Eritrea, without for a moment forgetting their ambitions in the Sudan, the longing for "the unity of the Nile" in the Egyptian phrase.

Saudi Arabia

More free than Egypt was the Arab kingdom of Saudi Arabia. It was presided over by the colorful and resourceful Ibn Saud, who in his original habitat of Nejd in the interior of the peninsula had, early in the 20th century, set about organizing nomadic Bedouins into settled communities. After the break-up of the Ottoman Empire, Ibn Saud fought and conquered the coastal district of the Hejaz, containing the Moslem holy cities of Mecca and Medina, and other territories. In 1932 he proclaimed the Kingdom of Saudi Arabia.

Over this dominion the self-styled lord of Arabia governed in the manner of the absolute patriarch. He strove to overcome the asocial traditions of his 5,000,000 subjects, roughly half the dwellers in the Arabian peninsula. Mecca served Ibn Saud as capital, and, as the birthplace of Mohammed, it gave him unique prestige among Moslems everywhere.

Aside from its importance as a religious center and the goal of hundreds of thousands of Moslem pilgrims annually, Saudi Arabia attracted small attention until 1936 when an American concessionaire struck oil in commercial quantities. To Americans Ibn Saud granted exclusive rights to open up oilfields because as he said, "The United States has no political ambitions in this part of the world." American investments grew rapidly and during World War II plans for great expansion were reported. The master of the land was enriched by loans, gifts, and generous royalties. Oil operations, the advent of the motorcar and plane, and other modern innovations shook the simple Arabians out of their Oriental complacency and indolence.

Along the southern coastal fringe of huge and largely desert Arabia

—half as big as Europe—two other states held sway, Yemen and Muscat-Oman. With the king (or iman) of the former, Ibn Saud negotiated an agreement in 1937 for the pacific adjustment of any dispute that might arise. Wandering Bedouins in the interior of Arabia eked out a bare existence wholly untouched by western ways and manners. By reason of treaties of one kind and another with the Arab lands, Great Britain exerted decisive influence in their international relationships.

Pan-Arab Stirrings

Of growing importance for world affairs was the upthrust of a Pan-Arab movement: an increased feeling of Arab solidarity grounded upon the common Arab language, historical traditions, and the Moslem creed and culture. Branches of this movement stretched from Egypt straight into Iran or Persia.

The immigration of Zionists into Palestine and the urge to present a united front against foreign domination fostered the Pan-Arab spirit among educated Arabs. In a sense the intellectual fountain-head of the cause was the American operated university in Beirut, and the logical headquarters was Egyptian Cairo, capital of the richest Arab country. So wrapped up were politically articulate Egyptians in their own struggle for real independence from Great Britain that they had neither time nor energy to promote the concerns of the Arab brotherhood.

But in the late thirties Egyptians assumed leadership among the Arabs, which caused no little jealousy elsewhere, not least in Saudi Arabia where Ibn Saud fancied himself as the predestined chief not alone of Pan-Arabism but of the Moslem religion in the bargain. Conflicting economic interests likewise tended to disturb the solidarity of the Arab peoples. No Messiah, no Gandhi arose to rally the scattered Arab forces. It is impossible to tell how deep, how genuine and widespread the longing for Arab unity really was. But that Pan-Arabism would be a factor for consideration in the world chancelleries of tomorrow could not be gainsaid.

CHAPTER IX

Republican France

France and America

WHEN word reached New York in August, 1944, that Paris had been liberated from the Nazi jackboot, an impromptu demonstration took place at Rockefeller Center. Tricolors of the Third Republic flapped at flag poles. Exuberant crowds embraced French sailors. A band let out with La Marche Lorraine and Lily Pons sang the Marseillaise. All of this harmonized with the epigram that every man has two countries: his own and France.

Of all the nations of continental Europe, France has doubtless enjoyed the widest popularity in the United States. If a foreign language is studied in school or college it is more likely to be French than any other. The French practice of social democracy and French ideals of liberty closely approximate our own. The memory of the indispensable assistance given the United States by royal France in the War of Independence created an enduring bond between the two nations. The security of France has seemed to many Americans to be linked with our own safety; the serious reverberations of the military defeat of France in 1940 upon American policy is described elsewhere (p. 555).

For many Americans Paris—brilliant, sophisticated, civilized Paris —is France; and tourist Paris is all Paris. But in fact each of the twenty arrondissements of the capital has peculiarities of its own. Paris plays a large part in French life, but is not by any means representative of all of France.

For the historically informed, France stands for strength and yearning for national glory. For, from the superficially great age of Louis XIV down to the hardly less superficially strong rule of Napoleon III, France was the leading military factor of Europe. Toppled from that proud eminence by Bismarckian Germany in 1870, France regained the commanding position upon the German defeat in World War I.

The Price of Victory

The war cost France dearly. For one thing, about 1,400,000 sons of the Republic were dead. Hundreds of thousands were more or less seriously incapacitated—the flower and more than the flower of the young manhood of the nation. From those terrible losses France never recovered, neither physically, psychologically, nor politically, for the war cut down men who would no doubt have given the nation fresh and vigorous leadership.

War casualties were felt more keenly in France than in other European countries because of the lower birthrate. Alone among the major nations France had gained only slightly in population since the beginning of the 19th century. As a result, whereas in 1815 France contained fully a sixth of the people of Europe, excluding Russia, by 1939 the French share had dropped to a twentieth. That radical demographic change had, of course, large bearing upon the French political position in Europe.

But the human cost was only the first part of the French price of victory. Fair northern provinces over which the war had been fought lay prostrate after the foreign invader had retreated. Farm-lands and peasant cottages were damaged or destroyed; flocks and herds had vanished; mining would require years before production reached pre-war levels; factories and means of transportation were in sad disarray. As standing reminders of the price of victory the national debt had risen to unimagined heights and France was heavily in debt to Great Britain and the United States.

Over against these liabilities the French had the inner satisfaction which the downfall of Germany brought—something intangible but for all that nonetheless real. Germany's military might had been broken, the ancient enemy could not be formidable for years to come; perhaps it could never menace France again. More, Alsace-Lorraine, with its rich resources of iron, had been recovered. For fifteen years, anyway, the coal of the Saar Basin would be flowing to France. The overseas holdings of the Republic had been extended in the form of mandated territories. Germany, furthermore, was bound to pay reparations, which popular French fancy supposed would remove the cost of the war from the French tax-payer. Allied arms would be stacked in the Rhineland for almost a generation at a minimum. If the French war gains were not commensurate with war losses, they were at least not without their gratifying features.

The Constitutional Structure

After a wide variety of constitutional experience and experimentation since the great Revolution of 1789, France adopted the "constitution" of the Third Republic in 1875, which persisted until 1940. France passed as a political democracy, even though the franchise right was jealously confined to the adult males. The French governmental system had special importance because it was imitated in other continental countries where free governments existed. In fact, in greater or lesser degree French constitutional forms were the prototypes for the new states of Europe.

Chief executive of France was a President chosen by the legislature and in practice very much a figurehead. Seldom was a popular personality named President, for French Republicans had an inherited aversion to the strong man who might make himself dictator. The real French executive was the ministry, headed by a Premier, whose tenure of office rested upon majority backing in both branches of the legislature; so long as a ministry commanded majority support, it managed the affairs of France and the empire. Quite commonly in the era between wars the Premier also held the portfolio of foreign affairs—one sign of the paramount importance of international affairs. Next to him in prestige was the Minister of the Interior, who nominated the most powerful local officials, especially the prefects of the departments.

The French legislature was made up of a Senate and a Chamber of Deputies. Senators, who were chosen by an indirect method, had to be at least forty years of age—in practice the average was around sixty—and the electoral law was so drawn as to give an overplus of influence to rural France, as in the Senate of the United States. For these reasons the French Senate displayed an unmistakable tendency toward conservatism on political and economic questions. Constitutionally the Senate had coequal power with the Chamber of Deputies, though money bills had to originate in the lower house.

After 1928 French deputies, of whom there were slightly more than 600, were chosen by districts as with Congressmen in the United States. The term of office was four years. A special feature of the French electoral law had large political significance; in the event that no candidate obtained an *absolute majority* in the first balloting—and seldom was a candidate so fortunate in more than one out of three of the districts—a second vote was required. Only a plurality was then needed for election. Someone has said that at the first balloting, French voters cast for the man they really wanted, and in the second, they voted against the candidate they most disliked. That custom invited a good deal of "horse-trading" and devious, corrupt bargaining between political "parties."

The tenure of a French ministry depended, as has been remarked, upon majority backing in both branches of the legislature. In the inter-war epoch France had no fewer than forty one ministries, the shortest of them lasting a mere four days, the longest contriving to hold on, with but a single change, for four years. Will Rogers, the American humorist, once remarked that after witnessing the changing of the Guards at Buckingham Palace he had flown to Paris to watch the changing of the ministry.

Quite often ministerial change involved only the withdrawal of the Premier and the more prominent cabinet personalities, and was in the nature of a re-shuffle, but change invariably brought a new course on some public policy. Some public men, to be sure, retained portfolios in a succession of ministries; Aristide Briand, for instance, presided over the Foreign Office for more than six years in a row. The great bulk of the French civil servants, who gave continuity to public business, were not affected by cabinet shuffles. But each ministerial shake-up generated considerable uneasiness in the business community, disturbing to economic well-being, and was likely to produce temporary paralysis in French diplomacy.

Sometimes personal rivalries and jealousies among cabinet members brought a ministry down. But ministerial instability was caused much more by a singular weakness in French constitutional usage: the Premier lacked power to dissolve the Chamber of Deputies and call for a new election in case of an adverse vote on a measure sponsored by the ministry. The British Prime Minister, in contrast, possessed that right. True, power to order dissolution, with the consent of the Senate, stood on the French statutes, but the right had been invoked only once, back in 1877. Thereafter the view prevailed that it was "unconstitutional" to dissolve the Deputies.

The chief cause of instability and the general inadequacy of the executive side of the Third Republic, as of other governments in which the multi-party system prevailed, was the coalition system. Since no "party" ever commanded a majority of the law-makers, French ministries depended upon the uncertain support of several "parties." Sometimes, indeed, a parliamentary bloc was formed simply to enact a specific number of laws and broke up once that was accomplished, compelling the ministry to resign.

*The many parties attacked each other with
propaganda – people had little faith in any of them
+ .·. there was a* Republican France *rapid turn* 223
of office

The Plethora of Parties

What made French politics puzzling to outsiders was the multiplicity of "parties," or rather of political groups, for party implies greater solidarity and discipline and organization than generally prevailed in France. At the election of 1936, for instance, nineteen political groupings managed to return representatives to the Chamber of Deputies. Names of groups were extremely fluid; they often belied the real outlook of the group, and many of them had a tortuous history of divisions and reunions. Frenchmen, more concerned with principles than with realities, had less taste for compromise than British politicians.

Although almost every conceivable shade of opinion on religious, social, economic, and political and international policies was represented by a faction in the French legislature, the groups may broadly be collected into three categories: the Right, the Center, and the Left. It would not be profitable nor is it necessary to sketch the features of all the groups, but a few of them require comment.

Speaking generally, the Right or conservative groups declined to accept the implications of the French Revolution and were wedded to Catholic clericalism; their outlook harked back more or less faithfully to the ancien regime. On the extreme Right was the royalist *Action Française,* which frankly preached the overthrow of the Third Republic by armed violence, and the restoration of a kingdom without a parliament. Léon Daudet, the loudest and most reckless advocate of royalism, summed up his creed as, "We don't wish to upset the Republic. We want to cut its throat. We are not a political party. We are a conspiracy." Though disdaining to take part in parliamentary elections the Action Française carried on an unrelenting and scurrilous propaganda against the republican democracy and professed to see its ideals realized in the Pétain administration which governed part of France after the German conquest in 1940.

The only Right group with a permanent organization was the Republican Federation, which was essentially the spokesman of big business, unsympathetic to all but the mildest social legislation. It was a warm partisan of Church interests, and leaned toward political authoritarianism. Intensely nationalistic, and without faith in the League of Nations, this faction once shouted loudly against the German peril, but supported "appeasement" after the Nazis had firmly established themselves in power.

Claiming to be "the party of Catholic youth and the parish clergy" the Popular Democrats voted for such social legislation as was in conformity with Vatican teachings and actively championed the cause of clericalism, notably church schools. Like other Rightist groups the Popular Democrats feared and distrusted Soviet Russia and French Communism.

Sometimes the Popular Democrats teamed up with Center groups of which the Democratic Alliance had the largest following. On religious issues the Democratic Alliance pursued a middle course between the friends and foes of clericalism; it resisted proposals savoring of economic collectivism, though it was not averse to state aid for capitalism. Deputies of this group were strongly individualistic, some voting with the Right, some with the Left, though priding themselves on belonging to the Center.

Down to 1936 the largest single French party was the leftward Radical or Radical Socialist group, recruiting its strength from small independent Frenchmen in village and city belonging to the lower middle class. Radicals conceived of themselves as the authentic heirs and apostles of the great French Revolution, believed passionately in individual liberty, political democracy, and social equality, and intransigently fought anything that smacked of clericalism. On economic questions the Radicals were a house divided, ranging from financial orthodoxy to Socialism, without however accepting the Marxian doctrine of class struggle. In foreign policy the Radicals were pacific without being pacifist, and favored the League. Arbitration, Security, Disarmament was a prized electoral slogan of the Radicals.

More clearly Left was the Socialist Party, which extolled Marxian principles of class warfare and the equalitarian state but in practice preferred to bring about changes in the prevailing economy by gradual parliamentary reforms after the manner of the British Labour Party. French Socialism was staunchly democratic in temper, fiercely hostile to clericalism, and a firm advocate of the League; along with political internationalism the party cherished anti-military, pacifistic convictions. Until 1936, when for the first time Socialism seated more deputies in the Chamber than any other group, the party stubbornly declined to participate in a ministry (except during World War I).

Bitter foe of Socialism was the Communist Party which broke away from Socialism in 1920 and remained completely apart until 1934. Both competed for the votes of class-conscious wage earners. In zeal and solidarity the Communists excelled the Socialists but in numbers they were far smaller. French Communism was affiliated with the Third International with headquarters in Moscow; it advocated physical revolution, "dictatorship of the proletariat," and international Marxism. Verbal warfare with French Socialism proceeded until after the victory of National Socialism in Germany; it was then apparent that the bitter cleavage between Socialism and Communism in Germany had helped Hitlerism to win through.

In order to check any likelihood of a parallel sequence in France, French Communists and Socialists drew together, though negotiations to merge the two groups fell flat. Both collaborated with the Radicals in the national elections of 1936, which assisted the Communist delegation in the Chamber of Deputies in jumping from a dozen to six dozen.

French Communism's Russophile orientation was amply reflected in the party outlook on foreign affairs. Ordinarily the Communists adopted a strictly international and anti-militarist line, but in the mid-thirties, on orders from Moscow, they lauded "immortal France," pressed for armament expansion and denounced Nazi Germany as a deadly European menace. When, however, Stalin trafficked with Hitler, and entered into the famous understanding of August, 1939 (p. 514), French Communism reverted to its anti-war themes, renouncing them only after the outbreak of the Russo-German war in June of 1941.

France in the Twenties

After World War I France was faced with heavy economic problems. Living costs had soared and continued to go up. The national debt had risen proportionately higher than in Britain, for the French government refused to impose heavy taxes and the outlay for the reconstruction of the devastated areas would be costly. Comforting, however, was the popular belief that German reparations would solve French economic perplexities.

Within less than a decade, all traces of the physical destruction caused by the war had been removed. Hundreds of new villages were laid out, and new factories with up-to-date machinery were erected, at a cost of almost four billions of dollars. According to the French reckoning not more than a third part of the reconstruction expenditures was covered by receipts from Germany, the remainder being met by public borrowing. Neither conciliatory methods nor the application of coercion in the form of the military occupation of the Ruhr valley in 1923 (p. 426) enabled France to secure the financial retribution from Germany that had confidently been expected.

The necessity of paying a large part of the reconstruction costs and interest on the national debt kept the French government budget in unbalance and the currency in a fluctuating state.

After World War I the National Bloc of Rightist groups, which had been managing French affairs, was continued in power. Although many of the Deputies elected in 1919 were war veterans—it was called the "horizon-blue" parliament—they were inexperienced in the ways of politics and the political veterans directed the course of events. The old war-horse Clemenceau presently shuffled off the public stage having been rejected for the presidency by revengeful critics of his diplomacy at Versailles. Dominant personality in the first phase of reconstruction was the ardent nationalist, Raymond Poincaré, under whose guidance France adopted the "hard" policy on German reparations which culminated in the march into the Ruhr valley.

Fiscal troubles and revulsion of feeling over the Ruhr policy, which involved a heavy strain on French finance, ate into the popularity of Poincaré and the Right and at the polls in 1924 the Left elements triumphed. Forthwith Aristide Briand assumed the portfolio of foreign affairs and held it into 1932; his policy toward Germany emphasized conciliation, not coercion.

The Prime Minister of the Left coalition, Édouard Herriot of the Radical Socialist Party, secured the adoption of laws against clericalism, but was incapable of remedying the monetary malaise, nor were his successors. In a little more than two years seven French cabinets in turn grappled vainly with budgetary tangles and the steady depreciation in the value of the franc. When in the summer of 1926 the franc dwindled to a tenth of its pre-war value—and promised to go lower—France appeared to be on the verge of complete financial chaos. Panic seized this nation of thrift and property and the flight of capital abroad was accelerated.

Out of the depths France was brought by a Poincaré Ministry of all the talents, a Ministry of national regeneration. By ruthless slashing of state expenditures, increasing taxes, and helped by reparation receipts under the Dawes Plan, Poincaré contrived to balance the budget and to stabilize the franc at four cents, or a fifth of its pre-war value. That rate was low enough to enable French wares to compete in world markets and to attract throngs of tourists to Paris.

On retiring as Premier in 1929 Poincaré was toasted as the savior of France and the franc. He could point with pride to the prosperity of the Republic; tourist traffic was booming; foreign trade touched an unprecedented peak; tariff legislation scrupulously protected domestic producers and gave them a virtual monopoly in French colonial markets; and large gold reserves had been accumulated in the vaults of France. It appeared that national prosperity was based upon unshakable foundations.

In the meantime, conditions in the recovered provinces of Alsace-Lorraine had taken an ugly, if not a positively dangerous, turn. As part of the German Empire these provinces had been granted (1911) a modest measure of home-rule, but French officials largely swept away Alsatian institutions in a resolute effort to assimilate the region to France and that quickly. Instead of treating local susceptibilities with the moderation that once had distinguished the French administration, France in the twenties tried to force the rising Alsatian generation—which was decidedly German in speech—to use French, beginning in the lower schools and on up to the historic University of Strasbourg. An attempt was made, but without success, to introduce secularization measures in schools such as prevailed in France. Civil servants who spoke only French were sent into the region. Economic hardships, for which the French government was held blameworthy, as is the way with men, intensified Alsatian resentment.

The upshot of it all was a vigorous revival of agitation for Alsatian autonomy. It was the official French view that Alsatian discontent was fomented and fanned by irredentists in Germany. Candid foreigners familiar with the facts hesitated to accept that interpretation, and the German government hotly repudiated the charge. Had not Germany in the Locarno Security Pact of 1925 implicitly renounced all pretensions to the provinces?

Legal action, taken by French officials against Alsatians suspected of separatist sympathies, embittered the situation. Openly, the unrest was trumpeted by election returns in which Alsatian autonomists scored heavily. At the voting for the Chamber of Deputies in 1936, for example, an Alsatian faction which demanded the abolition of the centralized French administration principally on religious grounds was victorious in fifteen constituencies. France, in a word, had scarcely succeeded better than Imperial Germany in reconciling the Alsatians to what many of them thought of as foreign domination.

A Time of Trouble

Poincaré's retirement, after almost three years as Premier, was presently followed by the return of fiscal distress in France and chronic instability of ministries. At the national election of 1932 the Left won a substantial majority of seats, owing in part to deals between Radicals and Socialists in the second balloting. But the Left proved unequal to organizing a durable cabinet. Frequent ministerial overturns fostered not only disgust with politics but growing dissatisfaction with the very fundamentals of the French political fabric.

France in these respects mirrored the pessimism concerning representative institutions of government that was prevalent throughout the continent.

The Great Depression, from whose evil ravages France for a time was immune, now darkened the French economic sky. Industry, foreign trade, and tourist revenues contracted abruptly. Prices of farm products fell sharply, and the high price offered by the United States for gold sent bullion flowing across the Atlantic. Repercussions of the slump adversely affected state finance, which now had to bear the additional burden of relief for the workless. Yet the French unemployment problem never became as severe as in other industrialized countries because many Frenchmen who were thrown out of work moved back to their natal villages and tens of thousands of foreign workmen returned to their homelands.

To combat the depression, the French government pushed through a drastic program of deflation; it stopped payment on war debts to the United States (after the flow of reparations from Germany had ceased), and it increased tariff rates and taxes. But those measures failed to brighten the economic picture. On the contrary, the lot of "little man," whether in city or country, steadily deteriorated. Protests and rioting caused by tax increases were matched by threats of civil servants, firmly entrenched in their positions, to walk off their jobs if their salaries were slashed in order to bring the state budget into balance. While these and related ills were upsetting French morale and gnawing away at national esprit, Hitlerism, beyond the Rhine, was thrusting into power and imperiling the very security of the Third Republic.

In harmony with the thinking of conventional French finance, and out of fear of runaway inflation, the government would not consider abandoning the gold standard or of devaluating the currency. As a result France became the most expensive European country in which to live or trade. To cover the recurrent deficit in the budget, borrowings were made from the Bank of France, whose directors exacted legislation, in turn, that was in keeping with orthodox economics. That course infuriated Left elements in France which favored less conservative financial policies. Cleavages between French Right and Left, between conservatism and "adventurism" in state economic policies, were sharpened by the Great Depression, and widened as the 1930's moved along, with baleful consequences for the international standing of the Third Republic.

Faith in France and her democratic order of society was being
 undermined at the very time that National Socialism was fighting its

way into control in Germany. At the end of 1933, the year of Nazi enthronement, France saw three ministries in as many months. As a kind of climax of the French national woes the malodorous Stavisky scandal was brought into the open. Even that affair was less gross than some other discreditable cases of corruption and financial jobbery which cropped up.

Alexander Stavisky, who emigrated to France from Russia, was a man of many parts, mostly reprehensible. For minor frauds he was arrested but set free on bail; by gifts to public officials, he bought immunity from the law. At the end of 1933 it was revealed that Stavisky had swindled the Bayonne municipal loan office out of huge sums and thereby brought thousands of Frenchmen to ruin. Evidence was adduced to show that highly placed French politicians were either witting or unwitting accomplices of the rogue. Excitement mounted to a new pitch when Stavisky was reported to be dead—by his own hand or by the police, in order to seal his lips.

About the same time sensational rumors asserted that French army funds had been misappropriated—money to complete the Maginot fortifications, for instance. Uncompromising enemies of the Republic, notoriously the Royalists, broke out in a rash of vitriolic articles whose object was to convince readers that corruption and bribery were synonymous with the already shaken French parliamentary regime. A Berlin newspaper jeeringly taunted France as "the sick man of Europe."

Accumulated political and social dynamite exploded in February, 1934, when Rightists and Leftists clashed furiously on the streets of Paris. Police intervention cost the lives of eighteen and several hundreds were injured. Simultaneously rioting broke out in provincial cities. To an American wit it appeared as though La Belle France was on the verge of degenerating into La Bellicose France.

In that critical moment in French affairs a strong Cabinet was formed of men with an unsullied reputation for personal probity and devotion to the national good. Former President Gaston Doumergue became Premier. His admirers hoped that he and his prestige would be able to duplicate the financial wizardry of Poincaré in the late twenties and thus restore popular confidence in the republican system. Fiscal reforms and administrative economies that were adopted improved the situation temporarily, but Doumergue's Ministry declined to move energetically against militant anti-republican societies which had recently grown in noisiness and, no doubt, in popularity.

It was Doumergue's personal conviction that the health of the Republic required that the Prime Minister should be clothed with authority to dissolve the Chamber of Deputies whenever it defeated a ministry, and order a new election. His open advocacy of that constitutional reform excited alarm in Left circles, which feared that Doumergue was sloping down the trail to dictatorship. When he requested extraordinary powers to try to lift the nation out of the financial morass, the Radical Socialists deserted him and the Ministry was obliged to resign. As was later appreciated that was the last chance to strengthen the governmental structure of the Third Republic—and the chance was missed.

After the downfall of the Doumergue Ministry, short-lived cabinets strove with only small success to produce betterment in the national economy. In 1935 the depression was at its worst in France when other countries were clearly on the way to recovery. That summer Pierre Laval, who twice before had headed French ministries, was made Premier and authorized to carry out fiscal reforms by decree. He issued over 500 orders, cutting state salaries and pensions and raising taxes.

That proved to be the last and most thorough-going effort to restore French economic health by deflationary measures. As before, critics on the Left declaimed against this policy and charged that Laval's rule by decree would end up in a dictatorship. In many ways Laval personified the singularly mercurial character of many a French politician of the epoch. Entering public life as a tribune of the industrial workers, Laval had shifted toward the Right as his fortunes rose, always with an eye to the main chance. His name, spelled the same whether left to right or right to left, furnished a clue to the fluidity of Laval's political outlook.[1]

Laval, as Premier, succeeded no better than his predecessors in effecting economic recovery or in restoring faith in the republican order. True, the externals of French representative government were unimpaired, but the inner life, the spirit, had decayed. And Laval was driven from office directly because of a bargain he arranged for the partition of Ethiopia (p. 478).

Outside parliament, in the meanwhile, the avowed enemies of the democratic Republic—protofascists—were gaining in numbers and in vehemence. Of them the most brash and formidable was the *Croix de Feu,* which was frankly modeled on Mussolini's Black Shirts. Financed by men of wealth this French version of Fascism attracted tens of thousands of disgruntled war veterans to its banners and claimed a membership of a million.

---

[1] After the defeat of France in 1940 Laval collaborated with the Nazi master, and, as a traitor to his country, was shot by a firing squad in 1945.

Founder and leader of the *Croix de Feu* was ambitious Colonel François de la Rocque, who came of a distinguished military family and was himself the wearer of eleven decorations for valor. Small, slender, and slightly lame, the Colonel had neither the primitive dynamism of Mussolini, nor the animal magnetism of Hitler. He was no mesmerist of the masses, yet he aspired to set himself up as dictator of France by a coup d'état, or as he said, "to put rotten parliamentarianism on a vacation." Fervently he and his henchmen denounced Marxism, democracy, and the electoral principle. But his battle cry that "40,000,000 Frenchmen can't be wrong" never attracted a mass following.

Other anti-democratic organizations published scurrilous newspapers and incendiary Fascist tracts, waved the bloody shirt of the "Red Peril," spread the poison of Judeophobia, and engaged in spectacular street demonstrations and occasional riots. Plainly, in the midthirties the forces of militant authoritarianism of the Right were on the march in France, and the government was disinclined to restrain them.

The Economic Framework

For an understanding of the course of French affairs it will be useful to sketch at this point and in a little detail the character and composition of the industry and agriculture of France.

In 1936 one out of every five Frenchmen was classified as an industrial worker. Most of them worked in small establishments but many in large factories, as, for instance, in the Citroën and Renault automobile works, patterned after plants in the United States. French national traditions of individualism long imposed legal barriers upon the formation of large corporations, but during the Great Depression, laws were somewhat relaxed, and large cartel combinations were organized to control prices and industrial production. Large scale industry was mainly concentrated in the north and northeast of France, and in cities such as Marseilles and Lyons. In the twenties the output of French manufactures and minerals more than doubled. Increasingly France relied upon foreign supplies of fuel and industrial raw materials, which in 1938 made up fully two thirds of the imports.

A significant facet of French economic history in the thirties was the rapid growth of trade unionism and the militant character of the unions. Before World War I, industrial workers—or rather the aristocracy of wage earners—were organized in the *Confédération Générale du Travail* (C.G.T.) and in the war years less skilled operatives were drawn in. The whole French unionist movement was profoundly affected by the Bolshevik Revolution and its aftermath in Russia.

Doctrinal dissensions within trade unionism culminated in an open rupture in 1922, the more radical workers founding a Communist union (*Confédération Générale du Travail Unitaire*), which allied itself politically with the Communist Party, much as the C.G.T. worked along with the belligerently anti-Communist Socialist Party. Quarreling between the two union organizations persisted until the mid-thirties when the growing peril of Right authoritarianism induced union leaders of all sects to submerge their differences and form a united front. Within three months—in 1936—membership in French unions jumped from 1,500,000 to 5,000,000. Organized labor was able to compel the adoption of social welfare laws, a department of government in which France had lagged far behind the leading industrial nations.

After World War I the traditional balance between French industry and agriculture shifted considerably. But France remained nonetheless preponderantly a rural nation. It had a population about a third that of the United States, compressed into an area smaller than Texas, and the majority of Frenchmen lived in villages and small towns.

The outstanding feature of rural France was the little farm owned and worked by the peasant and his family. More than half the farms had no hired workers, and in the entire Republic there were only about 250 large agricultural undertakings, mostly vineyards. The typical French peasant was noted for his conservatism, tough-mindedness, sobriety, and frugality—traits of the small landowner the world over. As confirmed individualists, in the main, the French peasantry looked upon state intervention in economic affairs with a hostile eye, unless projected legislation promised to benefit the rustic population directly. The outlook of the peasant, together with his strong desire for personal and national security, interpenetrated the policies of the whole country. Well has it been said that "the secret ambition of every Frenchman, whatever his class, is to own a little land and to watch in the twilight of his life his children and grandchildren go out into the world."

In the twenties there was a considerable migration from the French countryside to the cities. That trend, together with losses of men in the war, almost depopulated certain sections. To take up abandoned farm land—or to find employment in mills and mines—foreigners streamed into France in such volume that by 1930 the immigrant population approached 3,000,000 or triple that of 1913.

Among the French rustics, for all their individualism, economic cooperative societies had increasing popularity and political leagues were formed to secure legislation beneficial to farming interests. In response to peasant pressure the tariff, for instance, was repeatedly manipulated in a manner favorable to rural France and, by the same token, was injurious to French consumers. Laws were passed to raise farm prices and to furnish loans on easy terms.

In spite of all the vicissitudes of politics rural France remained the solid conservative mainstay of the Republic. Ministries came and ministries went, but the French peasant plodded along. Aligned with the peasantry was the greater part of the French urban middle class —not more than a tenth part of the population—but the controlling force in public affairs for generations by reason of wealth, intelligence, and ownership of the principal newspapers.

In spite of all the vicissitudes in economics France stood out in 1939 as the last major country of continental Europe in which comparative freedom of enterprise prevailed. There it was still permissible to form associations of workers or employers or consumers, free of state interference. There it was still possible to criticize economic policies that were pursued by the government. For all the legislation that was adopted by 1939 to bring about greater economic equality and security in France there was, nevertheless, a considerable area for individual initiative and private profit.

The Front Populaire and After

To ward off the rising menace of Right authoritarianism and to secure the passage of an ambitious schedule of financial and social welfare legislation and to reverse deflationary policies, the French parties of the Left—Radical Socialists, Socialists, and Communists— combined forces in 1935 in a parliamentary coalition called the Front Populaire. That combination promised "to defend democratic liberties . . . to give bread to the workers, work to the young, and peace to humanity as a whole."

At the national election of May of 1936, the Front Populaire captured six of every ten seats in the Chamber of Deputies, polling over a million more votes than all the other political groupings in the Republic.[2] Since the Socialists made up the largest party in the Chamber their chief, Léon Blum, was designated Premier. Blum, who was described as "a one-man brain trust," had had a brilliant career in

[2] Right groups attracted about 2,250,000 voters; the Center about 2,000,000; for the Left the Radicals had 1,500,000, Socialists 2,000,000, Communists 1,500,-000, and lesser groups 500,000.

almost everything except politics. His Socialism was of the evolutionary or reformist variety, but he disclaimed a Socialist program for his
coalition Ministry. "Our aim," he said, "is not to transform the social
system but to execute the promises of the Front Populaire." Communist deputies, while willing to back Blum in the Chamber with their
votes, would not take ministerial portfolios and assume the responsibilities that went with them.

Immediately upon the accession of the Popular Front to office,
the Blum Cabinet was confronted by two serious challenges. First,
men of the French moneyed plutocracy shipped funds abroad, either
fearful of Front Populaire legislation that would be detrimental to
their private interests or in order to aggravate the already heavy
financial difficulties of the Leftist Ministry. And, second, workers in
some of the large factories of Paris and other cities engaged in "sit-
down" strikes to oblige the Front Populaire to fulfill election promises
of social legislation and to coerce the conservative Senate into approving the desired laws. These events sharpened the tensions and antagonisms between Left and Right in French life.

In quick succession laws were passed by the Front Populaire which
made collective bargaining between management and men compulsory,
raised wages and salaries, granted holidays with pay, provided inexpensive recreational facilities for workers, and fixed the normal work-
week in industry at forty hours. Furthermore, the control of private
financiers over the powerful Bank of France was greatly curtailed and
the French armament industry was partly taken over by the state.
Twice the currency was devalued and the gold standard was at last
given up with the aims of promoting foreign trade and attracting tourists. For the benefit of discontented peasants the Blum Ministry carried
through far-reaching legislation to regulate the production and sale of
wheat and to furnish credit at low rates. And, lastly, political leagues,
such as the *Croix de Feu,* that were hostile to the Republic were
disbanded, though certain of them reappeared at once under new
names.

The Front Populaire economic legislation, socializing rather than
precisely Socialistic, was greeted with the same sort of praise and the
same kind of criticism that the program spoken of as the "New Deal"
elicited in the United States. The chief French innovation, the forty
hour work-week, provoked the most acrid debate. Proponents of the
measure held that a work-week of forty hours was both socially desirable and made jobs available for the unemployed. Critics, on the other
hand, charged that the law was responsible for raising the prices of
manufactured goods and for falling production. In any case, the

heated controversy over the forty hour week intensified the dissension and disunity in France and, in that sense, was a boon to the Republic's authoritarian neighbors, Germany and Italy.

Some of the laws adopted by the Front Populaire required large state appropriations and the budget for 1937 indicated another huge deficit. To grapple effectively with fiscal problems Blum requested the Chamber of Deputies to grant him plenary powers such as had earlier been given Laval, but on that issue the Radical Socialists balked, and the Blum Ministry yielded up the seals of office in June, 1937, after a mere year of power. Late in 1936 French business picked up considerably only to stagnate again in 1937 and to decline at year's end. Then bigger armament appropriations stimulated economic activity in general.

After the break-up of the Blum Cabinet the Radical Socialists occupied a commanding place in French affairs until after the onset of World War II. Grudgingly the legislature granted the new Ministry the semi-dictatorial authority it had denied to Blum. From April, 1938, until March, 1940, the Cabinet was headed by Édouard Daladier of the Radicals, who had served as War Minister in several cabinets, a grimly serious man, but unequal to sustained and decisive political action. For a time Daladier had the backing of Socialist and Communist deputies in the Chamber but they turned against him when the forty hour work-week was annulled by ministerial decree. And ideological controversies inside France were further embittered by international developments, particularly the Spanish Civil War (p. 485).

Civic decadence and class feuds within France, coupled with the growing military power of Germany and Italy compelled the Third Republic to follow in the diplomatic footsteps of Great Britain, with which, after April of 1938, France had a solid military alliance.

On the eve of World War II foreign observers saw (or thought they saw) a revival of the traditional French spirit of national solidarity and strength in view of the German-Italian menace to national security. But a French commentator was closer to reality when he wrote, "In 1939 the various elements of the French crisis had lost their virulence but the effects of the crisis had endured. The French body had not entirely recuperated. Time had been too short."[3]

Just before World War I France had been profoundly divided over domestic politics but as soon as fighting began, ranks were closed, justifying the old compliment that the French are "always excited except in moments of excitement." But in 1939 the division in the

---

[3] Pierre Maillaud. *France* (London, 1942), p. 103.

French mind ran deeper, much deeper. After seven years of acute controversy French Right and French Left were separated by a wall of mutual distrust; political leadership, moreover, was unresourceful and the memory of the crippling ordeal of World War I was all too green.

Before national unity could be achieved France went down before the furious onslaught of the mechanized armies of Hitlerian Germany.

The French Empire

Frenchmen have built two massive empires. Of the first, acquired by royal France, little still remains, most of it having passed to Britain as the result of world struggles in the 18th century. The second empire was largely the achievement and the pride of the Third Republic. Covering an area greater than the United States, and having a population half as large, the empire made France a "have" colonial power on which the sun never set. While the bulk of the French holdings were in Africa, stretching from the Mediterranean to the Congo, the Indo-Chinese colony was no mean dominion, and the Republican tricolor flew over small possessions in the Indian, the Pacific, and the Atlantic oceans. French colonial populations were very diversified on the level of civilization, religion, and race.

From the governmental standpoint the French empire may be divided into four classifications: the older colonies, such as Algeria, which sent representatives to the legislature in Paris;[4] areas which were under the direction of the Ministry of Foreign Affairs, (Tunisia and Morocco); regions under the Colonial Ministry with governors-general, such as West Africa and Indo-China; and the mandated territories of Togoland, the Cameroon, and Syria and the Lebanon (p. 439). Most of the French colonies had some degree of self-government and elective councils but little power, for French colonial policy allowed generally less latitude in government to natives than was true, for instance, in the British realm. In the Moslem-peopled provinces of northern Africa and in Indo-China the French in the period between wars had to contend with, and seek to repress or channel, a rising tide of nativist independence sentiment. France's African holdings, or many of them, attracted the avaricious gaze of colony-hungry Mussolini, which tended to weaken budding nationalisms and to strengthen native devotion to France.

It was standard French doctrine that the empire ought to redress France's deficiencies in Europe. Soldiers, for example, recruited in the

---

[4] At least three French colonials have been Cabinet members.

colonies would help to compensate for French inferiority in man-power. Senegalese tribesman did yeoman military service in World War I and natives of Indo-China served in labor battalions. Approximately a tenth part of the French military forces was drawn from the colonies. At Dakar in West Africa, only 1800 miles from Natal in Brazil, at Bizerte in Tunisia, at Djibouti in French Somaliland, and on Camranh Bay in Indo-China, France built naval and airbases of importance in world strategy. "Pacification" of unruly tribesmen in the colonies was a laboratory in which to train French officers and men.

France also profited from the material resources of her colonies, which were embraced within the national tariff system. By means of subsidies to shipping concerns, modest appropriations for roads and railways and other public works the French government undertook to develop the potentialities of the empire; but private capital was rather reluctant to invest in the colonies. In the late thirties France had almost a monopoly on the foreign trade of the empire, buying almost three quarters of the exports and supplying only slightly less of the imports; a third of French exports of manufactured articles found their way to the colonies.

Employment opportunities were made available for a few thousand French army officers, civil administrators, business men, and schoolmasters. But the French have been notoriously averse to settling in colonial possessions; in fact, the early migration to Canada, which was not large, is the only important example of permanent French settlement overseas.

Instead of pressing forward with the assimilation of the colonial masses to France, French policy in the epoch between wars was designed merely to convert native élites into Frenchmen. The French language was taught in the schools, the brightest youths were admitted to secondary schools, and the more promising of them finished their studies in France. Some of the European-educated natives assumed leadership in local nationalist agitations, but more commonly those who were assimilated thought of themselves as superior to the primitive masses.

In French Tropical Africa the traditional obligation of the blacks to perform compulsory labor was lightened and standards of hygiene and sanitation were bettered. Natives were encouraged to diversify their crops and to affiliate with cooperative societies, but individual land ownership was favored over the traditional tribal tenure.

To the colonies something of the flavor of social democracy which pervaded France itself was imparted. Ideals of equality and fraternity

—though not of liberty—obliterated the color line. And native colonial officials were compensated at the same rate as civil servants brought in from France.

Upon the outbreak of war in 1939 the colonies were almost unanimously loyal to France. After the French defeat in 1940 the African empire furnished not alone a theatre for an Allied counter-thrust against the Axis, but part of the manpower with which to deliver the blow. On the other edge of the globe, Japan's predatory penetration of the colony of Indo-China contributed materially to the oncoming of the Great Pacific War.

CHAPTER X

Spain and the Smaller States of Western Europe

The Importance of Spain

SPAIN in the 16th century was Europe's strongest, most feared, and respected nation. But her glory, like Ichabod's departed. For generations Spain had stagnated. It was customary for historians when making a generalization about western Europe to add "except south of the Pyrenees." It has been well said that "Spain, both economically and psychologically, differs so greatly from the other countries of Western Europe that the words of which most history is made—feudalism, autocracy, liberalism, Church, Army, Parliament, trade union and so forth—have quite other meanings there to what they have in France or England." [1]

Symbolical of Spain's impotence and decadence was the ease with which the United States had whipped her in 1898, wresting away most of the few remaining colonies of what in the 16th century had been a magnificent globe-girdling empire. Yet for all her weakness as a military power, Spain still exerted a not inconsiderable cultural and social influence in the lands of Latin America which once belonged to the Spanish crown, and to which Spaniards in appreciable numbers steadily emigrated. Next to English, Spanish is the most widely spoken of western languages.

Spain's location at the nodal point of trade routes in the Mediterranean and western Europe and her Balearic Islands, which command the French seaways to north African colonies, gave her unique strategic importance. And Spanish mineral wealth, in whose exploitation foreign capital was heavily involved, is agreeably varied: iron ore, copper, manganese, sulfur, potash, and mercury. Last of all, Spain's importance in the panorama of very modern Europe derives from the terrible civil war which broke loose in the summer of 1936 and threatened to draw all Europe onto the battlefield.

[1] Gerald Brenan, *The Spanish Labyrinth* (Cambridge, Eng., 1943), p. vii. This is a remarkably dispassionate and learned exposition of modern Spain.

Military Dictatorship

Spain managed to keep out of World War I and all elements in the nation profited materially by neutrality. But after the war, business recession invited a return of the political convulsions which had harried the country early in the 20th century. Strikes, rioting, and attempts on the lives of prominent officials were surface manifestations of deep discontent.

Across the Straits of Gibraltar Spain in 1912 had been allotted a protectorate over a small slice of Morocco. Native tribal chiefs not only declined to recognize Spanish authority but took up arms with the object of winning independence. Subjugation of the protectorate was marked by repeated setbacks for Spanish arms, costly operations, bungling on the part of Spanish commanders, heavy casualties and, in the end, French cooperation to crush the tribesmen. The job was completed in 1926.

The sorry military spectacle of Spain in Morocco, together with industrial worker and peasant risings at home, had in the meantime smoothed the way for a military dictatorship. Inspired by the success of Mussolini in Italy, General Primo de Rivera, whose record as a military man and as a provincial governor was not undistinguished, descended upon Madrid in 1923, and dispersed the existing parliamentary regime which was patterned on that of France and Britain. He had himself made chief of state. Backing him were the well-organized Spanish army officers. For almost seven years the military directed the course of Spanish affairs. King Alphonso XIII, an amiable man, whose prestige had been undermined by the disasters in Morocco, tamely acquiesced in the authoritarian system.

Rivera's rule was in line with the Fascist pattern, as shaped by peculiar Spanish conditions. Denial of fundamental civil liberties and the suppression of constitutional government antagonized liberal Spaniards; restrictions on labor organizations, espionage, and ruthless police repression infuriated wage workers and the down-trodden rustic millions. Bold critics of the dictatorship—and they were many and vehement—were unceremoniously jailed or forced to seek sanctuary abroad. For all Primo's avowed concern for the poverty-stricken Spanish peasants, nothing of significance was done to better their condition of squalor and distress.

Peasant discontent, in fact, lay at the very base of the restlessness and ferment in Spain. Over two thirds of the country's productive land was in the possession of two per cent of the population. Physical conditions rendered much of the surface of Spain totally unsuitable for cultivation. Although seven out of ten Spaniards depended on the soil for their livelihood, the bulk of them had no land of their own, but toiled for absentee landlords at pitifully inadequate wages and without security of employment. Chronically undernourished, this large rural population repeatedly indulged in attacks on landed estates and their leaders clamored for the dispossession of the aristocratic and ecclesiastical proprietors.

As monuments of the Rivera dictatorship there were only splendid automobile roads from the peaks of the Pyrenees to the warm Mediterranean coast, and the ending of the rebellion in Spanish Morocco— that and a swollen national debt together with an increase of republican sentiment. Upon the dictator's resignation and death in 1930, his power passed into less vigorous hands. With the departure of Rivera's rough spirit, republican agitation came out into the open and strikes broke out all over the kingdom. The Great Depression, moreover, reacted disastrously upon the national economy, bringing a slump in prices and widespread unemployment.

The Whirlpool of Politics

Currents and cross currents of Spanish political opinion were many and confusing. But it is possible to single out three broad groupings, Right, Center and Left, each of them with subdivisions, recalling the ancient observation of Strabo that the Iberians could never "put their shields together" for the common good.

. On the Right were the representatives of traditional Spanish conservatism and monarchism, who held (with Hegel) that "all that is is right, and all that is right is." That category embraced the Spanish landed grandees, a large proportion of the churchmen, the more affluent middle-class folk, and most of the top-heavy, expensive military caste, which was accustomed to play at politics—a kind of state within the state. While preferring the maintenance of the status quo, the Right held that if change could not be avoided it should be turned into authoritarian channels.

In the center of the Spanish political situation were men who had taken the liberal principles emanating from the French Revolution as their own. Believers in the supremacy of human reason, they were strongly anti-clerical and for the greater part advocates of republicanism, of which Spain had had a taste in 1873-1874. Spaniards of the lower middle class, intellectuals, professional folk and journalists notably, furnished the spark of the middle-of-the-way republican cause.

On the Left were aligned the elements favorable to far-reaching changes in Spanish institutions, social and economic, as well as political. There were Socialists of varied hues ranging from the revisionist variety of gradual reform, who dominated the trade unions of central Spain and of the mining districts of the north, through Stalinist Communists, who had only slight practical importance before 1936, to a small band of Trotskyite Communists, who thought of Spain as the headquarters for world revolution.

Quite apart from the Marxists of whatever school were the Anarchists and Anarcho-Syndicalists, who were more or less indigenous to Spain. Spokesmen of these ideologies contended that the State and the Church were the roots of all evil and ought to be destroyed and that property ought to be collectivized. Once State, Church, and landlords had been eliminated, a Utopia of plenty and freedom and happiness would prevail, Anarchist doctrine taught.

For the Spanish Anarchist the accent was on unfettered liberty. He bitterly resented authoritarian control of any nature or description. On that point he diverged irreconcilably from the Marxist, who desired a strong state. To achieve the overthrow of the existing society, Anarchism rested its faith in terroristic violence, sabotage, and strikes, culminating in a general strike of all workers. Industrial establishments and landed properties would then be managed by committees of workers.

Strongholds of Anarchism were the traditionally unruly city of Barcelona and the rural areas of southern and eastern Spain. Anarchistically-minded industrial workers, many of whom were peasants in origin and outlook, were unionized in the C. N. T. (*Confederación Nacional del Trabajo*). Rural Anarchism, which was an easily understandable reaction to the harsh conditions of life and labor among the Spanish landless and small-holders, was pointed toward the elimination of the landlord and a minimum of control by the central government. Strikes and physical violence, fomented by Anarchists, were familiar phenomena of modern Spanish history.

Fundamental, too, in the politics of Spain were the ardent strivings for home-rule in Catalonia and among the Basques. Catalonia, in fact, was spoken of as Spain's Irish Question. Having a language and a literature somewhat different from other Spaniards, with peculiar customs and being more hardworking and prosperous than the rest, Catalans for years had agitated for autonomy. A like cry sounded among the Basques. Rivera repressed Catalan aspirations with an iron hand, even forbidding local costumes and folk dances; by so doing he encouraged the growth of republicanism in the region.

Spaniards have a reputation for rugged, intense individualism.

Though many adults were politically inert, those who had opinions on public questions were noted for the obstinacy and fanaticism with which they held to their beliefs and the tenacity with which implacable passions held them. Spaniards tended to act as they thought (or felt) correct, with small concern for expediency and with little or no inclination to compromise. When their frenzy was fully aroused they were capable of shameless atrocities.

The Republican Democracy

Early in 1931 the Spanish dictatorship permitted the holding of elections in the municipalities. The vote went heavily republican— overwhelmingly so in the Catalan metropolis, Barcelona, and in Madrid, the capital. Indeed republican majorities carried forty six of the fifty provincial capitals. It was at once apparent that the alternative to a general political upheaval was the withdrawal of the unpopular king. Prudently enough Alphonso XIII, the unlucky, gave up the crown, as four of his predecessors had done since 1789.

Forthwith the Spanish monarchy was abolished and a Republic proclaimed. At an election for a Cortes, or assembly, to draft a new constitution, middle-class Republicans and their Socialist allies won by a big majority. In the constitution which they adopted, Spain was declared to be a "democratic republic of workers of all kinds," with universal suffrage, men and women alike, and a ministry responsible to a one-house Cortes. Catholicism was no longer the state religion; education was to be taken out of ecclesiastical control; and it was declared lawful for the state to assume ownership of productive property and to dispossess landlords. The first Republican Ministry was composed of middle-of-the-way men and moderate Socialists with Manuel Azaña, hitherto an obscure civil servant but an able and sincere republican and anti-clerical, as Premier.

Laws were promptly passed to implement the text of the Constitution. Public subsidies for the maintenance of religion were curtailed, Church estates were ordered cut up and Church industrial enterprises were closed down; certain monastic orders were banned and schools were to be reorganized under secular auspices.[2] A modest agrarian law authorized the division of grandee properties among peasants, the owners being given partial compensation. The pay of farm laborers was raised and hundreds of professional military men were put on the retired list. Rights of autonomy were voted to Catalonia, which appeased all save the more extreme home-rulers.

---

[2] For fuller treatment of the Catholic Church in Spain see Chap. XV.

While the Cortes was deliberating and making laws, Spain was upset by disturbances and risings engineered by Anarcho-Syndicalists and Socialists, who desired more drastic land legislation. Azaña struck vigorously at the malcontents, arresting many, and rigidly censoring publications. A Republican was heard to describe the new regime as one of "mud, blood, and tears."

That the Republican legislation had failed to satisfy appeared to be shown in a national election of 1933 in which the Left went down to spectacular defeat. Centrist strength increased but the most astonishing gains were made by the Right, whose strength in the Cortes was double that of the Left (though it had received fewer popular votes). That Rightist success was traceable to the peculiarities of the Spanish election law, to dissension between the Republicans of the Left and the Socialists, to the abstention of Anarchists from the polls, and to women voters who resented the anti-clerical laws.

Helpful to the Right was its excellent organization, whose spearhead was the party of Popular Action (*Acción Popular*), led by a youthful journalist, Gil Robles, who was married to a wealthy aristocrat. Staunchly clerical and conservative, Popular Action was dedicated to the defense of the interests of the Catholic Church and to a social order in harmony with Vatican principles.

The Spanish Republic now entered its second phase. Many innovations of the preceding administration touching Church and land issues were nullified by non-enforcement or frankly repealed. The grant of regional liberties to Catalonia was revoked, and querulous critics were severely dealt with. Risings and strikes attested growing discontent with the trends in government. Then, most unwisely three of Robles' henchmen were admitted to the Ministry, and army officers who had been pensioned off were reinstated. Whereupon, in the fall of 1934, the forces of the Left, scenting a Fascist dictatorship, launched general strikes and revolutionary risings.

As the Right saw it, these convulsions, attended as they were by much destruction of property and the loss of some lives, were intended to be the prelude to a Left revolution. On order of General Franco (p. 245), Chief of Staff, troops from Morocco were thrown against the disturbers of the peace, and they crushed the risings ruthlessly. The worst fighting occurred with miners in and around Oviedo. The heroism of their resistance made a marked impression upon Spanish workers and peasants everywhere. Thousands of rebellious spirits were thrown into dungeons and mass shootings removed many leaders. It appeared that Spain had been made safe for conservatism.

Spain's Civil War

Whether Spain, a country in which almost half the population was illiterate, a land of vigorous regional feelings, and economically backward, was ready for the kind of parliamentary democracy that was instituted in the early thirties must be a matter of opinion. In any case, some Rightist elements felt that the revolution had gone too fast and too far, while men of the Left were disgruntled because of the slowness with which the country was being made over. Street disorders, strikes, and murders committed by partisans of both factions, kept politically articulate Spaniards in a mood of constant tension.

Events moved at an accelerated pace after a crucial national election in February, 1936, at which the Left, united in a Popular Front as in France, polled a somewhat heavier vote than the Right, but secured a large majority of the seats in the Cortes. As the election law had operated to favor the Right in 1933, so on this occasion it had benefited the disparate forces of the Left.[3]

In the electioneering, Left orators had promised to liberate the thousands of political prisoners, to enact social welfare and agrarian reform laws, and to suppress Church schools. After the victory at the polls a Popular Front Ministry of Republicans was formed with Azaña, the chief architect of the Republic, at the head. Socialists and Communists declined to take portfolios. Amnesty of the imprisoned, a purge of the inflated army officer personnel, and the restoration of regional autonomy to Catalonia were the first items of business. Once more Spain was swept by a wave of strikes, peasant disorders, shooting affrays by both Right and Left sympathizers, and mounting political passions which seriously challenged the existing order.

At that juncture, with the connivance of Fascist Italy, Spanish Rightists, General Francisco Franco commanding, completed preparations for a coup d'état on a pattern familiar to the chequered history of Spain.

The forty-four year old Franco resembled more the dashing, ambitious general of Spanish tradition than the uncouth, volcanic dictator of contemporary Europe. At heart a monarchist and coming from a comfortable middle class home, Franco had spent almost thirty years in the Spanish military service. He had won his spurs in Moroccan warfare; he had ingratiated himself with the conquered Moors; and

[3] Left parties polled about 4,500,000 votes and obtained 265 seats; the Right including Basque autonomists slightly more than 4,000,000 votes but only 142 seats; the Center under 500,000 votes and 66 seats.

had earned considerable reputation as a philosopher of war. For a time, in 1933, Franco acted as Spanish Chief of Staff and he exploited that office to prepare the army for the approaching revolt against the Republic. After the Popular Front Ministry banished him in 1936 to the Canary Islands, Franco made his way back to Morocco, where he gathered troops together for a revolution which he seems to have thought, or wished, would make the army once more the paramount authority in Spain.

Fighting between Rebels and the government started in July of 1936. In the past, Spanish military insurrections organized by ambitious generals had seldom lasted very long. Within a few months, as a rule, either the insurgents had established a dictatorship or the rebellion ran out. But on this occasion, the appalling civil struggle raged for almost three years, leaving Spain prostrate at its close.

"The Spanish Civil War," writes Professor C. J. H. Hayes, distinguished American historian of nationalism and the war-time Ambassador of the United States at the Court of Franco, "was not a clear-cut struggle between democracy and fascism, or merely a first round in the Second World War. It was certainly not a conflict between 'pure black' and 'pure white'; there were admixtures of grey in each. Neither side was at all homogeneous, and shocking atrocities were committed on both sides." [4]

One reason for the length of the war was the widespread popular support which the duly elected government, called the Loyalists, enlisted. Though trained military personnel was scarce, a formidable and spirited Loyalist army was whipped into shape, and the small Spanish naval forces fought for the government. For another reason, foreign volunteers in small numbers, but many of them experienced, rallied to the cause of the Loyalists and aided them in the fighting. Limited quantities of war materials came from outside sources, chiefly through the agency of Soviet Russia, for which the Loyalists paid in cold cash.

The Basque autonomists, who as conservatives and devout Catholics were as hostile to social radicalism as any of the Right elements, aligned themselves with the Loyalists. And their claim to regional liberties was gratified by the Loyalist government. Thus, the important industrial establishments of the Basque country as well as the factories of Catalonia were available to turn out materials of war for the Loyalists.

On the other side, the Rebel or Nationalist armies under Franco

[4] C. J. H. Hayes, *Wartime Mission in Spain* (New York, 1945), pp. 45-46.

were not first-class fighting stuff. But they were reinforced, probably decisively reinforced, by troops and supplies from Fascist Italy and Nazi Germany.

Loyalist and Rebel alike fought with the kind of savage ferocity that was shown in the religious wars of 16th century France. Neither side expected mercy nor would be content with anything short of unconditional surrender. It was, in literal truth, a life or death struggle in which implacable hatreds and deep regional divisions were greatly intensified. Both sides displayed heroism and endurance which cannot be lightly dismissed with a contemptuous reference to "Red rabble" or "Rebel bullies." So ruinous was the destruction caused by the fighting that League of Nations investigators reported in 1938 that one out of every seven Spaniards was a homeless refugee.

What gave the Spanish ordeal its larger importance were the international implications and complications which are explained elsewhere (Chap. XIX). But it may be noted here that the Great Powers diverged profoundly on the Spanish conflict and that only by a narrow margin was a general European war averted—or better, postponed. While Italy and Germany backed the rebels, Soviet Russia befriended the Loyalists. Britain and France endeavored in all possible ways to isolate the conflagration behind the Pyrenees.

Division of mind within the conglomerate Rebel ranks of Franco interfered somewhat with the prosecution of the fighting, but the diversity and antagonisms inside Loyalism were even more pronounced and damaging. Nevertheless, it seems doubtful whether the Rebels could have won without assistance from Italy and Germany.

At the outbreak of the strife, revolutionary anarchists in Barcelona inaugurated a reign of terror and tried to refashion institutions in keeping with Anarchist doctrine. But troops at the command of the Loyalist regime crushed the Anarchists and forced them underground. Moderate Socialists filled the leading offices in the Loyalist administration throughout the civil war, but the Communists became in fact the driving force of the Loyalist cause. Well-disciplined, willing to follow a conciliatory and opportunistic course, with key positions filled by men trained and directed by Moscow, and above all the controllers of the war supplies shipped in by Soviet Russia, the Communists may fairly be said to have dominated the Loyalist scene until the spring of 1938. Their prestige dwindled after shipments of arms from Russia fell off. Of a Communist dispensation in Spain there seems never to have been a real likelihood. Many a prominent and respected Republican deserted the Loyalist camp in the course of the

fighting. And for no long period of time was it possible for the heterogeneous factions within Loyalism to work together consistently.

Early in 1939 Franco's armies and his German and Italian allies
captured the Loyalist strongholds of Barcelona and Madrid, which
had been besieged since November of 1936. They wiped out isolated
pockets of Republican resistance. Ferocious bombing of defenseless
civilians in populous Loyalist communities by Rebels and their foreign
allies appalled the conscience of civilized mankind and made vivid
the horrors which the ruthless use of aerial weapons had added to
war. After thirty two months of conflict the curtain descended on the
drama of Republican Spain.

When the bell tolled, Spain was in a melancholy plight indeed.
More than a million were dead; cities were shattered; industry was
paralyzed; wide expanses of the countryside were ravaged and
wasted; half the population was starving. Not soon would Spaniards
nor outsiders forget the torments and the destruction that the civil
war entailed. Thousands of Loyalists of all ideological faiths found
havens of refuge in foreign countries, where they talked and conspired
to overthrow the Franco victor when the time should be ripe for action.
Other thousands of Loyalists, unable to escape, were mercilessly
slaughtered by their vindictive adversaries, while much larger numbers were hurled into vile concentration camps for an interminable
stay.

The ironclad dictatorship which Franco set up, backed by a
fanatically nationalistic Falange Party, was largely patterned on the
Italian Fascist model and practice. Regional liberties which had been
accorded to Catalonia and the Basque province were revoked. It was
widely believed that if Europe again became immersed in a general
war the military resources of Spain would be placed at the service of
the Axis. Matters turned out differently. On the outbreak of World
War II Franco published a decree enjoining "strictest neutrality,"
and throughout the war he blew hot and cold according to the fortunes of battle. When the Axis appeared successful he aided it in
various ways without, however, becoming a full belligerent. When
the tide of war turned, Franco turned too—turned to thoughts of self-
preservation. Axis victory would have pleased him mightily.

Republican Portugal

Tiny Portugal rendered assistance to General Franco during the
civil war, less out of her own meager resources than as a funnel
through which the Axis powers poured men and materials into Spain.

By the Portuguese government, victory of the Franco rebels was held to be necessary for security and peace of mind. Officialdom professed to see in Spanish Loyalism nothing other than the Bolshevik bogey.

Since 1910 Portugal had been a republic, whose political history was studded with revolutionary risings—one eager student counted and endeavored to account for twenty one of them—depositions of presidents, and ministerial instability. But in 1926 a military coup installed General Antonio Carmona in power. An admirer of Rivera of Spain and of Mussolini, Carmona proceeded to hammer out a "new state," which in every respect was very old. All real authority reposed in the President and his Prime Minister, civil liberties were proscribed, and economic life was rigidly controlled by the state. Portugal was freed from the turmoil of rebellion, only to live with a noose round its neck.

Totalitarianism reflected the philosophy of the leading Portuguese politician, Professor Oliveria Salazar, who functioned as Premier after 1936. He was much concerned with "the civilizing mission" in Greater Portugal. As the her'tage from the great age of discovery, when bold and enterprising Portuguese navigators had claimed half a world for their king, 20th century Portugal lorded over one of the most extensive of empires, with some 11,000,000 inhabitants.

Vestiges of former Portuguese greatness were found in India, China, the eastern end of Timor, and the strategically placed Azores and Madeiras. But the bulk of the empire lay on either flank of the Dark Continent, Angola and Mozambique, huge holdings, though thinly populated, which Portugal had contrived to retain in spite of the covetous designs of larger European imperialisms.

Few Portuguese chose to settle in the colonies. Emigration, which in fact exceeded all records, was directed primarily to Brazil, once a Portuguese possession and cherishing linguistic and sentimental bonds with the old motherland. Legislation to raise native standards in the colonies and to remove the cruder abuses of exploitation was freely ordained in Lisbon but seldom executed. It was the intent of the government to keep foreigners out of the trade and shipping of the empire. An exception was made in the case of Britain, Portugal's ancient ally and protector, and the source of most of the capital for colonial development.

On Britain's request—and after repeated provocations from Germany—Portugal joined the general war in 1916. As compensation she reclaimed a small parcel of African territory from Germany and was assigned a share of reparations. But those gains seemed incommensurate with the cost of participation. In World War II Portugal, though making gestures of friendship to Great Britain, chose the way of neutrality.

Unique Switzerland

Switzerland is a small land where common sense is common and reasonably acceptable conditions of life make for political stability. The Swiss record for domestic concord is all the more remarkable because of the prevalence of four languages, differences in religion, in historical and cultural background, and in economic status. Yet the Swiss dwell together in amity, a short civil war of 1847 having been quite forgotten. Switzerland was an ideal environment in which to set up the headquarters of the League of Nations.

Something of the Swiss success derived from the governmental system which allowed free expression of the popular will and worked smoothly without frequent crisis. The central government was administered by a federal Council of Seven, chosen by a National Assembly for three years, with not more than one member from any one of the twenty-two cantons. Annually a member of the Council was elected President by the Assembly, and he was not eligible for immediate re-election. The Assembly itself was chosen by proportional representation which assured a membership corresponding closely to the strength of the different parties.

Considerable home-rule was permitted to the Swiss cantons, but national defense was a federal responsibility. Late in the thirties as apprehension over the designs of Nazi Germany grew, fortifications were strengthened and other measures of protection were taken. Switzerland's cherished neutrality was not infringed in World War II.

The Monarchical Democracies of the North

Small countries, contented and prosperous, make little political history unless they are cursed by misfortunes of geography. That was abundantly true of the monarchical democracies of Belgium, the Netherlands, and the Scandinavian trinity of Denmark, Norway, and Sweden. Lying in the path across which the German military chiefs intended to march to quick victory over France, Belgium had fought heroically in World War I and had suffered grievously. The Versailles Treaty awarded her small patches of territory in Europe, an impressive mandate in Africa, and a fair share of reparations, which assisted her in rapid recovery from the war's desolation.

Thereafter Belgium allied itself to France, sent troops on the reparations collection mission into the Ruhr in 1923, and signed the

Locarno Security Pact (p. 430). Apprehensive lest she should be involved in another war, Belgium in 1936 reverted to her traditional status of neutrality. Pledges to protect her independence were made by France and Britain. On another count Belgium's history differed from her small neighbors, for she had a grave linguistic problem. The population in the north spoke Flemish as distinguished from French to the south, and the Flemings insisted upon official rights for their tongue. After no little squabbling and the fall of more than one ministry over the question, Flemish was recognized as the standard language in the schools and public offices of the Flemish zone.[5]

In the main the record of the northern democracies ran parallel in the epoch between the wars. All of them preserved and strengthened the institutions of popular government and seemed immune to competing totalitarian ideologies. A small Fascist agitation in Belgium produced more noise than votes. All alike shared the economic fortunes and vicissitudes of the age and adopted measures intended to remedy social ills and equalize standards of living.

Sweden attracted world-wide attention by her extensive schemes of cooperation, which put her economy midway between the unregulated individualism of the 19th century and the state dominated economies of the totalitarian countries. Sweden, it is true, reeled under the impact of the Great Depression, a third of her industrial workers being forced out of employment, but owing to the tradition of state intervention in economic affairs, to a comprehensive program of government-financed work projects, and to astute monetary policies, Sweden made a quick and spectacular recovery. In 1939 national income was substantially higher than ten years before. The methods by which Sweden regained economic health were acclaimed as a general model for combatting business slumps in the future.

All the northern democracies were warm partisans of the League of Nations so long as that institution gave evidence of vitality in its supreme task of preserving the peace. Statesmen of the three Scandinavian countries met periodically to consider their common interests and mutual safety, but proposals for a solid regional agreement produced no concrete agreement. All these democracies were overrun by Germany in 1940 and yoked to the Nazi war-chariot—all save Sweden which managed to remain precariously neutral by putting her resources, especially her iron ore, at the disposal of Germany and by permitting passage of Nazi troops across her territory.

---

[5] Among Germans in northern Schleswig who passed to Denmark by plebiscite under the Versailles Treaty, there was some agitation for reunion with Germany.

Colonial Empire

Of these states three owned colonial empires: Belgium, Holland, and Denmark. The Danish holdings of Greenland and Iceland (which became virtually independent) had considerable strategic and scenic value, but almost no commercial importance.[6] It was another story with Belgium's Congo colony, eighteen times as large as New York State and with a population about equal to New York's. Before 1908 this vast Congo basin had been the private domain of the Belgian king, but in that year it was transferred to the kingdom. As a newcomer in colonial administration, Belgium learned much from the colonial policies of her Dutch and French neighbors. Many of the worst abuses in the treatment of the natives, which had once made the Congo a by-word for heartlessness and brutality, were abolished.

Belgian administrators, while retaining complete control of government, worked to elevate standards of living of the blacks as the prelude to giving them political rights. Health conditions were improved, rudimentary education was provided chiefly by missionaries, and elementary technical schools were operated by the government. Few white men lived in the Congo, and they were mostly officials. Forests and tropical heat confined white settlement to the capital near the coast and to the rich Katanga copper mines deep in the interior. Congo's foreign trade was largely monopolized by Belgians, a situation that was facilitated by state-subsidized shipping services.

Holland, like Belgium, was definitely a "have" colonial power, her possessions in the West Indies and the East Indies having been acquired by the 17th century. Even before the Americas were discovered the East Indies were fabled as one of the richest of territories and in the 20th century the output of quinine, kapok, rubber, tin, oil, pepper, sugar, and tea gave the Netherlands Indies world importance. For the greater part the capital used to open up the resources originated in Holland and it is estimated that at least five per cent of the population of the homeland depended on the colonies for their livelihood. Foreigners were permitted to carry on trade on equal terms with the Dutch, until Japanese commercial penetration assumed such dimensions that protective legislation was enacted.

Dutch colonial officials in the East Indies showed increasingly that they regarded themselves as trustees, not masters, with an obligation to promote the general welfare of the Indonesians. Living standards and public health were raised, and more and more attention

[6] Spitzbergen was regarded as part of Norway itself, but spots in the Antarctic were claimed as colonies.

was devoted to mass education. In keeping with a pledge made in 1918 educated natives were given a share in governmental affairs. In 1940 the Dutch government promised the archipelago dominion status. In spite of these forward-moving policies—partly as a result of them —rumblings of Indonesian discontent and clamor for freedom were heard. All the wealth of the rich Netherlands Indies fell into Japanese hands in the first months of the Great Pacific War. After the liberation in 1945 Indonesian Nationalists took up arms to prevent the restoration of Dutch sovereignty.

CHAPTER XI

Great Britain

Britain's Parliamentary Structure

BY REASON of an evolutionary process of parliamentary reform reaching over a century of time Great Britain had by 1919 become a political democracy responsive to the adult will. That evolution was marked by successive extensions of the suffrage right to different categories of the community, by adoption of the secret ballot, elimination of property and religious tests for members of parliament, and by the imposition of curbs on the authority of the aristocratic House of Lords.

Not a little of the general excellence of the British government was traceable to the superior civil servant corps, more particularly to the men in the higher administrative posts. Appointed on the basis of open competitive examinations, instead of for "service to the party," this permanent unobtrusive officialdom was noted for high standards of honesty and intelligence, for attachment to the traditional, and reluctance to accept responsibility. British public servants kept aloof from politics, and ministries, regardless of their political complexion, could rely upon loyal performance of duty. Civil service jobs were safe rather than exciting; to them was attached considerable social prestige. On occasion, charges of administrative tyranny and meddlesome grasping bureaucracy echoed in the kingdom, but these were electioneering phrases rather than positive fact. It has been said that no Englishman resents bureaucracy more than the bureaucrat.

Historical evolution has given to the British democracy some more or less unique features, such as a monarch who, though he reigns, does not rule. Standing aloof from party politics the king's essential political office for practical purposes is a symbol of national and imperial unity, the living personification of the kingdom and the realm. His solitary constitutional function is to designate a new prime minister upon the resignation or death of an incumbent.

Supreme executive of the kingdom and of the non self-governing parts of the British realm is the cabinet in London, headed by the prime minister. His tenure of office depends upon the favor of a majority in the popularly elected House of Commons. The authority of the House of Lords, which once was coequal with that of the Commons, has been so whittled down that it is very largely a high-grade debating society of accomplished statesmen and men of practical affairs. At any time the Commons by defeating a major measure sponsored by the ministry can turn the cabinet out of office or compel it to order a general election to ascertain whether the voters desire it to remain in power. In any case a parliamentary election must be held once every five years (except in war time).

If a ministry is defeated in the Commons or loses a national election it has to resign and the king invites the recognized leader of His Majesty's Opposition, or another statesman who is likely to command a majority in the Commons, to organize a cabinet and assume the management of the government, including the initiation of legislation.

By simple majority vote the Commons can alter any law, any precedent, any custom; and in England—or more accurately, the United Kingdom of Great Britain and Northern Ireland—no one holds power of veto. Nor is there any body comparable to the Supreme Court of the United States, possessing the right of judicial review, the right of declaring unconstitutional and invalid any enactment of the sovereign parliament. Britain's scheme of government is not enshrined in any single document like the Constitution of the United States but rests upon a succession of documents ranging from Magna Carta to the most recent parliamentary act of relevance.

British ministries represent parties or coalitions in the Commons. Parties, of which three have significance, Conservative, Labour, and Liberal, are organized in much the same manner and carry on the same kind of activities as American parties. Many British voters are deeply attached to one or another party; others, priding themselves on their independence, and, presumably, therewith the fluidity of their outlook and philosophy on public affairs, vote in accordance with conviction or emotion at a given time. The proportion of voters who actually exercised the franchise right in the era between wars ranged from fifty per cent in 1918 to eighty and six-tenths per cent in 1924. With the enfranchisement of women, which was completed by an act of 1928, the proportion of voters without strong party ties was much greater than before the war. These marginal, unattached voters frequently determined the outcome of ballotings, and to them party managers devoted particular attention.

British parties have their real differences, but they are somewhat less sharp than the enumeration of them may imply. Boiled down and added up, distinctions between parties have been in general differences of tempo, of pace, though that generalization requires reservation as is indicated below. British politics and politicians have small affection as a rule for fundamental ideologies, preferring a pragmatic instead of a strictly ideological approach to public questions. An effective parliamentary regime anywhere demands a willingness to compromise, a general attitude of fairness, and receptivity to opposing viewpoints—that the British have.

In continental countries the inability of public men to work out practical accommodations, for instance, between believers in private enterprise and exponents of state ownership, weakened democratic political institutions and opened the way to authoritarianism.

British politicians have a well-established reputation for ability to work out adjustments between divergent interests and points of view. When public controversy threatened to reach the point where violence might occur, then discussion, debate, and persuasion produced a settlement. In that tradition lies much of the explanation of the stability and solidarity of British politics in contrast to the turbulence in continental popular governments. Willingness to compromise goes far in accounting for the abiding faith in democratic processes and institutions, which permeates all British political parties that have practical importance.

Three Parties and Their Principles

Largest of the British parties in the inter-war years was the Conservative or Unionist, the lineal descendant of the Tories of an older day. While this party attracted followers from all levels of society, "true blue die-hards" among them, the main bulk of its support came from suburban districts and the countryside. Many an independently inclined voter, who, when the political atmosphere was comparatively tranquil, cast his ballot for Labour, moved to the Conservative side when prospects were stormy or uncertain.

The Conservative Party found the past and the present not unpleasing, and viewed the future with the eye of skepticism. It preferred existing ills to risking others, perhaps worse, that far-reaching change might bring. British Conservatism extolled private enterprise, opposed nationalization of the means of production and exchange, and resisted interference by government with the historic liberties of individual Englishmen. That is not to say, however, that Conservatism blindly and intransigently resisted change; it acknowledged, indeed.

that in certain areas of economic affairs state control was desirable and nationally advantageous.

Such social legislation as the Conservatives espoused between the wars was in keeping with time-tested precedents rather than based upon theory or having essentially idealistic purposes in view. As the spokesman of agricultural interests and of large industry, the Conservative Party favored policies which would keep taxes down for these groups. It likewise advocated broader powers for the House of Lords, so that that body might make revisions in laws adopted by the Commons.

After considerable bickering within party ranks, the Conservatives decided that tariff protectionism, at least for industries which faced stiff foreign competition, was necessary for national and imperial well-being. And they consistently pleaded for closer economic bonds with the self-governing Dominions by means of special preferences in trade and in tariffs.

Conservatism preferred the traditional rather than the adventuresome in imperial and foreign affairs. It harped upon the need of a powerful navy and of large fleet facilities—a first-class naval base at Singapore, for example—in order to defend the realm and its interests against any possible challenge. While not unfriendly to limitation of armaments, the Conservatives insisted that reductions should only be effected by agreement with other countries, requiring a comparable scaling down. On the issue of greater home rule for India, Conservatism pursued a cautious, evolutionary line of action.

Caution was writ large, too, on the broad Conservative outlook on diplomatic policies. Its faith in the League of Nations, for instance, as an institution to ensure international security and peace, was less lively than that of the other British parties. Until very late in the 1930's the controlling element in Conservatism frowned upon proposals for diplomatic commitments in Europe beyond those assumed in the Locarno treaties of 1925, (Chap. XVIII), and regarded the Soviet Union and the Third International with deep suspicion. Insofar as any British party was distinctly identified with the diplomacy of preserving peace by concessions to continental dictators in the 1930's, that party was the Conservative, over the shrill protestations of a Conservative minority, headed by Winston Churchill.

Smallest of the British parties was the Liberal, heir of the old Whig Party and for generations the sole competitor of the Conservatives. In the era between the wars Liberalism was riven by personal rivalries and factionalism, and fell from its proud place of prominence in British public affairs. But on two occasions, the Liberals were numerous enough to hold the balance of power in the Commons and the party contained several individual members, such as David Lloyd George, whose influence reached beyond Liberal circles. Historically, Liberalism had drawn its following from the middle-class and manufacturing elements, both management and men, but after World War I it appealed principally to a rather vague independent vote.

The late Archbishop Temple once wrote: "To a considerable extent, though by no means completely, the Conservative and the Labour Parties represent the 'haves' and the 'have-nots' respectively. That is politically unwholesome." Liberals agreed with that analysis and prided themselves on supporting national policies independent of class concerns, subservient neither to the propertied interests on the one side, nor the self-interest of trade unions on the other, seeking rather impartial justice.

Liberals in the main were enthusiasts for individual freedom and for international free trade, in order to keep down the price of goods, compel efficiency in production and as well to promote international tranquillity. They were opposed to monopoly or anything approaching monopoly in industry and shipping. They favored social welfare legislation on housing and schooling, but generally were unsympathetic to state ownership of productive property on the score that nationalization might lower instead of raise general standards of comfort.

Representatives of the Liberal Party never tired of pointing out that existing British electoral laws worked unfairly for their party interests. At the general election of 1929, for example, 512 candidates stood for the Commons under the Liberal emblem, and attracted over twenty-three per cent of the votes, but won in only fifty-nine constituencies, or under ten per cent of all the seats. Therefore Liberalism urged the adoption of proportional representation so that each party would be given seats in proportion to the vote cast for that party in the entire kingdom.

On foreign and imperial policies the larger body of Liberals was closer to the experimentation espoused by Labour than to the sober traditionalism of the Conservatives. Consistently Liberalism backed the League of Nations, and advocated friendly intimacy with Soviet Russia, progressive reduction of armaments, and betterment of native conditions in the overseas possessions.

Britain's second strongest party was Labour, whose roots run into the 1890's, but which attained large importance only after World War I. Its adherents were found very largely in industrial constituencies, particularly in the trade unions, which at their high point in 1920 counted 8,250,000 members. Built up mainly by hard-headed trade-union officials, the Labour Party advocated piece-meal social reform by parliamentary acts, not a swift and fundamental reordering of British society.

The long-term economic objectives of Labour paralleled those of Socialism the world over—state ownership, control, and development of the means of production. Yet Labour would not confiscate private enterprises but rather would purchase them for the state at a reasonable price. It was the Labour contention that state officials could manage production and distribution better than businessmen, and also could regulate prices more advantageously than the law of supply and demand.

Though holding these tenets of Socialism, the Labour Party avoided the Socialist label. It spurned the cut-and-dried ideology, the teachings of class warfare and violent revolution, and the militant materialism and atheism of strait-laced Marxian Socialism. Labour, moreover, stood squarely for democratic processes, the right of the opposition to be heard, and the preservation of civil liberties.[1]

The party was committed to such immediate goals as the extension of social welfare services, broader educational opportunities, and the acquisition by the state of all land, mines, transportation, and power facilities. Labour was not disposed to challenge the monarchical form of government; it was concerned with substance, not shadow.

Labour members in the Commons condemned protective tariffs, taxes on the necessities of existence, and argued for ever heavier levies on incomes that were not personally earned. With regard to the Empire, the party supported measures that would accelerate the preparation of colonial populations to govern themselves. Labour was devoted to the cause of universal peace, willing to adventure and run risks in international affairs, strong in support of the League of Nations. It advocated greater publicity, less secrecy in the conduct of diplomacy, and progressive reduction of armaments. General sympathy with Soviet Russia and a strong tinge of pacifism distinguished the Labour Party.

Compared with its more radical counterparts on the continent

---

[1] A small extremist faction, known as the Independent Labour Party, endorsed orthodox Socialism and agitated for revolutionary changes. Communism, on the Soviet Russian pattern, which Labour combatted energetically, never succeeded in seating more than two members in the Commons. Very likely, if unemployed workers had experienced the acute misery such as their counterparts had undergone after the Napoleonic wars, Communism would have grown to significant proportions. Public provision for the workless cut the ground from under Communism.

of Europe, the British Labour Party was conservative, attuned to British traditions and temperament, and devoted to constitutional procedures. Therein lay part of its success in attracting voters.

Allied to the trade-union interests in the Labour Party was an extraordinary company of British intellectuals, known as the Fabian Society of Socialists, which included such widely-known men of letters as G. B. Shaw, H. G. Wells and a brilliant set of scholars and writers. Outstanding among them were Sidney and Beatrice Webb, who wrote an impressive list of authoritative books on social and economic subjects.

These Fabians, taking their name from the imperial Roman commander, Fabius, who chose to make haste slowly and to conquer by attrition, devoted themselves to ferreting out facts, laying bare specific iniquities and inequities in British society, and to educating voters on the need for positive action by the law-makers. Preferring practical proposals of a reformist character to romantic dreaming, unresponsive to "short cuts to the millenium," the Fabians pleaded for gradual change by parliamentary methods. Sidney Webb hit off the outlook and the faith of the Fabians in his classic phrase "the inevitability of gradualism."

Trade unionism, and the cooperative societies as well, supplied organizing experience and votes for the Labour Party. The Fabian intellectuals furnished the brains, the higher strategy. A few adherents of the party were recruited from men and women of the aristocracy.

Post-War Economic Perplexities

Popular jubilation in Britain over the ending of the war in 1918 and a short-lived industrial boom tended to disguise the monumental economic problems which confronted the nation.

For generations, this little island off the coast of Europe had been the foremost workshop of the world, the world's principal banker, and the world's largest trader. Conditions arising out of four and a half years of grueling war profoundly upset old-established commercial connections, turned industry and workers into military production, and ate away a substantial slice of the country's overseas assets. Moreover, several million tons of British merchant shipping were sunk in the war, the national debt had multiplied twelvefold, and taxes were twice as high as in 1913. Costs of living had soared and four millions of soldiers and sailors restlessly awaited release from the King's service.

Homes fit for heroes to live in, such as had been extravagantly promised while the fighting progressed, were not available. A million Britishers, indeed, would require no homes, for they had perished in the war, three fourths of them from the British Isles. In the later stages of the conflict the government had intervened extensively in the economic affairs of the nation. Prices, wages, and profits were controlled; subsidies were allotted to certain industries; workers had been moved to places where their services were most needed.

Foreign competitors in manufacturing, conspicuously the United States and Japan, had greatly expanded their industrial establishments in the war years and continental customers after the war were in the doldrums. Germany, Britain's largest European market before 1914, was down, and Russia was out. Then, too, protective tariffs and other expedients to safeguard home industry were rising on every hand. British prosperity was fundamentally and inextricably intertwined with the prosperity of almost every other country in the world and only by increasing exports could the island kingdom pay for the huge imports of food and industrial rawstuffs upon which her very existence depended. For a short time after the Armistice the deeper consequences of the war upon British economy were obscured by a season of tinsel prosperity.

The Lloyd George Coalition

In the middle of the war, when Britain's fortunes appeared dark, the management of affairs had been assumed by a coalition ministry with David Lloyd George in the Prime Minister's office. This remarkable man who, by his personality, energy, and concern for the ordinary Britisher had risen from the obscurity of the Welsh countryside to the headship of the British realm, had led the country to victory.

Khaki election

In alliance with his Conservative colleagues in the coalition ministry, Lloyd George called for a parliamentary election. Held in December, 1918, while the electorate was still intoxicated by the triumph over the enemy or rendered apathetic by the horrors and trials of the war, the balloting resulted in an overwhelming victory for the coalition. By all odds the largest bloc of ministerial supporters were Conservatives, and, in the language of one British writer, it was "the wealthiest, the least intelligent, and the least representative House of Commons since Waterloo." Lloyd George held on to the prime ministership.

In the course of the electioneering, coalition orators had promised to make Germany pay the whole cost of the war. They also promised to carry out extensive social reforms. "Inhuman conditions and wretchedness must surrender like the German fleet," declared the

Prime Minister. While Lloyd George went off to Paris to arrange the peace, the Commons grappled with the grim tasks of demobilization and of economic reconstruction.

Not much preparation had been made for returning service men to civilian pursuits. Mutinies here and there among the troops spurred the authorities to rapid demobilization at the same time that munitions factory workers were being discharged. All who could not find work were eligible for financial assistance from the state, but throughout 1919 and well into the following year, few actually applied. As was the case in the world generally, business in Britain was feverishly active. Demand for consumer goods and capital goods at home and abroad, which had been pent up during the war, resulted in an unequalled export trade, rising prices, high wages, and an orgy of spending and speculation. The wheels of British industry were set humming.

It was the autumn of 1920 before the fierce energies of the postwar boom had spent themselves. In the meantime the Ministry had not devoted much consideration to social welfare measures, save for limited public assistance in the building of homes and legislation to consolidate the gains in agricultural production that had been made during the war.

Just as the British after-war boom reflected general world conditions, so did the heavy slump that followed—the worst on record to that time. Foreign trade and domestic demand for goods slackened, and correspondingly the number of the unemployed mounted. By the end of 1920 some 700,000 Britishers were out of work; 1921 was a year of unrelieved economic gloom and in the middle of 1922 about 2,000,000 were without employment.

A national unemployment insurance system, which had been inaugurated in a few selected industries before the war, was broadened (1921) to cover almost all workers. But since the resources of the fund were quite inadequate to care for the unemployed, the state was obliged to provide supplements, called "doles." Cuts in wages were made generally. The unemployed or discontented were urged to emigrate to the Dominions, which were romantically portrayed in terms of jobs for everyone, joyous outdoor living, no squalid streets or belching chimneys. Actually, while there were opportunities for ambitious agricultural settlers overseas, the chances for urban employment were limited, and the impulse to leave the homeland was less active than in the 19th century.

Rapidly the war-time measures for controlling economic affairs were given up, so that state authority in this area of life was not much greater than in 1913. At the same time, a Safeguarding of Industries Act granted tariff protection to establishments connected with national defense, and other industries in which it could be shown that foreign competition was inequitable. That act, along with duties imposed on certain classes of goods during the war, signified that Great Britain was drifting away from her free-trade moorings. Rates of taxation were raised to new highs in 1921, and Conservatives clamored for governmental economy, for reductions in expenditures for domestic purpose and for the empire.

Certain economies, not large, were made in the outlays for social welfare services and for national and imperial defense, particularly by reason of limitations on the fleet agreed to at the Washington Conference (Chap. XVIII). But that saving was counterbalanced by expensive military operations in Russia and the Middle East and costly repression of revolutionary ferment in Ireland. Arrangements were, however, completed for the establishment of a Free State in southern and central Ireland, which would have all the rights and privileges of a Dominion (Chap. XII). That settlement of the Irish Question antagonized part of Lloyd George's parliamentary coalition, and when it appeared that his Grecophile course in the Near East might involve war with Turkey, a majority of Conservatives indicated that they would no longer march with the "Wizard of Wales." He had no alternative but to resign. The astute Conservative party tactician, Bonar Law, Canadian-born and the first "colonial" to serve as Prime Minister, ruled in his stead.

Conservative Rule

For the national election of 1922 which followed the Conservatives adopted the slogan of "tranquillity"; "normalcy" was the American equivalent. They fought energetically against the Labour Party, for Liberalism was riven by feuds. A Conservative victory at the polls in 1922 confirmed Bonar Law in the prime ministership, but feeble health compelled him to resign after a few months in favor of Stanley Baldwin.

Of Baldwin, it was known that he had a reputation as a safe, enlightened, and successful industrialist, that his whole-souled patriotism was deep-rooted in love of the English countryside, that he had, as Chancellor of the Exchequer, arranged a treaty on war debts with the United States, and that he was an ardent believer in protective tariffs as one means of starting the wheels of idle British factories and giving employment to idle hands. This heavy set, square-jawed, slow-thinking, pipe-smoking product of heavy industry and sober politics aptly represented the Britisher—John Bull—of cartoon and proverb. No other British public man in the inter-war years more faithfully embodied the strengths and the frailties of Conservatism than honest, uninspired Stanley Baldwin, who was thrice prime minister.

It was the judgment of the Baldwin Ministry that a full program of tariff protection was necessary to set British industry and employment aright. Having no mandate from the electorate to enact legislation of that sort, Baldwin dissolved the Commons and waged an election in 1923 on the tariff question. That decision was gleefully welcomed by Liberalism, the historic champion of free trade, an issue on which it had administered a terrific defeat to the Conservatives in 1906. Labour, likewise, upheld the cause of free trade and preferred alternative remedies to cure unemployment. As more than once before, the merits and disadvantages of free trade and protection were paraded before the British electorate.

Baldwin was badly beaten and exponents of free trade were returned to Parliament in decisive majority, which made it plain that the voters were not convinced that tariff protection would restore prosperity. None of the three parties won a majority of the seats, but the Conservative Party was still the strongest. Liberal leaders, however, let it be known that they preferred, in an experimental sort of way, a Labour Ministry to a Conservative one. And so, in 1924, the Labour Party, though it held less than a third of the seats in the House, assumed for the first time the management of Britain and the British realm.

The Labour Interlude

The Labour Party chief, the Scotsman, Ramsay MacDonald, who was more the eloquent intellectual than the hard-headed, practical leader of trade unionists, moved into No. 10 Downing Street. This man who had opposed World War I from first to last also took charge of the British Foreign Office. Lacking a party majority in the Commons, the MacDonald Ministry had, perforce, to pursue a middle-of-the way course and it lasted less than a year.

On the home front, many of the policies of the preceding administration were amplified by the MacDonald Ministry. State aid for housing projects, for example, was increased and public grants to those unable to earn their daily bread were enlarged, but duties on some classes of imports were lowered. More impressive was the MacDonald achievement in external relations. The Prime Minister's talent for reconciling conflicting viewpoints assisted significantly, for instance, in securing the adoption of the Dawes Plan on reparations (p. 427).

For the purpose of encouraging British exports, the Labour Ministry negotiated a trade treaty with Soviet Russia, with which diplomatic relations, severed after the Bolshevik Revolution, had just been restored. It was agreed that the British government would guarantee a loan to Moscow to cover exports; the Bolsheviks in turn promised not to spread their revolutionary propaganda in Great Britain. Britishers who distrusted Russia for one reason or another protested heatedly against the treaty with the Soviets. Matters came to a head after a British Communist paper, hitherto obscure, appealed to soldiers to mutiny rather than shoot down strikers if they were called upon to do so and the Labour Ministry declined to prosecute the editor. Liberals in the Commons then withdrew their support from the Ministry. MacDonald had to order another national election, the third in two years.

As the electioneering was nearing its close, a letter was published in the British press, allegedly written by Zinoviev, the head of Moscow's Third International, summoning British Communists, a tiny minority, to prepare plans to overthrow the existing order by revolutionary violence on the Bolshevik model. Whether authentic or manufactured, the Zinoviev letter—with its threat to established British institutions—frightened some voters. It also helped to swell the totals of the Conservative candidates for Parliament, who had spent themselves in condemning Soviet Communism and its Socialist variants. Conservative orators soft-pedalled the politically dangerous protectionist issue in the campaign, promised tranquillity and stability and rigid economy. When the returns were in, their party had won an overwhelming majority in the Commons. The short Labour interlude was over, but the very fact that this young working class party had directed British public affairs at all in this period was a landmark in the homeland of representative government.

Tory Democracy—New Style

Unlike preceding cabinets, the Conservative Ministry, which took office in 1924, lived out the constitutionally allotted span of five years. Stanley Baldwin, Prime Minister a second time, liked to think of himself as the executor of the legacy of progressive social reform bequeathed to his party by Benjamin Disraeli in the 19th century. Like Disraeli, he accented the importance of the over-seas parts of the British realm for the United Kingdom.

In charge of public finance, as Chancellor of the Exchequer, was Winston Churchill, who after a variety of party experiences and three recent defeats for the Commons, had recently returned to the

Conservative fold. A hard-working and experienced Minister, with a flair for the dramatic, Churchill was a brilliant opportunist in politics, which is one of the hallmarks of the successful politician in a government responsible to the public will. Consistency, some one has said, is the hobgoblin of small minds, and, it may be added, if rigorously adhered to, consistency is likely to prove fatal to a public man in a democratically-ruled community.

Churchill, though sure, for example, that free trade was economically sound, readily submerged his personal convictions to the dominant view of the Conservative Party. Year by year, as Chancellor of the Exchequer, he sponsored measures which protected certain industries from foreign competition, without, however, pressing for thoroughgoing tariff reform. Much was said and little was done about safeguarding British agriculture, which had expanded during the war, with the result that the acreage given over to raising of crops steadily declined. Britain produced only about a third of her food requirements. Even so, British agriculture continued to be a substantial "industry," engaging well over a million workers, and keeping alive British traditions of skill in farming. Therefore it was possible for agricultural output to be rapidly increased when conditions demanded it—after the coming of war in 1939.

Under Churchill's guidance Britain returned (1925) to the gold standard on the basis of pre-1914 parity with the American dollar with the twin object of restoring London to its historic position as the world's first banker and of enabling the proud pound to look the dollar squarely in the eye. It was urged by a tepid opposition that the restoration of the gold standard was premature in view of the devaluation of currencies in European countries. In the light of the later record, the move must be set down as a piece of folly.

Throughout this period of the Conservative best, the tragedy of British industrial unemployment persisted, the army of workless holding rather steadily at about a million, or approximately double that of the years before the war. Since the national unemployment insurance fund was incapable of providing the necessities of life for the jobless, the state made up the deficit by borrowing on its own credit.

Employment conditions were worst in the "distressed areas" where production had shot up in response to war requirements, or where industries relied heavily upon exports, notably coal mining, shipping, shipbuilding, and cotton textiles. Critics of management in these types of business assigned British inability to compete with foreign concerns to obsolete equipment, unadaptability to changing world conditions, and to the uninspired character of merchandising techniques. Other critics ascribed much of the industrial malaise to trade-union resistance to innovations in production methods. Geographically, the "distressed areas" were located in northern England, the cities of Scotland, and, most serious of all, in Wales.

The British coal industry, which in the inter-war era came to be called the "black cancer" in the economic mechanism, was a perennial problem and gave rise in 1926 to the most acute industrial conflict in British history. Historically one of the mainstays of the export trade, British coal was confronted by special difficulties after the war, due to greater output and greater efficiency of production in the Ruhr valley and Poland, more efficient consumption of coal in steam engines, and the growing competition of oil as fuel. In the main, management of the British collieries was wanting in enterprise and competence.

For over a century a tradition of ill will between management and men had been built up. Miners of one generation in every family and village handed down memories of bitter disputes to the next. It was said indeed that British miners spent their leisure hours discussing three eternal themes: the dangers of the pit, the iniquities of mine owners, and the blessings that would flow from state ownership of the industry. Neither government subsidies nor remedies proposed by parliamentary investigations could solve the coal problem. MINE STRIKE

When, in 1926, owners cut wages, the miners went on strike. To their side, in a sympathetic strike, rallied about half of all organized British workers. Transportation facilities and several essential industries were paralyzed. Stoppage of work on this scale in the thickly-peopled British Isles created an extremely grave situation. Yet throughout the crisis all parties displayed a remarkably calm and sober spirit. Inexperienced hands volunteered to operate trains and the like, which was not without amusing by-products; the radio, very much of a novelty, attained popularity as a substitute for newspapers.

After nine unforgettable days the sympathetic strike collapsed, wrecked on the solid rock of British opinion. But the discipline and the solidarity of the striking trade unionists surprised friend and foe alike. To prevent the recurrence of a general industrial tie-up, Parliament in 1927 passed a law which declared a sympathetic strike illegal and imposed other limitations on the activity of unions—a law which stood on the statute books until 1946. As for the striking mine-workers, they held out until November of 1926, and then returned to the pits on terms offered by the proprietors. One solution of the coal problem, favored by the Labour Party and hotly debated in the inter-war years, was the nationalization of the mines. A hesitant, first step in that direction was taken by a Conservative-dominated Ministry in 1937. Legislation to replace private by state ownership was adopted in 1946, provision being made for reasonable compensation to the owners.

Although certain parts of British industry and trade were in the doldrums, other sections were busy to the point of prosperity. That was true of establishments which catered primarily to the home market or which displayed ingenuity and enterprise in meeting foreign competition and new economic conditions and appetites. In Britain as on the continent alert business men paid to American industry the sincerest form of flattery—imitation. By applying mass production methods, scientific research, improving techniques of salesmanship, and in general using "more brains," British concerns which were engaged in the manufacture of such goods as chemicals, tinplate, electrical goods, rayon yarn, staple fiber, and motorcars were able to enlarge output and provide new employment opportunities. Industrial activity in southern England, including the London area, contrasted sharply with the chronic unemployment in the distressed areas of the north.

Tory democracy cherished traditions of social reform and practiced them. State funds were made available for inexpensive housing, the pension laws for orphans, widows, and old age were liberalized, and the administration of local government was drastically overhauled. In a similar vein, the right to vote was extended in 1928 to women over twenty one on the same terms as men, which meant that female voters now outnumbered the men by some 2,000,000. Social welfare measures involved heavier taxes, and nullified the Conservative pledges of economy that had been made to the nation.

In the sphere of foreign affairs, the second Baldwin Ministry, which preferred conventional patriotism to the imaginative cosmopolitanism of Labour, could take pride in the making of the Locarno Treaty (Chap. XVIII) and took no little satisfaction over the rupture of diplomatic ties with Soviet Russia (1927). That decision was made after it was shown that Russians who were in Britain on commercial errands were engaged in fact in disseminating Bolshevik propaganda among the economically distressed. The "proof" of subversive activities was acceptable to those who desired to believe it true. With the United States, relations deteriorated because of the failure to come to an understanding on further naval limitation. The constitutional status of the Dominions with respect to the motherland was given new and important definition (Chap. XII).

By 1929 the term of the Parliament had run out, and accordingly a general election was conducted. The Baldwin Ministry faced the electorate without having fulfilled its promises of cutting down public expenditures and of creating full employment. It appealed for a renewal of its tenure on a platform of "safety-first," economy, and tariff reform. Liberals offered the voters an elaborate public works program and freer trade as the way of restoring general prosperity. The Labour Party had an even bolder scheme of public works, proposed the nationalization of certain industries, and ridiculed the Conservative thesis that prosperity could be purchased by public economy. It dwelt upon the intimate connection between international prosperity and security and Britain's own economic well-being.

Voters sent 289 Labourites to the Commons, 259 Conservatives, and 58 Liberals, so that for the first time Labour held more seats than its competitors. But, as in 1924, it did not command an independent majority. Baldwin at once resigned, MacDonald became Prime Minister a second time, and again his administration was dependent upon the good-will of the Liberals.

Labour Again

As with the first MacDonald Ministry the record of Labour in foreign affairs outshone its achievement on the domestic front, for Liberal support was more assured in the international field than at home. A readjustment of the German reparations problem; another international agreement on naval disarmament; the restoration of ordinary diplomatic relations with Soviet Russia; and the reassertion of the autonomy of the Dominions—all stand to the credit of Labour in its two year tenure of office.

It was the misfortune of the Labour Ministry that its assumption of office coincided closely with the financial debacle on Wall Street and the beginning of the Great Depression (Chap. XVIII). A party which had painted for the electorate a glowing picture of the manner in which it would restore prosperity watched the barometer of unemployment rise beyond all precedent; by the end of 1930, 2,500,000 British workers could not earn their daily bread, and the figure later swelled to nearly 3,000,000. As foreign trade declined, as the roll of the jobless lengthened, the state was obliged to borrow heavily, as previously had been done, in order to provide food and clothing and shelter for the unemployed.

Additional taxes were levied, and duties to safeguard certain industries were abolished, though not without loud protest from management and men whose livelihood was thereby adversely affected. Indeed, unequalled agitation for tariff protection, under the guise of "Empire Free Trade," arose from various strata of British society, most vigorously in the London mass-consumption newspapers.

In the summer of 1931 it was disclosed that the national budget for the year would show a $600,000,000 deficit. That announcement caused frightened foreign investors with loans in London to recall their funds and precipitated a grave financial crisis. Large sections of the British public feared that the very foundations of the national welfare were in jeopardy. How possibly might the financial obstacle be hurdled? How might the budget be brought into balance? By increasing taxation, said the bulk of the Labour Party leaders. By cutting down state expenditures for unemployment relief and the like, their Conservative opponents retorted.

Over a proposal to bring the budget into balance by reducing the appropriations for the unemployed, the MacDonald Labour Cabinet split asunder. The Prime Minister, who favored reduction, and a handful of his followers seceded from the Labour Party, and aligned themselves with representatives of Conservatism and Liberalism to form an all-party coalition or National Ministry. Never in peacetime was the inherent flexibility and elasticity of the British instrument of government more amply demonstrated.

The Record of the National Ministry

It was the assignment of the all-party Ministry to restore public confidence, to balance the budget, and to deal broadly with the national economic emergency. These tasks it accomplished. New or increased taxes were imposed, the salaries of public servants were cut by ten per cent, and the benefits to the unemployed were equally reduced. By suspending the gold standard, thus making British manufactures cheaper to foreign customers, exports were modestly encouraged. Whatever basis there may have been for the fear that the monetary system of Britain would collapse and that the nation would undergo the harrowing currency experiences of Germany in 1923 was swiftly dissipated.

While the country was still in a mood of panic the Ministry decided (October, 1931) to seek a vote of confidence from the electorate. For it was the judgment of the Conservatives that they could win a sweeping victory against the discredited Labourites, to whose administration was imputed responsibility for the financial plight. Without presenting a specific blueprint on its future policies, the National Ministry asked the voters to confirm its authority.

The outcome of the balloting surprised even the most sanguine Conservative prophets, for the opposition won less than a tenth of the seats in the Commons. Supporters of the National Ministry formed an almost unprecedented majority, and most of the majority was staunchly Conservative. Had the distribution of seats been proportional to the popular vote, as the Liberals desired, the disparity between opposition forces and the ministerialists would have been much less pronounced. MacDonald retained the prime ministership, but Baldwin held the reins until June, 1935, when he became Prime Minister in name as in fact. For the rest, the National Ministry was selected almost wholly from Conservative ranks.

Forthwith Britain embarked upon an essentially nationalist and imperialist program for combatting the ravages of the world depression with accent on tariff protection. Emergency tariff acts formed the merest preface to full-bodied protection which was adopted in 1932. Toward that "fiscal revolution" Britain, the pioneer in free trade, had been moving—not to be sure in a straight line—ever since 1914. The decisive tariff measures were piloted through Parliament by the Treasury chief, Neville Chamberlain, whose father, Joseph Chamberlain, had vigorously, though vainly, championed tariff reform, thirty years before.

The stock arguments for tariffs were once more thoroughly rehearsed. It was claimed that protection would reduce the excess of British imports over exports; add to the state revenue; defend home industry and the jobs of workmen; bind the members of the British realm with tighter economic bonds; and, of peculiar persuasiveness at the time, would enable the government to bargain with other nations for reciprocal tariff reductions. In its final form, the tariff legislation laid a duty on about half of all imported articles, except foodstuffs and goods produced in the Dominions. Subsequently, importation of agricultural products was regulated by a system of quotas.

All this prepared the way for an Imperial Conference at Ottawa, held in the summer of 1932, to establish special economic arrangements among the countries of the British crown. Shortly before the Ottawa parley the major Dominions had raised their tariffs and thus improved their positions for bargaining with the motherland. At Ottawa, in exchange for Dominion agreements to lower some duties, Great Britain obligated herself not to modify tariff laws for five years without Dominion concurrence. Dominion products, moreover, would be admitted to the motherland without duty. And the non-self-governing British colonies, which hitherto had kept the door wide open to commerce of all countries without discrimination, placed tariffs on imports, but granted special preferences to goods coming from the United Kingdom or the Dominions.

All in all, a sort of Pan-Britannic customs union, intended by its architects to benefit primarily the material welfare of the subjects of the British crown everywhere, had been fashioned. But the British realm was not a closed commercial monopoly. It could not be in the nature of things, for some essential goods were not produced in sufficient quantities within the customs union and in other lines there were exportable surpluses. It was formally asserted at Ottawa that the anticipated rise in the purchasing power of the British peoples would in time profit the trade of other nations.

But, on balance, by intensifying the evils of economic nationalism, British protectionism, however much it may have seemed desirable from the standpoint of inter-empire exchange, worsened world economic and political conditions. John Bull's somersault from comparative free trade to protectionism encouraged other countries to raise fresh barriers to international trade, just as American tariffs had earlier done.

Aside from the tariff revolution, the MacDonald-Baldwin coalition extended the program of slum clearance on an impressive scale; it granted small subsidies to companies which operated "tramp" steamers; and it carried through a vast debt conversion scheme whereby the interest on state loans was scaled down and a large saving in the annual appropriation for debt service was realized. Further savings were made by stopping payments to the United States on war debts, which British opinion justified on the score that Britain was no longer being paid by debtors on the continent.

Legislation on unemployment relief was revised and an improvement in national finance led the Ministry in 1935 to restore the cut in the benefits for the jobless and in salaries of civil servants. Unemployment figures, after reaching a peak in January of 1933, dropped off, being aided by the world economic recovery which got underway in that year. Naturally the Conservatives claimed that the measures which they had enacted were responsible for the betterment in national trade and finances. But their critics, especially those who were wedded to the free-trade philosophy, insistently argued that the improvement would have been ever greater if the protectionist heresies had not been allowed to poison British public policy.

Even shriller were the ceaseless indictments of the National Ministry's conduct of British foreign affairs. Most resolute and vigorous of the critics was Winston Churchill, who, surveying the course of events in 1938, described the preceding five years as "five years of futile good intentions, five years of eager search for the line of least resistance, five years of uninterrupted retreat of British power, five years of neglect of our air defences." [2] Instead of giving Europe courageous and resourceful leadership, such as was so urgently needed at a time when international relations were deteriorating and the specter of a recurrence of general war was growing more menacing, the National Ministry chose a passive and rather pacific course.

Instead of resisting the Japanese seizure of Manchuria, instead of pressing energetically for armament limitation, instead of checking the military resurgence of Germany under the driving force of National Socialism, the MacDonald-Baldwin Cabinet pursued the phantom of cautious Fabianism and even entered into a bargain with Nazi Germany on seapower which cancelled clauses in the Versailles Treaty. For believers in the principle of collective security, as represented in the League of Nations, Britain's supine diplomacy spelled inevitable and not unmerited disaster. And the wavering course in the Ethiopian crisis (p. 476) lent support to the strictures of the opposition. Concessions to Hindu Nationalism in an Indian Government Act of 1935 (Chap. XII) and a disagreeable tariff feud with the Irish Free State were the principal items in the imperial record of the period.

Shortly after the outbreak of the Ethiopian War in 1935 and just after an unofficial ballot had shown a preponderance of British sentiment in favor of collective international action to enforce peace, Parliament was dissolved and a general election was quickly conducted. At the moment the Baldwin Ministry was taking a surprisingly firm stand against Italy in the Ethiopian controversy. The assumption that this strong policy would be continued, undoubtedly swayed opinion in a Conservative direction. A hesitant Conservative pledge to build up the national armaments likewise carried weight with some voters, who were alarmed by the obvious growth of Germany's capacity for war and the beclouded international sky.

When the ballots were in—November, 1935—the Conservatives commanded another huge majority. This Parliament, as matters turned out, was to legislate for Britain and the realm until 1945.

Early in 1936, King George V, who had reigned since 1910, died. His son and successor, Prince Edward of Wales, adopted the title of Edward VIII. But he was never crowned. Rather than give up an American woman, Wallis Simpson, who had been twice divorced and

[2] Philip Guedalla, *Mr. Churchill* (New York, 1942), p. 272.

whom he intended to marry, Edward gave up all claims to the British throne. The scepter passed to his brother, who in May, 1937, was crowned as George VI with ancient pomp. By the unaccustomed vigor that he displayed in handling the ticklish transaction of Edward VIII's abdication, Prime Minister Baldwin somewhat revived his dwindling prestige.

Neville Chamberlain, Prime Minister

A matter of days after the coronation festivities, Baldwin at the age of seventy retired from No. 10 Downing Street in favor of his principal Conservative colleague in the Cabinet, Neville Chamberlain. A member of the aristocracy of commerce like Baldwin, the new Prime Minister, who had served as Minister of Health and as Chancellor of the Exchequer, shared his former chief's outlook on both domestic and foreign affairs There was small reason to suppose that domestic or foreign policies would be given a different orientation.

In the meantime the darkening international scene was producing a change in mood in the island kingdom. As early as 1935 Great Britain started to build up her defense services. Each fresh international crisis quickened British dread of the future and was followed by additional outlays for armament. Particular consideration was given to airpower and to contrivances to protect the United Kingdom and the life-giving shipping services against aerial attack.

Military and naval preparedness necessitated constant increases in British taxation and in public borrowing. With little protest, less as time progressed, the nation made the financial sacrifices that were required to provide teeth for British diplomacy or to fight if national and imperial interests and values were sufficiently endangered.

In the late thirties, international politics, it is not too much to say, shaped and colored British public life and thought. Yet at home there was steady improvement in economic conditions. Business activity increased in keeping with the rearmament program; the output of heavy industry and shipping surpassed all earlier levels, and, though the number of unemployed workers fluctuated, the general trend was downward. Disorderly political conditions on the continent and in Asia reacted injuriously upon Britain's foreign trade, but sales to Ireland rose after the six-year tariff war was ended. Exports to the United States also increased after a mutually advantageous trade agreement was negotiated (1938), requiring each country to lower tariffs on certain exports of the other.

As of 1938 just under half of Britain's foreign trade was carried on with other lands of the crown. But Britain was the best customer of thirty-one different countries and a valuable customer of ten more. Her imports, which consisted very largely of food—meat, dairy products, and grain in the lead—and industrial rawstuffs, almost equalled in value the imports of the next two largest importing countries, Germany and the United States. For goods brought in, Britain paid chiefly with exports of manufactured or partly manufactured articles, mainly cotton textiles, machinery, iron and steel, and coal. Funds derived from foreign investments, shipping—the British merchant tonnage was a quarter of the world's total—and other services rendered to foreigners also helped to pay for imports.

More and more, the authority of the state was extended over British economic affairs. By a series of acts the government took charge of foreign trade and finance, set up boards to market home-grown foodstuffs, and fostered monopolies in the iron and steel and cotton industries. A law of 1937 pointed toward the eventual state ownership of the coal mines. This trend toward "national capitalism" accorded with the wishes of the Labour Party and was brought about with the silent acquiescence, if not the hearty applause, of the British propertied elements.

In foreign policy the Chamberlain Ministry hewed close to the conventional and cautious lines of the Baldwin Cabinet. The central and guiding principle in foreign affairs was the appeasement of dissatisfied Germany and Italy by concessions. Until March of 1939, Chamberlain seems to have thought that course was the surest way to preserve Europe and the world from another catastrophic war. Since Britain's livelihood depended to a high degree upon a tranquil, orderly world, she was singularly concerned to maintain peace. British diplomatic history in the crucial second half of the 1930's is described in another connection (Chap. XIX).

Britain as a Social Service State

In the foregoing survey of Britain between the wars repeated reference has been made to legislation to improve the standards of living of the wage worker or to safeguard him against want due to forces beyond his control. Enactment of laws of that character was not the monopoly of a particular political party but was the handiwork of Conservative, Labour, and Coalition Ministries alike, in harmony with feelings embedded in the British consciousness of the age.

It is quite possible that the historian of a century hence will look upon Britain's record as a social service state as the most notable facet of British history of the inter-war years. What Britain attempted exerted an influence on other industrialized countries, not least the

United States. It is desirable, therefore, to summarize, and at some points to amplify, the story of British social legislation of the twenties and thirties.

Before World War I the tide of socializing legislation was rising in Britain. Laws had been passed that provided old age pensions and national health insurance; beginnings had also been made in self-sustaining, compulsory unemployment insurance. State intervention in economic affairs during the war helped to spread belief in the virtues of state action, and right after the war the unemployment insurance program was extended to cover all wage workers, except those engaged in agriculture or household service. But, owing to the chronically large volume of unemployment in the inter-war period, the insurance reserves were inadequate to meet the needs of the workless, so that the state stepped in and provided unemployment benefits or "doles," as this assistance was called. Without such relief the distressed areas of Britain would almost certainly have been the scene of violent social upheaval.

Other measures for social welfare were put into force. Old-age and widows' pensions, for example, were enlarged; children were given better schooling facilities and underprivileged children were fed and medically looked after. Very substantial improvements were made in British housing. In the twenty years between wars more than 4,250,000 dwellings were built or about half as many as existed in 1919, while the population of the United Kingdom increased by only ten per cent. The new homes were more comfortable, brighter, and much more easy to take care of than older ones.

Agencies of the state had an important part in providing these new living quarters. Almost a third of them were financed by local governments and another tenth by private companies with public help; the rest were privately built. Speaking broadly, British public housing projects were intended for the underprivileged. Private concerns constructed homes for the higher income families. The National Ministry, in 1933, launched a five year plan to replace 300,000 slum quarters with better dwellings; this program was practically finished when World War II began. Housing projects not only meant better health and more contentment, but they also furnished employment to many kinds of workers, which made the Great Depression less harrowing in Great Britain than in some other countries.

Enemy action and ordinary deterioration took heavy toll of British urban housing during World War II, but plans on an ambitious scale were drawn up for a resumption of construction when hostilities ceased. For greater London and its surroundings, architects designed a gigantic and comprehensive fifty-year rebuilding plan at the very time that the German Luftwaffe was busily performing its destructive work.

All in all, British social laws of the 20th century assured industrial workers of food, shelter, and treatment in case of sickness. No country surpassed, and hardly any rivalled, Britain in making provision for basic human needs due to the interruption of earnings, however caused.

A noteworthy British institution, outside the scope of government, which helped to hold steady the living standards of the British wage workers was the cooperative organizations for the sale of goods and the provision of credit. Started in 1844, the British cooperatives developed into a giant business resembling in some respects the chain stores and the retail outlets of mail order houses in the United States. Several thousand retail cooperative stores handled a large part of the grocery, meat and milk trade of the United Kingdom in the era between the wars. They had an important share, too, in the distribution of clothing, furniture, hardware, and electrical contrivances.

The central object of the consumers' cooperatives was to reduce the cost of goods by the elimination of the middleman's profit. Consumers themselves, of course, owned the stores. Prices as a rule were the same as in privately-owned stores, but profits were returned to each purchaser as dividends on the gross value of the commodities he bought.

As another means of paring down the cost of living, a central cooperative wholesale society was organized to serve as buyer and distributor of goods to cooperative retail shops. This society operated dairies, canneries, meat-packing plants, and factories for the manufacture of goods of various kinds. Also on a cooperative basis were a substantial banking system, an insurance company, a printing firm, and even a travel agency.

British cooperatives of one sort and another enrolled almost 9,000,000 members (1944). The success of the cooperatives persuaded many a Britisher that he would be materially better off if all the means of production and distribution were owned and managed collectively or by the state, rather than operated for individual profit.

The Case of York

Concrete evidence of the rising standards of British wage earners is admirably presented by B. S. Rowntree in two books: *Poverty and Progress* (1941) and *Poverty: a Study of Town Life* (1901). These books are case studies of social and economic conditions in 1939 and in 1899 in the old Roman city of York, a considerable manufacturing community of northern England. Rowntree's studies disclosed that whereas fifteen per cent of the wage workers at the time of the first survey (1899) lived close to the destitution level, the proportion had been cut in half by 1939. Workmen's income had risen almost forty per cent, due consideration being given to the advance in living costs.

The working week in York was reduced in the period between investigations by anywhere from six to ten hours on the average. When the first investigation was conducted almost none of the wage workers' homes had bathrooms and gardens; in 1939 a third of them was so provided. Popular schooling in the interval between surveys was impressively broadened; whereas no children of wage working families were attending secondary schools in 1899, about 1200 of them were studying on that level forty years later. And children were measurably healthier; the child mortality rate had fallen from 160 per thousand to 54. In spite of the marked improvements that had been achieved, Rowntree found in 1939 that a third of the wage workers was living below standards of decency, as he defined them, and that acute poverty harassed the aged in York.

Among other changes that came over the life of the industrial workers of York in the forty-year span, Rowntree reported that although taverns were still the principal places in which workers spent their leisure hours, the appointments of the "pubs" were better and the percentage of income spent on alcoholic beverages had dropped by forty per cent. Gambling was a more popular diversion than in 1899. The movies, the radio, and, for a minority of wage workers, bicycles and motorcycles afforded new and exciting recreational outlets. Attendance of workers at formal religious services had fallen off.

It was Rowntree's broad conclusion that workers' living standards had risen about thirty per cent and that the betterment was ascribable principally to the social welfare measures enacted by the state, not to the operation of any economic law. He ventured the opinion that the trend toward higher standards of comfort would be resumed after World War II was over.

In point of fact, Britain at war kept nearly all her public social services, and introduced new measures especially adapted to wartime emergencies. Beyond that, plans for further post-war social and educational reforms were worked out in considerable detail while the fighting proceeded.

CHAPTER XII

The British Commonwealth and Empire

The Nature of the British Realm

OF ALL the political institutions created by modern man, none surely is more strange, nor in its way more puzzling, than the complex that is popularly called the British Empire. In that "political family" is embraced a quarter of the globe's land surface, and as much of its population—all subject to, or influenced by, a little island off the shore of Europe, which occupies only a fifth of one per cent of the area of the earth. Within the British system are found every stage in human culture, an immense diversity of language, of creed, of custom, of race, and of conceptions of value. In truth the British realm is an international state, remarkably flexible, whose "constitution" has slowly evolved in response to changing circumstances and conditions.

Like Topsy, the British Empire "just growed," or in the sober language of Sir John Seeley, the most prized 19th century historian of the Empire, "we seem to have conquered and peopled half the world in a fit of absence of mind." That judgment neglects to give due account to historical fact. For in reality the Empire was in large part the creation of individual British initiative and private enterprise rather than of conscious state impulse.

Therein lies a distinguishing difference between the realm of the island kingdom and the empires of continental nations, for the latter owed their beginnings to state action and state support, and political authority was heavily centralized in the home capital. Britain, in contrast, allowed wider freedoms to her colonial possessions in their domestic affairs with self-rule as the avowed and ultimate goal.

Terms used in alluding to the British political complex have a certain ambiguity attached to them.[1] In an exact sense, the label

---

[1] An anecdote which has a folklorish tinge relates how Winston Churchill, talking with a group of American congressmen, allowed the word "Empire" to pop out, and then hurriedly added, "Or if you prefer, British Commonwealth—we have labels to suit all tastes."

British Commonwealth of Nations applies to all the self-governing parts of the realm: the United Kingdom itself, and the Dominions, Canada, Australia, New Zealand, South Africa, and the Irish Free State (Eire). Newfoundland, while officially a Dominion, was governed after 1933 by a commission appointed by the British crown; that unusual arrangement was set up in order to straighten out the tangled financial perplexities of Newfoundland.

And the title British Empire is (or should be) used for the non-self-governing, or dependent colonial territories: crown colonies, of which Hong Kong is an example; dependencies such as the Anglo-Egyptian Sudan; protectorates, like Nigeria, and mandated areas, such as African Tanganyika. The Empire, so conceived, is the primary concern of the United Kingdom and the executive director is a Colonial Secretary, who is a member of the cabinet in London.[2] British India must be thought of as an immense special case and complexity, whose government in the final analysis is under the jurisdiction of the London Parliament. The title British realm may appropriately be used for all the lands and territories subject in one way or another to the British crown.

The Great Dominions

Under the impact of world events and the secular currents of the age, the British realm, never static since its inception, underwent significant constitutional developments. Each of the self-governing Dominions has passed through an historical evolution peculiar to itself, so that a federal system prevails in Canada, and a unitary one in South Africa, but, in spite of differences, the structural pattern of the Dominions is surprisingly similar. Within the Dominions there was unmistakable evidence that the centrifugal force of nationalism was performing its accustomed work. Active participation in World War I and in the making of the Paris peace treaties encouraged the Dominions to sense their own strength and to seek full responsibility in foreign policy and in other ways to whittle down the legal attachment to the United Kingdom. As a sign of the times, the Dominions in 1923 were authorized to enter into treaties with foreign countries without reference to the government in London.

At an epochal Imperial Conference in London in 1926, the constitutional position of the members of the British Commonwealth of Nations was freshly defined. "Every self-governing member of the

---

[2] Certain of the Dominions have colonial responsibilities of their own. Australia, for example, holds a mandate for eastern New Guinea and administers the dependency of Papua.

Empire," the statement reads, "is now the master of its destiny. It is subject to no compulsion whatever." Making principle a binding law in the famous Statute of Westminster (1931), the legislatures of the several Dominions were formally asserted to be on a plane of equality with the Parliament of the United Kingdom, and supreme in foreign as well as in domestic affairs. In other words the only legislature that has any power or authority in Canada, for example, is the Parliament at Ottawa.

Just as there is no legislature which can pass laws binding on all the Dominions, so no executive can issue an order to them all. There is no common taxation and each Dominion is autonomous in tariff policies. Each maintains its own military services and exchanges diplomatic representatives with the motherland and some foreign nations. True, representatives of the several Commonwealths confer freely with one another and on occasion assemble in imperial conferences, but there is no permanent imperial organization. Conference recommendations can only be implemented by the independent action of Dominion governments. The reality of the independence of the Dominions in external policy was amply shown in World War II when one of them —Eire—exercised the privilege of declaring its neutrality and held to that course through the conflict.

The other Dominions loyally rallied to the support of the United Kingdom on the outbreak of war in 1939, though with varying degrees of enthusiasm. Canada, in spite of the unsympathetic attitude of the large compact French-speaking minority, together with New Zealand and Australia, at once declared war on Germany. Yet in Australia a proposal to send troops overseas to fight was passed only by a narrow margin, with the strong Labour Party unanimously opposed.

Reluctance to participate in the war was most pronounced in South Africa, which contains a Boer majority, descendants of the original Dutch settlers in the region, some of whom had never been reconciled to the connection with the British crown. Indeed, the Prime Minister, General Hertzog, the foremost champion of the unregenerate Boer farmers, was openly hostile to the union with Britain, and he strongly advocated neutrality for South Africa. But the partisans of intervention, headed by General Jan Smuts, a Boer who was a warm advocate of British imperial interests and values, and the Union's leader in World War I, carried the day for intervention in 1939.

Instead of instigating a civil war in South Africa, as had been the case in 1914, the defeated and disgruntled Hertzog and his nationalist allies carried on a campaign for peaceful separation from Britain and the establishment of a South African Republic. Partly to counteract the secessionist agitation, the Smuts faction made the outright annexation of German South West Africa, which had been mandated to South Africa in the Versailles Treaty, one of the supreme war aims of the Union.

Stronger than the centrifugal nationalist currents at work in the overseas Dominions were the traditional bonds of interest and value which linked them to the motherland. There was (and is) first of all a common sense of allegiance to the crown, a kind of super-patriotism, a dual political loyalty to one's own Dominion and to the greater British Commonwealth, reminiscent of the predominant outlook in the English colonies of North America before the War for Independence. All the Dominions, moreover, shared in a common and rich literary and cultural heritage, cherished similar conceptions of the political good life, judged men and institutions by the same scale of values. The Dominions were well aware of the advantages in finance and commerce which membership in the Commonwealth afforded, ties which were broadened at the Ottawa Conference in 1932 (Chap. XVIII). Finally, they were generally alert to the fact that their safety and independence rested heavily upon the military and naval protection which the United Kingdom afforded.

In the language of Winston Churchill, explaining the persistence of the British realm, "How are all these communities and races joined together? Why is it they wend their way along the stony uphill road in company? There is only one answer to that: it is because they want to. In fact they want to very much. If it were not so, there is no means to compel them. But they want to. They want to not only in the piping times of peace, but even more clearly they draw together in the most horrible shocks and agonies of war." That piece of Churchillian rhetoric, if open to question with regard to the Empire in the narrow sense, had solid foundations in historical fact so far as the thriving and energetic overseas Dominions were concerned.

Eire

Between World Wars, Ireland, or rather the greater part of Ireland, entered the circle of self-governing British Dominions, though staunch Irish Nationalists thought of their country as totally independent. For generations wrangling and controversy between England and Irishmen had been a persistent feature of European history, Irishmen insisting that they be given autonomy at least, since they constituted a distinct nationality. But England, for strategic, commercial, and religious reasons, balked at meeting the wishes of Irish nationalism. The feud embittered British relations with the United States, whither hundreds of thousands of Irishmen had emigrated, and typified many a minority problem on the continent of Europe.

Just before the outbreak of war in 1914, the government in London at long last voted to give Ireland home-rule, which gratified moderate Irish politicians, but the execution of the law was suspended by the war. During the war, leadership in Irish affairs was seized by the militant, intensely anti-English Sinn Fein or Nationalist Party, which desired an independent republic and actually published a republican constitution. Chief of the Irish Republicans was a singleminded revolutionary, Eamon de Valera, who preached revolutionary violence as the means to republican freedom. An Easter uprising at Dublin in 1916 was crushed by British soldiers.

At the Paris Peace Conference, an energetic Irish delegation, recruited partly in the United States, and appealing to the Wilsonian gospel of self-determination, sought to obtain international sanction for an independent Irish Republic. That effort got nowhere. The rejection of the Irish claim infuriated many a friend of Irish freedom in the United States and was a factor in the refusal of the Senate to ratify the Versailles Treaty.

Presently the Irish Republicans took up arms to win independence. Savage irregular war was waged between the followers of Sinn Fein and British troops, the notorious Black and Tans. Both sides were guilty of brutalities and bloody deeds as odious as the cruelties perpetrated on the continent in the era of the wars of religion.

To find a solution of the Irish Question, Prime Minister Lloyd George proposed a conference with Irish leaders. And after lengthy and ticklish negotiations, a compromise settlement was worked out to the satisfaction of a moderate faction of the Irish Nationalists, though not to the de Valera militants. By that understanding, which went into force in 1922, the southern, overwhelmingly agrarian, and Roman Catholic section of the Emerald Isle was granted the dominion status that Canada, for example, possessed. Called the Irish Free State, slightly more than half the size of Pennsylvania and containing about 3,000,000 people, the new state was given its own parliament, to which the ministry was responsible, and it had full jurisdiction over military, monetary, and tariff matters.

The establishment of the Free State represented a major stride toward the coveted goal of unfettered Irish freedom, though stubborn obstacles still stood in the way of complete independence. For one thing, the northern countries, spoken of as Ulster, inhabited chiefly by Protestants of Scotch descent, and a manufacturing and commercial region, were organically separated from the rest of the island.

Ulsterites in majority were uncompromisingly opposed to union with the Catholic south. Then, too, the authority of Britain in the Free State was not wholly eliminated, for the Crown through an appointed Governor-General still retained a voice—a small voice—in Irish affairs. Payments had to be remitted to London for loans that had been advanced to Irish peasants to purchase land and the British Admiralty retained fleet facilities in three ports.

Nevertheless, Irish moderates set the Free State in motion and the "new deal," incidentally, had a salutary effect on the relations of Great Britain and the United States. On the other hand, the intransigent Republican followers of de Valera fought the Free State compromise, first with arms and when that was seen to be fruitless, with tongue and pen.

That pacific course paid large dividends, for in the parliamentary elections of 1932, the de Valera forces, campaigning on an independence platform, were swept into power. Named Prime Minister, de Valera, once the champion of revolutionary violence, slowly graduated into an astute administrator and wily diplomat, resembling in these respects, the Soviet chief, Stalin. Under de Valera's leadership, the Free State proceeded to pass laws dismissing the British governor-general and in other ways cutting down the remaining ties to Britain.

As a climax a new Irish Constitution, in which the country was re-baptized as Eire and described as a sovereign and independent state, was approved in 1937 by a popular referendum. Meanwhile, de Valera's policies had revived the old bitterness with England, which had open expression in a mutually injurious war of tariffs. But, happily, in 1938, Eire and Britain hammered out an accommodation, putting commercial relations on a new basis, ending quarrels over repayment of land loans and cancelling British naval rights in Irish ports.

That last concession, which was intended as a special gesture of English good will, cost Britain heavily in World War II, for the ports were denied to British ships fighting German U-boats. Certainly the British Admiralty must have weighed carefully the significance of abrogating harbor privileges in Ireland, but apparently, it was never imagined that France could be conquered or that the Germans would convert French harbors into submarine pens. That, of course, is what actually happened.

Thanks to the Anglo-Irish arrangements of 1938 Eire was master in its own house, though not in all of Ireland, since the northern or Ulster zone remained constitutionally apart. For the de Valera Nationalists the partition of Ireland was a crime and a United Ireland the supreme object of politics. If Britain had acquiesced in the demand for unification, Eire might have abandoned its tense and precarious neutrality in World War II and have thrown its resources into the Allied scales—possibly, though not certainly.

The Dependent Empire

While the self-governing Dominions hoed their own political rows, enacted social and economic legislation to suit their own inclinations, the far-flung British colonial empire was administered by the Colonial Secretary in London. Reaching over the tropics from the West Indies across Africa to islands of the Pacific, the British Empire, in the narrow sense, embraced over fifty different territories, each with its own peculiarities, having a population of more than 60,000,000. Few of these colonials are of European origin, by far the greater part are primitive African blacks and the balance are Asiatics. West Africa, Nigeria principally, illustrated the diversity of the British colonial peoples. Along the coast and in forest belts lived Negroes, many of them Christian, pagan Negroes farther inland, and still deeper, Moslems, ruled by emirs on steppes that trailed off to the Sahara desert.

Within this widely diverse British Empire the variety of government is almost infinite, being determined by the state of native education, apparent capacity for political responsibility, and general economic and social conditions. It is fair to say that, uniformly, in the inter-war years, the British accent was on progress toward self-rule. Gradations in the evolutionary process ranged from the type of dependency in which the authority of the British governor was supreme, subject only to the Colonial Secretary in London, to the dependencies—Ceylon, for instance—in which political power belonged to local ministries which were directly answerable to the electorates.

In densely-peopled British tropical Africa "indirect rule" prevailed; that is, British officials governed by guiding and advising local chiefs and their local organizations. At every turn emphasis was placed on teaching the natives a sense of responsibility, and training native teachers, doctors, judges and the like. Before 1914, the British task and broadly the British accomplishment was to establish law and discipline, to stamp out tribal warfare, slavery, cannibalism, and kindred uncivilized habits. From 1920 onward, aside from giving natives actual experience in local government, British officialdom devoted itself to improving social welfare and developing economic resources and productivity.

At the same time, prized native customs and traditions were preserved with as little disturbance as possible. To be sure the labors of Christian missionaries frequently undermined pagan institutions, traditions, and prejudices upon which the old African morality was based and did not always succeed in creating an effective substitute. For it is much easier to inculcate the doctrine of Christianity in the minds of men than its spirit in their hearts. A couple of generations hence it ought to be possible to appraise the success of Christian missions in British tropical Africa.

It was standard British policy to look upon adequate food and housing, improved hygiene, education, and facilities of transportation as the indispensable preliminaries to broader political freedoms. Efforts toward those ends were intensified in the twenties and thirties, but much—very much—awaited the doing, and the development of anything like western industry lay in the future. British taxpayers footed part of the bills for demonstration farms, swamp drainage, the battle against disease, and facilities for vocational and professional education.

None of the taxes collected from native populations flowed into the London Exchequer, but British traders, of course, profited from sales of manufactured articles and imports of the agricultural or raw material specialities of the colonial areas. Young Britishers, too, found outlets for administrative and professional talents in the colonies. Some of the colonies possessed strategic importance for the entire British realm. While there was no system of military conscription, natives were enlisted in the armed forces for defense or police purposes.

On the whole, native populations in the British colonies were treated with greater consideration and more intelligence in the years between the wars than had been true in earlier periods; many an old abuse on the exploitation plantations, for instance, disappeared. By applying more enlightened concepts of imperial stewardship, the British wrote a record in their dependent colonies which compares favorably with that of any other European colonial power, with the possible exception of Holland in the Netherlands Indies.

India

The Indian member of the British realm stands in a class by itself, if for no other reason than its size—on an area half the extent of continental United States lives a population rapidly approaching 400,000,000, a fifth part of the human race. India's varied resources, its myriad varieties of animal and plant life, its variations in climate are matched by its human diversities and class stratifications. Dissimilarities in languages, cultures, castes, and creeds in India are not less profound than on the continent of Europe. Of fundamental importance are the Hindus, who comprise two thirds of the population, and the Moslems, less than a quarter, yet a minority of some 90,000,000 and proud of their religious and martial heritage. Between these two cultural-religious groupings—or at least between their politically articulate members—there was a long record of strife and jealousy, which if anything, was intensified between World Wars.

As if these intricacies were not enough, India was divided governmentally, the main part, three quarters of all, called British India, being the responsibility of the United Kingdom. The balance, made up of some 500 "agencies" and states, belonged to native princes. These native Indian states managed domestic matters to suit themselves, but their foreign relations were in the control of Britain under treaties.

Britishers benefited from employment in many administrative offices of the country, as skilled technicians, and from Indian trade and commerce, exchanging manufactured articles for jute, cotton, tea, wheat, manganese, and other commodities. But the economic importance of India for British prosperity changed with the passing of time, so that in the late 1930's Britain's total trade with India was less by some $50,000,000 than that with South Africa, and less by $35,000,000 than that with Australia. In other words, just before World War II the 400,000,000 Indians bought less from Britain than the 7,000,000 Australians. Potentially, to be sure, India like China was a limitless market, provided that means could be developed to pay for imports.

From London banking houses, capital was borrowed to build transportation facilities in India, to lay out irrigation systems and for general industrial and commercial purposes. But in popular fancy the extent of the British financial interest in India—and therewith the profits that were reaped—is grossly exaggerated. In 1939 private British investments of all kinds in India were probably not much greater than the British stake in Argentine railways alone—roughly about a billion dollars.

It must also be said that British administration established and enforced law and order, stamped out physical strife between Hindu and Moslem, knit the sub-continent together economically, and gave to India and the Indians the vision of future significance in the family of nations. Native manners and ancient customs were tolerated so long as they did not interfere with trade or transgress too violently British conceptions of morality. Taxes were levied for public services in a reasonably equitable manner on the whole. And Britain afforded India security against foreign invasion. It is the British contention, right or wrong, that both parties profited from the imperial connection.

Across the years, beginning with municipal administration in the 1880's, Britain allowed certain of the Indians to take part in the business of government. First, natives would have to gain experience in local government, western style; then gradually they would be admitted to provincial governments, and, eventually, to the central government. By allowing Indians to make recommendations or to criticize British administrative acts, a class of politically conscious and trained natives would grow up, who could, in time, assume the obligations and responsibilities in many departments of government.

Hindu Nationalism

Britain's cautious evolutionary course failed to satisfy—rather it irritated—an aggressive, European educated class of Hindu Nationalists, who would be content with nothing short of independence. The dominating genius of the Hindu independence cause came to be that strangely enigmatic and contradictory figure, Mahatma Gandhi, who symbolizes admirably the aversion of the Asiatic intellectual to the manners and the dominance of the western world.

Born into a top caste Hindu family, Gandhi was trained as a lawyer in England and spent twenty years of his life defending the rights and interests of his Indian countrymen who had settled in South Africa. He returned to India in 1914, a warm partisan of British methods in colonial matters. But the fratricidal European struggle of 1914 and the adoption of measures which strengthened the hand of the British administration in dealing with natives who were guilty of deeds of political violence, swung Gandhi into the anti-British camp. He joined up with the *swaraj* movement, which was agitating for home-rule for India.

This small, bespectacled, deeply religious ascetic discovered that he possessed rare talent for swaying a Hindu audience. The emotional hold that he established over his followers baffles the western mind. Was Gandhi saint or sinner? Divinely-inspired prophet or shallow charlatan? Whatever the answer, the fact is that Britain never before had to contend with so resourceful and so tenacious an Indian politician as Gandhi, one who counted his disciples in the millions, ranging from millionaires to Communists. For a quarter of a century, Indian political problems centered on the views and deportment of this "thin old man in the white dhoti." Time and again Gandhi was clapped into jail, each time emerging with his prestige heightened, if anything. In his personal philosophy Gandhi believed that "non-violent non-cooperation" with the British authorities would ultimately win freedom for India. What he preached he practiced but not all of his followers by any means preferred his passive and pacific path.

Such a person was Pandit Jawaharal Nehru, who after the close of

World War II, eclipsed even Gandhi as a force in the affairs of India. Son of a wealthy Brahman attorney, himself a Hindu nationalist, Nehru was educated in England and there was admitted to the bar. Of him, as of many another outstanding Hindu leader, it has been said that he discovered India when a student in England.

Upon returning to his homeland, Nehru allied with Gandhi and followed him through thick and thin, though except for their intense nationalism, the minds of the two men were far apart. For Nehru was a man of action, unsympathetic with pacifism, whose thinking was colored by collectivist ideologies of the western world. Advocate of far-reaching agrarian reforms and the development of manufacturing, Nehru had much in common with the British Labour Party.

An active figure in the Congress, the potent Hindu Nationalist political organization, Nehru was four times chosen President of that body. Repeatedly he was imprisoned for agitation against British authority. In jail he devoted himself to formulating his philosophy on public affairs more sharply, delving into India's past, and planning for her future. Books that he wrote as a prisoner reveal the sensitive quality of his spirit and the scope of his ambitions.

After World War II Nehru, fresh from prison, commanded strength in the Congress greater than the aged Gandhi, and once more he was chosen to head the Congress. Hailed as India's man of destiny, Nehru, the erstwhile incorrigible rebel, agreed in August, 1946, to take first place in an interim Ministry while British proposals for a constitution for a federal India were being worked out.

At this point, appropriately, may be summarized the burden of the Hindu Nationalist case against British rule, the fundamental bases upon which rested the agitation for Indian freedom. To the Hindu Nationalist's mind it was intolerable, morally wrong indeed, that one nation should lord it over another nation, especially a country with the proud cultural heritage of India. It is the Hindu Nationalist conviction that Indians are perfectly competent to look after their own affairs. Even as the Yankees, chafing under the British master had rebelled in 1776 and gained their freedom, so India similarly enchained must be rid of British overlordship.

To the Hindu Nationalist, Britain was nothing other than an economic vampire sucking the lifeblood out of the Indian population and condemning the natives to be hewers of wood and drawers of water. British civil servants filled positions which Indian natives ought to occupy and manipulated the economy of India so as to benefit Britain and the wider interests of the British realm. Such material and social changes as British administration had brought benefited the alien whites far more than the subject browns, the Hindu Nationalists contended.

Any way, western methods were destructive of India's ancient civilization. Against the materialism of the West and its bustling exuberance, the Hindu Nationalist posed the spiritual good and the pacific quietism which were of the essence of the historic Hindu habit of life. As for internal disunity in India—the conflict of creed and outlook between Hindu and Moslem, the stubborn aloofness of the native princes—that was due in the opinion of the chauvinistic Hindu elements to incitement by British agents. It would yield to conciliatory treatment if only British meddling were eliminated.

Upon these themes, with varying degrees of intensity, the Hindu Nationalists never ceased to play in rousing the political instincts of their fellow countrymen, in conferences with British negotiators, and in presenting the cause of independence to interested outsiders. Some among them harkened to the siren temptations of Soviet Russia. Whether they were persuaded by the merits of the Soviet ideology and practice, by the professed Soviet devotion to the idea of self-determination, or with the object of exploiting the good-will of the Kremlin in the campaign against Great Britain, it is impossible to state.

Constitutional Evolution of India

Indian risings, Hindu and Moslem alike, against British rule during World War I had elicited an official British pledge that natives would be more generously employed in the public services and that self-governing institutions would be gradually introduced. Deplorable post-war conditions, not least a devastating epidemic of influenza, were chargeable, so Hindu Nationalists asserted, to the alien British rule. Sporadic nativist outbursts were suppressed, brutally on occasion, as at Amritsar in northern India. There in 1919 followers of Gandhi brutally butchered five Europeans, and British troops retaliated by shooting down several hundred persons. The "massacre at Amritsar" supplied the enemies of Britain with ammunition that was to be fired for many a day.

In the meanwhile the British wartime pledge of greater self-government was implemented by the Government of India Act of 1919, commiting the sub-continent to a system of representative government. That Constitution set up a central government with a bicameral legislature, a Council of State, not more than a third of whose members might be British officials, and a Legislative Assembly, with forty appointed deputies and a hundred Indians elected on a very narrow franchise. Three matters of high importance—defense, religious affairs, and foreign relations—were reserved to the discretion of the chief representative of the British Crown, the Viceroy. Like the President of the United States, the Viceroy might veto any law passed by the legislature; but in India there was no right of appeal over a veto. He was also charged with protecting minorities and safeguarding the rights of the princely Indian states. Associated with the Viceroy in the conduct of the central executive was a Cabinet, part British, part Indian. The section of the Constitution of 1919 relating to the central government is still (1946) in force.

For Indian provincial affairs a considerable degree of self-government was granted in the Act of 1919 under a system of dyarchy; that is, provincial administrative responsibilities were separated into two classes. Certain important subjects, such as the maintenance of order and finance, were entrusted to the British provincial governor and his executive council. Other matters of lesser moment were assigned to a native ministry which was made responsible to an elected provincial legislature.

Instead of placating Hindu national sentiments the Government of India Act of 1919 simply whetted the appetite of *swaraj*. If Britain conceded so much, might not redoubled agitation secure more—even independence? Denouncing the new constitution as inadequate, Gandhi summoned his countrymen to quit doing business with Britishers, to manufacture their own cloth with ancient hand-techniques, and to boycott anything and everything of western origins—all to be sure without physical violence. When rioting and disorders arose, Gandhi was clapped into jail for years.

In provinces of mixed populations the execution of the Act of 1919 accentuated antagonisms between Hindu and Moslem, each accusing the other of tyrannical procedures. India indeed furnished fresh evidence for the thesis that representative government can only function when those who are represented desire much the same things. Political democracy even in an embryonic form imposed a heavy strain upon a community that was riven by creed and caste, and largely without training or experience in self-government.

In another attempt to find a workable and mutually acceptable pattern of government for India, Indian politicians in the early 1930's conferred with their British opposite numbers in a series of "Round Table" discussions at London. On several moot points amicable understandings were reached, but the bristling Hindu-Moslem animosities could not be resolved and the Indian princes would not consent to impairment of their power. Nevertheless, another constitution for India was adopted by the London government in 1935, in the face of vigorous protestations by Winston Churchill and other imperially-minded Britishers.

The Indian Government Act of 1935 ran into a bulky volume of more than 400 pages, testimony in itself of the complexities of the Indian problem. Among other things, it prescribed that Burma, which hitherto had been governed from India, should have separate political status.

For India itself, the Act of 1935 provided for a federal union of the provinces and the princely states, subject to the latter's concurrence. Although the Viceroy's powers closely paralleled those under the constitution of 1919, since he retained authority in foreign affairs and defense, all other federal matters were entrusted to a legislature of two branches, the majority of whose members would be chosen by a select electorate of about 6,000,000. In place of the dyarchy scheme in the provinces, which had proved unworkable, the provincial legislatures, and ministries answerable to them, were assigned complete autonomy in strictly provincial subjects. Something like 38,000,000 Indians were given the right to vote for provincial lawmakers.

In the event that a provincial government failed to function for any reason, the local British governor was entitled in the Act of 1935 to carry on public business. Seats in both the federal and the provincial legislatures were distributed in accordance with religious belief. In the province of Madras, to illustrate, nineteen groups were recognized. Hindus had a preponderance of the seats, but "untouchables," or outcasts, whose mere shadow poisons the food of a high-caste Hindu, together with Moslems, Christians, and Anglo-Indians were represented. And at Delhi a federal supreme court would be established to settle disputes between provinces and princely states.

The federal union provided in the Act of 1935 proved still-born. For the Indian princes, afraid that they might be victimized by zealous Hindu Nationalists, would not cooperate. Therefore the central administration that had been set up in 1919 continued to function. On the other hand, the new provincial arrangements went into operation at once, the Hindu Nationalists gaining control in seven of the eleven provinces.

That is not to say, however, that the Hindu Nationalists were appeased by the concessions of 1935. On the contrary, their supreme ambition was to wreck the scheme. When in 1939 the British Viceroy proclaimed that India was a party to the European War, without benefit of any democratic procedure, Hindu ministries in the seven provinces resigned. British governors then took charge and governed by decree.

Affairs of state in the other four provinces of India were conducted by natives with no more than modest success. Meantime, Indians were increasingly filling administrative positions, so that in 1939 over half of the senior civil servants of India and an overwhelming proportion of the subordinate ones were natives. The Indianization of the officer corps of the native army, too, except in top places, was very far advanced.

Not long after the coming of World War II the principal Hindu faction raised anew the cry for Indian independence, while the chief Moslem spokesman, Mohammed Ali Jinnah, demanded as he had before that the sub-continent be partitioned into two states, one Hindu, the other Moslem and called Pakistan. This Moslem state, which would be sovereign and autonomous, would embrace four or five provinces to the north in which Moslems were (or were claimed to be) the majority.

Thenceforth the Pakistan project occupied the very center of the Indian constitutional tangle. It was not revealed how this plan of partition could be reconciled with the requirements of Indian defense nor with the economic unity that had grown up in the course of two centuries. Moreover, Pakistan was flatly rejected by Hindu nationalism, which contended that the Indians were really one family of several members and must remain politically united. They wanted no "Ulster problem" in India.

The Economy of India

India to be sure did not live by politics alone. The vast majority of the Indian population eked out an extremely simple existence from the soil. They dwelt in tens of thousands of small self-sustaining villages, little touched by the swirl of politics, shackled by ancient burdens of caste and illiteracy, and living under conditions of really grinding poverty. From time to time, special natural calamities converted mass under-nutrition into famine. Surely the overarching social fact in Indian affairs was the amazing increase in population. In the decade of the thirties the net increase in numbers was slightly more than 50,000,000. The huge growth in population alone made any general elevation of living standards out of the question; the pressure of population on economic resources was heaviest in the rural regions. It was often suggested that education might check excessive reproduction, but relatively few Indian females were literate.

More Indian children than ever attended schools and that trend was reflected in the rising literacy, so that in 1941 about twelve per cent of all Indians could read and write, though literacy is of course only the beginning of education. Better irrigation facilities and sanitation, better transportation, light and power services marked the years between the wars. Those improvements made possible more effective control of plague and famine which, in turn, partly explained the astounding population increase. Yet the average Indian expectation of life was twenty-seven years in 1931 compared with the fifty-year average of the American Negro.

Between World Wars, too, machine production penetrated more deeply into the economy of India, a development that was stimulated by the adoption of tariff protection. After 1922, the Indian government was at liberty to fix tariffs in its own way, without reference to the interests of the British manufacturer and exporter. As one result, the share of the United Kingdom in the imports of India declined from about two thirds before 1914 to under three tenths in 1938. In spite of the overwhelming importance of agriculture in the country's economy, India pushed into eighth place among the manufacturing nations of the world, a growth that caused some perturbation among western competitors. The number of factories in India jumped from under 3,000 in 1914 to nearly 10,000 in 1939, of which 1,700 were described as "large industrial undertakings." Factory employees increased from under 1,000,000 to more than 1,750,000.

Popularly, industrialization was regarded as the primary method of maintaining or raising Indian standards of living. Some Hindu Nationalists gloated over the growth of factories as the way to escape dependence on the manufactured goods of foreign countries. Factories in India were engaged principally in the making of textiles, cement, soap, shoes, chemicals, and the refining of sugar; but heavy industry attained increasing significance, based upon the extensive resources of high quality iron ore and manganese. Under the pressure of World War II requirements, the steel capacity of the country rose to 2,000,000 tons, almost double the 1938 output. India indeed boasted the largest single iron and steel works in the entire British realm—the Tata concern near Calcutta. In response to industrialization primarily, Indian cities expanded rapidly. Calcutta, which grew at a fabulous pace in the thirties, took first rank with a population of 2,000,000 while Bombay, showing a mere twenty-eight per cent growth in the 1930's, dropped into second place, with 1,500,000 residents.

Nature provided splendid protection for India with her teeming millions, myriad cultures, and intransigent social problems—the towering Himalayas, arid plateaus, trackless jungles, and two thousand miles of surrounding seas. British arms on the sea, in the air, and on the land reinforced the works of nature. Natives were enrolled in the fighting services and Indian treasuries bore part of the expenses for national defense. Together nature and man in World War II frustrated the designs of conquest cherished by the military masters of Tokyo. Whether the memory and the advantages of British protection would count much with Hindu Nationalists, intent upon freedom for their country, must be left to the future to unveil.

Dark shadows of Hindu unrest in 1939 beclouded the British imperial sky. At other places in the far-flung realm, evolving British policies had succeeded in reconciling Dominion and colony to membership in the imperial system. If in the colonial empire the change-over from customary ways and thought to western ones was less rapid than critics desired, the standard official British rejoinder was that the transformation could not be hurried without courting disaster. But Hindu nationalism was not, perhaps could not, be appeased short of Indian independence. Within the United Kingdom itself in 1939, no politically strong body of opinion favored the break-up of the British realm. The dominant view seemed to be crystallized in the wartime eloquence of Winston Churchill, "I have not become the King's First Minister in order to preside over the liquidation of the British Empire . . . We mean to hold our own."

CHAPTER XIII

Germany: Democratic and Hitlerian

THE defeat of the German armies in the autumn of 1918 came as a surprise and a shock to a nation that had been drugged by propaganda of eventual victory, reinforced by a long succession of military triumphs in eastern Europe and the smashing advances in France in the spring of the year. Military defeat intensified popular animosity toward the established political order.

Before the Armistice was signed revolution cleansed Germany of her semi-autocratic rulers from the Hohenzollern Emperor on down. Sailors at Kiel set the ball rolling toward the end of October by mutinying and hoisting the Red flag of Communism over the German men-of-war which had been built at such incalculable diplomatic cost. From Kiel the tide of revolution swept across the industrial communities of the west and south. Socialist governments compelled petty kings and princes to renounce their powers. In Berlin Social Democratic spokesmen demanded that Kaiser William II should retire from the scene. That he did, fleeing to Holland and there announcing his formal abdication. All the princely heads of the German states—more than twenty of them—followed suit. The German Revolution of 1918 was a dully undramatic business.

Forthwith a German Republic was proclaimed and Friedrich Ebert, chairman of the moderate Social Democratic Party and an ex-saddler by trade, was invested with the supreme authority in a provisional government. Ebert's appeal for the maintenance of discipline was generally obeyed. German soldiers and sailors streamed back to their homes, welcomed by their fellows as heroes. Billboards carried red placards of the Ebert Socialist government: "Only Hard Work Can Save Us," showing an emaciated child stretching out its hands for the products which only hard work would bring forth.

But a sharply cacophonous note was struck by Marxist extremists, whole-souled German Communists, before whom the intoxicating example of the Bolshevik Revolution in Russia gleamed. Called the Spartacists, this faction, headed by Rosa Luxemburg and Karl Liebknecht, doctrinaire Marxists, contemplated the establishment of a proletarian dictatorship and the nationalization of all the means of production. They reacted violently to a proclamation of the Ebert Ministry promising merely socializing changes and the election of an assembly to draw up a constitution. The Ebert program was endorsed, however, by a Congress of Councils of Workers and Soldiers, representing all sections of Germany.

And the Spartacists attested their faith by recourse to arms. Berlin and other large cities were rocked by civil war in which the insurgents were beaten. Their leaders were shot and the challenge of Left extremism was temporarily stifled.

As had been promised, elections for a German Constitutional Assembly were held in January, 1919. All Germans over twenty—women as well as men—were eligible to vote and about ninety per cent actually exercised the right. Representation was accorded to parties in proportion to the votes each polled. Moderate Socialists, accordingly, obtained 185 seats, and members of bourgeois parties ranging from Democrats through Centrists—the Catholic Party—to unregenerate, stubbornly monarchical Nationalists, elected 236 representatives.

The Weimar Constitution

At Weimar, famous cultural center, the Constitutional Assembly worked out a frame of government for the new Germany. The constitution that emerged from the deliberations was an extremely democratic document, calling for more popular control over public affairs than prevailed in any other populous nation. The making of laws was entrusted to a Reichstag whose deputies would be elected by all Germans who had reached the age of twenty. The Ministry, to be presided over by a Chancellor, would hold office only so long as it commanded the support of a Reichstag majority.

As head of the Republic, the Weimar Constitution provided for a President who would be elected for a seven year term by all qualified voters. But the President's powers were more nominal than real, except in two important particulars: in time of serious emergency the President might issue decrees which would have full force of law and might suspend the fundamental civil liberties of the citizens; second, on the recommendation of the Ministry, the President might dismiss the Reichstag and order a general election.

To the Weimar Constitution was attached a declaration of the rights belonging to every citizen, simply because he was a German. That declaration resembled the American Bill of Rights, for it recognized the right to say what one felt, to print what one wanted, to

assemble for peaceful purposes at will, and to worship in accordance
with one's preference. It was also prescribed that private property
should not be expropriated without due process of law; on the other
hand, the state was authorized to assume ownership of private business enterprises or landed estates if that seemed desirable. Any and
all special privileges which titled folk had traditionally enjoyed were
cancelled.

It appeared that the Weimar document had made Germany safe
for democracy. From one viewpoint the extensive voice in public affairs given to the German electorate and the broadening of personal
liberties represented a logical evolution of tendencies which had been
at work in Germany even before the war. From another angle the
Weimar system involved too sharp and too sudden a break with the
dominant political traditions of the country. Germans had little
experience or training in the exacting art of democratic government.

Furthermore, varieties of opinion on public policies were legion.
The multiplicity of political parties, which was encouraged by a proportional representation scheme, was one of the besetting difficulties
of the Weimar democracy throughout its short life. As in France,
the great variety of parties meant that ministries were coalition bodies,
susceptible to the same diseases as French cabinets. Certain German
political elements, the extreme Left, were hostile to the Weimar order
because not enough had been done in the way of social and economic
change. The Right, on the other side, held that the new system
deviated too far from accustomed German paths and longed for a
return to the "good old days." Men of the Right, who were influential
in the armed services and in the higher bureaucracy, bitterly resented
the military defeat and national inferiority, bitterly resented the
democratic society which the friends of the Weimar Republic were
bent upon creating, eagerly awaited a favorable opportunity to emas-
culate democracy and firmly reestablish German military and national power.

The Weimar Republic in its infancy had other weighty handicaps.
The makers of the Constitution were precisely the men who had reluctantly accepted the Treaty of Versailles. Germans of all ranks in
large majority detested the Treaty as too drastic and too far removed
from the popular expectations that had been evoked by President
Wilson's original program for world settlement Extremist, grossly
tortured interpretations of what had been promised and what had
been delivered deepened disgust—and worse—with the statesmen of
Weimar. The taint of Versailles stuck to the Weimar democracy.

Beyond all that, the German experiment in democracy was launched amidst social distress and political travail. Irreconcilable monarchists and militarists founded terroristic societies for the purpose of overthrowing the Republic, and, thinking the pear was ripe, sought to pluck it in March, 1920. An armed force swooped down on Berlin, compelling Ebert, who had been formally chosen President, and the Ministry to flee. But on an appeal from Ebert the workers of Berlin paralyzed the capital by a general strike and the insurgent regime quickly crumbled. That sequence seemed to argue that the Weimar order was fundamentally popular. What happened in Berlin incited Left malcontents in the Ruhr valley and other areas to rise against the Republic. However, they were swiftly put down by the troops of the national army, the Reichswehr.

At the first election under the Weimar Constitution—in June, 1920 —the strength of the Right was increased and that was followed by sporadic Rightist attacks on partisans of the Republic. Among the scores of victims of the murderous condottieri were Matthias Erzberger, a Centrist statesman of vision, and Walther Rathenau, organizer of the national economy in the war who was hated as a Jew. Like Erzberger, Rathenau was considered by many a "traitor" because of his advocacy of fulfillment of the Versailles Treaty and of international reconciliation.

The Economic Malaise

This political ferment matched—reflected in fact—the troubled social and human situation. When the Armistice was signed, large masses of German city dwellers were on the verge of physical collapse after months of under-nourishment and unrelenting war work. The Allied blockade, moreover, kept out food until March, 1919, and was not completely lifted until after the peace treaty was accepted. Hard enough in cold fact, the ravages of the "hunger blockade" were exaggerated by propaganda, and left memories never wholly effaced from the German mind.

The heavy heirlooms of war—the national debt, for instance, had grown thirtyfold during the war, and plants and equipment had deteriorated from intensive use—together with the losses suffered at Versailles were bound to dislocate German economy. Yet the unhealthy conditions were for a time somewhat disguised by hectic industrial activity, induced by steady inflation of the currency. Owing to the currency depreciation, costs of production, wages included, lagged behind selling prices, and liquid funds were plunged into plant expansion. By 1922 there was practically no unemployment. Prosperity, however, was lop-sided and artificial. While industrial production failed to regain pre-war volume, it still kept well ahead of consumption.

Failure of Germany to meet reparations, as prescribed in the Versailles Treaty, led to French occupation of the Ruhr valley as is elsewhere explained (Chap. XVII). That brought with it the total depreciation of the German mark. Printing presses poured out so much paper money to cover the requirements of the government as to reduce the currency to utter worthlessness. In the end the government had borrowed 191,000,000,000,000,000,000 paper marks from the issuing Reichsbank! The mark had fallen to a third of a thousandth-billionth part of its 1913 value.

That grim catastrophe was due principally to Allied pressure for reparations. It was also brought about by unwisdom and indecision on the part of the German political authorities, as well as the speculative maneuvers of German financiers and industrialists.

Germany economy was churned from top to bottom bringing financial gains for some and crushing losses for others. Debtors, for example, were suddenly freed of their obligations and the entire government debt was cancelled. Many a financier who had bet accurately on the inflation improved his fortune. Low wages afforded excellent prospects of profit for the industrialist. On the other hand, to a substantial degree, the solid, stable, middle and lower middle classes, which in the main had regarded the Weimar experiment sympathetically, were economically guillotined. From the impoverished and embittered, recruits were enlisted for versions of chauvinistic nationalism, not least National Socialism, or for Left radicalism. More than ever the Weimar Republic was identified with national humiliation, personal hardships, and misery.

The striking contrast between the impotent and disorderly Germany of 1923 and the rich, flourishing, and powerful German Empire of ten years before worked more effectively, no doubt, for the cause of authoritarianism than the most impassioned propaganda. Vengeance upon France for being chiefly responsible for Germany's plight was written on the heart of many a German. It was in the midst of the Ruhr occupation that Field Marshal Ludendorff and an obscure Austrian expatriate staged a comic opera revolution in Munich, the Bavarian capital. Labelled "The Bavarian Mussolini" at the time, the actual name of the insurgent chief was Adolf Hitler. But, like other risings against the Weimar government, the Ludendorff-Hitler revolt was swiftly suppressed by the Reichswehr.

The Stresemann Era

Just before Germany surrendered on reparations and the Dawes Plan on reparations was worked out (Chap. XVII), a new ministry was organized with Dr. Gustav Stresemann as Chancellor. It was made up of Democratic Socialists, Centrists, and other middle-of-the way politicians. Until 1929 Stresemann directed German diplomacy in ten different cabinets. He loomed so prominently in affairs of state that his name was pinned to the period.

In physical appearance Stresemann as fully satisfied the cartoonist's conception of the typical German, as Stanley Baldwin served for Great Britain. He had a thick neck, a small bullet head, and eyelids that were fringed with pink. His frame was massive, his shoulders broad, his whole architecture of the heavy order, save for his hands which were the hands of a woman. The total impression that Stresemann made was that of a bulldog, a lithe, tense bulldog.

Admittedly Stresemann the diplomatist is something of an enigma. He was hailed by admirers as a man genuinely desirous of fulfilling Germany's international engagements, as the prerequisite to national reconstruction, and of working for a durable European understanding. But he was reviled by foreign critics as an artful deceiver whose real aim was to reinvigorate his country in preparation for another war, and to that end was hoodwinking credulous foreigners, such as his French opposite, Aristide Briand.

Stresemann, who came of lower middle class stock, had risen on the prosperity of the Hohenzollern empire. As an outspoken German nationalist and imperialist he had made a name for himself in the Reichstag. But did he change his spots after the war and accept German defeat as final? It is significant in this connection that the German Right vilified Stresemann for his avowal of a Versailles fulfillment policy, for signing the Locarno treaties, and for leading Germany into the League of Nations (Chap. XVII). The hatred with which the Nazis honored his name argues, if it does not prove, that he honestly tried to behave as a good European.[1] Stresemann's premature death in October of 1929 removed from the German stage the one man who might have averted the victory of the Nazis.

National Recovery

Almost all phases of German economic activity recovered and expanded in the years from 1924 to 1928. Railways and highways were

---

[1] Nazi detestation of Stresemann stemmed in part from his marriage to a Jewess; their daughter and her husband committed suicide after Hitler's accession.

improved; electricity was supplied to many new consumers and rates were pared down. German industry experienced boom conditions, so that by the end of 1928 most branches of the economy were at least as active as in 1913. Output of mills and factories indeed surpassed the pre-war volume and Germany regained her old leadership in the manufacture of chemical, electrical, and optical supplies.

Germany's merchant marine topped 4,000,000 tons, only slightly under that of 1913, and the great liner *Bremen* captured the mythical blue ribbon of the Atlantic as the fastest and most luxurious ship afloat. An airplane capable of accommodating 169 passengers was put into service and a Zeppelin girdled the globe. By a bit of financial alchemy and some foreign financial assistance a new monetary structure was set up, which retained its stability.

For large sections of the Reich's population, living standards had bounded back to the levels of 1913 or better, though there was an unhealthy amount of unemployment—seldom less than 1,000,000, usually more—and groups of the middle class who had been impoverished by the inflation of 1922-1923 lived in straitened circumstances. Germany's export trade, moreover, failed to regain pre-war dimensions. Dearth of capital, Versailles Treaty losses, high tariffs in foreign countries, and stiff competition by foreign manufacturers hampered recovery in external commerce.

State finance was stabilized by discharging surplus officials, cutting salaries, and levying heavier taxes, which prosperity made practicable. Obligations on reparations as set in the Dawes Plan were paid in full and punctually. It had never been intended that the Dawes program should be anything more than temporary and in 1928 talk of a new and definitive settlement cropped up in political and financial circles.

Extension of public services in accord with established German traditions accompanied the return of prosperity. Cities vied with one another in providing homes for the wage workers, something that had been neglected since 1914. Between 1919 and 1932 over 2,500,000 dwellings were constructed in Germany, half of them by public enterprise. Airy, architecturally attractive apartment blocks dotted the urban landscape, and schools, hospitals, and facilities for popular diversion were increased.

In the national field an ambitious scheme of compulsory unemployment insurance was adopted. An elaborate system of judicial inquiry and mediation was set up to adjust disputes between management and wage workers. Inside factories works-councils of elected workers were formed to promote industrial concord, and to increase industrial efficiency. In some of the larger German firms, elected workers had seats on the board of directors. That interesting innovation had little time to prove itself before it was submerged in the Great Depression.

Germany's economic renaissance in the late twenties verged on the miraculous and was traceable to the operation of several forces. First of all, productive energies which the war and the after-war had diverted into other channels were now turned into traditional directions. The more rational handling of reparations under the Dawes Plan reacted beneficially upon national morale and encouraged an atmosphere of confidence in business circles. Furthermore, German corporations paid to American industrial technology the most sincere form of flattery—imitation. They studied American methods of mass production, learned of more efficient factories and equipment, and applied their findings.

German governmental agencies, both national and local, stimulated the upswing in business by furnishing generous subsidies to shipping lines and to heavy industries. At the same time that plant expansion and intensive rationalization were increasing the output of goods, they also raised the war potential of the country should the Versailles limitations on armaments ever be removed.

Supporting the phenomenal recovery at every point were loans which foreigners poured into Germany. In the belief that Europe was on the way to stability, foreign investors—American mainly, but Dutchmen and Britishers too—felt that loans to Germany would be safe and they liked the lucrative interest rates that were offered. In all, approximately $7,500,000,000 were lent to Germany (about half on short term) or triple the amount paid as reparations in the Dawes epoch.

To what ends were these funds put? Some loans were made to German industries for purchase of machinery, improvement of plants, and the like; part was spent in public improvements; the balance made its way abroad to cover reparations dues. What happened was something like this: Germany borrowed from foreigners, Americans preferred; a part of the loans passed to the French, British, and other creditor governments; they in turn shipped some part of what they received to Washington to liquidate their war debts. It was a grand international merry-go-round: the place was rapid, the music gay—as long as it lasted.

But the tempo of foreign investment in Germany slackened ominously in 1928, and in 1929 the flow virtually ceased. Foreign financiers had grown skeptical of Germany's ability to repay, and the fabulous profits which Wall Street was promising made an irresistible appeal to capital. Since Germany's domestic prosperity and reparations payments were dependent on foreign loans, their cessation threw the country into a dangerous financial plight once more.

The Tide of Politics

Through the years of surface prosperity the German political barometer rose from stormy to fair, and the forces of political extremism dwindled in popularity. At the outset, to be sure—in May of 1924—only half a year after the peak of the currency inflation, the extremist fringes demonstrated impressive strength in a national election. In 1925, on the death of President Ebert, whose popularity had been an asset in keeping moderately minded workers loyal to the Republic, Field Marshal von Hindenburg, aged hero of the wartime armies, was elected in his stead. That choice was a clear victory for the Right, and for the exponents of monarchism and chauvinism, as the Marshal was their candidate too. In foreign capitals the election of Hindenburg was spoken of as the forerunner of the restoration of the Hohenzollerns and a war of revenge. Those apprehensions, however, were soon generally dispelled. Despite his personal monarchical convictions, the old "Rock of Gibraltar" steadfastly upheld the Weimar democracy until 1932.

With the much-respected Field Marshal in the presidential chair the fidelity of the German army to the Weimar regime was assured. The Reichswehr, which was tailored to meet the Versailles specifications, had unflinchingly stood by the Republic. It had crushed armed challengers whether from Right or Left. Except for the loyalty of the Reichswehr the German democratic experiment must have succumbed years before it did.

Although the German General Staff was officially abolished by the Versailles Treaty, it had a worthy successor in an ordinary department of state containing almost a thousand "staff officers" and no fewer than fifty-five generals. Professional soldiers, scions of aristocratic and military families, made up the officers corps of the Reichswehr and preserved the Prussian cult of officer solidarity. Commander-in-Chief after 1920 was General Hans von Seeckt, under whose resourceful direction the small German army was molded into a highly efficient force, capable of swift expansion in the event that conscription was revived. Seeckt typified the aristocratic Prussian military caste to which he belonged. He was precise, inscrutable in countenance, broad-shouldered, and spider-waisted. More than once in the distracted twenties this man might conceivably have set himself up as German dictator had he desired so to do.

By arrangement with the Soviet Union, German military men went to Russia to gain experience in the manipulation of weapons, such as warplanes and tanks, which were forbidden to Germany in the Versailles Treaty. In return German experts put their technical knowledge at the disposal of the commanders of the Red army. In China, too, German theorists of war tried out their ideas. Factories to manufacture military equipment for the Reich were built in foreign countries. Germany's small navy, featuring pocket battleships, commanded respect among naval technicians as did the Reichswehr in foreign army circles. Respect—but scarcely more than that—for Allied troops until mid-1930 garrisoned key cities in the Rhineland.

Staunch German Republicans intended to deliver a decisive blow against monarchism by arranging a referendum in 1926 calling for the expropriation of princely estates without compensation; the proposal was heavily defeated. That outcome could be—and was—interpreted as meaning that Germans in majority were ready to have their old monarchs back. Nevertheless, the parliamentary democracy continued to function and at the balloting for the Reichstag in 1928 the Social Democratic friends of the Weimar Republic won an encouraging victory. It seemed that the future of Germany belonged to the moderates and that democratic principles had firmly rooted themselves.

Fall of the Weimar Republic

Germany's hectic prosperity of the late twenties was succeeded by a terrific slump and financial crisis. First, tens of thousands, then hundreds of thousands, then millions were unable to earn their daily bread. An American journalist who prowled around the Reich estimated that a quarter of the population was without enough to eat; a family of three living on state aid had the equivalent of a little more than four dollars a month for food, after paying for rent, heat, and light.[2]

To a large degree the grim and desperate German malady was intertwined with the globe-wide depression (Chap. XVIII). It wrought disastrously upon German foreign trade. But conditions inside Germany aggravated and deepened the calamity. The national economy had never really recuperated from the dislocations caused by the war,

[2] H. R. Knickerbocker, *The German Crisis* (New York, 1932), pp. 19-24.

the peace settlement, and the subsequent currency inflation. To provide for the workless and other forms of social welfare and to finance public works, the German government spent beyond its income from taxation. Heavy budget deficits resulted.

Even before the onset of the Great Depression a downward revision of reparations had been agreed to by Germany's creditors in the Young Plan (Chap. XVIII). After a debate of unprecedented intensity the German Ministry succeeded in securing Reichstag acceptance of the new plan, to which was tied an Allied pledge to evacuate the armies of occupation from the Rhineland. That was itself an earnest of Allied faith and hope in Weimar Germany. It was carried out five years before the minimum time prescribed at Versailles.

In the meantime budget difficulties and exasperation over the Young Plan had forced the resignation of the Cabinet and the appointment of the leader of the Centrist or Catholic Party, Dr. Heinrich Brüning, as Chancellor. Brüning accepted the thankless assignment on the understanding that he might form a Ministry above parties and that President Hindenburg would back the new Cabinet to the full, as he had thrown his weighty support in favor of ratification of the Young Plan.

Brüning combined to a nicety the qualities of the statesman with the knowledge of an expert economist and the devotion of a patriot to the common welfare. His Ministry, comprising moderate conservatives and middle-of-the-road politicians, held sway from March, 1930, to June, 1932, plagued though it was by rabid attacks from the Right and the extreme Left and by insoluble economic problems. When the deputies defeated a ministerial proposal for straightening out state finance, the Reichstag was dissolved and a general election was ordered for September, 1930.

Conducted while popular emotions were still excited by the struggle over ratification of the Young Plan and while the country was falling deeper into the pit of depression, the September election resulted in a sensational success for the extremist National Socialist Party. Previously the Nazi movement, though noisy and vociferous, had had only small practical importance. For almost a decade the supreme leader of Nazism, Adolph Hitler, had shrieked and conspired and written. But in the election of May, 1928, his party had captured exactly twelve seats in a Reichstag of nearly 500.

Into the professed intentions and goals of National Socialism and the sources of its popularity we shall explore later on. It is sufficient here to remark that in the electioneering of 1930 Nazi spellbinders exploited the lean times through which Germany was passing.

They demanded the cancellation of the peace treaties; they reviled Jew and Communist as the twin scourges of the Fatherland; and they generally promised all good things to all good men. When the ballots were tallied the Nazi Party had polled over 6,400,000 votes. It had won 107 seats, nine times as many as in 1928 and almost a fifth part of the deputies. At the opposite end of the political spectrum the Communist delegation in the Reichstag rose to seventy seven. In Berlin the Communists attracted over a quarter of the electorate. Communism, like National Socialism, made rich political capital out of the harsh economic conditions and prospects.

Worried by these political trends, foreign money-lenders in panic recalled as much of their loans to Germany as possible. That intensified the desperate financial situation, especially for banks which had borrowed on short term and had then reloaned to industrial concerns. Unemployment which stood at 2,250,000 early in 1930 passed the 6,000,000 mark two years later. Since the newly adopted insurance system could not care for the unemployed, the state stepped in with a meager dole.

The Social Democrats, still the largest party in the Reichstag and the mainstay of the Republic, alarmed by the double peril of National Socialism and Communism, supported Brüning. So did Hindenburg, who allowed him to govern in a semi-authoritarian fashion and to issue one emergency decree after another. The Brüning Ministry endeavored to fight the depression by a rigorous program of deflation in spite of the social and political repercussions which that policy entailed. Prices were fixed, wages were regulated by the state, and in other directions government controls over economic affairs were extended. To protect the currency at a time when flight of capital had assumed dangerous dimensions, the Cabinet clapped on severe control over capital exports. Devaluation of the currency as a way of stimulating foreign sales was ruled out by popular apprehension of a recurrence of the run-away inflation of 1923. With the object of raising its prestige and of increasing trade the Brüning Ministry negotiated a customs union with Austria but the project was still-born (Chap. XVIII).

Financial confusion on the continent in the meantime had raced from bad to worse. The collapse of the great Austrian *Kredit Anstalt* bank shook confidence in banks generally. In Germany, the severe crisis was combatted by a moratorium on bank deposits together with greater state authority over the banking structure and industrial and commercial concerns which were interlocked with banks.

It was patent that Germany could no longer fulfill the Young reparations commitment. Postponement of payments for a year under the Hoover moratorium was presently followed by a new understanding with Allied creditors which scaled down the German obligation to next to nothing (Chap. XVIII). Even so, Nazi propagandists never ceased to exploit popular grievances over reparations—and that effectively.

In spite of the achievement in lowering reparations, the popularity of the Brüning Ministry declined outside the ranks of the Center Party. It was the Chancellor's conviction that the Weimar Republic could only be saved from engulfment by the Nazis if Hindenburg was reelected to the presidency when his term expired in 1932, and if preparations were made to restore the monarchy. After no little coaxing "the old Gentleman" consented to run a second time, with Hitler as his principal opponent. At the first balloting Hindenburg fell short of the necessary majority by a hair, but at the second election he came through with a modest victory, thanks to the votes of the devoted friends of the Weimar regime.

Encouraged, Brüning moved to suppress Hitler's trouble-making private army, though nothing of consequence was done to alleviate the growing economic distress. The large Communist bloc in the Reichstag vied with the Right in assailing Brüning's administration and in seeking to wreck the Weimar edifice in the naive belief that collapse would inevitably mean the enthronement of Communism. By their tactics the Communists played squarely into the hands of their most deadly enemies, the Hitlerites. Brüning, moreover, could not point to any fresh success in international politics that might have steadied his prestige.

The year 1932 was one of mounting street brawls, terroristic activity, political murders, economic paralysis, and a succession of elections. With the wave of disorders reaching unparalleled heights, President Hindenburg, who had quarreled with Brüning over a project to split up large landed estates, suddenly dismissed the Ministry. Franz von Papen, another Centrist and a nationalist, the darling of German big business and a wily intriguer, was placed at the head of a cabinet made up of Hindenburg's friends. In reality, it was a presidential dictatorship. The election of a new Reichstag was ordained.

Before that election was held, the von Papen Cabinet executed a coup d'état in the Prussian government, superseding the hitherto dominant Social Democrats by a set of conservatives subservient to the national Ministry. That act heralded the liquidation of the Weimar Republic. Social Democratic leaders were severely criticized for tamely allowing von Papen to take over the Prussian government. They retorted that at elections to the Prussian Diet in April, 1932, the Left coalitionists who supported the Weimar regime were put in a minority, and they had continued to govern simply because the opposition majority could not form a cabinet. It was the Socialist contention, furthermore, that recourse to a general strike or to armed resistance to prevent the coup in Prussia would only have benefited the extreme Left or the extreme Right.

At the national polling in July the Nazis, who applied the appeals and the tactics that had been winning friends and influencing people since 1930, took 230 seats, a gain of 123. Their popular vote exceeded 13,750,000, and the Communists got over 5,250,000.

No party was large enough to organize a ministry, so another election was staged in November, 1932. In the interval, economic conditions slightly improved. On that occasion, the Hitlerites sustained an unmistakable decline in fortunes, which seemed to indicate that the movement was on the downgrade. On the other hand, the Communist voting strength nearly reached the 6,000,000 mark, encouraging fears of a proletarian revolution, with or without the assistance of Soviet Russia—a theme preached by Nazi evangelists morning, noon, and night.

No cabinet could function in a parliamentary manner without the backing of the National Socialist deputies. Hindenburg, therefore, chose to retain the presidential dictatorship. There was, however, a change of staff. Von Papen retired as Chancellor in favor of General Kurt von Schleicher, who had been Minister of Defense and who professed to believe that he could harness and drive the Nazis. In that he failed and he quit after fifty seven days.

Thereupon Hindenburg, now a living fossil, named the forty-four year old Nazi chief as Chancellor, with a Cabinet composed mostly of conservative satellites of the President. Von Papen and the rest of the Hindenburg clique imagined that they had taken Hitler and the Nazis into camp. This was the twenty-first ministry to hold office since the adoption of the Weimar Constitution. "Vorwärts mit Gott," Hindenburg cried, but the echo flew back, "Vorwärts mit Hitler."

It was understood that another national election would be held to test popular confidence in the Hitler-von Papen combination. Preparatory to the voting, Leftist elements in the Reich were subjected to savage persecution by excited and confident Hitlerites. Just before the vote was taken, Berlin's massive Reichstag building was gutted by fire. The Nazis pinned responsibility for the conflagration on the Reds, charging that the fire was part of a Communist plot to take Germany along the road to Moscow. It is almost certain that the fire was set by the Nazis themselves to justify the proscription of the Communist Party, the suspension of constitutional liberties, and to frighten the timid and the gullible in the German electorate.

To the alarm among moderates and conservatives occasioned by the ominous growth of Communist voting strength and the piece of arson, add the fact that all available instruments of propaganda were monopolized by the Nazis and their friends. Add, too, Nazi terrorism, and one has the immediate setting for the decisive German election of March 5, 1933. In the deeper background were the economic chaos, misery, unemployment, and the inability of former administrations to produce political stability or material improvements.

To the polls trooped eighty-nine per cent of the electorate as against seventy-five per cent in the Reichstag election of 1928, mathematical evidence of the immense political excitement that prevailed. The National Socialist Party got nearly forty-four per cent of the votes and with their Nationalist allies commanded a slender majority of all. Nonetheless, the adversaries of Hitlerism, given the huge limitations under which they had campaigned, had done reasonably well. True, the Communist poll slumped considerably, but the Social Democrats dropped only a single seat and the Catholic Center actually gained three. In fact, the votes cast for non-Hitlerian parties exceeded by about 1,000,000 the National Socialist poll.[3]

At last the parliamentary deadlock had ended. The victorious Hitlerians swept the Weimar democracy into oblivion more swiftly than the monarchy had been discarded in 1918. Counter-revolution had triumphed. Germany entered the Third Reich.

Whatever its shortcomings, whatever its handicaps, the Weimar Republic could take just pride in several services it had rendered to Germany. After the monetary debacle of 1923 it put the currency on a stable basis; it carried Germany into the League on terms of equality with other Great Powers; it secured the withdrawal of foreign garrisons from the Rhineland five years ahead of the assigned date; it practically liquidated the reparations problem in 1932. Whether under more favorable circumstances popular government could have endured in Germany has been the subject of much speculation, which, of course, lies outside the orbit of history.

[3] Votes were cast in the following proportions: National Socialist, 17,265,000; Nationalist, 3,132,000; middle-of-the-way Republicans including the Catholic Center, 6,260,000; Social Democrats, 7,176,000; Communists, 4,845,000. The assumption that Hitlerism was "natural" to the German temperament is challenged not alone by this voting record but by the drastic measures subsequently taken by the Nazis to crush all criticism and opposition.

The Nature of National Socialism

Many political movements have deceptive names but not so National Socialism. It was aggressively nationalist and strongly anti-capitalist—an amalgam of the two most powerful currents at work in very modern Europe.

As early as 1920 the party, which had been founded the year before, published an elaborate "unalterable program." That profession of faith and hope was a hotch-potch of principles and prophecies drawn from many strands of the German past and shaped in the light of Germany's sorry present. Here was a glittering assortment of ideas and a great deal of obviously hysterical tosh, calculated to appeal to various strata of German society.

In conformity with the "National" term in the party title, the platform of 1920 demanded the cancellation of the Versailles Treaty in its entirety, the union of all German-speaking folk in a Greater Germany, the acquisition of new land for the surplus German population, and respect for Germany as an equal among the Great Powers. It called for the rehabilitation of the armed forces of the Fatherland on the basis of compulsory military service and an authoritarian form of government in which all concerns of public and private life would be subordinated to the will of the state.

And the Nazi program was "Socialist" too, asserting belief in socializing changes that would enhance the economic power of the state and would presumably lift up the status of the ordinary citizen. More specifically, the platform of 1920 prescribed broader social welfare legislation, restrictions on the accumulation of capital, confiscation of war profits, public ownership of large industries and stores, and the parcellation of big landed estates for the benefit of the peasantry.

Though markedly anti-capitalist in tone National Socialism was equally antagonistic to complete state ownership of productive property and to the international solidarity of wage workers, principles that were cherished by the Marxian version of Socialism. In matters of religion the Nazi platform bespoke the need for "positive Christianity"—whatever that might be—and the relegation of Germans who belonged to the Jewish "race" to the rank of guests, without the normal rights of citizens. Bavaria was the spawning ground of National Socialism and Munich "die Haupstadt der Bewegung."

Party organization followed strictly military lines, requiring absolute obedience to the supreme chief, the Führer. Alluring slogans such as "Deutschland Erwache!" (Awaken, O Germany!), "Aryan" swastika emblems, brown shirts, and flaming banners in red and white and black were adopted as Nazi insignia.[4] Meetings of the faithful were conducted with mystical ceremonial and camp-meeting fervor. For the preservation of order at public gatherings and to combat opponents, an inner corps of Black Guards (*Schutzstaffel*) was created, which grew into a Nazi elite.

In its early history the National Socialist Party recruited followers from disillusioned war veterans, unemployed workers, frustrated "little men," youths for whom the future looked black and foreboding, and university intellectuals. Eventually the Nazi gospel won converts in every rank and stratum of society. In 1926 only 50,000 names were on the party rolls, but six years later membership had swollen to 1,000,000.

Like totalitarian crusades in other countries National Socialism possessed an invaluable asset in its leading personality, Adolph Hitler. Yet Hitlerism was bigger than Hitler, the supreme exemplar in very modern times of the little man with big ideas and a small soul who was inflated into a world force. The successful exploitation of Hitler's perverse genius was the product of the peculiarities of the time in which he happened to live.

Son of an impecunious Austrian official, Hitler in his school-days became obsessed with the notion of German "racial" superiority. Aspiring to be a painter he wandered to Vienna—for many a city of gaiety and festive merrymaking—where he spent five miserable and unhappy years. Poverty of talent frustrated his artistic hopes and ambitions, but Hitler never ceased painting and fancying himself a connoisseur of art and architecture. In Vienna he contrived to eke out a wretched existence performing the most menial tasks and living in flop houses.

It was during the interlude in Vienna that Hitler acquired many of his enduring convictions: aversion to cosmopolitanism; contempt for the affluent bourgeoisie and the masses; neurasthenic hatred of the Marxian Socialist and the Jew, detestation of parliamentary government. At the age of twenty three Hitler drifted to Bavarian Munich where he spent two good years and in 1914 he joined a Bavarian regiment. He fought on the western front, was thrice a casualty, and was awarded the coveted Iron Cross, though he displayed no particular military talent, for at war's end he was merely a corporal—a lance-corporal at that.

---

[4] The Nazi flag had a red field symbolizing the anti-capitalist ideology, a white circle recalling the fervent nationalism, and a black hooked cross representing the superiority of the "Aryan" over lesser breeds of humanity.

For the Weimar democracy which rose out of the ashes of military defeat Hitler had only scorn and derision.[5] Joining the newly founded Nazi Party Hitler by his energy, animal magnetism, beguiling manner, will power, and oratorical talents quickly made himself top-man in the organization. No small part of his prestige he owed to his ability to lash an audience into an impassioned frenzy. His themes were simple, his language unpretentious, his faith compelling, his ardent sincerity bewitching. Like Napoleon before him, Hitler came to think of himself as a veritable man of destiny, an immortal, an anointed German Messiah.

After much demagogic talk about the need for a second German revolution to restore German might and greatness, Hitler in alliance with Field Marshal Ludendorff staged an opera-bouffe rising at Munich in 1923, which was frankly imitative of Mussolini's "march into Rome" a year before. Hitler was cast into prison. This afforded him an opportunity to start writing or dictating his notorious autobiography, *Mein Kampf*.

In that volume the disappointed painter painted a portrait of himself, his inner beliefs, his soaring ambitions at the age of thirty five and elaborated the doctrines of his party. *Mein Kampf* poured vituperation upon the Jew as the scourge and destroyer of German society and extolled the virtues of "racial purity." The German nation must be cleansed of all alien impurities and racialism must be made the religion of the German "master-folk." Hitler's exaltation of the notion of the certain triumph of the "Herrenvolk," as the precursor to the establishment of an earthly paradise, recalled, as did the Marxian teaching of the divine destiny of the proletariat, the ancient Jewish concept of the chosen people.

This villager who had tasted the disappointments and the delights of urban life lauded the advantages of rural living in *Mein Kampf*, the traditions and the satisfactions of the great-outdoors. The Germany of tomorrow, he went on, must have a simplified form of government, from which quarrelsome factionalism was absent, and in which the direction of public affairs rested with an all-wise, all-knowing, all-powerful Führer, responsible to himself alone. This superman would do what the "Herrenvolk" wanted and would do it before they knew what they wanted. To the necessities, interests, and purposes of the state, obligations of morality must be subordinated and to those same ends all rival institutions must be submerged.

So far as the rest of the world was concerned Hitler's testament

---

[5] "I regard the present German Reich as neither a democracy nor a republic, but a Marxistic-Jewish-international pigsty," he declared.

reasserted the central Nazi international objectives of 1920 with addenda. He accented, for instance, the stock national doctrines of hydra-headed Pan-Germanism. France, which so recently had descended upon the Ruhr valley, was Germany's implacable foe and her "lust for dominion" must be destroyed. In places *Mein Kampf* recommended a diplomatic alliance with Britain and/or Italy to attain German national ends. Territorial expansion would be achieved above all at the expense of Soviet Russia. "If we speak of new soil we can but think first of Russia and her subject border States." "Only the might of a triumphant sword," Hitler cried, "will in the future assign us territory and with it life for our nation."

All the vials of Hitler's wrath were poured out upon the Soviet Union: "the most frightful regime of tyranny of all time;" 'a mixture of bestial horror with an inconceivable gift of lying"; a government which "feels called upon to impose its bloody oppression on the whole world."

And *Mein Kampf* closed with the resounding assurance: "A state which in an age of race poisoning, dedicates itself to the care of its best racial elements must one day be lord of the earth."

For every devout Nazi *Mein Kampf* served as the law and the prophets. In a short time it became a best seller, the most discussed of books, and the author, the world's most talked-about man. After the victory of National Socialism passages from the book were read aloud in school and barrack. German industrialists were ordered to bestow gift copies on their workers, and every duly wedded "Aryan" couple was given a copy at the expense of the state.

Upon release from prison Hitler resumed his political agitation. He strengthened the party organization, or brooded grimly over the future amid scenes of Alpine beauty in his chalet at Berchtesgaden. But the climate of opinion in Germany in the late twenties was not particularly favorable for popular acceptance of the doctrines he espoused. One mark among many of the insignificance of Hitler in the twenties is the almost complete absence of any reference to him or his movement in the American press after the Munich Putsch of 1923. All that, however, was changed by the astonishing gains of the Nazis at the polls in September, 1930. Two and a half years later the Hitlerian dictatorship was firmly established.

Why National Socialism Crowded to the Fore

Without the economic tornado that swept across Germany in 1930 it is scarcely likely that the Nazis would have come into power. Mass unemployment and misery provided fruitful soil for the impassioned demagogue, and the ardent Nazi minority was lavish with promises of the millenium that would dawn, once their crowd was given charge of German destinies. But that attraction alone would not have carried the Nazis to triumph. After all, the Communists flaunted a like vision.

Whence came then the 17,750,000 votes cast for the Nazi Party at the crucial election in March of 1933? Some unemployed Germans were attracted by assurances of jobs; some hard-beset countryfolk liked the Nazi pledges to dissolve the large Junker estates and to break the "bonds of interest slavery." Some propertied and religiously-minded men and women discerned in National Socialism the heroic warrior that would slay the menacing dragon of Communism.

Impoverished German middle class folk, moreover, all the bewildered little men, desired to give rein to their hatred, envy, and remorse and longed for safe anchorage in the fierce economic storm. Some Germans had grown weary of the fumbling Weimar democracy which seemed incapable of curing economic maladies or of restoring Germany to a place among the Great Powers. Besides, whole-souled German monarchists and professional soldiers who had never reconciled themselves to the Weimar regime envisaged in National Socialism a tool that could be turned to their special purposes.

Many a German was swayed by the Nazi promise of a Greater Germany, embracing all folk of German speech, of a Germany that would be able to avenge the defeat of 1918, the "shame of Versailles," and the memory of the Ruhr humiliation. It was undoubtedly the stress on nationalism which explains the Nazi success in outdistancing international versions of Socialism in this time of cruel social distress.

To the young German voter Hitlerism appealed with peculiar force. Full of courage, obedient, despondent over personal and national prospects, steeped in love for the Fatherland, adolescent Germans flocked to Hitler's standard as the children of Hamelin to the Pied Piper. Many a woman developed a mystical adoration for the Führer and his cause which had a quality of religious devotion about it. The Nazi racial mythology, too, struck responsive emotions in some German breasts, and the oft-repeated pledge to expel Jews from the professions and business opened up the prospect of jobs for discontented "Aryans."

For hosts of Germans, National Socialism, in a word, appealed as a kind of panacea, which would put all things right. In any case, for many, a Hitlerian regime was preferable to any alternative program that was on the horizon. Some part of the comparative strength of the movement was due to the rough tactics and brutal terrorism with which Nazis cowed or silenced opponents and to paralyzing disunity and lack of spirit among political groupings which despised the Nazis and all their professions. It was the multiplicity and variety of appeals, no one cause alone, which carried the Nazis to victory.

The Totalitarian Reich

Once in command the Nazis swiftly pushed to completion the authoritarian institutionalism toward which Germany had been drifting. All real political power was vested in the Ministry, presided over by the Chancellor, Hitler. Final decisions on questions of large importance were made by him, and after the death of President Hindenburg in 1934, the presidential prerogatives too were transferred to the Führer. To Hitler, personally, the German armed forces took an oath of allegiance.

Hitler dominated his team of hard-driving Nazi associates, bent them to his imperious will or broke them. Though the form of the old Reichstag was preserved, the substance had vanished; it merely echoed amen to Hitler's exhortations. On infrequent occasions the dictatorship solicited the opinion of the electorate by means of plebiscites, but the manner of their conduct, the employment of every device of propaganda and intimidation, and the absence of organized opposition nullified the significance of these referenda.

One by one the older German political parties were suppressed, leaving the National Socialists alone in the field. Social Democrats in the Reichstag courageously voted against the Nazi proposal to give Hitler full power, despite threats of vengeance. Very few of those eighty nine Socialist deputies were alive a year later and their organization was broken up. State monopolies on press and radio made it impossible to diffuse views at variance with Nazi orthodoxy. All the regular police forces of the Reich were placed under the administration of Berlin. They were supplemented first by the military police of the party, the Blackshirted Elite Guard, and by a hateful body of secret political police, the ruthless and brutal Gestapo, whose scope knew no bounds. Law courts were shorn of all semblance of independence and the impartial administration of justice, once the pride of Germany, became a dim memory. "The judge," as General Goering put it bluntly, "must be an active supporter of the National Socialist viewpoint."

Liberty of oral as well as of written expression disappeared. Thousands of influential Germans suspected of hostility to the Nazi tyranny were summarily hustled off to loathsome concentration camps or confined in ordinary prisons; there they languished with no pretence of legality so long as it suited the whim of the authorities. In the concentration camps, of which Dachau and Buchenwald were the most infamous, perhaps as many as 20,000 inmates were placed at the beginning of Nazi rule under ingeniously cruel guards; the bestial horrors persisted until invading Allied armies stopped them twelve years later. Draconian terroristic tactics of the Nazis intimidated all save the most hardy foes of Hitlerism and the brutalities of the concentration camp acted as a tremendous damper on any anti-Nazi reflexes in the German mind.

With the object of uprooting sentiments of loyalty to the individual states of the Reich, historic boundary lines were erased by the Nazis. The nation was refashioned into provinces. All civil servants, provincial, municipal, and other, were subjected to the rigid rule of Berlin.

It would have been unusual indeed if a "revolution" of the scope engineered by the Nazis had been accomplished without a violent counter-movement. But open, organized resistance to "the new order" came not from German elements which suffered under the heavy hand of dictatorship but rather from within Nazi Party ranks. Certain Nazis grew irritable because the economic planks in the official party platform were not promptly carried out, not at least as had been expected; they held that a second and socially radical revolution was necessary. Inside the party, too, dissension arose over the allotment of public jobs and from a desire to elevate the status of the Nazi storm troopers in relation to the regular army. Rumblings of discontent were attended by rumors that an armed rebellion against the Hitlerian regime was being prepared.

Whether the reports were true or not, Hitler and his "conservative" henchmen struck savagely at the dissenters. In June, 1934, almost a hundred Nazi leaders were "purged," done to death in cold blood. Some of the Führer's oldest and most trusted companions perished, among them the chief of the Brown Shirts, Ernst Roehm, who may have contemplated making himself the master of the army as well as of the storm troopers.

That blood bath, which incidentally removed all doubt from Hitler's mind as to his own greatness, evoked loud outcries abroad, where humanitarian sentiments had already been turned against the totalitarian Reich by the callous abuse of Jews, political adversaries, labor leaders, and economic radicals. Following the purge the Brown Shirts were reorganized and strictly subjected to the state, though not merged with the Reichswehr. From time to time thereafter individuals holding responsible public positions who were believed to be less than total in their devotion to the Nazi scheme of things were superseded by men of unquestioned fidelity to the Führer and his monolithic state. Exactly ten years elapsed after the June, 1934, purge before another really serious challenge to Hitlerian mastery appeared in Germany and that too was crushed ruthlessly.

Nazi Economy

Totalitarianism in the sphere of government was matched and buttressed by the almost complete subjection of economic processes to state control.[6] Opportunism and pressure of circumstances rather than preconceived dogmas determined the pace at which the Nazi state established its authority over economic activities.

To be sure, the principles and practices of free enterprise had never struck such deep root in Germany as in other western countries. German railways and other means of communication, for example, had been largely owned and operated by government for decades. In the closing stage of the Weimar era state control over banking and foreign exchange was almost complete and over industry extensive. Those precedents and practices from World War I, when German economy had been wholly state-directed, were applied with vigor by National Socialism.

On a larger view the Hitlerian dictatorship made state control over economic affairs—wages, prices, profits, investment, and capital export—and a planned economy more thorough than ever before. That was a sort of natural culmination to state ascendancy over German economic life which had been in course for some time. It is the age-old experience that government control feeds on itself. Regulations required more regulations until everyone was reduced merely to a small cog in a gigantic machine.

By 1939 the nationalization of large German industrial establishments was effectively completed. That was accomplished, not by taking properties away from their private owners, but by subjecting them to meticulous state regimentation. Owners retained title to their plants, but government bureaucrats managed them and the Nazi state appropriated a share of the profits, if any. Business concerns were told what to manufacture; they were allotted fuel and industrial rawstuffs; they were informed what they should pay for commodities and the prices at which their products should be sold.

---

[6] Tsar on the economic front until 1936 was Dr. Hjalmar Schacht, a clever monetary wizard, who leaned toward orthodoxy in his economic thinking. When Schacht stepped down, Field Marshal Hermann Goering of "guns not butter" fame undertook the supreme direction of national economy.

In the first flush of the Nazi regime German business interests which had helped Hitler to gain power benefited both financially and by the elimination of the frightening prospect of a "Red" revolution which many a capital owner thought of as imminent. But in the long run Hitlerism dictated to capitalism, not the other way around; competition and private initiative were pared to the minimum. There was more than mere wit in the observation that on the economic plane the difference between Hitlerism and Stalinism was that in Russia it was colder.

At a time when the prevalent commercial policy in all of Europe was to export as much as possible and to import as little as possible, German foreign trade was brought wholly under the sway of the state and planned by the state. Public officials decided what should be imported, how payments should be made, what goods should be sold abroad and whither they should be sent. Exports were promoted by an elaborate system of government subsidies and by barter agreements with small foreign countries, which afforded German commerce peculiar advantages in those markets.

The character of foreign trade was determined in keeping with the Nazi resolutions to make the country economically self-sufficient and to meet the requirements of armament production. The Third Reich intended, in short, to make itself as little dependent as possible upon foreign supplies of food and industrial raw materials, so that if war came, the nation would be less vulnerable to blockade than in World War I.[7]

Accordingly, the state fostered the manufacture of synthetic oils, motor fuels, and wool, of substitutes for natural rubber and other articles normally purchased abroad; and the state financed projects for the more efficient exploitation of domestic resources of rawstuffs (low grade iron ores, for one). Citizens were ordered to eat home-grown foods and obliged to curtail the consumption of commodities which customarily were imported.

As one safeguard against a possible enemy blockade the Nazis endeavored to bring the small countries of central Europe and the Balkans under their dominance. They succeeded remarkably well. That success was ascribable to the willingness of Germany, alone among the Great Powers, to buy the agricultural surpluses of the Balkan nations at remunerative prices. By 1938 roughly half the foreign trade of the Balkans was carried on with the Reich; and the proportion increased after the outbreak of World War II.

[7] The magnitude of that undertaking is accented by the fact that coal was the sole industrial commodity which Germany did not import.

As the economic coils of the Nazi octopus wrapped themselves round the Balkan states, the political influence of Berlin mounted correspondingly. Next to the Balkans, Latin America was the principal objective of the German trade expansion, but the gains there were not nearly so complete as in southeastern Europe.

An essential feature of the Nazi drive for self-sufficiency was the agricultural program. During the Great Depression prices of German agricultural products had fallen disproportionately low, so for social reasons as well as in the name of autarchy and in token of the ideological party interest in the countryside, the Nazis were intent on raising rural standards of living. Tax remissions were granted to farmers and they also benefited from lowered interest rates, higher tariffs, and cheap labor furnished by Nazi youth organizations. By strict regulations it was made difficult for farm workers to change their place of employment. For the purpose of checking movement from country to city, the Nazis tried to make rustic living gayer. Cheaper electricity, the building of moving picture houses and of model peasant communities were aspects of that policy.

German agriculture like German industry was controlled and planned in Berlin. Peasants were told in detail what to plant, the fertilizer to be used, prices to be charged, and the distribution of farm products was made a state responsibility. No longer was it permissible for the peasant to sell, mortgage or divide up his farm, if it was smaller than 300 acres (which meant the vast majority of holdings). By Nazi law farm property had to be bequeathed intact to one son or other "first heir" in conformity with local custom. Although the Nazi pledge to carve up the big estates of the Junker aristocrats in northern and eastern Germany was not carried out, the proprietors were converted into agents of the state, managing their lands as parts of the Nazi-directed economic mechanism.

Rural standards of comfort improved modestly under the dictatorship, but except for increased output of sugar-beets and potatoes little had been accomplished by 1939 in the way of agricultural self-sufficiency. On the other hand, by then, large reserves of imported foodstuffs had been accumulated.

Along with the industrial plants, industrial manpower was rigidly regimented by government. At the start of Nazi rule trade unions were suppressed without serious difficulty and strikes and collective bargaining were prohibited. Wage workers could not freely seek employment, though some were pushed around to places where there was a labor shortage. Workers could not arbitrarily be discharged by their employers.

Wage earners and employers (their associations were equally abolished) were united in the "Labor Front," a branch of the National Socialist tree. Agents of the Labor Front fixed wages, hours of employment, and settled disputes between management and men. The Labor Front extolled the honor and dignity of toil and special "courts of honor" were set up to punish violators of these principles. To furnish "approved" educational opportunities, recreational facilities, and vacation trips to wage workers at low cost or none at all, a "Strength through Joy" organization was established. All the social welfare legislation of the older Germany was preserved and in some directions extended.

National Socialism prided itself on whipping the ogre of unemployment. When the Nazis took command well over 6,000,000 names stood on the workless registers, but by 1939 there was an actual shortage of skilled men and workers were being brought in from other countries. Looked at from another viewpoint, whereas at the end of 1932 slightly more than 12,500,000 Germans were at work, in 1939 the figure had risen to beyond 22,000,000. That phenomenal achievement was due partly to the improvement in general world economy after 1933, but more so to the policy of the Nazi government in stimulating economic activity by a variety of "work-creation" schemes, of which the upbuilding of armaments had the largest importance.

At the outset the Nazi administration fostered employment by cutting the work week and compelling management to hire more men. And in line with the Hitlerian dictum that woman's sphere was "Kirche, Küche, und Kinder," women were forced out of factories or induced to quit by loans which made it feasible for them to marry and have homes of their own. A modest impetus, moreover, was given to new business undertakings by tax concessions, state subsidies, and similar devices.

Under state auspices huge public works projects were organized, as a rule schemes that were non-competitive with existing enterprise. Young men, marshalled in compulsory labor corps, were set to work reclaiming wasteland, draining swamps or building a network of magnificent super motor highways—"autobahnen," they were called, serviceable alike for tanks or commercial trucks. Something like 1,500,000 housing units were erected and in Berlin, Munich, and other large cities spacious public and Nazi Party buildings and broad boulevards were constructed.

For all the Nazi housing enterprises an acute shortage in homes existed in 1939. It was conservatively estimated that 2,500,000 dwellings were urgently needed. Over-crowding was especially serious in the industrial communities of central Germany which boomed after Hitler came to power. Materials and workmen, which might have been applied to housing, were employed in building barracks and the long military rampart in the Rhineland called the Siegfried Line. The revival of compulsory military service in 1935, likewise, thinned the ranks of the unemployed.

From that point onward German industrial activity (and therewith employment) was enormously accelerated and kept humming by a vast rearmament program, on land, on sea, and in the air. In a remarkably short time Germany was converted into one gigantic arsenal of war. An incomparable military machine was fashioned which very soon enabled the Nazis to ride rough-shod over most of Europe.

Feverish activity in industry and greater employment put more money into circulation. That in turn heightened the demand for consumer's goods and led to greater production of wares of that kind. All combined to create a "psychology" of confidence and facile optimism which encouraged still greater production. On an overall view German industrial output rose about 100 per cent between 1933 and 1938, and volume substantially exceeded the level of 1929. Heavy industry registered the largest gains but some types of production— clothing and textiles, for instance—increased only modestly.[8]

By 1939 Germany was using all her manpower, most of her material resources, most of her productive capacity. For wage workers the work week had by then been lengthened ten per cent or more and the tempo of work intensified. Taking industrial workers as a whole, standards of living had somewhat improved over the dark year of 1932. Small wonder that Hitler was popularly thought of as a miracle-worker. Jobs and security of employment in fact go far to account for Nazi popularity among German wage earners. Jobs, aggressive nationalism, glittering triumphs in the diplomatic arena, the standing menace of the Gestapo and the concentration camp—these were the varied pillars upon which the Nazi dictatorship rested.

Foreign observers commented on the artificial nature of Germany's economic resurgence and confidently predicted an eventual and inevitable collapse—if and when the pace of rearmament slackened and no other employment for the mighty industrial engine was devised.

Little mystery surrounds the manner in which the Nazi government

---

[8] Statistics on steel and iron tonnage speak eloquently on the general state of German industry. During the Weimar period when steel mills were working almost entirely for peace purposes, peak output was reached in 1929 with 18,500,000 tons; during the Great Depression the figure fell to half that, but under the impetus of the Nazi rearmament, production in 1939 passed 23,000,000 tons.

financed its all-important part in the economic upswing. First of all
—and in defiance of reiterated Nazi promises—customary taxes, already steep, were upped and new taxes were introduced. Rising money
incomes in the late thirties pushed up tax receipts so that probably
as much as two thirds of the state appropriations were met out of
taxation.

Beyond that, government loans were disposed of to investors or
forced upon banks, business firms, and fraternal orders and special
assessments were imposed from time to time upon corporations and
societies. Confiscations of Jewish property, likewise, netted some
revenue for the public treasury. The virtual repudiation of debts to
foreigners was a money-saving measure. Funds also were obtained by
the simple expedient of printing paper currency, though strict government manipulation of the financial mechanism forestalled runaway
inflation such as Germany had undergone in 1923.

Cultural Uniformity

Cultural institutions tend sharply to mirror the political and material environment in which they flourish. Under the swastika banner
German culture underwent considerable modification both as to quality
and direction. Schools, literature, art, and theatre were thoroughly
coordinated and regimented into sterile uniformity. That was a phase
of the Nazification program designed to keep 67,000,000 Germans
moving in a common groove from cradle to grave.

Dictatorships strive above all else to indoctrinate the oncoming generation. Shouted Dr. Bernhard Rust, Nazi Minister for Culture and Education, "The whole function of all education is to
create a Nazi"—an apt epitaph for the tomb of German learning.
Schools at all levels were degraded into nurseries of Nazi beliefs and
practices; teachers and textbooks inculcated the mythology of the
innate superiority of the German "race"—the master-man idea of
society—and the solemn duty of dominating inferior folk. Schools
glorified the achievements of the German past, presented in a warped
fashion, and extolled the martial virtues. Walls of schoolrooms were
placarded with pictures of Hitler and his chief associates; prayers
were offered up for the Führer's health, and Nazi political songs
were sung. So that sound bodies might match "sound" minds and
spirits special attention was given to physical training in the primary
and secondary schools.

Of particular significance in the Hitler school regime was the
Napola or institution of national political learning, a straight Nazi
innovation. Cadets at the age of twelve were sent to these schools for

training as a tough, determined elite from which to recruit future party and state leaders. This was the incubator of Nazi "supermen," par excellence; their school houses were sometimes romantic medieval castles, whose very walls spoke of the military glories of feudalism, and were operated on military lines. Teachers and students wore Hitler Jugend uniforms and the curriculum stressed physical and moral hardihood, unquestioning allegiance to duty, fanatical, unswerving loyalty to state and Führer.

Germany's famous universities, once the envy and the admiration of the world of scholarship, were merged into the fabric of the *Führerstaat* as much as the army, or the Brown Shirts, or the steel mills. Prized German traditions of academic liberty were swept into oblivion, and the state annulled the self-governing rights of learned institutions. University professors gave the Hitler salute at the beginning and the close of their lectures as faithfully as did pugilists entering or quitting the prize ring. And professors had to be on guard lest in their teaching they should betray the slightest criticism of Nazi policies and have an ardent student report the fact to police authorities. Schoolmasters and university professors who were unwilling to hew close to totalitarian Nazi dogmas were ousted from their posts with scant formality.

For more mature German youths, labor in the harvest fields was a patriotic obligation and all male youths were required to serve a term in compulsory work organizations. Instruction in the dogmatic Nazi gospel formed a central feature of the Hitler Jugend, a tightly knit youth league in which membership was virtually compulsory from the age of ten on. Similar indoctrination was imparted to young men who were conscripted for military service.

Supervision over literary and theatrical productions was entrusted to Doctor Paul Goebbels in his capacity of Minister of Public Enlightenment. An "Old Guard" Nazi, academic son of an industrious and saving middle class family, Goebbels boasted that he played upon the emotions and thoughts of his countrymen as a master at the piano. His "thought control" technique represented a curious blend of censorship and propaganda.

Writing of any sort that deviated from National Socialist principles was banned. Copies of internationally renowned books which did not fit the Hitler pattern were gleefully tossed into bonfires, and libraries kept books containing "dangerous thoughts" under heavy lock and key. A lynx-eyed censorship scrutinized literature of all kinds, newspapers included, before publication and it was hazardous to smuggle forbidden books into the country. On the positive side, a matchless propaganda service with branches in key cities of the Reich and manipulated by the shrewd and ingenious Goebbels, effectively indoctrinated the mass mind. Propaganda had a large part in assisting the Nazis to win power and thereafter they relied on propaganda to further their ambitions.

By diverse agencies, from school through barracks to newspapers and radio, Nazi interpretations of men and affairs were insinuated into the minds and emotions of the German millions. Legends, half-truths (and less) were driven home with consummate skill as psychological preparation for whatever might befall in international relations. Among the beliefs which Germans were induced to accept were that their country had no responsibility at all for the coming of World War I; that for four years their fighting forces had waged an Homeric contest against the entire world; that the German army was not beaten in 1918, but rather surrendered to hunger, to want, and the treachery of internationally minded marplots on the home front; that Germany had been beguiled by Wilson's "Fourteen Freckles" which the Versailles Treaty grossly violated; that the harsh Treaty was itself a frank compliment to German strength; that the Allied blockade wantonly starved millions of Germans after the fighting was over; that reparations—and reparations alone—were responsible for the economic tribulations of Germany; that the peace-loving Führer was striving for international cooperation, but greedy, jealous foreigners thwarted him at every turn; that if another war came it would be forced upon Germany, which would fight in self-defense against rapacious encircling enemies.

For the Nazi, truth was not to be found in the nuances, in shades of grey. Rather truth was either white or black, good or bad, and conscious, calculated dishonesty made it so.

Nazidom and the Churches

When the Nazis presumed to coordinate religious organizations with the *Führerstaat* in the name of total national solidarity they met formidable resistance. Indeed the most defiant challenge to the new order came from German clergymen. Only in a Christian pulpit might a man publicly upbraid Hitlerism and perchance remain free to do so again. Try though it did the Nazi swastika failed to conquer the Christian cross completely.

A battle royal raged between the Nazi regime and ideology and some of the Protestant pastors, whether of the Lutheran or the Calvinist creed. Yet the state compelled the Protestant bodies to merge (officially at least) and robbed them of much of their traditional spiritual freedom. That roused violent protestations from a militant Protestant minority, but the great majority of Protestant clergy and laity seem to have drifted with the surging national tide.

Bold souls who persisted in their condemnation of the intolerance of the authoritarian state or who raised their voices against Caesar's intervention in the affairs they held to be God's were taken care of by the Gestapo. Some pastors were driven from their parishes or forbidden to preach; some suffered salary cuts or were transferred to obscure villages. The more outspoken among them, of whom stout-hearted Pastor Martin Niemöller, minister in the wealthy Berlin suburb of Dahlem, was the best-known, were hustled off to concentration camps with small ceremony. Acrimonious controversies between rebellious Protestant clergymen and the Nazi dictatorship persisted until a surface truce was arranged after the outbreak of war in 1939.

Not less than Protestantism, possibly more, Roman Catholicism whose greatest strength lay in the Rhineland and Bavaria, resented and resisted Nazi efforts to regulate every aspect of human life. Under a Concordat signed in 1933 by Nazi officials and Cardinal Pacelli— subsequently Pope Pius XII—for the Vatican, German Catholic clergy were forbidden to engage in politics. But Catholic confessional schools and church societies, youth leagues included, might carry on their customary functions, and religious journals might be published and circulated without restraint.

Fierce quarreling between the rival faiths of Catholic Christianity and National Socialism broke loose when the state coerced Catholic children to enter the Hitler Jugend and laid restrictions on the educational and press liberties of the churchmen. It was the avowed aim of the Nazis to monopolize the training of all youth. Catholic bishops in letters to their flocks protested firmly against infringements of the Concordat and other transgressions of Catholic conceptions of the good life. In 1937 Pope Pius XI in an encyclical "mit brennender Sorge" ("with burning anxiety"), which was read from every Catholic pulpit in the Reich, strongly condemned the spirit and doctrines of Nazidom. Michael Cardinal von Faulhauber, Archbishop of Munich, was a tireless protagonist of Catholic rights and an uncompromising and courageous critic of Nazi wrongs.

The Hitlerian government, on its side, railed against clerical political meddling and alleged evasion of foreign exchange regulations by monastic orders having international connections. However, the disputes lost their vigor in the autumn of 1939 when the guns commenced to roar.

Earnest German Christians were alarmed by the growing popularity of neo-pagan cults among ardent Nazis. These exotic sects of "blood, race, and soil" preached a gospel of German "racial superiority" and practiced pagan rites in imitation of primitive Teutons before the advent of Christianity. In lieu of the Old Testament they adopted Nordic sagas and fairy tales and they purged the New Testament of "Syrian superstitions."

Instead of Christian universality, intensely nationalistic German pagans exalted tribal exclusiveness. They demonstrated their hostility to the historic faith by asserting that " Nazi Germany and Christianity are incompatible" and that "the Cross must fall if Germany is to live." Even a new trinity was created with the Führer as one of the three! "We believe," explained a prominent disciple of paganism, "that the Lord God has sent us Adolph Hitler, so that Germany should be established for all eternity."

Pagan propaganda, together with the systematic campaign against Christianity, roused considerable if sporadic complaints from German Christian spokesmen. Although the cultist agitation subsided with the coming of World War II, its very existence, and Nazi interference with religious independence, enflamed devout Christians in the outside world against the Hitlerian regime.

Persecution of Jewry

Similarly, Nazi racial fanaticism and persecution of Jewry infuriated men and women of good will in foreign countries and helped to bring about the eventual downfall of the Hitlerian regime. Hostility toward the children of Israel, whose roots run deep into the German and the European past, was an original, a persistent, and a poisonous tenet of the Nazi creed. Hitler once exclaimed, "The Jew is the implacable deadly enemy of all light, the hater of all true civilization," but in reality the old-established Jewish population of Germany was the most cultured and civilized Jewish community found anywhere in the world.

Silly, nonsensical doctrines about "race," about the inherent superiority of the "Aryans," resentment against Jewry on political and economic grounds, social antipathy toward Jewish newcomers who had moved in from eastern Europe, the need for a convenient and conspicuous scapegoat upon which could be saddled responsibility for the ills that afflicted the German nation—these items made the Jew a ready target for Nazi orators and pamphleteers. The campaign of vilification and denunciation conducted by the newspaper, *Der Stürmer*, even outdid the maniacal ravings against Jewry in Hitler's *Mein Kampf*. All the old monstrosities about Jews, and some novelties as well were served up week after week in lurid articles and hideous cartoons.

By a Jew the Nazis meant any individual who had as much as a single grandparent belonging to the Jewish religion. Yet even by that comprehensive definition Jews comprised less than one per cent of the German population.

Laws that were ordained as soon as the Nazis acceded to power (and subsequently broadened) severely restricted "non-Aryans" in business operations and in the learned professions. Legislation debarred them from the civil service and drastically regulated their attendance upon institutions of learning. By law "non-Aryans" were denied the status and normal rights of citizens.

From some of these measures Jews, it is true, who had seen service in World War I were exempted, but otherwise they were applied indiscriminately. And "cold pogroms"—social ostracism—were intensified by the attitude and action of the state. Sadistic outrages and other manifestations of physical violence against Jewry were merely a foretaste of the incredibly cruel victimization of this people, after World War II started, wherever the Nazi jackboot descended.

Within religious circles of Germany the Nazi reversion to primitive intolerance provoked considerable moral protest. Vastly louder was the furore excited abroad, accompanied in places by boycotts on goods made in Germany. Jewish refugees, among them men and women who were respected wherever civilized culture was honored, streamed into foreign countries, where they helped to give wide currency to the ugly and brutal aspects of the Nazi regime. Plans for the removal of all Jews from Germany were being considered when World War II began.

The Nays

By 1939 few competent observers doubted the inner strength of National Socialism or its firm grip on the great mass of the German nation. Fabulous successes in international politics, recounted elsewhere (Chap. XIX), reinforced the domestic prestige of Hitlerism and fostered a blind superstitious belief in Hitler's personal infallibility. In Germany, as in any country, a substantial share of the community passively acquiesced, of course, in the prevailing regime. Yet the existence of concentration camp and Gestapo testified that not all the articulate had succumbed to the dictatorship. It would be inaccurate to imagine that allegiance to the Nazi way of life was of equal intensity in all German minds and hearts.

It is permissible simply to list the German groupings in which antipathy to the *Führerstaat* was found. First of all, intellectuals and humanitarians for whom Nazi deeds at home and in foreign affairs meant the destruction of cherished ideals and hopes; next, wage workers dissatisfied with conditions of life and labor or who held to rigidly Marxian views of society; and certain industrialists and churchmen who resented the intrusion of the state into their particular preserves.

Inside the Nazi Party, "left-wing" folk who felt that the economic reformation had not gone far enough may be reckoned among the dissenters. Last of all, professional military men begrudged the penetration of their potent and exclusive circle by young, ambitious Nazi "upstarts." The higher officers who rejoiced over the return of conscription in 1935, and to whose ears the whirring of armament plants was sweet music, reacted hostilely in 1938 when Hitler dismissed fourteen top-members of their caste and took for himself supreme command of all fighting services. The older men, or some of them, resented the loss of traditional army independence. Put together, these dissidents made up a minority—no doubt a slender minority—of the politically minded in the Third Reich.

★

THE
HIGHER LIVING

★

CHAPTER XIV

Society and Science

A Time of Change

SET against the long expanse of the past and the limitless range of the future, the cycle of twenty years between World Wars, to whose social and cultural history we now turn, seems puny indeed. Yet these years were fraught with large meaning for those who chanced to live through them. For these were their times: times of torment and trouble in politics and economics, the inescapable sequel to the upheaval of 1914-1919; times of rapid modification in the social heritage; times of bewilderment in thought and confusion in sentiment as the continuation of the changing pattern of civilized existence begun with the Renaissance; times in which the findings of patient mostly unacclaimed scientists and the wider diffusion of learning beckoned society on to the greener pastures of the future.

Harmony in the intellectual and cultural spheres was notoriously absent. Those who longed for unity and concord cast wistful glances at the 13th century. New threads, or older ones more thoroughly appreciated, in the affairs of the mind and the spirit interwove themselves with strands as ancient as organized society itself to form contemporary culture. The wave of the higher living might on occasion recede, but the tide kept rolling, rolling on, whither no historian was competent to say.

Population

Despite the large human losses suffered in the war and caused by famine and disease after the conflict had ended, Europe's population stood substantially higher in 1939 than in 1913. A careful estimate put the figures at 542,000,000 and 468,000,000 respectively. These figures may be compared with 188,000,000 in 1800. In western and northern Europe there was a marked tendency toward stabilization of the population. At the same time the pre-war trend from countryside to city, from farm to factory persisted. The increasing popularity of apartment-dwelling, the growing cost of raising children, numbing disquiet concerning the future, the dwindling authority of the churches, the greater freedom and employment of women—all contributed to the prevalence of smaller families. But even more important, no doubt, was the spread of the practice of family limitation.

The size of a family tended to be in inverse ratio to the household's ability to command education, leisure, and comfort. Before 1914 knowledge of methods of limitation had been confined largely to the well-to-do, but during and after the war such information was disseminated among all social ranks, with the result that "planned parenthood" increased. Certain governments, the French and Italian among them, enacted drastic legislation to curb the spread of birth control information, and religious and moral groups were active to the same end.

Eastern and southern Europe, in contrast to the west, recorded huge accessions to the population. Soviet Russia, as the most populous of the countries, paced the field with a net annual increase reported in the thirties to be of the order of 3,000,000. The growth of Poland was proportionately as great. Under Fascism, crowded Italy's population shot up by about 5,000,000, due in part to the sharp reduction in emigration.

Positive though not particularly fruitful efforts were made by authoritarian governments to encourage large families on the ground, to use the words of an Italian writer, that "only a regular increase (in population) can guard against the dangers of a rapid decrease. . . . A diminishing population at least in the case of a civilized country is invariably a bad thing in itself and a bad omen." To reasoning of that sort, critics retorted that official population campaigns, if successful, would press down living standards, intensify social discontent, and create a larger human reservoir for aggressive military purposes.

Socialization and Education

Not new but much enlarged all across Europe in the inter-war period was the activity of the state to safeguard and improve the social well-being of the community as a whole. The principle that nothing with social implications lay outside the sphere of government —which was strengthened by public policies in the social sphere during the war—had ever wider acceptance and application. On the specifics of this tendency in the several countries we have elsewhere remarked. It is sufficient here simply to list a few of the more obvious social services which governments supplied: schooling; assistance for needy mothers and children (medical assistance, vacation camps); insurance programs for industrial workers covering accidents, sickness, unemployment, and old-age; housing projects; and measures to protect the public health.

Conspicuous among the social earmarks of the time were the diffusion of learning and the ideal of compulsory schooling for all children up to the age of fourteen. Popular participation in public business, either actively or passively, required a literate citizenry. The onward sweep of industrialism demanded a trained citizenry. Progress in methods of production made possible a prolongation of the period of childhood and youth. Uniformly, public education, with free tuition and free school supplies, was provided by government, though in some countries churches continued to maintain schools and in other places the clergy furnished religious and moral training in the state schools. The existence of "public schools" in England, which were really exclusive and expensive private institutions, tended to deny equality of educational opportunity and to perpetuate a caste system to a degree unequalled on the continent.

Although considerations of cost and the indifference of uneducated parents prevented complete attainment of the goal of universal literacy, the advance that was made in some countries, especially in eastern Europe, was nothing less than prodigious. Soviet Russia, traditionally a land of heavy illiteracy, recorded an amazing change. In 1939, eighty one per cent of the inhabitants over nine years (ninety one per cent for males) were reported to be able to read and write as compared with fifty one per cent in 1926, the most striking improvement having been made among rural women. If the struggle against illiteracy had been virtually won in Russia, the battle for more advanced schooling had still to be fought, for eighty per cent had received only the veriest rudiments of education. Turkey embarked on a program of universal and required schooling and her policy was more or less imitated in neighboring countries of the Middle East.

Along with the extension of schooling there was an expansion in the scope of education and a large amount of experimentation in learning techniques. It was held that children should no longer be sent into active life equipped merely with the three R's. Rather, they must be given—and were given—some acquaintance with the fundamental arts and the fundamentals of science. They were intensively taught the ideological beliefs of their particular country, instructed in physical education and personal hygiene, and trained in skills necessary for vocations. The doctrine that formal education was—or ought to be— a lifelong process found increasing acceptance. For the very young, crèches, kindergartens, and day nurseries were provided in ever larger numbers. For those who had completed elementary schooling, continuation programs were made available in many countries. For adults special courses of instruction were arranged. In the service of mass education, libraries, museums, the movies, and the radio were extensively utilized.

Education at the higher levels attracted and expanded as never before. After the war European university halls were crowded with ex-soldiers, subsidized by government, who had learned in the army that higher education was an asset in advancing from the ranks. Something like thirty new universities and high-standing technological institutes were established in the era between the wars. In Russia the number of such institutions jumped from seven to twenty and practically all the European universities introduced summer sessions, some of which attracted troops of foreigners.

University instruction was offered in subjects little taught, if at all, before 1914. These included the newer branches of science, vocational subjects such as journalism, foreign literatures, and history, though the culture and traditions of the United States were notoriously neglected. Not until 1945 did Cambridge University appoint an American scholar to lecture on United States history. Particularly marked was the increase of courses (and of special institutes) for the "scientific" study of international politics. This was a field of knowledge in which prejudice and ignorance were woefully common. Interest in it had been fostered by a war in which the traditional distinction between soldier and civilian had been blurred to the vanishing point, making the conduct of diplomacy of personal concern to every citizen.

European university enrollments experienced no growth comparable to that in the United States at the time, but attendance everywhere, except in Germany, went up. The increase of students in Russian and in British "provincial" institutions, as distinguished from the ancient foundations of Oxford and Cambridge, could only be described as phenomenal. More generous provision of scholarships for university study contributed to the growth of student bodies. In 1938 probably two out of every five university students in England and Wales were helped financially.

Totalitarian regimes revoked the right of academic freedom, perhaps the most prized tradition of European higher learning. They strictly regulated the subjects to be taught and the teachers who taught them, to the grievous detriment of sound learning.

Helpful in the communication of information and ideas to the masses and the classes was the growth of the press. Newspaper circulation increased as did the number of papers in most countries. Many of the new ones were mouthpieces of national minorities. But in Britain and in Weimar Germany amalgamations, crushing to individuality, concentrated power in a comparatively few hands. Innovations were made in the press by the coming of the radio, which speeded up the dissemination of news, and the transmission of illustrations by photographs (1928). In the authoritarian states newspapers lost whatever freedom of expression they had formerly possessed; correspondents of international news-gathering agencies were subjected to censorship and suppression and newsmen were expelled.

Dozens of new periodicals made their appearance. Very popular indeed were fiction magazines in the nature of narcotics and also those with pictorial illustrations. A German magazine, *Querschnitt,* first set the fashion for periodicals with a profusion of photographs, silent satire, and amazing omniscience. In the form of inexpensive reprints, books were supplied to the public at unusually low prices. Millions of copies of some of the best literature—fictional and non-fictional—were printed by publishers who more and more catered to readers of small incomes.

Feminism

The emancipation of women, one of the social nallmarks of the 19th century and a phase of the general movement for broader human rights, made considerable gains after 1918. Soviet Russia abolished discriminations and inequalities of all kinds between the sexes. As one aspect of the transformation of Turkey, the new civil code (1925) removed discriminations against women and obliged towns-women to abandon their traditional veils. Whereas down to 1914, only the small Scandinavian nations had admitted women to the suffrage, by 1928, as a reward for wartime services and in response to democratizing sentiments, women were allowed to vote for parliamentary candidates on the same terms as men in all the large countries of Europe, except France, Spain, and Italy.[1]

Where women were permitted to vote, some representatives of their sex were returned to parliament. One out of fourteen German deputies, for example, in 1929, was a woman; one out of six in Russia. A growing proportion of women filled civil service positions, though not in the highest ranks. It was prescribed in the Covenant of the

---

[1] Repeatedly the French Chamber of Deputies granted votes to women, but invariably the more conservative Senate turned down the legislation. Spanish women were given suffrage privileges under the short-lived Republican constitution of 1931.

League of Nations that "All positions under or in connection with the League . . . shall be open equally to men and women."

During the war, military requirements drew women into war industries, taught them that they had individualities of their own, and pointed out economic independence to them. To an unprecedented extent women competed with men in factory and office—defying the ancient convention that the role of the housewife was the only legitimate occupation for their sex. Even in heavy factory work, women matched their sisters who toiled in the harvest fields. Rarely, however, were women given equal compensation with men doing the same job.

Once allowed to study in the universities on the same terms as men, women in growing numbers entered the learned and liberal professions. Women were admitted to the bar in Britain in 1921 for the first time, but few entered the clerical profession. In the Church of England, for instance, only the humblest rank, the deaconate, was opened to women. They could conduct services and preach, but they could not administer the holy sacraments. In continental Protestantism women clerics were conspicuously rare.

The increase in feminine participation in traditionally masculine pursuits along with secularising currents and the social dislocations occasioned by the war modified the status of women within the family and brought about some alterations in inherited morality. Changing attitudes were illustrated in one way by greater frankness in speech and print. It was everywhere apparent that the institution of marriage had lost something of its stability as the multiplication of divorce statistically attested. Divorce laws in most European countries were relaxed. The rate of divorce, largely an urban phenomenon, related to the growing independence of women, moved upward.

Nowhere were relations between men and women altered so much as in Soviet Russia. After the November Revolution, the conventions of sexual morality and of religious sanction for marriage were tossed aside; the ease with which divorce could be procured in Russia became the subject of proverb. But in the late 1930's the government intervened and compelled a return to something like pre-war fashions in marital ethics.

America's Impact Upon European Habits and Manners

How rich and diversified European influences have been upon living in the New World is a matter of common knowledge. Far less appreciated was the impact of the United States upon many fronts of life in the Old World, a subject which has engaged the imagination of many writers of fiction. As yet it has failed to attract much serious investigation by professional students of society.

The American impact, which has been operative for a century at least, gathered force in the epoch between the wars. Thanks to American participation in the war, to the presence of American troops on European soil, to the tourist throngs of the 1920's, and to the philanthropic activities of Americans in relief and rehabilitation, many a European underwent a process of Americanization. By no means novel, but perhaps intensified, was the Americanizing influence of repatriated emigrants upon their home communities scattered across the continent.

European authors were wont to portray the United States as a land of huge cities swiftly built, a land of soaring skyscrapers and whirring machines—worthy of emulation, some believed; a land of the eternal melting pot, and of dull uniformity—to be shunned, others thought. Works of popular American fiction which were translated into European tongues afforded readers some acquaintance, frequently unreal, with the buoyant atmosphere and the strange paradoxes of the American way of life. For the European masses, ideas of New World existence were derived more largely from the popular press, which played up the exciting and the dramatic—and the unimportant—or from the celluloid products of Hollywood, again with the accent on the untypical, the sensational, and the neurotic. Quaint European misconceptions of the United States paralleled distorted American notions of Europe.

Americanization involved, among other things, an acceleration of the tempo of European living as is illustrated by swifter transportation and frenzied publicity. City-dwellers in western Europe, at any rate, imitated American customs in cooking and laundering, in eating a greater variety of canned and bottled foods, and in wearing clothing and shoes turned out cheaply by mass production methods. On the British table porridge had long been the staple breakfast food; "Quick Quaker Oats" cut the time for preparation to a few minutes, and increasingly cereals eaten with milk in the American style competed with porridge. "Force" and "Grape-Nuts" were the first to cross the Atlantic, soon to be followed by a bewildering profusion of "flakes" and puffed grains. Also popular were "milk bars" in which tasty drinks with glamorous American labels were dispensed.

The length of time that feminine fashions were fashionable was shortened, after the manner of the United States. Touring Americans made popular lipstick, rouge, and other beautifying aides which were once the monopoly of ladies of easy virtue. Chewing gum, which was hawked on the streets as a novelty, seems never to have captured the European fancy. Europeans danced and drank cocktails a l'Americaine. In many places American bars, cafeterias, jazz bands, Negro blues and spirituals, midget golf, and even American football had their followers.

Who can measure the importance of the success of American athletes at the Olympic games in quickening the interest of Europeans in sports? For the humbler folk and the haughty, the machines, the household utensils, and the ingenious gadgets of American technology —available in Woolworth stores—were a source of endless wonderment.

So pervasive, in fact, was the influence of America upon the British pattern of living that a social chronicler felt constrained to write, "By 1937 it was taken for granted not only in business but in all departments of everyday life that the United States would set the pattern and the pace and Great Britain would follow." [2] Taking a broader sweep, C. E. M. Joad, an English popular philosopher wrote, half in earnest, half in jest (it may be), "The fact that any American novelty from jazz to low-heeled shoes is immediately snapped up and exploited by the nations of western Europe suggests that in superficial things, that is to say, in the things that matter, it is the ambition of other peoples to be as like America as possible. We may infer, therefore, that both the pace and the standards of western civilization are likely to be set for some time to come by the United States and that as regards England, the only change that seems probable in the near future is the change that makes us more, not less, like the America of today." [3]

The March of Science

The advances in natural science during the last four centuries of western history represent the most marvelous accomplishments of the human intelligence, ingenuity, and imagination. Cumulative in character, one generation of workers building upon the techniques and conclusions of its predecessor, scientific progress played havoc with the doctrines of social thinkers who interpreted human history in terms of emergence, maturity, and inevitable decay. If the era between wars brought to light no scientist of the transcendent genius of Galileo or Newton, no Darwin or Pasteur, it could boast the splendid achievements of such men as Einstein and Rutherford in physical science,

[2] R. Graves and A. Hodge, *The Long Week-End* (London, 1941), p. 434.
[3] C. E. M. Joad, *The Babbitt Warren* (London, 1926), p. xii.

Einthoven, Fibiger, and Fleming in biological science; and the loss to learning by death in the war of promising investigators—such as Moseley, physicist, Schwarzchild, astronomer, and von Prowasek, parasitologist—can only vaguely be conjectured.

So numerous were the additions to scientific knowledge, so technical and specialized was so much of the research that one scientific pundit was tempted to observe: "Each department of science has its own society of votaries who meet, as it were, in a Masonic Temple and converse in a jargon that has little, if any, meaning for the general ear." Titles alone of original articles in a single year were reported to fill seventeen closely printed volumes and it was estimated that 25,000 publications were devoted to scientific findings, intelligible only to highly specialized specialists. A large amount of the newly-disclosed data was, to be sure, trivial in character, filling in details without contributing to advances in theory or interpretation.

While a good share of the systematic research was carried on within the walls of European universities or allied institutes, an increasing amount was done in the laboratories of industrial concerns, especially investigation directed toward technical improvements and greater efficiency. Much research was sponsored by governments, eager to make discoveries of value in national defense, though by no means for that purpose alone.[4]

Since science knew no political frontiers, the germ of a productive idea was quickly "cross-fertilized" by alert minds in laboratories located in widely separated parts of the world. So it was with the most dramatic occurrence of 1939 in science: the splitting of the atom of the heavy element uranium and its transmutation into barium and other light elements. That achievement was foreshadowed by research in Rome and finally accomplished in Berlin, Paris, Copenhagen, and the United States.

Similar was the history of the development and application of sulfanilamide, a drug possessing properties useful in treating various infectious diseases among men and animals. German investigators discovered prontosil in connection with study in the chemistry of dyes and scientists at the Pasteur Institute in Paris resolved prontosil into its molecular components and inspired a chain of experiments in England and the United States which resulted in one of the most beneficial medical remedies of the century.

Customarily and properly, scientific investigation is divided into two broad types, though the boundary between them is frequently

---

[4] The famous Rockefeller Foundation in 1939 provided grants for co-operative research in forty seven lands, including Java and the Fiji Islands.

blurred to the point of unreality: "pure research," commonly a long-term abstruse proposition concerned with the discovery or elucidation of fundamental hypotheses and facts, and often carried on in the laboratories of educational institutions; and applied science, the employment of basic principles and facts emanating from them for social needs and purposes. However important the novelties in scientific theory—Einstein's refinements of the doctrine of relativity, for instance—they appeal less to the student of society than developments which had direct social significance. It is principally the contribution of science in altering habits of living and in ministering to man's material requirements that we shall consider here.

For some intellectuals—a minority within a minority—the philosophical implications of scientific hypotheses had immediate significance. But the "man on the street" was too deeply immersed in the cares and concerns of day-to-day living to bother much with these matters, even if he had the native gifts to understand them. True, facile popularizations of scientific theories by means of semifiction, or graphic representations in movies and museums conveyed something of the import of pure science to the masses, but the resourceful explorations into the structure of the atom, for example, meant little for them as compared, say, with the perfection of radio transmission.

It is significant that the materialistic philosophy and outlook—assuming that purposeless material was the only kind of reality and deliberately depreciating or quite excluding the force of human aspirations and ideals—which were ascendant in scientific circles late in the 19th century, lost considerable ground in the 20th century. The attendant dogmatism experienced a parallel decline. As scientific measurements grew more precise, as more and more facts were accumulated—both requiring amendment or abandonment of older hypotheses once thought of as unassailable—some men of science displayed greater humility regarding their disciplines and were less inclined to confuse conjectural theory with ascertained fact. It came to be rather generally accepted that in the scientific realm the only dogma was that there was no dogma, that nothing was fixed and unchanging save the law of probability.

For the student of natural phenomena, no less than for the student of society, two crisp aphorisms of the great Darwin have enduring wisdom and application: "It is a golden rule which I try to follow, to put every fact which is opposed to one's preconceived opinion in the strongest light," and again, "I have steadily endeavored to keep my mind free, so as to give up any hypothesis, however much beloved, as soon as facts are shown to be opposed to it."

In the epoch between wars it was more fully recognized that science possessed social roots and had vast social implications. The belief grew that science should not develop independently of social values, that studies into the secrets of nature and their application formed part of the general human pageant rather than something separate and distinct. Human values and social considerations, it was increasingly acknowledged, should take priority over the mere advance of science for science's sake. Genuine apprehension was expressed in some learned quarters because technological advances proceeded far more rapidly than changes in the social order.

Remarked Sir Alfred Ewing, in 1932, when president of the British Association for the Advancement of Science, with regard to technological progress: "Admiration is tempered by criticism; complacency has given way to doubt; doubt is passing into alarm. There is a sense of perplexity and frustration, as in one who has gone a long way and finds he has taken the wrong turning." It was deplorable in Ewing's opinion that society had been equipped with material powers and productive capacities which it was ethically unprepared to handle. Hints were thrown out that it might be the part of wisdom to declare a "holiday on research" in order to allow society to adjust its inherited habits to the altered conditions which science had brought to pass.

No one could doubt that science applied to the arts of peace had brought a rise in the standards of creature comforts, had shortened hours of toil, and had made possible popular leisure without precedent. But how was the leisure time employed? Was joy in work diminishing? Had the social consequences of men's enlarged mastery over the forces of nature grown too complex and too formidable for mortal control? Applied to the art of war, had not science retarded the onward march of civilization? Whatever misgivings along these lines social thinkers might have on the merits of science, this incorrigible revolutionary would not be restrained but relentlessly and inexorably pushed along in the modification of ways of living, thinking, and fighting.

The Physical Sciences

Ever since the discovery of the X-rays in the mid-1890's there has been tremendous activity in the physical sciences, centering chiefly on the phenomenon of radiation and the structure of the atom. It was even imagined that once the atom was really understood, science would be well on the way to an understanding of the ultimate nature of material things. By splitting the atom, it was believed, a new source of productive energy to supersede coal and petroleum might be discovered which would have truly revolutionary social consequences.

That exciting possibility, the vision, for example, that "airplanes would shoot round the world with a few grains of split atoms," fascinated the popular imagination. Cautious investigators engaged in theoretical research on the atom decried such fanciful speculations and pointed out that in any case before atomic energy could be exploited, new machines would have to be constructed to utilize it.

Experimentation on the atom upset many established principles of physical science, opened up a new realm for inference and conjecture, and tended to merge physics and chemistry into one branch of study. The outstanding figure in the field of atomic exploration was no doubt the Britisher, Lord Rutherford, who succeeded in disrupting the atom by atomic projectiles, thereby revealing knowledge of nuclear structure. Where Rutherford pioneered, a host of other clever minds, physicists, chemists, mathematicians, followed in resourceful efforts to unravel the mysteries of the complex atom. Their labors were crowned during World War II with the successful release of atomic energy and its application in the manufacture of the atomic bomb.[5] On every hand, engineering and invention made abundant use of the findings of physical science.[6] Machines were constantly being replaced by more automatic and more efficient ones, for the machine evolved like a living organism. Habits of living were altered by electricity in furnishing artificial illumination and power to drive labor-saving machines and locomotives. Huge hydroelectric stations were constructed; generators to produce electricity were vastly increased in size; and lines to transmit electric power were enormously extended. The rapid growth in the use of electricity dethroned old King Coal. But between 1913 and 1938, industrial research, responding to the competition of electricity and oil, doubled the available energy tapped in a ton of coal.

During World War I the exploitation of the internal combustion engine in motorcars, tanks, and airplanes popularized that contrivance. After the war the gasoline engine largely replaced the horse in road transportation, except in eastern Europe. It was used extensively in the mechanization of agriculture, particularly in Russia, and in the

[5] See Arthur Eddington, *The Nature of the Physical World* (London, 1932); M. L. Oliphant, "The Release of Atomic Energy," *Nature*, CLVII (1946), 5-7.

[6] How huge the advancement was in applied science was suggested by the number of patents for inventions granted throughout the world. The figure for 1939 was 147,396, with seven countries, one of them Italy, neglecting to report. Fully two thirds of the patents were registered in Europe but the total did not mean an equal number of new inventions, for in the absence of an international patent, inventors had to secure patents in all countries in which they desired protection for their devices.

propulsion of vessels. The airplane emerged in the twenties as the swiftest carrier of mails and passengers. Regular air transportation services linked up the principal cities of Europe. On June 21, 1919, two British aviators, Captain Alcock and Lieutenant Brown, completed the first successful flight between America and Europe, flying from Newfoundland, and covering 1,880 miles in a matter of fifteen hours and fifty seven minutes. That trans-Atlantic flight was quickly forgotten, so that when Charles Lindbergh made an epic crossing to Paris in 1927, it was popularly believed that this trip was the first of its kind. Yet actually over a hundred people, counting the crews of planes, had previously flown the Atlantic.

The caterpillar-track truck and the automobile virtually eliminated the camel as a means of transport on the desert. Progress in the automotive industry also made military mechanization—the manufacture of fast units of armored combat vehicles—an actuality. All in all, the astonishing growth in the use of the gasoline engine and its steady improvement must be set down as one of the more outstanding developments in the era between wars. The satisfaction of the demand for petroleum or an effective substitute became a major worry of European nations.

Remarkable advances were registered in the photographic art, an invaluable aid to scientific research as well as serviceable in more utilitarian and familiar ways. In astronomy, for example, photography made possible more accurate verification of observations. For biological science, photographic use of ultra-violet light of short wave length more than doubled the power of the microscope. Interesting, too, was the advent of microphotography wherewith books, for instance, could be reproduced on films.

Infra-red photography penetrated haze in a way that was valuable for aerial photography and for the navigation of ships in foggy weather. The problem of underseas photography with a submersible camera attracted study. Photoelectric cells were made to behave like "automatic eyes", capable of opening doors, setting off burglar alarms, and even of rejecting discolored beans as they passed along on a conveyor belt. The history of radio and television will be discussed in another connection (Chap. XVI).

Creative chemistry continued to pour forth an endless succession of marvels and to provide the basis of new industries. More than ever before, the chemical laboratory functioned as the heart of the factory. When in the 1930's European countries emphasized public policies that were designed to make them more economically self-sufficient, applied chemistry was summoned to create goods which ordinarily had been imported. The results verged on the miraculous, notably so in the case of Nazi Germany. From coal, scores of products were distilled, ranging from benzene, through aspirin to materials for explosives, plastics, and insecticides. By subjecting coal to the action of hydrogen at a high temperature and a high pressure, an acceptable alternative to gasoline was obtained, a discovery of the highest military importance for Germany, for example.

Other wonders of chemistry included new medicines and pharmaceuticals—antiseptics, synthetic remedies, vitamins. There also appeared "rare earths" for electric filament lamps, synthetic precious stones and perfumes and dyestuffs, an amazing array of cellulose articles—artificial textile fibers, vegetable parchment—artificial fertilizers and rubber, luminous paints, and the discovery of a host of forms in which the simple soya bean could be made to serve the needs of man. Chemists also learned that solid carbon dioxide provided refrigeration that was much more efficient than ice.

Frequently it was asserted that World War I had been a "chemist's war" and that if international strife were renewed civilians as well as soldiers would be quickly destroyed by the chemist's wizardry. Publicists spread popular consternation by their dire prophecies of the wartime use of poisonous gasses; one of them even predicted that all the inhabitants of Paris could be wiped out in an hour by a hundred planes discharging gas-laden missiles if there were no wind. More sober writers held that casualties from gas warfare would be kept low because of the rapidity with which gas was diffused in the atmosphere and by protective masks; far greater, military experts warned, would be the destruction caused by gas let off by high explosives. Chemists, physicists, and other scientists were reported to be at work in all the major countries contriving "secret weapons" which would be unloosed should Europe experience another war. The event did not belie the predictions.

Of necessity, astronomy, most ancient of all the sciences, remained largely inferential because so much of the data could be checked only imperfectly, and even more speculative was cosmogony which endeavored to account for the origin of the celestial universe. Greater precision in instruments,[7] refinements in the methods of studying the solar and stellar systems, and multiplied astronomical observations brought an impressive increase in empirical knowledge of the heavens and inspired daring, sometimes fantastic hypotheses concerning the

---

[7] Searchers of the heavens were in 1939 eagerly awaiting the completion of a gigantic 200 inch telescope being manufactured at Corning, New York for use by American astronomers.

findings. The most amazing developments occurred, no doubt, in astrophysics, that branch of astronomy which studied the physical nature of sun, planet, and stars.

The vastness of the stellar system as compared with the solar system was more fully appreciated in the interval between wars, as was the utter insignificance of the earth when compared with either. Only when graphically put, do astronomical assumptions become intelligible; let an ordinary living-room represent the stellar universe, then a ball an inch in diameter would correspond to the sun, and the earth itself would have the likeness of a grain of mustard seed. However wounding to human self-esteem such a representation of the earth might be, there was compensation in the thought that the conception itself had been reached by the free operation of human intelligence.

Telescopic research proposed that whereas the human eye could detect at best 3,000 stars, the actual number of stars was probably as great as all the drops of water in all the oceans of the globe. The astronomer casually asserted that the nearest known star was 25,000,-000,000 miles distant. The immensity of the realm in which the astronomer worked was further suggested by the supposition that the light by which one of the remoter nebulae is seen has taken 150,000,000 years and more to reach us, traveling at the rate of 186,000 miles a second. Or, stated otherwise, the distant nebula is seen as it existed over 150,000,000 years ago and all but one per cent of its journey was completed before the advent of man on this earth. One may fairly wonder what the poet Addison would have thought if someone had told him that this was what he described as "the spacious firmament on high."

In the higher ranges of astronomical experimentation and thinking, distinguished authorities indulged in much learned speculation on the age of the universe and on whether the universe was continually running down or steadily expanding. The latter view appeared to be the more probable, a conclusion not discomforting to the laymen whose imagination had been stirred by the grandiose flights of the astronomer into the infinite.

The "Earth Sciences"

Geology and its companion meteorology supplied new information and new ideas on the structure and growth of the earth and on the atmosphere above the earth. Much speculative ingenuity was shown in efforts to determine the length of geologic time. It appeared that the age of the earth exceeded a billion years and was less than ten

The Higher Living

billions, an estimate of about five billions finding rather general approval in learned quarters. Traditional hypotheses on the origin of the earth were subjected to continuous scrutiny and revision. Study of the nature of the happenings between the "birth" of the earth and the first appearance of life yielded persuasive theories.

Considerable research was devoted to earthquakes. The services of the trained geologist were more and more prized in the search for mineral wealth, petroleum particularly. Instruments and techniques of professional prospecting became more precise and reports of fabulous discoveries of subterranean wealth issued from Soviet Russia and southern Asia, though they were not fully verified.

Aviation and the coming of radio encouraged more intensive meteorological study; study, for example, of the problem of atmospheric visibility, a subject hitherto largely ignored. Better equipment and the establishment of new meteorological stations brought about refinements in weather charts; weather information was collected and collated in London from fully 600 stations scattered about Europe as well as from ships on the high seas and from the outer world by radio.[8] On the basis of factual studies the art of weather forecasting slowly became more exact, though much remained to be learned before it could take rank as a science. The skies awaited charting in the meticulous manner that the perils of the oceans had been marked out.

As of 1919, very little of this earth, apart from the polar regions, contained unknown areas of sufficient interest to invite exploration. That little engaged the energies of restless and curious mortals between the wars. After several vain attempts the Norwegian explorer, Amundsen, in 1926, flew a plane directly over the North Pole and landed on the Alaskan coast seventy two hours after leaving Spitzbergen. Much livelier was the interest in Antarctica, where aviation was also pressed into service. Parties flying the flags of several countries carried on explorations in this area of snow and ice. They laid claims for their governments to what they had discovered in the belief that the lands contained mineral wealth or had strategic importance or would be useful to the whaling industry. It was proved, among other things, that Antarctica was much smaller than the vast continent of early modern imaginings which had lured a long succession of dauntless European mariners into Pacific exploration.

Soviet expeditions greatly enlarged knowledge of Arctic and Si-

[8] Since Europe's weather was directly affected by conditions in the polar region, several governments in 1933 set up stations near the Arctic Circle which furnished useful data.

berian geography, and transportation over the Arctic became practicable at certain seasons. The Arabian desert was crossed (1931)
for the first time by a non-native, the desolate Simpson desert in
Australia (1939) was similarly explored, and airplane and camera
mapped the trackless forests of Brazil. Several groups of explorers
busied themselves in the mountain area of central Asia, and more
than one party almost managed to reach the summit of Mount Everest.
The interior of the large island of New Guinea was systematically surveyed and expeditions which were engaged in collecting museum-
pieces in Asia and Africa added slightly to geographical lore. Now
that the land surface of the globe had been almost completely explored, now that virtually all the blank spaces on world maps had
been filled in, adventuresome souls turned to underseas exploration,
and marvelous instruments were devised to chart the ocean deeps.

The Sciences of Life

Systematic experimentation in laboratories amassed fresh evidence
to strengthen the Darwinian hypothesis that living creatures, man
among them, had gradually evolved out of earlier forms. A vigorous
controversy raged, however, as to whether the process of organic
evolution had come to pass continuously by infinitesimal steps, or
discontinuously by sudden leaps. Rival theories were supported by
relevant observations. The particular theory a given investigator espoused seemed largely a matter of the particular branch of study he
claimed as his own.

By unearthing new fossil remains, anthropologists increased knowledge of the antiquity of man and human fortunes in pre-historic times.
Sensational indeed was the discovery of a human skull in Rhodesia
(1928) which was allied in some respects to the famous Neanderthal
skull; other bones uncovered nearby suggested that the Rhodesian
creature walked upright, and was possibly a forerunner of "our" man.
Fossilized fragments of Neanderthal man were found beside the Sea
of Galilee and in Uzbekistan, and a Yugoslav anthropologist in 1928
happened upon a massive cave in his country containing artifacts
believed to have been used fifty to 100,000 years ago.

Near Peking in China portions of skulls of several large-brained
primitive individuals together with evidences of the use of fire and
well-shaped artifacts were discovered (1929-1939). This *Sinanthropus
Pekinensis,* who lived from 300,000 to 500,000 years ago, was probably an ancestor of man as known to us. Additional fragments of the
"erect ape-man" (*Pithecanthropus erectus*) were found in Java, which
made it possible to reconstruct a complete skull as it was 500,000

years or so ago. Bits of evidence pointed to the conclusion that "our" man may have arisen from the primitive primate stem in very remote times, prior to the branching off of the anthropoids.

Scarcely less interesting than the anthropological disclosures between the wars were the rays of light shed upon western man's oldest communities by scientific archaeology in numerous excavations all over the ancient Near East, in the Greek and Italian peninsulas as well as in other parts of Europe. Agencies responsible for the excavations published elaborate reports of their finds and in a popularized form the press made the information available to the general reader.

Illuminating were the discoveries made in the 1920's by the opening of the sepulchre of the Egyptian monarch, Tutankhamen. Furniture, objects of art, an ornamental throne, and other wealth were brought out of the tomb. Excavations in Palestine revealed a hitherto unknown civilization antedating 5000 B. C. Digging near the royal palace of Jericho uncovered evidence to substantiate the Biblical narrative of the siege and capture of that ancient capital. At Byblos in Syria, an unusual temple, containing gold and silver relics, which may have been destroyed as long ago as 2250 B. C., was uncovered.

Further work at Ur, in southern Babylonia, proved that community to have been a city of canals, a Venice of 2,000 years ago, and an extensive area of fine sculpture was unearthed at Persepolis, once the capital of the mighty Persian empire. Not far away a remarkable and remarkably well-preserved Stone Village, possibly 6,000 years old, was found. Inside the houses mural decorations and tables with dishes and flint knives could be seen.

Aware of the value of classical memorials in fostering popular patriotism, Fascist Italy made generous appropriations for the restoration and discovery of antique Roman remains. In Rome itself the plan of an entire city quarter of the imperial epoch was brought to light and excavations at nearby Ostia disclosed three pagan temples with refined sculpture, wall paintings, and mosaics. Archaeological research in Moravia produced enlightening information on human achievements in central Europe 20,000 and more years ago and, in England, fresh light was thrown on man's doings before the Roman conquest.

Biology, in its main divisions of zoology and botany, made notable advances which had direct bearing on social welfare. The idea was accepted to a greater extent than ever, perhaps, that biological research of a "practical" character was just as important, and presented just as fundamental problems for investigation, as study inspired by no utilitarian motives. Applied biology had exceptional vogue in Soviet

Russia where facilities for research were provided on an imposing scale; after 1928 studies from Soviet laboratories attracted international scientific attention.

By means of bulletins and popular educational facilities scientists placed their special knowledge at the disposal of the agriculturalist. The wartime discovery that nitrogen, invaluable as fertilizer, could be synthetically manufactured from the air, was applied extensively. New varieties of plants were perfected—wheat and the soya bean, for example. Powerful electric gas-filled lamps were used to accelerate plant growth and the cultivation of plant crops in water and in sand was put on a commercial footing (1937). Valuable work was done in Italy and Japan in improving silk-worm culture.

Striking gains were made in plant pathology. Epidemics of cereal rust diseases were traced directly to wind-blown spores and vigorous war was waged upon pests—cinch bug, locust, grasshopper— and noxious weeds. By improving insecticides and discovering parasites which dutifully preyed upon destructive insects, the annual loss to agriculture from pests, reliably estimated at ten per cent of production, was sharply reduced. In 1926, for the first time, airplanes were pressed into service in dusting and spraying crops. A good deal of scientific energy was expended on the betterment and protection of orchards and forests, on the prevention of soil erosion, and on flood control.

Several problems connected with the raising of animals yielded to research. Ways were found, for example, of immunizing chickens against fowl plague and of cattle against tuberculosis (temporarily against hoof and mouth disease).[9] Russian specialists made an interesting innovation in breeding by the artificial insemination of cattle and sheep. Much study was devoted to the inheritance of characters that had economic value in food animals.

As never before, scientific skill was applied to the cultivation of seafood. Fishing was extended into new areas in the Arctic region and a better method of salting fish by brine injection was worked out. Preservation and storage of foodstuffs were greatly improved and it was demonstrated (1938) that satisfactory nutrition was possible on a diet of stored food exclusively.

The progress in scientific nutrition stood out as one of the cardinal advances of the years between wars, being encouraged by food shortages during World War I. Just before 1914 it was learned that certain food factors in addition to the ordinary elements of diet were

[9] Dogs were successfully inoculated to prevent distemper.

vital for physical well-being and to these "accessories" was given the name of vitamins. A great amount of research was done on the distribution, testing, and artificial preparation of vitamins and knowledge of them constantly grew. By 1929 vitamins had made their way into textbooks—and advertising copy.

Consider the case of vitamin B1. Two "pure" scientists, Jansen and Donath, in 1926 isolated B1 in minute quantities from rice polishings; team work by three sets of investigators resulted in a practical method of synthesizing it. Whereas the first gram of B1 is said to have cost over $200,000, the price was rapidly scaled down to an infinitesimal sum; during World War II, manufactured vitamins had no inconsiderable part in keeping the peoples of belligerent countries in singularly good health.

Also essential for bodily welfare were the newly discovered hormones, or chemical substances secreted by ductless glands and carried by the blood to another organ which was thereby aroused to activity. By 1938 several vitamins and hormones were being prepared commercially. Nutrition approached the status of an exact science; debate on the salient principles of nutrition was largely silenced, though more knowledge was needed on methods of assessing malnutrition. It was clear that if existing nutritional information were practically applied, much disease and human misery could be overcome, and it was proposed that the abolition of malnutrition should be the next major social reform. That there was room for betterment was apparent, for even in Britain, wealthiest of European countries, a third of the population was officially reported to be improperly nourished.

In the epoch between wars impressive progress along several lines was made in the prevention and cure of human ailments. To the aid of the medical art were brought all the pertinent findings and resources of the experimental sciences: instruments of precision and illumination in diagnosis, vaccines against communicable diseases, and chemistry to attack occupational diseases and hazards. For the ailing westerner, laboratory tests were available at every turn. It is probably not too much to say that the advancement in medicine and surgery in the last quarter century eclipsed that of any preceding period of equal length.

Rapid was the advance in radiology for both diagnostic and therapeutic purposes. After 1925 excellent X-ray negatives could be easily made and the danger of the X-ray to patient and operator was minimized. Potent remedies for the alleviation or prevention of venereal diseases, diphtheria, tetanus, meningitis, and diabetes were standardized, and typhus and typhoid fever became rarities wherever western hygiene and medicine were extensively practiced. Surgery grew less painful and safer, much of value having been learned by treatment of injuries during the war. The study of the bacilli which destroy dental enamel was pushed vigorously.

Penicillin is spoken of as the world's most wonderful drug and is believed to have almost limitless possibilities in attacking bacterial diseases. Already it has fought successfully—and swiftly—blood poisoning, pneumonia, gonorrhœa, streptococcus infections, and promising results are announced in combatting other diseases. The discovery of penicillin resulted from years of patient search by many investigators for just this type of germ fighter. Quite "accidentally," in 1929, Professor Alexander Fleming blundered upon penicillin while engaged in routine bacteriological researches at St. Mary's Hospital of the University of London. He chanced to observe something new, something different, about a glass culture plate. On the plate was a fleck of green mold, surrounded by a clear fluid where, by all experience, there should have been the milky presence of hundreds of bacteria. Fleming recognized that something was killing the germs on the plate; it was the mold carried in by the air. Out of that mold, penicillin was extracted. Injected into the body, the drug assisted the body in destroying deadly bacteria.

Research on penicillin and its applications seems to have languished until after war began in 1939. Then scientists in Britain and the United States went to work on the problem in earnest, seeking a new and, as it proved, invaluable weapon against infectious wounds in battle. The production of a sufficient quantity of penicillin to treat a single patient required an inordinate amount of time and work. What was needed was a method of making the drug by large-scale processes. Presently pharmaceutical companies set about preparing penicillin synthetically. Knighted for his discovery, Fleming was rightly hailed as one of the Olympian personalities of the 20th century, whose fame promised to outlive that of his more glamorous contemporaries in politics, war, or industry, who captured the headlines in their lifetime.[10]

Diseases peculiar to the tropics such as sleeping sickness and yellow fever, which plagued white man and native alike, were brought under more thorough control. A German drug, Bayer 205, was successfully used to overcome sleeping sickness and a safe and effective method of immunization against yellow fever was discovered (1934).

[10] See Jane Stafford, "Penicillin," *The American Scholar*, XIII (1944), 469-478.

War upon the malaria-carrying mosquito cut down the death rate of Singapore by a quarter. Wherever in the Orient western hygienic techniques were introduced, the death rate dropped substantially.

Governmental agencies took an increasingly active share in the maintenance of public health by bringing sources of infection like water and milk under control, by publicity concerning ways of avoiding or remedying ills, and by providing medical care for the industrial worker and the indigent. The number and facilities of institutions dedicated to medical research increased notably. Nations, in fact, vied with one another in boasting of the manner in which average life expectancy had been lengthened by the application of scientific knowledge. Yet, however much medicine had accomplished, large areas of illness awaited conquest. Little enough was known of the causes and cure of cancer, rheumatism, measles, influenza, and the common cold. Research on all of them was intensive and extensive.

On the edge of science perhaps should be placed the study of eugenics whose province it was to find ways and means of perpetuating and improving desirable physical and mental qualities among people and of eliminating defectives. This study led to investigations in human heredity. It was learned that many conditions were more complex genetically than once had been assumed and that collections of pedigrees furnished only inadequate data.

Many crude unverifiable theories on eugenics were advanced and therewith much stupidity about races, masquerading in the guise of science. Actually this was little else than silly rationalization of personal and political prejudices. There was much to be said for the contention that the improvement of humanity was peculiarly a biological problem, but much seemingly sound eugenic knowledge could not be applied because of humanitarian or religious resistance.

If psychology—the exploration of mental phenomena—had not attained the full dignity of an exact science by 1939, it was moving toward that goal and was the subject of a huge volume of tough-minded research. An array of discordant bodies of psychological doctrine existed, puzzling to all but the fully initiated. Both scientifically and popularly, psychology had been given an impetus by World War I. The use of propaganda had disclosed much concerning thought and behavior which was subsequently applied in governmental and business publicity. Mental tests, for instance, which were designed to measure aptitudes and personality traits, attained considerable popularity. After 1934, workers on Swedish state railways were selected with the aid of psychological tests and they were used in Hungary for

determining military promotion. In World War II accumulated knowledge and testing techniques placed the selection of personnel for military assignments on a more scientific basis than ever before, with
results that must have far-reaching applications in civil life.

Psychiatry was increasingly serviceable as medicine for the mind.
Before 1914 psychiatry implied little more than care of the insane.
In the course of the war specialists showed that "shell-shock" and
allied mental disorders were psychological, not physical. That discovery helped to enhance the value of psychiatry. Moreover, in 1917,
the distinguished Viennese scientist (and later Nobel prizeman),
Julius Wagner von Jauregg, demonstrated that general paralysis of
the insane could be therapeutically treated by malarial injection.
Other psychiatrists found subsequently that certain common forms
of insanity could be curbed or at least relieved by convulsions brought
on with insulin, drugs, or electric shocks; and by a subtle operation
on the brain distracting obsessions could be eradicated. Beyond all
this, psychiatry had a good deal to say about the mental care of injured workmen, about juvenile delinquency, crime, and alcoholism.[11]

Studies in the psychology of the child had value for the educator,
and men of letters were profoundly influenced by novel theories on
sex and the vagaries of psychoanalysis. This latter "science of unconscious mental states," which attained considerable vogue in the
1920's, seems to have made a great impression on popular thinking,
and spread abroad many wild and fanciful doctrines. The pretensions
of psychoanalysis to recognition as a science were hurt by the fact
that leading European practitioners founded personal and divergent
schools of interpretation. It appeared that psychoanalysis would
profit from fewer dubious theories and more solid factual investigations.

To Sum Up

Until the discovery of the Aladdin's lamp of science, the great
majority of men lived on a treadmill. Production rarely reached beyond the minimum of food, clothing, and shelter required for bare
existence. Life for the many was brutish, meager, short. But in the
19th century, applied science acted with revolutionary force upon
the theory of economic scarcity.

With no little confidence, informed men anticipated a time when
the magic of science would gratify all society's material needs without
the expenditure of much human energy. It was not unusual, for ex-

---

[11] See P. M. Lichtenstein and S. M. Small, *Handbook of Psychiatry* (London,
1944), an enlightening and comprehensive manual.

ample, to read in a book of sober scholarship that "A group of la-
bourers equal numerically to an Army Corps in time of war, if properly equipped and working on suitable lands, could produce yearly the
amount of wheat which is now consumed by the whole of the human
race."

All that enterprising science had learned about man's earth, the
heavens above it, and the waters around it, all the headway that had
been made in elucidating the mysteries of human origins and of early
civilizations, all that had been accomplished in improving bodily well-
being and in the quest to understand how the mind worked—all
these gains failed to satisfy the ambition of science. For science, there
was no finality.

But there was another side, a staggering unanswerable question
which loomed larger with World War II. Would the breath-taking
advancement of science prove the means of promoting or of ruining
civilization? Would the machine master man or man the machine?
It was Emerson who wrote, "Things are in the saddle and ride mankind."

CHAPTER XV

Religion and Religious Organizations

Place of Religion

IT IS unnecessary to urge on the student of history the importance of religion in the human past or its central role in the evolution of the western mind. However religion may be defined—and without extensive research a hundred and one conceptions may be discovered—it has been one of the larger facts and forces in the human record. Man's interpretation of the universe about him and its relation to himself has wrought powerfully upon his ways of living.

Nor is it necessary to labor the point that religion has not been a static phenomenon in western life, but an evolving, a changing one, in response to secular shifts and to the progress of the human mind. From the intellectual and emotional stirrings let loose by the Renaissance down to the impact of the most recent findings in science, the record of religious change is straight if not narrow.

For the largest part of European society, religion historically has been associated with the ideas of ancient and medieval Christianity, modestly modified for many by the doctrines of the innovators during the Reformation. The totality of opinions covering such items of belief as a transcendent Deity trinitarian in personality, the unique divinity of Christ, personal immortality, punishment for sin in a world beyond this world, the Bible as the inspired record of the Almighty's acts, wishes, and commands—these made up the creed of historic Christianity.

Faith's Challengers

Upon orthodox convictions, newer ideas and newer secular interests made inroads in the 20th as in the late 19th century. Most powerful, no doubt, were the growing preoccupation of people with the affairs of the work-a-day world, the attractions of the newer forms of amusement, the lure of the motorcar and of golf, the satisfaction of religious cravings offered by literature and the fine arts, the absorption in practical programs of moral and social reformation, and the urge to create a new heaven on the old earth.

Staunch Socialists, and some who were not, frankly avowed a crassly materialistic philosophy, from which the idea of a Supreme Being was absent; for them organized religion was anathema. For many a super-nationalist the worship of the state supplanted the creed of supernaturalism; by them the state was invested with the emotional and spiritual attributes once reserved for the Supreme Being. The cumulative effects of the scientific advance from the astronomy of Copernicus to the biology of Darwin and beyond strongly affected the religious thinking of the epoch.

World War I, moreover, left its mark upon Christianity, strengthening its hold upon some minds, diminishing it upon others—especially those which found difficulty in reconciling belief in a benevolent and omnipotent Deity with the anguish of mind and heart and with the destruction of young life the fighting brought in its train. Many earnest men in wartime and after were puzzled and perplexed by the ancient riddle: Why does the Almighty allow such iniquities as this?

Several sources, then, fed the streams of atheism (disbelief in any Ruling Power), of agnosticism, (doubt as to such an Existence) and of complacent apathy regarding conventional religion. Agnostics drifted toward a version of naturalism spoken of as neo-paganism and indifference reinforced the feeling that religion was superfluous, of small or no relevance for "the good life." Not immoral, but leading upright and honorable lives, their outlook on life's purpose had a purely naturalistic character.

Some restless souls, chiefly among the well-off, sought mental and spiritual tranquillity in novel or substitute faiths. Christian Science, for example, transported to Europe from its American birthplace, spiritualism, psychoanalysis, and cults of Oriental origins, all attracted significant European followings in the twenties. Late in the decade, in France—and not in France alone—there was a revival of interest in the 19th century creed of positivism or the religion of humanity with its cult of inevitable progress. For a short time, the French statesman, Aristide Briand, was the acknowledged high priest of the faith.

So respected a figure as the Abbé Loisy, the principal exponent of Catholic modernism, gave a new twist to the idea of progress by writing that the League of Nations "implied a religion of humanity and that in the fullness of time, it would itself be the outward and visible form of such a religion." Toward the end of his argument, quoting the Apocalypse, Loisy optimistically identified Geneva with the new

Jerusalem—"that universal city, open to all men, a city of light and life for which the earth will be fruitful in peace."

Many religiously minded men—Jew as well as Christian and even some Moslems—chose to revise the inherited faith in the light of the fuller understanding of nature and her ways, the discoveries of comparative religion, and the challenge of an industrialized and urbanized order of society. For such people the concerns of this world and the social implications of organized religion had as great an appeal—if not indeed a greater—as theological speculations on the unknowable and the infinite.

After due and proper allowance has been made for the trend away from religious orthodoxy, the fact remains that the generality of Europeans, aside from the Russians, continued in the era between the wars, to seek religious satisfactions and assurances in one or another branch of Christianity. Despite the universal decline of religious influence on politics and social affairs and learning, the Christian churches proceeded to perform their functions day by day, year in and year out. In town and country, in slum and village, thousands of parsons, pastors, and priests unobtrusively carried on their appointed tasks. New houses of religion were built, missions and educational enterprises were launched, and theological scholarship was cultivated.

Roman Catholicism

Roman Catholicism claimed the allegiance of one out of seven inhabitants in the world, distributed all over the globe but found principally in continental Europe. The superb organization of Roman Catholicism, ever a source of strength, centering in the papacy at Rome, and maintained by over 1,500 archbishops and bishops and hosts of lesser clergy in various ranks, gave that church a stability and a solidarity denied to other religious communions. In combatting the assaults of irreligion, anti-clericalism, and the pretensions of secular governments, Catholicism benefited from its compact intellectual system, which had been marvelously re-invigorated in the late 19th century, and from the experience which long generations of rivalry with political authority had taught.

Though it is impossible to compute mathematically, it would appear that in spite of losses in some quarters, Catholicism's following in Europe was greater in 1939 than it had been at the turn of the century. To the masses this venerable institution which had outridden the buffetings and vicissitudes of nineteen centuries of time, appealed powerfully in an age of material confusion, social stress and distress, and intellectual tumult. World War I and its aftermath drove men to meditate on fundamental values, of small concern in times of peace, and to seek reassurance that the disturbed secular world was not the whole of reality. The wide-open arms of Mother Church offered comforts, consolations, and certitudes which the world could not give, and which the creeds of the Reformation could provide only with limitations.

For intellectuals, too, Catholicism had peculiar attractions: the satisfactions of definiteness and certainty, the emotional appeal of the sacramental rites, the lure of an international religious fellowship, which stood majestically above the wrangling of competitive national-isms. Writers and thinkers represented by G. K. Chesterton [1] in England, Sigrid Undset in Norway, and students of the French philos-opher, Henri Bergson, if not indeed the master himself, formed the vanguard of the return of the intellectuals to the Roman faith.

The activities of the Vatican during the war, such as attempts to restore peace by diplomacy and to alleviate the hardships of war prisoners and refugees, raised Catholic prestige in some places. To the same end the selfless wartime labors of eminent prelates contrib-uted, above all, those of Cardinal Mercier of Belgium, whose enheart-ening pastoral letters and fearless intervention on behalf of his com-patriots, while Belgium was occupied by German troops, earned for him and his church the deathless devotion of a grateful nation.

The Anglo-Catholic movement within the bosom of the Church of England, which had been underway for a century, gathered momentum after the war, winning the allegiance of a quarter of the Anglican clergy, it was reported. Some Anglican divines and laymen preferred to enter the Catholic faith completely.

Catholicism gained ground steadily in England. Parochial schools enlarged their enrollments and papal beatification of English martyrs who had perished for their faith during the Reformation had a quick-ening effect upon Catholicism in the island kingdom. Cardinal Hinsley, who was enthroned as Archbishop of Westminster in 1935 and died in 1943, attained a special place of respect among his countrymen, un-equalled since the restoration of the Catholic hierarchy in England at the middle of the 19th century. Warmly patriotic, a man of all

---

[1] Chesterton's *The Everlasting Man* (London, 1925), a brilliant and widely read exposition of Catholic viewpoints, contained a vigorous assault upon "aca-demic" theories on the evolution of man and on religion. He was the best known Englishman of his age to be converted to Roman Catholicism, and when four years later his wife imitated him, a Catholic paper placarded the event all over London. At Chesterton's death, Cardinal Pacelli, later Pope Pius XII, eulogized him as a devoted son of the Church and a gifted defender of the Catholic faith.

around competence and varied experience, Hinsley prized the universal Christian values. Loyalty to his church was united with a deep humanity and generosity that reached out to all men, especially to the poor and the afflicted.

Minor English discriminations against Catholicism, such as laws banning bells in Catholic religious structures and prohibiting priests from wearing their vestments in public, were repealed. At the coronation ceremonies of King George VI in 1937, the antique formula, "defender of the [Anglican] faith" was dropped from the ritual, out of deference to Catholic sentiments in Britain and the British realm. The adjustment of the thorny Irish Question in 1922, whereby the essentially Catholic section of that island obtained Dominion status (Chap. XII), bettered the relations between the British government and world Catholicism.

In France, "the eldest daughter of the Church," Catholicism recovered something of the standing it had enjoyed before a wave of anti-clericalism swept over the Republic early in the 20th century. Catholic acquiescence in the secularization legislation and the loyal participation of the clergy in World War I softened the fierce zeal of the anti-clericals; while clerics in other continental countries had seen service as chaplains and medical attendants, French clergy had been obliged to bear arms as well. Not a few priests were killed or crippled and some even rose to responsible positions in the military forces. After the war there was a scarcity of French priests, for seminaries had been closed while the fighting was on, and that shortage created a more serious problem for French Catholicism than the destruction of noble cathedrals and parish churches by the artillery of rival armies.

Catholicism enlarged its hold upon the French by organizing its own educational institutions and clubs for women and children, by fostering Christian trade unions, and by an aggressive religious press. Among the obvious symptoms of Catholic vitality were the vigor of French religious literature—the writings of the philosopher-theologian, Jacques Maritain, particularly—and the erection of a hundred churches in the Paris area alone. Popular allegiance to the Church mounted as popular faith in politics and politicians declined, for Catholicism stood forth as the defender "of the moral heritage of humanity, the dignity of the person, and the Christian order in the world." [2]

Formally Catholic political organizations played only an unim-

[2] For a searching analysis of French Catholicism by an eminent French intellectual, see Jacques Maritain, "Religion and Politics in France," *Foreign Affairs*, XX (1942), 266-281.

portant role in French affairs before World War II, but the Catholic
party of Germany, the Center, exerted a large and sustained influence
upon German public life, until dissolved after the enthronement of
National Socialism. In Austria the Catholic Christian Socialists dominated the Republic during the greater part of its free existence; their
onetime leader, Monsignor Ignaz Seipel, one of the most astute European politicians, and his successors undertook to remold Austria as a
cooperative Christian commonwealth in keeping with the social principles that the Vatican espoused. In other countries, Belgium, Slovakia,
and Poland, for example, parties founded upon Vatican precepts
shared actively in the march of political events.[3]

With the unquenchable zeal of St. Paul, Roman Catholicism in the
inter-war epoch pressed forward in the task of evangelizing the
heathen. Special attention was devoted to building up a native priesthood and a corps of religious workers by establishing training schools
in mission fields and appointing converts as bishops. Six Chinese
bishops, for instance, were consecrated on one occasion. Competing
with Islam and Protestantism in Darkest Africa, Catholic missionaries
brought tens of thousands into their religious fold and in the 1930's
claimed 7,000,000 followers there.

Over against the gains which Catholicism registered must be set
the losses which were suffered in continental Europe. Under the impact
of the secular currents of the age, some intellectuals forsook the faith
of their fathers and none were so bitter toward the Church as those
who left it. Moreover, in Czechoslovakia, a mass secession, in the
spirit of the pre-Reformation Czech reformer, John Huss, took place.
Over 1,000,000 believers, though only about 200 priests, withdrew
from Catholicism, soon after freedom of worship was proclaimed, and
founded a Czech National Church. For the most part, the seceders
adopted the Unitarian position, but a minority affiliated with the
Orthodox Church of Yugoslavia. To appease Czech national senti-

---

[3] In eastern Poland and neighboring areas the Uniate Oriental Church counted
about 5,000,000 adherents, almost all Ruthenians or Ukrainians in nationality.
Certain of the ceremonies and the liturgy of this church were identical with those
of the Orthodox Church, the language of the services was Old Slavonic, but the
faith and doctrine were Roman Catholic and the headship of the Pope was acknowledged. This hybrid religion was set up originally (1596) as a Polish device
with political implications, intended to separate the Ruthenians from their Russian
cousins. Membership was confined almost entirely to peasants who were subject to
Polish or Polonized landlords. The church served as a spawning bed of Ukrainian
nationalism and supplied, no doubt, the chief dynamic of anti-Polish feeling among
the Ukrainians.

ments, the papacy appointed a patriotic Czech archbishop of Prague in place of a German and Slovak bishops were substituted for Magyars in the Slovak counties. Catholicism in Germany, as is recounted in another place (Chap. XIII), encountered a resourceful and arbitrary competitor in National Socialism.

Republican Spain, where anti-clericalism was rampant, sharply reduced the traditional prerogatives of Catholicism. Ever since the campaigns against the Moors in the twilight of the medieval epoch— crusades, really—Spanish Catholicism had been somewhat different from Catholicism in other parts of Europe and the divergence deepened in very modern times. Church and State were allied more intimately in Spain than in any other European nation and the clergy were frequently an influential factor in public affairs.

By the Republican regime, which was set up in 1931, State and Church were separated and no longer would the government furnish subsidies for the maintenance of religion, nor permit churchmen to participate in public education. Under a series of laws the Jesuits were expelled and other monastic orders were required to pay taxes and dispose of their business enterprises; some ecclesiastical properties were expropriated. Not all of this anti-clerical legislation, to be sure, was fully enforced and the whole situation was thrown into confusion in 1936 upon the outbreak of civil war in Spain, (Chap. X).

In the course of that sanguinary struggle much church property was sacked and destroyed. Many clergymen were abused or done to death by partisans on both sides of the barricades. No Spanish institution was quite the same after that fratricidal contest as it had been before, though the Church revived much of her ancient splendor.

Roman Catholicism in Russia, where adherents were comparatively few, underwent the fate common to all religious organizations in the Soviet Union. Catholic chapels and seminaries were closed and the number of churches available for divine services dwindled to a mere fraction of the 1914 figure.

From an essentially political viewpoint the role of the Vatican— as a world force—was definitely enhanced in the period between wars. All the concordats or treaties which the Vatican had arranged with European governments, defining the rights and the limits of Catholic activity, were nullified during World War I, and new ones had to be negotiated. These treaties fortified the position of the faith in "Catholic" countries and broadened Vatican authority over the churches. In a limited way, the treaties recalled the medieval alliance between Church and State, for they allowed the clergy to share in public education on the lower levels,[4] and assured them of financial subsidies. On the other hand, the clergy were required to take an oath of allegiance to the state and to abstain from participation in political affairs.

The concordat with Mussolini of 1929 had peculiar significance, not alone for its content, but because it formed part of a wider settlement adjusting the relations of Church and State which had been gravely troubled ever since the soldiers of the Italian king occupied the Holy City in 1870. On the moot question of marriage, the Italian concordat recognized the validity of unions performed either by the clergy or by civil authorities. It was prescribed that Christian doctrine should be taught in the state schools "according to Catholic tradition" by teachers and from textbooks which had the approval of the bishop in each diocese. Though bishops and archbishops had to be individuals acceptable to the Italian government, the right of appointment was reserved to the Vatican.

Italian clergy were exempted from ordinary military service; full freedom for monastic orders was acknowledged; and the Church was declared at liberty to administer its own properties. Moreover, Catholic secular organizations, such as Boy Scouts and circles of girls, which were dedicated to the diffusion and application of religious principles, might function without molestation on the understanding that they would not engage in political activities.

By the epochal Lateran Treaty, signed at the same time as the concordat, a tiny territory about a mile square was set aside in Rome as the city of the Vatican over which the Pope was the independent temporal sovereign. Thus the Pope ruled this area in essentially the same way that his predecessors had governed the Papal States for hundreds of years before the unification of Italy in the 1860's. As token compensation for the territory which the papacy had lost at the time that Italy was united, the Fascist government agreed to pay the Vatican about $150,000,000 and to set up a fund of about $200,000,000, on which the interest would be turned over to the papacy annually.

The Holy See was permitted to have its own communications system and to publish the one uncensored newspaper in the Fascist kingdom. A long string of Italian anti-clerical laws was cast into oblivion. These arrangements restored the Holy See to the list of sovereign states and reconciled many a devout Italian Catholic to the kingdom.

[4] Roman Catholicism believes not only that the doctrines of the faith, but that other subjects should be taught to Catholic children against a Catholic background by Catholic teachers. It is held that the religious view of life affects more than just the teachings of religion itself and that for Catholics wholly secular education is not only inadequate but morally wrong.

On his side, the Pope validated the king's title to the old States of the Church, and to other territories that had been taken over by the State. Altogether a new chapter was begun in the history of Church and State in the Italian peninsula.

It was difficult, however, for the Catholic Church and the totalitarian State to work in close harmony in Italy or anywhere else. Bickering developed over marriage questions and, more seriously, over the Fascist claim to monopolize the education and social organizations of youth. As a rule the Church was obliged to yield. Papal condemnation of Fascism's anti-Jewish laws evoked angry rejoinders from Mussolini.

As concessions to the national religion, the Fascist regime imposed a ban on public Protestant propaganda, though not on Protestant churches, and prohibited the circulation of literature which for any reason was distasteful to the Catholic clergy.

The heightened prestige of the papacy in secular affairs was suggested in one way by the increase in diplomatic missions accredited to the Vatican. France, for example, resumed the political ties which militant anti-clericalism had severed a generation earlier. British and Dutch ministers were sent to the papal court for the first time since the Reformation. Without restoring formal diplomatic relations, which had lapsed in 1867, President Roosevelt appointed (1939) a special envoy to Rome. Altogether thirty-seven countries maintained legations at the Vatican and the Vatican in turn had diplomatic representation in almost all of these nations. It was standard Vatican policy to treat with any government, whether democratic or totalitarian, provided it met the minimum demands of the Church on subjects having religious implications.

For much the greater part of the era between the wars, from 1922 to 1939, the ancient and spacious chair of St. Peter was occupied by Pius XI, the 260th in his line. He was an old man of sixty five when he began his pontificate, but his reputation for vigor was amply sustained in the papal office. It was under his direction that treaties were negotiated with "Catholic" countries, the knotty "Roman Question" was adjusted, and a relentless campaign was conducted against the materialist doctrines and atheistic propaganda of Communism in general and the Soviet Union in particular.

Distrust and dread of the spread of the Soviet way of life colored papal policies in Europe generally and caused the Vatican to look upon anti-Soviet political movements as bulwarks of order and discipline. On more occasions than one, Pius XI vigorously assailed Communism as a "destructive force which menaces everything and has a program of social ruin." He exhorted the Catholic faithful to "pray, pray, pray, because truly it is only by the intervention of God that we may hope to see better days, and days free of a threat against everything we hold most sacred and most dear." By reason of the Pope's exalted spiritual office, his every utterance and deed carried special weight with his worldwide flock, both clergy and laity, though Catholics were not in conscience bound to agree with his views or to act upon his recommendations. But churchmen in several countries responded to the appeal to lead an offensive against atheistic godlessness, all of which did not fail to intensify ill-will in Moscow toward the Vatican.

While he thundered against Communism and all its works, Pius XI proclaimed a gospel of social justice and of greater consideration for the propertyless wage earners. In 1931, on the fortieth anniversary of Pope Leo XIII's celebrated pronouncement on capital and workers, Pius XI published an eloquent, seventy page encyclical restating and amplifying official Catholic teachings on social and economic subjects.

He roundly condemned unfettered competition in trade and industry and the principle that government should keep hands off economic processes. No less emphatically he denounced social creeds which taught class warfare and militant hostility to religion. Well aware of the maladies' which afflicted highly industrialized societies—the encyclical appeared in the midst of the Great Depression—the Pope was confident that the medicine of materialistic Socialism would make the patient worse rather than effect a cure. "No one," the encyclical asserted, "can be at the same time a sincere Catholic and a true Socialist," and by Socialist was meant, quite evidently, one whose social philosophy was grounded upon a secular, non-religious interpretation of life's purpose.

Pius XI was not guilty of indulging merely in exposition and destructive criticism. On the contrary, the teachings of the Church on social issues were explained with precision and in detail. Private property, for instance, while held to be a "natural" right was not without responsibilities: "In the use of property, men must take into account, not only their own advantages, but also the common good." Employees had a right to a living wage, and upon government devolved the responsibility of enforcing the duties implicit in property ownership and of safeguarding the general welfare of workers. It was asserted in the encyclical of 1931 that the greedy few who had accumulated financial and industrial power in their hands transgressed moral law and by their behavior fostered conditions which encouraged the diffusion of Communism. State action, animated by concepts of social justice, the return to "the teachings of the Gospel," obedience to "the eternal law of God"—that was the way of salvation for sorely-afflicted society, recommended by the Supreme Pastor of Catholicism.

And the words of the Pope were unlike seed sown on stony ground. In several of Europe's Catholic countries, political parties, as has been seen, adopted the Vatican code on social questions as their own, and pressed for the adoption of legislation to give the principles effective application. Among Catholic leaders in the United States, the views of the Vatican exerted a strong influence on behalf of social reform laws. On more narrowly social subjects, as well as on political and economic problems, Pope Pius XI spoke out in no uncertain terms. An encyclical on marriage, for example, extolled the divine character of Christian matrimony and condemned divorce, companionate marriage, family limitation by unnatural methods, and kindred practices of the 20th century, as "hateful abominations which reduce our cultured nations to the barbarous standards of savage peoples."

An appeal, too, was issued to all Christian believers to enter the Roman Catholic communion without reservations. That utterance put an end to conversations between Church of England theologians and Catholic scholars in which the differences that kept the two faiths apart were being quietly explored. To the Orthodox Church, the papacy addressed a special overture to reunite, but like similar entreaties across the centuries, this one failed of its purpose.

The revival of "racial" fanaticism in the thirties and the intrusion of governments into areas of life which Catholicism regarded as outside the sphere of Caesar, provoked strongly worded protests from the Pope. Exhortations urging arbitration of international quarrels and appealing for limitation of armaments, admonitions to statesmen that their policies were leading inescapably to war, poured from the Vatican in a steady stream. Amidst the stormy confusion of secular politics, Pius XI proclaimed a Holy Year in 1933, inviting the faithful of all the world to Rome to organize a spiritual union for peace.

Pius XI was not unmindful that his primary duty was to safeguard the purity of the faith, over which he was the final and infallible authority. Doctrinal and intellectual controversies which had troubled Catholic circles at the turn of the century were stilled. Papal letters to the faithful dwelt upon the high virtue of scholarship, provided that it kept within the framework of historic Catholic belief.

Pius XII, a gentle and mystical soul, although experienced in the ways of secular diplomacy, acceded to the papal throne early in 1939. He pleaded eloquently for the maintenance of peace among the nations and made energetic efforts, within the limitations imposed by the impartial character of his office, to keep the powers from flying at one another's throats again. His coat-of-arms depicted a dove holding an olive branch in its beak and the device, "Opus Justitiae Pax," (The Work of Justice is Peace). Truly Pius XII remarked: "The sword can impose peace, but it cannot preserve peace."

In some quarters it was believed that papal diplomacy might contribute importantly to ending World War II. That, however, did not come to pass. Yet Pius XII frequently set forth his convictions on the way to peace and on how to maintain peace. His Christmas address of 1939 anticipated the Atlantic Charter (Chap. XXII) by almost two years. The Pope's cautious, even-handed neutrality during the war, as befitted the shepherd of all Catholics, brought down on his head the maledictions of critics in both belligerent camps. Each of them held that the Pope should publicly denounce the acts and methods of the enemy, and enjoin devout Catholics on the opposing side against taking part in the war effort.[5]

Protestantism

Always a house divided against itself, though free from the fantastic sectarianism of the United States, Protestantism in Europe predominated in Great Britain, in Holland, in the Scandinavian countries, and in Switzerland. It was also the faith of two out of three of the Christians in Germany and had the allegiance of active minorities in France and Hungary.[6] Much more than the older forms of Christianity, Protestantism, whether Anglican, Lutheran, or Calvinist, felt the impact of the secular philosophy and currents of the age. The Protestant principle of individualism, moreover, encouraged religious indifferentism and the fact that Protestantism prevailed in countries where industrialism and commerce were most developed was not without its bearing upon religious notions and devotions.

Where Protestantism was officially linked up with government, as in England and Scandinavia, there was some agitation for disestablishment. How close State and Church were may be illustrated by the case of Sweden, where almost everyone belonged, at least nominally, to the national faith, Lutheranism. Over the Church, the Swedish king exercised certain administrative powers, though he was not its ruler in any exact sense; no legislation on church matters was valid without parliamentary sanction and an ecclesiastical assembly might veto any law on church affairs that the parliament passed. In friendly cooperation with the church authorities, the Swedish government furnished reli-

[5] See S. S. Hayden, "Foreign Policy of the Vatican," *Foreign Policy Association Bulletin*, XIX (January 15, 1944).

[6] The world over, Protestantism counted about 175,000,000 members, about half of them in the United States.

gious instruction in the public schools. Relations between state and Protestant church between the wars were not particularly troubled in any European country except in National Socialist Germany. (Chap. XIII).

During World War I the officials of the Church of England imagined that conditions bred of the conflict would foster a lively spiritual reawakening. A national "mission of repentance and hope" was planned in 1916, but the popular response to the enterprise was described as "most disappointing." Anglican theological schools which had been closed during the war reopened very slowly; some remained bolted and barred for lack of candidates. Whereas in 1900 the Church of England had over 21,000 clergymen, in 1928 there were just a few more than 16,000. Attendance upon divine services in the non-conformist churches as well as in the official national church fell off. England's "Free" churches, of which the Wesleyan Methodist was the largest, were credited with over 2,000,000 members. They were noted for their intense spiritual vigor and simple gospel. They looked askance at plans for Christian unity.

It was often said that only ten per cent of the British attended places of worship with regularity. Still the well-off regarded themselves as bound to the church, by whose rites they were baptized, confirmed, married, and buried. Spirited evangelists could usually attract a following in London, though the American revivalist, Aimee Semple McPherson in 1928, somehow failed to strike fire. Children receiving religious instruction in British Sunday Schools in 1928 were a fifth less numerous than a generation earlier. Nor was the decline in religious interest a purely urban phenomenon, for in not a few English villages, many countryfolk entered the church only for baptisms and other rites. The rural church had all the appearances of a dying institution. Strong views in favor of the disestablishment of the Church of England were expressed, and the separation of Church and State in Wales was actually effected in 1920.

Out of line with the currents of the age was a novel version of Christian simplicity called the "Oxford Group" movement. The child of a hearty, amiable, mystically minded American, Frank Buchman, this movement held that the Almighty had a guiding plan for the life of every man. It placed great emphasis on "quiet times," in which, Quaker-like, believers listened for guidance that would help in settling their own and the world's perplexities. At "Group" week-ends in the English countryside "Buchmanites" sought mutual aid by freely sharing confessions of their shortcomings. The Group enrolled some Anglican clergymen and well-to-do folk, and for a time it had a vogue in

Oxford and other university communities, but Buchman's plans for attracting industrial workers came to grief.

Future students may look upon the labors to bring about greater unity among non-Roman Catholic Christians as a major feature of Christian history in the era between wars. Even more ambitious was the hope of gathering all Christian communions together in one comprehensive organization, under the emblem of "Unity in Diversity, Diversity in Unity." Time had worked to soften the theological differences among the sects that had emerged from the Reformation and the growing concern for the social application of Christianity healed many an old wound.

During the war, furthermore, members of divergent confessions had been thrown into closer contact, which, on the whole, fostered mutual sympathy. Perhaps the most compelling of all the forces that were conducive to Christian solidarity was the belief that a united front was imperative if the struggle against pagan naturalism and materialism was to be fought to a triumphant victory.

Sectarian divisions within Scotch Presbyterianism and English Methodism were closed, and four Protestant groups joined forces in China (1927) to establish the Church of Christ in that missionary field. The lines which separated Lutheran and Calvinist in Germany were largely erased by the merger, in 1928, of the two faiths in twenty-eight of the German states into the German Evangelical Church Federation, and subsequently by the pressure of the National Socialist regime. Similar coalitions brought together Protestant bodies in Switzerland and France. The Anglican Church established intercommunion with the Old Catholics, a tiny anti-papal sect which appeared in the 1870's, and put out feelers for union with the Churches of Sweden, Finland, and Estonia and with Orthodox Catholicism.

Even more interesting were conferences of international Protestantism, at which points of difference were explored and points of agreement evaluated in the hope of facilitating more unity of understanding and action.[7] This movement reached its high point at a conference in Oxford (1937), the most nearly worldwide Christian

[7] The leading spirit of this movement was Dr. Nathan Soderblom, head of the Swedish Lutheran Church, who combined the lofty idealism of a religious thinker with the energy and ability of a practical statesman. As a liaison man he brought together Christian leaders of former enemy countries after the war, and in 1935 his dream of a world Protestant congress was realized. Held in Stockholm, this "Universal Christian Conference on Life and Work" attracted delegates from thirty-seven countries and most of the Churches. For the first time Protestant leaders sat down together with Orthodox Catholic divines.

assembly of non-Roman Catholics in history. German Protestants were not represented, due to the refusal of the National Socialist state to grant passports to delegates, but prominent representatives from the Orthodox Catholic Church took part. Discussions at Oxford ranged over a wide variety of topics—topics with political, economic, and social implications and little time was spent on doctrinal and theological issues.

Resolutions of the Oxford conference denounced national egoism, the abuse of minorities, unfair treatment of the underprivileged and anti-religious movements. One by one the shortcomings of the existing economic order, as seen through Protestant eyes, were listed. Attention was called to the intimate connection between international economic rivalries and international war. On the position which the Churches should take if and when the nations were again immersed in armed conflict, there were wide diversities of opinion and no agreement could be reached, though the League of Nations was endorsed as an ideal institution. To arrange for similar meetings later, a world council of churches, embracing all non-papal Christians, was established.[8]

By Protestant leadership the whole complex of foreign missionary enterprise was subjected to a process of re-evaluation. The evils of competition in mission fields were acknowledged and understandings to remove them were arranged. On foreign fields greater care was devoted to aiding converts in improving their material and social conditions on farms and in towns. Schools and hospitals, social betterment organizations, and agricultural stations reflected the intention of Protestantism to apply Christianity in practical ways among backward peoples.

For continental Protestantism in the era between the wars, the name above every other name in the realm of religious thought was Karl Barth, whose thinking was vividly colored by the secular environment in which it was done. Swiss by birth and a liberal in religious and social outlook by training, Barth experienced a profound conversion during the war and its disillusioning aftermath. Fresh study of the ideas of the Reformation and of the Bible diverted him from the liberal tradition and into the hard patterns of historic Calvinist thought. Barth's "theology of crisis" was grounded upon a pessimistic conception of human nature which made man puny in the

---

[8] At Dutch Utrecht in 1938, Protestant Christians drafted a charter for the world council of churches, providing for a central executive committee and a general assembly to discuss matters of universal concern and to consider plans for organic union. At once seventy-three church bodies ratified the charter.

scales of the Almighty. The Deity, he thought, was a relentless sovereign, whom men could not discover by mere thought, but only by means of divine revelation.

Instead of the inductive approach to the eternal verities to which Protestant liberalism was attached, Barth preferred the anti-intellectual deductive method, utterly repudiating any appeal to pure reason. The Bible should not be treated like other literature, sacred or profane, but rather, Barth thought, it should be accepted as an authentic revelation of the Almighty to human beings. Instead of busying itself in an attempt to establish the Kingdom of God on this earth, Christianity should summon men to repentance for their sins of omission and commission, and to prayer. For the social action of liberal and applied Christianity, Barth substituted a militant orthodoxy of meditation and reflection.

Opponents assailed Barthianism as "theological fascism," but none could deny the impact of Barth's doctrines upon the Protestant thought of the age. Indeed, the degree of assent or dissent from his views was accounted the surest touchstone of a Protestant's theology in Germany and neighboring countries. Rational and socialized Protestantism in Germany, which had penetrated the minds and pens of theological professors far more than it had affected German pastors and laymen, almost disappeared in favor of this Barthian reversion to the older molds of belief and of other competing versions of the creed of Luther or Calvin. After holding chairs of theology in several of the most distinguished German universities, Barth was expelled from the country because of his outspoken condemnation of National Socialism for interfering in the spiritual sphere.

Orthodox Catholicism

For the greater part of Russia and the Balkan Peninsula the historic faith had been Orthodox Catholicism, often miscalled Greek Catholicism, which in the 11th century had formally separated from the western or Roman Catholic Church. Wherever it existed, Orthodoxy was intimately allied with government, for the idea of a free Church in a free state had no place in eastern thinking. The Church was regarded as subordinate to the State in secular affairs, and superior to the State in spiritual matters, though in practice it was not always easy to tell where ecclesiastical authority ended and the authority of government began.

As has already been explained (Chap. V), the Orthodox Church of Russia, together with other religious organizations, experienced very serious hardships on the morrow of the Bolshevik Revolution, and only under great difficulty did the faith survive at all. Emigré Orthodox clergymen, who found refuge in Paris, frankly acknowledged the faults and shortcomings of their Church in the past and set to work vitalizing the thinking and social attitudes of Orthodoxy against the day when religious freedom might be proclaimed in the USSR.

Political convulsions in Turkey, too, wrought upon Orthodox Catholicism. If the Turkish government of Mustapha Kemal had had its own way, the ancient Christian patriarchate at Constantinople would have been abolished, but the Great Powers of the west intervened and blocked that. The patriarch's authority was, however, curtailed by the transfer of Greeks from Asia Minor to Greece, and by the grant of autonomy to the Church in Albania, so that his communicants did not exceed 300,000.

As the national faith of the several Balkan countries, Orthodoxy, a curious blend of mysticism, ecclesiasticism, and patriotism, preserved its pre-war position as the State Church. Popular attachment in the Balkans to the faith was generally strong and deep, for the Church, her monasteries, and her clergy had kept alive national cultures and hopes in the long centuries of Turkish domination. In places, the Church had furnished the inspiration for wars of liberation, political independence, and expansion. In the light of what had happened to the faith in great Russia some Orthodox divines in the Balkans discussed the desirability of separating Church and State, but nothing positive was accomplished.

At a great Orthodox Congress in Athens (1936)—the first in more than two centuries—and another in Bucharest in 1939, scholars debated on theological and administrative questions. Most of them preferred to follow traditional paths; only a few contended for revision in the Orthodox creed and polity, for more emphasis on the sermon in public worship, and on Bible study for laymen. The Orthodox Church never experienced a Reformation, so that there was no tradition of conflict with Protestantism, and therefore the clergy were not unreceptive to approaches from the Church of England for "reunion." Repeated consultations with the object of arranging a consolidation were held, without, however, making much progress.

Judaism

Though it has repeatedly been attempted, no really satisfactory census of the Jewish population in the world has yet been made. Much depends upon the scope of the enumeration—whether it includes the followers of the Hebrew religion in one or another of its versions, or whether it is broadened to cover those who have shared in the social and cultural heritage of Judaism, but who have abandoned the religious faith of their fathers. In any case, the total must have been somewhere in the vicinity of 20,000,000 before World War II.

Jews living in eastern Europe, in Poland, in Rumania, and the Soviet Union made up the larger part of the European Hebrew constituency. Where free exercise of religion was permitted (which was not true, of course, in Soviet Russia), the Jewish faithful tended to follow traditional patterns of belief, of custom and costume, little affected by the ebb and flow of new ideas. To the west—in Germany and the large cities of other countries, Jewry formed only a small minority and the tendency to assimilation there was promoted by considerable intermarriage with Gentiles. Individual Jewish synagogues reformed their theology in the light of Biblical scholarship, the advancement of science, and related intellectual currents.

The cherished dream of a Zionist state for Jews seemed on the way to fulfillment when Palestine was opened to Jewish settlement (Chap. XVII). Aided by the large section of Jewry which was Zionist in conviction and by others not Zionists but who desired to see a Jewish center created in Palestine, tens of thousands of Jews sought a new freedom in that ancient land. Waves of anti-Jewish feeling rolled over central and southern Europe with portentous rapidity, especially after the Great Depression of the thirties, swelling the tide of emigration to Palestine.

Islam

Islam, once the dread terror of Christendom, has fallen far from its former estate. So far as Europe is concerned, the followers of the Prophet are confined to narrow districts in the Balkan peninsula. Outside of Europe, however, Mohammedanism is the creed of at least one tenth of the world's population with adherents in Turkey, in the Arab lands, in southern Asia, notably the huge Moslem community of India, and in Africa. In the central regions of the "Dark Continent," Moslem missionaries energetically competed with Christians for the allegiance of the Negroes. Since it was the faith of millions of colonial subjects of European countries, Mohammedanism was a spiritual force that had constantly to be taken into account by imperial administrations.

In connection with the history of Turkey (Chap. VIII), it has been explained how the Turkish caliphate was abolished and religious reforms were effected in Turkish Mohammedanism. True, some learned Turks and the peasant masses held to Islamic orthodoxy, but other intellectuals, under the influence of western science and secularism, pleaded for theological reconstruction. Only sentimental ties bound the more zealously nationalistic followers of Mustapha Kemal to the creed of Mohammed.

It seemed apparent that Islam needed a new prophet to reinvigorate the faith, but Moslem doctrine taught that there could be no prophet after Mohammed. For all that, Moslemism could not be lightly dismissed. As a religion and a way of life Mohammedanism in its great centuries had contributed to the renaissance of western civilization, and by reason of its tens of millions of adherents, its total lack of racial discrimination, its missionary fervor and its internationalism, Islam had an indisputable claim to be called a world faith.

CHAPTER XVI

Literature and the Fine Arts

Literary Trends and Traits

IF A man dwelling on Mars gazed down upon Europe in the tumultuous interval between wars, he must have been appalled by the ferment, the dissent, the uncertainty, in creative literature and the fine arts, no less than in politics and economics. For whether one thinks of the novels of competence which poured in a flood from the presses, or the essays and literary criticism, or the poetry and the drama, the essential impression is one of perplexity and complexity. Literature faithfully mirrored the unhappy tension, the general political and social unrest, in which it was produced, and it had immense value for an understanding and interpretation of the thought and feeling of the inter-war period.

Once publication costs had receded after the war, the literary output of Europe surpassed all records in quantity. The quality, to be sure, must be determined by the winnowing processes of time rather than by the immediate estimates of contemporary critics. Men of letters in nations which had been enchained before 1914 had fuller and freer scope for their talents, as the writers in the Czech language sufficiently illustrate. With the realization of the dream of an independent Czech nation a diversified literature expressed a virile self-confidence and a glowing optimism for the future—a future generally envisaged along democratic and socialized lines.

For their materials, European writers commonly turned to subjects that were all around them and to the urgent problems of contemporary civilization: the sharpening industrial conflict, the vision of a radically reordered society, real or imagined incidents from the war, the quest for religious and philosophical certitude, the manner of life of the rustic and the proletarian. The speculations and findings of science, especially psychoanalysis, which emphasized the less than conscious in human nature, made a deep impression upon imaginative literature between the wars, as had been the case earlier in the 20th century.

376

Historical romances, apart from those with war themes, lost something of their former popularity, but fictionalized biography, in which established fact was mingled with conjectural fancy and trivialities were treated melodramatically, appealed to a large circle of readers. The Englishman, G. Lytton Strachey, pioneered in this "new biography" with witty and satirical portraits of *Eminent Victorians;* André Maurois cultivated this form of literature successfully in France and Emil Ludwig made a business of it in Germany. Not less favorable was the reception given to mystery and crime stories, the doings of dauntless detectives, which appeared in a positive torrent to meet an eager demand. Anthologies of various literary categories were abundant and served as beacons or gleaners.

Literature in Britain

For sheer diversity and international influence the palm among European literatures in the era between wars must, no doubt, be awarded to Britain. Authors with well-established prestige vied with younger writers in exploring the virtues, the faults, and the peculiarities of the British mind and spirit, in interpreting the present and forecasting the future. H. G. Wells, probably the most widely read author of the time, created stimulating reading for those who could and would look forward. The theme of advancing civilization by means of a planned world order, administered by men of intelligence and good will, found in him its most consistent and versatile exponent. Wells' *Outline of History*, which presumed to record the past from the origins of the globe to A.D. 1920, and contained a blueprint for the future, had considerable influence in arousing popular interest in history and in inspiring similar surveys of other fields of knowledge.

In other works of distinction, brimful of ideas and information— *The Salvaging of Civilization, The World of William Clissold, The Work, Wealth and Happiness of Mankind,* and *The Anatomy of Frustration*—a colossal interview with himself in which allusion was made to every cause for which he campaigned—the indefatigable and inexhaustible Wells implored his readers to allow full scope to reason in the reformation of society. Although disillusioning events dimmed the extravagant idealism of his wartime publications, Wells continued to be ever the optimistic crusader, the confident prophet of better days that were yet to be, once enlightenment and active intelligence were enthroned.

The contributions of G. B. Shaw, iconoclastic and controversial as usual, sustained his reputation as a world figure, the Voltaire of his century. From the barbed arrows of this dogmatic skeptic, no tradition

nor institution, whether state, church, or society in the broad, escaped
and what Shaw thought and wrote captivated readers who longed for
a nobler and more rational way of life. In *The Apple Cart* Shaw
launched out with customary ridicule against political democracy and
pleaded for a government managed by experts. The variety of conceptions which men have come upon in their quest for the Almighty
he elucidated in a deeply thoughtful parable, *The Adventures of a
Black Girl in Search of God.* The spiritual abyss reserved for those
who put their trust in mere riches alone Shaw depicted in *The Million-
airess.*

The unrest and uneasiness of the age, the literature of dissent and
bitterness, were admirably represented by D. H. Lawrence, novelist
and poet. His fundamental approach to life, the ceaseless strife between the animal traits and the finer spiritual sensitivities in man, his
unmitigated contempt for the smug comfort of the bourgeoisie, his
peculiarities in style and subject matter—all these Lawrence exhibited
in his last novel, *The Virgin and the Gypsy.* Imitators of Lawrence,
though lacking in the master's subtlety and artistry, flourished in
many countries.

Aldous Huxley exploited his encyclopedic knowledge of science in
the penetratingly satirical *Brave New World,* and his mordantly cynical view of human nature and his advocacy of greater enlightenment in
everyday living were well revealed in *Eyeless in Gaza.* John Galsworthy completed a richly detailed chronicle of the wealthy English
middle class, *The Forsyte Saga,* condemning the contented complacency of the class without reserve and exciting sympathy for the
victims of discrimination and social injustice. *A Passage to India,* by
E. M. Forster, analyzed racial prejudice with rare understanding, and
was acclaimed as "the greatest novel of the century." Out of step with
staunchly realistic fiction was Joseph Conrad, one of the foremost
masters of the English language, though born a Pole. Tales of the sea
and of high adventure written in an engaging narrative assured him
a secure niche in the twentieth century literary hall of fame.

Toward the end of the 1920's, after Britain had begun to recover
from the weariness which the war had imprinted on thought and emotion, story-tellers recounted episodes from World War I which were
more often than not pacifistic sermons on the futility of the ghastly
struggle. With passion and fidelity, Richard Aldington's *Death of a
Hero* arraigned and satirized the generation that marched to war, and
furnished glimpses of the grim conflict itself. H. M. Tomlinson in *All
Our Yesterdays* recaptured the poignancy of the war in distinguished
and sensitive prose. And two notable dramatists reproduced the spirit

of wartime: R. C. Sheriff's *Journey's End,* a remarkably faithful portrait of life in the trenches, and Allan Monkhouse's *The Conquering Hero,* a penetrating study of a conscientious objector who emerged a hero in spite of himself.

Noel Coward, the leading English theatrical personality of the inter-war period, achieved distinction with a play on social types devoid of all moral sense, *The Vortex.* He was probably best known for the spectacular patriotic drama, *Cavalcade,* which was an immense success on both stage and screen. The plays of the whimsical James M. Barrie —*The Boy David,* for instance—did nothing to enhance the international fame he had gained before 1914.

Outstanding in British polemical, literary criticism was Gilbert K. Chesterton, a devotee of paradox and a militant defender of Catholic Christianity against the assaults of materialism. His friend, Hilaire Belloc, belonged in the same class for he, too, ranged far and wide in the literary categories and had an undisguised bias for the values of religious medievalism.

On his eighty-fifth birthday, England's poet laureate, Robert Bridges, issued *The Testament of Beauty*—expressing the mellow wisdom of old age—which seemed likely to be an enduring monument in English literature. In this work Bridges wandered extensively over the realms of ·knowledge, touching upon matters of transient as well as permanent concern—from French painting to intimations of immortality—and he tried to fashion a satisfactory synthesis out of it all. His successor as Poet Laureate, John Masefield, mingled verse and prose in *The "Wanderer" of Liverpool,* an appreciation of shipping, man, and beauty. He composed, too, some animated pictures of rural sporting life.

The Torchbearers, an elaborate epic inspired by the marvels of astronomical research, brought fresh fame to Alfred Noyes, who hitherto had confined himself largely to verse on happy familiar topics. Every emotion from pleasure to disgust, from hope to despair was explored in new patterns and rhythms by a little appreciated poet, L. Aaronson, in *Christ in the Synagogue.* The leading poet of pessimism and disillusionment was T. S. Eliot, Missouri-born but a naturalized British subject. Much that he wrote, as *Ash Wednesday* bears witness, was rich in illusion and shrouded in obscurity, requiring careful analysis of phrase and form. He contrived to reduce to verse the despairing mood and moral sterility of the time and was scrupulously studied by younger poets. Toward the close of the epoch Eliot's verse, *Burnt Norton* for example, became less captious and more hopeful in tone, with a tendency to mysticism.

Three first-rate literary craftsmen of Irish origins, James Joyce, George W. Russell, and Sean O'Casey, made distinguished contributions. Joyce caused a great sensation with *Ulysses,* a vast psychological survey of the tumultuous physical and mental life of a group of Dubliners through a single day. Written as a reaction against formalized patterns in the novel, *Ulysses* was distinguished by its gusto, great vitality, and odd vocabulary; for its obscenity, as some judges interpreted it, its coarse frankness in the eyes of others, the work was long legally banned, but its technique and content exerted a considerable influence upon aspiring fiction writers and a kind of *Ulysses* cult came into being.

G. W. Russell, better known by his pen name AE, participated actively in the Irish Nationalist cause and busied himself with issues of social significance as *The Interpreters* reveals. As a poet—*The House of the Titans and Other Poems*—Russell wrote lyrics, strongly tinged with mysticism. *The Plough and the Stars* by O'Casey, another crusader for Irish freedom, was a beautifully written drama, interpreting characters that participated in the Irish rebellion of 1916, in which high comedy was exquisitely blended with stark tragedy.

French Literature [1]

In the wider perspective of time, historians of comparative literature may accord French writing first place in the era between the wars, for variety, verve, novelty, and artistic craftsmanship. French literature was exceedingly diversified, notably cosmopolitan, and defeatist, sounding the sharp staccato of a disenchanted, war-weary generation. French men of letters cared for human values of universal significance, interpreted the manners and morals of the hour, ruthlessly probed the inner springs of behavior, and candidly judged the virtues and weaknesses of Frenchmen in particular and of mankind in the large. Because they neglected to warn their countrymen of national political dangers in the 1930's, because of the deep accents of pacifism and international fraternity in much of their writing, French authors have been charged with a measure of responsibility for the military humiliation of France in 1940.

From the legion of French writers who inquired into the manner, motives, and distresses of society, it is possible to select only a few, distinguished for originality and cleverness. Marcel Proust, supremely

[1] In this survey, literature in continental languages has been largely restricted to books which, on the basis of artistic merit or popular appeal, publishers have judged suitable for translation into English.

a novelist's novelist, may some day be recognized as the foremost of the lot. In his many-volumed classic, *Remembrance of Things Past*, Proust reproduced in one spacious, satirical, and philosophical interpretation the complex material and spiritual strands of French civilization during the half century in which he lived. While all social groups were represented—over 200 characters made up the cast—the central figures were exceptional and erotic folk (some of them acquaintances of the author) removed from the ordinary run of mortals in their passions and prejudices, in their vices and abnormalities, and in their concentration on social affairs. Remarkable for brilliant analyses of human behavior and for masterly descriptions of mental states, Proust's masterpiece firmly established the psychoanalytical technique in French story-telling.

André Gide, the leader of the French literary anarchists in the 1920's, has been described as "a cynic with a conscience." Conceiving of man in amoral and non-ethical terms, Gide insisted that truth and sincerity were the cardinal virtues and hypocrisy, the darkest of vices. His *The Counterfeiters* stood high among the books necessary for an understanding of French public morals and private manners in the years after the Armistice. In it Gide derided convention for convention's very own sake in no uncertain language and gave a patent of literary respectability to eccentric individualism and moral vagaries. Convinced that private property was socially wrong, Gide eventually wheeled into the camp of Communism, though a visit he paid to the Soviet Union and first hand acquaintance with the Stalinist version of Communism proved signally upsetting.

The authentic mouthpiece of the youth of France, distracted and driven to cynicism by the war and its sequel, was the aristocratic Henri de Montherlant, whose *The Dream*, an autobiography from World War I, resembled a score of similar books by writers of lesser genius. As a physical equivalent and substitute for the trenches, he recommended athletics and vigorous sports, as *The Bull Fighters* testified. A mocker of patriotism and humanitarianism, Montherlant could write, "It is equally foolish to die for humanity and one's country, for these will eventually become as obsolete as God." In the novels of François Mauriac, *The Desert of Love, The Vipers' Tangle*, the baser traits of the provincial French bourgeoisie were unconventionally exposed. Rough passions predominated, which sometimes led men back to the mystical religion of their fathers. An exponent of Catholicism as the social savior, though hardly a proselytizer, Mauriac sponsored an entire school of Catholic novelists.

An almost unique optimism and aloofness from the world of reality pervaded Jean Giraudoux's romantic *Suzanne and the Pacific*. In an essay contest a rural schoolgirl won a ticket for a world cruise; shipwrecked in the Pacific, Suzanne had a grand time playing at Robinson Crusoe, living with nature on a desert isle for three years, yet she protested not at all when a party of British scientists rescued her and carried her back to civilization. Unconvinced that the world as he knew it was the best of all possible worlds, Giraudoux still doubted whether much improvement could be effected, at least not swiftly. In *My Friend From Limousin*, a tale of a French soldier who, as a victim of amnesia, eventually emerged as a German politician, Giraudoux drew a deeply thoughtful contrast between French and German national character. A sensitive and warm-hearted nationalist, Giraudoux sympathized with the Vichy regime after the German victory over France in 1940.

Like Giraudoux, Paul Morand was a minor French diplomatic official who saw much of the world and what he saw he interpreted in serious, dispassionate, and distinctly pessimistic novels. In two books which created a major literary sensation, *Open All Night* and *Closed All Night*, he described pathological human specimens, here and there in Europe, who had been tossed up in the ugly confusion of the war's aftermath. Well acquainted with the United States, Morand in *World Champions* trenchantly traced the vicissitudes of four companions, students and graduates of Columbia University, and penned lively comparisons between his French homeland and the exuberant New World. It was his despairing belief that intermingling of peoples, instead of promoting understanding and good will, fostered distrust and antipathy.

Literary critics groaned under the sheer weight of huge family sagas and historical novels running into many volumes which poured from the pens of some eminent French writers. Besides Proust, there was Romain Rolland's *The Soul Enchanted*, much of which reflected the contemporary currents in French national culture; here were the years of the war, the years of corruption and despair together with a large amount of revolutionary propaganda. Inbued with a lively sense of social responsibility, Rolland, once a warm admirer of Count Leo Tolstoi and Gandhi, shifted his allegiance to Lenin and his ways.

Men of Good Will, by Jules Romains, scientist as well as philosopher, was a massive sociological panorama of French and Parisian society during and before the war. Almost every facet of human activity was minutely analyzed: politics, economics, nationalism, the tragic imbecilities of war, the higher living, all were grist to Romain's mill and he ground exceedingly fine. He was a man of good will, an advocate of progress and justice in human relations, though precisely what Romains meant by such terms was concealed in mystery.

Not dissimilar in scope was George Duhamel's masterwork, *Pasquier Chronicles,* a family saga which expounded the theme that regimented existence in an intensified machine-economy threatened to submerge utterly the emancipated individualism of the forepart of the 20th century. Duhamel emerged from the fires of World War I with his faith in civilized ways badly shaken. In *The Heart's Domain,* he preached a gospel of pacifism, brotherhood, and the renunciation of corrosive materialism. *Scenes from the Life of the Future* recorded impressions Duhamel picked up on a quick visit to the United States; "Americanism" signified for the sensitive Duhamel, the mastery of the machine over man and the degradation of the finer values of living.

For *The Thibaults,* a colossal and intensely realistic portrait of a prosperous French middle class family early in this century, Roger Martin du Gard, a kind of 20th century Zola, was given the Nobel literary prize. Centering upon the career of a young insurgent in revolt against his elders, the work was given power and distinction by the author's discriminating understanding of the eccentricities of human nature, his sage philosophizing about war, and his unswerving devotion to truth as he saw it. An intense hater of armed conflict, Martin du Gard believed strongly in peace at any price, as did so many of his literary contemporaries.

Strongly left-wing in outlook among the prominent French novelists were Henri Barbusse and André Malraux. Author of *Under Fire,* at once a brutally matter-of-fact narrative of the war and a moving pacifist tract, Barbusse went over to militant economic radicalism as *The Inferno* and an eulogistic tribute, *Stalin,* exhibit. Revolutionary Marxism in action furnished the inspiration and the materials for *Man's Fate,* by Malraux, a gruesome, exhaustive account of the doings of foreigners who heroically sacrificed themselves in a futile effort to liberate the toiling Chinese masses. The fortitude and faith of a Communist who secretly intrigued against Hitlerism was depicted in another of Malraux's stirring proletarian novels, *Days of Wrath.* Arrested, cast into a dark cell, subjected to gross physical abuse, the disciple of Marx contemplated taking his own life, but throughout the grim ordeal he was sustained by his confidence in the ideal of human fraternity—a faith that was confirmed when a comrade took his place in prison, enabling him to escape. Life among French villagers was instructively defined by Alphonse Chateaubriant in *The Peat Cutters* and by Jean Gione in *Hill of Destiny,* a novel of unusual distinction telling of elementary folkways in Provençe.

French dramatists of the period leaned toward psychological themes rather than the sociological topics which had been popular before 1914 and frequently they chose pathological cases for depiction. *The Weaker Sex* by Edouard Bourdet and Paul Raynal's *The Unknown Soldier,* a sprightly satire on war, may be cited as typical French dramatic productions.

Of the French poets, Paul Claudel and Paul Valéry, both outstanding as stylists, promised to have enduring value. Claudel, sometime ambassador to Japan and later to the United States, revealed in his verse the profound influence of his conception of metaphysical Catholicism, to which he had been converted after an extraordinary Paul-like experience. His lyrical pieces—*Feuilles des Saints* and *La Père Humilié*—medieval in thought and majestic in composition, have been likened to "a cathedral in an age of jazz." Called a poet-mathematician, Valéry was noted for emphasis on intellectualism, the absence of sentimentalism, and purity of form in his verse. He published little but the collection *Charmes* contains one of the finest pieces of French poetry, *La Cimetière Marin,* in which Valéry attempted to reconcile somehow problems of living and dying.

Literature in Spain

Part of the intellectual background of the Spanish revolutionary turmoil of the 1930's (Chap. X) was the literature of that country. Though inferior to the French in quality and quantity, it was not undistinguished and displayed more originality, color, and vigor than Spain had known for three centuries. Spanish writers pleaded for thoroughgoing reform in Spanish ways of living and upbraided the ruling elements for neglecting to put Spain abreast of the nations beyond the Pyrenees. In José Ortega y Gasset and Miguel de Unamuno, Spain possessed two intellectual publicists whose writings also appealed to an international audience. Professional philosophers both, they directed their learned exhortations primarily to the thin layer of educated Spaniards.

A liberal conservative in viewpoint, Ortega y Gasset observed his times through Spenglerian glasses (p. 391) and caustically assailed the Spanish Bourbon monarchy and Spanish degeneracy. For the unlettered multitude, his detestation was boundless, and in *The Revolt of the Masses,* he dwelt upon the evils of mob dictatorship. He much preferred a progressive democracy and for a time in fact served as a deputy of the Spanish Republic. *Invertebrate Spain* mirrored Ortega's mind when his country was in the throes of revolution and reconstruction.

So critical was Unamuno of the Bourbon tyranny that he was sent into exile, where he expressed in sonnets the bitterness he felt in his heart. Very popular with the rising generation of intellectuals, Unamuno discoursed vigorously at one time or another on all manner of subjects and reposed greater confidence in the common man than Ortega, provided he had intelligent leadership. Unamuno's generally liberal outlook was queerly colored by a kind of anarchic mysticism which scorned scientific materialism and searched ceaselessly for the way to personal immortality; *The Agony of Christianity* recounted the difficulties, present in any age, of reconciling the ideals of the Christian creed with the practical exigencies of everyday existence.

Immensely popular in the English-reading world was the prolific Spanish novelist, Blasco Ibañez, whose international fame stemmed from a war-epic, *The Four Horsemen of the Apocalypse*. From Argentina the reader was carried to France where battle actions were described and the four horsemen, symbolical of the ravages of war, slaughter, conquest, famine, and disease, galloped roughshod. Essentially a political manifesto lauding the Allies and spewing forth hatred of Germany, this novel possessed every quality required for a best-seller and as a film it became world famous. For participation in revolutionary conspiracies, Blasco Ibañez repeatedly felt the heavy hand of the Spanish government, yet he persisted in his propaganda. In 1924 he issued a violently republican polemic, *Spain Under the Terror: Alfonso XIII Unmasked,* and then took refuge in France.

Though Blasco Ibañez wrote picturesque sociological novels on manners in Valencia, his talent as an interpreter of Spanish life was doubtless inferior to that of Pío Baroja. Sympathetic with the poorer and downtrodden section of Spanish society, though with small faith in Utopian patterns for social betterment, Baroja loved to irritate the staid bourgeoisie with dispassionate portraits of the lower orders. *Red Dawn,* for example, told of a vagabond who grew weary of aimless adventuring and settled down to a prosaic existence, while his young brother, after preparing for service in the Church, abandoned religion for Anarchism; every version of Anarchism had full and free exposition at public meetings marked by doctrinal turbulence.

Baiting the middle class likewise appealed strongly to Ramón del Valle Inclán, who composed vividly realistic narratives of literary "Bohemians" and wrote of the barbaric cruelties and sensual degeneracy of South American revolutionaries; *The Tiger* was a representative example of his art. Valle Inclán staunchly supported the Spanish Republican cause.

It may be that Ramón J. Sender most accurately captured the spell of revolutionary Spain. His best book, *Seven Red Sundays,* brilliantly illuminated the Spanish mind and reflected the author's warm humanitarianism; in it the course of a worker's uprising in Madrid in a week of time was faithfully traced. Much information was disclosed on the ideals and aims of the revolutionary factions and more about the selfless individuals who upheld them in this epic, but unsuccessful, proletarian struggle. Sender, who fought on the Loyalist side in the Spanish civil war, fled abroad when he realized that defeat impended and described cruel and gruesome episodes from the fighting in *The War in Spain.*

Italian Literature

Pronounced emphasis on realism, crude eroticism, and scientific materialism which featured Italian literature early in the 20th century was reinforced by the events of World War I and the disillusionment and torments which followed the peace settlement. Later on, conspicuously after Fascism had firmly established itself, Italian writers reverted to classic traditions, to "constructive idealism," and the fervent exaltation of the Fascist state.

High priest of Italian amoral realism and surely one of the most versatile literary figures of this or any other century was Gabriele D'Annunzio, poet, dramatist, novelist, soldier, nationalistic free-booter, and ardent Fascist. He was appointed prince of the realm by Mussolini and next to il Duce was the most prominent Italian of his time —all of which he recounted in his formidable autobiography. Except for a few exquisite war-poems, D'Annunzio after 1915 was an exhausted literary volcano, but the younger set which had gathered round him perpetuated his style and his traditions. Foremost among them was Guido da Verona, the most popular Italian author during and just after the war, who portrayed with amplitude the glamorous passions, the primitive instincts, the absence of moral toughness in the pleasure-seeking Italian middle class (*Mimi Bluette*).

Newer tendencies in Italian literary art could be detected in the novel, *Rubè* by Giuseppe A. Borgese, a tale of the disintegration of Italian youth, written with warmth and understanding. The hero, his mind tortured by unattainable intellectual ambitions, joined the army and shared abundantly in the military life and love affairs of the soldier. When the fighting ceased, he returned to his home and, while watching a proletarian disturbance, was killed. In a sort of sequel, *The Living and the Dead,* as yet untranslated, a fighting man found satisfying inner peace, despite external confusion, by contemplation of the mysteries of life and death. Borgese, incidentally, moved to the United States in 1931, taking the chair of Italian literature in the University of Chicago.

Marino Moretti's *The Throne of the Poor* drew a striking contrast between human conditions in the tiny Republic of San Marino and in the large countries of Europe. While life there was circumscribed it had abundant compensations: a military man, by reason of his sheer goodness and humility, obtained the top place in the poor republic. In *Confessions of Zeno,* Italo Svevo, a successful paint manufacturer who turned to literature under the influence of his tutor, James Joyce, presented a rollicking satirical burlesque on the fashionable cult of psychoanalysis.

Two propagandistic tracts directed against Fascism, *Fontamara* and *Bread and Wine,* earned international renown for Ignazio Silone. The first, one of the greater novels that these troubled times provoked, retold the grim happenings in a southern Italian village which had the temerity to resist the Fascist authorities; it was a profound commentary on the character of the Italian peasantry and on the rapacity and cruelty of Fascist officialdom. *Bread and Wine,* rooted in village life, also, pictured an enthusiastic idealist, who, having fled from Italy—Silone was himself a refugee, returned in disguise and learned to his sorrow that the rustics were unready to strike a blow to free themselves from the chains of the dictatorship.

Even more prized in discriminating foreign literary circles were the writings of Luigi Pirandello: volumes of short stories—*Better Think About It Twice,* which has the flavor of Boccaccio, and *A Character in Distress*—and dramas. As a playwright Pirandello's reputation was made with *Six Characters in Search of an Author,* in which six men crossed the stage as material to stimulate the dramatist's imagination and the life-story of each made up the body of the play. At his best in the delineation of bourgeois types and traits, Pirandello's underlying philosophy rested on the Hamlet thesis: "There is nothing good or bad, but thinking makes it so." Giovanni Papini, an earnest and passionate Italian intellectual best known for his engaging and eloquent *Life of Christ,* was once a violent anti-clerical, preaching the necessity of a transforming revolution. But after the war Papini found release from his mental anguish in religion of a mystical variety, as the *Life of Christ* and other religious studies revealed.

Literature in Germany

For an understanding of Weimar and Hitlerian Germany, the literature of the time is a rich mine of information and suggestion. A spate of novels on the grueling experiences of World War I, gripping and unforgettable stories in the spirit of *What Price Glory?* acquainted the outer world with something of wartime ways in Germany and the disillusionment, disgust, and despair that followed military defeat and revolution. Then, too, that novelty for Germany, freedom of the press, introduced by the Weimar democracy, invited daring and uninhibited expression of opinions, criticisms, and dreams. There was, for example, Arnold Zweig's series, *Young Woman of 1914, the Case of Sergeant Grischa,* which captured the spirit of the fighting on the little known Russian theatre of the war; *Education Before Verdun,* a super-tragedy on the western front; and *The Crowning of a King,* in which political intrigues in eastern Europe in the closing phases of the conflict were recalled. Taking the series as a whole it was a sermonic indictment of militarism and dwelt upon the cheapness of human life, the malice in some hearts, the everlasting struggle between the forces of good and evil in the affairs of men.

More restrained and dispassionate was Ludwig Renn's *War,* a faithful record of the sentiments of a German fighting-man who had been blown about like a leaf before an angry gale, and containing an excellent description of the final debacle of Germany's great armies. Erich Maria Remarque's semi-autobiographical *All Quiet on the Western Front* graphically portrayed the futility of war and attracted a tremendous international audience. In it the horrors and the pathos of the battleline were much exaggerated; a film version of this work provoked riots in Germany. After the victory of National Socialism, Remarque escaped from Germany and eventually reached the United States, a piece of the *Flotsam* of which he later wrote.

Renn in *After War* and Remarque in *The Road Back* detailed the harsh experiences of German war veterans who found it extremely difficult to re-enter civilian society. More successful was the hero of Ernst E. Wiechert's *The Baroness,* who, returning home a decade after the Armistice, managed with the aid of his patroness and the healing powers of Mother Nature to regain something akin to ordinary human composure. Wiechert, an officer whose bravery in the war won him the highest military decoration, was esteemed in the late 1930's as the leading author of Germany, though he fell afoul of the Hitlerian regime and was obliged to spend some time in a concentration camp.

The larger aftermath of World War I and the ravages of the economic depression brought forth several enlightening novels: Lion Feuchtwanger's *Success,* a lengthy, realistically vulgar, but nonetheless admirable recreation of the fever of the inflation years; the dramatic and exciting *Grand Hotel,* by Vicki Baum; Rudolph Ditzen's *Little Man, What Now?* which had a universal appeal since it dealt with the fate of "little men" the world over during the Great Depression; and, for ways and manners in a provincial German town, *Katinka,* by Irene Forbes Mosse.

As a representative of the conservative German story-tellers who contrived to write after 1933, Hans Carossa may be selected. Deeply interested in everyday events, the common man and the welfare of Germany, he preached national regeneration in *Dr. Gion.* Later, in *The Secrets of Rich Living,* Carossa elucidated his inner reflections on the rule of National Socialism. The central character in the latter story, a man given to thought rather than action, cultivated the friendship of a band of Hitler Jugend, whom he admired for their frankness, courage, and carefree spirit; but he found them quite unteachable and utterly devoted to material values. The scene of the book was laid on the borders of Austria and the work was pervaded with a longing for the serenity of that rather nonchalant, charming, and easy-going land of Germans. Yet Carossa eventually made his peace with the Nazi regime.

Certain German novelists penned books on eternal themes, comprehensive in philosophy and expertly written. Here the towering figure was Nobel prize winner, Thomas Mann, whose *The Magic Mountain,* a caustic parable on the institutions and ideas of pre-1914 Europe and an elaborate epic of *Joseph and His Brothers,* based upon the Biblical narrative, confirmed the world renown he had attained before the war. Interwoven with profound understanding of ancient cultures in the *Joseph* series were acute observations on the heritage of the contemporary world from the deeper and darker past. Vividness of imagination and beautiful prose distinguished all of Mann's writing.

In almost the same category may be placed Jacob Wassermann's *The World's Illusion,* in which the two extremes of pre-war European society, the ruling caste of landed aristocrats and of industrial barons and the lowest class in the social pyramid, confronted one another. Man himself, Wasserman thought and taught, was responsible for the evil which existed, and the way of salvation must be sought in doing good for others. He pleaded for more rationality and sweet reasonableness in man's dealings with man, but concepts of abstract justice were the world's great illusion.

In a perplexing but excellently written novel, *The Castle,* which has been likened to *Pilgrim's Progress,* Franz Kafka portrayed the workings of an inferiority complex and dealt deftly with universal issues of right and wrong. Kafka, who wrote to clarify his personal philosophy, exerted no small influence upon authors writing in the English language. Disregarding the terms of Kafka's will, his executor published several of his novels posthumously, among them *Amerika,* which disclosed the author's lively enthusiasm for the transatlantic Republic—Benjamin Franklin's *Autobiography* and Walt Whitman's poetry were among his favorite books—and traced the evil career of an unsophisticated German youth who sought Dame Fortune in the United States and found rather her unlovely daughter, misfortune.

Drama and poetry written in German attained less international distinction than novels in that tongue. Hermann Sudermann, a favorite of an earlier generation, turned out plays which were always realistic and often satirical. Technically and philosophically unusual was the playwright, Ernst Toller, who, upon recovery from wounds suffered in the war, stood forth as the leading exponent of proletarian drama, an arch-apostle of anti-militarism and of a radical re-ordering of the German economic system.

No more bitter castigation of the corrosive effects of war upon warriors was written than Toller's *Hinkemann.* Imprisoned for subversive political activities, Toller produced *The Machine Wreckers,* a case study of the age-long struggle between human fraternity and brutalized tyranny in economic relationships, and *Man and the Masses,* an indictment of war and of machine civilization. Like many another prominent German man of letters, Toller, after Hitlerism assumed power, fled abroad, dying by his own hand in New York City.

Among the poets writing in German there was the Swiss, Carl F. G. Spitteler, whose epics, such as *Olympian Spring,* gained him the Nobel Prize; and Rainer Maria Rilke, a wanderer over the face of Europe, who voiced his reflections on the riches of poverty, the destiny of mankind, and love of nature in strangely mystical verse (*Sonnets to Orpheus.*) Stefan George's poem, *The War,* and lyrical pieces which were attuned to authoritarian political principles and condemnatory of anything savoring of radicalism made him a favorite of National Socialism; yet after the Hitlerian victory, George moved off to Switzerland. Abroad, the novelist Carossa, who regarded Goethe as the finest expositor of the noblest traits in the German character, was looked upon as the foremost German poet of the later 1930's.

Last to be mentioned, but by no means least in influence among German writers of the time, is Oswald Spengler, best known for *The Decline of the West,* an encyclopedic work of marked originality, which interpreted the past and sketched the future in very somber colors. History, it may here be interpolated, has been variously explained as a record of gradual decline from a golden age, or as progress toward an unknown destiny; as a drama of salvation or the unfolding of a "World Spirit"; as determined by material forces or by philosophical ideals. No interpretation of history universally acceptable has been found and it may be doubted whether any ever will be discovered.

Spengler's central doctrine of the imminent collapse of western civilization was extremely popular in the dank atmosphere of pessimism which hung over Europe after the Armistice. Though *The Decline* had been planned and partly composed before 1914, avowedly as a protest against the prevalent European optimism, it was not published until the summer of 1918; by 1930 it had run through more than ninety editions in Germany alone.

Spengler surveyed the higher living of the European nations and their Oriental predecessors, singling out for detailed examination Graeco-Roman, Arabian, and Western societies. Civilizations, like organic beings, he concluded, passed inevitably through discernable stages: youth, maturity, old age, and death. Western civilization, which started about A. D. 1000, was virtually exhausted and doomed to extinction. "Western civilization," Spengler proposed, "is the latest but not the last of the recurring cycles which advance and recede like the tides of the sea."

There was nothing especially novel about Spengler's theme of cycles and decadence, for several other modern minds had anticipated it in part, and the notion of "eternal recurrence" had its proponents as long ago as Greek antiquity. What Spengler did was to present a wealth of illustration for his theory, to draw many persuasive analogies between one civilization and another and in many aspects of living—political structure, literature, science, architecture, and painting. Under ordinary circumstances this monumental literary adventure would probably have appealed to philosophers and historians alone, but in the mood of post-war Europe, it had wide general reading and left its mark on the speculations of an entire generation. Quickly a whole library on "Spenglerism," part in support of the gloomy prognostications of the "Jeremiah of Munich," part in condemnation, came into being.

Encouraged by the success of *The Decline,* Spengler, in short books and pamphlets, elaborated his doleful prophecies, warning specifically against the perils of proletarian dominance in western society and the engulfment of the whites by the colored races. All over the West he discerned evidences of impending doom, coupled with an arrogant superiority complex, and arrant disbelief in tradition and religion. Scorn for Marxism, contempt for democracy, admiration for captains of industry, and confidence in dictatorship figured in Spengler's writings. They helped to prepare the ground for the triumph of National Socialism, though Spengler personally had certain reservations regarding the Nazi regime.

After the Nazis had triumphed, German literature underwent drastic changes, as has been hinted. A draconian censorship, more rigorous by far than in the Empire of Bismarck or William II, determined and regimented the output of men of letters. For another thing, the totalitarian regime silenced the pen of Jewish writers who were responsible for a very high production of the post-war literature. And hitherto obscure authors produced a Hitlerian "court literature" conforming to the National Socialist outlook. Such an one was Hanns Johst, who was showered with high honors for *Schlageter,* a drama of the state of affairs in the Saar Basin, at the time still outside the Third Reich. Johst indeed was dubbed the poet laureate of Nazidom.

Russian and Lesser Literatures

Two sets of writers in the epoch between wars created literature in the Russian tongue: representatives of the older Russian generation who lived abroad after the Bolshevik Revolution and produced little of importance except for Ivan Bunin's *Arseniev's Life* (a splendid panorama of pre-revolutionary Russia in the nature of autobiography), and those who wrote inside Russia. The latter group included orthodox Communists, commonly authors without literary pretensions who exploited the abundant materials thrown up by the Soviet experiment, and their fellow travelers, not professed Bolsheviks, whose style was likely to be more polished and who ranged more widely in subject matter. All imaginative literature in the USSR tended to be optimistic in tone and was, of course, obliged to conform to the official orthodoxy of the state. More than one writer was silenced as a "literary kulak."

In very modern Russian literature the Olympian figure was Maxim Gorki, versatile in vocations as a youth, versatile in writing in maturity, a lifelong advocate of the cause of revolution, the friend of Lenin and Stalin. On his pages the rank and file of the Russian melange of peoples came alive. As an interpreter and a prophet of Russia and its inhabitants Gorki indeed had no peer. He was a prophet fully honored in his own country; for one thing the great and historic city of Nizhni Novgorod, his birthplace, was renamed in his honor. Gorki's final contribution to fiction appeared in the 1930's, a long, complex, historical novel which recounted the evolution of Russia from the 1880's to the Bolshevik upheaval, and was calculated to appeal to the socially minded. (*The Bystander* and *The Magnet*, leading on to the risings of 1905, *Other Fires*, the stormy stage of 1905-1906, and *The Specter*, on the decade before 1917.)

Many aspects of revolutionary Russia attracted fictional interpretation of sufficient value to be translated into English. Isaak Babel's *Red Cavalry*, wild stories of personal experiences in the campaigns against the anti-revolutionary "Whites" and the Poles, recreated the heroisms and the horrors of those struggles. A. Fadayev's *The Nineteen* described the emotional atmosphere that prevailed in little-known Siberia during the civil war. *The Naked Year*, by Boris Pilnyak, skillfully analyzed the life of the several social strata in a small Russian city during the famine of the militant Communist era.

With understanding and detachment Michael Ossorgin in *Quiet Street* delineated the changes brought about in the lives of cultured Moscow intellectuals by the revolutionary storm and stress. And the violent submergence of middle class intellectuals was treated in Alexei Tolstoi's *Darkness and Dawn*. Ilya G. Ehrenburg, rollicking critic of the bourgeoisie, manufactured thrilling melodramas, as in *A Street in Moscow*, a ferociously brutal tale revolving round a shopkeeper who tried to kill young vagabonds guilty of thievery. Bolshevism's messianic mission was proclaimed in *The Beginning of the Century* by Andrei Beli, an engrossing portrayal of the intellectuals of Moscow, written in a style that was widely imitated.

Rich talent in portraying the impact of the Soviet way of life upon the peasant millions was displayed by Mikhail Sholokov in *And Quiet Flows the Don*, a grimly Bolshevik interpretation of life in a Cossack village during the decade of 1910, and in *Virgin Soil Upturned*, a convincing reproduction of the agonies and the hopes aroused by the Soviet collectivization of agriculture. Another literary champion of Bolshevism, Leonid Leonov, effectively described the titanic rural reconstruction in *Soviet River*. Representative of the fiction dealing with industrial progress under state-planning was Valentin P. Kataev's *Time, Forward!* a dramatic story of a single day in a concrete plant in which workers exerted every energy to exceed the output of a rival factory.

Portraits of the bewildering vicissitudes in Soviet education were sketched in *The Diary of a Communist Schoolboy* and *The Diary of a Communist Undergraduate,* by a teacher, N. Ogynov. Panteleimon Romanov's writings, *Three Pairs of Silk Stockings* and *Without Cherry Blossom,* retold with wit and accuracy the shifting moral standards by which the Russians lived.

Typical samples of the productions of Soviet playwrights, mostly with a propagandistic tinge, and dealing with vital "slices of life," were edited by Eugene Lyons in *Six Soviet Plays* (1935). Communist Russia's foremost poet, Alexander Blok, eulogized the Red Army in a curious piece, *The Twelve;* the mystical figure of the Christ is shown carrying a Red Banner at the head of a dozen boisterous, devoted Red Guardsmen (the Twelve Apostles), as they patrolled the streets of demoralized Petrograd. Apparently overwhelmed by the tragic accompaniments of the Revolution, Blok, who died in 1921, inscribed his last poem to Pushkin, greatest poet of Imperial Russia.

Soviet officials endeavored to create an "orthodox proletarian poetry" by encouraging young workers and peasants to compose appropriate verse, but much of the product, as the writings of the peasant, Sergei Essenine, illustrate, rose no higher than ephemeral propaganda. Disappointed in time with the ways of the Soviets, Essenine in one of his unpublished poems, *Nomarkh,* lauded a bandit chieftain who fought the Soviet regime because it disappointed the expectations of the countryfolk. Unable to drown his personal disillusionment in dissipation, Essenine finally killed himself. Spoken of as the poet laureate of the November Revolution, Vladimir Mayakowski ardently proclaimed the dawn of the new life in Russia. But gradually he, too, drifted into criticism of Soviet actualities, not least the rigors of the censorship, and was subjected to persecution, which, along with an unfortunate affair of the heart, caused him to shoot himself.

Other Soviet poets contrived to guide their pens in keeping with shifts in official policy, as was the case with Demyan Bedny. Yet he also fell afoul of the censors for a time, because in *Bogatyri* he sang in captious tones of mythical heroes of the Russian past and of the men who had brought Russia into the Christian communion. During the war with Germany, Soviet poets exalted Russian patriotism and voiced their praises of the infallible Stalin.

Among the smaller European nationalities, creative literature emphasized distinctly national interests and character, though touches of cosmopolitanism were not entirely absent. Especially noteworthy was the emergence of a literature of international importance in the Yiddish language, an amalgam of German and Hebrew. Sholem Asch, a Polish Jew, who thought and wrote in Yiddish, gained recognition by plays and stories dealing with patriarchal Jewish life in eastern Europe particularly. In *Three Cities,* a bulky novel of Jewish life in St. Petersburg, Warsaw, and Moscow before, during, and after the Bolshevik Revolution, affluent Jews were shown purchasing social distinction while their poorer fellows debated the pros and cons of Zionism or schemed and fought to establish a classless proletarian society. *Salvation* explained how Jews in a Polish village a century ago found in their religion compensation for the discriminations and humiliations inflicted upon them. *Uncle Moses* artfully presented folkways in a self-contained sweat-shop community created by Polish Jews in New York City. Israel J. Singer's *The Brothers Ashkenazi* pictured the manners and conditions of Jewry in Lodz, the expanding "Polish Manchester," just before 1914; some of these harried folk attained financial eminence, while others resorted to industrial warfare in order to assure themselves of the merest necessities of existence.

The first author in the Czech language to achieve wide popularity outside of his native land was Karel Čapek, playwright, novelist, essayist. Strong social consciousness and feeling for the masses were reflected in his writing, and his Utopian romances revealed an obligation to H. G. Wells. Čapek's famous drama, *R. U. R.* (Rossum's Universal Robots), in which machines were converted into beings having all the powers of men except capacity for thought, added the word "robot" to the vocabulary of western languages; and the same motif was exploited in the fantastic *War with the Newts.* Muchprized was a trilogy of novels—*Hordubal, Meteor,* and *An Ordinary Life*—in which Čapek depicted the eager quest of Slav types in search of ultimate reality.

Another Czech man of letters, Jaroslav Hašek, produced the supreme "comic opera" of World War I: *The Good Soldier: Schweik.* This grotesque and humorous narrative of the Hapsburg monarchy riding to destruction centered upon a cowardly dog thief of Prague, who was dragooned into military service but managed to pass through the fighting unscathed. Hašek expatiated at length on the cruelty, the silliness, and the pretensions of war as it affected an unwilling participant and thereby created a rich and hilarious satire on militarism.

A somewhat similar saga of the life of a private soldier, a simple Polish peasant, was told by the Pole, Joseph Wittlin, in *Salt of the Earth.* His fellow countryman, Ferdinand Goetal, composed an instructive diary of a Polish prisoner who, after the war, became a civil servant in Cracow (*From Day to Day*).

For Finland, the leading novelist was Frans Eemil Sillanpää, who was awarded the Nobel Prize for his epic portrayals of the tragedies and the beauties of his native land. *Meek Heritage,* for instance, traced the career of a rugged Finnish peasant, from his birth in the hard 1860's until he fell before a "White" firing squad during the Revolution of 1918.

Aino Kallas' matter-of-fact stories of the hard-pressed peasantry of Estonia under Imperial Russia—*The White Ship*—afforded valuable insights into the way of life of a lovely but little known corner of Europe. Yugoslavia's most eminent living author, Miroslav Krleza, dramatized the decline and fall of the Croatian aristocracy in *The Lords Glembayevs.*

Hungary boasted two excellent novelists in Lajos Zilahy and Lajos Hatvany. The former's *The Deserter,* an instructive social and political document on the first quarter of this century, depicted the life of a sturdy Magyar patriot who deserted from the Hapsburg army, organized Communists for a time, and then perished in a riotous brawl. *Bondy Jr.,* by Hatvany, entertainingly chronicled the history of a Hungarian Jewish family which fought its way out of rustic obscurity and contrived to amass great wealth; the father, a successful grain merchant, struggled to make his sensitive and artistic son into another business man. Universally popular were the light, not always conventional plays of the Hungarian, Ferencz Molnár, such as *The Swan, The Play's the Thing,* and *Girl Unknown.*

The reputation of Norway as the mother of wise, serious, and singularly imaginative composers of fiction was amply sustained by Knut Hamsun and Sigrid Undset, both winners of the coveted Nobel Prize, and Johan Bojer. Hamsun's *Growth of the Soil* told of the way in which a humble peasant hacked a farmstead out of the forest primeval. Before very long the holding had marvellously blossomed into a "civilized" community. After the manner of Rousseau, Hamsun warned that "civilization" inevitably brought on human degradation and that only those who lived close to Mother Earth would grow in beauty and character. Curiously enough, after the German occupation of Norway in 1940, Hamsun identified himself with the traitorous Quisling.

Studies in the history of medieval Norway converted Sigrid Undset to Roman Catholicism, and her writings teem with ideas of universal religious and moral import. The thought and feeling of medieval Christianity were freshly defined in two large, frank, almost photographic reproductions of life and labor in the Norway of the 1200's and the 1300's, *Kristin Lavransdatter* and *The Master of Hestviken*. After that, Undset undertook a series of novels, *The Faithful Wife* among them, full of acid criticism of contemporary manners and morals. In *The Great Hunger* and its sequel, *The New Temple*, Bojer analyzed the competition within the human soul between the longing for material prosperity and the desire for inner contentment and assurance; the way to approach the Almighty, the principal character learned through much travail, was through service to humanity.

The Fine Arts: Architecture

Among the fine arts, architecture most faithfully responded to the mechanistic keynote and the socializing currents of the time, and had the most widespread social significance. No similar period perhaps witnessed so much construction: dwelling places, industrial and commercial structures, buildings for educational and civic purposes, and war memorials of many varieties. Although ecclesiastical architecture lagged behind the secular, a few notable cathedrals, as in Liverpool, and some fine churches were erected.

National governments and municipalities vied with one another in building efficient low-cost housing. In Britain something like a third of the population was re-housed in the era between wars, and in Germany and Soviet Russia, a large proportion of the population were similarly provided with new homes. Great cities, such as Vienna, Rotterdam, and Barcelona, constructed huge apartment blocks, occasionally communities in themselves, with parcels of land reserved for recreation. An increasing proportion of the urban population lived in these multiple dwellings, equipped with up-to-date conveniences. Construction was financed by public agencies. Greater attention than ever before was devoted to city planning; magnificent boulevards flanked by new architectural monuments were laid out in the great capitals of Europe.

Creative, unconventional architects made full use of materials which industrialism provided. Steel, for example, which brought radical changes in construction, reinforced concrete, metals of various sorts, glass, plastics, and, here and there, colored tiles were effectively exploited. More than ever before perhaps architectural thinking was affected by the purposes for which buildings were primarily intended; functionalism that tendency was called, yet utility and efficiency were not wholly sacrificed to beauty. Indeed, the emphasis on the aesthetic appeal of apartments, factories, railway stations, office buildings, and stores represented a welcome change from the characteristic architecture of the late 19th century.

Outstanding among the architects who set the pace for contemporaries was the Frenchman Le Corbusier, the pseudonym of Charles Edouard Jeanneret. Famous as a designer of private dwellings and one of the prize winners in the competition for the palace of the League of Nations, Le Corbusier was an indefatigable exponent of functionalism in architecture and of the value of good housing in making the urban masses contented. His German counterpart, Walter Gropius, presided over a famous school of the building arts at Dessau, and designed workships and school buildings which made much use of glass panes as surfacing materials for walls.

Erich Mendelsohn and Ludwig Miës van Rohe were two other influential figures in German architecture. The former was one of the pioneers in factory and store construction in which lavish use was made of plate glass and steel work. For the purposes of the scientist Einstein, Mendelsohn designed (1920) a laboratory and observatory at Potsdam, having the appearance of optical instruments, and intended to keep the vibration caused by the wind at a minimum. After the National Socialists came into power, Mendelsohn carried his architectural theories to Palestine and Britain. Miës van der Rohe achieved international distinction for skyscrapers in which metal and glass were extensively exploited and for an exquisite pavilion erected for an exhibition in Barcelona (1929). In that structure, space rather than mass was stressed. The roof was one great concrete slab, resting on metal columns, with the area beneath partitioned by marble wall screens.

While the techniques of these innovators had considerable imitation, some European architecture reflected older, more conventional patterns. Classical formality, for instance, with emphasis upon the regal splendor of buildings had full scope in Italian structures, such as the postoffice of Naples and the railway station in Florence. It was also seen in the town hall of Stockholm. Strongly reminiscent of a Gothic cathedral with fine symmetrical arches was the Crematorium of Vienna, one of the European architectural gems of the period.

During the first decade of the Soviet Union, builders paid little attention to style in architecture. The immediate urge was to construct buildings for all manner of purposes in the great Russian cities and indeed to build wholly new cities, in which the virtues of planning were practised. In the 1930's desire for more beauty manifested itself; and there was much borrowing by Russians from the ideas of Le

Corbusier and other westerners, as was illustrated in the splendid, rather simple Moscow subway stations and the cubistic pattern of Lenin's mausoleum.

Painting

If architecture had the liveliest social significance among the fine arts, painting competed with music for the distinction of most accurately portraying the unrest, the inquietude, the intellectual uncertainties, the struggle between the traditional and the novel in the epoch between wars. Any generalizations about artistic productions are bound to be misleading, for newer patterns jostled with older conceptions. In other words, the devotee of abstract design worked in the same age with the master of photographic realism. Rampant individualism brought forth a chaos of schools of painting, many of them short-lived, with Paris, as usual, their nursery and their battleground. There was much ado about surrealism, for example, which gave scant consideration to technique, allowed the artist to put mental and emotional impressions upon canvas with riotous individualism, and in minute, quite overwhelming detail.

The revulsion against photographic accuracy in favor of novelty and experimentation was best exhibited, no doubt, in the compositions of the Frenchman, Henri Matisse, leading advocate of simplicity in painting, and of Picasso, the pseudonym of the Spanish-born Pablo Ruiz. Picasso, a fertile and versatile artist, doubtless the most influential painter of the time, popularized, if he did not invent, "cubism," in which emotional experiences were suggested in an abstract art reminiscent of mathematics. Characteristic was his *Portrait of M. Kahnweiler*, in which only tiny bits of objects were to be seen; in this "puzzle picture," the observer noticed a vest with a watch-chain, above it, hints of an eye, an ear, and nose, but the rest of the subject was smothered with business documents. Color counted for little and at the point where Picasso stopped innovating, in order to paint in more conventional and objective ways, lesser artists carried on to extravagant and rather bewildering extremes.[2]

Representative German painters who endeavored to lay bare the inner essence of men and things, to tear away the mask of external appearance, were Alexander Kanolt, noted for his singularly grotesque landscape compositions, and George Grosz, who devoted his talent

[2] The eminent Spanish artist, Ignacio Zuloaga, continued to paint throughout the period, but his best work was behind him. A prolific painter, Zuloaga was hailed by some critics before 1914 as "the most brilliant painter alive" and he was extremely popular among art collectors in the United States.

to satirical propaganda against militarism, capitalism, and bourgeois stuffiness. Abstract art of that character had lavish expression in Soviet Russia, but in National Socialist Germany it was ridiculed as artistic Bolshevism (*Kunstbolschevismus*) and placed under the censor's ban.

The art of portraiture was carefully cultivated along conservative lines by Sir William Orpen, Britain's official artist of World War I. He painted wartime personalities and a much-prized picture of the peacemakers at the Paris Conference, as well as brilliantly colored scenes of the fighting in France.[3] John Singer Sargent, too, recorded impressions of the battlefront in *Gassed*. Born in Florence of an American family, and a European by preference, Sargent's larger reputation rested on his vivid portraits of prominent men and women—Theodore Roosevelt and the Duchess of Portland, for example—and the famous mural decorations in the Boston Public Library, depicting the evolution of religion.

Art critics praised Orpen and Sargent for their technical abilities and insight into character, but questioned whether they deserved to be classified with the foremost masters of the art of portraiture. The Hungarian, Philip A. de László, was acclaimed as the painter of Edward VII of Britain, Mussolini, and other conspicuous celebrities. His portraits were notable for draughtmanship and coloring.

Sculpture

Like painting, sculpture between the wars was infinitely diversified and showed an inclination to depart from older forms of representing real or imagined objects in natural materials. Demand for statues of war-heroes, including Unknown Soldiers, and ornamentation for public places, apartment houses, and the like offered unusual opportunities for artistic workers in stone, bronze, and other metals. From a host of sculptors, four geniuses of rare merit stood out; Aristide Maillol, Ivan Méstrović, Jacob Epstein, and Alexander Archipenko.

Maillol's statues in stone and bronze had about them something of the simplicity and serenity of Greek art, and earned him the place in French sculpture vacated by the great Rodin. His reclining *Goddess of Fame*, for a monument to the artist Cézanne, revealed his tal-

[3] His portrait of the statesmen of 1919, Orpen matched with an imaginative tribute, *To the Unknown British Soldier in France*. In that realistic piece, set in the splendor of the Versailles Palace, not the pen but the rifle was mightier. Two ragged miserable young soldiers kept watch over the coffin of a fallen comrade, while imaginative symbols, including the Cross, recalled the devotion of the men whose lives were snuffed out in the war.

ent at its best; the design was extremely natural and simple. The larger cities of Yugoslavia were adorned with statues and memorials commemorative of South Slav unity from the studio of Méstrovič, once upon a time a herder of sheep. After serving as an apprentice to a stone mason, Méstrovič studied in foreign art centers, selected Michelangelo as his master, and displayed remarkable ability in a variety of forms of sculpture. A devout Roman Catholic and active in politics, his genius was well illustrated in the fine bronze statue of the Croatian ecclesiastical and patriotic leader of the 19th century, Bishop Strossmayer, at Zagreb, the principal Croatian city. Many galleries in the United States acquired small figures, smooth and simple, from Méstrovič's workshop.

Though born on Manhattan's East Side, Jacob Epstein is often considered European. By some authorities he is regarded as the supreme sculptor of the century, equally distinguished in conception and in execution. For his ideas Epstein frequently sought what was most virile, colossal, and mystical in Jewish tradition and Eastern art.

Whereas Maillol preferred small compositions, Epstein revelled in the mammoth, as is seen in his masterpiece, *Adam*, which is seven feet tall and weighs three tons. This representation of primitive man, with powerful arms and the head of an Assyrian, hewn from English alabaster, gives the observer a feeling of monumental force, energy, and purpose. Bronzes, busts of celebrities, and heads of children revealed Epstein's superb talent as a modeler. Severely criticized for sensuality and his mystical quality little understood, Epstein was a storm center of London's artistic controversies; to his foes he boldly made answer in a unique autobiography, *Let There Be Sculpture* (1940).

Archipenko, claimed alike by Lithuania and Russia, more or less copied Epstein in a heroic *Moses,* representing the Hebrew lawgiver bearing a tablet and toiling laboriously upward in search of a new revelation from heaven. This figure of massive dignity was inspired by the tragic plight of the refugees from Hitlerian Germany and to them it was dedicated. In earlier work Archipenko attempted to freeze the shapes of ideas and subconscious impressions into abstract sculpture, done in marble, terra cotta, and metals. Elongated torsos, figures merely suggested, with parts of the body frequently missing, characterized much of Archipenko's art. The curious piece, *The Metal Lady*, in copper, brass, and lead, which was shown all over the western world, may be taken as typical. As a teacher of sculpture and drawing he eventually established himself in New York City.

Among independent critics protests were voiced over the decline
in the minor arts, since machinery turned out standardized products
at a price with which the creative individual craftsman could not
compete. Whether that estimate was valid may properly be left to
the judgment of posterity, for certainly in etching, wood-engraving,
lithography, and other pictorial arts there was much that was skillful
and esthetically attractive in the between-wars period.

Some students of the fine arts bewailed the indifference of the age
to creative art, while others—and they would appear to be the more
accurate observers—exulted over the growing popularity of painting
and sculpture as a diversion. They called attention to the growth of
galleries and other facilities for exhibitions, to the droves of visitors
who thronged museums (the writer almost had to fight his way into
galleries in Soviet Russia, so great was the press of workers and peasants), and to the provision of funds from public and private sources
to encourage young artists of promise.

Music

All that has been said in a general way about the other fine arts
in the inter-war period applies with equal force to music, the supreme
language of the emotions. Compositions, in a profusion of forms,
ranged from the conventional—the Wagnerian romanticism in the
ascendant late in the nineteenth century—to the non-conformist,
"modernistic" styles, which professed to be starkly realistic in their
attempt to interpret the tempo, the cacophony, the actualities in
everyday living of a war-riven and machine-dominated generation.

Classification of accomplished musicians into strict schools is
not permissible, for the musical critics were hopelessly at odds on
the way in which composers should be grouped, and artists expressed
themselves differently at different times. Considerable care was devoted to craftmanship after the manner of the 18th century, and
composers of originality sought to infuse their works with the impersonal, intangible, and abstract qualities prized by painters and
sculptors. Neo-classicists insisted that music should be simplified,
restricted to essentials, and they introduced certain innovations in
technique.

By many pundits the supreme place among composers was assigned to Igor Stravinsky, a Russian-born modernist, who reproduced his environment. All the orthodox rules of writing he spurned,
without following any set pattern of his own, and he was aped by
many younger artists. Stravinsky's music was distinguished by the
absence of what is commonly regarded as rhythm and harmony, by

brilliant coloring, and sensational momentum. *Pulcinella* and *Oedipus Rex*, an opera, may be selected as characteristic works of Stravinsky in this period.

Stravinsky's countryman, Sergei Prokofieff, wrote in a variety of forms: music for movies, a very popular opera, *Love of Three Oranges,* and a whimsical fairy tale for children of all ages, *Peter and the Wolf,* in which each character was portrayed by a different instrument. These compositions were robust, primitive in their impetuosity and simplicity and not particularly calculated to stir the emotions. After wandering around Europe a great deal, Prokofieff finally settled down in Moscow; not a Bolshevik by conviction, it would appear, he was nonetheless authorized to create a vast cantata to celebrate the twentieth anniversary of the November Revolution.

The title of "composer laureate" of Soviet Russia was conferred upon Dmitri Shostakovitch, a young artist of unusual creative talents. Outside his homeland he was best known perhaps for the sociological opera, *Lady Macbeth of Mzensk*, whose plot was a narrative of total depravity: an old-fashioned adulteress commits murder for passion, flees to Siberia and there perishes by her own hand. In spite of the vivid orchestral music, the opera scandalized western audiences; in Russia itself the official censorship branded it as too formalistic and smacking of bourgeois decadence.

After being performed only a few times, *Lady Macbeth* was banned and a like fate befell *The Nose*, a satirical opera, inspired by an imaginative fantasy written by Gogol almost a century earlier. Shostakovitch also composed several symphonies and music to accompany moving pictures, all vigorous and with a tendency to boisterousness.

For sheer radicalism in composition, top place, it would seem should go to Arnold Schönberg, a Viennese, who was given the dubious distinction of being "king of the cacophonists." Always a storm center of musical controversy, he wrote many piano pieces and songs, technically skillful but filled with sounds which grated on the ears of all except the thoroughly initiated. His pupil, Alban Berg, softened the master's revolutionary bent in an operatic masterpiece, *Wozzeck,* highly imaginative and original. Adversely criticized at first, *Wozzeck* gradually won widespread appreciation and, together with songs and a violin *Concerto*, earned Berg international acclaim.

Another German, Paul Hindemith, after following modernistic inclinations, turned in later work to more traditional, neo-classic forms. Both for the quality of his music and its variety, Hindemith was greatly admired, and he pioneered in what the Germans called

Gebrauchsmusik, or simplified workaday music for use in the movies or on the radio or by amateurs and children. *The Days' News* was a characteristic example of this type of composition. Quite markedly romantic in feeling was *Mathis the Painter* by Hindemith, a symphony of three parts, each related to a panel in a famous altar-piece, and prized for its elements of grandeur. One of many artists who fell under the frown of National Socialist censorship, Hindemith withdrew from Germany in 1934 to teach music appreciation and composition in Turkey and subsequently in the United States.

Noteworthy among French modernists was Maurice Joseph Ravel, who succeeded Claude Debussy, in a real sense the father of modernism, as the foremost composer in France. The reputation which Ravel made before 1914 was sustained in the stylistic ballet, *The Child and the Enchantments,* and the exceptionally stirring *Boléro;* if this work failed to win unanimous applause from the critics, it surely solidified Ravel's popularity with the musical laity. Ravel also wrote meritorious pieces for the piano and a few songs. Though reluctant to teach, he nevertheless had many imitators among younger musicians.

Another Frenchman (by choice), Arthur Honegger, in one phase of his career found lively themes in the stormy atmosphere of the age. *The World Crisis,* (1930-1931), a sort of cantata, realistically imported into music the disquietude and the pessimism of the hour in which it was written. *Pacific 231* described the steam engine and *Rugby* captured the energy and exuberance of contemporary athletics. For music of a more austere and conventional character, Honegger was inspired by historical subjects: the oratorio, *King David,* which made the composer known to music lovers everywhere, and *Joan of Arc at the Stake.*

Modernism in Italy had its leading exponent in Ottorino Respighi. His internationally renowned *Fountains of Rome,* rich in color and beauty, related the impressions which four fountains in the Eternal City left upon the artist's spirit at different hours of the day. Similar in character and content was *Church Windows.* Britain was represented among the modernists by Ralph Vaughan-Williams (*Old King Cole, Job*), a pupil and disciple of Ravel. Bela Bartók, at once a creative composer, an accomplished pianist, and gatherer of Hungarian and Rumanian folk tunes, stood first among the Hungarian modernists.

Distinguished among the musical artists who revived more or less traditional forms was Richard Strauss, the last of the line of musicians of that name who called Vienna their home. Ranked among the leading composers of his time, the heir of Richard Wagner indeed in operatic compositions, Strauss coasted along after World War I on the immense popularity he had already achieved. *Whipped Cream,* for instance, enhanced not at all the reputation of the author of *The Rose Cavalier* (1911), a really charming operatic classic; the *Alpine Symphony* and the *Day of Peace* were unmistakably inferior productions. Sir Edgar Elgar was hailed as the dean of British musicians and the man who brought Britain into the front rank in orchestral music. Apart from choral works he wrote *Nursery Suite,* acclaimed for its delicate charm and grace.

Rather the traditionalist, like Elgar, was the Finnish master, Jan Sibelius, who translated the ancient national folk legends of his dour countrymen into the international language of music. Most famous for symphonies, Sibelius also produced many pieces for violin and piano, several operas, and a good deal of workaday music. His mighty and profoundly moving *Finlandia* (1899), ever an inspiration to his Finnish fellows, attained international popularity in the 1920's.[4]

While it cannot be proved statistically, it appears probable that music touched the lives of a higher proportion of Europeans in the era between wars than ever before. The enlarged interest in music and in some measure of appreciation of music can be traced to the appearance of the radio, to the perfection of the phonograph and the recording piano, and the popularity of the movies, in which music had a part and for which accomplished artists did not disdain to write. Very popular with a wide public was primitive syncopated music inspired by folk melodies or plagiarized and adapted from old classics.

A large share of this "jazz" music—characterized by melodious themes, syncopated rhythms, and diversified orchestral coloring— had its source in the United States, the New World's one original contribution to the music of the Old. American jazz bands toured Europe, attracting droves of young listeners who were ignorant of the fact that the music was intended for dancing. American tourists were pleasantly tickled—some of them—to hear gondoliers on Venice's canals warble, *Yes, We Have No Bananas,* and other pieces of syncopated music. Discerning critics detected jazz patterns in the works of some of the most respected composers of the generation, and certain observers warned that popularization and the intrusion of the jazz spirit might have debasing influences upon the musical art.

[4] Among European musicians, essentially performers, were Enrico Caruso, Fedor Chaliapin, and Frieda Hempel, singers; Ignace Paderewski and Serge Rachmaninoff, pianists; and the famous violinists, Fritz Kreisler and Mischa Elman.

Movies, Radio, Television

Whether moving pictures deserve to be considered among the fine arts is debatable, though the eminent English scholar, Allardyce Nicoll, has hazarded the opinion, comforting to Hollywood, that the commercial movies have produced a drama comparable with the achievements of Elizabethan England. Along with the radio, the movies furnished the masses with styles of entertainment unequalled before; literally, miles upon miles of celluloid were turned out.

In the early days of the movies, reels of fact had the greatest popularity. But after 1915, without entirely disappearing, they were replaced in rank by pictures having plots. Indeed the making of newsfilms was fostered by European governments which appreciated their value in the service of propaganda or education (the line between them is ill-defined), and the appearance of *The March of Time* (1935) in the United States brought fresh prestige to this type of picture. That remarkable Russian picture, *The General Line,* describing the advances in Soviet agriculture, illustrated the way in which the film diffused knowledge that was comprehensible even to the most illiterate person.

Though film fashions were largely set in the United States, "Hollywoods" were established in all the major countries of the world. In the twenties, the love story theme held first place; in the thirties there was a strong bias in favor of colossal historical subjects and pictures satirizing war. Animated cartoons, in color after 1932, created a new and popular form of the film art. Technicolor was applied to feature pictures as well.

But color as an innovation was dwarfed in importance by the advent of the "talkies" in 1925; within four years they had begun to crowd the silent picture off the screen. This "revolution" necessitated changes in many directions; old studios were no longer usable, players had to have good voices, the thousands of show-houses had to be re-equipped. And linguistic problems were created for American producers who up to then had enjoyed an immense superiority in the export of films; only partly was the linguistic difficulty overcome by inserting passages spoken in the tongue of the country in which the picture was to be shown. Films in the French language found new markets in Belgium and North Africa where the American product was no longer intelligible. Pictures imported into Britain from the United States were placed on a quota basis which proved to be the commercial salvation of the British film industry. After the coming of the talking picture, nothing new was added between wars to the

"the world's most popular entertainment," except technical improvements.

What the movies did for the eye of society—and later the ear—in the way of entertainment and enlightenment, the radio did for the ear alone. Soon after the war, "the wireless telephone" progressed rapidly, a message being transmitted from England to Switzerland in 1920. In that year, in the United States, Station KDKA broadcast the results of the presidential election to those who had assembled their own sets. Two years later a British concern was set up to broadcast news and concerts. So rapid was the improvement in transmission that in 1923 a musical program was broadcast from Pittsburgh, relayed to London, and thence all across Britain.

After that, the expansion of radio could only be described as sensational. Private companies and governments set up broadcasting stations and receiving sets were sold by the millions. With this contrivance a statesman could address his nation and the wider world more readily than a yeoman of the preceding century could communicate with his neighbor on the next farm; a man of religion could speak to hundreds of thousands of listeners, and the press of the world was confronted by a formidable competitor.

Back in 1661 one Joseph Glanville had boldly prophesied, "The time will come and that presently, when by making use of the magnetic waves that permeate the ether which surrounds our world, we shall communicate with the Antipodes." The realization of that dream came true in 1932 when Britain started to broadcast to Australia.

Macaulay, the English historian and essayist, once remarked that of all inventions, the printing press alone excepted, those which abridge distance have done most for the advancement of civilization. Had he lived in the 20th century, he might well have placed the radio above printing, for it carried its message to the unlettered and the literate alike. No one could escape the radio; it got them all.

After radio came television, which communicated optical images of moving objects by wireless. Real television dated from 1926, though a few years earlier the Scotch inventor, John L. Baird, obtained televised images of simple fixed objects, and by 1930 his company was giving public demonstrations at the London Coliseum. Images in color were sent across the Atlantic in 1931. The transmission of the British coronation procession in 1937 was the first example of a truly successful relay of an outdoor event by television, and in 1941 colored television was being shown without blur or flicker. Scientists in many countries promised that before very long, distant scenes could be reproduced in one's home as readily as radio brought

in voices from afar and that school children would be "transported"
to other countries to learn their geography lessons.

In Sum

Looking at the epoch between the wars as a whole, it is apparent
that in the esthetic province of European civilization, the twenties
were rich in experiment and vitality. In literature, drama, architecture,
painting, sculpture, and music—in all the fine arts—production was
large and innovating talents came to the fore, without, however,
eclipsing the pre-1914 era. The traditional cultural centers, Paris,
London, even Berlin and Vienna, with Moscow moving in, supplied
fresh evidence of the ability of man to create and appreciate the
higher esthetic forms.

But with the onset of the Great Depression and the sweep of totalitarian regimes, which shackled the free, creative spirit, decline set
in. Yet the finer pleasures, even in the thirties, were far from being
neglected—a point not to be missed in any quest for a balanced
understanding of Europe during "the long armistice."

*

INTERNATIONAL
AFFAIRS

*

CHAPTER XVII

Groping Toward Stability (1919-1928)

Economic Aftermath of the War

FROM a broad point of view the European economic record written just after the war paralleled that after the Napoleonic warfare a century earlier. On both occasions, while the fighting raged, public debts multiplied enormously and governments issued printing-press money to cover their deficits, causing prices to rise and confusing business transactions. At war's end came a feverish economic boom to be followed by severe depression and widespread human distress.

A full quarter of a century elapsed after the downfall of Napoleon before Europe was restored to something like economic health, but in the 20th century, national and international economic relationships were vastly more intricate than a hundred years before. The "way back" was correspondingly more tortuous, if, indeed, it could be found at all. Nowhere did the general public appreciate that the transition from the ordeal of war to conditions of peace would be a tedious and painful process.

In the latter half of 1919 Europe and the wider world experienced a phenomenal boom in industrial activity. Demand for goods which had been postponed in wartime appeared, orders from overseas piled up, and in some countries credit was rapidly expanded. Scarcity of goods forced prices to shoot up and employment was excellent; the feverish prosperity of the time seemed to fulfill the confident wartime assurances that the soldiers would return to "homes fit for heroes." Only gradually did it dawn upon men that the post-war prosperity resembled an Arabian Nights' Entertainment: exciting, wonderful, unreal.

By the summer of 1920 prices were dropping almost as quickly as earlier they had risen. Foreign purchases slacked off; fantastic fluctuations in currency values, industrial strife, crises over German reparations, famine in Russia—these and other factors extinguished the short unhealthy season of post-Versailles prosperity. Manufacturers and merchants found themselves stocked with wares which could not be disposed of at the cost of production. Compulsory liquidations were forced upon insolvent concerns, business activity declined, and unemployment mounted.

Round the globe the year 1921 was one of universal economic gloom. It was estimated that a third of the world's factories was smokeless. Millions of tons of shipping rode idle at the wharves, mutely testifying to the paralysis of international commerce. By the end of the year prices had fallen to just over half their maximum in the post-war boom, and wages had dropped to about two thirds of their top figures. Price declines meant in effect that the heavy heritage of recently contracted debt, both public and private, had virtually doubled. That was a weight too heavy for debtors to carry and had to be lightened, sooner or later, by reducing the gold-value of the national monetary units or, more drastically, by thoroughgoing repudiation of debts.

It is very easy to exaggerate the importance of the destruction caused by the fighting itself, whether human or material, for the melancholy economic plight that prevailed in Europe just after the war. Actually the wartime damage to productive capital in the form of land, ships, buildings, and civilian property was small compared with the total that was available in the world. Even those physical losses were quickly repaired. Science applied to warfare had made destruction easier, science applied to reconstruction made rebuilding easier as well.

Within two years, after all had been declared quiet on the western front, the devastated areas of France and Belgium looked very much as they did in 1913, except for the absence of tall trees; even ruined districts of battered Poland were restored with surprising rapidity. Merchant tonnage soon topped the 1913 level, industrial plant and equipment soon exceeded in productive capacity that of pre-war days and transportation systems betrayed few signs of the strain which wartime requirements had imposed upon them.

Europe's deeper malady, the colossal legacy of economic maladjustment, was not visible to the naked eye. Demobilization of war veterans and the dismissal of workers who had been engaged in war industry swelled the army of the jobless. Deeper than that, the delicate international credit mechanism which had evolved in the 19th century was thrown out of gear during the war. Debtor nations had been transformed into creditor countries and vice versa. In neither case were the nations involved prepared for their new status, and economic statesmanship either would not or could not drive home to the public the lessons implicit in the change.

Certain governments furthermore perpetuated the dubious wartime practice of meeting public expenditures that were in excess of taxes and loans by printing additional paper currency. As a result, exchange rates of national currencies flapped about like flags in a strong breeze. Under normal conditions fluctuations in exchange rates had been kept within the limits where it was advantageous to ship gold, but in the war years, one country after the other had forsaken the gold standard. Because of currency confusion business confidence was impaired, and uncertainty tended to dry up the exchange of commodities between the nations.

Outside of Europe—in the United States, Japan, Australia, and other countries—productive facilities, factories and farmlands, which had been artificially encouraged by war requirements cut into markets which previously had been supplied by European exporters. And, inexorably, the economic consequences of the Paris peace settlements worked themselves out. New boundary lines in Europe disrupted traditional commercial and communication connections, and new countries or enlarged ones enacted high tariff legislation, eager to protect infant industries and farm producers. In addition to all that, as the British economist, Keynes, had foretold with literary brilliance and uncanny accuracy,[1] the execution of the reparations provisions of the Versailles Treaty wrought with evil consequences upon the material welfare of Europe at large.

Diplomatic Turmoil

Unfinished business left over by the Paris Conference gave rise to bitter disputes over territory and to actual clashes of arms at several places. Among the Turkish nationalists, for example, there was no intention of accepting the verdicts of the peacemakers written into the Treaty of Sèvres. Above all else, the Turks resented the assignment of the coastal city of Smyrna (Ismid) and its environs to the hereditary Greek enemy. Aided and comforted by France and Italy, Turkish troops drove the Greek army of occupation, which had British backing, out of Asia Minor, and a new treaty settlement was demanded.

At an international conference at Lausanne in 1923, the Turks secured from the wartime enemies a treaty which was generally grat-

---

[1] J. M. Keynes, *The Economic Consequences of the Peace* (New York, 1920).

ifying to Turkish ambitions and national interests. Not only was unfettered Turkish sovereignty over Asia Minor acknowledged, but in
Europe Turkey retained the area that had been hers in 1914.[2] No
limitations were imposed upon the fighting services, but Turkey was
forbidden to construct military defences along the Straits leading to
and from the Black Sea; Italy gained full sovereignty over the Dodecanese chain of islands in the Aegean. As is elsewhere related (p. 434),
the Arab-inhabited provinces which formerly belonged to Turkey
were either parcelled out as mandates to Great Britain and France
or were given independence.

At the Paris Conference the boundaries of resurrected Poland
had not been wholly fixed—the frontier facing Russia for one—and
there a settlement was reached only after a sharp melodramatic Polish-Russian war in 1920 which accentuated the traditional hatreds of
the two peoples. At a time when Russia was wracked with civil strife,
hastily improvised Polish armies had marched into the Ukraine as
far as Kiev. Then Russian forces swept westward to the very threshold
of Warsaw and threatened to inundate Poland entire, but the Poles
with some assistance from France and Britain effected a remarkable
recovery and drove the Russian invader back. A treaty defining the
Polish-Russian frontier was signed at Riga in 1921. It was as freely
negotiated as any treaty is likely to be after a bitter war and Russian
negotiators expressed themselves as satisfied with the Riga terms.

Although the Riga boundary excluded from Poland extensive
tracts that had been hers at her medieval height, it incorporated in
the Republic large minorities of White Russians and Ukrainians. Previously, the Supreme Council of the Allies had recommended the
famous "Curzon Line," some 150 miles to the west of the Riga frontier, as the temporary Polish-Russian frontier. That proposal had
been advanced because the area to the east of the line was mixed
in speech and religion and a hurried decision might be unfair. The
future should determine whether or not the Curzon Line should be
the permanent boundary. The military defeat of Russia led to the
fixing of the Russo-Polish border in the Riga Treaty.

Policymakers in Moscow keenly distrusted Poland, regarding it as
the spearhead of the capitalist world 'pointed against the Soviet
Union. Yet for almost a generation the Russians refrained from
raising the question of a change in the Polish frontier. Indeed, in a
Non-aggression Pact of 1932, they actually reaffirmed the existing
boundary. It was not until 1939, a matter of days after the start of

---

[2] Arrangements were made for an exchange of populations between Turkey and
Greece.

war between Poland and Germany, that Soviet Russia demanded a new frontier with Poland and sent armed forces into the coveted eastern section. Poland and her eastern frontier became, in time, the largest political barrier to full concord in the Grand Alliance which fought and destroyed Nazi Germany.

In the territorial settlement of Upper Silesia, Poland fared less well than her more optimistic patriots had anticipated. Special interest attached to this province because of its varied mineral resources and its factories and rolling-mills; both Poland and Germany, the owner before 1914, claimed that the population was predominantly of their nationality. It was prescribed in the Versailles Treaty that the inhabitants of Upper Silesia should themselves decide under what flag they should live. In 1921, amidst stormy circumstances, the plebiscite was held.

In the province as a whole Germany received much the higher vote, about sixty per cent, but in certain sections Poland commanded a majority; in the industrial area, communes which voted for Poland were inextricably mixed with communes that voted for Germany. In some places town-dwellers favored Germany, while most of the peasants in the surrounding countryside preferred Poland. Here, obviously, was a situation not susceptible of easy solution; and while British diplomacy believed that the whole province should be retained by Germany, the French with equal ardor insisted that it should be awarded to Poland.

After acrimonious controversy, Upper Silesia was finally partitioned (under the auspices of the League of Nations), tens of thousands of Poles remaining with Germany, and many Germans becoming Polish citizens. So that the industrial complex might be preserved, an elaborate German-Polish treaty was negotiated and the arrangements worked with considerable satisfaction. But inside Germany the partition of Upper Silesia was reviled as a gross transgression of the principle of self-determination and Polish nationalists were equally aggrieved. Besides, a year before plebiscites held in two small districts on the southern fringe of German East Prussia had gone almost solidly against union with Poland.

On the other side of the territorial ledger irregular Polish troops, secretly aided and abetted by the authorities in Warsaw, swooped down upon Vilna and its environs, to which Lithuania had strong claims. Possession, however, was nine points of the law. In 1923 Polish ownership was given formal international sanction, though Lithuania declined to concur and the Vilna question kept the two countries at bitter enmity.

Frankly imitating Polish tactics, Lithuania sent forces into the Memelland, German before 1918 and containing the small but serviceable harbor of Memel. While the city itself was overwhelmingly German in national sentiment, the country round about was heavily Lithuanian. Eventually the Allied powers recognized Lithuania's ownership, solemn assurances having been given that the residents would be permitted considerable freedom in managing local affairs. That arrangement stood until March of 1939, when Hitlerian regiments "reclaimed" the Memelland for Germany.

Farther along on the Baltic, Soviet Russia in 1920 acknowledged the independence of the Republics of Latvia, Estonia, and Finland. And after an arbitration decision by the League of Nations—the only example in Europe of that kind of settlement of an international dispute in the era between wars—Finnish sovereignty over the strategically valuable Åaland islands, which was contested by Sweden, was recognized, with the proviso that the population should enjoy home-rule.

By the Treaty of Trianon the Kingdom of Hungary had lost land to Czechoslovakia, to Rumania, and to Yugoslavia. These countries were resolved to hold what they had gained. On two occasions just after the war the deposed Hapsburg monarch, Charles, tried to regain the Hungarian throne of his ancestors, which the neighboring states successfully resisted, afraid lest the restoration of the king would be the prelude to efforts to reclaim territory that had fallen to them. These "succession states," Czechoslovakia, Rumania, and Yugoslavia, bound themselves by treaty (1921) to keep Hungary from recovering her former territory by force. That alignment, which was known as the Little Entente, and which became diplomatically associated with France, preserved its integrity until 1938.

Off to the south, the seaport of Fiume and adjacent territory at the head of the Adriatic was an arena of sharp competition between Italy and Yugoslavia. It was the focus, in fact, of all the accumulated antagonisms and political passions of the Adriatic coast. At Paris the peacemakers had recommended that Fiume should be internationalized and serve the commercial and shipping interests of both contestants, but that judicious proposal roused the fierce wrath of ambitious Italian nationalism. Suddenly a filibustering expedition in charge of the militant Italian author-warrior, Gabriele D'Annunzio, seized Fiume and set up an authoritarian regime. No inducement could persuade the Italians to pull out. It was not until 1924 that a definitive compromise was concluded, leaving Italy sovereign over most of the disputed Fiume area but giving Yugoslavia special rights in the use of harbor facilities.

Glancing back over this troubled story of economic and diplomatic turmoil just after the war, one might conclude that Europe was hopeless. Surely these episodes were symptomatic of the fact that Europe was a sick man, wounded and enfeebled by war to a degree that physicians of a brave new world did not always perceive.

The Washington Conference

While the Paris Peace Conference "left-overs" were being adjusted in Europe, a patch of blue in an otherwise somber international sky emerged from the Washington Conference, summoned by the United States. The central purposes of that parley were to seek international agreement to limit seapower and to work out understandings on questions involving the Pacific area and China that were of general concern. Programs for naval expansion which were underway in the major seapowers, tension between the United States and Japan over the latter's predatory course in China and the abuse of Korean patriots augured ill for the preservation of peace. Furthermore, at the end of "the war to end wars" the cry arose for economy in public expenditures. Curtailment of the fighting services seemed an easy and ready way to make savings, as well as a means of mitigating international suspicions and mistrust. More than once before 1914 proposals for an Anglo-German understanding to restrict navies had been canvassed, but nothing had been accomplished. It was otherwise in 1922 when the five greatest sea powers: the United States, Great Britain, Japan, France, and Italy, bound themselves to limit the number and size of the largest battleships and aircraft carriers.

At the Washington Conference Great Britain agreed to equality with the United States in capital ships, which was no small matter in view of the historic supremacy of Britain on the blue water. To be sure, if Britain had been unwilling to accept parity, the gigantic shipbuilding program that was in course in the United States would quickly have outdistanced that of the British fleet. It was arranged, too, that Japan should have sixty per cent as much capital ship tonnage as the Big Two, and France and Italy thirty-five per cent as much.

Although it was attempted, no understanding could be reached at Washington to impose limitations on cruisers, submarines, or other auxiliary craft. Sharp dissension between French and Italian naval chiefs which appeared at Washington was a grim portent of the fiercer rivalry in the years which followed. Yet the agreed restrictions on capital ships removed the prospect of a race in that category, such as had so disastrously poisoned Anglo-German relations earlier in the century. And substantial savings were effected in national budgets.

The capital ship treaty was only the beginning of the work of the Washington Conference. Japanese suspicions of American intentions in the western Pacific had been aroused by the announcement of plans to improve American fleet stations in the great ocean. Indeed, if the United States had not been willing to cancel those projects, it is unlikely that Japan would have ratified the fleet limitation treaty. But the United States, Britain, and Japan promised at Washington not to enlarge their fighting facilities in specified zones of the Pacific, which meant in reality that Japan was naval master of the Far Pacific, and could not be challenged without a costly and perhaps a long war. Outside the barred zone, at Singapore, on the tip of the Malay Peninsula, Britain decided to lay out a huge naval station, as protection for British and other European interests in southern Asia and the Pacific Ocean generally.

Another troublesome Pacific problem was the Anglo-Japanese Alliance, signed originally in 1902, to safeguard the Oriental interests of the two island empires against Imperial Russia. It was serviceable also against Imperial Germany and was due to expire in 1921. That Anglo-Japanese Treaty had never been popular in the United States which let it be known that it would prefer to see the alliance dissolved; the British Dominions in the Pacific registered similar views in London. Bowing to these wishes, Great Britain proposed at Washington that the partnership with her faithful Japanese ally should be replaced by a Four Power Pact, with the United States and France as members.

Accordingly, a treaty was arranged. The four countries bound themselves to respect each other's rights in the Pacific vastness and to confer jointly on any dispute that might arise. Highly applauded at the time it was made, the Four Power Pact had next to no practical value, save as it provided Britain with a decent way to bury the alliance with Japan without too gravely wounding the *amour propre* of intensely sensitive Nippon.

Of vastly more importance was a Nine Power Treaty on China. It was entered into at Washington by all the nations with large interests in the Pacific region, except the Soviet Union, which was regarded as a sinister menace to everything decent in international affairs and was not invited to Washington. By signing the Nine Power Treaty, the several nations committed themselves to respect the political independence and the territorial integrity of the young Chinese Republic

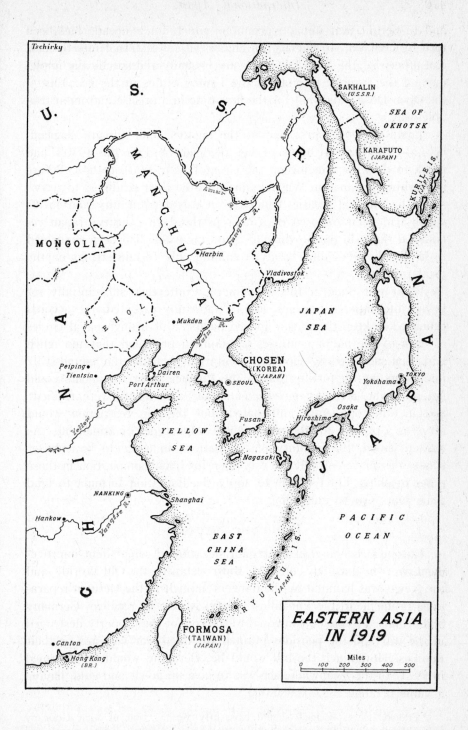

Tschirky

U. S. S. R.

MONGOLIA

MANCHURIA

JEHOL

Harbin

Mukden

Yalu R.

Sungari R.

Amur R.

Nonni R.

Vladivostok

SAKHALIN
(U.S.S.R.)

SEA OF
OKHOTSK

KARAFUTO
(JAPAN)

KURILE IS.

JAPAN
SEA

CHOSEN
(KOREA)
(JAPAN)

SEOUL

Fusan

Nagasaki

Peiping
Tientsin

Dairen

Port Arthur

Yellow R.

YELLOW
SEA

Osaka

Hiroshima

Yokohama TOKYO

JAPAN

PACIFIC
OCEAN

NANKING

Hankow

Shanghai

Yangtze R.

CHINA

EAST
CHINA
SEA

RYUKYU IS.
(JAPAN)

FORMOSA
(TAIWAN)
(JAPAN)

Canton

Hong Kong
(BR.)

EASTERN ASIA
IN 1919

Miles
0   100   200   300   400   500

and to permit that unhappy country, which for a decade had been torn by civil war, to manage its affairs without external interference. Put otherwise, the Nine Power Treaty formally and specifically implemented the favorite formula of the United States in the Far East— the Open Door—and that for the first time in a precise and unmistakable way.

Japan was of course one of the signers. And Japan's flagrant, crystal-clear transgressions of her pledged word in the 1930's had much to do with bringing on the Great Pacific War of 1941. Before adjourning, the men at Washington indicated their readiness to reconsider the unequal treaties touching on extraterritoriality and tariffs which had been imposed on China in the 19th century. Japan renounced rights in the province of Shantung which had been confirmed to her in the Versailles Treaty, retaining only certain strings on the local railway.

What was done at the Washington Conference substantially relieved international tensions, and, if faithfully executed, the accords promised to keep the Pacific indeed pacific. But in high naval circles of each of the major countries the opinion prevailed that too much had been sacrificed by the naval limitation pact and the "stand-still" understanding on fortification in the Pacific. Their arguments could not, however, convince governments; the agreements were ratified; and it was confidently anticipated that big-ship restriction would serve as a pattern for the reduction of other types of armaments. As matters stood, the inability of the nations to agree to limit lesser classes of war vessels left the way open for lively competition in those types of ships. Later efforts to apply the limitation formula to land armaments proved unavailing.

Economic Stresses

Europe's economy, in the meantime, showed some slight improvement over the dark days of 1921. But constantly, the Old World—and the New—was haunted by the dangers implicit in the German reparations problem. In the Versailles Treaty, it may be recalled, Germany had promised to pay a sum equal to the cost of the property destroyed in the war and the pensions granted to Allied war veterans or their families. How much the bill would be, Germany would be informed in 1921. In the meanwhile, she was to give up goods and gold, having a value of about $5,000,000,000.[3]

[3] France, it was decided, should have fifty-two per cent of what Germany paid; Britain twenty-two per cent, Italy ten per cent, Belgium eight per cent, and the final eight per cent would go to other claimants.

Whether Germany actually met that initial obligation it is difficult to tell. In any case, in 1921, the Allied Commission which had charge of reparations informed Germany that the gross bill would be about $31,500,000,000, to be liquidated in installments over a lifetime. Under duress Germany accepted the heavy verdict—or heavy then it seemed—but soon fell behind in payments and requested the postponement of part of the obligation—a moratorium, it was called. To that the Allied creditors consented. A conference of all the powers was convened at Genoa (1922) for the avowed purpose of finding ways of stimulating trade between the nations. From the Genoa meeting emerged stillborn resolutions summoning all countries to put government finance in balance and to bring order out of the currency confusion.

Delegates from Soviet Russia attended the Genoa gathering, but proposals to get them to promise compensation to foreigners for losses suffered by the confiscation of property after the Bolshevik Revolution fell flat. The Russians, indeed, stole a march on the West by negotiating a promising bargain with Germany, a political outcast like herself. In that agreement, the Treaty of Rapallo of 1922, arrangements were made for the resumption of normal commercial transactions between the two Ishmaelites, and for provisional cancellation of all German financial claims on the Soviet Union. That deal paved the way for military contacts between representatives of the two countries.

News of the Russo-German bargain fell upon an unsuspecting Europe with the explosive force of a bomb. It was widely believed that the German-Russian alignment presaged joint action to undo the territorial and political settlements which World War I had brought. Such fears turned out to be groundless, though something akin to friendship persisted between Berlin and Moscow until the enthronement of National Socialism in Germany (1933).

If on the financial and trade fronts little was accomplished toward restoring Europe to economic health, several of the smaller nations contrived to strengthen themselves within by parceling out large landed properties among peasant families. Yet that gain was considerably counterbalanced by the action of the United States in severely limiting immigration. Ever since 1890 hundreds of thousands of unhappy European rustics had set off to the New World to better their fortunes. Some of them remained permanently in their new homes, though sending part of their earnings to relatives in Europe; others went back to their native countries with a tidy pile of American dollars (sometimes) and a stock of ideas and habits which they had picked up in the strange land of mines and mills beyond the Atlantic.

After World War I, a combination of circumstances in the United States—half economic, half political and social—raised legal barriers to prevent a tidal wave of immigration from Europe. Preliminary and temporary measures of restriction preceded the definitive Act of 1924 which set an annual immigration quota of two per cent of the number from any country residing in the United States in 1890.[4] The measure wrought with peculiar force upon the "peasant" countries of Europe and the results were readily apparent.

Whereas in 1921 over 800,000 newcomers had been admitted to the United States, in 1930 the number had dwindled to under 50,000. In the darkest years of the Great Depression more aliens returned to their European homelands than entered the United States. The British Dominions likewise enacted legislation to limit immigration. All these restrictions damned up enterprising commoners in the Old World, making the struggle for existence harder than it would otherwise have been.

One clause in the American immigration law of 1924 discriminated sharply against Japan—and all Asiatics—by wholly excluding Japanese workers instead of admitting them on the quota principle that was applied to Europeans. That heavy blow descended upon sensitive Japan before it had started to recover from a catastrophic earthquake (1923) which ruined the fine port of Yokohama, destroyed large sections of Tokyo, and snuffed out about 100,000 lives. So weakened was Japanese finance that a few years later there was a profoundly upsetting panic. That and other internal stresses strengthened the conviction of certain members of the Japanese military caste that the solution of their country's plight must be sought in the establishment of Nipponese political ascendency over China, which would be converted into a reservoir for raw materials and a market for Japanese manufactured articles.

Britain and France

Frightened by the growing might of Imperial Germany, Britain and France had fashioned a cordial political understanding in 1904. In the diplomatic crises of the decade that followed, the links between the Channel neighbors were drawn tighter. They fought shoulder to shoulder in World War I until the German enemy was crushed.

Then the bonds of solidarity were seriously weakened, as is the way with coalitions after victory. At the Paris Conference British and French policies and interests collided head on and the dissensions and

[4] After 1929, immigration might not lawfully exceed about 150,000 in any one year.

recriminations after the Versailles Treaty was signed threatened more than once to disrupt the entente utterly. Indeed, there was no full meeting of British and French minds until the late thirties, months after the military resurgence of Nazi Germany. Then the reappearance of the peril that had originally brought the two countries together produced a diplomatic reunion.

The fundamental explanation of the cleavage that developed between France and Britain after the defeat of Germany in 1918 is not hard to discover. Apprehensive of the recovery of the hereditary enemy beyond the Rhine, fearful of a war of revenge, and mindful of the swift invasions in 1870 and 1914, France insisted upon the literal execution of the Versailles Treaty, which would hold Germany in leash economically and militarily. Beyond that, as prerequisites for national safety, France kept her army large and entered into alliances with Poland and Czechoslovakia, beneficiaries like the Third Republic of the Paris settlements, and afraid too of a war with Germany. France, moreover, studiously sought to inveigle Britain into a solid military alliance. Animating the French policy, too, was the determination to obtain reparations from Germany to rebuild war-devastated areas, to pay pensions, and to liquidate foreign debts that had been contracted during the fighting.

Between the French outlook and the predominant view in Britain a wide gulf yawned. The essential difference rested less, much less, on any divergence in international ethics than on stark geographical fact: the Rhine River is narrower than the English Channel. Behind that moat Britain had a feeling of safety which was denied the French. More, the British navy was ruler of the waves, the European waves at any rate, while the once menacing German High Seas fleet was resting on the ocean floor and German airpower was only a memory.

In those circumstances Britain could afford to deal moderately with the fallen foe. Then, too, it was in the British interest that Germany should get back on its feet economically, which would be advantageous to Europe entire, not least to British foreign trade. And all thinking on full employment in the island kingdom eventually reverted to means of expanding foreign commerce.

For that element in British public life, broadly the non-Conservatives, who had faith in the Weimar experiment in democracy, it was of capital importance that the treatment of Germany should be designed to nourish the infant and thus to discourage the unregenerate German groups which desired the restoration of the monarchy and German military power. Therefore the unwearied agitation in non-Conservative British circles for revision of the Versailles Treaty and unflagging resistance to French overtures for a military alliance. Britain, it was said, must neither bind her diplomatic hands, nor consent to undisputed French hegemony in Europe. It was also held by some Britishers that a solid diplomatic alignment with France would surely invite a counter diplomatic combination, likely enough in the form of a German-Russian partnership.

Given that fundamental cleavage—the French accent on security, the British emphasis on economic recovery—the post-war strains and stresses in Anglo-French diplomacy assume an intelligible pattern. On only a single issue did the two governments present a united front; namely, the enforcement of the military specifications of the Versailles Treaty. By the spring of 1922 these terms had been very nearly executed, but delays ensued and the Allied Military Control Commission was not withdrawn from Germany until 1927. After that there was no permanent Allied body to keep an eye on the state of German armament. British opinion, more than French, seemingly, resented the failure to try the Kaiser, as prescribed in the Versailles Treaty, because of the unwillingness of the Dutch government to yield up the imperial refugee. It resented, too, the German evasion of the Versailles clause calling for the trial and punishment of other German war criminals.

On policy in the Near East British and French statesmen clashed sharply, even more acridly on the disposition of Upper Silesia, and most violently of all on German reparations. Whereas Britain was inclined to relax the reparations terms, France brushed aside any such proposals as suicidal and calculated to encourage the late enemy to repudiate other items in the Versailles Treaty.

Occupation of the Ruhr

We have seen that in 1922 Germany had been given a partial moratorium on payments due the Allies on reparations. Even so, Germany fell behind and presently asked her creditors to grant a complete moratorium. That request precipitated an illuminating intergovernmental debate on the whole intricate maze of reparations and of the debts which the Allies owed the United States government for loans that were advanced after America's entry into the war and following the Armistice.[5]

The sums involved ran into astronomical figures, baffling to the general public and puzzling even to the candid among the financial

[5] Germany had no reparations obligations to the United States, but it had to reimburse the government for the costs of the army of occupation in the Rhineland and for damage that German agents and their accomplices had done in the United States during the war.

experts. For Americans, an essential point was that in the course of the war, the United States, which had been a debtor nation, shipping goods abroad to meet its foreign borrowings, was converted into a creditor country. If the United States was to be repaid for the war loans, then huge quantities of goods would have to be imported, an idea that cut straight across the widely cherished American tradition that tariffs should protect industrial concerns and wage earners against foreign competition. Indeed, by act of Congress in 1922 tariffs were raised to a new high level, making payment even more difficult; yet Americans on the whole expected the European debtors to "come across."

Just how did the war debts due the United States link up with German reparations? The nations which Germany owed were precisely those that had financial obligations to the United States. Great Britain, France, Italy, and the smaller debtors were reluctant, unwilling indeed, to pay America unless Germany first paid them. Otherwise the "war victors" would be paying, while the vanquished nation would not.

When the Allies inquired the terms upon which the United States would settle the war debts, they were informed that the government was ready to consent to what amounted to *partial* cancellation. Accordingly, between 1923 and 1930 most of the European debtors signed contracts with the United States to make annual payments on their obligations over a span of sixty-two years. In each instance, in arranging the contracts, the ability or capacity of the debtor nation to pay was taken into account. Britain's total obligation, for example, was reduced by about twenty per cent, France's by fifty per cent, and Italy's by more than seventy-five per cent.

In spite of these concessions the benevolent Uncle Sam of the war period seemed to some Europeans to have taken on the character of a greedy, grasping, avaricious Uncle Shylock. Some Americans, too, notably professional economists, who were familiar with the niceties of international economics, contended that the national interest would, in the long run, be best served by a greater, if not indeed the complete, cancellation of the war debts.

What the European governments contracted to pay the United States they intended to collect from Germany; so that war debts and reparations were in fact Siamese twins. For reasons already explained, Frenchmen, regardless of political outlook, adamantly insisted upon strict enforcement of the reparation claims. Within France the conviction had gained general acceptance that Germany, or at any rate the German industrialists, were not making an honest effort to meet obligations. Therefore it was felt that the fraudulent debtor must be physically coerced.

Sharing that view was Premier Raymond Poincaré, no doubt the ablest if not always the most farsighted statesman of the Third Republic. His exceptional juristic talents found ample scope in the bitter reparations dispute both with Great Britain and with Germany. It seems quite unlikely that Germany could in fact perform the reparations commitments until after the country had been financially and economically rehabilitated. Nor could Germany float loans abroad to pay her debts as France had done in the 1870's, for the reason that foreign banking interests lacked confidence in German ability to repay.

When, in 1922, Germany technically defaulted on reparations, Poincaré, solidly supported by French nationalism, arranged with Belgium to undertake collections by military force. Whether that operation was legally permissible under the Versailles Treaty was a hotly debated international question. In any event, the British government frankly dissociated itself from the Franco-Belgian course, assumed an attitude of benevolent neutrality, and Anglo-French cooperation ceased temporarily to exist. To many Britishers it seemed that France was taking an unfair advantage of a defeated and impoverished Germany and that the invocation of armed force to obtain reparations would rouse fierce and lasting resentment in a nation that one day would surely be strong again.

Early in 1923 French and Belgian armies marched into and took over the administration of the Ruhr valley, incomparably the greatest industrial district of Germany, an area of steel mills and blast furnaces and of the richest German coal fields. In a real sense the Ruhr was the industrial heart of the German nation, pumping blood through all the arteries of the Republic. Germany beyond the Ruhr was only a country of potato fields, someone was heard to remark.

Instead of cooperating with the French to enable them to secure goods for reparations the Ruhr population—from coal-miner to ballet dancer—went on vacation and would not do a tap of work. That course of passive resistance was recommended by the German government itself which promised to compensate idle workers and property-owners who balked at executing French commands. To all outward seeming, coercion in the Ruhr was a renewal of the war.

Until September, 1923, the agonizing struggle of national wills dragged on: the French bent upon getting reparations, the Germans obstinately (if passively) resisting. Then the German government, their country torn with as many wounds as Caesar's body, yielded, surrendered without conditions, for there was very grave danger lest the state would crack asunder and the national economy would be ruined beyond repair. The German currency was doing a St. Vitus' dance; winter was approaching; there was no coal, and millions of Germans were living close to the starvation line.

What consequences the Franco-Belgian occupation of the Ruhr had for German domestic history is recounted elsewhere (Chap. XIII). Here it may simply be repeated that it weakened the democratic regime, intensified the hereditary German hatred for France, and fostered the growth of political extremism.

For France, this fresh humiliation of Germany brought undoubted psychological gains, for no one could doubt who was "boss" in Europe. But in so doing France antagonized influential elements in Great Britain and the United States, which, since the making of the Versailles Treaty, felt sure that France was selfishly and short-sightedly advancing national interests at the expense of larger considerations of European stability and convalescence.

Since German economy was intimately connected with the material welfare of Europe as a whole, the Ruhr episode aggravated economic woes all around, precipitated the disintegration of several national currencies, and generally postponed the return to something like normal economic activity. The currency of France itself started down the toboggan slide, and for the reparations account little had been secured. The coal of the Ruhr just could not be dug with bayonets.

As a sign of a changing mood in France, parliamentary elections in 1924 installed the conciliatory Herriot in the place of the pugnacious Poincaré. Never again did France undertake to compel execution of the Versailles Treaty by force, whether because of inner weakness or the feeling that the certain costs would exceed the probable gains.

The Dawes Plan

Germany had submitted without reservations and so the way was opened for a "new deal" on the whole question of reparations. With the consent of all the interested powers, a committee of international financial wizards was created to study Germany's capacity to pay and to offer recommendations for the future of reparations. That committee, which was headed by an American, Charles G. Dawes, devised a reparations program known as the Dawes Plan.

The Dawes Plan specified the exact sources from which the German government was to obtain funds to meet all foreign obligations, reparations and the cost of armies of occupation. It indicated the amounts that should be transmitted each year, and it set up a network of agencies to supervise German economic affairs. Nothing was said about the full reparations sum to be paid; that fixed in 1921 stood as official. A loan would be floated on the international money market to provide Germany with gold to be used as backing for new currency, or to provide a small amount for reparations. It was assumed in the Dawes Plan that French and Belgian soldiers would be promptly withdrawn from the Ruhr. All the governments accepted the Dawes proposals and they were immediately put into operation (1924). Foreign troops evacuated the valley of the Ruhr.

The Dawes settlement, while not final nor intended to be final, afforded Europe a breathing spell, a chance for popular passions to cool, and international feuds to lose something of their ardor. General improvement in international relations followed. Virtually all the major problems inherited from the treaty settlements of 1919 had by now been adjusted, and Europe's statesmen were at last in a position to concentrate on the challenging task of stabilizing peace.

A Great Renewal

Edward Gibbon in his famous volumes on the Roman Empire selected the second century of the Christian era as the happiest and most prosperous in human annals. With no less hesitation the student of very modern Europe will choose the years 1925-1928 as the brightest and most promising known to the 20th century.

Germany, which in 1923 had fallen so low, made a remarkable economic recovery (Chap. XIII), and in other countries improved conditions were generally apparent. The process spoken of as rationalization had wide application, which meant more goods for more consumers at lower prices. Automobiles and commercial aircraft were used more extensively and for the smaller pocketbook there were artificial silk, the radio, the cinema, and a wide array of household electrical appliances.

European prosperity would have been more widely diffused and more firmly based if governments had not felt constrained to grant tariff protection to native industry and agriculture. Tariffs, in fact, were steeper, more numerous and more frequently changed than before 1914. The continent was criss-crossed by a score of customs barriers, and agitation for even higher tariffs was lively, due in part to the penetration of Japan into world trade on a large scale.

Partly to combat the rising tide of protectionism and to ensure economic recovery, a World Economic Conference was organized by the League of Nations at Geneva in 1927. Representative financiers, industrial magnates, and professional economists of all nations attended. Discussions at Geneva centered on the vices of tariff competition and the virtues of freer international trade. It was resolved that the time had come for the nations to start lowering the trade barriers which handicapped the exchange of commodities. With unanimity the delegates endorsed the opinion that "economic conflicts and divergence of economic interest are perhaps the most serious and the most permanent of all the dangers which are likely to threaten the peace of the world." •

For a time, a short time, after the Geneva parley tariff rates ceased rising and the prospects for expansion of international trade seemed bright. But no large country was willing to take the initial step for really drastic lowering of duties. The smaller nations believed that agrarian protectionism was indispensable for peasant stability, if for no other reason. Thus the hopes of an increase in international commerce swiftly vanished into thin air.

Locarno

The years of the Great Renewal witnessed positive betterment in the political relations among the powers of Europe, and efforts were made to heighten the sense of security as a prelude to disarmament. Security, it must be said, is an extremely elastic and comprehensive term. In the language of a distinguished French diplomatist, Jules Cambon, "The word (security) signifies more indeed than the maintenance of a people's homeland or even of her territories beyond the seas. It also means the maintenance of the world's respect for them, the maintenance of their economic interests, everything, in a word, which goes to make up the grandeur, the life itself of a nation."

Since the League of Nations did not provide security to the point where nations felt it safe to cut down their armaments, statesmen considered a proposal obligating nations to submit any international controversy to arbitration before going to war. That principle of compulsory arbitration was incorporated in the ill-starred Geneva Protocol of 1924, prepared under the auspices of the League. It was also prescribed in the Protocol that a nation which declined to settle a quarrel by arbitration would, by that very fact, be regarded as an aggressor, and would be restrained by the physical force of the other countries.

For this ambitious project considerable enthusiasm was generated especially in France, but it failed of international acceptance. For one thing, a change in ministries in Great Britain, which brought the cautious Conservative Party into office, helped to ruin the Protocol, and the British Dominions expressed disapproval, half in fear that it would lead to complications with Japan over immigration, half because they preferred to avoid entanglement in the politics of Europe. Without British participation no scheme of compulsory arbitration had any chance of success.

Upon the death of the Geneva Protocol, European diplomacy turned to the idea of special security arrangements, more limited in scope, agreements to meet "a specific danger in a particular area." Initiative in this matter was taken by the German Foreign Minister, Dr. Gustav Stresemann (Chap. XIII), who seems to have believed that his country should genuinely try to fulfill the Versailles Treaty and to contribute to a greater feeling of safety. He also desired to get foreign soldiers out of the Rhineland. His overture led to consultations between the British Foreign Minister, Austen Chamberlain, and his French opposite number, Aristide Briand. The outcome of these deliberations was the historic Locarno agreements, so-called from the idyllic Swiss village in which the three statesmen concluded the pacts in October, 1925.

The principal Locarno treaty, spoken of as the Rhineland Security Pact, was intended to give France a greater sense of safety from German attack. It stated that the Versailles boundary between Germany and France (Belgium, too) should stand permanently. Germany, in other words, freely consented to her existing western frontier, and implicitly renounced all pretensions to Alsace-Lorraine. Germany promised not to send troops into the Rhineland zone which had been demilitarized by the Versailles Treaty.

These undertakings, Great Britain and Italy guaranteed to uphold by force of arms if need be. This meant, in effect, that for Great Britain the Rhine had become the national frontier. Further, France and Germany bound themselves to submit disputes that arose in the future to judicial settlement.

At Locarno, Stresemann entered into similar engagements with Belgium, and in treaties with Poland and Czechoslovakia agreed to arbitrate any quarrels that might occur. But Germany would not bind herself to regard the status quo in eastern Europe as fixed and final. Rather, Stresemann asserted that Germany hoped to bring about boundary revisions in the east by processes of peaceful change. So that Poland and Czechoslovakia might feel more secure vis-à-vis Germany, France promised military help in case either should be attacked by Germany and the Slav states in turn gave reciprocal pledges to France.

The French and their allies were eager to have Britain assume a commitment to preserve the eastern boundary of Germany, paralleling the obligation in the Rhineland, but British Conservative conviction, which thought of eastern Europe as beyond the range of British security interests, defeated that hope. Not until 1939, indeed, did British policy in eastern Europe undergo modification. Without positive assurances of British military assistance neither France nor her allies were willing to curtail their armaments. For the French, the recurrent theme was "security before disarmament"; while the British held that security depended, first of all, on armament reduction.

At the Locarno meeting German diplomatists for the first time since the war had negotiated with representatives of the victor powers on a footing of equality. Yet at home nationalistically-minded Germans declaimed violently against the Locarno understandings. President Hindenburg, however, urged that the accords should be ratified and Stresemann, by hinting at forthcoming concessions from the Allies, succeeded in persuading a majority in the Reichstag to vote favorably.

Locarno was one of several promising signs of European recovery. Austen Chamberlain cheerfully characterized the Locarno treaties as "the real dividing line between the years of war and the years of peace." But he hastily and properly added that only a beginning had been made. During the next three years, the Locarno statesmen, Briand, Chamberlain, and Stresemann, collaborated effectively in smoothing out problems of mutual concern. Allied soldiers were evacuated from Cologne, for example, and the size of the occupying armies in the rest of the Rhineland was scaled down. Stresemann pressed for complete withdrawal, to which Briand was not unsympathetic provided reparations payments were guaranteed. Before negotiations on these points were completed, however, Chamberlain had resigned and Stresemann had died. By 1930 the magic of Locarno had lost most of its luster, though not entirely until 1936, when Hitler consigned the treaties to the waste basket.

Germany had accepted the Locarno arrangements on the explicit understanding that it would be permitted to enter the League of Nations and would be assigned a permanent seat on the Council. Formal application for admission provoked a sharp controversy among some of the lesser nations over the distribution of Council seats. But after some difficulty, the issue was satisfactorily resolved and in 1926 German representatives took their chairs at Geneva alongside the victors in World War I. With moving eloquence, Aristide Briand welcomed the Germans to Geneva, declaring that France and Germany had had their fill of military glory and could now work together in the heroic task of preserving international tranquility. Another milestone on the highway to enduring European peace had been passed, it appeared.

The League in Action

The League, in the meantime, had been increasing in wisdom and stature, and seemingly in favor with the generality of mankind. What exalted hopes worshipful admirers in 1919 reposed in the League! This was the central agency of what was enthusiastically labelled "the new diplomacy". This international organization was to keep the peace and to supplant the historic, hateful, and discredited method of settling international disputes by physical force. At the initial session of the League of Nations on January 16, 1920, the presiding officer, Léon Bourgeois, declared, "This day will go down in history as the date of the birth of a New World. For the first time in history, all the free nations have leagued themselves together to substitute right for wrong." That expression of faith reflected the high hope that the League would preserve peace and put international wrongs to rights.

It was fondly imagined and logically proved by ardent believers in the League that in the new world born of the "war to end war," old international rivalries and passions would be conspicuously absent. Had not the war shown that armed quarrels were ruinous for victor and vanquished alike? Would not sheer material self-interest override chauvinistic ambitions in the future? Would not world opinion throttle any challenger of the peace? Was it not now practicable for nations to scale down their burdensome, fear-inspiring armaments? But, when all was said and written, the effectiveness of the "new diplomacy" depended upon the willingness of the Great Powers (and the near-Great) to work together in making the League perform its covenanted responsibilities.

Meetings of League bodies started in 1920. A large secretariat of experts on a wide variety of human and international problems was assembled and set to work. As of 1926 League membership embraced all the nations of military significance, except the United States—whose defection handicapped the international organization from the beginning—and Soviet Russia, still militarily weak and distrustful of the League as an instrument of predatory capitalism, positively menacing to the security of the Soviet seventh of the earth.

Already the League had participated in the adjustment of several international disputes: the status of the Åaland islands, Polish boundary tangles, and the delimitation of Albanian frontiers. In connection with the last the League had suffered a setback, or to speak more generously, had failed to fortify its prestige. In 1923 several Italians, a general among them, who were engaged in laying out the boundary between Albania and Greece were slain, allegedly by Greek bandits or irregular soldiers. When Greece hesitated to redress the crime, Italian seaforces, on order of the blustering Mussolini who had recently become Premier, bombarded the Greek isle of Corfu and landed troops. A Greek appeal to the League to resolve the quarrel presented the Council with the most dangerous political controversy with which it had yet had to grapple.

Mussolini challenged the competence of the League to intervene in the dispute, if for no other reason than that the murdered men were the agents of the Conference of Ambassadors, set up by the Peace Conference to fix boundaries. Nevertheless the League Council, without pressing the question of jurisdiction, recommended a plan of settlement to the Conference of Ambassadors, which that body largely adopted. Italy was obliged to leave Corfu but only after securing from Greece a stout sum to compensate for the slain men and to appease Fascismo's sense of national honor.

Assuredly the Italian bombardment and occupation of Corfu was a flagrant violation of the Covenant. If the Council had acted with determination, il Duce, who was as yet not firmly in the saddle, could scarcely have withstood concerted international pressure. But at the moment the powers were immersed in the Ruhr imbroglio and were wanting in resolution. The Corfu episode showed that the League could be deterred from dealing effectively with a strong nation; the young institution to preserve the peace had missed a golden opportunity. Mussolini's prestige profited.

More encouraging was the success of the League in nipping in the bud a war between Greece and Bulgaria. Ever since the making of the peace, Bulgaria had been at odds with her neighbors because of depredations committed by violent Bulgarian bands which aspired to regain territory lost by the war. Border incidents between Bulgar and Greek in particular were endemic and matters came to a head in 1925, when two Greek soldiers were killed along the Bulgarian frontier. Right away Greek troops were moved onto the soil of Bulgaria; the latter appealed to the League and the Council ordered the belligerents to cease fighting—a command which both obeyed.

Then a League commission investigated the quarrel on the scene, absolved Bulgaria of responsibility for the killings, and Greece was compelled to indemnify Bulgaria for the invasion. That swift settlement of an actual war heightened the reputation of the League though, of course, only two small countries were directly involved. A real test of League effectiveness would arise when a major state was implicated in a dispute in which the League clearly had competence.

The Saar Basin

Under the Paris peace settlements the League had jurisdiction over the Danzig Free State (Chap. VI), the Saar Basin, and the mandated colonial areas; all of this furnished tough, exacting work for League officials. Although under League trusteeship, the German-inhabited Saar district was actually governed by a commission made up of a Frenchman, three other foreigners, and a native German, which reported to the League periodically. The importance of the area derived from its strategic location and from coal fields and heavy industries, both of which had been assigned to France in the Versailles Treaty. Disputes arose between the inhabitants of the Saar and the administrative commission, French-dominated, which failed to govern in a reasonably impartial fashion. More than once French troops were used to quell disturbances.

Changes in the composition of the Saar governing body in 1926 brought some improvement in the district. In 1930 French soldiers were wholly evacuated and the task of preserving order was taken over by the local police. Under the Versailles Treaty the residents of the Saar would decide in 1935 the future political status of their homeland. Perhaps the largest item on the League's record of achievement was the administration of the Saar and the successful conduct of the plebiscite, to be described later.

The Mandated Territories

By the peace treaties the former German colonies and territory wrested from the Turkish empire were placed under the guardianship of the League. These regions, called mandates, were parceled out among the victor nations, and the country holding a mandate was required to render an annual account of stewardship to a League body, the permanent Mandates Commission. So the way was opened for possible innovations in the administration of backward areas and betterment in the life and labor of the native populations.

Mandated territories were classified in three groups, in conformity with the political and economic maturity which they had attained. In the most primitive class, the former German Southwest Africa and the ex-German holdings in the Pacific, the authority of the nation holding the mandate was practically complete. It was less so in the rest of the ex-German possessions on the Dark Continent. In the third type of mandated area, the former Turkish lands—Iraq (Mesopotamia),

Syria and Lebanon, Palestine, and Trans-Jordan—the inhabitants were promised a broad degree of home-rule.

To the Mandates Commission, the mandatories reported each year. If the Commission thought the account of activities in the mandate satisfactory, it merely gave its approval; otherwise the Commission censured abuses or recommended changes to be introduced, and by pressure of publicity endeavored to force improvement. But the Mandates Commission was not clothed with executive power; it could neither propose positive administrative action nor investigate native conditions on the spot.

Palestine

Of all the mandated territories none had larger international importance than Palestine, which before World War I formed part of the Turkish province of Syria. British armies had conquered the area in the war and to Britain was assigned this mandate. Palestine's population was overwhelmingly Arab, mostly Moslem, but with a substantial Christian minority. Among the Arabs a spirit of nationalism had made some headway; and certain Arab chieftains interpreted wartime promises given by British agents to mean that Palestine would be permitted to merge in an extensive independent Arab state.

On the other hand, the British ministry in the midst of the war had promised the Zionists that Palestine should become a Jewish homeland, a place of asylum for the harassed sons and daughters of Israel living in Europe. That goal had for years been the central objective of a well-organized Zionist movement among Jews in Europe and the United States. Jewish spiritual ties with the ancient land of Palestine may be likened to the affection of Moslems for Mecca or of Roman Catholics for Vatican City.

In the British pledge to Zionism—the Balfour Declaration of 1917 —it was asserted that Britain would view with favor the establishment of a Jewish national home in Palestine, and at the same time the civil and religious rights of the Arab population would be protected. It was a commitment, in other words, to create a Jewish sanctuary in Palestine, not to transform the region into a Zionist commonwealth. Zionist spokesmen were insistent that Palestine should be a place where Jews who needed to, or wished to, might freely emigrate without restriction; a place where Jews would be liberated from the disabilities and oppressions which had long been their lot, and where Jews might live in peace and security. Zionists claimed all this as the inherent right of any nationality.

Into Palestine after the war poured Jews from the central and eastern parts of Europe. The pace of immigration was accelerated after the rise of the National Socialist Party in Germany and the Nazi reign of terror against Jewry. Whereas in 1919 the Jewish population in Palestine was under 60,000, many of whom were unsympathetic to Zionism, by 1942 Jews were estimated at almost 500,000, and four fifths of the increase was due to immigration.

From the material standpoint the accomplishments of Zionist initiative, capital, enterprise, and hard work, whether of brain or brawn, verged on the miraculous. On land purchased from Arabs, much of which had to be reclaimed before it was suitable for cultivation, Zionist colonists raised excellent crops. Oranges, grapefruit, melons, and figs were marketed widely. Arab peasants, or some of them, raised their own living standards by imitating Zionist farming techniques.

Machine industry, too, penetrated Palestine, where hitherto manufacturing had been confined to handicrafts. Food and clothing factories and cement and brick works were established, chemicals were extracted from the Dead Sea; and the historic river Jordan was harnessed to supply hydroelectric power. What so recently as 1909 had been a desert region blossomed into the thriving city of Tel Aviv, an Aladdin's lamp creation, which in time was home for three out of ten of the Jews in Palestine. And Haifa on the coast grew only less rapidly. As the terminus of the pipeline from the oil fields of Iraq, Haifa contained large refineries and storage plants, and on the infant merchant navy in the harbor of Haifa fluttered the blue and white Zionist flag. It was contended by Zionism that plans for agricultural and industrial expansion would furnish a livelihood for a vastly larger population, though Palestine is only a trifle larger than Vermont.

In Palestine, too, a Hebrew cultural renaissance flowered. The ancient Hebrew tongue was employed by men of letters and into that language were translated the choicest treasures of world literature. Education was properly honored with public schooling for virtually every Zionist child; the educational system was crowned by a Hebrew University on Mount Scopus in Jerusalem, whose library contained 400,000 volumes. It became a center for the diffusion of Jewish culture the globe around. Zionists boasted, likewise, a symphony orchestra of their own, made up of seventy resident Jews. Hospitals, dispensaries, and institutions for social welfare were generously provided.

All in all, Palestine, by reason of Zionist grit and Zionist brains, developed into the most progressive region in western Asia, an oasis of comparative well-being. But the influx of Zionist settlers roused angry resentment in Arab breasts, though the Arab community itself almost doubled in numbers between the wars owing largely to the high birth rate. Between individual Arabs and Zionists normal human relationships were not uncommon, but between the two national groups fierce tension prevailed, expressing itself in chronic and bloody riots and other varieties of violence. To put the matter bluntly, Arab nationalism clashed with Zionist nationalism. Arab peasants resented the sale of land by absentee landlords or responded to the urgings of zealots who were afraid that the Zionists would become preponderant both economically and numerically.

The other constant factor in the Palestinian situation was Great Britain, which could not please both national groups. Nor could Britain induce them to work harmoniously together for the common good. Britain, to be sure, had her own imperial interests to look after. Because of proximity to the Suez Canal and Egypt and because of the air routes, railways, and oil lines that traversed Palestine, the region was a kind of land-bridge of the British realm. Then, too, Britain had to move warily lest the whole Arab East be set in flame by the Palestinian contentions. Such a fire might spread among British-ruled Moslem populations in India and other places.

Under the Balfour Declaration Britain had assumed specific obligations to Zionist and Arab alike, and it could not be unmindful of the Christian stake—of nearly 125,000 Christian inhabitants and the Christian holy places in Palestine. Jerusalem was a holy city of Jew, Christian, and Moslem. Always the British government was subject to twin pressures: pressure from rulers of Arab states and Moslem spokesmen; and pressure from Zionists and their friends in Britain and the United States.

Over Palestine a British High Commissioner was set who was, of course, answerable for his administration to the Mandates Commission of the League. British proposals for the establishment of an autonomous government failed to attract the approval of the leaders of the rival nationalities. A specific British plan to divide Palestine into a Jewish state and an Arab state, while restricting the mandate to the holy cities and a narrow frontage on the Mediterranean was coldly rejected by both sides. Arabs clamored for an independent state or political union with their neighbors; Zionists, on their part, pushed for the creation of a Jewish Commonwealth, and reacted militantly when Britain in 1939 imposed strict limits on immigration.

Recurrent outbreaks between armed partisans kept Palestine in a stage of tension and British bayonets constantly had to hold down the lid on the boiling cauldron. It seemed evident that until a definitive settlement was come to there could be no peace in this region of rising world importance; evident, too, that settlement would have to be imposed in the absence of willingness for practical compromise.

Eastward from Palestine lies Trans-Jordan, an extensive, primitive and sparsely-peopled region of impoverished peasants, which was embraced in the British mandate for Palestine, but expressly excluded as a possible Jewish settlement. The economic ties of Trans-Jordan with Palestine were close. Some Zionists contended that if Jewish immigration were allowed, the economic record in Palestine would be duplicated in so far as natural environment permitted. A Mecca-born Arab chief, the Emir Abdullah, was installed as ruler in 1921. He had his own army, tariff, and diplomatic representation abroad, but at his elbow was a British resident and Britain had military rights in the area. By action of Parliament Britain, in 1946, converted Trans-Jordan into an independent Arab kingdom, but British military rights were retained.

Iraq

Just as British forces had occupied Palestine during the war, so they had captured the valley of Mesopotamia from the Turks. Under the title of Iraq this region, with abundant oil resources and strategic frontage on the Persian Gulf, was assigned to Britain as a mandate. That decision set off an Iraqi insurrection, fomented by nationalists who desired full and immediate independence, in conformity with British wartime promises. Without much trouble British troops crushed the insurgents and a trustworthy Arab, King Feisal, whom the French had expelled from Syria, was seated on the Iraqi throne. A territorial dispute over the Mosul oil district in which Great Britain championed the interests of Iraq against Turkey was straightened out by the League in 1926 in a manner that was favorable to the British position—the League's sole success, incidentally, in a first-rate quarrel involving a Great Power.

Iraq made significant progress both politically and economically. In form and standards the government which was set up in once fabulous Bagdad conformed to western ideals. At the side of the monarch was a conventional parliament, elected to be sure by a favored few, for the mass of the Iraqi population were uneducated peasants and shepherds, illiterate tribesmen or urban workers. The population was far from homogeneous; tension between two Moslem factions, the Shia and the Sunni, the latter in command, was never allayed.

More serious was the friction with the Kurdish minority who are distinct in language and sympathy from the Arabs, and who are kinsmen of Kurds in Persia (Iran) and Turkey. The Bagdad government would not entertain the idea of giving the Kurds the autonomy they wished and tried to appease the chiefs with mere promises.

Wealth in Iraq increased about as much as could be expected in a country having large desert areas and a generally low quality of agricultural production. Arabs and British agents got along with reasonable smoothness. Native police and military services were organized and a native officialdom was trained. The Iraqui administration had reached such maturity by 1932 that Britain granted the mandate political independence, while retaining certain military rights, to protect oil fields, pipelines, and airplane bases.

Syria

To France, whose interest in the Levant dated from the Crusades, was given a mandate over Syria and the coastal district of the Lebanon, which had a predominantly Christian population. From the beginning the presence of French officials and troops was keenly resented by nationalistically-minded natives. Isolated clashes led on to a serious armed uprising in 1926, in which bitter fighting occurred in the capital, Damascus. The French put down the insurrection with shocking severity.

Under French rule there was some progress in the improvement of Syrian highways and irrigation facilities, and plans were worked out for ultimate independence, with safeguards for French economic and cultural interests and guarantees to preserve communications with the French overseas empire. That program, which promised to go far in meeting the insistent demands of native patriotism, was put aside because of World War II, but was carried out after hostilities had ceased.

Lesser Tasks of the League

While the principal concern of the League was with political matters, it performed many subsidiary tasks beyond the range of any single state, all too little known or appreciated. We have already remarked on the assistance of the League in bringing order out of the financial chaos in Austria and in Hungary and on the international economic conference convened at Geneva in 1927 (p. 428). An International Labor Office, parallel to the League organization, was created with a view to raising and equalizing the conditions of the workers of the world. That bureau organized annual conferences on labor questions, secured the passage of more than a score of international agreements on sanitary regulations, and collected and distributed information about industrial and working conditions in many countries.

Several humanitarian enterprises carried on before 1914 by separate international bodies were brought under the League roof in Geneva and new ones were added. The League, moreover, shared actively in the transferal of Greek refugees from Turkey and in the repatriation of men and women uprooted by the war. Agencies were created to facilitate communication between scholars and other intellectuals. Conferences were organized and resolutions adopted to improve international communication services, to curb tropical diseases, and to combat the traffic in opium and kindred social evils. Some observers held, indeed, that if the League had accomplished nothing more than the enlargement of the number of internationally-minded men and women, the toil and sweat which its establishment and operation entailed were amply rewarded

As prescribed in the Covenant, the Council of the League organized, in 1921, a Permanent Court of International Justice, whose judges were chosen from the finest legal talent in the world. In a sense the supreme tribunal of the globe, the Court was popularly spoken of as the World Court. In case of a dispute between two nations, the quarrel *might* be transmitted to the Court for a decision in conformity with accepted international usage. Many countries, Britain and Germany among them, agreed to submit any controversy involving the meaning of the text of treaties or of international obligations to the Court for judicial decision.

As authorized by the Covenant, the Court handed down advisory opinions on moot questions that were submitted to it by the Council or Assembly of the League. On several occasions in the inter-war epoch it appeared as though the United States would join the World Court. But the force of inertia and of downright hostility to a tribunal which some Americans regarded as a pendant to the League prevented the passage of the necessary legislation. Like so many other organs set up to deal with international problems after World War I, the Court was included in machinery of peace established after World War II.

Armament Limitation

Among other responsibilities which devolved upon the League was that of preparing the way for a general reduction in the fighting establishments of the nations. Of course, the countries which were defeated in the war had been compelled in the peace treaties to limit their armies and armaments severely and the victors had morally promised to do likewise. Armament reduction, it was urged, would not only make possible financial savings but would also tend to diminish distrust and suspicion among the nations. Competition in armaments, as every informed student knew, was one of the deeper sources of war in 1914.

After the signing of the Locarno treaties and the admission of Germany to the League, which tended to increase the feeling of international security, the League could turn to the task of scaling down fighters and military equipment. A preliminary commission was appointed to study existing armaments and to devise a program which would serve as a basis for international limitation discussions.

Optimistic laymen, prone to oversimplify, were disappointed for the technicalities of armament limitation exceeded the imaginings of all but the most imaginative. The root of the difficulty lay in the French fear that the Third Republic was not sufficiently safeguarded against the ancient foe beyond the Rhine. France was perpetually haunted by the specter of a rejuvenated Germany, larger in population and greater in industrial strength, which might one day engage in a war of revenge. So French representatives in the preliminary conference on armament limitation brough the consultations to a deadlock by raising the almost insoluble issue of "war potential."

The fighting capacity of a nation depends not alone on soldiers and their equipment, but also on such things as the quantity and quality of a country's industry, transportation facilities, the size of the population, and the like. How could these matters be regulated and limited by international agreement? No convincing answer was forthcoming. In 1928 Soviet Russia, hitherto absent from the deliberations, sent a delegate to the conference who blandly recommended that the nations should abolish all their armaments. Few realists regarded the Russian proposal as seriously or sincerely advanced and still fewer thought it at all practicable.

No progress was made in curtailment of land forces and pessimism reigned concerning further naval limitation. Since the Washington Treaty of 1922 had set no restrictions on warships other than capital craft, lively international competition developed in the building of cruisers and auxiliary ships. For the purpose of limiting these types of vessels a parley of the leading seapowers was called at Geneva in 1927. But France and Italy, deeply distrustful of one another, declined to attend. Japan participated but took almost no part in the deliberations. And diplomatic preliminaries between the United States and Britain were far from thorough or even adequate when the meeting convened.

At the Geneva Conference, debate centered on the manner in which American and British *cruisers* should be restricted. The naval requirements of the two nations differed greatly, for each had to maintain a fleet in keeping with its own peculiar strategical needs and interests. In the end, Anglo-American compromise having proved impossible, the delegates agreed to disagree. The breakdown of the Geneva Conference caused bad blood between the two greatest naval powers. Anglo-American relations deteriorated further when it was disclosed that Britain had struck a secret naval bargain with France for pooling the seaforces of the two countries. This angered American naval chiefs.

Already the Congress of the United States had under consideration a bill for a substantial expansion of American seapower, which occasioned suspicion and mistrust in Britain. In the tense atmosphere that was generated, the pacific leader of the British Labour Party, Ramsay MacDonald, could say that a war between Great Britain and the United States was "not unthinkable."

The Latin Sisters

Just as French diplomacy was constantly colored by dread of another war with Germany, so also French policies were influenced by bickering and competition with the fractious, war-mongering regime of Mussolini. On three fronts the Latin sisters were at odds: in ideology, in the Mediterranean, and in the Balkans. Antagonism rising out of these differences inspired competition in naval armaments, which had a worsening effect on diplomatic relations. As noted, neither France nor Italy sent delegates to the abortive naval parley at Geneva.

The cleavage between the dominant political ideals and practices of France and Fascist Italy requires little comment. It was a conflict between the everlastingly opposed ideas of liberty and authority. As the heir of the great Revolution and sponsor of representative government on the continent, France was far removed from the compulsory authoritarian police state of Fascismo. Mussolini's unbridled denunciations of the democratic dogma evoked rejoinders in kind from Frenchmen, and fierce criticism of Mussolini and his regime by Italian refugees who found sanctuary in France heightened ill-will.

But France was more than the champion of "the ideas of 1789." She was equally the prime defender of the European status quo, while Italy bombastically—and not without truculence—preached the necessity of territorial revision, not, it is true, in the South Tyrol which Austria had bequeathed to Italy in 1919 and where Germans were subjected to rigorous Italianization. Not there, but covetous Fascist eyes were riveted upon the French protectorate of Tunisia, upon Nice and Savoy, upon Corsica, and tropical colonies in French Africa.

"We are hungry for land," Mussolini exclaimed, "because we are prolific and intend to remain so." To be sure, France and Britain transferred modest parcels of territory in Africa to Italy in the twenties, and by diplomatic obduracy Mussolini contrived to gain a place in the administration of Tangier, at the mouth of the Mediterranean. But those gains failed to appease the Fascist appetite, and noisy pretensions to French possessions naturally roused resentment in the Third Republic.

Very lively, too, was the competition of the Latin sisters for primacy in the affections of the Balkan countries. The French won a commanding position by negotiating alliances with Rumania and Yugoslavia and by making loans to straitened Balkan governments. But Italy cut in, signed pacts of friendship, attracted dissatisfied Bulgaria into its orbit for a time, and Italian finance and trade silently penetrated into the peninsula. Of particular interest to Italy was strategically valuable Albania, and il Duce in 1926 converted that tiny and tormented principality into a Fascist protectorate. The growing power of Italy in the Balkans frightened Yugoslavia more than ever, and led it into a military alliance with France (1927). In sum, the Latin sisters, who had fought as allies in World War I, were drifting farther and farther apart.

Paris Peace Pact [6]

In the era of good feeling induced by the spirit of Locarno, it was felt in some quarters that the time had come to pronounce international war forever "outlawed." Visionary though the idea was in the light of the traditions of international relationships, outlawry of war captured the imagination of large sections of opinion in the western world, and reflected the popular longing to have done with violence in the settlement of quarrels between countries.

Cautiously governments bowed to the popular will and in 1928 a solemn pact was signed in Paris by almost every independent country including Soviet Russia. That document asserted that nations would settle disputes of all kinds only by pacific means. Understood, however, was a reservation that the commitment would not debar a nation from fighting to defend itself, and there was no provision for the application of force in case of violation. Since, in 1914 and in earlier wars, the belligerents uniformly contended that they were fighting in self-defense, the much-acclaimed Paris Peace Pact was without much practical importance, a treaty that had little more significance than the paper on which it was written.

[6] This document is frequently referred to as the Kellogg-Briand Pact, in honor of the American and the French statesmen most active in bringing it into being.

As of 1928

What then was the outlook for the maintenance of international peace after a decade of groping toward stability? Reconstruction had progressed so fully as to erase the physical damages of the war and economic activity at the time promised well for the future.

For Europe the supreme fact as of 1928 was the ascendancy of France, in spite of the irreconcilable friction with Italy and inner French dread of Germany. Because of her large army and stocks of heavy war material, France was strong in her own right at the end of the first decade of the Versailles system. True, the term of French military service was reduced to one year in 1928, but that was compensated for by the beginning of construction on massive fortifications—the famous Maginot Line—along the frontier facing Germany. And France had a set of allies: Poland, and the Little Entente, whose armies, the strategists calculated, would suffice to contain Germany on the east if the need arose. More than that, France had such security as the Rhineland Security Treaty of 1925 and the League of Nations afforded.

Great Britain, aside from commitments under Locarno and the Covenant of the League, preserved a free hand so far as Europe was concerned. Britain was bent, in 1928, on strengthening the bonds with the Dominions and on rebuilding friendship with the United States, which controversies over naval armaments had somewhat impaired.

As for Germany, she was faithfully meeting the Dawes reparations annuities and looked forward to a final settlement on payments arising from the war. Her armaments were small, as prescribed in the Versailles restrictions. But Germany was not exactly in diplomatic quarantine, for she had assumed obligations in the Locarno treaties and as a League member. To the east Germany had the line to Moscow laid by the Rapallo Treaty of 1922 and confirmed by a treaty of 1926, wherein the Germans assured the USSR that they would not be party to an economic or aggressive military war against the Soviets. German loans were being advanced to Russia to purchase manufactured goods or to pay salaries of German technicians who were in the employ of the Kremlin. Military technicians of the two countries were exchanging information.

By 1928 Soviet Russia was looked upon with rather less mistrust and suspicion in the official circles of the west than had been true in the first tumultous years of the Bolshevik regime, but the menace of the Communist gospel of world revolution still dominated western thinking about Russia. On their part, the men in the Kremlin, never forgetting the Allied military intervention immediately after the November Revolution, were obsessed with the notion that a capitalist conspiracy was afoot to destroy the USSR.

Yet Russian representatives had participated in international conferences, and Moscow had strengthened diplomatic ties with small neighbors in Europe and in southern Asia. Soviet commercial intercourse with foreign countries had grown modestly, but in 1927 Great Britain broke off diplomatic relations, on the score that Soviet citizens had been guilty of circulating. subversive propaganda in the island kingdom.

British antipathy toward the Soviets was partly traceable to the activity of Bolshevik agents in the Orient. These agents abetted Chinese Nationalists in their heroic struggle in the mid-twenties to unify their country and to abolish the special rights and privileges which foreign powers, not least Britain, possessed in China. With the assistance of Russian military and political advisers, the Nationalist armies, General Chiang Kai-shek commanding, marched from southern China up to and beyond the Yangtze valley.

Then Chinese Nationalist leaders, alarmed by signs of revolutionary radicalism, dismissed their Soviet counsellors and proceeded with the heavy task of unification and reconstruction on their own. Pro-Russian elements in China, often spoken of as the Chinese Communists, were harried and driven to the northwest by Nationalist forces. With Japan, Soviet Russia had many points of friction, and Japanese officials repeatedly charged Moscow with responsibility for the insignificant Communist movement in the "land of the cherry blossom."

If by 1928 the Soviet Union had not been fully restored to a place in the family of nations, neither was she in the state of ostracism of the early twenties. The program of planned economic development on which the Kremlin embarked in 1928 (Chap. V) transformed Russian productive power radically and heightened Soviet prestige in international affairs.

On an overall view, the international machinery for the preservation of peace was, in 1928, impressive: the League of Nations, apparently growing in strength and authority, the Locarno treaties, and the vague illusory Paris Peace Pact. To the last document was attached the signature of the United States, which symbolized in one way the American interest in world peace, as did the presence of American delegates at many international conferences. If homilies on international good will and high-sounding paper pacts could purchase peace, the United States would buy it. But the United States was unwilling to pay in the tangible coin of cancellation of war debts, the lowering of tariffs, or in definite commitments to employ American armed forces to restrain or coerce a violator of the peace.

Surveying the world scene at the end of 1928, one did not need to be endowed with a super-optimistic temperament to conclude that the outlook for lasting peace was brighter than at any time since all had been declared quiet on the western front. Unhappily, after the Great Renewal came the Great Depression.

CHAPTER XVIII

The Great Depression and the German Resurgence (1929-1935)

The Crash on Wall Street

AT LEAST two dates in the history of the United States readily identify themselves: October 12, 1492 and October 29, 1929. On the latter day shares exchanged in the New York market exceeded 16,-400,000, gilt-edged securities sharing the fate of worthless mining stocks; paper losses for the single session approached $9,000,000,000. In a span of two months security values of $30,000,000,000 were washed away—a sum greater than the direct cost to the United States of participation in World War I.

The Great Depression, which forms the watershed in the economic history of the world between wars, had started. Yet business and political leaders in the United States confidently asserted that the recession was technical and only temporary. Certain that the fundamentals of the national economy were sound, they explained that greater prosperity than ever before known lurked just around the corner; Wall Street, in fact, was a one-way street leading inevitably upward.

Those comforting assumptions were presently torpedoed by stark fact. The swift and dramatic crash on the New York Stock Exchange heralded a world-wide depression which put an end to the fabulous dreams of the late twenties. Prices of goods dropped perpendicularly —agricultural and rawstuff prices faster than prices of manufactured articles—and the progress that had been made since the war in the economic recovery of Europe and the wider world was quickly canceled.

Once more the burden of debts, government and private, grew too heavy to bear, and painful readjustments had to be made. In the face of the economic blizzard, economic nationalism fastened its grip upon nations large and small. All alike struggled to save themselves by neo-mercantilist expedients pointed toward national self-

447

sufficiency. Economic misery fostered political authoritarianism all across the Old World, fatally undermining the brave new democratic experiments born of World War I. Few people in the world, if indeed any, were exempt from the material impoverishment and the demoralizing psychological consequences which attended the Great Depression.

Giddy America

At the heart of the global calamity, though not to be unduly exaggerated, was the giddy America of the late twenties. For the traveler returning to New York from abroad, the first object to strike the eye was the towering skyscraper, the second, the rush of motorcars. Both symbolized the American atmosphere of the time: the feverish boom in urban building, the hectic tempo of the exuberant American way of life.

The automobile, which in the twenties became the possession of most of the families in the United States, attested the national zest for speed and roving, the yearning for wider freedom. For Americans a car was nearly as important as a home; among city-dwellers in fact many more owned automobiles than owned homes. From being a "nation in arms" during the war the transatlantic giant had quickly become a "nation on wheels." The annual showing of new car models grew into a unique American institution and was surrounded with ceremonialism bordering on religious ritual. Not only did the United States mine about three quarters of the world's output of petroleum products, but it consumed as much. One's car might be the sorriest of equipages—even a "jalopy" held together by wire, string, and faith —but if it moved, it moved, and unquenchable optimism gave assurance that some day the "old bus" would have a sprightly successor. Buoyant public men indeed suggested the building of two-car garages.

No large country ever approached the prosperity which the United States experienced in the late twenties. Once the nation had emerged from the slough of the short post-war depression the popularity of the motorcar, the improvement of highways, efficiency in manufacturing techniques, amalgamations of business concerns, frenzied speculation in city land and buildings, an enormous expansion of credit, frantic gambling on the stock market, the appearance of scores of novel household appliances—available like everything else on the installment plan—all these combined to create an atmosphere of feverish and joyous well-being.

But in this epoch of the raccoon coat, the gardenia, and the ticker tape it was not all carefree enjoyment. The American landscape was dotted with consolidated rural schools and spacious high schools. The prevailing prosperity was mirrored in fact in the phenomenal growth in the numbers attending institutions of learning. Standards of comfort were generally raised, hours of work declined, and for most workers the purchasing power of wages moved up. Wage earners, who had learned the way of the investor by buying Liberty Bonds during the war, joined their more comfortably situated fellows in the exciting speculation on Wall Street.

Yet the American economic sky was not wholly blue. Farmers, for instance, who produced for export were in a depressed state. Burdened by debts contracted during the lush wartime expansion, they could not find profitable markets abroad. Prices fell, huge surpluses piled up, and farmers were advised to beat their plowshares into fishing rods and golf clubs. The textile, shoe, shipbuilding, and coal mining industries had little share in the intoxicating prosperity, while technological innovations in industry cost many workers their jobs. With the resounding crash of fictitious values in the autumn of 1929, the 1,000,000 or so who had been out of work rapidly swelled into a vast army, exceeding 13,000,000 in the depth of the depression.

It would be idle here to weigh the legion of explanations which have been plausibly proposed to account for the catastrophic slump in American economic activity. Interpretations range all the way from the collectivist indictment of the fundamental tenets of capitalism, through the inevitable business cycle of boom and depression, to the folly of voters in rejecting in 1928 the presidential candidacy of Governor Alfred E. Smith.

Among the obvious factors which brought on the collapse were the repercussions upon business of the prolonged "hard times" in Middle-Western agriculture, the failure of national banking authorities to impose checks on the nation-wide speculative orgy, the wasteful extravagance of consumers, the overexpansion of some industries, the decline in exports which was related to the decline in investments abroad, and the cumulative impact of the dislocations in the world's financial and economic mechanism resulting from World War I. Different students of the depression assign different weights to each of these and to allied phenomena.

In the wake of the stock market hurricane in the United States, prices collapsed round the globe, international trade shriveled up, the wheels of industry slackened, and unemployment spread like a prairie blaze. According to the calculations of League of Nations experts, 100,000,000 persons soon found that society had no use for the services by which they had been accustomed to earn their living.

Neo-Mercantilism Triumphant

Great though the depression was, it became even greater by further flight from the ideal of freer international trade. In that trend the United States paced the field. Several months before the debacle on Wall Street, Congress began tinkering with the tariff, primarily with the object of bringing relief to agricultural exporters. In its ultimate form, the Hawley-Smoot Act of 1930 advanced duties on about 1,000 items, carrying them to unprecedented levels. Distinguished American economists by the score and spokesmen of companies engaged in world trade cried aloud in protest, but theirs were voices in the wilderness. In Europe, resentment over the Hawley-Smoot measure was undisguised and unanimous. A Frenchman compared the new tariff to a declaration of war, while to an English journalist, it was similar to the German attack of 1914.

Promptly forty nations imitated the tariff legislation of the United States and the war of livelihoods was on. As is elsewhere explained (Chap. XI), Great Britain, historic citadel of free trade, was the most important convert to the gospel of full-bodied protectionism. The British course had a profound psychological influence upon other nations. It seemed to set the final stamp of approval upon the wisdom and virtue of protective tariffs and lent an impetus to the mad race for economic self-sufficiency.

Not only did nations raise tariff barriers higher, but other measures affecting commerce were adopted which contributed to the strangulation of free multilateral trading. When Great Britain suspended the export of gold, most of the countries on the continent (but not France) followed suit; and to control shipment of goods from nations with cheaper currencies a system of fixed quantities of imports—quotas—was established. In some cases reciprocal agreements on trade and even outright inter-nation barter arrangements were negotiated.

Importers were obliged to secure permission from state officials before bringing in foreign wares. Governments, that is, took charge of the financial mechanism of international business, each and all seeking salvation by making themselves as independent as possible of foreign sources of supplies. Export of capital from the wealthy nations to the needy countries dried up. And the sequel? Exchange of goods slumped all down the line. By 1933 international trade had fallen sixty per cent by value—and economic paralysis spread correspondingly. Neo-mercantilism had triumphed!

Reparations Again: The Young Plan

Evil as was the impact of the Great Depression upon other countries, the consequences for Germany were most dramatic. Industrial unemployment and allied ills proved to be the Achilles' heel of the Weimar Republic and precipitated the National Socialist revolution.

Even before the onset of the depression, Germany's creditors had canvassed the desirability of a downward revision on reparations. Foreign Minister Stresemann welcomed the idea and insisted that arrangements should also be made for the withdrawal of Allied troops from the Rhineland where they had been stationed since the Armistice of 1918. Negotiations on both questions were initiated at the end of 1928, the making of "a complete and final settlement" on reparations being assigned to a committee of financial experts, whose chairman was an outstanding American business man, Owen D. Young.

That committee prepared the Young Plan of 1929 which fixed German reparations at less than a third of the maximum figure that had been set in 1921; it also abolished foreign supervision over German financial and economic affairs. Until 1988, Germany was to make annual payments equal to the cost of restoring the French and other Allied areas that had been devastated in the war and to the debts which the Allied creditors owed the United States for wartime loans. It was also stipulated in the Young Plan that the Allies would make further reductions in the reparations bill if the United States would whittle down her claims on them. Stated otherwise, Britain, France, and the others would forgive their debtor in proportion as their debts were forgiven. It was a reassertion of the familiar Allied thesis that reparations and war debts were one, but that idea found little more public favor in the United States than the first time it was broached. As for the United States government, it stood firm on the proposition that the two forms of intergovernmental financial obligation were entirely separate and distinct.

It was no light task to secure Reichstag acceptance of the Young Plan because of the stubborn opposition of the Right. But President Hindenburg threw his bulky support behind it and that carried the day. Outside of Germany it was popularly assumed that the reparations tangle had now been settled forever, and that Germany, having met the Dawes annuities on schedule, would fulfill the lighter burden of the Young program. But to do so, the minimum prerequisite was a steady expansion of German trade. That the Great Depression made impossible.

As a reward for the ratification of the Young Plan and as a gesture of faith and hope in the Weimar Republic, the Allies pulled their garrisons out of the Rhineland in June of 1930, five years before the minimum time set in the Treaty of Versailles. After that, the Allies were without any means inside Germany of enforcing the military prohibitions or the territorial settlements in the Treaty; from that point indeed may be dated the re-emergence of Germany as a strong military power.[1]

Foreign optimism concerning Germany was soon and rudely blasted. At the polls in September, 1930, the National Socialists captured 107 seats, nine times as many as after the 1928 voting. That startling development, which reflected the debauched economic situation in Germany, naturally occasioned alarm and dread in foreign nations and frightened capitalists recalled as much of their German investments as possible, thereby adding to the national plight (Chap. XIII).

Apprehension among Germany's near neighbors rose higher, in March of 1931, when the Cabinet of Brüning announced that a customs union had been arranged with the Austrian Republic. The agreement would remove Austro-German tariff barriers, but it was explicitly stated that the political independence of the signatories would not be affected. Alarmed spokesmen for France and for the neighbors of Germany in central Europe protested that a customs union between the two German states would be the merest preface to the formation of a Greater Germany, and, on their insistence, the legality of the customs accord was submitted to the World Court for an opinion.

By a vote of eight to seven the Court decided that the customs treaty would violate a pledge given by Austria in 1922 in connection with reconstruction loans. In the opinion of some observers the ver-

---

[1] An interesting, if premature project for a United States of Europe was broached by the French Foreign Minister, Aristide Briand, in the summer of 1930, a super-sovereignty that would command military power, planes especially. The plan was predicated upon French security; "all possibility of progress toward economic union," the Briand memorandum asserted, "being strictly determined by the question of security, it is on the political plane that constructive efforts should first of all be made." Security first, last, and all the time dominated French diplomatic thought and that meant the perpetuation of the existing treaties; for France the very thought of treaty revision was heresy. Unsympathetic critics branded the Briand union a wily stratagem to ensure the ascendancy of France. Mussolini's demand that revision of treaties must precede federation postponed the "United States of Europe" to the Roman calends.

dict of the Court appeared to have a political, not a judicial, flavor, inasmuch as the judges from France and countries allied to her had voted against the treaty; while others held that the judges "listened like judges, deliberated and decided like judges, and differed like judges." In any case, Germany and Austria had officially abandoned the project before the Court's decision was disclosed to the world. This episode, while it meant a loss of face for the Brüning Ministry, was a boon to Hitlerism. Already Brüning had revealed that Germany's distraught economy could not meet the prescribed reparations.

The Wreck of Reparations

With depression deepening on every hand, with black clouds of despair and gloom hanging low over the entire globe, the United States dramatically intervened and somewhat cleared the atmosphere. It was proposed by President Hoover (June, 1931) that payments on all intergovernmental obligations, reparations, and Allied debts to the United States be stopped for one year. Such an accommodation, it was believed, would encourage a general revival of confidence and promote economic recovery all around. After no little haggling on the part of France, which was reluctant to see Germany go scot free, the interested governments approved the Hoover moratorium. As matters turned out, that act marked the end of reparations for practical purposes.

Before long it was evident that Germany would be unable to resume payments when the year of grace had expired. If the Allies invoked coercive measures of collection they would simply benefit the Nazis whose spellbinders were making political capital out of reparations—tribute, in their phrase.

Under the circumstances it was the course of wisdom to modify the reparations bill once more. So at Lausanne in 1932 the Allied creditors scrapped the Young Plan and scaled down their claims on Germany to a paltry $714,000,000; but that settlement would become operative only if the Allies could negotiate a "new deal" with the United States on war debts. Since the transatlantic Republic stubbornly declined to modify its traditional stand, the Lausanne agreement was never ratified. But no more reparations were forthcoming from Germany, not a pfennig in fact was paid after the Hoover moratorium. Similarly Germany soon stopped payments on almost all private loans that had been extended in the twenties, or redeemed them at heavy discounts.

No wholly satisfactory accounting of what Germany paid in reparations from first to last has ever been drawn up. One Nazi statistician claimed that the Allies profited to the tune of over $55,000,000,000, while the official French figure was less than a tenth of that sum; probably the actual amount was in the neighborhood of $7,000,000,000. Whatever Germany paid after 1924, after the inauguration of the Dawes Plan, really came out of the pockets of foreigners, Americans mainly, who invested in German securities. Nevertheless the Nazis never ceased to exploit the national grievance over reparations, harping on the colossal sum originally set, and neglecting to mention that it was never paid or that Lausanne was the cemetery of reparations. Almost certainly the Hitlerian government extorted more from occupied countries in any single year of World War II than Germany remitted altogether as reparations.

The wreck of reparations was presently followed by the cessation of Allied installments to the United States on war debts. After 1933 Finland alone somehow contrived to fulfill its contract. Twice a year the United States presented bills to the debtors, but that was no more than a legalistic gesture. At the outbreak of World War II, because of accumulated unpaid interest, the sums due the United States exceeded the advances that had originally been made. For the purpose of avoiding a repetition of this melancholy chapter of history the United States in World War II furnished the Allied nations with war goods and services under the program spoken of as "Lend-Lease."

The London Naval Conference

With the world in the grip of paralysing depression and financial stringencies plaguing all nations, the time seemed propitious for a renewed approach to the intricate task of restricting national armaments. Failure of the Geneva Conference of 1927 to limit seapower embittered British-American relations, as has been noted, and led to fresh naval construction. To halt that trend the British government invited the four leading seapowers, the United States, Japan, France, and Italy, to a meeting in London to tackle anew the question of naval limitation. All of them accepted.

Growing tension and jealousy between France and Italy beclouded the London Conference of 1930. Driven by desire for Fascist prestige Italy demanded the right to have a fleet as powerful as that of France. The French retorted with the arguments that the frontage of their country on three bodies of water and the widely scattered French empire required naval superiority over her Latin neighbor. No compromise arrangement could be found so these two powers had no part in the more important accords reached at London. Nor were French tempers sweetened by a bellicose speech of il Duce in which he declared that "although words are beautiful things, rifles, machine guns, ships, aeroplanes, and cannon are more beautiful."

Taught by the unhappy Geneva experience of 1927 the British and American governments carefully prepared for the London parley by advance diplomatic exchanges, and Britain indicated willingness to cut down her claims for large cruisers. On the other hand, the Japanese delegation put in a bid for seventy per cent as much tonnage in non-capital warcraft as the United States instead of the sixty per cent ratio fixed for capital ships in the Washington Treaty of 1922. In the agreement that was finally hammered out Great Britain and the United States were given essential parity, though Britain was allotted a somewhat higher tonnage in small cruisers. In destroyers and submarines the navies of Britain and the United States would be identical. The Japanese were placated by being allowed seventy per cent as much light cruiser and destroyer tonnage as the United States, sixty per cent as much heavy cruiser tonnage, and equality in submarines.

Since France and Italy had failed to accommodate their differences and because of the possibility that these nations might build warships to the point where Britain's safety might be endangered, a "safeguarding" or "escalator clause" was written into the tripartite treaty. That article authorized any one of the signatories to expand its fleet beyond the level prescribed, if security should require it; in that event, the other two powers might make proportionate increases in their naval strength.

At London, too, all five delegations accepted definitions concerning the equipment of submarines and their use in time of war. It was also agreed that for the next five years no capital ships should be built; in other words, this feature of the Washington Treaty of 1922 was extended to 1936.

What diplomacy had achieved at the London parley was subjected to considerable criticism in the five participating countries, the sharpest protests issuing from the Admiralties, which contended that vital national interests were being put in jeopardy for the sake of false economy. Yet the governments in each instance looked upon the understandings as advantageous, on balance, and they were duly ratified. Achievement in the matter of fleet limitation, modest though it was, encouraged the popular belief that analogous restrictions could be effected in other branches of the fighting services.

The "Disarmament" Fiasco

No international problem was attacked more frequently after World War I, none was more complicated, than that of armament limitation, or "disarmament" as it was commonly called. Under the Covenant, the League of Nations was charged with the responsibility of preparing the way for disarmament, and in 1930 after five years of arduous and tedious labor a League Commission brought forth a skeleton treaty for general limitation and reduction. That was the prelude to the calling of a world "disarmament" conference at Geneva in February, 1932, with the Soviet Union and the United States represented as well as League members—fifty-seven countries in all.

Hailed as the most important gathering since the Paris Peace Conference, it was hoped that the Geneva deliberations would produce an understanding that would at once improve the prospects for enduring peace and curtail world expenditures for armaments, which then stood at about $4,000,000,000 a year. Unhappily, world political conditions had deteriorated sharply just before the Geneva Conference assembled. Nazi chauvinism was on the march in Germany; Mussolini's verbal bellicosity had not slackened a whit; and in the Far East the guns of Japan were actually blazing away in Manchuria. The atmosphere, in a word, was not conducive to positive accomplishment in the sphere of disarmament.

From almost the beginning, the sessions at Geneva were dominated by a fierce and unrelenting tug-of-war between two sets of nations. One group, headed by France, desired to preserve existing international arrangements and to maintain the status quo. On the other side were the nations which insisted upon treaty revision, for whom Germany was spokesman. As matters stood, the French bloc commanded an overwhelming preponderance of power. It would not consider reduction of armaments without solid guarantees of help in case Germany should go to war to alter boundaries in Europe. On no issue was French political opinion so unanimous as on the priority of security over disarmament.

With no less obduracy Germany demanded the right to have armed strength equal to that of France. In German thinking it was intolerable that the military forces permitted under the Treaty of Versailles were scarcely superior to those of Belgium and less than those of Czechoslovakia or Poland. On the solid rock of French-German antagonism all plans for armament limitation were shipwrecked. A precious opportunity was missed in the spring of 1932 when Brüning's moderate German Ministry coexisted with one in France that was favorable to a bargain. Thereafter, no show of intelligence and good will, no display of ingenuity in devising compromise formulas could overcome the radical divergence between the ancient Rhine rivals. True, eventually the French advanced a proposal for German armament equality at the end of eight years, but the scheme was hedged round with qualifying, if not nullifying, reservations.

That was utterly unacceptable to a Germany in which the Nazis had already taken charge. Hitler bluntly demanded armament equality; either other nations must scale down or Germany would build up. Then with dramatic suddenness Hitler, in October, 1933, not only withdrew from the Geneva Arms Conference, but quit the League of Nations as well. The die was cast for German rearmament on the grand scale in total disregard of the Versailles clauses. Appropriations for military purposes were greatly enlarged and the German military industry was soon working at capacity. These developments heightened fear and alarm in France, which was in the midst of a desperate economic and political crisis. French diplomacy bestirred itself to tighten bonds with her Slavic friends and even to draw the Soviet Union to her side.

Deadlock, despair, failure, funereal were words that pressmen employed to describe the disarmament fiasco. On into 1934 conversations proceeded. British diplomacy in the interval tried to lure the Germans back to Geneva through private channels, but was unwilling to commit itself to effective guarantees of French security. London stood solidly on the principle that security for all depended fundamentally on armament reduction. Special committees were named at Geneva to examine special military problems but the fervent expectations of an international understanding to control armaments were as dead as Ptolemaic astronomy.

Debilitating pessimism gripped the nations. All prospect of cutting taxes vanished as large and small powers alike hastened to increase armament expenditures. And, as in the first years of the 20th century, armament competition was accompanied by manifestations of national insolence and rising mistrust and suspicion. Once more the doctrine of unfettered force was being enthroned.

War in the Orient

Outbreak of war in the Far East, as has been said, cast a somber shadow over the Geneva Arms Conference. Japan in the fall of 1931, defying her international engagements, unsheathed the sword against China. Quarreling centered upon the region called Manchuria by westerners. There, the explosion of a bomb on the chief rail line furnished the Nipponese with a flimsy pretext for launching a war without so much as a diplomatic warning. To understand this clash, which the Japanese lightly described as the "China incident," but which many outsiders came to regard as the beginning of World War II, it is necessary to digress a little into Far Eastern affairs.

For a quarter of a century Manchuria had been an arena of friction between Japan and China; there Japanese imperialism clashed with the rising surge of Chinese nationalism. As a handy region, potentially rich in foodstuffs and raw materials, Manchuria appealed to Japan as an area that would help to supply the requirements of the fast-growing Japanese population; and it would afford an outlet for manufactured goods and for surplus population, if not of Japan herself then for the heavily-peopled colony of Korea. From the strategic angle Japanese control over Manchuria would strengthen the Nipponese position vis-à-vis the Soviet Union and China.

On its side, the Chinese government was naturally intent upon keeping its own, of preserving the territorial integrity of the Republic.

In 1905, at the end of a war with Imperial Russia, Japan had taken over a Russian-built railway in southern Manchuria and had the right of posting guards along the track. China, moreover, had bound herself in a vague manner not to lay down competing railways in Manchuria. Ten years later, Japanese privileges in Manchuria were extended to ninety nine years; her subjects were given the right of settlement and of carrying on business in Manchuria. Many Koreans moved in. Their presence antagonized Chinese residents, millions of whom had streamed into Manchuria to escape civil war in other parts of China.

Numerous were the street scuffles, riots, and similar incidents involving Chinamen and foreigners. These affairs could no doubt have been settled by negotiation had Japan desired a peaceful solution. But moderately-minded politicians in Nippon had given way to the dominance of the arrogant military caste which preferred the sword to the pen.

Disorderly conditions inside China proper and anti-Japanese agitation militated against Japanese trade with China. At the same time new railways were started in Manchuria, which would compete with the established Japanese road. The Great Depression, moreover, dealt a staggering blow to the large Japanese silk trade, and foreign commerce generally was handicapped by the neo-mercantilist policies pursued by other countries.

Against that background, and with social discontent and economic distress mounting, Japan's military chiefs resolved to assert their mastery over China and expel western businessmen in the bargain. Heedless of League warnings, deaf to the protestations of nations with interests in China, Japan plunged ahead in the conquest of Manchuria and by February, 1932, felt able to proclaim a puppet state, baptized as Manchukuo.

Sentiment in China flared up violently over the invasion and the depredations committed by Japanese troops. Patriotic boycotts on Japanese goods were made more effective and some Japanese resident in China were maltreated. Half in reprisal, half to coerce the Chinese government to "cooperate," Japanese troops were thrown into the wealthy metropolis of Shanghai and into sections of northern China proper. In a kind of atavistic frenzy they slaughtered Chinese soldiers and civilians without distinction. When it appeared that Peking was on the verge of capture by the invader, China reluctantly signed an armistice (May, 1933), leaving the Nipponese dominant over Manchuria and over an extensive belt of north China. Seemingly, the latest Japanese adventure in unabashed imperialism and militarism had earned decent profits.

Manchuria and the Outer World

The magnitude of Japan's triumph was underscored by the inability of the League of Nations to restrain her in this first major trial of the collective security institution to keep the peace. China appealed to the League for protection, which caused the despatch of a commission of distinguished experts, with the British Lord Lytton as chairman, to inquire into the Sino-Japanese imbroglio on the scene. That body scrupulously studied the wide range of disputed points, winnowed away an enormous mass of legend, asserted the legitimacy of Chinese sovereignty over Manchuria, and denied the Japanese sophistry that it had taken up arms in self-defense. And the Lytton Commission prepared a set of recommendations which offered a basis for reasonable accommodation. When Japan flatly declined to accept international guidance in reaching a pacific settlement, the League Assembly unanimously condemned her; whereat Nippon walked out of the League—the first country of first rank to do so.

No one could doubt that the legal case against Japan was complete. She had flouted the League Covenant and wantonly trampled upon the Nine Power Treaty signed at Washington in 1922. Yet no government was prepared to exert economic force, not to say military, to compel the law-breaker to come to terms. Put otherwise, no great power was convinced that its own vital interests were sufficiently jeopardized by the seizure of Manchuria to take risks that might lead to war with Japan. Every available agency for mobilizing moral pressure against Nippon was invoked but only the application of force, not appeals to moral virtue or the sanctity of treaties, could have taught Japan to behave.

The Manchurian crisis dealt a mortal blow, as was later fully appreciated, to the League idea that the safety and integrity of one nation was the selfish responsibility of all countries. Here was an evil omen of more serious setbacks in the future. At the time of the League defeat in the Orient, Mussolini was prating about his invincible legions, but he had not yet ordered them into Ethiopia. National Socialism was not yet in command of Germany. But the League failure in the Far East encouraged challenges by the Axis later on.

Friends of the League consoled themselves with the thought that it would prove its real mettle in a quarrel geographically nearer to Europe. On larger perspective, a more judicious estimate would be that the League was too young to shoulder the heavy responsibilities entrusted to it. Only if the member states freely and fully cooperated could anything effective have been accomplished. It was the nations rather than the League that had failed.

The United States and Soviet Russia, neither of them League partners, displayed a lively concern over the Japanese spoilation of China. On legal, moral, and economic grounds, the United States government protested indignantly against Japan's course. Within six months the New York *Times* carried 1,707 columns of Manchurian news, evidence in itself of the deep American interest in the Oriental dispute. When the State Department formally charged Japan with violation of the Paris Peace Pact, Japanese diplomacy temporized, but Japanese militarism proceeded on the work of conquest. In the very first test, the anti-war treaty was shown to be valueless as critics had prophesied when the project was under discussion.

The United States, like the members of the League, refused to recognize Manchukuo as an "independent" state; that position was never changed. Thus, from the viewpoint of international law Manchuria remained Chinese territory. Twice, at least, the government in Washington seriously considered trying to restrain Japan by means of an economic boycott. But in fact the United States was no more inclined than any of the big European nations to take effective measures against the Nipponese marauder. The passage of a law promising independence to the Philippines in 1946, though reserving certain naval rights in the archipelago, appeared to mean the end of the Yankee adventure in Oriental imperialism.

More alarmed than the United States by the thrust of Japan into

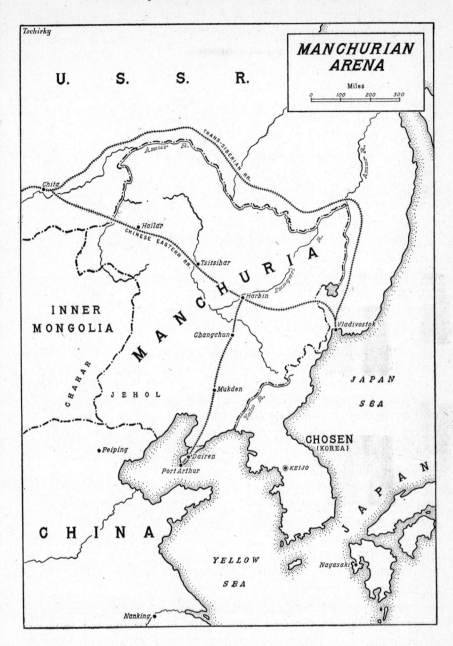

Tschirky

MANCHURIAN ARENA

Miles
0   100   200   300

U. S. S. R.

TRANS-SIBERIAN R.R.

Amur R.

Chita

Hailar
CHINESE EASTERN R.R.

Tsitsihar

M A N C H U R I A

Sungari R.

Harbin

Amur R.

INNER
MONGOLIA

Changchun

Vladivostok

CHAHAR

JEHOL

Mukden

JAPAN
SEA

Yalu R.

Peiping

Dairen
Port Arthur

CHOSEN
(KOREA)

KEIJO

C H I N A

J A P A N

YELLOW
SEA

Nagasaki

Nanking

Manchuria was the Soviet Union. Would the soldiers of the Mikado drive into eastern Siberia which they had occupied for many months after the Bolshevik Revolution? Nobody knew, but everybody knew that imperialistic appetite grows with eating, for that was the lesson of experience.

Soviet-Japanese clashes of a minor sort along the 1,500 mile Siberian-Manchurian border accentuated ill-feeling, which was already inflamed by standing disputes over Japanese fishing rights in Siberian waters. There were charges and counter-charges of subversive propaganda. Quarreling over the Chinese Eastern Railway which crossed Manchuria en route to Vladivostok, and which the Soviets had inherited from Imperial Russia, threatened to wind up in armed conflict. On behalf of its protégé, Manchukuo, Japan negotiated with Moscow to buy the line. Haggling over the price, and fights between Russians and Nipponese in Manchukuo, gravely embittered relations. But the men in the Kremlin decided to cut their losses and struck a bargain with Tokyo in 1935, transferring the railway rights to Manchukuo-Japan. The diplomatic tension relaxed somewhat.

Trouble with Japan caused Soviet Russia to speed up the construction of railways in Siberia and in other ways to improve its defenses in the Far East. The possibility of war in the Orient at the very time that Hitlerian Germany, arming rapidly, loomed up as a potential menace to Soviet security, prompted the rulers of Russia to give their foreign policies a different orientation (p. 470).

Another London Conference

By mid-1933 the economic fates had relented, the worst fury of the Great Depression had spent itself, except in the notable instance of France, and multiplying signs pointed toward general world recovery. To accelerate that process by international action, a World Monetary and Economic Conference was convoked at London in June. Sixty four nations were represented.

It was the consensus of thought among European delegates that the first needful measure was the stabilization of currencies by international agreement. Unless that were done, any tariff reductions to stimulate commerce might be nullified by declines in currency values. Another view, however, was taken by the United States, where the newly-installed Roosevelt Administration was launching the country on the protean program called the "New Deal."

Sympathetic at first to international monetary stabilization, Roosevelt suddenly reversed himself, for he had another objective closer to his heart. That was the raising of the price level of American commodities by depreciating the value of the dollar. In that way, it was believed, recovery on the home front would profit. Accordingly, the United States announced that stabilization of currencies would be untimely. That decision ruined whatever chance there may have been for general economic improvement by stabilizing currencies. Without any substantial achievement to their credit, the delegates to the London conference folded their tents and stole away. The trend toward economic autarchy, much favored in the totalitarian states, was intensified.

Glancing back over the epoch of the Great Depression, the immediate consequences of that catastrophe, which started openly in the United States, are seen to be world-wide and calamitous. Even remote fishermen in Labrador and pearl-divers on the shores of the Indian Ocean felt the impact of the convulsion which brought such widespread unemployment, misery, and bankruptcy in its train. Although the vexing problem of intergovernmental debts bequeathed by World War I was interred, nations universally took the road to economic self-sufficiency and Japan took the road to war. The League sustained a fateful, though scarcely a fatal, defeat. Exalted hopes of armament limitation by international agreement were only modestly realized in the Three-Power London Naval Treaty. In the United States, under the "New Deal," economic affairs were subjected to a degree of state direction without precedent, while in Germany, National Socialism bowled over the Weimar Republic. Indeed everywhere, except in Soviet Russia and Fascist Italy, new administrations had taken charge as the result of peaceful or violent change.

National Socialism and Europe

On the eve of Hitler's advent to power, Germany's diplomatic situation was not without its favorable aspects. True, no international formula permitting Germany to build up its fighting machine had been discovered and there was little prospect of any revision of prevailing boundaries by peaceful processes. Yet reparations were a thing of history. The Soviet Union was not unfriendly; Fascist Italy felt more akin to Germany than to France; within the United States and Great Britain and even in France itself, substantial blocs of opinion were disposed to grant further concessions to Germany. But the victory of Hitlerism brought radical modifications in foreign attitudes.

Though the outer world resented many aspects of Nazi domestic policies, it was the Third Reich's military potentialities, and in time its deeds in foreign affairs, which roused profound mistrust and fear. The declared aims of Nazi foreign policy, as traced in the official party program and elaborated in *Mein Kampf*, have already been set forth (Chap. XIII). Here it may be repeated that the Nazis were pledged to cancel the "slavery" of Versailles, territorial, military, and financial clauses alike. They asserted that pre-1914 frontiers would not suffice for the new Germany, so Austria and other areas of German speech must be gathered into a Pan-Germania; that the hereditary enemy, France, must first be isolated by alliances with Britain and/or Italy, and then France must be destroyed; that living room for expanding German millions must be gained in Soviet Russia and her borderlands; that military force alone could achieve these ends; that peace was despicable—or "first, fight—and then perhaps pacifism."

Many a foreigner in official positions and outside, familiar with unexpurgated versions of *Mein Kampf,* accepted that book as an accurate blueprint of the purposes and contemplated action of Nazi Germany. If that interpretation were correct those aims could not be attained by free negotiation and methods of peaceful change. As early as June, 1933, the United States Consul-General in Berlin, G. S. Messersmith, warned Washington that the Nazis were "capable of actions which really outlaw them from ordinary intercourse," and that they planned to "make Germany the most capable instrument of war that has ever existed."

Other foreign experts and commentators begged to differ and to look upon the stated principles of Nazi international policy as a vote-catching device, replete with the irrational fancies of an irresponsible extremist and agitator. Once faced with the exacting responsibilities of office the Nazis by moderate acts, it was urged, would invalidate the rash words that had been written and spoken. Both schools of interpretation found evidence to fortify their judgments in early Nazi diplomacy.

As we have seen, only six months after making himself master of the "master-race," Hitler retired from the Geneva Arms Conference and from the League of Nations. A popular German plebiscite overwhelmingly ratified those decisions. Right away German rearmament was greatly accelerated and carried on in full light of day. Plans were formulated for a submarine fleet and for the enlargement of the small but formidable surface navy. At least one responsible British commander recommended serious consideration of Allied reoccupation of the Rhine bridgeheads in retaliation for German rearmament, but no major power was prepared to dispute effectively the flat abrogation of the Versailles military restrictions.

Deals with Poland and Britain

True, Hitler and his top aides delivered speeches full of soothing and pacific sentiments. Those assurances satisfied some foreign minds. Apprehensions in Poland and Britain were somewhat allayed by diplomatic accords which those countries arranged with the Third Reich.

Lying between Germany and Soviet Russia—each of which coveted territory in the Polish Republic—Poland was in an uncomfortable, not to say precarious, spot. Ever since the Paris peace settlements, responsible German leaders—and others—had insisted that some day the "Polish Corridor" and Polish Upper Silesia would be reclaimed by Germany; and agitation for the recovery of the Danzig Free State was incessant and vehement. On the other flank, the Soviet Union cherished ambitions in eastern Poland. To all and sundry, the Poles replied that existing boundaries accorded with the wishes of the populations involved. They reinforced their words by League membership, by military alliances with France and Rumania, and by a large standing army.

Nazi spokesmen, after the triumph of their party in 1933, breathed fire and flame against Communism and the Soviet Union—if anything with greater bellicosity than previously. It was not fanciful, therefore, for Polish leaders to imagine that their country as in World War I might serve as a German-Russian battleground. There is some evidence that, in 1933, the Polish government recommended military intervention in Germany for the purpose of unhorsing National Socialism. If such a Polish proposal was broached, it was vetoed in Paris and London.

Instead the Poles made a surprise move by entering into a Non-aggression Pact with Germany (January, 1934), both states promising that force would not be invoked to settle any quarrels that might arise in the next ten years. Outsiders suspected that a secret treaty was signed providing for Polish and German territorial gains at the expense of Lithuania and the Soviet Union, but no authoritative confirmation of that assumption has been revealed. More than once after the making of the Non-aggression Pact Hitler professed his affection for Poland with disarming suavity; in 1937, for instance, like a beguiling sorcerer, he affirmed that the agreement was proving mutually advantageous.

All Europe was astonished by the Polish trafficking with the Nazi regime. In France it was feared that the Poles might be getting ready to discard the existing alliance. Yet in reality the Polish-German understanding had not removed a single outstanding cause of friction. True, the treaty released Nazi Germany from total diplomatic quarantine, but it was only a truce, not a sign of reconciliation.

Even more startling was a naval limitation treaty which Britain signed with the Nazis in 1935. Alert to the peril of another naval race, such as had preceded World War I, and anxious to conciliate the Hitler state, British diplomacy secretly negotiated with the Germans on seapower. The upshot was a German pledge to hold fleet tonnage at about one third that of the British realm with the proviso that in submarines the two nations should have equal strength. With a navy of that size Germany could command the Baltic and a sea-attack across the North Sea would be exceedingly risky business.

Without bases abroad the German navy would necessarily be massed in the North and Baltic Seas, the Kiel Canal forming a safe and quick connecting link. Britain's fleet, however, was distributed over the seven seas, and ordinarily not more than half of it was in convenient reach of the North Sea, so that locally, the ratio with Germany would be closer to two to one than three to one; and German warships would be the latest word in naval architecture. Nonetheless the British were now fully aware of what was under way in Germany and that was preferable to the unheralded appearance of a German High Seas fleet two or three years later.

However advantageous the naval treaty might appear in the eyes of Britain, her continental friends, France especially, condemned the deal as base treachery, wanton acquiescence in a breach in the Versailles Treaty. The ancient cries of "Perfidious Albion" and "You can't trust England" filled the French press. Very shortly the French who had placed their naval faith in submarines primarily resumed the construction of capital ships. Mussolini, on his part, rather welcomed the prospect of a strong Germany on the blue water, for that would compel Britain and France to remove warcraft from the Mediterranean, to Italy's gain. Not improbably the deterioration in Anglo-French relations which followed the publication of the British naval treaty with Germany, encouraged il Duce to go forward with his ambitions in Ethiopia.

Recovery of the Saar

If Hitler contemplated adding Austria to Germany in 1934, the project had grossly miscarried (p. 155). German spirits, however, were buoyed up by the recovery of the Saar Valley, which the Versailles Treaty had placed under the aegis of the League. Almost the entire Saar population of 800,000 was German in speech, customs, traditions, and culture, dependent largely on coal mines and steel mills for their livelihood, and in great majority, Roman Catholics.

It was stipulated in the Peace Treaty that, in 1935, the Saarlanders should freely decide whether their homeland should rejoin Germany, remain under League administration, or be united to France. For the third option there was never much sentiment, but the pro-League solution appealed to elements in the Saar which disliked the prospect of National Socialist rule—Social Democrats, Communists, and Catholics resentful of Nazi religious tactics. On the eve of the balloting the Saar was deluged with Nazi propaganda; waverers were threatened with dire punishment if the vote should go against reunion with Germany. To further Nazi interests Hitler sent in a trusted agent, Joseph Bürckel, who, under the banner of "Deutsch ist die Saar," worked with local Nazis. They set as their goal a 100 per cent pro-German vote.

So as to ensure independence and secrecy in the plebiscite, the League Council specified just how the voting should be conducted. An International Plebiscite Commission of foreign technical experts and supervisory officials was sent in and also an international police force made up of British, Italian, Dutch, and Swedish soldiers.

Under those model arrangements the Saarlanders trooped to the polls in January of 1935. There was complete secrecy in the voting and no untoward disturbances. Over ninety per cent of the voters cast for union with Germany. This was strong evidence of the potency of nationalism when pitted against dislike of Nazi authoritarianism or against economic advantage, for materially the Saar Basin would have been better off if League authority had been perpetuated. Quite likely, many voters who cast for Germany believed that Nazi ascendancy would be nothing more than a passing episode in German history.

Presently the Saar region was officially incorporated in the Third Reich and there was wild rejoicing in Germany over the return of the lost sheep.[2] Invaluable lessons had been learned from League management of the Saar and from the conduct of the plebiscite. Indeed, the voting arrangements there set a standard below which no appeal to self-determination may fall if it was to be acceptable to world opinion.[3]

Revision Marches On

The month of March holds a peculiar place in the annals of National Socialism. That was the month in which the Nazi Party took full command of German affairs and that was the preferred month for staging sensational coups with international implications. March of 1935 was the occasion for an announcement that the German army of the future would be raised by conscription. It was also revealed that

[2] France was compensated, as provided in the Versailles Treaty, with coal shipments in lieu of the output of the Saar mines.

[3] Plebiscites staged by Hitler's henchmen in Austria in 1938, and in Luxembourg in 1942, as well as those held under Soviet auspices in the Baltic Republics and eastern Poland in the course of World War II, were unconvincing, inasmuch as one of the parties having an interest conducted them.

German youths undergoing training at any time would exceed 500,000, a force larger than that of France.

Against this flagrant and epochal infringement of the Versailles Treaty the victor nations of World War I protested, though without particular vehemence, for France and Britain had resigned themselves to the reappearance of Germany as a top-notch military power. Reproofs which the League administered to Nazidom had an air of routine formality about them. A League committee set up to study measures that might be applied in case of further repudiation of the Treaty of Versailles never amounted to anything. Success in the matter of conscription encouraged the belief in top Nazi circles that other treaty clauses would yield to a little sapping and mining, a little bluster and blandishment.

As if to calm the alarm provoked by this fresh manifestation of rearmament on the grand scale, Hitler in May, 1935, addressed the world with pacific assurances. Not only, declared he, was Germany prepared to negotiate on limitation of armaments, but it intended to uphold the Locarno accords, not excluding the ban on German troops or fortifications in the Rhineland. So far from harboring designs on Austria, as was being said abroad, Germany desired an international pact binding countries against interference in the home affairs of other nations.

Few realists placed much confidence in these professions of a peace-loving Nazidom. But at the moment Britain, France, and Italy were linked up in a diplomatic entente, spoken of as the Stresa Front, and France had a loose diplomatic tie with the Soviet Union. Here was an alignment of power which, it was believed, was capable of frustrating any Nazi attempt to redraw Europe's map by rattling the sword or unsheathing it.[4]

Clamor for further revision of treaties mounted in fury within Germany. Agitation for the return of territory lost to Belgium and Denmark was restrained, though strident with regard to the cessions to Poland and the pre-war colonial holdings in Africa. Hitler in *Mein Kampf* had repudiated overseas expansion, holding colonies to be a liability, and feeling that any move in that direction would surely alienate Britain and ruin any chance of arranging a British alliance. But an active German Colonial League kept green the memory of the former African colonies and Nazi spellbinders strummed vigorously upon the colonial chord.

Overseas holdings were demanded as a symbol of German national

[4] It was precisely at this point that the Anglo-German naval bargain was published.

greatness, of her stature as a world power, and to refute the accusation that Germans were unfit and unworthy to administer backward peoples. It was also urged that colonies would provide an outlet for surplus German population and places in which tropical products might be purchased with German currency. Various proposals were canvassed in Britain and France to appease German colonial appetites, but apparently none of them was seriously discussed in official quarters.

Reversing himself, Hitler in 1936 made restitution of colonies standard Nazi doctrine. Whether that was intended as a genuine bid for "the redistribution of the riches of the earth" or rather for purposes of diplomatic bargaining is still unclear. Speaking in the name of the German Colonial League, General von Epp declared, early in 1939, "We demand the abolition of the ridiculous guardianship over our overseas property. But over and above this, we demand, as one of the leading civilized nations of the world, our share in a coming planned distribution of world space, which is necessary for the future of a nation of 80,000,000 people." [5] What the German claimants neglected to mention was the serviceability of colonies as naval and air bases or as troop reservoirs. That consideration alone assured an Allied veto for Nazi colonial pretensions. [6]

France and Slavdom

In face of the rising military might of Germany, France set to work to strengthen her diplomatic fences, as befitted the supreme guardian of the territorial status quo. German rearmament had in fact robbed France of the military superiority that had been hers since the Armistice of 1918. True, there was the Maginot line of fortifications, a symbol of the desire of France to tend her own garden, and to retain her comfort, her elegance, and her empire. But the Maginot Line tended to create a false sense of security, as some French diplomatists appreciated. French arms and fortifications alone were not enough.

Soon after the end of World War I, France had sought to protect herself through military alliances with Belgium, Poland, and Czechoslovakia. Rumania and Yugoslavia were also drawn into the orbit of Paris, though they were of secondary concern in the network of French security. The alignment with eastern Europe accorded with long-established French diplomatic tradition; these states were a

[5] Quoted in L. S. Amery, *The German Colonial Claim* (London, 1939), p. 127.
[6] Out of hand in 1936 Hitler abolished the international commissions which had regulated shipping on the great German rivers under the Versailles Treaty.

substitute, up to a point, for the alliance with Imperial Russia before 1914. France's allies, on their part, with some reservation to be made in the case of Poland, were not unmindful that their own safety depended in the last analysis upon the French fighting services.

French diplomacy applauded the formation of a Balkan Entente in 1934, containing Yugoslavia, Rumania, Greece, and Turkey. The central purpose of that "league" was to preserve the status quo in the Balkans. More exactly, it was an invitation to the great powers, not least Germany, to keep hands off southeastern Europe and a warning to discontented Bulgaria that an appeal to force to rectify boundaries would meet with overwhelming resistance.

If the French Foreign Office had had its way an "Eastern Locarno" would have been formed to freeze existing frontiers in eastern Europe and to pledge mutual assistance in case of attack. This project, which would embrace Soviet Russia, Germany, Poland, and Czechoslovakia, and would of course strengthen French security, was taken up energetically by Foreign Minister Louis Barthou in 1934. But Germany and Poland responded unsympathetically, calculating that the disadvantages of the scheme outweighed the prospective merits; perhaps Polish opposition was due to German inspiration. In any case the Nazis were themselves bent upon boundary revision and were completely hostile to any plan to preserve the status quo.

The idea of an eastern Locarno perished when Barthou, in company with King Alexander of Yugoslavia, was assassinated at Marseilles in October, 1934. His passing removed from the French stage the last strong foreign minister that the Third Republic produced.

Meanwhile France cast about for some kind of a closer understanding with the Soviet Union, with which in 1932 a Non-aggression Treaty had been negotiated. Both nations distrusted Germany. The men in the Kremlin were alarmed by the freely avowed Hitlerian ambitions in the Ukraine and resentful of the abusive denunciations of Communism. Besides, Japanese imperialism in the Far East had quickened Soviet fears for the future. Elementary prudence, therefore, argued the desirability of cultivating friendlier relations with the West, so that the work of Socialist construction in the USSR could be pressed forward with greater confidence.

Stalinism in Foreign Affairs

As one mark of a new orientation in foreign policy, Russia applied for, and was welcomed in 1934 to membership in the League of Nations. Hitherto the Soviet chiefs had denounced the League as a hypocritical contrivance of cunning capitalistic countries inimical to the USSR. Given a permanent seat on the League Council, Russia stood forth as a staunch champion of collective security.

Then, in May, 1935, a Franco-Soviet Pact of Mutual Assistance was completed. Each country promised to aid the other in the event of an attack. That understanding was far weaker than the pre-1914 Franco-Russian Alliance, since there was no provision for armed co-operation and there were qualifying reservations. France hesitated to seek a full-fashioned alliance for one reason because of the resent-ment that too intimate an alignment might cause in Britain, and also in Poland and Rumania, which mistrusted the Soviet Union. Influ-ential sections of Rightist French opinion, fearful of Communism, condemned the pact with Russia from the start. The Soviet-French treaty was never a living reality and after the Munich Conference of 1938 it was relegated to the dusty archives of the French Foreign Office.

In 1935, Czechoslovakia, another of the French allies, entered into a supplementary Treaty of Mutual Assistance with Russia. It was, however, explicitly stated that the USSR would be obligated to aid the Czechs should they be the victim of an attack, only if France carried out her commitment to help Czechoslovakia.

Another sign of the new course in the Kremlin was the restoration of normal diplomatic relations with the United States, effected in the autumn of 1933. Not since the Bolshevik Revolution had these two giants exchanged ambassadors, though a small but fluctuating trade had grown up. Profound ideological differences, mutual mistrusts and suspicions kept Russia and the United States apart. Yet they had common bonds in their dread of Japanese expansion and the desire to restrain it, and the United States in a time of depression was keenly anxious to profit from Soviet commerce. To an overture from Wash-ington in 1933, Moscow responded with unmistakable cordiality. After concessions on outstanding grievances, such as expropriated American property rights in Russia and the diffusion of Communist propaganda, formal diplomatic relations were resumed. Somewhat later a Soviet-American commercial treaty, hopefully intended to enlarge trade, was negotiated.

The Stresa Front

France not only moved toward Soviet Russia but sought an under-standing with Italy as a potential bulwark against Germany. The sudden emergence of Germany as a strong and defiant military power had enhanced Italy's diplomatic worth, may even have led Mussolini to think of himself as indispensable. In these circumstances, after years of bickering and polemics, the Latin sisters managed to bury the hatchet—though not too deeply.[7]

Under an agreement completed in January, 1935, France was given assurances of Italian support against Germany in exchange for concessions in Tunisia and Tangier; the bargain may have been sealed with mutual pledges of military aid. It appears that Mussolini now assumed that France would not interpose any obstacles to the gratification of his expansionist ambitions in Ethiopia.

In April, 1935, just after the resumption of conscription in Germany, representatives of France and Italy conferred with British diplomatists on the preservation of Austrian independence and on a common line of conduct toward Germany. Agreements on those points were reached. Italy seemed in this way to have identified herself with the west and a conference that Mussolini previously had held with Hitler appeared to be nothing more than an innocent flirtation. Since the three-power meeting took place at Stresa, Italy, the world press talked of the Stresa Front, but Italy's attachment proved of short duration.

As of 1935

In the early summer of 1935 the European diplomatic alignment clearly favored the nations which desired to maintain the territorial status quo and to keep the peace. Except for the Non-aggression Treaty with Poland, Germany was still isolated, though something more than mere sympathy may have bound her to Japan. Over against Germany was the Stresa Front representing a formidable array of strength: Britain, France, Italy, and, by reason of the French Mutual Assistance Treaty with Russia, that combination was reminiscent in a sense of the Allied coalition of World War I prior to the Bolshevik Revolution. In this camp, too, should be counted the allies of France in central and eastern Europe.

A damaging blow at the solidarity of the Stresa group was struck by the British naval treaty with Germany. The combination was soon to be irreparably destroyed by Fascismo's war upon Ethiopia.

Nationalism on the political as on the economic plane was at least as intense in 1935 as in 1914. There were now twenty-six varieties of

---

[7] Mussolini in the spring of 1933 had brought forth a plan for a super-sovereignty of Britain, France, Germany, and Italy to keep the peace for ten years, which recalls the alliance compact after the downfall of Napoleon. His proposal that treaty revision would be an object of the "Peace Club" met with a completely frigid reception. Much watered down, a Four Power Pact was signed (June, 1933) but it had no practical importance.

national honor and national interest to be served. Europe, moreover, was more heavily armed than ever before in history. New and swifter weapons of war were rising on every hand. In spite of all efforts to curb it, power politics—a penchant for resorting to military threats to win diplomatic disputes—remained the predominant factor in the high politics of the world.

It was a Europe in which fear was paramount and the well-spring of that fear was brusque, impetuous, aggrieved, unsatisfied Germany. "Perhaps the worst factor of all," wrote a perceptive American journalist, "is the sense of fatality that pervades Europe, the uncertainty about the future, the bewilderment about the present, the sense of having stood for two decades on shaky ground. The war destroyed something in Europe which has never been restored. It might be called social stability." [8]

[8]Harold Callender, "Europe Gropes for a Way Out," New York *Times*, March 31, 1935.

CHAPTER XIX

The Road to War

The Problem of Recent History

IT IS a truism that no historian is better than the sources of information that he relies upon. Much of the material in this chapter and the next, as in earlier ones relating to the diplomacy of the European powers, is based upon fragmentary and unofficial evidence. The data which is indispensable for definitive study is at present under lock and key in the diplomatic archives of the several governments or in the notes or memories of men prominent in the high politics of the Old World. Until that evidence is made available, the historian must warn that his narrative makes no pretense of being wholly authoritative or complete.

Yet another limitation weighs upon the historian who ventures to write of his own times. However lofty his ideals of impartiality and honesty may be, his own convictions, even his own prejudices, doubtless, are bound to cast a shadow across his pages. Diplomatic history at best can hardly attain anything more than approximate truth.

On behalf of the statesmen whose public deeds pass under review, let it be said that they pursued policies which they felt desirable from the standpoint of national or imperial interests or ideological values at a given moment. The historian, coming after the event, has the very real advantage of hindsight and acquaintance with consequences in assessing the elements of wisdom and folly in the courses of action which policymakers chose to follow.

Fascist Conquest of Ethiopia

Among the milestones on the road to World War II one of the larger was the success of Italy in conquering African Ethiopia—known too as Abyssinia—over the tepid efforts of the League of Nations to restrain and discipline her. The Italian course was inspired partly by the dynamics which are familiar to the history of very modern imperialism—greed for national glory, commercial and strategic advantage, and aggressive altruism or the yearning to shoulder more of the "White Man's Burden" in the Dark Continent. For the Fascist regime, for Mussolini, moreover, victorious foreign adventure would tend to divert the popular mind from domestic perplexities which the Great Depression had aggravated; put otherwise, Ethiopia would be an "Ethiopiate" for the Italian masses. Beyond that, Mussolini's prestige rested squarely upon his ability to convince the Italian nation that the Fascist dictatorship could win impressive successes. Heavily-peopled Italy had long been taught that a greater African empire—ancient Rome reborn—would relieve the grim struggle for existence at home.

Ethiopia, never a province of imperial Rome, was a country made up of a rather loose confederacy of tribes, some of which indulged in slave-trading. That furnished Fascismo with a ready moral excuse for imperial expansion. In the 1890's Italian soldiers had tried to annex Ethiopia but the adventure was frustrated by native arms with some aid from outside. The Italians had sustained a crushing defeat at Aduwa, leaving a stain on the national escutcheon, which many a Fascist felt ought to be wiped off.

The economic worth of Ethiopia is a matter of considerable conjecture, but it is not irrelevant, perhaps, to suggest that if the material resources had been large, the area would have been seized by one or several of the Great Powers at the time of the general partition of Africa in the late 19th century. Ethiopia had joined the League of Nations in 1926, Italy and France standing as sponsors, which seemed to imply that Italy had renounced ideas of conquest. The British government, on the other hand, was disinclined to admit Ethiopia to the League because of native marauding raids into adjacent British colonies.

When Fascist Italy's strategy of winning mastery over Ethiopia by peaceful commercial penetration failed, the fateful decision was taken to achieve the objective by physical force. True, the League of Nations might resist. but the League had not prevented Japanese aggression in Manchuria, the League had not prevented Germany from rearming, nor had it been able to call a halt to a war in South America.[1] Mussolini, moreover, relied upon the undercover support of France, with which relations had just taken a more friendly turn. And at the Stresa Conference (p. 472) British diplomacy had not officially raised the question of Italian intentions in Ethiopia. Mussolini evidently

---

[1] That war, fought by Bolivia and Paraguay over the ownership of the Gran Chaco, raged from 1928 to 1935, when exhaustion compelled both parties to sign an armistice. Both states belonged to the League, but proposals made by the League Council to stop the fighting, had borne no fruit.

assumed that France and Britain would not sacrifice his friendship for the sake of a backward African principality.

For justification of an appeal to force, Italy found a pretext in recurrent and disquieting raids of Ethiopian tribesmen into Italy's east African empire. In the most serious encounter (at Ual Ual, December, 1934), sixty Italians and 200 natives were slain. Italian national honor, it was shouted, required adequate atonement. Efforts of third parties to work out an accommodation were indignantly spurned by Mussolini, and, in October, 1935, Italian divisions crashed across the Ethiopian frontier. Hostilities were on.

The issue thus raised was not merely an Italo-Ethiopian issue but one challenging the whole future of the League of Nations as an agency to preserve security and peace. As a League member, the Ethiopian King, Haile Selassie, besought assistance against the invader. After comprehensive and judicial study of the evidence in the case Council and Assembly alike adjudged Italy guilty of violating the Covenant. How now should the League aid the victim of aggression?

It was prescribed in the Covenant that in a case of this sort, League nations should apply economic, and possibly military, pressure upon the aggressor. But wide divergence of opinion prevailed in League circles as to just what should be done. The French government conceived the League to be chiefly an instrument of protection against Germany. It was disinclined to jeopardize the rapprochement with Mussolini, so recently realized, by backing effective sanctions against the law-breaker. If the British Ministry had been willing at this time to enter into a solid military alliance with France, the French might well have considered strong action more sympathetically.

The British were not only unready to make new commitments to France, they were reluctant to take too great risks of war with Italy. Mussolini's blusterings to the effect that the imposition of sanctions other than those of an economic character would mean war were not without effect on the Cabinet in London. As in France, so in Britain anti-war sentiments were widespread. It was feared that Germany might intervene in a war and that the conflict would spread like a prairie fire into a general European conflagration. There was real doubt whether Britain's fighting services—rearmament had only just started in earnest—would be equal to such an ordeal.

True, in the first stage of the acute tension over Ethiopia the British Foreign Minister, Sir Samuel Hoare, had taken a firm stand against Italy and Conservative spokesmen in the election campaign of 1935 had pledged to uphold the Covenant. But that attitude was

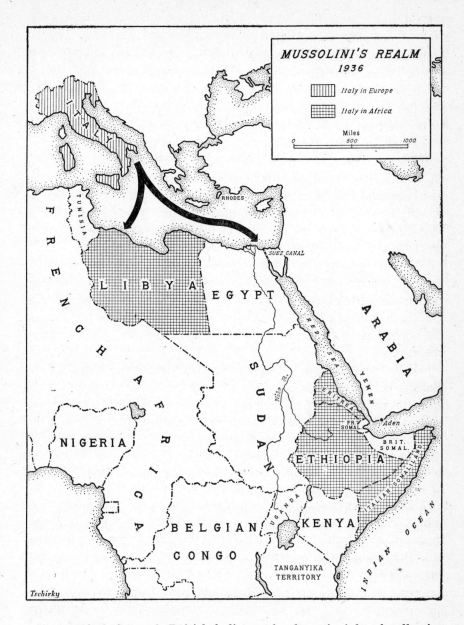

soon modified. Staunch British believers in the principle of collective security demanded that the screws should be turned tightly on the aggressor, but they were without decisive influence.

French and British diplomacy really determined the character of the League measures against Italy. League members were instructed not to sell armaments to the covenant-breaker, not to permit the flotation of loans for her, nor to purchase any goods from her. A limited number of key-goods, besides arms, might not be sold to Italy, though oil, so essential for the war-machine and for ordinary industrial uses, was not included on the list of forbidden articles. The nominal reason for the omission of oil was that non-League nations, the United States, for example, might furnish oil if Italy were denied supplies by League members. Apparently Britain favored adding oil to the list, but France would not go along out of fear that it would mean war, in which Germany would line up with Italy.

Western diplomatic and military pundits calculated that the struggle in Ethiopia would be prolonged and exhausting as the Boer War had been, and that partial sanctions would in time prove sufficient to throttle the Fascist marauder. In other quarters it was imagined that Mussolini might seize the occasion of the capture of an enemy city to proclaim a glorious victory and then seek peace by diplomacy.

All but four of the League states complied with the sanctions program. But no attempt was made to blockade Italy nor even to keep Italian ships from passing through the Suez Canal, which would have gravely handicapped the prosecution of the war. What the League did embarrassed Italy without seriously inconveniencing military operations.

While the fighting in Ethiopia proceeded, British and French diplomatists, behind the scenes, concerned themselves with several stratagems to restore peace. The final scheme—the Hoare-Laval plan—invited Italy to cease fighting in return for a substantial slice of Ethiopia and a large measure of authority over much of the remainder of the kingdom—virtually a protectorate. The disclosure of that "plan for peace" roused a storm of contemptuous indignation from partisans of the League. For his share in it, the British Foreign Minister, Sir Samuel Hoare, was hounded out of office by an infuriated public. The standing of his French opposite number, Pierre Laval, was fatally undermined. Young and affable Anthony Eden, known for his devotion to collective security and stiffer sanctions, succeeded Hoare at the Foreign Office.

Almost oblivious of the League and its sanctions, Italy pushed ahead with the war. Il Duce exhorted his countrymen to prize the mailed fist. Mass demonstrations against the League, the alacrity with which Italian women handed over their wedding rings to help finance the campaigns, and the whole-souled support which the clergy gave to the war reflected the popularity of the Ethiopian undertaking. Difficulties of topography and climate, difficulties of transport and commissariat hampered Italian military operations though not to the extent that western experts had predicted.

Italy, of course, had an immense superiority in armaments and resources of every kind. The Italian forces revolted the conscience of mankind by the wanton bombing of villages, the slaughter of civilians, and the use of poison gas. By the early summer of 1936 Ethiopia was overrun except for inconsequential guerilla nests. Whereupon Mussolini proclaimed the annexation of the country and amidst much fanfare the hollow honor of Emperor of Ethiopia was conferred upon King Victor Emmanuel III.[2] Apart from thousands of lives, it was estimated that the conquest had cost Italy a billion dollars, without reckoning the material losses because of sanctions.

Confronted by actual annexation, the League revoked the bans on commercial dealings with Italy—an act which signified the humiliating collapse of collective security. Friends of the League system insisted that the Covenant should be reformed so as to salvage as much as possible from the wreckage and a commission for that purpose was appointed. Since the League could provide no assurance of safety, nations reverted to the time-honored devices for guaranteeing their security; that is, more armaments and more alliances. A gloomy sense of despair gripped Europe more tightly than ever.[3]

As for Mussolini, he wore the kind of smile traditionally associated with the cat that has swallowed a canary. For the Italian nationalist, Fascismo had demonstrated its might and the national capacity for enduring sacrifice when pitted against fifty nations in the League. Italy now deserted the League as Japan and Germany had done before her. Presently Mussolini was shouting that though he "held out a great olive branch to the world, this olive branch springs from an immense force of 8,000,000 bayonets well sharpened and thrust from intrepid young hearts."

There were other immediate consequences of the Ethiopian crisis. Nazi Germany exploited the situation by ordering troops into the demilitarized Rhineland area, while German trade ate into Balkan markets of Italy. And in the autumn of 1936 Germany joined with Italy in a momentous diplomatic entente spoken of as the Axis. Thus the way opened for German-Italian collaboration in Spain and Austria, leading on to a genuine military alliance in May, 1939.

[2] For the war see Pietro Badoglio, *The War in Abyssinia* (New York, 1937). The author was made supreme commander when De Bono failed to go forward fast enough to suit il Duce.

[3] The extent of defense preparations is indicated by the outlay for armaments of about $13,000,000,000 in 1936, well over five times the appropriations of 1913, when Europe was described as "armed to the teeth." For the period 1932-1939 it is soberly estimated that the armament expenditures of the nations approximated $90,000,000,000—once an unimaginable sum.

Since British resistance to the Italian aggression had been more vigorous than that of any other major state, Italian official and popular hatred of the island kingdom rose to intense proportions. Britain and Italy, whose relations had been friendly since the eve of the unification of Italy, had come to the parting of the ways, though later there were attempts to patch up differences and resurrect the old cordiality. One by one, finally, the governments of Europe extended official recognition to Italian sovereignty over Ethiopia.

Rhineland Occupation

The year 1936, which opened with Italians battering down Ethiopia, closed with Spaniards engaged in fierce and wasting civil war. In between, the Nazi dictator sent armies and armaments into the Rhineland in bold defiance of the Versailles and Locarno Treaties and the victors of World War I. The Rhineland move had enormous significance for the diplomatic and military events that subsequently unfolded.

Frenchmen for generations had been taught to think of the Rhine River as the natural boundary of their country. Down the corridors of time echoed the doctrine proclaimed by Danton to the National Convention in January, 1793: "The limits of the Republic are marked by Nature herself. We shall reach them all, towards every point of the compass, the Rhine, the Atlantic, and the Alps. That is where the frontiers ought to end." At the Paris Conference in 1919, Clemenceau fought manfully to detach the left bank of the Rhine from Germany but compromised for a treaty clause excluding the Rhine area from the German defense system permanently. At Locarno in 1925, Germany of her own free will had reaffirmed the demilitarization of the Rhineland and more than once Hitler had expressed his approval of the Locarno commitment.

But in March, 1936, when Europe was preoccupied by the controversy over Ethiopia, the Führer tossed Locarno into the wastebasket by ordering about two divisions of soldiers, equipped with all the paraphernalia of contemporary war, into the picturesque Rhineland. That surprise action was a kind of logical sequel to German rearmament and was taken on a Saturday. Hitler had quit the League on a Saturday; he had proclaimed the revival of conscription on a Saturday; each at a time when British and French statesmen were taking their week-end ease. To excuse the Rhineland move Hitler argued that the Mutual Assistance Treaty which France had just ratified with Soviet Russia nullified Locarno and absolved Germany from her engagements, but outside Germany that legalistic sophistry found small acceptance.

Hitler coated the bitter Rhineland pill by presenting Europe with vague proposals for keeping the peace. It was even intimated that the Third Reich might return to the League if the Covenant were revised, divorced from the Treaty of Versailles, and Germany's colonial claims were taken under advisement. Here for the first time Hitler publicly raised the issue of colonial restoration. "We have no territorial demands to make in Europe," the Führer remarked.

It is reasonably certain that the German troops would have been withdrawn from the Rhineland if France and Britain, or indeed France alone, had threatened to apply force to uphold the Locarno and Versailles Treaties.[4] But, as a matter of fact, neither government was in a mood for decisive action. They squirmed, they uttered stern verbal protests, suggested negotiation, and Britain threatened to fight if German soldiers stepped upon French or Belgian soil, but no more. So, also, the League of Nations condemned the Third Reich for willfully breaking her international engagements—and there the matter was allowed to rest. Armament appropriations, however, were enlarged all around.

Inside Britain a considerable section of opinion held that Germany, in occupying the Rhineland, had merely reasserted full sovereignty over her very own territory, while other Britishers took the view that France was not imperiled, since she was protected by the massive Maginot bastion, the most splendid achievement of military architecture the world had ever known. Some Britishers even hailed the Rhineland coup as merited retribution to France for refusing to support more thorough sanctions against Italy in the Ethiopian dispute —all of which reinforced the pacific, do-nothing mood of the London policymakers. Britishers who saw in the Rhineland act the unfolding of a strategic plan dangerous for British national and imperial welfare raised warning voices but failed to carry conviction to their countrymen. Britain's acquiescent response to the occupation of the Rhineland unleashed the most acrimonious anti-British campaign in the French press since Fashoda and the Boer War.

At the moment that the German troops moved into the Rhineland France was undergoing one of her recurrent ministerial crises. The initial thought of the French Ministry was to employ armed force to

---

[4] The Locarno Treaty expressly committed Britain and Italy to come to the aid of France in the kind of situation that had been created. Embroiled in Ethiopia, il Duce was completely frigid to any suggestion of action.

drive the Germans out, but that course was vetoed by the dominant opinion in the French democracy which was averse to any warlike step, and the financial cost of military intervention appears to have influenced the decision of the Ministry to acquiesce in a *fait accompli.*

For the Hitlerian dictatorship the occupation of the Rhineland was at once a boldly successful stroke and the inspiration for a more aggressive course in diplomatic affairs generally. "I go my way," Hitler broadcast to the world—with the assurance of a somnambulist—"the way which Providence has sent me." He could point out what had already been accomplished by way of "shaking off the chains of the slavery of Versailles," as the Nazi phrase ran: withdrawal from the League, recovery of the Saar, remilitarization of the Reich, all crowned now by the march into the Rhineland. More than that, Germany had a formal truce with Poland, a naval understanding with Great Britain, and signs multiplied of growing cordiality with Italy and Japan.

Called upon to express an opinion on recent foreign policies, the German electorate gave Nazi diplomacy a thundering vote of confidence, just short of 100 per cent "Ja." To be sure, the only way to express dissent was to spoil the ballot or cast a blank vote. Proclaimed the Führer in a speech extolling the Nazi attainments on the home front and disavowing any desire for war, "The German people have in the year 1936, in the fourth year of the National Socialist regime, ended the period of their historic dishonor." By year's end all the Versailles clauses imposing limitations on the Reich's domestic sovereignty had been swept away by unilateral Nazi action.

Once more in command of the Rhineland, the Third Reich seriously impaired the sense of security in France and Belgium particularly. Belgium indeed soon renounced the military alliance it had with France and reverted to the pre-1914 status of neutrality. It was the Belgian hope that if war engulfed Europe again she would be neither a partner nor a pawn in the conflict. And Belgium was assured of protection by France and Britain should she be the victim of German aggression. Already the military staffs of the three nations were conferring on plans for military cooperation in the event of an unprovoked German attack.

Within a year, Nazi fortifications in the Rhineland area were well advanced and the existence of that rampart, spoken of as the West Wall or Siegfried Line, made it feasible for German diplomacy to adopt a much more aggressive tone in dealings with neighbors in central and eastern Europe. So long as the western flank of Germany had lain open to easy French invasion, a German "Drang nach Osten" was hardly within the realm of the practicable. But the West Wall and the garrisons behind it—as well the rising strength of German air power—wrought a profound and swift change. In proportion as the capacity of the Third Reich for war mounted, the prestige of France declined. Historically, British diplomacy had displayed only a limited concern in the lands watered by the Danube and the Vistula, and the Chamberlain Cabinet was as yet unready to assume new commitments out there. A continent in a state of equipoise, permitting Britain to pursue its traditional role of balancer *par excellence,* seemed of all diplomatic alternatives the least undesirable from the standpoint of London.

A "New Deal" at the Straits

Italy's imperial expansion in Ethiopia caused genuine alarm in Turkish governing circles. Who could tell whether Mussolini's appetite might fasten upon Turkey next? Already the Italian flag flew over the Dodecanese archipelago in the Aegean off the Turkish coast and naval and air bases of sorts were built there. That Italy in the past had tried to establish itself in Asia Minor was all too well known by the Turks.

Prudence, therefore, dictated seeking international approval for rearming the Straits area leading into the Black Sea, which had been demilitarized in the Treaty of Lausanne of 1923 (Chap. XVII). A Turkish proposal to that end raised the large issue of international transit through the Straits, a perennial storm center in European politics. But the very fact that the Turks desired to change a treaty by peaceful negotiation in an hour when Italy and Germany were revising treaties by brusque unilateral action assured a sympathetic reception for the appeal.

With the solitary exception of Italy all the nations that had signed the Lausanne Treaty sent delegates to a Straits conference held in 1936 at Montreux, Switzerland. To that gathering the Turks presented a program for the Straits area that would be distinctly beneficial not alone to their own country but likewise to the Soviet Union, with which Turkey was on terms of friendly intimacy. That bill of particulars provoked an acute conflict between British and Soviet diplomatists. Britain desired to keep Russian warcraft cooped in the Black Sea without right of passing through the Straits into the Mediterranean, where they might imperil British shipping. The Kremlin, on the other hand, recalling the Anglo-French naval intervention in the Black Sea after the Bolshevik Revolution, wanted the Straits closed to the navies of potential enemies. In the end, happily, a compromise arrangement was worked out.

By the Montreux Convention Turkey was authorized to rearm the coasts of the Straits and adjacent islands. In peace or war, merchant vessels of all nations might freely use the Straits if Turkey was neutral. But severe restrictions were laid on the passage of warships through the Straits in peacetime, except that Soviet fighting craft other than submarines and airplane carriers might go through without hindrance. On the other hand, in time of war, the Straits would be closed to all belligerent ships unless (in effect) Turkey allowed them free transit.

Promptly Turkish soldiers moved into the formerly demilitarized zone and defense armament was rapidly installed. Whatever the Montreux Convention might assert, the Turks were again masters of the Straits and Soviet security on the Black Sea littoral was better assured so long as Turkey loyally upheld the agreement. By assenting to the Convention Britain and France built up political capital in Turkey, leading on to a Treaty of Mutual Assistance in October, 1939. Even Italy, reluctantly to be sure, came round and formally acknowledged the "new deal" in the vital Straits area.

Spain and the Powers

World attention, in the meantime, had shifted from the eastern Mediterranean to the western, to Spain, where civil war had broken out in July of 1936 before the shock of the Fascist conquest of Ethiopia had subsided. The environment in which that sanguinary Spanish struggle matured and the course of the conflict have already been treated (Chap.X). It is the international aspects of the Spanish fratricide that must here be reviewed.

Europe's Great Powers diverged radically on the conflict in Spain, partly in the name of ideological values though more fundamentally, no doubt, in the light of differing political, strategic, and economic interests. More exactly, Fascist Italy and Nazi Germany, foes of the status quo, encouraged the Rebels under General Francisco Franco to fight, and then lent them military assistance with the hope of winning a friend, if not indeed an ally, in case of a general European war. Both states stood to profit by Spanish trade and mineral resources.

Just as the Axis backed the Rebels, so Soviet Russia threw its weight to a modest extent behind the Loyalists. The object of the policymakers in the Kremlin was less to spread Stalinism than to further the broad interests of Soviet foreign policy. It may be—the evidence is cloudy—that the Russians hoped that out of the Spanish tragedy a European war would evolve in which the deadly Soviet foe, Hitlerian Germany, would have to fight on two fronts. That expectation, if expectation it was, failed to materialize, and the Soviets, disappointed, inclined toward a bargain with Germany which bore fruit in the historic understandings of August, 1939 (Chap.XX).

Unlike the totalitarian regimes, the governments of Great Britain and France eschewed taking a hand in the Spanish struggle, over the merits of which their publics were bitterly divided. The point was that the profusion of factors and issues in the civil war could be and were variously interpreted in countries where freedom of opinion and expression prevailed. Therefore neutrality in the Spanish turmoil appeared to be the least evil of alternative evils.

Aside from that, the British and French cabinets feared that if they actively intervened the conflict might grow into a continent-wide war, and British policymakers doubted whether the Dominions would cooperate in a struggle arising out of the Spanish War. Advocating a policy of aloofness the French Premier, Léon Blum, newly come to power as leader of the leftist Front Populaire coalition, declared, "Once competition in the delivery of arms has been installed in Spain heaven only knows what it will lead to." He reflected the sentiments of millions. It seemed the part of wisdom to seek to localize the war and to preserve Spanish territorial integrity.

Therefore France and Britain proposed an international understanding obligating the nations to keep hands off Spain and to lay an embargo on assistance to both of the Spanish belligerents. To that program of non-intervention all the Great Powers and over twenty smaller ones gave formal assent, but from the beginning non-intervention was a mockery and a farce. An international committee which was created to implement the pledge of non-intervention quarreled endlessly and provocatively. To enforce a ban on foreign "volunteers" going to Spain, an international naval cordon was thrown round the peninsula but its effectiveness was limited. The torpedoing of merchantmen in the Mediterranean, said to be hauling war supplies to the Loyalists, was almost certainly the work of Italian submarines. When an international piracy patrol was organized the attacks ceased.

The non-intervention policy staved off—or in the light of a longer perspective, deferred—a general war, but it failed utterly to prevent the sending of assistance to the Spanish combatants. In the first months of the war outmoded weapons were shipped to the Spaniards, but in November, 1936, first-line Russian planes were supplied to the Loyalists. Italy and Germany then forwarded equipment of equal grade to the Rebels. Along with guns, tanks, and planes, large contingents of

Italian and German troops were shipped in. When they proved unable to carry the Rebels to quick victory, reinforcements were hurled into the Spanish struggle; their presence was the subject of official boastings in Berlin and Rome. Soviet Russia, geographically remote, despatched technicians and special agents to assist the Loyalists, but sent no military units. For Soviet materials of war the Loyalists paid spot cash. Even they fell away in the spring of 1938.

For varied reasons, doctrinal predominantly no doubt, volunteer fighters from France, Britain, the United States, Italy, and other countries fought alongside the Loyalists. Some war goods from western sources found their way into Loyalist hands. From France, for instance, went airplanes and military supplies, and Loyalist planes were frequently refuelled and repaired at the French military aerodrome at Toulouse.

The outside aid delivered to the Loyalists was small and uncertain, compared with Axis contributions to the Rebels. The assistance to the Rebels was of invaluable, if not indeed of decisive importance in carrying General Franco to victory. Later on, Mussolini called upon Franco to pay $275,000,000 for the help that had been furnished.

Into the spring of 1939 the fierce Spanish contest dragged on. Early in the uprising the German and Italian governments had extended formal diplomatic recognition to the Franco regime, which subsequently attested its gratitude to the Axis by signing an anti-Comintern pact, directed against "international Communism." Yet the German and Italian hope that in the event of a European war Franco would throw in his lot with the Axis was never fulfilled, though some unneutral aid was given in World War II and Axis victory would undoubtedly have suited Franco's book.

For Britain and for France, the course of events in Spain, and the outcome, meant a humiliating loss of face, even though the peace of Europe had not been shattered and the political independence and territorial integrity of Spain were preserved. Just before the Loyalists capitulated, the London and Paris cabinets recognized the Franco government as legitimate. It was not difficult for the Axis plunderbund to conclude that the western nations were either too proud or too weak to fight. In that sense the Spanish business was an encouragement to further Axis adventures. As for the Kremlin, the suspicion was deepened that what the West really desired was a clash of arms between the Soviet Union and Germany in which Britain and France would stand on the side-lines and profit by the mutual destruction. The Spanish affair, in other words, intensified Soviet distrust of the diplomatic intentions and the military capacities of the capitalist democracies, and, as has been remarked, that formed part of the larger background of the Kremlin's decision to make a diplomatic deal with the Nazis in 1939.

Japan on the Warpath Again

As if the international perplexities of Europe were not more than enough to exhaust the patience of a modern Job, and while the Spanish imbroglio dragged along, Japan reopened the war upon China. In the summer of 1937, the armistice in the Orient, arranged four years before, was brusquely ruptured. A minor incident—skirmishes between Chinese and Japanese troops—provided, as usual, the occasion. By now, aggressive military oligarchs wholly dominated the affairs of the land of the cherry blossom. Reckless, headstrong men, neither controlled nor restrained by the popular will, would not be content until they had established a *Pax Japanica* over eastern Asia at least. A military putsch of February, 1936, had driven every moderate policymaker from office and set the seal to Japanese imperial aims.

Symbolical of the mastery of the Nipponese extremists was a Japanese demand, made in 1935, for naval equality with the United States and Great Britain. At that point the Washington and London naval limitation treaties (1922; 1930) were due for renewal. Holding that established fleet ratios were adequate to ensure Japan against successful attack, the American and British governments declined to concur in the Nipponese claim. So the whole fabric of naval limitation, as it bound Japan, was tossed into the discard, and with it went the prohibition, agreed to at Washington in 1922, on the construction of fighting facilities in specified areas of the Pacific.[5]

The passing of the limitation treaties was the signal for furious naval construction. Britain celebrated New Year's Day of 1937 by laying down the keels of two 35,000 ton battleships, in addition to some 200,000 tons of vessels already on the ways. Appropriations by the United States provided for over 250,000 tons of naval shipping. Germany was striving to reach the fleet level fixed in the treaty of 1935 with Great Britain; Japan, France, Italy, and Soviet Russia were building or planning to build as rapidly as their resources and their treasuries permitted. A competitive naval race, costly, psychologically fear-provoking, and politically dangerous, was on.

Inside China, meanwhile, unprecedented national unity had been achieved. The Nationalists of Chiang Kai-shek had joined with the Chinese Communists, after years of internecine fighting, to present a

---

[5] The United States, Great Britain, and France agreed in 1936 on the size and equipment of war vessels without setting any maximum on the total tonnage.

united front against Japan. If China became firmly united in spirit and in purpose, if China created effective fighting services and a large armament industry, as she was by way of doing, it would be no light task for Japan to subjugate the country and convert it into a monopolistic Nipponese preserve. For the Japanese military caste, the time to strike was now or never.

Thunderclouds of war hanging lower and lower over Europe—and anti-war sentiment at a peak in the United States—encouraged Japanese ambitions. As more than once before, Europe's adversity was Japan's opportunity. Given the European tension, Britain, for example, could not reinforce her seapower in eastern waters to any considerable extent, and could scarcely do more than protest verbally if her large commercial stake in China were imperiled by Japanese aggression. Nor could Britain readily protect her far-flung strategic and imperial interests in the southern Pacific area. In like case, the Asiatic empires of France and Holland might be placed in jeopardy.

To make matters even more perilous, Japan openly aligned itself with Nazi Germany by signing, in November, 1936, a treaty directed against the spread of "international Communism." For the Japanese patriot that accord, which in some sense was a substitute for the alliance with Great Britain that had expired in 1922, was extremely gratifying; it argued equality with a Great European Power and equality was something dear to the proud Nipponese heart.[6] Mussolini put his signature to the anti-Comintern document in November, 1937. It was natural for Soviet statesmen to look upon the pact as a mask for contemplated aggression. Russia's ambassador in Japan told the American envoy, Joseph Grew, that the anti-Comintern combination "was undoubtedly directed against Britain . . . it envisaged the division of various British overseas possessions and the Dutch East Indies between Japan and Germany in case of war." (December 3, 1936).

In the manner of eating an artichoke, Japanese armies kept picking off parts of northern China and then, in 1937, frank, though undeclared, war started and did not cease until 1945. Superior weight of metal enabled the Japanese to whip the Chinese on battlefield after battlefield. There was no question of the stubborn valor of Chiang Kai-shek's forces, especially the guerilla warriors, but without quantities of up-to-date weapons the Chinese were outpowered. Losses on both sides were large, vastly heavier for the Chinese because of cruelties which the invader inflicted upon civilians. Yet it was widely held

[6] It was believed that the two nations had made a secret deal to split up the richly-endowed Dutch East Indies.

in the outer world that Nippon was being bled white, economically if not in manpower.

By the opening of World War II the Japanese controlled almost the entire Chinese coastline, the larger part of the Chinese heavy industries, and the most productive agricultural provinces. Tokyo declared its intention of extending to China entire the sort of puppet administration that had been set up·in Manchuria. It appeared that the army of the Mikado was very largely, and the airforce partly, tied down by the war on China, though that was not the case with the impressive and restless Japanese navy.

The government of Chiang Kai-shek organized headquarters at Chungking on the Yangtze river, deep in the interior of the country. Communications with the outside world were confined to three routes: a railway running in from French Indo-China; a motor highway— the Burma Road—quickly constructed from a railhead at Lashio in Burma; and indifferent roads leading to the Asiatic realm of the Soviets. But the war supplies which reached Free China through these channels could not meet the requirements of the desperately embattled nation. Nonetheless the Chungking government, still the nominal authority over the greater part of China, kept up the unequal struggle, hoping for foreign intervention against the Japanese aggressor.

Inescapably the war in the Orient had repercussions in foreign countries which had interests and values at stake. Much foreign property was damaged, foreign nationals were insulted and assaulted, foreign commerce was virtually paralyzed, and Japanese forces wantonly fired upon small foreign warships. The injured governments were profuse with expostulations; and Japan, equally profuse with apologies, by legalistic casuistry tried to explain—or explain away—the misdeeds.

Not long after the onset of the fighting, China applied to the League of Nations for protection, precisely as had been done in 1931. Although· Japan had clearly violated the Covenant—as well as the Nine Power Treaty of 1922 and the Paris Peace Pact—and although the legal case against Japan was as airtight as in the spoliation of Manchuria, no Great Power wished to invoke armed force against the transgressor. Therefore the League was capable of nothing more efficacious than amiable resolutions of sympathy for straitened China and strident condemnations of Japanese brigandage.

Soviet Russia manifested friendship for Free China by sending in limited quantities of war matériel. Several sharp disputes along the Siberian-Manchukuoan border produced fresh strains in Russo-Japanese diplomacy, but they were promptly ironed out. Against any eventuality, Russia went on improving its capacity to fight in the Far East. The Japanese, on their part, took military precautions where the USSR was concerned, which pinned down a substantial contingent of Nipponese troops.

The United States and World Affairs

No government registered sterner protests in Tokyo over the deliberate infringements of rights and treaties than the United States, China's long-time and particular champion. Under law on the statute books President Roosevelt might, in his discretion, have cut off all commercial intercourse with both belligerents, merely by proclaiming that "a state of war" existed. That he would not do for it would have handicapped China far more than Japan.

At Chicago, in October of 1937, the President delivered a memorable indictment of aggression and declared that it might be well if the peace-loving nations combined to "quarantine" disease-spreading Japan. The unsympathetic response in the Congress punctured the President's trial balloon. Tension between the two nations mounted when Japanese airmen, bombed, strafed, and sank the American gunboat *Panay* in Chinese waters in December, 1937. That, by any definition, was an act of war, though after an exchange of diplomatic notes the Tokyo government expressed regret, promised to make financial retribution, and did so.

During the *Panay* crisis the United States Congress showed neither signs of bellicosity nor any disposition to collaborate with other governments—had they been inclined to do so—to call a halt to Nipponese aggression. Yet American resentment over Japan's course was concretely expressed by the laying of an embargo upon the exportation to Japan of certain goods useful in carrying on the war and by serving notice of the abrogation of the American-Japanese trade treaty—an act which hinted that the United States might seek to restrain Japan by the weapon of economics. To Free China frank gestures of American friendship took the form of small but enheartening loans.

Looked at broadly, the policy pursued by the United States with regard to the Orient paralleled its course in Europe. That chapter of American foreign affairs requires the briefest possible exposition. With national energies in the United States heavily concentrated on the New Deal trinity of "relief, recovery, and reform", the prevalent mood in the Republic was one of abstention from extra-American affairs. True, President Roosevelt had dedicated the nation to a world policy of the "good neighbor," but the practical application of the doctrine was confined to the Western Hemisphere. Good neighborliness in dealings with the nations of Latin America induced a more cooperative attitude on their part toward the northern colossus. In 1938 Canada was assured that the United States would act if the security of the neighbor to the north were imperiled.

It is true, too, that in Europe the United States had quit treating the Soviet Union as a pariah and entered into ordinary diplomatic relationships. At the several naval and disarmament conferences the United States was competently represented and, in 1934, it assumed membership in the International Labor Organization. On the economic plane, moreover, the Hull reciprocity tariff policy, inaugurated in the same year, which allowed the President to cut duties by as much as fifty per cent in return for comparable concessions by other nations, paved the way for new trade treaties with twenty one states. Of those agreements, the one with Great Britain, the largest customer of the United States, covered the widest field. American sales to the United Kingdom exceeded purchases from her, but the United States bought more from the British colonies, particularly rubber and tin, than she sold. Here then were the elements for a mutually advantageous commercial bargain; and each party contracted, in 1938, to lower tariffs on a broad range of commodities which benefited the flow of commerce on both sides.

These matters apart—and they were hardly of the first order of importance—took place as grave events unfolded in the Old World: the resurgence of Germany, the Italian seizure of Ethiopia, the virtual demise of the League, and the Spanish Civil War. The transcendent opinion in the United States was something like this: "Look at Europe: the same old shop with the same old evils; power politics paramount; headed for inferno on roller skates; nothing of real and lasting value accomplished by our participation in World War I. Better steer clear of the mess."

By the mid-thirties the feeling that the United States had blundered egregiously in entering World War I was reaching flood tide. Disillusionment was fostered by revelations of pre-1914 European diplomacy and by investigations conducted by the Senate, which disclosed the huge profits coined in wartime by certain "merchants of death." Corrosive cynicism and preachments of negative pacifism made an incalculable dent upon the American mind and emotions. Speaking to the Italian ambassador in November, 1935, Secretary of State Cordell Hull remarked that "with the extremely disastrous and unsatisfactory experience of the American people in going to Europe and aiding Italy and other countries to the extent they did, they are almost wild in their demand that we not only avoid being drawn into the war but that we stay entirely away from the same."

Hostility toward Europe was accentuated by the refusal of war-debtors to "come across"—which American tariff laws made difficult—though they found funds to pile up armaments. As a mark of displeasure the Johnson Act of 1934 was passed, which closed the American money market to defaulting debtor nations. The next year a presidential recommendation to join the World Court was beaten in the Senate, albeit by a narrow margin.

American aversion to involvement in war matched similar sentiments then to the fore in Britain and France. These three nations were content with the status quo, nations in which the public will shaped the course of international policy.

That is not to say that liberty-loving America was unmoved by the dark tyranny, the uncouth barbarities of the dictatorships, particularly the Hitlerian abuse of minorities and threat to enduring peace. The world would be well rid of Hitler, it was generally felt. The doughty Mayor Fiorello La Guardia of New York City proposed that an effigy of the Führer should be exhibited in a chamber of horrors. Advocates of retaliation upon Germany organized a boycott which caused a sharp falling-off in German imports. Nazis countered with propaganda in support and vindication of the Hitler regime, making use of knots of friendly sympathizers with National Socialism in the United States, who were more noisy than numerous.

Given the ruling climate of opinion in the United States the enactment of the Neutrality Acts of 1935-1937 is readily understood. Sponsors of these measures believed that by surrounding the Republic with an impenetrable hedge of olive branches the United States would be able to keep out of war. On the assumption that certain practices had facilitated involvement in 1917, the Neutrality Acts prescribed that, whenever the President declared that a state of war existed, it would be unlawful for Americans to sell war matériel of any description to any belligerent; to make loans to a nation that was fighting; to travel on a ship flying a belligerent flag; nor might American vessels carry any munitions or any goods whatever to a nation at war—the famous "cash and carry" provision.

In the beginning these laws were applicable only in conflicts between sovereign nations, but soon after the onset of the civil war in Spain they were broadened to cover domestic strife as well. The legislation in fact was put in force against Italy and Ethiopia, and against Spain, but not in the Sino-Japanese struggle.

Many a voice was raised against the Neutrality Acts and the

philosophy that underlay them. It was pointed out that they were a boon to nations intent on aggression; they were decried as incompatible with American national honor and freedom of the seas, and as positively perilous from the standpoint of national safety. But the dominant state of mind favored aloofness from extra-American affairs. That mood persisted, though with diminishing popularity, until months after the start of World War II.

The Anglo-French Alliance

In the early months of 1935 Britain embarked upon a program of building up its military establishment, special attention being given to air defenses. Once the island kingdom had possessed a mighty air armada of some 30,000 planes—that was in 1918, but almost all of them were scrapped by order of the then Secretary of War, Winston Churchill. In 1930 Britain had a mere 770 first-line planes as compared with Italy's 1,100.[7] To pressure for expansion in airpower the Baldwin Ministry bowed. Plans for the making of the giant bombers which carried on mass raids against the Third Reich from the spring of 1942 until the downfall of Nazidom were drawn up in May of 1936—just after the German occupation of the Rhineland. Apparently by the autumn of 1937 the Royal Air Force was on a par with the German Luftwaffe. When war actually came, Britain had the two best night-bombers in existence, the *Wellington* and the *Whitley,* while the British *Blenheim* in the light-bomber class and the *Spitfire* fighter acknowledged no superior anywhere.

Appropriation bills for British rearmament met with steady opposition from Labour and Liberal M.P.'s, who only hesitantly and reluctantly admitted the necessity of greater capacity to fight. Anti-war feeling and downright pacifism had the same kind of popularity in Britain that they had in the United States and France. Many a British youth of the thirties had come to regard patriotism as an absurdity, military discipline as a stupid and archaic tyranny, and war as the supreme social crime. For that body of thought, preparations for war were detestable and inherently dangerous as leading inevitably to a clash of arms. No British ministry could be oblivious of the strength, the sincerity, nor the intensity of the "peace movement."

The fact that Britain had engaged in military expansion at all reflected the growing anxiety over the international turbulence and the British resolution to implement the words of Prime Minister

[7] For the story of the upbuilding of British airpower, see Marquess of Londonderry, *Wings of Destiny* (London, 1943).

Baldwin, uttered in 1934, that Britain's frontier was no longer the chalk cliffs of Dover but the Rhine river. For British diplomacy the implications of that new frontier pronouncement attained a significance not unlike that of the Monroe Doctrine in the public thought of the United States. "Hands off France," was the British counterpart of "Hands off the Americas."

The year 1937 was one of comparative calm in the diplomatic annals of Europe, though not, of course, of the Orient. It was the year of the massive purges in Soviet Russia which were upsetting to the foreign friends of the great Eurasian power, to some of whom Russia seemed to be a gigantic madhouse. In that year, moreover, it was revealed that Britain intended to lay out the stupendous sum of $7,500,000,000 for armaments over the next five years. A huge naval base at Singapore, a "Gibraltar of the Pacific," conceived of as a stubborn obstacle to Japanese expansionism, was rushed to completion; outlays for British warships were stepped up; reforms were made in the British army and plans for peacetime conscription were matured. Each fresh international crisis quickened British fears for the future and was followed by an acceleration of armament construction.

Britain's foreign policy in this crucial period was determined in the final analysis by Neville Chamberlain, Conservative Prime Minister after June, 1937. For him the guiding principle of policy was the "appeasement" of dissatisfied and arrogant Germany and Italy, by concessions, as the surest alternative to war. It was assumed that solutions of international disputes could be found by diplomatic negotiation and in the light of reason rather than by an appeal to force. Critics, however, reviled that course as a supine attempt to buy off the Axis by acquiescence in wanton breaches of international commitments.

The Chamberlain policy of concessions could work in only two circumstances. First, if there was solid reason for believing that one more mark of appeasement would bring Axis demands to an end, rather than invite fresh demands. Or, if the conceder was prepared to go on conceding forever in order to avoid armed conflict. The latter was not the case with Chamberlain, for there were certain definite British interests on which there could be no compromise, no more retreat.

Time must elapse, ardor cool, and clearer perspectives emerge before anything approaching a dispassionate verdict can be rendered on the virtues and the vices of the diplomacy Chamberlain espoused. Few public men in modern British history have been the objects of

more rancorous attacks by opponents or of more unrestrained lauda-
tion by supporters. At his death in 1940 one impassioned admirer
declared, "Next to our Lord, I think Mr. Chamberlain is the greatest
man who has ever lived in the world."

Not all the British Conservatives were willing to follow the diplomatic path pursued by the Prime Minister. In fact, an open breach in
the Chamberlain Cabinet occurred in February, 1938, when the Foreign Minister, Anthony Eden, resigned on the score that further negotiations with the dictators would be not only futile but dangerous for
the national interest. It was Eden's conviction that vigorous diplomatic
action would compel the dictators, specifically Mussolini, to meet British terms and so prevent war. Out of office, Eden aligned himself with
the Churchill "ginger group" which clamored for greater speed in
rearmament; thenceforth into 1939 the Conservative Party was seriously divided on diplomatic policy.

Weakness, ferment and dissension inside France, coupled with the
growing armaments of Germany and of Italy, obliged the French government to take its cues in foreign affairs from London. Step by step,
in response to the rising European tension the bonds between the
two nations were drawn tighter. For instance, reciprocal pledges of
military assistance were exchanged after the remilitarization of the
Rhineland in 1936, and provision was then made for periodic conversations between the General Staffs. Immediately after the annexation
of Austria to the Third Reich, presently to be described, a genuine
Anglo-French Alliance was worked out in April, 1938; it was agreed
that in case of war there should be complete unity in the command of
the fighting services on land, on sea, and in the air. By signing that
full-fledged and unprecedented alliance, Britain was committed to fight
jointly with France if hostilities broke out on the continent. And
just as in 1936 the two governments had promised to protect Belgium
from invasion, so in January, 1939, they committed themselves to
assist Holland and Switzerland if German forces should move against
either country.

Until 1935 France, as has been noted, was the dominant military
power of Europe and peace on the continent was upheld by French
armed preponderance. But the swift expansion of German armaments
ended the French ascendancy, though France steadily built up her
capacity for war. Communist deputies in France, on order from Moscow apparently, soft-pedalled their traditional anti-military sentiments
and matched the conservative Right in supporting bigger armaments;
but love of peace and aversion to preparations to fight pervaded all
layers of French society, being especially strong in Socialist ranks.

The feeling that France was safe regardless of what might happen was stiffened by the Maginot fortifications along the eastern border facing Germany. The chief sponsor, André Maginot, sometime Minister of War, however, had never thought of them as complete or even adequate protection against a German onslaught. His plan for extending the defense rampart along the frontier of Belgium was seemingly vetoed by the Belgian government. Maginot calculated, too, on powerful supporting forces of tanks and planes, especially planes, and it was precisely in that department of war that France lagged notably behind Hitlerian Germany.

As late as 1934 France led Europe in military aviation and appropriations that year were voted for the expansion of airpower. But technical innovations reduced French planes to obsolescence almost as soon as they were finished, and France drained her factories of workmen in order to keep up her large army. It appears that the output of planes while Léon Blum's Front Populaire Ministry was in office surpassed that in the early part of 1939. In any case French plane production was far below that of Germany and the quality of the French planes—in speed, maneuverability and fire power—was inferior to the best machines in the Luftwaffe. Frantic efforts were made to procure first-grade aircraft from American factories.

Subordinate French army officers, Colonel Charles de Gaulle among them, pleaded with their military superiors to speed up the mechanization of the fighting forces in readiness for mobile warfare. But the older and conservative French commanders, who thought of a new conflict in terms of the equipment of World War I, preferred the types of armament that had brought ultimate victory in 1918. Therefore, instead of an army of machines France had a large army of men, inadequately equipped by the exacting standards of World War II. In the testing time of combat French military might was exposed as a deceptive façade.

So far as the French were concerned the diplomatic solidarity of the Channel neighbors was popularly confirmed in the summer of 1938 by rapturous ovations given King George VI and his Queen on a visit to Paris. The French President was welcomed with hearty acclaim by Londoners at the beginning of 1939. Throughout the nerve-wracking period just before the outbreak of World War II, the French government acquiesced without notable dissent in British diplomatic leadership.

CHAPTER XX

The Last Phase

Nazi Annexation of Austria

BETWEEN March of 1938 and April of 1939 Hitlerian Germany strode from one "bloodless" occupation of territory to another. The Nazi goal of unmaking the Treaty of Versailles was almost completely reached. Independent Austria, the Czech Sudetenland, then the remnant of Czechoslovakia and the Memel district passed swiftly under the sword of the Third Reich. Greater Germany, though not yet Pan Germania, had become reality. That radical transformation in Europe's map followed unerringly from the master coup of 1936 in rearming the Rhineland.

First act in the awesome drama and the first territorial revision undertaken by the Nazis was the annexation of Austria in March, 1938. To that climax the path had actually been smoothed two years before when Hitler, reversing his earlier Austrian policy, had signed a treaty with Chancellor Kurt Schuschnigg of Austria in which the independence of that country was affirmed and each party promised not to interfere in the domestic affairs of the other. Hard times economically were grist to the mill of those Austrians who believed that in union with Germany salvation would be found. Anschluss sentiments were stimulated by Austrian Nazis and by a huge volume of propaganda issuing from the Reich.

Through bullying pressure at the beginning of 1938 Hitler secured freer scope for the Nazis and their activities inside Austria, and forced the appointment of three prominent Nazis to posts in the Schuschnigg Ministry. Thereafter street demonstrations and political disturbances in Vienna and other Austrian cities increased ominously. Hitler let it be known in no uncertain language that German-speaking folk outside the Reich, Austrians included, must be allowed to determine under what flag they preferred to live.

Unwilling that his nation should lose its independence by default, Schuschnigg suddenly decided to seek the views of the Austrian electorate on their future destiny. He surrounded the right to vote in the projected plebiscite with regulations which tended to favor the status quo. Unquestionably, the Nazi policymakers in Berlin believed that the referendum, if it were held, would damage the Anschluss cause. Therefore Hitler roughly demanded that the plebiscite be canceled and that Schuschnigg give up the Chancellorship. Nazi troops were massed along the frontiers of the little country.

Preparations were fully matured for military invasion when Schuschnigg, deeming discretion the better part of valor, resigned. Then German armies rolled in and occupied the land; Austria was proclaimed a part of the Third Reich. That declaration was confirmed in a plebiscite a few weeks later. Forthwith practically all the institutionalism and laws of Germany were introduced into the former Austrian free-state. No one knows nor ever will know whether the union with the Reich reflected the real will of a majority of the Austrian population. That an impressively large anti-Anschluss faction existed is undeniable, but the outcome of the plebiscite in favor of union cannot be wholly ascribed to Nazi pressure and intimidation.

The death of Austria caused a profound stir in western capitals, at least on the surface. Many a Britisher, many a Frenchman felt that what had happened was right and in harmony with the self-determination dogma, even though the method of achieving the union was reprehensible. France at the moment was in the familiar throes of a ministerial upset, yet she joined with Britain in an emphatic protest on the annexation as endangering the peace of Europe. All things considered it is probable that nothing short of war could have induced Hitler to disgorge his Austrian birthland. Soviet Russia, in alarm, recommended the summoning of an international conference to work out plans to resist Germany in the future. The British government greeted the idea unsympathetically, remarking that "it might seem like organizing Europe into two ideological blocs."

Union of the two German-speaking lands extended the Third Reich to the border of Italy but, in complete contrast to his attitude in 1934 when he had threatened to fight to prevent Anschluss, Mussolini placidly gave his blessing to the annexation as befitted a partner in the Axis alignment. Austria added to Germany's manpower and material wealth, for it had a fund of foreign currency, a substantial industry, timber reserves, and some iron and other mineral resources.

Master of Austria, Nazi Germany was in a position to control more thoroughly the trade of the Danube valley and of the Balkan peninsula, and proceeded to do so. On the strategic side, too, the German situation was immensely bettered. The Third Reich now stood cheek to jowl with Hungary and Yugoslavia, while Czechoslovakia was converted into a peninsula thrusting into the German sea. A cartoon in the London *News Chronicle* picturesquely described the perilous position of Czechoslovakia: Germany was represented in the form of a wolf's head with the upper or Silesian jaw closing over western Czechoslovakia on one side, while the Austrian lower jaw encircled the area from below. "The jaws of the German wolf are closing in," the caption warned. Six months later the jaws had snapped shut devouring a choice chunk of the Czech Republic.

The Doom of Czechoslovakia

By blotting Czechoslovakia from the map, Nazi Germany very nearly precipitated an European war and brought the approach of world catastrophe much nearer.[1] Once Austria had fallen into the spacious German basket, the Sudeten "autonomists" in the Czech Republic redoubled their tumult, waxed more arrogant, and a torrent of invective and frenzied nationalism swept over the frontiers from the Third Reich.

Suspicious German army maneuvers along the Czech border in May, 1938, and exciting frontier incidents roused panicky fears of war. The Prague government partly mobilized its fighting services. Britain and France clearly warned that they would fight if German troops moved into Czechoslovakia. If, as can scarcely be doubted, Hitler intended to "settle" the Sudeten controversy by force at that time, the courage displayed by the Czechs and assurances of Anglo-French backing caused the German sword to be replaced in the scabbard. The task of completing the Siegfried Line against France was pressed forward with maximum despatch.

Throughout the summer months demonstrations and disorders in the Sudetenland attained such a pitch that the Czech government placed the troubled areas under martial law. Enflaming Hitlerian propaganda grossly exaggerated the mistreatment to which the Sudetens were subjected. When the Czechs at long last brought forth proposals giving the region autonomy, the Sudeten leaders, Konrad Henlein in the van, now frankly intent on secession and union with the Third Reich, cavalierly brushed them aside. Not improbably that attitude reflected the desires of the majority of the Sudetens old

[1] The history of the Czechoslovak Republic and the emergence of a Sudeten German Party are treated in Chap. VI.

enough to have an opinion, though it was by no means unanimously applauded.[2]

At that juncture, in September, 1938, Hitler caused the most dangerous international crisis since World War I by defiantly threatening to seize the Sudetenland by force. France and Russia, as has been noted, were explicitly bound by treaty to defend the integrity of Czechoslovakia and if it came to war Britain would surely be involved, directly by virtue of commitments to France. To avert the "awful arbitrament" of a general conflict the British Ministry worked for the maintenance of peace by direct diplomatic negotiation with Hitler.

To that end, the elderly Prime Minister Chamberlain made two hurried flights to Germany by air to confer in a straightforward manner with the Nazi dictator. At the second parley the Führer made his conditions stiffer, though so far as could be judged the German civilian population desired peace.

In concurrence with France, Britain promised that the Sudeten areas which were peopled mainly by folk of German speech should be ceded to the Reich. But Hitler truculently demanded that Nazi soldiers should occupy the aforesaid districts at once under pain of war. Therefore the Czechs started to mobilize their fighting forces, French troops took up positions in the Maginot Line, the British fleet was ordered to North Sea stations, trenches were hurriedly dug in London's parks and open spaces, and gas masks were distributed. Chamberlain warned that Britain would resist any nation that tried "to dominate the world by fear of its force." The Soviet Union officially though vaguely proclaimed its solidarity with the Anglo-French coalition. Nazi legions were drawn up along three sides of Czechoslovakia. Europe's peace hung by a gossamer thread.

Munich

The climax of the terrifying and confusing Sudeten crisis took the form of a meeting in Munich called by Hitler for the purpose of fixing the manner and the methods by which the Sudetenland should be transferred. In attendance were the Führer, his ally Mussolini—whose pressure for a peaceful solution of the controversy was reinforced by telegraphed pleas from President Roosevelt, Chamberlain, and for France, Premier Daladier. They signed an agreement, which was less a negotiated settlement than a surrender to the dictates of the Führer. By the Munich pact the dread prospect of war was deferred at the last

---

[2] Many Germans, conspicuously Socialists, courageously demonstrated their loyalty to the Czech state until the Nazi occupation, whereupon some sought refuge in the Czech interior.

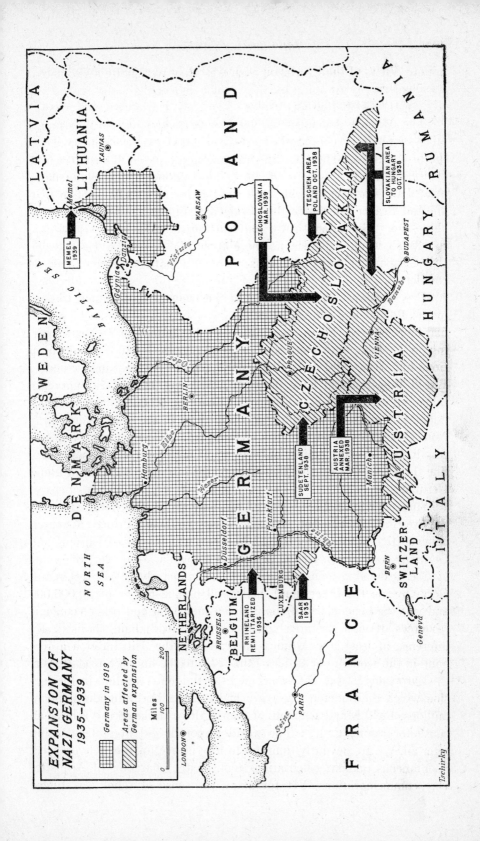

EXPANSION OF
NAZI GERMANY
1935–1939

Germany in 1919

Areas affected by
German expansion

Miles

0   100   200

MEMEL 1939

KAUNAS

LITHUANIA

LATVIA

Memel

BALTIC SEA

SWEDEN

Gdynia

Danzig

WARSAW

Vistula

P O L A N D

CZECHOSLOVAKIA
MAR. 1939

TESCHEN AREA
POLAND OCT. 1938

SLOVAKIAN AREA
TO HUNGARY
OCT. 1938

R U M A N I A

Oder

BERLIN

Elbe

Hamburg

PRAGUE

C Z E C H O S L O V A K I A

BUDAPEST

Danube

VIENNA

G E R M A N Y

DENMARK

NORTH
SEA

Weser

Düsseldorf

Frankfurt

SUDETENLAND
SEPT. 1938

AUSTRIA
ANNEXED
MAR. 1938

A U S T R I A

H U N G A R Y

Munich

NETHERLANDS

BRUSSELS

BELGIUM

RHINELAND
REMILITARIZED
1936

LUXEMBURG

SAAR
1935

Rhine

SWITZER-
LAND

BERN

Geneva

I T A L Y

LONDON

Seine

PARIS

F R A N C E

Tschirky

minute. Views of the Czechs on what was afoot were not even solicited; they had simply to abide by the verdict delivered by the representatives of the Great Powers.

The Munich document assigned to Germany over 11,000 square miles of territory containing more than 3,000,000 residents, and left the broken Czech state at the strategic mercy of the Third Reich. A clause calling for a plebiscite in some sections of the Sudetenland proved still-born and it was small comfort to the Czechs to have Britain and France guarantee the abridged Republic against unprovoked aggression. Characteristically and categorically Hitler asserted that the Reich would advance no more territorial claims in Europe and that German colonial pretensions were not a matter to provoke armed conflict.

Czech sorrows did not end with the transfer of territory to Germany. Poland and Hungary filched away fringes of land which they had long coveted, Poland getting a valuable industrial region, centering on Teschen, with more than 200,000 people. If Hungarian aspirations had been fully met, all the land ceded to Czechoslovakia after World War I would have been recovered, but instead Hungary obtained an area about equal to Connecticut and Rhode Island having a population in excess of a million. In all three of the districts cut away from Czechoslovakia lived tens of thousands of folk who did not profess to be German, Polish, or Magyar in national feeling; something like three quarters of a million Czechs, for instance, had passed under German rule.

Surrender at Munich involved not only diplomatic humiliation for the western powers but strategic losses to boot. Prince Bismarck believed that whoever controlled Bohemia was master of Europe, and Germany was now in virtual control of Bohemia. Moreover, the value of Czechoslovakia as a military power was sharply reduced; Greater Germany, on the other hand, had swollen to a nation of 80,000,000 and was the beneficiary of the Sudeten industrial and other economic resources, though the area consumed more food than it raised. By inference at least, the Munich pact allowed the Third Reich a free hand in the economy of eastern Europe up to the line of Soviet Russia.

Europeans in the mass welcomed the sudden relaxation in the tension which the Sudeten war scare had created. Speaking the mind of millions, Field Marshal Smuts of South Africa declared, "We have all cause for rejoicing. . . . The world is not devoid of statesmanship after all. We are devoutly thankful to Providence for this deliverance." Spontaneous popular celebrations took on the character of Armistice Day commemorations. Yet for many the sense of relief was tinged with pangs of pity for Czechoslovakia. The House of Commons endorsed the Munich settlement by a majority of 222, Eden and Churchill being among the dissenters. And in the French Chamber of Deputies the vote on Munich stood 350 to 75; almost all the adverse votes were registered by the Communists on orders no doubt from Moscow. At the end of 1938 Lloyds quoted odds at thirty two to one against a war within the year.

But in Prague among the Czechs a spirit of sullen despair and humiliated anger reigned which was captured by a poet:

> The sources of our streams have gone from us,
> Only our walls are left us,
> And the starry sky
> And disgust.
> Stabbing the blue, the Castle,
> Loftier than ever it was,
> And in our eyes is shame, for those who stripped us
> And from our sorrows patched themselves a peace.

The Debate Over Munich

Over the elements of wisdom and folly in the Anglo-French acceptance of the Munich terms, controversy has been rancorous and promises to remain so. Yet the alternative to submission to the Hitlerian demands would almost certainly have been to plunge most of Europe into war. Some critics at the time, and others wiser after the event, hotly upbraided the British and French policymakers for "selling Czechoslovakia down the river," for retreating in cowardly fashion before the bullying menaces of Hitler, and for impairing the chances of preserving peace in the future. One British journal reproached Chamberlain for having "turned all four cheeks to Hitler." Rather than accept the Munich conditions, critics contended, the British lion should have stood firm, growled ominously and then, the cocky Nazi eagle, frightened, would have dropped its prey and flown off to Berchtesgaden.

On a broad view the Munich accord was indeed the culmination of the diplomacy pursued by the western powers ever since the withdrawal of the occupation forces from the Rhineland in 1930. In explanation of the Anglo-French Munich policy a broad array of arguments has been adduced in which fact is intricately entangled with hypothesis. It is argued, first, that approval of the annexation of the Sudetenland to Germany tallied with the democratic principle of self-determination, since the inhabitants were overwhelmingly German in speech and in the main desirous of union with the Reich. And by accepting Hitler's terms an international conflict had been avoided in which Czechoslovakia would have been swiftly crushed by the encircling and massive German war machine.

Not only had a general conflagration been avoided but, in the language of Chamberlain, Munich meant "peace in our time," an interpretation that appealed to men with an invincible capacity for hope. Certain partisans of the accord, moreover, were skeptical as to whether the Soviet Union would have fought if it had come to a showdown, or could not perceive how Russia would have been of much military value, for one reason because so many top commanders had just been liquidated in the wholesale purges. It was further believed by some Britishers and Frenchmen that clashing Soviet and German interests and ambitions would in the natural course of events cause the two nations to fly at each other's throats. Such a conflict, mutually exhausting, some westerners would have welcomed as a providential removal of the world's strongest totalitarianisms that would have assured security for the rest of Europe. For such minds the Munich chapter in the history of appeasement deserved unqualified applause.[3]

The dominantly pacific temper of British and French opinion, as manifested, for example, in the votes in the parliaments on the Munich compact, had no little part in leading to the decision at Munich. In both countries the desire for peace at almost any price was pronounced; in fact M. P.'s of the British Labour Party voted against peacetime conscription as late as the spring of 1939. British diplomacy —French too—at Munich and before must be judged in the light of the mood in parliament and among the electorate. Munich illustrated vividly the advantages which an aggressive militarized state under authoritarian direction possessed, when face to face with governments which were responsible to the popular will.

Another weighty consideration that contributed to the acceptance of the Munich pact was the weakness of the Anglo-French fighting

---

[3] Not unrepresentative of those who thought that a Russo-German clash lay in the offing was the sober and respected English diplomatic historian, H. W. V. Temperley, who wrote, "Everything suggests that Hitler purposes in the future the maintainance of a defensive in the West, while his active designs are in the East. . . . His desire for eastward expansion remains unchanged. . . . If Germany wants the Ukraine she will ultimately have to fight the Soviet Republic. But her line of penetration may be peaceful and economic, at any rate for some time, and it at least avoids all conflict with either England or France. . . ." A. J. Grant and H. W. V. Temperley, *Europe in the Nineteenth and Twentieth Centuries* (New York, 1939), pp. 684-685. Written in November, 1938.

services compared with those at the command of Hitler. The disparity appeared most dangerous in airpower; as matters stood London and Paris were open to aerial bombardment by the Luftwaffe. The ease with which the Japanese had bombed Shanghai, and the ill-fortunes of Madrid and Barcelona in the Spanish Civil War had deepened popular horror of bombing. And it was believed that a swift overwhelming stroke from the air might decide a war in a matter of days. Therefore it was elementary wisdom, some men thought, to yield to Hitlerian demands and gain time to build up capacity for fighting.

A definitive judgment as to whether the anti-German bloc was militarily more powerful in the autumn of 1938 than when war actually broke out a year later must await fuller information, but one or two relevant points are clear. On the one hand is the fact that the West in 1939 no longer had the Czech war potential on its side, Czech soldiers, matériel, and the extensive armament industry. But British power in the air was greater in 1939 than a year earlier. Was it, however, stronger relative to the Luftwaffe? Tentatively it may be ventured that the Anglo-French partnership was somewhat more battleworthy in 1939 than in 1938. And it is apparent that national unity and popular readiness to fight in Britain and France had grown in the intervening year. To the strengthened will to fight the repeated Anglo-French diplomatic efforts to save the peace, crowned by Munich, had definitely contributed.

By accepting the Munich accord and by refusing to invite Russia to share in the prefatory deliberations, the western nations estranged the policymakers in the Kremlin. Though it is debatable, it may be that the Soviet Union would automatically have taken up arms if war had resulted from the Sudeten crisis. At any rate it seemed to the Russians that extravagant concessions had been made to the Third Reich at Munich with the sinister aim of encouraging a Nazi attack on the Socialist Commonwealth. Russia now reverted to her older posture of diplomatic aloofness and the Franco-Russian "alliance" of 1935 crumbled.

Last of all, the Sudeten crisis accented the eclipse of the League. All that the Assembly attempted was a pious declaration that the dispute could be pacifically adjusted and an expression of hope that no nation would fight to achieve its objectives.

After Munich

In spite of the comforting "peace in our time" hypothesis, Munich might prove no more than the merest truce, a respite, as was intimated by the general upbuilding of armaments that ensued. Italy resounded with intensified agitation over irredentas, stimulated by the belief that the Anglo-French combination was effete and helpless. For fifteen solid minutes the Fascist chamber rang with wild shouts of "Tunisia, Corsica, Savoia."

After Munich, constitutional changes were effected in the truncated Czech Republic which gave home-rule to Slovakia and to Carpatho-Ukraine (Ruthenia), but that accommodation lasted only a few short months. Polemics between Czech and Slovak politicians, separatist commotion among some of the Slovaks, and alleged abuse of the small German minority by Czechs supplied Hitler with pretexts for breaking the Munich compact and the utter destruction of Czechoslovakia.

Out of a clear sky in March, 1939, German troops swooped down upon and occupied the Czech land without encountering any resistance. Most of the area was then defined as a German protectorate under the direction practically of German officials; once more the Nazis had followed:

> The law of Nature we all know
> The good old rule; the ancient plan,
> That he should take who has the power
> And he should keep who can.

By that deed Germany had taken control over a region inhabited almost wholly by non-Germans, in flat transgression of the principle of self-determination to which the Führer had previously appealed when pushing out Reich boundaries. The Czech Protectorate contained industries capable of an armament production almost equal to that of Italy.

At the same time a status of nominal independence was bestowed upon the Slovak counties, though in reality policies would be decided in Berlin, and Carpatho-Ukraine was annexed to Hungary, which had ruled it before World War I. Those startling events wrought with revolutionary force upon European diplomacy, more exactly upon the policy of Britain which had now learned that appeasement had not appeased. Presently Hitler compelled Lithuania to surrender the Memelland, adjoining East Prussia, and under the German flag before 1919.

The Axis Stiffens

Common interests and common ambitions—prestige and power— had impelled Germany and Italy in 1936 to form the Berlin-Rome Axis. That bond was reinforced in the next year by a treaty directed

avowedly against "international Communism"—the Anti-Comintern
Pact, the original version of which bore the signatures of Germany
and Japan. The Axis, as has been explained, worked in assisting
Franco's Rebels to victory in Spain. Mussolini smiled upon the phenomenal extension of German territory in central Europe and cast
about for suitable compensation for himself.

British diplomacy in the meantime bestirred itself to loosen if not
to disrupt the bonds which linked Italy to Germany and to mitigate
the bitter antagonism which the Ethiopian controversy had provoked.
Mussolini welcomed British overtures for he preferred greater freedom
of diplomatic activity than exclusive reliance on German friendship
permitted. On Britain's initiative friendly official letters and visits
were exchanged, gentlemen's agreements respecting Mediterranean
and African questions were initialled, Fascist transgressions of the
non-intervention understanding on Spain were winked at, and Foreign Minister Anthony Eden, who advocated stiff resistance to the
Italian dictator, walked the political plank. Anglo-Italian rapprochement reached a high point in a pact of April, 1938, in which Mussolini
disclaimed any desire to annex Spanish territory; he promised to reduce the Italian garrison in Libya, which menaced Egypt, and Britain
agreed to press for international recognition of Italian sovereignty
over Ethiopia. It was stipulated that both nations would respect the
territory of the other and refrain from hostile propaganda. Since
France also initiated diplomatic conversations with Italy it was possible for publicists to believe that the Stresa Front of pre-Ethiopian
days was by way of being resurrected.

That, however, was not on the cards. Tension developed afresh
when Italy in April, 1939, invaded Albania. Since 1927 the two countries were linked in defensive alliance and commercial activity had
quietly drawn the Balkan state into Fascismo's coils. Then on Good
Friday of 1939, with little or no warning, Fascist forces descended
upon the tiny realm of artless King Zogu. To conquer Albania presented no serious problems and Mussolini soon added the title of
Albanian King to the crown of Italy.

Mastery over Albania made Italy more thoroughly the ruler of
the Adriatic than ever, increased Italy's timber resources, and brought
Italy small Albanian oil fields. Beyond that, Yugoslavia's strategic
position was weakened and Greece looked with genuine alarm upon
the Fascist troops along her frontier. As for Britain and France, they
formally acquiesced in the ill-fortune that had befallen Albania, while
Hitler was fervent with his applause.

Nazi ties with Fascismo were drawn tighter in May, 1939, when the two states completed a precise military alliance that was to run for ten years. Among other things, the treaty bound each signatory to support the other with all its fighting strength in case of war, though there may have been a secret codicil allowing Italy to expand her armaments before carrying out the pledge. Confident of Nazi support and friendship, Mussolini could press his demands upon France and Britain in the Mediterranean area more vigorously; and the alliance encouraged Hitler in his still unfulfilled territorial ambitions. As if to seal the pact arrangements were made for the emigration of the German-feeling folk in the Italian Tyrolese province who desired to leave.[4]

Britain's New Course

From the crowded diplomatic chronicles of the late spring and summer of 1939 it is possible to deal only with the more essential developments which reached their fateful culmination in the outbreak of World War II.[5] The total dismemberment of Czechoslovakia, and after that the Italian occupation of Albania brought the Anglo-French policy of purchasing peace by appeasement crashing to the earth. Promptly, British diplomacy was given a radically different orientation and France followed along afterward.

The outward signs of Britain's new course were three: guarantees of assistance to certain east European nations whose independence and integrity might be challenged by the Axis partnership; an attempt to organize a "peace-front" of the European countries which desired the maintenance of the status quo, the Soviet Union among them; and the intensification of British preparations to fight, one of whose remarkable features was the adoption of peacetime conscription and popular acceptance of that innovation with surprisingly little grumbling.

Not long after Czechoslovakia was destroyed, Nazi diplomacy and propaganda concentrated on the Danzig Free State and the districts of Poland inhabited by men of German speech, perennial "danger spots" ever since the making of the Versailles Treaty. With customary gusto Hitler renewed demands earlier made upon Poland for the recovery of Danzig and the cession of a strip of Polish territory for transportation purposes across to East Prussia—a corridor across the Polish Corri-

---

[4] By a plebiscite, whose outcome was reported in January, 1940, a substantial majority expressed a desire for citizenship in the Third Reich and presently many moved off bag and baggage, being compensated by the Italian government for their properties.

[5] For a short German version of the coming of the war, consult Alfred von Wegerer, "The Origins of this War: a German View," *Foreign Affairs*, XVIII (1940), 700-718.

dor. If Poland concurred then Germany would allow her rights of way to Danzig and would guarantee Poland's boundaries against abridgment.

To the Polish policymakers it seemed that surrender to Germany on these points would invite a repetition of the ancient fable in which the camel, permitted to thrust his nose into the master's tent, eventually crowded the master out. To accept the Danzig demand would have placed Poland eternally at Germany's mercy. Had not Frederick II of Prussia observed that "he who rules Danzig and the mouth of the Vistula has more power than the king in Warsaw?"

The somber fate of Czechoslovakia, as indeed the dominant trend of Hitlerian diplomacy in general, supported the Polish reasoning that one concession to Germany would be succeeded by another demand. The Poles, therefore, declined to acquiesce. Whereupon press and radio of the Third Reich filled the atmosphere with lurid tales of persecution systematically and ruthlessly inflicted upon the helpless German-speaking minority dwelling under Poland's flag. Superheated propaganda worked its evil work upon the undisciplined emotions of Germans everywhere.

At that point Great Britain promised to render all the support in its power to Poland if she decided to fight to preserve her integrity. That pledge symbolized the end of appeasement, though it would not be possible for Britain to go far in honoring the commitment without the cooperation of the Soviet Union.[6] The guarantee to Poland, which was in the nature of a "blank cheque," came after the Warsaw government had rejected Nazi demands concerning Danzig and the Corridor according to the British view; and testimony from the Polish side substantiated that as fact. But in the Nazi interpretation the British pledge preceded the Polish reply and to a considerable extent encouraged Polish obduracy and bellicosity and therewith further mistreatment of the German minority in Poland.

Presently Poland gave a reciprocal promise of aid to Britain in time of need and just before the onset of World War II those assurances were incorporated in a conventional Anglo-Polish Treaty of Mutual Assistance to be valid for five years.[7] After Italy seized Albania, Britain working jointly with France, guaranteed the independence of Greece, of Rumania and, in a more limited manner, of Turkey. Brit-

---

[6] The French government gave Poland a similar pledge of assistance.

[7] An unpublished supplement obligated Britain to aid Poland only if her boundaries were violated by Germany—not the Soviet Union—and called for mutual cooperation in case German forces attacked Danzig, Lithuania, or the Low Countries.

ain provided credits, having the character of political subsidies, to certain of the "guaranteed" countries for the purchase of military equipment.

These special and binding commitments in eastern Europe represented a revolutionary departure from the diplomatic policies which Britain had persistently followed. In point of fact the only precedent in British history for these guarantees of boundaries in eastern Europe was a pledge to defend the frontier of the Ottoman Empire against Imperial Russia given in 1878 and never put to the test. Inside Germany Britain's new course was officially construed as a stratagem to fence the Reich in by an armed coalition, preparatory to an attack— the same doctrine of encirclement that had attained such wide currency before World War I.

But from the British standpoint the reversal of policy was necessitated by the challenge to "the just equilibrium of Europe," made by a swollen and still unsatisfied Nazidom. After the German march into Prague the tug-of-war in Britain between the "appeasers" and their opponents had given way to a mood of grim but united apprehension. The conviction had deepened in all circles of the British community that Germany aspired to dominate Europe by physical force and therefore endangered Britain's power and security and liberties, not less than had Hohenzollern Germany or the France of the Revolution and Napoleon, or the France of Louis XIV, or the Spain of Philip II.

Popular British distrust of and ill-will toward the Third Reich was heightened by the manner in which Hitler had repeatedly broken promises and flouted international engagements. "We neither intend nor wish to annex Austria." "All we ask is the Sudetenland." "We assure all our neighbors of the integrity of their territory." Thus the Führer had spoken but deeds spoke so much louder. Small wonder that Britishers concluded that Hitlerian Germany was utterly untrustworthy and perfidious. The British mind revolted, too, against the philosophy and many of the domestic practices of National Socialism which clashed so violently with the British democratic outlook and tradition.

Britishers who feared for the safety of kingdom and realm clasped hands with their countrymen who were imbued with a lively sense of democratic and humanitarian mission. Nationalist and ideologue alike —the one antagonistic to the German state, the other full of hatred for Hitlerian cruelty—subscribed to diplomatic measures which involved real hazards of war with the voracious Axis coalition. Not since 1914 had Britain been so nearly of one mind, united in the resolution that no more territorial changes should be brought about in Europe by force or threat of force under peril of armed conflict with Great Britain itself.

If the Chamberlain Ministry had hesitated to implement that national determination by appropriate diplomatic undertakings, such as the guarantee to Poland, it would almost certainly have been hurled from office and that swiftly. Inescapably the British pledge bucked up Poland, so that, unless the mood in Germany modified, pacific settlement of the Polish-German dispute was not to be expected.[8]

The "Peace Front" Quest

In the quest for a "peace front" to discourage further German expansion, Britain solicited an understanding with Soviet Russia, such as had been contrived with Imperial Russia 'under somewhat similar circumstances in 1907. Throughout the late spring and summer of 1939 negotiations for a political agreement and exploratory military conversations were undertaken in Moscow by representatives of the two countries, with Frenchmen sitting in. What the British had in mind was a treaty of mutual assistance requiring each signatory to aid the other in case of war resulting from support given to "victims of aggression." At the same time, under cover, the Soviets were being wooed by Germany. In the end the Kremlin spurned the Anglo-French overtures and yielded to Hitler.

On the failure of British diplomacy to attract the Soviet policymakers into the "peace-front," a huge volume of speculation, learned and popular, has accumulated. In the absence of anything like complete official evidence in the case only a tentative appraisal may be ventured.

Deep dissimilarities between Britain and the great Eurasian power, as well as specific issues, played their part in frustrating the design for a grand alliance against the Axis, or better the Triangle, for Japan too must have figured in the exchanges and the decisions. A generation of open or scarcely veiled antagonism, a fog of distrust, could not be dispelled overnight and replaced by a trustful partnership. Between the Soviet Union and the Anglo-French bloc a wide ideological chasm yawned; the men in the Kremlin regarded capitalist democracy with a suspicious eye just as policymakers in the West mistrusted Soviet Communism.

Given such wide disagreement, such tensions, distrusts, and fears,

---

[8] It is the writer's opinion, grounded in part on the Polish climate of opinion as he observed it in July, 1939, that even without western assurances of help the Warsaw government would have repulsed Hitler's demands to the end.

it is not hard to understand why each camp questioned the good faith of the other. The Russian assumption that the West aimed at deflecting German military energies eastward—an assumption that had been heightened by Anglo-French diplomacy in the Spanish Civil War and by the Munich accord—was evidently not modified by the Anglo-French guarantee to defend Poland. "We will not pull other people's chestnuts out of the fire," shouted Stalin in March, 1939, and that theme with variations was iterated and reiterated by top Soviet spokesmen and the official press.

In western circles there was skepticism concerning Soviet fighting power and indeed regarding the very stability of the Stalinist regime. Russians, on their part, had real doubts about the quality of the Anglo-French military machine.

These differences might have been by-passed if the diplomatic negotiators had been able to reach an accommodation on particular questions. The Soviet leaders set as their price for a treaty a free hand in the Baltic Republics and Finland and the right to move troops across Poland in the event of war with Germany. Consulted on that point the Polish government withheld its approval; in spite of the gravity of the German peril the Poles would never voluntarily allow a single Russian soldier to set foot in the Republic. Temperamentally unsympathetic to Russians and the Soviet way of life, Polish policymakers could not rid their minds of "old unhappy far-off things and battles long ago."

As for the Russian claim to the Baltic nations, that was too much for Britain to accept. Standing forth as the champion and guarantor of small nations, British diplomacy could hardly have consented to the domination of the Baltic states by their old Russian master. Such were the direct causes of the breakdown of the effort to establish an understanding between the Soviets and the West, and to form an overwhelming peace front against the Nazi-Fascist menace.

Culmination

The light along the German-Polish highway had changed in the meantime from the yellow of caution to the bright red of imminent danger. German demands for Danzig and the Corridor had been repeated in shrill tones, the ten-year Non-aggression Pact of 1934 with Poland and the British naval limitation treaty had been tossed into Hitler's wastebasket with scant ceremony. Poles were warned of the doom in store for their country if they refused to come to terms but Polish policymakers firmly declared their intention to hold what they had.

Neither disputant was in a mood to budge. The press, the radio, the movies in each nation harped upon the atrocious outrages visited upon their fellow-nationals in the other country; mutual animosities and old deep-seated hatreds rose to fever heat.

Pointed reminders sped from London (and Paris) to Berlin warning that an attack upon Poland would automatically mean war with the western powers. For example, Lord Halifax, Foreign Minister, frankly declared on June 29, 1939:

> We know that if the security and independence of other countries are to disappear, our own security and our own independence will be gravely threatened. We know that if international law and order is to be preserved, we must be prepared to fight for its defense. In the past we have always stood out against the attempt by any single power to dominate Europe at the expense of the liberties of other nations and British policy is, therefore, only following the inevitable line of its own history if such an attempt were to be made again. . . . In the event of further aggression we are resolved to use at once the whole of our strength in fulfillment of our pledges to resist it.

That was a bald reassertion of the ancient British dogma that to safeguard Britain's own security no single country would be permitted to dominate the continent, stated in language that even the humblest intelligence could understand. Nothing there about a Machiavellian plot to encircle the Axis, a subject on which German propaganda was loudly beating the tom-toms of war.

To all representations the Germans retorted that British diplomacy was interfering in the affairs of eastern Europe where Britain had small direct interest. If Britain were sincerely desirous of keeping the peace, instead of seeking grounds for the destruction of the Third Reich, then she would compel Poland to yield to the Nazi demands, it was said. And, it was added, if Germany took up arms it would do so only to redress intolerable wrongs and to defend herself against provocative and covetous enemies.

Little suspected by outsiders, diplomatists of Nazidom and of the Soviet Union were secretly carrying on momentous conversations on commercial and political topics. Anyone at the time who suggested that these nations might arrange a rapprochement was apt to be labelled a fool or a knave. Had not spokesmen of each nation been delivering venomous verbal attacks on the other power for years? Was the conviction not well-grounded that the Nazis cherished designs upon the fat lands of the Ukraine and the rich mineral wealth of the

Soviet state? That had been schematically described in bold characters in *Mein Kampf* and in many utterances of the Führer.[9] Was it not Hitler's paramount conviction—or fanaticism—that the Soviet Union was the supreme danger to European civilization?

In spite of all that, the Nazis eagerly desired an arrangement with the Kremlin that would assure them of the neutrality of the great Eurasian power in the immediate future. If such a deal were made Britain and France might conceivably be frightened into abandoning Poland—another Munich in fact. Or, if not—and war came—the benevolent neutrality of Russia would brush away the Nazi nightmare of serious hostilities on two fronts.

The basic line of Soviet strategy in negotiating a "pact of friendship" with Germany is susceptible to more than one interpretation. Two main strands of interpretation have had respectable partisans. In the thinking of some observers the Soviets chose an understanding with the Nazis on the hypothesis that Germany and the western bloc would go to war, mutually deplete their resources, and leave Russia in an unchallengeable position in Europe. Another group, however, believes that the Kremlin policy was predicated on the conviction that sooner or later Russia and Germany would fight and, since the Soviet chiefs lacked confidence in Russia's ability to make war with Germany successfully, it was simply wisdom for them to procrastinate and gain time in which to improve the capacity for war—for a war in which Japan might attack on the east while Germany thrust in from the west.[10]

Whatever the motives, the Berlin and Moscow governments startled the world, not least their own publics, on August 21, with the spectacular news that trade and non-aggression treaties had been completed. Secret agreements apparently provided territorial gains for each signatory in the lands lying between them. Seemingly highly gratified over the outcome of the bargaining Soviet Foreign Commissar Molotov exclaimed that the agreement "eliminates the danger of war between Germany and the Soviet Union." Whether intended to do so or not the Soviet government by making the accord with Germany encouraged Hitler to plunge ahead in his Polish ambitions.

[9] At a Nuremberg party Congress in 1936, for instance, Hitler said, "If Germany possessed the Ural Mountains with their immense wealth of raw materials, Siberia with its vast forests, and the Ukraine with its extensive wheat fields, the country and the National Socialists would be bountifully supplied."

[10] It is said that Stalin initiated conversations with Hitler for a partnership as early as mid-1934 and that diplomatic exchanges continued spasmodically until the making of the August, 1939 pact. J. Alsop and R. Kintner, *American White Paper*, (7th ed., New York, 1940), p. 52.

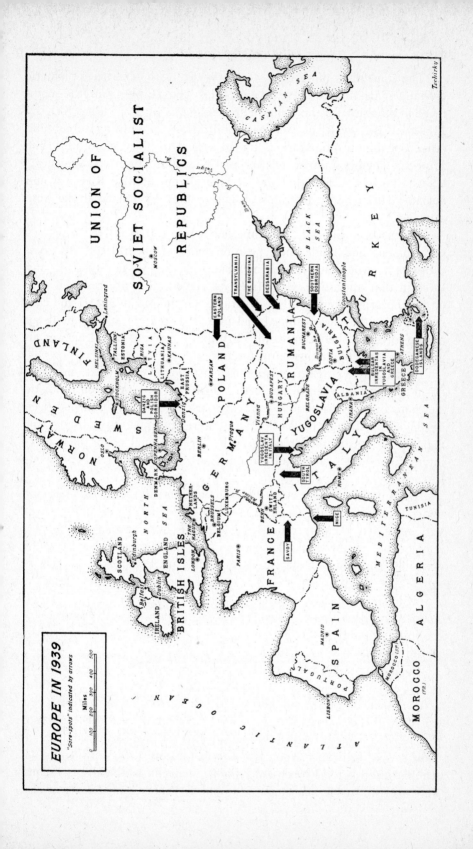

EUROPE IN 1939

"Sore-spots" indicated by arrows

Miles
0   100 200 300 400 500

UNION OF SOVIET SOCIALIST REPUBLICS

FINLAND

NORWAY

SWEDEN

BRITISH ISLES

SCOTLAND

IRELAND ENGLAND

NORTH SEA

DENMARK

NETHER-LANDS

BELGIUM

LUXEMBURG

FRANCE

SPAIN

PORTUGAL

GERMANY

SWITZ-ERLAND

ITALY

POLAND

EAST PRUSSIA

LATVIA

ESTONIA

LITHUANIA

HUNGARY

YUGOSLAVIA

RUMANIA

BULGARIA

ALBANIA

GREECE

TURKEY

CASPIAN SEA

BLACK SEA

MEDITERRANEAN SEA

ATLANTIC OCEAN

MOROCCO (SP.)

MOROCCO (FR.)

ALGERIA

TUNISIA

DANZIG AND POLISH CORRIDOR

EASTERN POLAND

TRANSYLVANIA

THE BUKOWINA

BESSARABIA

SOUTHERN DOBRUDJA

DODECANESE ISLANDS

IRREDENTAS IN YUGOSLAVIA AND GREECE

SOUTH TIROL

YUGOSLAV IRREDENTA IN ITALY

NICE

SAVOY

Moscow

Leningrad

HELSINKI

OSLO

STOCKHOLM

TALLINN

RIGA

KAUNAS

WARSAW

BERLIN

Prague

Vienna

BUDAPEST

BELGRADE

BUCHAREST

Sofia

TIRANA

ATHENS

Constantinople

Edinburgh

Belfast

Dublin

LONDON

THE HAGUE

BRUSSELS

BERN

PARIS

MADRID

LISBON

ROME

TUNIS

Tschirky

The final days of August were crowded with feverish diplomatic exchanges, passionate press polemics, last-chance pleas for the maintenance of peace by the King of the Belgians, by Pope Pius XII, by President Roosevelt, as well as mobilizations of fighting forces and other last minute preparations for an appeal to physical force. Prime Minister Chamberlain in a letter to Chancellor Hitler of August 22 made it perfectly clear that the German alignment with Russia would not affect in any way Britain's pledge to stand by Poland if she were attacked.

"It has been alleged," Chamberlain wrote, "that if His Majesty's Government had made their position more clear in 1914 the great catastrophe would have been avoided. Whether or not there is any force in that allegation, His Majesty's Government are resolved that on this occasion there shall be no tragic misunderstanding. If the case should arise they are resolved and prepared to employ without delay all the forces at their command." Britain, in a word, would answer an appeal to force by an appeal to force.

People all over Europe, in those last hours of August, marched down the familiar road to war with surprising calmness, even fatalistic stoicism. But the exuberance and eagerness for the fray that had been displayed on the eve of World War I were conspicuously absent. For many a European, rendered jittery by international crisis piled upon international crisis, a fearful end must have seemed preferable to endless fears.

A scant ten days separated the conclusion of the Berlin-Moscow understanding from the German invasion of Poland. Poles, in the interval, intimated their readiness to negotiate in a normal diplomatic manner, but Hitler would not consent. Having drawn up a new set of demands, containing more extensive claims on Polish soil, Hitler asserted that the Warsaw government would not comply with them. At dawn on September 1, Germany's mighty forces were sent hurtling against Poland without so much as a declaration of war. Hitler's was the initiative and it was he who spurned the diplomatic pen in favor of the sword.

Poland summoned her western guarantors to carry out their promises of assistance—and that they did. Britain on September 3, faithful alike to her interests and her values, declared that a state of war existed with Germany. The self-governing Dominions with the exception of Eire loyally rallied to the support of the motherland, as in World War I. France, too, promptly withdrew the sword from the scabbard, for as the French ambassador in Berlin had said, "If Poland were overrun by Germany now, it would be France's turn next; or else

France would have to decline to the level . . . of Germany's vassal."

Italy, after a last-minute gesture to avert hostilities, about which there is still a good deal of mystery, chose to stand on the side-lines in a manner reminiscent of 1914. Soviet Russia, the United States, and Franco's Spain likewise proclaimed their neutrality.

So once more the fate and future of Europe's nations and peoples depended upon the uncertainties of war. Men remembered the melancholy prophecy uttered by Sir Edward Grey just before World War I, as he stood at the window of the Foreign Office, "The lamps are going out all over Europe; we shall not see them lit again in our lifetime."

★

WORLD WAR II

★

CHAPTER XXI

World War II: The Ascendancy of the Axis

The Call to Arms

THE martial enthusiasm that had greeted the European war in 1914 was notably lacking in 1939. Just as the war started the present writer happened to be in Berlin and in London. The spirit in both capitals, as he observed it, was apathetic, bewildered; and there was grim resignation to what had come to pass. World War I had taught large masses of Europeans something of the havoc and horror another struggle would entail for individuals and for society. Progress in weapons of combat implied greater sufferings than the struggle of a quarter century earlier had involved.

Besides, the idea of resorting to physical force to solve international problems was more widely regarded as a mark of unenlightenment and savagery than at any time since the emergence of the European national state system, some four centuries ago. And yet, once the call to battle had sounded men and women willingly bore sacrifices in the national cause, though only slowly did the western belligerents reawaken to the realities of total war. Almost six years were to elapse before the grueling contest was over. More fully than ever before in history the whole globe was drawn into the maelstrom and because of the destruction of life and the devastation of property continental Europe was reduced to a state that defied description.

The Defeat of Poland

Reversing the broad strategy of World War I Germany struck first in eastern Europe, against Poland, while standing on the defensive in the west. For all their spirit and bravery the Poles were utterly incapable of halting the great Nazi war-machine unless effective pressure was exerted upon the enemy by France and Great Britain, and such help failed to materialize.

The Germans opened the Polish campaign at a furious tempo.

The Luftwaffe, screaming destruction from the skies, smashed aerodromes; planes near the ground strafed Polish troops; and tanks and
armored columns rolled rapidly over the dry Polish soil carrying everything before them. Stunned and demoralized, the Poles fought heroically, an epic of rare gallantry being written in the stubborn defense
of Warsaw. In a surprise move Russian troops marched into eastern
Poland proclaiming themselves liberators of the populations of the
eastern provinces. After three weeks of fighting formal Polish resistance ceased. The governmental authorities escaped abroad, coming to
rest eventually in London, where they set up a government in exile,
which the Allies recognized as legitimate.

At the end of October a German-Soviet treaty was presented to
the world, which once more dismembered the Polish state. Germany
appropriated the lion's share of Poland, half of it being annexed outright to the Third Reich and the remainder was organized as a "Protectorate." The USSR was acknowledged as sovereign over about
two fifths of the erstwhile Republic.

Inside the conquered nation the alien occupiers ruled without pity.
The agonies of hell descended upon the hapless Poles. Nazis compelled
their Polish subjects to produce for war purposes or hauled them off
wholesale for compulsory work in the Reich, evacuating in all perhaps
as many as 3,000,000. So enormous and revolting were the Nazi crimes
against the Poles that a new word was coined to describe it: *genocide,*
that is, the studied and cruel extermination of a nation. Poland's educated classes were the focal point of barbarity, for they largely provided public leadership and organized underground resistance to the
conqueror.

Similar, though on an even more gruesome scale, was the lot of
Polish Jews. Herding them into indescribable reservations was only a
minor form of Jewish persecution. Sadistic massacre was the preferred
Nazi method employed against Jewry and massacres in time raged
from western France to eastern Ukraine. It seems probable that fully
4,000,000 Jews, Polish citizens for the greater part, died as the result
of starvation, disease, and murder in every terrible variety. It would
be hard indeed to find in European annals a blacker page of man's
inhumanity to man.

Soviet procedures in eastern Poland were less outrageous, but
death was the penalty meted out to resisters, and hundreds of thousands of Poles were deported to the USSR. In spite of all (or because
of all), in spite of the national reputation for romanticism, the Poles
displayed a valor and a conscience unsurpassed in the war. Secret
underground forces, which in time permeated the whole country,

vexed the conqueror, supplied useful information to the Allies, and in July, 1944, organized a heroic though futile insurrection in Warsaw.[1]

The USSR Expands

Seemingly in connection with the dismemberment of Poland the Nazis assigned the Kremlin a free hand in the republics along the Baltic. At any rate the USSR arranged treaties with Estonia, Latvia, and Lithuania which brought the Soviets naval and air stations in each country. To allegations that Russia contemplated full control in these areas Molotov bluntly retorted, ". . . we declare that all nonsense about sovietizing the Baltic countries is only to the interest of our common enemy of anti-Soviet provocateurs."

Demands made upon Finland for bases and Finnish territory adjacent to Leningrad were sturdily rejected. Whereupon the Soviet Union declared war on Finland, a neighbor, in the words of President Roosevelt, "so infinitesimally small that it can do no injury to the Soviet Union." For more than three months the unequal Russo-Finnish struggle persisted, the Finns fighting amazingly well and earning the sympathy and applause of the outer world. Britain and France indeed made preparations to assist the Finns and had the USSR expelled from the League of Nations as an aggressor—the last futile gesture of the League—which, inescapably, heightened Soviet hatred of the Atlantic powers.

In time the Red fighting machine overbore the Finns and in March of 1940 imposed a victor's peace. The USSR secured the coveted bases and pressed the frontier one hundred miles back from Leningrad; Finns in the ceded district moved across into Finland. While the Russians set to work remedying the defects in their military organization which the campaign had revealed, the Finns nursed hopes of revenge and recovery of lost territory when conditions were propitious.

After the defeat of France in June of 1940 (described below), the USSR organized farcical elections in the southern Baltic Republics and then completely incorporated them into the Soviet realm. At the same time Rumania was induced to transfer Bessarabia and the northern section of the Bukovina. Except for the Bukovina, these areas had belonged to Imperial Russia, but in none did the Soviets have a clear case for possession or anything like a clear case, by the test of the nationality of the populations involved. Rather it was the contention of the USSR that these districts were needed for national security.

[1] The Polish resistance, which may be taken as characteristic of similar movements in other countries that fell under Axis rule, has been graphically depicted by Jan Karski, *The Story of a Secret State* (Boston, 1944).

The West and the Sea

Not long after the destruction of Poland, Hitler offered a peace plan proposing mutual guarantees of security in Europe, limitation on armaments, and the restitution of the German colonies taken away at Versailles. But the Allies answered that overture with a prompt and brusque negative. The Nazi diplomatic record and the lengthy list of broken promises had utterly destroyed faith in the German word. Britain and France, who evidently believed that a domestic insurrection against the Nazis was in the making, had no wish to negotiate a peace which at best would be an uneasy truce. The august London *Times* ridiculed the Hitlerian "olive branch" as "terms of no peace." The governments of Belgium and Holland a little later offered to serve as mediators between the belligerents, but their initiative yielded no positive results.

So uneventful was the war on the western front that it was labelled a "phony" war. French troops took up their positions in and along the Maginot fortifications and a British expeditionary army, almost identical in size with that of 1914, was landed in France and placed under the supreme direction of the French commander-in-chief, General Marie Gustave Gamelin. Supplies and munitions flowed across the Channel without interruption and measures were adopted to integrate more fully the fighting resources of the two nations.

But except for aerial "dogfights," artillery duels, and occasional sorties toward or over the German border the western theatre was ominously quiet in the first half dozen months of the war. Neither side undertook a major offensive. Nor were there heavy Nazi air raids on British and French cities, against which elaborate precautions had been taken, such as the annoying and dangerous nightly blackout. True, Nazi planes bombed British naval stations repeatedly and Britain retaliated on enemy fleet bases, but the expected lightning war in the air failed to develop.

On the sea, the British fleet clamped a blockade on shipments of all kinds to Germany, starting the slow but deadly process that had contributed so vitally to victory in World War I. But through the first eight months of the new war, ships were allowed to pass to small European neutrals and to Italy and part of their cargoes eventually found their way into Germany. In the hope of keeping Italy neutral, the British blockade was especially lenient on the commerce of that country.

Germany appealed immediately to the U-boat weapon of which she had about fifty seven, only half of them fit for operations beyond the North Sea. In the first week of the war submarines sank eleven ships, though the British convoy service effectively safeguarded the transit of goods from the United States. Submarines also torpedoed a heavy British battleship—the *Royal Oak*—at anchor in the fleet base at Scapa Flow, and the airplane carrier, *Courageous.* Magnetic mines, intended primarily to paralyze traffic to London, blew up several ships and endangered every vessel that moved in British waters.

German surface raiders did considerable damage to shipping on the high seas, one, the formidable "pocket battleship," the *Graf Spee,* sinking 50,000 tons in the South Atlantic. Pursued by three British cruisers, which inflicted heavy damage, the *Graf Spee* took refuge in Montevideo harbor; four days later (December 17, 1939) the ship was scuttled to avoid total destruction or capture. It was Britain's first naval triumph of the war. The German liner, *Columbus,* committed suicide in the Atlantic after sighting British men-of-war. In an act of courageous daring British sailors raided the German prison ship, *Altmark,* tender of the *Graf Spee,* in Norwegian coastal waters, and released some three hundred imprisoned British merchant seamen.

Blitzkrieg in Western Europe

The uncanny calm in the west was violently ruptured in April of 1940. To prevent German ore ships from steaming along the coast of Norway, the Allies announced on April 8, that mines were being laid, despite the protest of the Norwegian government over infringement of its neutrality. That night, the Germans heavily attacked the British fleet station at Scapa Flow, causing considerable destruction. Next day German land, air, and seaforces stormed into neutral Denmark. Without any show of resistance, the Danish government acquiesced in the status of a Nazi protectorate.

Simultaneously, the Hitlerian forces moved against Norway, on the pretext that the Allies were contemplating seizure of the country. The Norwegians, who received some aid from Britain and France, sturdily resisted the invader. Sharp naval encounters took place, and very stiff fighting occurred in the north, around Narvik, but German command of the air doomed Norway to defeat.

Allied forces left Norway under circumstances that were reminiscent of the Dardanelles fiasco of World War I, though the larger part of the splendid Norwegian merchant marine passed to the Allies. Chivalrous King Haakon transferred his government to London. The Nazis installed as chief executive of Norway, Vidkun Quisling, whose name promptly was adopted as a synonym for self-seeking traitor. For five years Quisling ruled in full glory, though not without resistance to his nazified regime, only to perish at the hands of a Norwegian firing squad when the Hitlerian realm crumbled.

For the Allies, the Nazi conquest of Norway was a bitter pill. German shipping could now traverse the Norwegian coast with little fear of molestation and strategic points could be exploited as submarine lairs and plane bases from which to harass Allied cargo carriers. Moreover, Sweden, though continuing to remain neutral, placed her resources, of which iron ore had the highest importance, more fully at the disposal of Germany. Lest Iceland be seized by Nazi strategists, British forces occupied that island.

Bad as was the Norwegian affair for the Allied cause it was soon dwarfed by the sledge-hammer blows delivered by the Germans in the spring of 1940 upon the Low Countries and France. Charging the Netherlands, Belgium, and Luxembourg with conduct unbecoming to neutrals, Hitler, on May 10, hurled his armies against those small, weakly-armed nations. Military tactics repeated those that had worked with such spectacular success in Poland—screaming dive-bombers, swift-charging panzer divisions, followed by swarms of parachutists and foot soldiers.

At that critical point in the war Neville Chamberlain, forsaken by many of his consistent supporters, turned over the British Prime Ministership to Winston Churchill, who surrounded himself with an all-party Cabinet, among others, the Labour chiefs, Clement Attlee and Ernest Bevin. Pugnacious, unconquerable, and eloquent, Churchill, who had long prepared himself for just such a challenge, infused fresh energy into the rather lackadaisical British war effort and inspirited the faint-hearted in a manner without close parallel in modern history. To defend the island kingdom against possible Nazi invasion, a volunteer Home Guard was hastily enrolled. Sensing to the full the dark perils that lay ahead, Churchill bluntly told his countrymen, "I have nothing to offer but blood, toil, tears and sweat."

Allied forces dispatched to the relief of the Low Countries availed little against the onrushing German torrent. That diversion was no doubt a strategic blunder for Allied military plans were predicated on an essentially defensive war, making full use of the admirable Maginot fortifications and obliging the enemy to take the offensive at every point. After the Nazis mercilessly bombed Rotterdam at a cost of some 30,000 civilian lives, active fighting in Holland came to an end. The Belgians held out longer, fighting desperately in places, but the weight of the enemy forces was overwhelming, and on May 28, King Leopold surrendered with the bulk of his army.

The Dunkirk Evacuation

In the meantime, the Germans had struck into France, piercing (May 12) the French defenses near Sedan, and a panzer column raced westward through Amiens to Abbéville on the English Channel, reaching it on May 21. By that bold German maneuver, British, French, and Belgian troops to the north were wholly separated from the main French armies. General Maxime Weygand, who had superseded the defense-minded Gamelin as supreme commander of the Allied forces, and who was spoken of as Marshal Foch's finest pupil, found himself in an exceedingly uncomfortable predicament. French counterthrusts from the south scarcely dented the German lines. Millions of French civilians in panic-stricken flight choked the highways which the troops needed for orderly withdrawal.

Allied armies in Flanders, British mostly, pulled back to Dunkirk, the sole port that the enemy had not captured or invested. Their situation appeared beyond redemption. Then occurred "a miracle of deliverance," one of the thrilling evacuations of history, though it was nothing new for British troops to find salvation on the seacoast.

While the skies over Dunkirk were dark with fighting planes and billowing clouds of smoke, while shell-fire converted the city itself into an earthly inferno, British naval men collected ships of every vintage and description (even rowboats) to remove the battered soldiers from the continent. Making thousands of trips to and from Dunkirk, British seamen, between May 29 and the night of June 3-4, hauled away some 225,000 Britishers and half as many other Allied soldiers.

The discipline of the Allied troops, the magnificent valor of the Royal Air Force (R.A.F.), and the superb cooperation of the British fleet robbed the Germans of their hope of enveloping the Dunkirk armies and indeed gave the evacuation the quality of a "glorious defeat." Yet behind them, the British left almost all their military equipment and stores and about 13,000 dead and 40,000 prisoners.

In the Dunkirk operations the Royal Navy lost ten destroyers and seventy five more were severely damaged—which were soon to be made up by the transfer of "over-age" destroyers by the United States. Admiral Bertram Ramsay, who had overall responsibility for the Dunkirk withdrawal, gained a fitting reward four years later, when, in his capacity of Supreme Allied Naval Commander, he directed the ferrying of Allied invasion armies back to France.

The German campaign in the west was skillfully planned and executed with amazing smoothness and coordination by the several branches of the armed services. German soldiers fought intrepidly and were little restrained by dictates of humanity or established customs of war. The comforting assumption cherished in British circles that the Hitler regime would crack up in a testing time was proved an utterly false and pernicious illusion. And worse was still to come.

The Conquest of France

Without pausing, the battle-happy Germans opened another offensive against the French on the Somme river, intending to knock the Third Republic completely out of the war. The Somme itself, full of water, stood as a natural barrier to armored columns, though the Germans had seized bridgeheads at several points. In the fighting to the north much of the French mechanized equipment, never large in comparison with the German resources, had been sacrificed but the French still had quantities of seventy five millimeter guns, which, if properly directed, could disable almost any enemy tank.

The Battle for France, a far vaster contest than any of World War I, began on June 3. Perhaps as many as 2,000,000 Germans were engaged, and about the same number of Allied troops, French overwhelmingly, but small, tough British detachments too. For a couple of days, the outcome seemed in doubt, both sides fighting desperately. But the Germans threw in reinforcements of men and matériel, especially tanks which fought in clusters of 200 or more, and the Luftwaffe attacks from the sky never slackened.

Then on June 10, Mussolini, thinking the war was virtually over, served notice that Italy had become a belligerent. The Germans, stepping up the tempo of fighting, smashed across the Seine. While three parts of the Nazi hosts converged irresistibly upon Paris, a fourth pushed toward the Maginot Line from the west.

Ten days after the beginning of the Battle of France, the Germans had crossed the Marne river in force. Broken and demoralized the French reeled southward in retreat. Parisians forsook their homes in a mass exodus and the French government moved first to Tours and later to Bordeaux. It would have been suicidal to try to defend Paris, so it was declared an open city, and the Germans poured into it.

On June 14, the soldiers of Hitler, accompanied by all the mechanical paraphernalia of the mightiest of military machines, marched triumphantly down the noble Champs Elysées. Over Napoleon's Arc de

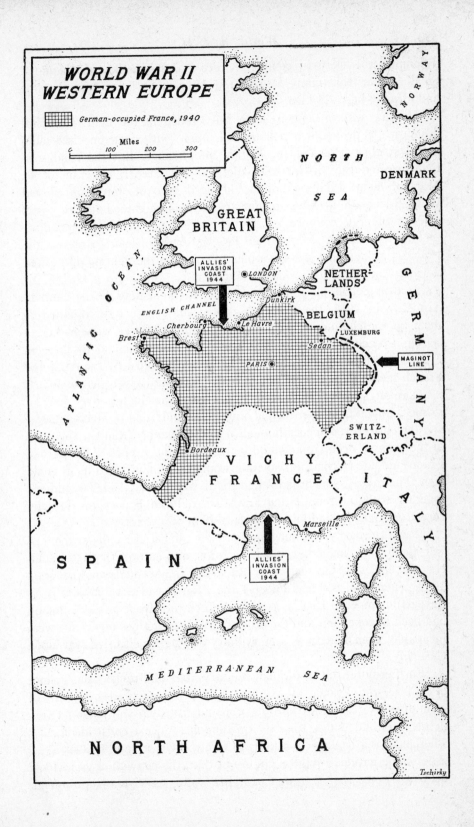

WORLD WAR II
WESTERN EUROPE

German-occupied France, 1940

Miles
0   100   200   300

NORWAY

NORTH
SEA
DENMARK

GREAT
BRITAIN

ALLIES'
INVASION
COAST
1944

LONDON

NETHER-
LANDS

GERMANY

ENGLISH CHANNEL

Dunkirk

BELGIUM

Cherbourg

Le Havre

LUXEMBURG

Brest

Sedan

MAGINOT
LINE

PARIS

Bordeaux

SWITZ-
ERLAND

VICHY
FRANCE

ITALY

ATLANTIC OCEAN

S P A I N

Marseille

ALLIES'
INVASION
COAST
1944

MEDITERRANEAN   SEA

N O R T H   A F R I C A

Tschirky

Triomphe the German conqueror raised the swastika of Nazidom. Small wonder that many men shared Mussolini's belief that the war had already been decided.

Hoping against hope to keep the French in the fight, Churchill dramatically proposed a real federal union, with common citizenship and a single parliament for Britain and France. But the conditions that inspired the British offer dictated the French rejection of it. Marshal Henri Philippe Pétain, the aged hero of Verdun in World War I, was made Premier on June 16, and he thought, as did Weygand, another veteran commander, that France must seek an immediate cessation of hostilities. By the close vote of thirteen to eleven the French Cabinet turned down a plea to continue the fighting and asked the victorious Axis for terms of surrender.

At Compiègne, on June 22, the site of the signing of the German Armistice in 1918, the French accepted the severe terms handed to them by the conqueror. All German prisoners of war were to be released, French military forces were to be disarmed and discharged, French warships were to anchor in harbors controlled by the Axis, and French merchantmen were not to leave port until given permission.

German soldiers, moreover, would garrison slightly over half of France, including the principal industrial and food-producing areas, and the entire French coastline down to the Spanish frontier; the costs of the army of occupation would be borne by the French. That part of France outside German jurisdiction would be administered by Frenchmen. The defeat, which had taken the lives of about 150,000 soldiers, together with the humiliating armistice, reduced France to a sorrier condition than she had known in more than 500 years.

It was primarily German superiority in almost every department of war, manpower, machines, esprit de corps, and enterprising commanders, coupled with the tactics of blitzkrieg, that beat down France in 1940. Then, too, whereas in 1914 the French had a valuable ally to the east in Imperial Russia, there was no eastern front in 1940. Poland had been knocked out and the other small eastern allies of France were incapable, even had they been willing, of waging effective war upon Germany.

Furthermore, the traditional military élan of France—the France of Valmy, the France of Verdun—had been impaired by years of civic disunity resulting from rancorous partisanship and personal vendettas in public affairs, from the unwillingness of extremist ideologues, whether of the Right or the Left, to forget their private, special interests for the national welfare. On top of that, the conviction was widely held in France that war was irrational folly, as so many prominent

French men of letters had persistently preached in the interval between World Wars, and it was also felt that France with her stationary population could not endure a repetition of the costly blood-spilling that had taken place from 1914 to 1918.

Upon the French mind, too, corrosive and bewildering Nazi psychological warfare played with no small effect—now warning of social revolution, now appealing to French pacific instincts, now charging that the French were the stupid cat's-paws of Britain, which would fight to the last drop of French blood. No inspired or inspiring French leader, no Clemenceau, or a Churchill emerged to counteract divisive influences. Yet when due allowance has been made for French internal weaknesses, the fact still stands that France was beaten principally because of the military advantages which the enemy possessed and exploited with consummate skill and boldness.

Vichy France

Under the leadership of Pétain, who was vested with the power of dictator, and a conservative junta, an authoritarian regime was set up at Vichy and a "Révolution Nationale" was put in motion. It was proclaimed that "work, the family, the soil, and the fatherland" would be "the sinews of the new national existence" of France. Here was an undisguised police state, manipulated part of the time by Pierre Laval, ex-Premier, and an avowed Naziphile. Left in a state of stupor and confusion by the swift march of events many Frenchmen acquiesced in the "new order" because they genuinely believed that there was no feasible alternative.

The men of Vichy framed their administration in keeping with the political philosophy and practice of Axis totalitarianism. Among the features of the regime were a gagged press and radio, state-controlled youth associations, the application of the Nazi laws on Jewry, and the dissolution of trade unions and associations of employers. A system of economic "corporatism" similar to Mussolini's was introduced and strikes and lockouts were declared unlawful.

French factories were set to work producing for the traditional national enemy, though many plants were stripped of their installations for the benefit of Germany. Crushing financial tribute was exacted. About 1,000,000 Frenchmen, furthermore, were shipped to Germany to work under compulsion, and some were even impressed into the German army. All males from sixteen to sixty and childless women from eighteen to forty five were conscripted for labor service. In Alsace-Lorraine, policies of Germanization and colonization from beyond the Rhine were methodically executed.

Elaborate prescriptions attempted to subject French agriculture
to state control, but in one way and another the peasantry largely
evaded the regulations. Though repressive and restrictive, the German
administration avoided a deliberate and systematic program to destroy
the French nation as was done among Poles and other "inferior folk"
in eastern Europe. In November, 1942, France was deprived of the
last vestige of independence when Hitler ordered the occupation of the
Vichy-ruled zone.

French hostility to the invader, tepid in the first months after the
Armistice, grew more and more vigorous and confident with time.
Increasing sabotage, increasing circulation of anti-Nazi literature,
and the formation of secret underground armies, testified that the
indomitable spirit of France was reviving. Terroristic abuse of French
resisters by the Gestapo—the concentration camp and the execution
of hostages—fostered rather than stifled enmity toward the Germans.[2]
In the end collaboration had narrowed to such a degree that the Vichy
regime found itself in isolation, hated and despised by most Frenchmen.

Outside France the supreme personification of national redemption
was General Charles de Gaulle, professional soldier, Undersecretary
of Defense just before the capitulation to Germany, who from his
London sanctuary summoned his countrymen to remember the revolutionary legacy of liberty, equality, and fraternity. "France," he assured them, "France has lost a battle, she has not lost the war."

De Gaulle organized the "Free French"—called later the "Fighting French"—movement and was recognized as chief of state by a
third of the French colonial empire. In time, after no little friction
with the United States, he was acknowledged by the Allies as the
first leader of France. In Africa a new French army was gathered
together. The prestige and authority of de Gaulle mounted as the war
wore on and upon the liberation of France, in 1944, he was welcomed
home as the foremost Frenchman of the hour, large in stature and
equally large in faith and courage, though somewhat deficient in diplomatic finesse and political acumen.

[2] Illustrative of German treatment of civilians was the case of Henri Maspero,
one of the most brilliant French scholars on Chinese affairs. Unable to find Maspero's son, who was an active Resister and eventually died fighting in the ranks
of the United States army, the Gestapo arrested and deported the scholar to
Buchenwald concentration camp. Half starved, sick of dysentery, Maspero nonetheless lectured to fellow inmates on Taoism, Chinese Buddhism, and Tibetan
Lamaism. A matter of weeks before Buchenwald was captured by the Allies,
Maspero died.

Italy Enters

Hitler's main ally, Italy, proclaimed neutrality in September, 1939, or rather non-belligerency, whatever that meant. Despite Mussolini's undisguised hostility to the Allies, the blockade was not applied upon Italy until March, 1940, when vital shipments of coal from Germany were cut off. By picturing the blockade as designed to strangle Italy, the tightly controlled Fascist press whipped up popular hatred of Britain.

Diplomatic conversations meantime were carried on by London and Paris with Mussolini, for the purpose of ensuring Italian neutrality. Both before and after he became Prime Minister, Churchill addressed friendly overtures to il Duce, once declaring that he had "never been the enemy of Italian greatness nor even at heart the foe of the Italian law-giver." The United States government offered to act as mediator between Italy and the Allies on matters that were in dispute, and promised to see that any understandings that were reached would be fulfilled after the war. At the same time the United States frankly warned the Fascist regime that if Italy fought alongside Germany, the United States might furnish material assistance to the Allies, and might even align itself with them in the fighting. But these moves profited nothing.

After conferring with high Fascist dignitaries in February and March, 1940, Sumner Welles, Undersecretary of State of the United States, reported that Italian antagonism toward Hitlerian arrogance was general, and so was aversion to involvement in the war. That was not, however, the attitude of il Duce.

Mussolini's personal lust for combat had, of course, been heralded from the housetop. Had he not written, for example, "War alone brings all human energies to their highest tension and imprints a stamp of nobility on peoples who have the courage to face it?" For all that, the Duce portrayed in the diary of Count Ciano, his son-in-law and Foreign Minister, vacillated, and had a hard time making up his mind to fight and holding fast to it. When the fatal decision to intervene was taken, the response of the Italian nation, Ciano wrote, was not enthusiastic.[3]

Arch-Fascists could, of course, rationalize that national interests would be furthered by successful war. Lavish imperialistic ambitions in French and British Africa might be realized; Corsica, Nice, and

[3] Hugh Gibson (Ed.), *The Ciano Diaries*, 1939-1943 (New York, 1946), p. 264.

Savoy might be gained; British naval ascendancy in the Mediterranean might be overthrown, and the Middle Sea might become, as in antiquity, a Roman lake. Beyond that, the Italian position in the Balkans might profitably be expanded. Fascist spokesmen occasionally referred to their country as "the greatest Balkan power."

Fascist chauvinism, moreover, was eager to repay Britain for its hostility during the Ethiopian conquest and to cut a larger figure in the high politics of the world. Conceivably, too, a brief bold adventure would divert the mind of discontented Italians from domestic tribulations. Mussolini waited to take the fatal leap until France was reeling and it seemed a sound calculation that Britain singlehanded could not long withstand the German and Italian totalitarianisms. Victory would mean not alone a triumph over the "pluto-democracies," but would set the seal upon "the new order of Fascism" of which il Duce had so often and so truculently spoken.

Crying, "It is the hour of destiny! To arms!" Mussolini ordered the nation into the war on June 10. Small land contingents were at once dispatched against France, and modest aerial warfare was waged against the Allies, who promptly retaliated. When France gave up, an armistice was arranged, broadly similar in content to the German document; it contained no promise of the cession of French territory. With France out of the fray Fascist arms turned to North Africa and the Balkans.

Britain Fights On

After Dunkirk, after the calamitous collapse of France, Britain stood alone, exposed to invasion and sea encirclement by the Axis, while Japan wrested away concessions in the Orient. In that perilous hour Churchill, strong in the strength which familiarity with Britain's past gave him, told his nation—and the world, "We shall fight on the beaches. We shall fight on the landing grounds. We shall fight on the fields and in the streets. We shall fight in the hills; we shall never surrender." Those clarion words caught the popular British fancy.

Pre-war political wranglings were submerged. Rival idealisms were tucked away as British factories hummed to repair the Dunkirk losses. The United Kingdom was transformed into a mighty fortress and arsenal. Against the peril of imminent German invasion Britain relied confidently upon the English Channel, upon the great navy, upon the R.A.F. whose fighting qualities had been convincingly demonstrated over northern France and Belgium. It was believed that the resources of the Dominions and world empire, together with prospective support from the United States, would somehow enable the island kingdom to win through.

Fearful lest the Axis would appropriate the strong French sea forces, the British navy, on July 3, blazed away at a large French squadron anchored off Algerian Oran and sank or damaged several ships. Before opening fire the British commander invited the French admiral in charge to order his vessels to go to British ports or to the French West Indies or, as an alternative, to scuttle them. The Frenchman made no answer, and most of his ships were either destroyed or seriously crippled.

French warcraft in British harbors were seized, though a spectacular attempt, in league with General de Gaulle, to capture the port of Dakar in west Africa went awry; the battleship, *Richelieu*, stationed there was, however, rendered useless. Untouched was the considerable part of the French navy based on Toulon, which was augmented by men-of-war that escaped the British assault at Oran. Britain's campaign against the French fleet roused bitter outcries from the men of Vichy, but they went unheeded in London, where the operations were justified by the elementary instinct of self-preservation.

The Spain of General Franco, now a "non-belligerent," exploited the international situation by seizing the international zone of Tangier, over the straits from Gibraltar, and by whipping up agitation for the recovery of the British-owned fortress of Gibraltar itself. Just why the victorious Axis refrained from occupying the Iberian peninsula, which would have brought them valuable strategic assets at small cost, is one of the unexplained mysteries of World War II.

It was a boon to Britain that when her fortunes were at their nadir Spain (and Portugal) kept out of the fighting. Three reasons appear to have dictated a course of "neutrality": the price which Spain asked of the Axis in exchange for intervention exceeded Hitler's willingness to pay; Franco's calculation that Britain could inflict heavier damage on Spain than vice-versa; and Spanish war-weariness after the bloody and harrowing civil strife of the late thirties.[4]

Shortly after the conquest of France, on July 19, Hitler came forth with an appeal to Britain to "listen to reason" and to arrange a "common-sense" peace through negotiation. Not for a moment was the gesture seriously considered in Britain even though the realm was in as precarious a plight as ever in its history. Replying for the nation,

[4] For a valuable report on Spain during the war, consult C. J. H. Hayes, *Wartime Mission in Spain* (New York, 1945). Hayes, a distinguished American historian, served as ambassador to Generalissimo Franco.

Foreign Minister Halifax asserted, "We realize that the struggle may cost us everything. . . . But we shall not stop fighting till freedom, for ourselves and others, is secure."

Nazi strategy of aerial warfare on the island kingdom, meanwhile, had passed through its initial phase: methodical though not particularly effective attacks upon Channel shipping. On August 8, 1940— anniversary of the blackest day for the German army in World War I —the fury of the Luftwaffe was at last loosed upon Britain itself and proceeded until the end of October. From airdromes in occupied western Europe, on the threshold of Britain, the German High Command planned to destroy British fighter aircraft and then to devastate London after the manner of Warsaw and Rotterdam. That accomplished, invasion of Britain would be undertaken.

Even though the Germans enjoyed a large numerical advantage in planes, British defenses ruined the grandiose Nazi calculations and shattered the myth that the Luftwaffe was invincible. Wave after wave of German fighters, or fighters escorting bombers, assailed the island kingdom. While the teeming metropolis of London was the primary target, provincial and seaport communities were badly hit by Dorniers and Henkels and the manufacturing city of Coventry was almost demolished. On one raid the Luftwaffe started 1,500 fires in the heart of London, wrecking or gutting many old and famous buildings. That was the most dramatic night of the air blitz of the capital, a night not soon to be forgotten by Londoners. (December 29, 1940.)

British Hurricanes and Spitfires and anti-aircraft guns robbed the Germans of their exalted ambitions. On the single day of September 15, 185 enemy planes were brought down at a cost of twenty-five British fighters. During three months of operations the Germans lost 2,375 aircraft and comparably appalling losses in flying personnel.

Very soon, however, the German raids ceased to be grave perils, and were looked upon in the nature of nuisances. The first Battle of Britain had been won. The threat of annihilation had been warded off, and time had been earned to manufacture implements of war and to rally allies to Britain's side. More than that, the R.A.F. caused destruction along the French invasion coasts, bombed Berlin six days in a row, attacked German manufacturing cities, and struck at the industrial north of Italy in reprisal for futile Fascist participation in the aerial assault upon Britain. Detailed Nazi plans for the invasion of Britain, uncovered later in a Brussels garage, remained, perforce, in the blueprint stage.

While the terrors of the blitz were horrible enough for British civilians, the dimensions of the attack fell below expectations. Rather than impairing morale, the bombings stiffened the national backbone and the resolve to have due revenge when conditions were opportune. A proposal from the German side, honestly intended or otherwise, to arrange a truce on city bombing, found no favor in the British Isles. Aside from dock areas, the damage done by the Luftwaffe to British factories and communication facilities was decidedly negligible.

Saluting the skill, the discipline, the toughness of the British airmen, Churchill declared that, "Never in the field of human conflict was so much owed by so many to so few." It was Britain's "finest hour."

North Africa and the Middle East

Until the intervention of Italy, the Mediterranean region was an obscure and quiet theatre of war. Large bodies of Allied troops had been accumulated in the Middle East in case the enemy attempted a thrust toward the vital Nile valley or the oil-lands of the Middle East. Upon the surrender of France and the withdrawal of Frenchmen from the Allied pool, fresh British troops, especially Anzacs, were hurried in.

In a manner reminiscent of Napoleon, Mussolini contemplated the humiliation of Britain by overpowering Egypt and the Anglo-Egyptian Sudan. If successful, another stride would have been taken toward restoring the glories of ancient Rome and the imperial British thoroughfare over the Mediterranean would have been wholly blocked. At the outset fighting was confined mainly to the rival airforces, the British raiding airdromes in Libya, Eritrea, and Ethiopia. The *Regia Aeronautica,* of which the Fascist chief had orated so vaingloriously, was no match for the Dominion flyers with the R.A.F.

In November, 1940, Italian armies from Libya drove sixty miles inside the border of Egypt and also seized British Somaliland. Their stay, though sweet, was short, for in 1941 the British cleaned the enemy out of Eritrea, the Somalilands, and Ethiopia. The picturesque sovereign of the last, Haile Selassie, whom Italian marauders had chased away in 1936, moved back to his capital, flanked by British advisers.

Along the Mediterranean coast meanwhile the prolonged see-saw contest between the Axis and the British had turned favorably for the latter. At the end of December, 1940, British armies, General Archibald Wavell commanding, counterattacked in Egypt, driving the Italians pell-mell across Libya and by February reaching Bengazi, a march of 500 miles. The colossal casualties which the Fascists had suffered together with their failure to snatch the prize of the Nile convinced the Germans that they must take a hand in the African business.

Aside from mastery at the Nile, which would render communication between the United Kingdom and India and the British Dominions in the southern Pacific more difficult, successful operations in North Africa would open up dizzy vistas of power to the Axis. For beyond Egypt lay the rich oilfields of the Middle East, and beyond them lay India, into which the forces of Japan might thrust from the east. All in all the stakes in North Africa were high.

Into that theatre was dispatched an able, up-and-coming Nazi commander, General Erwin Rommel, with German tanks, planes, and troops. Striking hard at Wavell's men, Rommel drove them in headlong, though orderly, retreat back into Egypt, and for a time it seemed an open question whether the Nile could be saved. But the Germans soon exhausted their energies and appeals of Rommel for reinforcements that might have enabled him to win through went unheeded in Berlin—a fateful blunder as the event proved. Fighting languished until November, 1941, Wavell in the interval piling up troops and matériel, much of which originated in the United States. Then the British harried the enemy from his advanced positions, fought desperate tank battles on desert wastes, and by Christmas Day of 1941 the Union Jack was again flying over Bengazi. It was in no sense a decisive victory, but it gave a moral lift to an Allied world which had just suffered disheartening disasters in the Soviet Union and in the Pacific.

In the Middle East the Allies by a series of unorthodox maneuvers in 1941 established their authority on firm foundations. In April the ruler of Iraq, Rashid Ali, who had usurped the throne and who had distinctly pro-Nazi leanings, summoned the British to evacuate their troops and mobilized his Iraqi warriors. Instead of complying the British fought the natives, overcame them with little difficulty, and installed an administration in Iraq friendly to the Allied cause.

It may be that pro-Vichy officials plotted with Germany to hand over the French mandated territory of Syria and the Lebanon as a base for Axis operations against the Suez Canal and the Nile. At any rate to forestall any such possibility, in June, 1941, British and Free French forces invaded Syria. The Vichy administration protested strenuously and French soldiers on the spot fought to prevent the occupation, but they were easily subdued.

Finally, the Kingdom of Persia (Iran) whose monarch, Riza Shah Pahlevi, had been hearkening to the siren voice of German agents, was jointly taken over by British and Soviet troops in August, 1941.[5] Long a theatre of Anglo-Russian rivalry, Britain and the USSR in a

[5] The involvement of the Soviet Union in the war is discussed in Chap. XXII.

treaty signed in January, 1942, promised "to respect the territorial integrity, sovereignty, and political independence of Iran," and to evacuate their troops "not later than six months after all hostilities" with Germany and her associates were suspended. To these understandings the United States became a party at a conference in Teheran, December, 1943 (p. 593).

By occupying Iran the Allies not only eliminated a potential ally of Germany, but secured another and valuable "bridge of victory" over which war supplies could be transported to the hard-fighting armies of Marshal Stalin. Immediately upon the conclusion of the war the destiny of Iran caused a serious rift in the Grand Alliance and supplied the first major test for the United Nations.

Axis Mastery of the Balkans

Radical territorial revisions, in the meantime, had come to pass in the Balkan peninsula. Under duress, after the collapse of France, Rumania was compelled to cede Bessarabia and the northern Bukovina to the USSR, to return the southern Dobrudja to Bulgaria, and, perhaps the unkindest cut of all, to relinquish northern Transylvania to Hungary. Jovial King Carol, who was held blameworthy for these disasters, was obliged to resign the crown to his son, Michael.

These losses did not end Rumania's ill-fortune. It had to grant permission to Nazi technicians to enter the country for the twin purpose of building up the national military establishment and of increasing the output of the oilfields upon which the German war-machine and industry were so heavily dependent. Before long Rumania openly aligned itself with the Axis coalition—as did Hungary and Slovakia.

From the dependency of Albania Italy made ready to push farther into the Balkans. Greece was summoned to hand over to Albania (technically) certain districts of strategic importance, and when it manfully demurred, Mussolini, on October 28, 1940, ordered his armies against the stout-hearted Greeks. Evidently il Duce expected a quick victory, but in that he was entirely deceived for the Greeks not only halted the Italian invasion but themselves assumed the offensive into Albania.

As promised in the pre-war treaty of guarantee, Britain dispatched some aid to Greece, land forces and units of the RAF, which bombed fleet stations and other targets in southern Italy. Most spectacular was a raid upon the Fascist navy in the harbor of Taranto. Moving in with torpedo-carrying planes, on the night of November 11, 1940, the Royal Navy delivered a crippling blow to the sheltered Italian ships; three battleships and four or more smaller men-of-war were severely damaged. And two weeks later in an encounter off Sardinia, British torpedo-planes and naval gunfire badly punished a large Italian capital ship and five other vessels.

Those bold attacks at a critical stage in the war dispelled doubts about the supremacy of the White Ensign in Mediterranean waters. In March, 1941, Britain scored again in the Battle of Matapan off the southern coast of Greece. Two Italian squadrons were heavily pummeled; five cruisers or destroyers were sent to the bottom and other ships were put out of action at a cost of only two naval airplanes. Italy ceased to be a serious counter on the surface of the sea.

Since Italy unaided had been incapable of defeating Greece, Germany rallied to her support, annihilating Yugoslavia in the process. To the Belgrade government, Berlin presented a demand for free passage, which was accepted. A pact of neutrality was signed with the Axis. But two days later (March 27, 1941) Yugoslav military chiefs repudiated the bargain, led their troops in an uprising, deposed Regent Prince Paul and his Ministry, and proclaimed the young Peter as king. It was heroic but futile. German stukas and panzer divisions smote the Yugoslavs like lightning and on April 17 formal surrender took place. Whereupon Yugoslavia was carved into a dozen slices, some passing under German authority, some Italian; even Hungary and Bulgaria shared in the spoils, and what remained was administered by Yugoslav puppets of the Axis.

Out in the Yugoslav villages and forests and mountains daring guerilla bands were rallied to carry on the resistance, to interrupt enemy convoys and to make the life of the conquerors as miserable and as dangerous as possible. One group, the Chetniks under General Draja Mikhailovitch, believed that when Axis rule was broken, the Yugoslav monarchy of King Peter should be restored, while another faction, the Partisans, headed by Joseph Broz, whom history knows as Marshal Tito, favored a Yugoslav republic and a Communist order of society. Between Chetnik and Partisan a fierce, unrelenting feud developed, but Allied backing in time was thrown to Tito's side. His insurgent army attained the larger military significance and had an important part in the later phases of the war in the Balkans against Germany. When victory was attained Tito assumed control of Yugoslavia, and Mikhailovitch, accused of collaborating with the enemy, was hunted down, captured, and shot as a traitor in 1946.

Long since, Greece had succumbed to the Axis. Striking swiftly across the kingdom, Nazi mechanized divisions entered Salonika on April 8, 1941 and took Athens less than three weeks later. Britain's

R.A.F. offered valiant resistance but they were hopelessly outnumbered, and with ground troops were withdrawn to Crete. Publicists likened the quitting of the Greek mainland to the evacuation from Dunkirk, four out of five of the Britishers getting away safely.

Conquered Greece suffered the gruesome tragedies of Yugoslavia and Poland. Bulgaria, which had yielded to Nazi blandishments and glittering prospects of territorial aggrandizement, and had entered the Axis fold, was rewarded with Greek eastern Macedonia as far as Salonika—and the whole of Yugoslav Macedonia to boot. Greek peasants were expelled from their homes and fields and their places were taken by Bulgarian immigrants. Warring gangs of *komitadjis* rendered life and property precarious in the extreme.

As in other conquered nations, underground organizations of patriotic Greek guerillas mushroomed into being, fought the good fight as best they knew how, inflicting heavy casualties and keeping some 120,000 German troops tied down. As Greeks of antiquity had taught mankind how to live, so modern Greeks taught men how to die. Famine ravaged the kingdom, making conditions of bare existence more desperate, if anything, than in other countries which had fallen before the Axis.

From Greece proper the Germans carried the war to the Anglo-Greek haven of Crete. To effect its conquest a spectacular airborne invasion was employed. Despite the fact that Britain held command of the sea, enemy troops in gliders and parachutists were easily deposited in Crete. At first the invaders were slain wholesale, but then they established footholds from which they could not be dislodged; and after ten days of battle, the British, under relentless machine-gun fire and bombing from the sky, were obliged to withdraw on May 31.

The reverse on Crete, falling as it did just when Rommel's arms were rolling Britishers back into Egypt, provoked a storm of criticism in the British press and Parliament. Might not airborne corps descend upon the United Kingdom as they had upon Crete? Would not the eastern Mediterranean be more hazardous than ever for British merchant tonnage? Would not Syria be pounced upon with the object of striking at the Suez from the north? That last question at least was answered by British occupation of Syria, as has been noted.

By reason of diplomacy and conquest the Axis bloc now lorded it over the Balkans except for Turkey, whose diplomacy underwent violent contortions. In October, 1939, the Turks had bound themselves in alliance with the Atlantic powers, though insisting upon a clause exempting them from going to war against the Soviet Union. That treaty was toasted in the West as a diplomatic coup of high magnitude and presently was cemented by an Anglo-French loan to the Ankara government.

But the Turks warily declined to abandon neutrality and freely sold their surplus products to both sets of belligerents. Properly impressed with the Axis victories in the Balkans, the Turks, on June 18, 1941, signed a treaty of "mutual trust and sincere friendship" with Germany. It seemed as though the Turks were on the verge of marching with the Nazis—a prospect that was not unnoted by policymakers in Moscow.

The Sea War

French withdrawal from the titanic struggle and the entry of Italy had far-reaching implications for naval operations. British fleet action, as noted above, knocked out part of the French navy in order to prevent its employment by the Axis and the Italian surface navy was effectively throttled by the encounters at Taranto and off Cape Matapan. Thereafter Mussolini relied chiefly on his submarines, which torpedoed at least one British cruiser and a few steamers, while German U-boats injured or sank three or more major British units in the Mediterranean toward the end of 1941. And holes were blown into the hulls of two large warships—*Valiant* and *Queen Elizabeth*—by "limpet" bombs, affixed by daring Italians in Alexandria harbor. Taken together, these British naval misfortunes were extremely serious.

Yet the British accounted for several Italian undersea craft, interrupted transport between the Fascist homeland and North Africa, and, in spite of heavy attacks from air and sea, convoyed supplies across the Mediterranean. Malta, British way station in the Middle Sea, was pounded continuously and ferociously, without, however, running up the white flag of surrender.

More perilous was the intensification of the German undersea war upon British merchant shipping. Possession of France and North Sea harbors furnished the Nazis with admirable facilities for campaigning against commerce-carriers. Speedy motor torpedo craft—E-boats—darted out from French bases and the coastline was studded with U-boat pens and airdromes.

Traveling at full speed on the surface by night, German U-boats worked their way into assembling grounds of British convoys. With the support of the air-arm they took a heavy toll of British cargo vessels, reported at almost 5,000,000 tons in the first eighteen months of the war. A really grave shipping crisis—one of the two most acute in World War II—developed in the spring of 1941, when British vessels were being torpedoed several times faster than new ships were sliding down the ways. After that, the losses appear to have slacked off for a time.

German surface raiders were also remarkably active. They sowed mines as far away as Auckland, New Zealand, damaged or captured a couple of Allied merchant ships. In November, 1940, the battleship, *Admiral Scheer,* attacked a convoy bound for Britain, destroying four of the vessels.

Diversion of warships to the Mediterranean to fight the Italians, German control of the European coastline, and the refusal of neutral Eire to allow her ports to be used for servicing imposed very real handicaps upon British naval operations. But, in September of 1940, the United States transferred to Britain fifty "over-age" destroyers that had been built during or just after World War I. In exchange, the United States obtained leases on sites for military purposes in British possessions in the Atlantic and the Caribbean. That transaction, which was an omen of vastly greater assistance soon to come from the United States, aided Britain signally in combatting the German effort to paralyze shipping. Helpful, too, was the completion of long-range British planes to patrol the principal sea-lanes.

Apart from fighting the Battle of the Atlantic, British men-of-war and planes struck at German bases along the French and Belgian coasts. The rigors of the European blockade were intensified. Merchant vessels of all continental nations, France included, were ordered in July, 1940, to secure British permits, or "navicerts," before setting out to sea. Ships without the required document laid themselves open to capture and expropriation.

Impressive though the Axis conquests were, the occupied countries yielded few of the raw materials in which Germany and Italy were deficient and they were badly off in food production. It was reported in 1940-1941 that acute shortages in oil, due to the blockade, were imposing limits on Axis military plans. In addition to the blockade, British bombers smote industrial targets and so cut down output. Yet it was a fair assumption that with such methods of war it would take a long, long time to defeat the Axis.

On the ocean, major naval engagements were fought in May, 1941. Germany's big battleship, *Bismarck,* and the cruiser, *Prinz Eugen,* on the loose, came upon the *Hood,* a great British battle-cruiser, off Greenland, and destroyed her. Whereupon a British squadron took after the German ships. It chased them 1,750 miles, sent the *Bismarck* to her grave, and damaged the *Prinz Eugen*, though not sufficiently to prevent her from reaching port. That success at sea, occurring at the moment of the British evacuation of Crete, brought comfort and consolation to the sorely-tried island kingdom.

CHAPTER XXII

Enter the Giants

IN THE early morning of Sunday, June 22, 1941, the Germans and their allies struck furiously into the USSR at many points along a front of 1,600 miles. That invasion imprinted a radically different complexion on World War II in almost all its aspects. As Charles XII of Sweden and Napoleon, in their epochs, had met their Nemesis in Russia, so would Hitler and the superb engine of war whose throttle he held.

Less than six months after the beginning of the German invasion of the great Eurasian power, terribly destructive months for the USSR, Japanese planes delivered their blow upon the American base at Pearl Harbor, and the United States joined the global conflict. How the giants of the Old World and the New became active participants in World War II is the material of this chapter.

Soviet Policy and the War

Upon the outbreak of war, the policymakers in the Kremlin pursued a diplomatic course that has been divergently interpreted. While for Churchill, Russian policy was "a riddle wrapped in a mystery inside an enigma," Stalin asserted that "our policy is simple and clear." After the conclusion of the Non-aggression Pact with Germany in August, 1939, (p. 545) and the coming of the European conflict, there was indeed simple clarity in the Soviet course. Although the war was officially condemned as a typical capitalistic-imperialistic clash [1] —and that interpretation was echoed by Communists in other nations, the Soviets sided with Germany and against the Atlantic powers. In more than one speech Commissar for Foreign Affairs V. M. Molotov said that "a strong Germany is an indispensable condition for durable peace in Europe."

Molotov, who was put in charge of the Soviet Foreign Office in

---

[1] Official Soviet interpretations on the war varied from time to time, but in February, 1946, Stalin reverted to the orthodox Marxist concept that ". . . the war arose in reality as the inevitable result of the development of the world economic and political forces on the basis of monopoly capitalism."

May, 1939, was spoken of as Stalin's "man Friday." Of humble parentage, Molotov—the name is an alias deriving from the Russian word molot, meaning hammer—was given a technical education and as a youth joined the Bolsheviks, collaborating with Stalin in the publication of *Pravda*. As a Soviet writer and speaker on political and economic affairs, he was noted for his pedantry and verboseness. A member of the powerful Communist Politburo, an astute, tough-minded, and stubborn bargainer, hard-working and unassuming, Molotov mistrusted the capitalist world and was wary of foreign diplomatists and their stratagems.

Russo-German commercial treaties led on to fairly extensive barter transactions between the two countries. Soviet wheat, fodder, and oil were sold to the Reich and commodities originating in Japan, soy beans and military wares, for example, were hauled across the USSR to Germany. Foreigners wondered, indeed, whether the Soviet Union would become a gigantic economic reservoir for the Nazis. On the other side, German technicians, machinery, and plane designs were supplied to Russia, though Soviet requests for German warcraft and naval designs were turned down.

Germany kept hands off the Soviet-Finnish War of 1939, though Italy, Axis partner, sent the Finns a little assistance. It appears that Nazi military chiefs, no less than professional soldiers in other countries, drew false conclusions on Russian fighting capacity from the Finnish conflict. Undoubtedly the rapid German conquest of France in 1940, and the Nazi power that triumph demonstrated, surprised and alarmed the men in the Kremlin. If they had been proceeding on the assumption that the belligerents to the west would ruin one another, leaving the Soviet Union supreme in Europe, that reasoning had been proved erroneous. Given the loudly trumpeted Nazi plans for eastward expansion, there was danger that Russia might be the victim of an attack at any time.[2]

The German naval attaché in Moscow reported (June 10, 1940) a "noticeable cooling off and technical difficulties on the part of the Russians." But Hitler observed (July 21, 1940), "Even though Russia views Germany's great successes with tears in her eyes, she herself has no intention of entering the war against Germany. . . . The German fuel situation is most difficult, but as long as Rumania and Russia deliver, and hydroelectric works can be safeguarded against [British] air attacks, it is not critical."

[2] On the immediate background of the Russo-German war new light was thrown by documents presented at the Nuremberg trial (1945-1946) of Nazi leaders, but official testimony from the Soviet side is very scanty.

For reasons of state the Soviet Union (p. 523), took possession of the Baltic Republics, reclaimed Bessarabia, and annexed the northern Bukovina. Though the Nazis raised no official objections, these Russian acquisitions heightened tension between the two capitals. In August, 1940, Germany started to make overt preparations for war with the Soviets by transferring ten infantry and two armored divisions from the west to Poland, "in case rapid action should become necessary to protect Rumania oilfields."

British diplomacy, meanwhile, was studiously courting Soviet good will and friendship. As ambassador to the USSR, Prime Minister Churchill, himself a relentless critic of Communism, appointed Sir Stafford Cripps, an accomplished lawyer and prominent politician of leftist outlook. Publicly Cripps' mission to Moscow was described as exploratory, intended merely to arrange for commerce between the two nations. Whatever diplomatic advances Cripps may have made were rebuffed by the Kremlin and the USSR held faithfully to the understandings with Germany.

Great Britain declined to recognize the Soviet annexation of the Baltic Republics, though some time before the German invasion, British statesmen gave Moscow "clear and precise warnings" of what impended. Officials of the United States likewise dispatched warnings of the forthcoming attack to the Kremlin.

After the making of the Treaty of the Triple Alliance in September, 1940, which welded Japan more firmly to the Axis (p. 558), uneasiness mounted in the Kremlin, even though war with the Soviet Union was explicitly excluded from the published purposes of the tripartite treaty. Soviet policymakers were eager to arrange an accommodation with Nippon that would lessen the likelihood of a war on two fronts. That objective was attained in a Soviet-Japanese neutrality pact of April, 1941, which was to run for five years.[3]

On the other side, Foreign Commissar Molotov and a suite of Soviet experts journeyed to Berlin in November, 1940, to confer with Nazi leaders. Much uncertainty surrounds the Berlin conversations, yet it appears that the Germans invited the USSR to enter the Triple Alliance, to lease sections of the Ukraine, and suggested that Russia should expand into the Middle East. Recurrent rumors had it that Hitler and Stalin were dickering on a gigantic transaction to divide up the Near and Middle East.

Molotov at Berlin apparently raised no objections to German mili-

[3] As part of the rapprochement, the Russians recognized the Japanese position in Manchuria, while Tokyo similarly acknowledged Soviet lordship over Outer Mongolia.

tary plans to succor Italy in the Balkans. He was assured of Nazi sympathy with Soviet aspirations to bases on the Turkish Straits and rectification of the Soviet-Turkish frontier. Certain border questions touching the Baltic Republics and Poland were adjusted at the Berlin parley and a joint official communiqué declared that the negotiations had reached agreement on all points of common interest. In January, 1941, new and far-reaching Russo-German pacts were signed concerning economic, resettlement, and frontier matters.

Even so Hitler and his aides were evidently convinced that the USSR could not be drawn into a status of vassalage like that of Italy. At or about this time the Nazi policymakers finally decided to lay away the designs for large-scale invasion of Britain in favor of a frontal attack on the Soviet Union.

While making gestures of appeasement to Hitler, the Soviets intensified preparations for the defense of the Socialist Fatherland. Faults in the war-machine which the Finnish campaigns had revealed were rectified and measures were adopted to improve the morale and the discipline of the Red Army; to raise the dignity of army officers they were authorized to wear swords. Through decrees lengthening hours of employment, tightening factory discipline, and the like, the output of mills and factories, especially those engaged in war production, was improved. A million Russian youths were conscripted for training as mechanics or railway workers, and steps were taken to accumulate reserves of strategic raw materials. Rationing was restored and increasing quantities of food were taken from the peasants. Russia, in short, was getting ready for any eventuality.

Nazi conquest of the Balkans and the alignment of Rumania, Bulgaria, and Hungary with the Axis marked a turning point in Soviet-German relations. Disquietude in the Kremlin now gave way to genuine alarm. Stalin, in a surprise move (May 6, 1941), assumed the office of Soviet Premier. He is said to have remarked, "Hitler is striving for world domination. This we cannot tolerate."

Military operations in the Balkans, the unexpected vigor of Yugoslav and Greek resistance, upset the Nazi timetable for war on Russia, necessitating the postponement of the projected invasion for several weeks. That delay contributed, up to a point, to the failure of the Germans to realize the dream of capturing Moscow by Christmas of 1941.[4] Requests which the Kremlin presented to Turkey for a leasehold on the Straits appear to have been turned down because of Nazi

[4] Apparently the attack on Russia had originally been planned to begin on May 15, but fighting in the Balkans caused a change to June 22, that date being selected on June 1.

diplomatic pressure at Ankara. Presently the news was heralded round the world that German and Turk had entered into a treaty of friendship. For the rulers in the Kremlin that pact was an extremely unkind cut.

From the Balkans, moreover, German armed forces were transferred to the Russian border and a Nazi mechanized division was dispatched into Finland. The USSR, on its part, conducted military maneuvers in the west in May instead of in the autumn as was the custom, and Soviet armies, variously estimated at 150 to 160 divisions, were drawn up along the German frontier.

The German-Russian War Begins

Then, without more ado and seemingly without demanding concessions of the Kremlin as the price of peace, German and satellite armies, in June, 1941, stormed into Soviet territory. The motives behind that momentous Nazi gamble are not far to seek. First of all, the Germans desired to crush the USSR, which was growing ever stronger militarily, as the prelude to a concentrated assault upon Great Britain; or possibly, if Russia were eliminated, Britain in despair might sue for peace. The Russian adventure, next, would keep the Nazi military machine occupied. It "cannot stand idle. . . . It must be in continual motion," Churchill remarked.

Then, too, mastery over European Russia would provide coal and oil substitutes, which Germany and her allies desperately needed, grain and ore to counteract the British blockade, and perhaps areas for German settlement—the *Lebensraum,* in a word, of *Mein Kampf.* From Russia a drive could be conducted into the Middle East and mayhap into the Suez Canal zone and India. Expansionism of that order had long been preached by the Nazi cult of geopolitics, whose high-priest was a learned general, Karl Haushofer. His writings, which accented the importance, economic and strategic, of the vast interior of Eurasia, colored to a degree the thinking of Hitler and his intimate colleagues.

As a rival totalitarian creed, finally, National Socialism hated Communism with religious fervor. By means of a "crusade" against the Reds not only would the Stalinist regime be overthrown, but the stock of Nazidom would rise among Germans and westerners who abhorred and dreaded the Communist way of life.

Allied with Germany were Italy, and Finland and Rumania, both of which had been despoiled of territory by Russia and both of which aspired to unredeemed lands in the USSR. Hungary and Slovakia likewise dispatched troops into Russia and contingents of volunteers (thinly disguised) were enrolled in Spain, France, and Belgium for the Russian war. Only Bulgaria among the Axis confederates in Europe hung back, chiefly because of the strong Russophile sentiments among the Bulgar population. Like Bulgaria, Japan held aloof from the Russian struggle, as indeed it was committed to do under the neutrality compact with the Soviets. On instructions from Berlin, the German ambassador in Tokyo besought Japan to attack Siberia, but in vain.

As soon as the invasion started, Churchill identified the fortunes of Russia with Britain, promised assistance, and shipped tanks and planes. Anglo-Soviet military and economic missions were exchanged. Britain, reluctantly, issued a declaration of war on Finland.

It seems to have been the opinion in top Nazi circles that the USSR could be overrun in the same speedy fashion as Poland, France, and the Balkans. "We will cut through Russia like a knife through butter," one German refrain ran. An early revolt inside the Soviet Union was counted on, such as Trotsky and other critics of Stalin had confidently believed would follow Soviet involvement in war. And Ukrainian émigrés in the German baggage would be exploited in rousing the Ukrainians to insurgency, much as in 1917, when Ludendorff had used Lenin to deliver the *coup de grâce* to an older Russia. Not much impressed with the military capacity of the USSR certain German commanders thought that the hardest fighting would be over in a matter of months.

Soviet leaders, on their part, looked for a prompt rising of German industrial workers in the "universal proletarian revolution" of which Lenin, years before, had written with confidence. But in that expectation the Russians were as deceived as the Nazis who imagined that the Soviet war power would crumble easily. International Communism, hewing to "the Moscow line," now interpreted World War II as a struggle to save the pioneer Socialist Commonwealth against predatory "Fascism." Communists everywhere rallied to the defense of Soviet interests, with not less zeal than previously they had hindered the Allied war effort in their home nations.

The Massive German Drive

To defeat Russia the Germans may have set in motion 150 crack divisions of their own—some 5,000,000 men—together with fifteen Rumanian divisions and perhaps twelve Finnish. Plans of campaign paralleled those that had humbled Imperial Russia in World War I with the elaborations required by the heavily armored divisions, the Luftwaffe, and the more far-reaching objectives that the Nazis had in mind. So far as military resources went, the USSR alone among the European powers had anything approaching the German mechanized equipment.

At the start of the campaign the invader pressed into the Soviet Union according to schedule. The northern army (von Leeb) struck out for Leningrad, the central army (von Bock),[5] whose appointed goal was Moscow, moved upon Smolensk, while the southern army hammered into the Ukraine. Week after week the Wehrmacht swept victoriously forward and the prophesies of another lightning Nazi triumph seemed by way of fulfillment. Would it be France all over again?

Casualties on both sides of the battlefront were enormous, though the rival statistics stand in such violent conflict that no satisfactory computation is possible. Repeating the historic strategy invoked against Napoleon, the Russians pulled into the interior, fighting fiercely as they did so. As the Red armies retreated, they laid bare the countryside, ruined industrial establishments, and dynamited the proud Dniepropetrovsk Dam. Soviet factory installations and operatives, though not much agricultural equipment, were transported to the interior away from the path of the invasion.

The southern armies were commanded by the elderly General Gerd von Rundstedt who, like Hindenburg in World War I, had been recalled from retirement. Far abler than Hindenburg and no doubt the most competent of all the old-line German commanders in the war, this tall, ascetic, Prussian aristocrat despised the Nazi upstarts and their social objectives. But as a professional soldier Rundstedt dutifully carried out assignments. With him in charge, the Germans conquered the valuable Ukrainian districts. Kiev fell; Odessa fell; Kharkov fell; Rostov-on-Don fell—ahead lay the route to the oilfields of the Caucasus and the Middle East. Then the Russians counterattacked in force and regained Rostov. That reversal, the first serious one the Wehrmacht had encountered, was a foretaste of others to come.

With the support of the Finns, Nazi troops in the north penetrated into the suburbs of Leningrad, major manufacturing center and headquarters of the Red Baltic fleet. The old capital of Peter the Great was invested and the factories and warehouses heavily bombed.

But the main German offensive was directed, as was Napoleon's, at Moscow, to obtain winter quarters and to crack Soviet morale. Smolensk, key-point on the way, was captured after desperate fighting. On October 1, a breathing-space for recuperation having

---

[5] Field Marshal Fedor von Bock typified the Prussian commander of history and legend—hard-boiled, a hard driver of his men, bent upon victory regardless of physical costs, and not a skillful strategist.

been taken, the Luftwaffe, panzer divisions, and motor-borne infantry drove hard upon Moscow. "Russia is broken and will never rise again," shouted Hitler in high exultation (October 3).

Soviet government bureaus were hurriedly removed to Kuibishev, well to the east on the Volga. Women and children were evacuated, and a state of siege was proclaimed in the capital. At one point a German spearhead thrust to within fifteen miles of the goal. But Moscow did not fall. In fact, in December the Russians, commanded now by Marshal Georgii Zhukov, delivered a counter-offensive in the teeth of a harsh Muscovite winter. The suffocating pressure on Moscow was relieved, and Zhukov advanced another stage in a career that was to make him the greatest Russian soldier of the war.

Glowing Nazi boastings of an easy triumph in the East went a-glimmering. The Red armies, though they had vacated an area ten times the extent of Pennsylvania, had neither been entrapped nor annihilated. Bitterly chagrined, Hitler relieved several top commanders, for one the Commander-in-Chief of the army, Walther von Brauchitsch, while Rundstedt was shunted to France. Hitler, himself, ex-corporal that he had been, obsessed with his own intuitive genius as a strategist, took command of the Wehrmacht as, since 1938, he had had supreme direction of all the German fighting services.

The Russian climate, the dreaded Muscovite winter, incomparable German supply problems over great distances, "the brutish tenacity of purpose," with which the Soviet troops fought in the "Great Patriotic War" (as the Russians then called the struggle), the deadly work of Soviet saboteur and guerilla warrior—each and all contributed to the frustration of the grandiose dreams of Nazidom. Like his Napoleonic forerunner, the German invader neglected to reckon sufficiently with the inhospitality of the Russian host.

So certain were the Germans that the enemy would swiftly crackup that only preliminary preparations had been made against the rigors of the Russian winter and German civilians were ordered to ransack their wardrobes to provide warm clothing for the shivering Nazi legions. German morale, too, was impaired by the "fearful flood of Nazi blood" that had been spilled. Still the prodigious conquests of Soviet soil promised, in due time, to yield foodstuffs that would relieve the monotonous diet on the German home front and to furnish rawstuffs for war industries.

On the other hand, the USSR had suffered terrific losses in fighting personnel, in equipment, in territory, and in material resources. Assistance flowing from Britain and the United States could not begin to compensate for the Russian losses caused by enemy destruction or

WORLD WAR II
EASTERN EUROPE

Allied supply routes to
Russia

Territory under Axis
domination

Depth of Axis penetration
as of Dec. 1941

Depth of Axis penetration
as of Dec. 1942

Miles

0   100   200   300   400   500

FROM U.S. AND BRITAIN

Murmansk

Archangel

N O R W A Y

S W E D E N

F I N L A N D

HELSINKI

Leningrad

STOCKHOLM

TALLINN

ESTONIA

RIGA

LATVIA

LITHUANIA

KAUNAS

MOSCOW

S.   S.   R.

Smolensk

EAST
PRUSSIA

Danzig

BERLIN

WARSAW

P O L A N D

U.   S.   S.   R.

Kiev

Kharkov

Don   R.

Stalingrad

GERMANY

Prague

Vienna

BUDAPEST

HUNGARY

R U M A N I A

Rostov

FROM IRAN

Novorossisk

Sevastopol

BUCHAREST

YUGOSLAVIA

BELGRADE

SOFIA

BULGARIA

ALBANIA

TIRANA

G R E E C E

Istanbul

B L A C K   S E A

ANKARA

T   U   R   K   E   Y

I R A N

ATHENS

S Y R I A

I R A Q

Tschirky

occupation of factories and farmlands. Bleak though the prospects were, the Russians took comfort from the facts that, as 1941 drew to its end, the Red armies had stemmed the Nazi onslaught and the United States had entered the titanic struggle as a full-fledged belligerent.

The United States and World War II

On the outbreak of war the United States government declared neutrality. But the mood in Congress and in the country regarding this struggle diverged substantially from the war in 1914. Press and radio for years had acquainted the American nation with the march of events in Europe—and in the Orient—infinitely better than a quarter century earlier. Except for frank admirers of National Socialism—a negligible company and without much influence in the councils of state—America detested Hitlerism because of inhumane and undemocratic practices at home and because of the aggressive foreign policy culminating in the general war.

Aversion to Hitlerism was, however, tempered by unhappy recollections of the outcome of American participation in World War I and by a lively desire to avoid embroilment a second time in a quarrel not of America's making. That outlook remained a constant factor in the public life of the United States until the bombs of Nippon rained down on Pearl Harbor.

As early as January, 1939, President Roosevelt gave it as his judgment that a European war would have perilous implications for the security of the United States and all the Western Hemisphere. When war actually came he laid an embargo on the shipment of arms or munitions to the belligerents, as the Neutrality Laws enacted in the mid-thirties prescribed. Then Roosevelt requested the Congress to alter the neutrality legislation, and after full debate, appropriate action was taken by the Congress. By the revision the ban on the export of war-goods was lifted, though goods had to be paid for before leaving American ports and had to be hauled away in vessels not owned in the United States. Ships, furthermore, flying the Stars and Stripes might not enter combat zones, nor might citizens of the United States travel on ships of belligerent nations.

Large orders for weapons were at once placed by Britain and France with American firms. There was, however, a sharp diplomatic exchange with the British over the stoppage and search of United States ships on the high seas and over the British navicert system which required a vessel to obtain a clean bill of health from a British official before setting off for Europe. In that way Britain intended to make certain that cargoes would not reach the enemy. But the resentment that flared up over British policies on the high seas proved temporary and never seriously affected general American policy toward the Allies.

With the object of keeping the war away from the shores of the Western Hemisphere, the United States in collaboration with the other New World republics, proclaimed "sea-safety zones" around the Americas, into which belligerent warcraft were forbidden to enter. To assist Finland in her struggle with Soviet Russia, the United States extended a small credit for the purchase of agricultural products. Then, too, Roosevelt named Myron C. Taylor, a prominent steel manufacturer and Episcopalian, as his personal representative to the Vatican. Presumably that appointment was made in order to facilitate cooperation for bringing hostilities to an end at a propitious time.

Early in 1940 the Undersecretary of State, Sumner Welles, was dispatched to Europe to confer with the governments of Britain, France, Germany, and Italy on "the present possibilities of concluding any just and permanent peace." Welles' instructions forbade him to offer proposals for the restoration of peace and, so far as its central objective was concerned, the mission was fruitless.

The dramatic military developments of 1940—the German occupation of western Europe, the entry of Italy into the struggle, the thrilling spectacle of Britain standing up boldly to the aerial blitz—had impressive reverberations in the United States. Conquest of France and Holland, moreover, and the British concentration on the war in Europe, opened up exciting vistas of Oriental aggrandizement for imperially-minded Japanese. There was also a possibility that the Axis might interfere in the New World colonies of the defeated nations.

The government of the United States sent firm warnings to Japan to keep hands off the lucrative Netherlands Indies. Repeated protests were registered in Tokyo over the movement of Nipponese soldiers into French Indo-China and because of economic concessions granted to Japan in that colony by Vichy France. Washington reacted in a hostile manner when Britain, under pressure from Japan, closed the Hong Kong route and temporarily shut the Burma Road over which small quantities of war goods were being transported to the Chinese Nationalists. More credits, small, though not without diplomatic implications, were extended by the United States to the embattled regime of Chiang Kai-shek.

To forestall the transfer of European colonies in the New World to the Axis, a Pan-American Conference at Havana (July 27, 1940) resolved to place them under the joint trusteeship of the American Republics should there be an Axis threat of seizure. The United States not only reaffirmed its pledge to protect Canada from attack but arranged with the Dominion for a board of defense to prepare plans for mutual assistance.

Interventionists and Non-Interventionists

Up and down the Republic, meanwhile, in the halls of Congress, in the press, over the radio, wherever men and women congregated, the diplomatic policies of the nation were being debated with mingled reason and passion. Division of mind paralleled to a remarkable degree the cleavage that had appeared in the American democracy during World War I. Discussion roused some of the deeper instincts and emotions of men and feelings ran as hotly as in the controversies between contending versions of Christianity in early modern Europe. Throughout the great debate relations with Japan received scant attention, for it was upon the national course vis-à-vis Europe that the public interest was focused.

Two broad climates of opinion shaped up in the United States: the interventionists, either eager or reluctantly willing to take a full part in the war; and the non-interventionists, who for one or another emotion or reason would keep the nation out of the conflict. Under the impact of events viewpoints shifted. Yet there was a solid core of consistency and stability in both positions.

Warmly disposed to intervention were Americans who were convinced that the Axis and Japan were bent upon world domination, and that if the Axis triumphed in Europe, it would sooner or later fall upon the New World. At first, it was reasoned, the Axis might pursue a program of peaceful commercial penetration of Latin America and that done, it would seek to conquer the richest prize on earth, the United States. If Britain should go down in defeat might not the Axis appropriate the British fleet and immediately jeopardize the safety of the United States? At the very least, an Axis victory would necessitate the maintenance of a huge and an enormously expensive defense establishment in the United States for an indeterminate period.

Also interventionist-minded were Americans who conceived of the European struggle as a life-or-death contest between the free and democratic way of life and the authoritarian ideology of the Axis. Defeat of democracy in the Old World would inescapably impair the prestige of free institutions the globe over, while a British victory, on the other hand, would tend to strengthen the democratic cause. So, also, Americans who admired Britain, whether for her large and varied contributions to the sum of civilization, or for British pluck and tenacity in standing up to the Axis war-machine, were inclined, with differing degrees of fervor, to espouse American intervention.

That was the attitude, too, of many Americans who were strongly wedded to the principle of collective security to preserve international peace. Lastly, many an American, scandalized by the inhumanities and bestial horrors of Axis rule, both before the war started and after, believed that the United States should exert its power to eliminate the Nazi and Fascist challenge to the ways of civilized living.

It would be elementary prudence, it would be an act in the practical spirit of self interest, the interventionist logic ran, for the United States to merge the national resources, material and human, with the British, and together extinguish the common Axis menace. Some Americans who were ready to intervene to the extent of aiding Britain economically or even with naval and air forces, flinched from approving the dispatch of expeditionary armies to European battlefields.

As in the interventionist fold, so among the non-interventionists there were varieties of opinion and differences in the tenacity with which convictions were held. There were Americans, for instance, who were quite indifferent to what happened beyond the borders of the United States, in continents a full ocean away. These "diehard isolationists" preferred to turn their backs on the troubles and torments of the outer world and to offer up thanks that the United States was not as other sinners.

To other Americans it seemed that the sequel to participation in World War I had demonstrated the unwisdom or the futility of risking a second involvement, however appealing the ideological and humanitarian considerations, unless the territorial interests of the United States should be threatened beyond reasonable doubt. Such men drew sardonic contrasts between the high purposes for which the United States had enlisted in 1917 and the bleak realities of the aftermath. War with Germany and her confederates, they held, would entail heavy American sacrifices, without prospect of curbing "the senseless cyclical struggle for power in Europe."

It was also argued that any financial losses resulting from Axis trade invasion of Latin American and other markets would be far smaller than the expenditures that would be required to carry the war through to victory. Certain individuals were of the opinion that intervention in the war, far from saving democratic freedoms and free institutions abroad, would imperil their very continuance at home.

Arrayed in the non-interventionist group, too, were men who out of conviction or mere prejudice bore deep grudges against Britain, or who liked Axis totalitarianism. There were still others who believed that Japanese discipline and efficiency would bring benefits to the yellows and browns of Asia, or who were absolute pacifists or Communists adhering to the views of Moscow.

Through the whole complex and illuminating spectacle of a great democracy desperately groping its way to a decision, there ran elements of political partisanship. Democrats in Congress tended to back Administration proposals that might lead on to belligerence. Indeed, many an American, who cherished a grudge against Britain, so revered Roosevelt that he unhesitatingly followed the President in aiding Britain. On the other side, Republicans in Congress in majority voted negatively on measures which the Administration sponsored having a bearing on the war.

Cooperation with Britain

In the autumn of 1940, with the United States in the vortex of a heated presidential election, Germany, Italy, and Japan announced a military alliance, pledging to assist one another, if any signatory were attacked by a nation then at peace. Since the Soviet Union was expressly excluded from the scope of the treaty, this new Triple Alliance was pointed squarely at the United States. It meant that if the United States took up arms against the Axis, then Japan would fight America. It meant, likewise, that if Japan and the United States clashed, then Germany and Italy were bound to go to war with America. So far as the Axis was concerned, the minimum advantage flowing from the Alliance was the assurance that the United States would have to hold a large part of her naval resources in the Pacific. Secretary Hull reviled the Tripartite Alliance as "monstrous" and he echoed the conviction of tens of millions.[6]

During the presidential canvass of 1940 both major candidates—Franklin D. Roosevelt and Wendell Willkie—pledged aid to "Britain short of war," but gave assurances against participation in the conflict. By presidential order of September 3, 1940 the United States, as has been said, transferred fifty "over-age" destroyers to Britain, in exchange for eight naval sites on British territory in the New World. And substantial stocks of weapons of various descriptions were re-

[6] The British ambassador to Japan, Sir Robert Craigie, believed that but for the Allied military disasters of 1940, Japan could have been deterred from aligning with the Axis and could have been persuaded to make a decent peace with China. In view of the imperialistic ambitions of the Japanese military caste, Craigie's surmises are dubious to say the least. Robert Craigie, *Behind the Japanese Mask* (London, 1946).

leased to Britain to compensate in part for the losses suffered in the Flanders disaster.

Elected for a third term, Roosevelt presently declared to the Congress that the United States would not acquiesce in an Axis-dictated peace and eloquently expounded the "Four Freedoms" upon which the security and happiness of the nations depended—freedom from want, freedom of worship, freedom of speech, freedom from fear. Before long he was calling upon the United States to become "the arsenal of democracy" and to supply material assistance to nations whose independence was held to be necessary for the safety of the American Republic itself.

Lend-Lease

A specific plan to implement that idea was handed to the Congress in January of 1941. Called Lend-Lease, the act authorized the President to sell, transfer, exchange, lend, lease or otherwise dispose of ships, aircraft, implements of war and other commodities to the government of any country whose defense the Chief Executive thought vital to the defense of the United States. Recipients of help under this proposal would not be obligated to make repayment in cash, but reimbursement might be made in any other manner that the President approved.

So devised as to fall within the range of practical politics at the time it was presented, Lend-Lease was sufficiently elastic to meet contingencies if the United States should become an active belligerent. It was designed primarily to provide aid to Great Britain, but with time Lend-Lease became the very cement of the entire United Nations, the most important single invention of the war except for the atomic bomb.

Although Britain had not wholly exhausted the financial resources upon which she might draw to purchase war goods in the United States, the sponsors of Lend-Lease felt that the British required moral encouragement and believed, too, that passage of the Act would stiffen the backbone of other nations not yet the victims of Axis appetite. Prime Minister Churchill hailed Lend-Lease as "an inspiring act of faith," "a monument of generous and far-reaching statesmanship," "the most unsordid act of history."

It was now that debate in the United States over foreign policy rose to a crescendo. It was urged by certain friends of Lend-Lease that adoption of the proposal would help to keep the war away from the Republic; had not Churchill appealed, "Give us the tools, and we'll finish the job?" Opponents of the measure, on the other hand, played upon the theme that Lend-Lease would be another stride on the road to full involvement in the war. For more than two months the advantages and disadvantages of Lend-Lease were exhaustively argued in the Congress and in the country. In the end the bill was enacted into law by comfortable majorities in both Houses.

Promptly Congress authorized an appropriation of $7,000,000,000 to carry out the objects of Lend-Lease. Credits were used to supply Britain with aid of almost every description—munitions, industrial rawstuffs, food, tobacco—and with facilities for repairing damaged British merchant and naval vessels. British man-power, materials, factories, and ships which previously had been engaged in the export trade, in order to earn funds to pay for American-made goods, could now be diverted to war purposes.

It was not until 1942 that Lend-Lease assistance was moving across the Atlantic in large volume. By then, goods and services were being supplied to the armed forces of the United States by Britain—Lend-Lease in reverse, or Mutual Aid, as the British called the whole complex transaction.

Goods had not only to be promised to Britain; the cargoes had to be safely delivered to their destinations. Otherwise, the principle that the survival of the United Kingdom was a national American interest would be nullified. When German submarines torpedoed cargo carriers en route to Britain, the old issue of the rights of neutral commerce on the high seas was revived. To protect Lend-Lease merchantmen on their errands the United States navy set up "neutrality patrols" on the water and in the air across the Atlantic.

Nonetheless U-boats attacked American ships. The freighter, *Robin Moor,* for instance, was sunk off the coast of Brazil, in June, 1941, with no provision to rescue the crew. In September the destroyer *Greer,* carrying mail to Iceland (and signaling the presence of a German submarine to the British), was unsuccessfully shelled. Whereat Roosevelt ordered the vessels of the United States navy to shoot Axis craft on sight, which meant, in substance, an undeclared naval war upon Germany and Italy.

By that time supplies were moving from the American arsenal to the USSR as well as to Britain. Russo-American relations, bad after the Bolshevik Revolution, had improved in the mid-thirties, but they deteriorated sharply with the making of the Soviet-Nazi pact of 1939, the Finnish war, and Soviet absorption of territory along her western frontier. Relations hit bottom when Moscow arranged the neutrality treaty with Japan in April, 1941.

But after Germany invaded the Soviet Union, the mood changed, in spite of widespread antipathy to the Communist way of life in the United States. On the assumption that aid to the Soviets would contribute to the defeat of the Nazis, Lend-Lease assistance was extended to Russia. There were two widely different ideologies, but one uniting purpose. Although the Red armies at the time were falling back before the mighty German onslaught, Roosevelt confidently asserted that the USSR would not be knocked out of the war.

The Atlantic Charter

Off the coast of Newfoundland, in mid-August of 1941, Roosevelt and Churchill held a three-day conference which had been in preparation since January. Accompanying the chiefs of state were military advisers and economic experts to deliberate on matters of high strategy and material cooperation. Among the subjects that came under review were the Lend-Lease shipments to Britain, aid to Soviet Russia, and the policy to be pursued with Japan in the hope of restraining her ambitions. It seems probable, too, that military and naval specialists elaborated plans for collaboration in the event that the United States should become a full-fledged belligerent.

Out of the dramatic Atlantic meeting came "a rough and ready war-time declaration" on the general purposes for which the struggle was being waged. Spoken of as the Atlantic Charter, the document proclaimed universal principles for the future which served as a sort of platform for the foes of the Axis and Japan. Disclaiming all interest in territorial aggrandizement for their countries, Roosevelt and Churchill expressed "a desire (not will) to see no [territorial] changes that do not accord with the freely expressed wishes of the people concerned," and stated that "they respect the right of all peoples to choose the form of government under which they will live." These articles seemed to say that countries overrun by the Axis and Japan would one day live their own lives again and that if other nations were conquered they, too, would be given the gift of freedom.

Another point in the Charter asserted, "They will *endeavor*, with due respect for their existing obligations, to further the enjoyment by all states, great or small, victor or vanquished, of access, on equal terms, to the trade and to the raw materials of the world which are needed for their economic prosperity." No doubt a bid to minds that believed that commercial rivalry and "have-not" status invited an appeal to arms, this clause held out the promise of better times for all and sundry.

The Charter carried a stock reaffirmation of the "freedom of the seas" principle, and another point expressed the conviction that force must be abandoned in the adjustment of international quarrels. After the aggressor nations had been overpowered and disarmed the United States and the United Kingdom would "aid and encourage all . . . practical measures which will lighten for peace-loving peoples the crushing burden of armaments." The Charter also hinted at "the establishment of a wider and permanent system of security."

The Soviet Union and nine governments in exile presently endorsed the Atlantic Charter. Sometimes likened to the Wilsonian Fourteen Points agenda of World War I, the Charter diverged from that utterance on two main counts: first, nothing was said about specific territorial changes, and second, this was a joint statement of the heads of the United States and British governments and assented to by the duly constituted authorities of ten other Allied nations.

America Girds for Defense

Ever since the lightning defeat of France in 1940 the United States had been busily preparing men and machines for national defense. In the summer of 1940 Congress enacted the first peacetime conscription law, making men between the ages of twenty one and thirty six liable for a year of military service; a maximum of 900,000 would be selected for training. Appropriations for huge expansion of the armed forces were quickly adopted, and by November, 1940, expenditures of approximately $11,000,000,000 had been voted, a large part for the construction of a "two-ocean" navy. To coordinate preparedness measures, an Office of Production Management for Defense (OPM) was created (January, 1941) and stockpiles of strategic rawstuffs, albeit small ones, were accumulated.

By April, 1941, private industry in the United States was turning out the first tanks (ahead of schedule) and it was reported that the production of aircraft was approaching the British and German output of 1,500 planes a month. In July the first Flying Fortresses—bombers capable of carrying a four ton load and mounting seven machine guns —reached Britain and fighter craft, too. Steel production was soon running at a rate of nearly 80,000,000 tons a year, or more than all the rest of the world. Shipyards were humming in the building of warcraft and merchantmen. "Two ships a day will keep the Germans away" ran a popular slogan.

As another way of overcoming the shortage in shipping, vessels in United States ports belonging to Axis nationals or to countries that had been overrun, were commandeered. United States troops, moreover, occupied Greenland in April, 1941, and largely replaced the British garrison in Iceland a short while later.[7]

By presidential order cargo ships flying the United States flag were authorized to enter Egyptian ports—technically a neutral country— passing through the combat zones in the Gulf of Aden and the Red Sea. Civilian pilots ferried war planes to British armies in the Near East by way of South America and Africa. In mid-August of 1941, after a particularly stormy debate, Congress, by a majority of one in a total vote of 405, instructed the army to keep drafted men in the service for eighteen months longer.

Directly because of renewed U-boat attacks on United States ships, Roosevelt requested further modification in the Neutrality Law, so as to permit the arming of American cargo carriers and to legalize their entry into certain maritime war zones and belligerent ports. Supporters of the measure advocated passage on the ground that the proposed revision followed unerringly from the adoption of Lend-Lease. In the midst of the debate Roosevelt made the startling revelation that he had documentary evidence to prove that the Nazis had prepared plans to carve South America into five vassal states and to supplant all existing religions by an international Nazi cult in which *Mein Kampf* would serve as the scripture. Revision of the Neutrality Act was carried in the Senate by a vote of fifty to twenty seven and in the House by 212-194, a narrow margin, indeed, for a shift of ten votes in the House would have defeated the bill.

Pearl Harbor

While the mind of the United States was largely concentrated on the European struggle, relations with Japan had steadily deteriorated. As has previously been indicated, animosity and suspicion between the two great Pacific nations, between two divergent patterns of life, reached grave proportions after the Japanese conquest of Manchuria. On the one side, Japan was embittered by discrimination against her nationals and her trade, by American aid to Nationalist China to prevent its conquest, and, above all, by what the Tokyo policymakers regarded as unwarranted American interference in the Nipponese design of monopolistic empire in eastern Asia.

The United States, on its part, aside from detestation of bare-faced Japanese imperialism, keenly resented the growth of Nipponese

[7] The importance of Greenland was twofold: it lay on the direct air route from North America to Britain, and weather stations on the island furnished meteorological data for the direction of the aerial offensive against Germany and the occupied countries of western Europe.

seapower and airpower, the depredations and brutalities committed in the undeclared war in China, and the alignment of Nippon with the Axis through the treaty of September, 1940.

The very core of the antagonism, however, was the cleavage over China, which protracted American-Japanese diplomatic negotiations could not resolve. Whereas the United States adamantly insisted that Japan should stop fighting China, pull her armed forces home, and abide by the "Open Door" principle, the Japanese obdurately called upon the United States to cease encouraging Nationalist China to fight and to allow Japan to mold the destinies of the East with a free hand.

Not only did the United States refuse to betray China, it continued to send token assistance to the government of Chiang Kai-shek and that for three main reasons. First, it was established American policy to succor victims of aggression. Then, the United States had committed itself to keep the Chinese door open and, in the Nine Power Treaty of 1922, to uphold "the sovereignty, the independence, and the territorial and administrative integrity of China." The third and most elemental reason proceeded from the fundamental instinct of self-preservation; if Japan should become master of eastern Asia she would be a standing menace to the territorial interests of the United States.

Incidental developments in the autumn of 1941—the imposition of a virtual Anglo-American blockade on trade with Japan, Nipponese pressure into French Indo-China and threats to Siam (Thailand), British assurances of cooperation with the United States if war came, the dispatch of additional Anglo-American fighting forces to the East —intensified suspicions and fears on both sides. No doubt the fact that Soviet Russia was locked in mortal combat with the armies of Germany exerted a decisive influence upon the time the Japanese warlords chose to unleash hostilities.

On the morning of Sunday, December 7, 1941, some 300 planes of the Mikado, carried from a base in the Kuriles, delivered a surprise and shockingly successful series of attacks upon the great mid-Pacific station of Pearl Harbor. It resulted in over 4,500 American casualties and completely crippled the main Pacific fleet. In all, the Japs sank five of eight battleships, a target ship, a minelayer, and a floating drydock. Three destroyers, the three other battleships in the harbor, cruisers, and several other ships were damaged, and 187 planes were smashed to smouldering wrecks. It was a shock to the United States almost as stunning as the shock of the atomic bomb upon Hiroshima forty two months later. The Pearl Harbor treachery cost the enemy only five two-man submarines and twenty eight aircraft.

Japan's formal declaration of war was couched in medieval gran-diloquence: "We, by the grace of Heaven, Emperor of Japan, seated on the throne of a line for ages eternal, enjoin upon you our loyal and brave subjects: we hereby declare war on the United States of America and the British Empire."

Pearl Harbor cut short the debate in the United States on war or peace. With only a single dissenting voice the Congress voted hostilities upon Imperial Japan. The war of words was replaced by a war of arms. When Germany and Italy in keeping with the alliance treaty hurled war declarations at the United States the nation picked them up in the spirit in which they were sent.[8]

Speaking for a nation united as it had never before been united for war, Roosevelt said, "We are now in this war. We are in it all the way. Every single man, woman, and child is a partner in the most tremendous undertaking of our American history."

Nine nations of the West Indies and Central America likewise en-tered the struggle, to be joined in 1942 by Mexico and Brazil. The other Latin American states broke off relations with the Axis, Chile and Argentina holding back until 1943. Not until March, 1945, did the Argentine declare war on Germany and Italy, while Russia re-frained from fighting Japan until August, 1945.

[8] To the Reichstag in an elaborate address Hitler proclaimed, "A historical revision of unique scope has been entrusted to us by the Creator." And he said that it was the job of the Third Reich to revise history to some purpose. He went on with characteristic denunciations of "the unholy trinity of capitalism, Bolshe-vism, and Jewry." What the United States sought, Hitler was sure, was "to take over the British Empire."

CHAPTER XXIII

The Swing of the Pendulum

Birth of the United Nations

THE dawning of the year 1942 was heralded by the foundation of the United Nations, sponsored by President Roosevelt. At Washington on January 1, twenty six nations, the United States, Great Britain, and Soviet Russia among them, solemnly pledged to wage war together until victory, and then to establish a peace based, not on selfish advantage for themselves, but on freedom and mutual collaboration for the common good. The signers explicitly subscribed to the purposes and principles of the Atlantic Charter, and before the holocaust was over fifty one states had accepted the Washington declaration and entered the United Nations circle.

Presently Soviet Russia and Great Britain arranged a conventional alliance binding themselves to work together in war and in peace. When victory was won the two nations would eschew territorial aggrandizement and would not meddle in the domestic affairs of other countries. Unless replaced by an international institution for the maintenance of security the Anglo-Russian partnership would run for twenty years. Stalin was moved to describe the British alliance as "an historic turning point," and the USSR now formally identified itself with the Allied economic program of mutual aid.

Mighty though the Grand Alliance was in manpower and physical resources, the task of whipping the Axis and Japan promised to be formidable and prolonged. As matters stood, the Axis bestrode the continent of Europe like a colossus. The Soviet Union had been so severely wounded that it was an open question whether she could contribute much to the common effort. On the sea the effectiveness of German submarines in intercepting cargoes to Britain and to Russia by way of the Arctic had increased. In the Orient Japan held a strong defensive position, had a battle fleet of first-class quality, and land and air forces which had not seriously been impaired by over four years of combat with China.

If the Allied strategists contemplated strangling Nippon by blockade that plan was thwarted by the furious offensive operations to the south undertaken by the enemy. The main reliance of the United Nations was the United States, its immense reserves of energetic manpower, its vast industrial and food-producing capacities, remote from aerial bombing, its rapidly expanding armed services, its facilities for ship-construction.

Japan at Flood-Tide

The crippling blow dealt to the United States navy at Pearl Harbor was only the first and most audacious of a succession of Japanese triumphs across the vast distances of the largest of oceans. Other Pacific possessions of the United States were attacked with impunity and many of the smaller ones, such as Guam and Wake, were seized by Nipponese troops. Moreover, two great British men-of-war, the *Prince of Wales* and the *Repulse,* incorporating the latest innovations in naval architecture and manned by picked crews, though lacking aircraft protection, were hit and sunk off Malaya. On Christmas Day, 1941, soldiers of the Mikado gleefully hoisted the flag of the Rising Sun over historic Hong Kong. Not since the retreat from Flanders had British pride and prestige been so severely wounded.

Fighting fiercely, capably led and profiting from an immense local advantage in men and equipment, the Japanese forces swiftly overpowered the colonial holdings of the western nations in and off southeastern Asia. The Philippines were conquered after a few, grim, heartbreaking months of war, rich in glorious and tragic episodes. On Bataan peninsula, tattered, ill-fed American and Filipino troops made an heroic stand, but without naval or effective air support they were defeated—the heaviest setback suffered by American arms in the whole war.

At the fortress of Corregidor, like Bataan previously known to only a few Americans but now on every tongue, the American garrison fought against hopeless odds for twenty seven days, and at the end watched glumly as the Japanese lowered the Stars and Stripes in token of surrender. General Douglas MacArthur, commander-in-chief in the Philippines, swore as he was evacuated to Australia that one day he would return, a promise that he made good in the fullness of time.

Thailand (Siam) yielded to Japan after a few hours of token resistance. Down through the Malay peninsula, the Nipponese advanced recklessly and rapidly, and then over into Singapore, formidable British naval station, reputed to be invulnerable. The capitulation of Singapore, on February 15, 1942, the greatest setback for British arms in

World War II, cast a cloud of gloom over the Allied world. Almost as much mystery surrounded the sudden collapse of the Singapore island fortress as the Pearl Harbor disaster.

On into the fabled Dutch East Indies the enemy pressed his relent- less drive, there repeating the earlier successes against the western empires. Up in Burma, meantime, Allied armies were compelled to retreat and by May, 1942, that kingdom was practically in Japanese possession. The greater part of the British troops operating in Burma were safely evacuated, but they left their heavy equipment behind and the Burma Road over which supplies had been transported to Nationalist China was sealed off.

For anything like a parallel to the swift Nipponese victories, the page of history must be turned back to the dazzling career of Ghenghis Khan. Vast territories with teeming populations and rich mineral, rubber, and agricultural resources had fallen to the enemy. Their exploitation, if properly organized, would greatly assist Japan in the prosecution of the war, while the loss of tropical products im- posed serious handicaps upon the Allies. So situated were Japanese forces after less than half a year of violent campaigning that the security of both Australia and restless India were in jeopardy.

Small wonder that Prime Minister Churchill secretly confided to the Commons that "the violence, fury, skill and might of Japan had far exceeded anything that we had been led to expect." At the time he spoke Japanese air and surface forces had already attacked Ceylon, destroyed 100,000 tons of cargo shipping in the Bay of Bengal, and gained effective command of the Bay. There was reason to fear that India might be invaded in the not distant future.

To safeguard the seaways to the East by way of South Africa, British forces occupied the French island of Madagascar, and to coun- teract political dissensions in India which were laming the war effort, Sir Stafford Cripps was flown there to confer with Indian leaders, Hindu, Moslem, and others. At the beginning of the war Hindu leader- ship had expressed sympathy with the Allied cause, while reiterating the stock demand for independence. But in the fall of 1940 open resist- ance to British authority started and thousands of rebellious Hindu Nationalists were imprisoned.

Cripps offered the Indians eventual Dominion status and promised that India could "decide in the future its relation to other member states of the Commonwealth." But the Hindu chiefs, bent upon fuller political responsibilities for India immediately, and obsessed with the idea that Britain was on the verge of defeat, flatly spurned the over- ture. Spokesmen of the Moslems, firmly wedded to the partition of

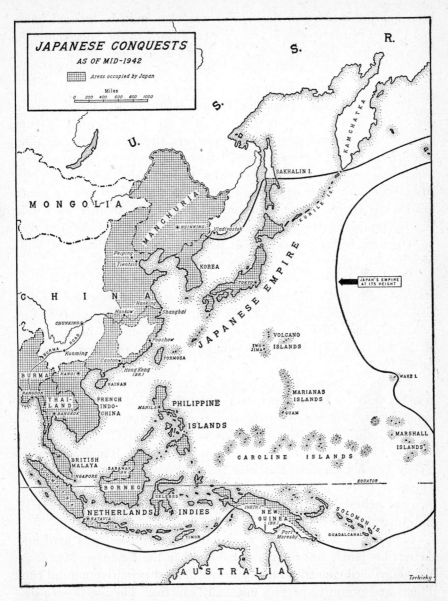

JAPANESE CONQUESTS
AS OF MID-1942
Areas occupied by Japan

India into a Moslem and a Hindu state, were equally unbending. Old
stubborn obstacles, the heritage of long Anglo-Indian bitterness, could
not be surmounted and the Cripps mission yielded no beneficial results.
Presently Hindu leaders were clapped into jail, Gandhi among them,
and the familiar cycle of violence and repression reappeared.

Australia's safety was directly threatened by Japanese landings on
New Guinea, by violent air raids upon its southern ports and indeed
upon Darwin in Australia itself. Soldiers of the Antipodes who had

been fighting in African theatres of war were quickly brought home
and United States troops in convoy were rushed to the huge continent
"down under." Happily, two major sea engagements, in which the
Nipponese were soundly thrashed, relieved the peril to Australia and
virtually put a stop to Japanese expansion.

The first of these engagements, the Battle of the Coral Sea, in
early May, 1942, lasted six days, without the Japanese or American
surface fleets so much as seeing one another. Airplanes did the fighting.
The United States suffered losses, but the Japanese naval expedition,
which was pointed for southern New Guinea, abandoned the plan.
About a month later a Japanese squadron was discovered en route
to Midway Island. Again rival aircraft fought one another, each side
heavily punishing the other, but so badly mauled was the Jap that
he retreated. In the perspective of time the American victory at Midway loomed up as the turning point in the Great Pacific War.

Making a bold surprise jump Nipponese forces occupied the west-
ernmost isles of the Aleutian archipelago, which represented, potentially at least, a threat to Alaska and North America proper. But
practically that adventure had no more bearing on the broad course
of the war than a spectacular "Doolittle" bombing raid over Tokyo in
April, 1942.

Among the many archipelagoes in the Southern Seas which had
been occupied by the Japanese were the Solomons. Firmly entrenching
himself there, the enemy intended to use the Solomons as a base for
bombing missions to Australia. But in August, 1942, United States
marines effected landings at various points on the islands and after
bloody fighting captured the prize Henderson airfield on Guadalcanal.
Try as it would, Japanese seapower could not prevent the passage of
men and materials to the Solomons or to New Guinea, where American
and Australian forces had dug in.

Fighting on New Guinea, as on other Pacific isles, was hard and
the terrible jungle was often a worse foe than the Japanese. Men from
highly civilized countries found warfare against primitive natural conditions and primitive peoples unusually exacting. They were at a dis-
advantage until the employment of the products of western industry
tipped the scales in their favor.

The Japanese flood was checked. But the campaigns to conquer
Guadalcanal and to win footholds on New Guinea, as starting points
for the expulsion of the enemy from the southern Pacific, had consumed fully six months. If that were to be the pace of reconquest, long
years of war would be required to drive the Japanese from the regions
which they had seized with such startling dispatch.

The Russian Front: Stalingrad

As the Americans in the autumn of 1942 had called a halt to Japanese progress in the Pacific, so with gathering might the Russians had turned the tide in the Soviet motherland. But before that point was reached, the soil of the USSR had borne as destructive, as pitiless, and as savage fighting as modern history records.

Throughout the early months of 1942 specially equipped and trained Soviet troops bit into the long German front at many sectors and Russian guerilla fighters gnawed unceasingly at enemy lines. General Winter too was enlisted on the Red side. It was perhaps the most bitter winter in half a century, and the ill-prepared Wehrmacht suffered terribly—the Russians only less so. It was almost miraculous that the invader avoided complete disaster in early 1942.

When weather conditions turned favorable, the Germans resumed their hammer blows, striking at the Crimea, which was taken after an heroic defense at Sevastopol. Then the Nazi offensive was concentrated in two main routes, first, toward Voronezh to the south of Moscow, with the objective of outflanking the Soviet capital. That thrust was halted in July. Second was a series of slashing drives at the Don river, which was crossed, and once more the Germans and their allies swept into Rostov.

At that juncture the Nazi offensive branched off, the main weight of energy being focused upon Stalingrad on the lower Volga, while another drive was pointed in the direction of the Caucasus and vital Soviet oilfields. In the latter sector the Nazis pressed victoriously forward, winning the oil-wells at Maikop, but falling short of larger ones at Grozny, on the northern edge of the Caucasus. It would appear that the inability of German transport to keep panzer divisions supplied with fuel, which meant three weeks of enforced idleness, was one of the critical failures in the Nazi war with the Soviets.

The Battle of Stalingrad stands out as one of the great epics of modern military history, to be compared in many ways with the desperate struggle around Verdun in World War I. A typical Soviet "boom-town," containing the greatest tractor plant of the Union and other large factories, Stalingrad had been the scene of a decisive struggle in the Russian civil war and thereafter had been renamed in honor of the Soviet dictator, who had participated in the strategy that brought victory at Stalingrad to the Red forces.

In August the Nazis started their third massive lunge upon Stalingrad which carried them in a fortnight to the fringe of the city; in a single day of heavy bombing three quarters of Stalingrad were flat-

tened. Throughout September and October and on into November the
Nazis and their allies pounded away with all the skill and resources at
their command. They took most of the city and they were desperately
anxious to hold it as a suitable wintering-place for the troops, as a
strong point, and as a safeguard for communication lines to the south.
Stalingrad was the high-water mark of the German conquest.

Tactically Stalingrad was hard to defend, for it sprawled out for
thirty miles or more and backed upon the mile-wide Volga, over which
Soviet troops and supplies had to be ferried. Subjected to constant
bombardment the Red troops were given no rest, but they battled on
bravely and with tenacity. Munitions workers, nurses, even house-
wives fought alongside the men of the Soviet army. Factories were
converted into fortresses, and reinforcements were poured in from
the east.

German commanders threw tank and infantry division after tank
and infantry division into Stalingrad only to have them stopped by
great rubble barricades on alternate sides of streets and caught in
the raking fire of anti-tank guns. Fighting raged in alleys, court-
yards, shops, from house to house, even from room to room. Once
great Stalingrad was transformed into a monstrous graveyard of
ruined buildings, shattered walls, and rotting flesh.

Rumblings in the Reich over the time that was required to capture
Stalingrad elicited from Hitler the reassuring statement that "we are
taking so long because we do not want mass murder." He proclaimed
in fact that the fall of the coveted city was imminent.

But the indomitable Russians would not have it thus. Having denied Stalingrad to the enemy, the Red armies in turn launched a powerful counterattack on November 19, relieving the city and taking
droves of prisoners and masses of war booty. In the fierce fighting ten
Rumanian divisions were cut to pieces and seven of Mussolini's
divisions suffered almost as severely. Unable to withdraw their encircled troops, the German commanders, on February 2, 1943, surrendered with 330,000 men.

Stalingrad ranks among the decisive battles of history. It was the
worst catastrophe that German arms had suffered since the victory
of Napoleon at Jena in 1806. The Russians now felt themselves the
equal of any power in the world and they were eager to make sure
that other nations were conscious of their strength. As for Hitler, he
ordered a first-class funeral for his lost legions, with four days of
public mourning and plenty of appropriate music.

Stalingrad was followed up by a violent Red offensive in the
vicinity of Voronezh. From that point down to the Caucasus the for-

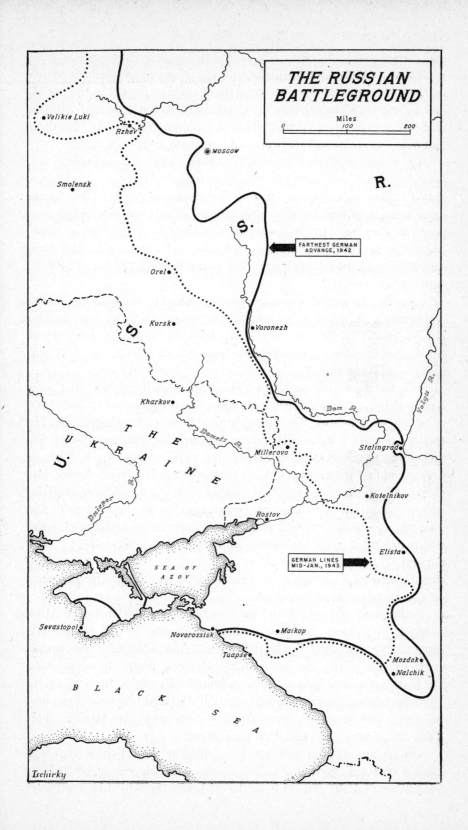

THE RUSSIAN
BATTLEGROUND

Miles
0   100   200

•Velikie Luki

Rzhev•

•MOSCOW

R.

Smolensk•

S.

FARTHEST GERMAN
ADVANCE, 1942

Orel•

S.

Kursk•

Voronezh•

Don R.

Volga R.

Kharkov•

T H E

Donets R.

U K R A I N E

Millerovo•

Stalingrad•

U.

Dnieper R.

•Kotelnikov

Rostov•

GERMAN LINES
MID-JAN., 1943

Elista•

SEA OF
AZOV

Sevastopol•

Novorossisk•

•Maikop

•Mozdok

Tuapse•

•Nalchik

B L A C K   S E A

Tschirky

ward lines of German and satellite were cracked. By now the initiative on the vast plains of the USSR had unmistakenly passed to the Soviets and the struggle in the east had definitely inclined toward Marshal Stalin. Yet there were no signs that the German armies would break up and disintegrate as had the forces of Napoleon in 1812 and 1813.

The larger strategic pattern of the Soviet High Command was now evident. In keeping with old Russian tradition, the Red armies had delayed the advance of the invader by ceaseless attrition, but at the same time they had steadily pulled back, until conditions were most propitious for a powerful counter-thrust. Then huge reserves of Soviet manpower and weapons were hurled into the contest. Excellent Russian staff-work kept supplies moving to the front in the face of almost superhuman obstacles.

In spite of terrible suffering among Russian civilians and acute shortages of the bare necessities of life, Soviet factories kept turning out the goods of war. In the midst of the fighting new armies were raised and trained, a prodigious achievement which has few parallels in military annals.

In a survey at the outset of 1943 Stalin stated that the Red army had inflicted 9,000,000 casualties upon the invading hosts, 4,000,000 of which were deaths. That unquestionably was an exaggeration, but enemy casualties were very large, and besides, Stalingrad had disillusioning repercussions upon the mind of Germany. Instead of the propaganda of impending victory that hitherto had been dinned into German ears, the themes of fear and the dread consequences of defeat were emphasized. Germans were warned that if they faltered now "Asiatic vandalism" would engulf the Fatherland and the miseries which prevailed after the defeat in 1918 would seem small by comparison. What hitherto had been a war of Axis conquest had been transformed into a struggle for Axis survival, as any informed German or Italian must have perceived.

Throughout the spring and summer of 1942 agitation for an Allied invasion of western Europe—a "Second Front," it was called—was intense in Britain and the United States. And Marshal Stalin openly criticized the Allies for not doing something more efficacious than the mass aerial bombing of German industrial centers, to draw off the German hordes hammering eastward. But Allied strategists doubted whether their resources were equal to storming the Atlantic Wall. They did, however, venture an experiment.

On August 19, a contingent of Canadians and British struck at Dieppe on the French coast. Planes fought the biggest air-battle since September of 1940 and for a matter of hours the Allied expeditionary forces held a precarious toehold on the shore. But the German defenses were proved more formidable than armchair strategists had imagined. The Dieppe raid collapsed, and the cries for a Second Front subsided somewhat. Churchill undertook a hurried flight to Moscow to explain to the Soviet leaders why a Second Front was impracticable and to lay before them the plans of strategy that had been decided upon. But Stalin and his fellows were not placated and complained bitterly and captiously that the Red armies were bearing the whole brunt of the war.

Allied aid to the USSR in the shape of war supplies was being delivered, to be sure, in growing volume and over two principal routes. The more important way was from British ports to Archangel and Murmansk in northern Russia, a trip of 1,500 miles. To convoy merchantmen along the Arctic, where attacks from German coastal craft and planes had to be fought off for days on end, where icebergs were a constant peril, and where in winter ships become topheavy with ice imposed added and terrible strains upon the resources of the Royal Navy.

Less hazardous was the transport of goods to the Soviet Union around Africa to landing places on the Persian Gulf. Protection on that route had to be provided by the guns of the Royal Navy against possible Japanese forays; besides, the sea-voyage from Britain to Persia (Iran) was 11,000 miles (12,000 from New York), and once supplies reached Persia they had to be hauled hundreds of miles overland or across the Caspian Sea to their Soviet destination. Yet in the face of all obstacles the flow of munitions, vehicles, foodstuffs, and the like to Russia steadily mounted and was an invaluable asset for the Red armies.

Russia, moreover, benefited from Allied military operations in North Africa which compelled the Germans to divert squadrons of the Luftwaffe and some other war equipment away from the Soviet theater.

Allied Victory in Africa

Axis fortunes in North Africa were entrusted to the dashing, scientific soldier, General Erwin Rommel, one of the very few first-class commanders that Hitler brought to the fore. A professional warrior, though not of the Prussian military caste, Rommel was long a personal friend of the Führer and that facilitated his rapid ascent of the military ladder. A deep thinker on strategy, Rommel displayed genius as leader of an armored spearhead in the French campaign, and he worked out the coordination of tank, plane, and infantryman to a nicety. He held a low opinion of his Italian allies and was always in hot water with Mussolini's generals.

At the beginning of 1942, Rommel and his famous Afrika Korps started an offensive on Tripolitania and kept it going at a whirlwind pace for months with only brief let-ups. Desperate battles of tanks studded the hot desert warfare. Though the British were superior at sea and held a slight advantage in the air, their equipment for land fighting was inferior. Therefore the Axis armies were able to run the foe out of Tripolitania and on into Egypt once more, the British digging in only when El Alamein was reached. It was a mere sixty five miles from that point to Alexandria and the crucial Suez Canal. For his glittering exploits Rommel was awarded a marshal's baton, and he picked a choice white stallion for his prospective entry into the historic cities of Egypt. Some students of strategy hold that if Rommel had been reinforced by half a dozen new divisions he could have attained his Suez and Middle East objectives.

As the British dropped back, fresh supplies of weapons were rushed to Egypt and Generals Bernard Montgomery and Harold Alexander—the latter had directed the trying evacuations of Dunkirk and Burma—were placed in command. Montgomery, perhaps the most capable British soldier of World War II, though an exceedingly difficult personality to get along with, cherished Oliver Cromwell as his idol and was noted for the Spartan methods he applied in training troops.

On October 23, 1942, the British started a great and decisive counteroffensive which the Afrika Korps was powerless to stop. Artillery smashed Rommel's defenses at El Alamein and then tank and plane drove the enemy in precipitous retreat back along the Mediterranean; in these operations the ships of the Royal Navy collaborated brilliantly with the R.A.F. in destroying a third of the Axis supply vessels and bombarding Nazi coastal positions. That decided the issue. Within three months the British progressed 1,350 miles. That gratifying success, synchronizing as it did with the Soviet victory at Stalingrad, and the American occupation of Guadalcanal, heralded the end of the beginning for the Allied cause.

At the other extremity of the Mediterranean, in French North Africa, meantime, American and British forces, General Dwight D. Eisenhower commanding, had been successfully put ashore in the biggest land and sea operation of history. Resistance by the Vichy French forces, which at first outnumbered the invaders, was little more than token in character. Allied troops drove hard upon Tunisia, which according to plans was to be subdued by Christmas. That expectation

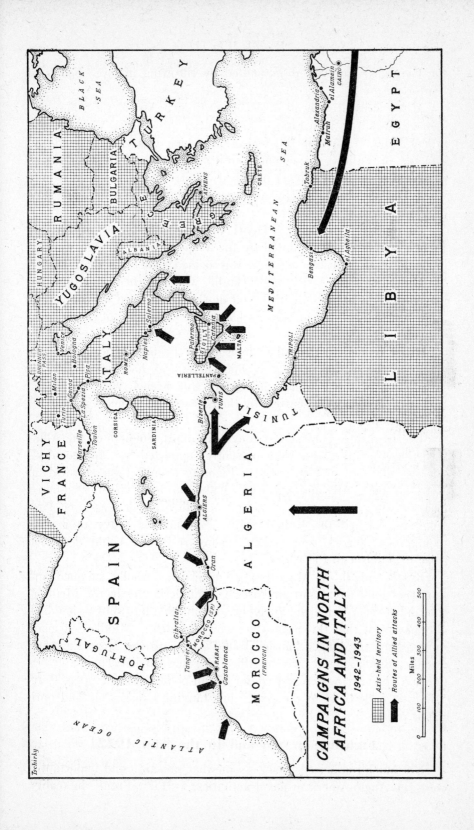

CAMPAIGNS IN NORTH
AFRICA AND ITALY

1942–1943

Axis-held territory

Routes of Allied attacks

Miles

0   100 200 300 400 500

the Germans, however, disappointed by throwing in large bodies of reinforcements.

As administrative head of occupied French Africa, the Allies recognized Admiral Jean-François Darlan, a prominent Vichyite and ardent hater of Britain. The selection, which was frankly made on grounds of military expediency, infuriated General de Gaulle and provoked a storm of protest in Allied countries, which subsided only when Darlan was killed by an assassin's bullet on Christmas Eve of 1942.

To replace him General Henri Giraud, gallant and picturesque French soldier (and untainted by the Vichy brush), though wanting in qualities of political sagacity, was named. No more than Darlan did Giraud suit the tastes of de Gaulle, who felt the nomination belonged of right to himself. Bit by bit de Gaulle crowded his competitor aside and gained recognition as the supreme leader of Frenchmen abroad.

Hitler replied to the Allied invasion of French Africa by taking charge of the section of France which heretofore had been under the jurisdiction of the Pétain-Vichy group. But French warships in the harbor of Toulon were scuttled by their crews and so made useless for Nazi purposes.

The road into Tunisia was rough and hard. Soldiers of the Allies thrusting from the west were presently supported by Montgomery's "desert rats" out of Libya, and a Fighting French force stormed up from the south. Ally and Axis each chalked up local victories, suffered local defeats; a sharp reverse for American arms at Kasserine Pass violently shocked the United States. But neither heavy rains, nor mountainous terrain, nor skillful enemy resistance could deny the prize of Tunisia to the Allies.

By the middle of May, 1943, Tunisia was wholly subdued and soon the small naval and air base of Pantelleria, set in the Mediterranean between Africa and Sicily, was bombarded into submission. The elimination of that threat to Allied shipping in the Middle Sea made unnecessary the longer journey round Africa to the Near East and Pacific, adding significantly to Allied carrying capacity.

And the way was prepared for a full-bodied assault upon Italy, "the soft underbelly of the Axis," in Churchill's masculine and optimistic prose.

Fighting on Sea and in the Air: 1942

Not much publicized because somewhat prosaic—and important— were the Anglo-American naval activities, a "First Front" in reality.

Vehement was the British press outcry in February, 1942, when the Nazi warships, *Gneisenau, Scharnhorst,* and *Prinz Eugen,* slipped out of the French harbor of Brest, and, under cover of airpower, threaded their course through the English Channel and the North Sea and into the Baltic. Linking that spectacular episode with the disheartening capitulation at Singapore, British opinion caused Churchill to shake up his Cabinet and inject some new and more vigorous blood into it.

As in World War I the Germans pinned great faith on the U-boat. Month by month the fleet of undersea marauders increased and in 1942 may have reached 530, despite considerable sinkings. Not only were U-boats more numerous and bolder but new tactics, the tactics of "the wolf-pack," were put to the test; that is, clusters of eight to sixteen submarines operating under a single commander slipped into the center of an Allied convoy, loosed torpedoes in every direction, and then dashed off at top surface speed. As had been true since the onset of war, Allied weapons to fight the submarine were so limited that U-boats came to the surface with impunity even in daylight, fired at cargo carriers with their guns or charged their batteries.

After the outbreak of the Great Pacific War Allied shipping difficulties took on an extremely grave character. For a time the United States lost tankers and merchant vessels faster than they could be replaced and, for 1942 as a whole, Allied sinkings through submarine action exceeded 6,000,000 tons—the peak destruction came in November—or almost half the losses because of U-boats in the whole war.

To answer the serious challenge of the submarine, ship construction in American yards was greatly speeded up and the situation was saved.[1] Soon after the United States became a belligerent an Anglo-American Shipping Allocation Board was created so that cargo tonnage might be used most efficiently in the broad Allied strategic pattern. The Board was conspicuously successful and in 1944 it was widened to cover the shipping resources of seventeen Allied nations and one neutral, Sweden.

American naval units, furthermore, assumed an increasingly more prominent role in the crucial Battle of the Atlantic. More extensive use was made of aircraft patrols and of escorts to protect convoys. That worked. It was officially disclosed that only one out of every 200 Allied vessels in convoy failed to complete the voyage; every convoy that reached port was a battle won. Britain put a strange new

---

[1] To combat the U-boat menace and to provide a landing field for the invasion of western Europe, Allied technicians experimented with a project to build a 2,000,000 ton aircraft carrier out of ice-blocks. The idea was not abandoned until December, 1943, and by then the submarine danger had been considerably reduced.

ship into convoy duty—the escort carrier, a merchantman with a flight deck built on. American and Britisher vied with each other in devising instruments and weapons to fight the submarine: sonar buoys, magnetic detectors, and the like. Nazi assurances that U-boats would effectively intercept American troop-transports on the sea were blasted, as the presence of Americans in North Africa—and before that in the British Isles—eloquently testified.

On any day of the year, 600 British warcraft of all types were operating on the blue oceans. Regularly they patrolled 80,000 miles of seaways, keeping watch over as many as 3,000 ships and keeping Axis Europe blockaded, too. Regularly British units were at work clearing mines from 14,000 miles of ocean. On the average, three real naval engagements were fought each week, not to mention endless encounters with submarines. Here was indeed a First Front, which was all too little appreciated by those who loudly clamored for a Second Front.

In the air, too, activity mounted in tempo, the Allies in the west seeking to draw off German planes from the Russian theater and to smash industrial targets and U-boat bases in Axis Europe. At the end of May, 1942, Cologne was struck by a thousand British bombers, which caused great devastation; it was said that the destructive power was fourfold greater than anything previously undertaken. Essen, Bremen, and other German cities were likewise subjected to fearful poundings, a foretaste of worse that was to come.[2] On the 4th of July, the first airmen of the United States made flights over German-occupied territory. Axis raids were largely restricted to spectacular sneak attacks on British seaports and the damage inflicted was slight.

Counter Strokes in the Pacific

Building upon the gains won toward the end of 1942, Allied arms, predominantly American, gnawed away in 1943 at the fringes of the fabulous Japanese conquests. Growing superiority in the air enabled the United States to expel the Nipponese from some strategic points and as the year moved on the Japs were cleared out of eastern New Guinea, New Georgia, Bougainville, and most of the Solomon archipelago; but "island-hopping" was slow, tedious business, uncongenial to the national temperament of the United States.

In June, 1943, the Australian Prime Minister, John Curtin, assured his countrymen that the danger of invasion no longer existed. Still, the

[2] Sir Arthur Harris, chief of Bomber Command, said confidently, "If I could send 20,000 bombers to Germany tonight, Germany would not be in the war tomorrow." But competing calls upon air resources prevented so massive an assault upon the industries of the Third Reich.

enemy held strong defensive positions in the western section of New Guinea and at Rabaul in the Solomons.

In May American forces started to drive the invader from the western islets of the Aleutians, another omen of rising American naval strength in the Pacific. The task was accomplished in three months amidst hazards of weather and terrain difficult to exaggerate. With the freeing of the Aleutians, it became feasible for American bombers to attack Nipponese positions in the neighboring Kuriles.

Far to the south, in the central Pacific, the Americans in November advanced upon the Gilberts. Operations focused on the small but ingeniously defended island of Tarawa, which was subdued after a short though bloody struggle. Lessons learned in the conquest of Tarawa would be splendidly applied in subsequent amphibious campaigns up the ladder of Pacific islands to the very heart of Nippon itself.

The Japanese, meantime, had "dug in" in the areas they had conquered, exploited the material and human resources, and maneuvered adroitly to enlist the cooperation of the native populations in the war effort. To the Burmese, for example, a nominally independent government was granted and persistent and shrewd propaganda was employed to intensify native Asiatic resentment against the white man. Though partly successful, Nipponese tactics failed to attain their objectives fully, for some natives, who took Allied wartime utterances such as the "Four Freedoms" and the Atlantic Charter seriously, formed guerilla bands of resistance. They waged unceasing war against the Japanese and dreamed of a day when they would be liberated from all alien control, yellow and white alike.

Along the extensive front of Manchuria, Japanese and Soviet armies were massed each in readiness for any warlike move on the part of the other nation. None was made; indeed a pre-war treaty granting Japanese fishing rights in Siberian waters was renewed, and the Japanese navy did not interfere with small quantities of Lend-Lease materials that were hauled from the United States in Soviet ships to Vladivostok.

The Invasion of Italy

Collapse of Axis power in North Africa laid Italy open to Allied invasion. That prospect roused nervous fears in the Axis countries and stimulated special unrest and disaffection in Italy; mass strikes which recurred in the industrial North were probably instigated by the anti-Fascist underground and quarreling increased inside top Fascist circles. Therefore Mussolini made changes in his cabinet and by dictatorial decrees endeavored to improve discipline among factory workers.

Outside of Axis Europe it was believed that conquered peoples would spring at the throats of their oppressors once the forces of Allied invasion were set in motion.

On July 9, 1943, a huge Allied expedition of some 3,000 ships set off from Africa for the conquest of Sicily; "Operation Husky" it was called. That was the first large scale amphibious assault upon Axis territory. Landings were effected on Sicily with surprisingly little opposition at first, beaches were in many cases unmined, pillboxes were deserted, and many Italian soldiers melted away into civilian clothes.

Presently the resistance stiffened, though not sufficiently to halt the Allied advance. Messina was taken after violent fighting and that victory virtually finished the Sicilian campaign. Italy's mainland could now be invaded, while airfields in Sicily furnished bases to intensify the aerial bombardment upon the Axis.

On the Italian political front, meantime, a volcano had erupted, blowing Mussolini off his pinnacle. While the Allied advance across Sicily proceeded, il Duce held earnest consultations with Hitler, who frankly admitted that Germany was incapable of rendering more aid than already was being given. When that verdict was transmitted on July 26 to the Fascist Grand Council, the members on a vote of nineteen to seven deposed Mussolini and had him arrested.

Supreme authority was vested in King Victor Emmanuel III and Marshal Pietro Badoglio, perhaps the foremost Italian soldier at the time. Mussolini's downfall thrilled the Allied world. By the same token, it depressed the Germans, who were informed that a clique of Italian traitors and conspirators was responsible for the repudiation of Fascism.

Nazi parachutists in a bold adventure rescued Mussolini from prison. He set up a "Fascist Republic" in northern Italy and proclaimed his intention of carrying on the war to the bitter end. His new regime was of course the merest puppet of the Germans. General Albert Kesselring took charge of military operations and governmental affairs in the central sector of the peninsula, while the ubiquitous Rommel commanded the situation to the north. Sporadic risings, organized by Italian partisans, testified that war-weariness coupled with anti-Fascist sentiment were on the rise.

With the approval of the King, Badoglio entered upon secret negotiations with the Allies for an armistice, and on September 3, 1943, it was revealed that a settlement had been signed. Although the detailed conditions of the armistice were not divulged, for reasons of military security, Badoglio, nonetheless, surrendered unconditionally. Italian soldiers were instructed to turn in their arms. Most of what remained of the Fascist fleet, merchant marine, and airforce were handed over to the victors. It was agreed that until the Allies had captured Rome, an anti-Fascist Ministry would look after Italian affairs under Allied supervision. Fascist institutions were scrapped and Fascists were purged from public offices. Presently the Badoglio Ministry assumed the status of co-belligerent by declaring war on Germany.

The Allied offensive in southern Italy had meanwhile not been developing as fast as Allied leaders and peoples had anticipated. True, early in September Allied armies gained footholds in Italy proper and an amphibious landing was made at Salerno, below Naples. Grim and desperate struggles ensued there with the enemy thrusting hard in an effort to drive the invaders into the sea; but, supported by naval bombardment, the Allies held the dearly bought ground doggedly. Stout German resistance frustrated the Allied plans for a quick drive into Rome.

British troops advanced into Naples on September 30. The Allied line by then stretched across the peninsula from sea to sea. The islands of Sardinia and Corsica were captured. Airfields in southern Italy were readied for an intensified assault upon north Italian cities and "Hitler's Fortress," including the Balkan peninsula. But progress to the north was irritatingly slow, being hampered less by the enemy, vigorously though he fought, than by formidable natural obstacles and adverse weather conditions. Yet some thirty five German divisions were kept busy on the Italian front and thus were not available for the fighting in the Soviet theater. As the Germans yielded ground they devastated the abandoned areas, but the destruction of famous Italian architectural and artistic treasures was less thorough than had been feared.

Over against the gains in Italy, the Allies had to post a reversal in the Aegean area. British landings in the Dodecanese in September, 1943, were hailed as the preface to a thrust into Greece. But the Germans counterattacked in force, compelling the British to relinquish their precarious positions on the Aegean islands.

Sea and Air: 1943

As on land, so Allied superiority on the sea and in the air grew apace in 1943. At the start of the year Grand-Admiral Karl Doenitz, a veteran submariner, who firmly believed that the U-boat could save the Third Reich from defeat, was named commander of the German seaforces. Inasmuch as Doenitz was the architect of the *Rudel-system*, the wolf-pack strategy, his appointment heralded an intensification of undersea warfare. Official Allied spokesmen frankly acknowledged that shipping was the Achilles heel of the war effort.

In the early spring of 1943 the Nazis carried on the U-boat campaign with renewed violence and no small success, and sinkings touched a new high in March. But Allied counter measures were improved; patrol craft assigned to convoy duty were much increased and a kind of "air umbrella" was raised for transatlantic sailings. By June the worst was over in the Battle of the Atlantic, ship casualties that month being smaller than at any time since the entry of the United States into the war.

More efficient patrolling compelled Nazi wolf-packs to stay underwater in daylight. They could cruise at only two to four knots an hour, for higher speeds would have exhausted their batteries. Patrols, the placing of Leigh lights on night-flying planes, the use of radar instruments and other ingenious anti-submarine contrivances made surfacing perilous, but that had to be done once daily, as a rule, to replenish the supply of fresh air and to charge batteries.

Through the final third of 1943 German submarines were reported to have been sunk in greater numbers than Allied cargo carriers. For the year as a whole, ship losses were only two fifths of 1942 and only a quarter of the 1943 total was torpedoed in the second half of the year. Bold attempts of Japanese seamen to break through the blockade to Germany were brought to a standstill. In a word, Doenitz had fallen far short of his objectives. Yet his prestige with Hitler remained undiminished and in the Führer's last testament Doenitz was named as successor in place of Goering.

Helpful in the job of hunting down the submarine was a British deal with her ancient ally, neutral Portugal, which permitted Allied use of certain naval facilities in the Azores Islands. At year's end convoys were proceeding across the Atlantic as over the Mediterranean almost without fear of molestation. As a crowning naval stroke, off the northern tip of Norway, a British squadron fell upon the great German battleship, *Scharnhorst,* which was attempting to destroy a convoy en route to Russia, and sent her to join the *Bismarck* (December 26, 1943). Mastery of the seas which the Axis had seized in 1941 had been fully regained by the Allies.

Bombing assaults upon the Reich and the occupied countries, which had risen in magnitude in 1942, attained such heights in 1943 that air enthusiasts confidently predicted that bombing alone could crush the enemy. Harmonious cooperation between British and American airforces made possible round-the-clock operations, the former raiding by night, the latter by day.

In the spring months the aerial campaign was concentrated on the vital war industries of the Ruhr valley. In July the great seaport of Hamburg was thoroughly pummeled; at the end of the year Berlin gained the unenviable distinction of being the most bombed city in the world. In all, Allied airmen were by way of destroying forty major German centers and fifty more of lesser significance. Germany and with it occupied Europe were being methodically softened up as the prelude to invasion across the Channel. During 1943 the R.A.F. alone dropped twice the tonnage of bombs dropped in the first three years of the titanic struggle.

Never in all history had men possessed so devastating and so destructive a weapon as the great bombers. Casualties of airmen, to be sure, ran high, the British alone losing some 18,000 of her keenest young men, either killed or imprisoned. Yet the losses were fractional compared with the casualties in the trench fighting of World War I; to win three and a half miles in the bitter fighting on the Somme in 1916, 21,000 Britishers had been sacrificed in a single day.

The mounting Allied air offensive resembled in a way the sea-blockade for, like the mills of the gods, they both ground slowly. But grind they did. Saturation raids, military disasters in Russia, in Africa, in Italy, the failure of U-boat warfare intensified alarm and despondency in many a German heart and worsened the economic plight of the nation.

Food rations in Germany were cut down in May, 1943, and clothing and housing steadily deteriorated. To keep the war going the total mobilization of the Reich's human resources was decreed. Efforts were made to spur on the populace by reiteration of the dread consequences of defeat; the alternatives offered were simply victory or annihilation. Neither political parties nor trade unions were available in the monolithic Reich to channel popular longing for the end of hostilities as in 1918. Symptomatic of the impending doom of Germany were the cooler attitude adopted by Sweden toward the Reich and the intensification of the mass brutalities in the conquered countries, for which one day the Germans would be made to pay dearly.

The Liberation of Russia: 1943

On the Russian front, the brilliant Soviet triumph at Stalingrad ushered in a year of immense, almost uninterrupted military gains for the Red army. Moving inexorably westward the Russian commanders by shrewd timing and astute coordination of resources liberated about two thirds of the territory which the invader had seized.

At the outset of 1943 the long blockade of Leningrad was broken though the siege was not lifted, and the Nazi keypoint of Kharkov was retaken only to be lost a month later. By bombing enemy lines the Red airforce forced the Nazis to postpone offensive operations, which got under way finally in July but the Germans were halted before the month was over. Then the Russians launched a full-scale and impetuous counteroffensive on the south and center which irresistibly swept the enemy before it. Kharkov and Kiev were taken by storm; Smolensk and Gomel were reclaimed, and at Christmas time the Red armies started an impressive winter campaign.

For the Germans it must be said that, though they fell back, the Stalingrad entrapment was not repeated. No troops ever responded with more valor, more endurance, and technical perfection than the Germans in Russia. Without high standards of discipline, leadership, and administration the retreating German armies would have duplicated the French debacle of 1940. Despite disheartening reverses army morale seems not to have faltered.

Throughout the year, or at least until the Allied conferences described below, Soviet spokesmen and press complained that the western Allies were not carrying a fair share of the military burden; operations in North Africa and Italy were dismissed as "side shows." What Moscow imperiously demanded was an invasion of western Europe, for which the Allied commanders were as yet unready. It was, however, disclosed that General Eisenhower would be Supreme Commander of the invasion forces, with Montgomery in command of the British divisions. Britain's air Vice-Marshal, Sir Arthur Tedder, would be Eisenhower's deputy and British Admiral Sir Bertram Ramsay would have charge of naval operations.

More and more, the Soviet Republic took on the character of a conventional military state and old martial traditions of the Russian nation were resurrected. Comrade Stalin, who was exempted from service in World War I because of a physical infirmity, assumed the dignity of Generalissimo. Brilliant marshals and generals, who replaced the dubious commanders of the first stage of the war, were showered with privileges and lavish publicity. Young soldiers earned rapid military promotion by the talents and the loyalty they displayed in battle. The defender of Stalingrad, for example, General Alexander Rodimtsev, who had fought in the Spanish Civil War, was only thirty-six.

Members of the Russian officers' corps were permitted to sew epaulettes on their uniforms, which since the Revolution had been forbidden as tsarist symbolism. To reward gallantry Soviet military decorations, named for tsarist generals such as Suvorov and Kutuzov, were struck off, and ceremonies of investiture, as under the old regime, were held within the walls of the Kremlin. Historic Russian Guard regiments and the colorful Cossacks, forgotten since the Revolution, were restored to their old-time glamor.

Orthodox notions of army discipline and order were more fully applied and the office of political commissar, whose duty it was to watch over the behavior of the officers, was abandoned. The Red army enjoyed immense numerical superiority over the Nazis and their satellites, recruiting troops from a population almost double that of the enemy, and the Russian rear was protected while the Germans were being attacked in heavy force elsewhere. Those advantages, along with the flexible tactics of the Russian commanders, counted heavily in the Soviet smash westward. On the open plains, the tank was given free rein; to reduce enemy strongpoints, artillery was brought up, while cavalry harried the foe out of swampland and forest. Aircraft in Russian strategy held second place to ground operations.

On the Soviet home front, life in the war-areas was incredibly hard. Fields were laid waste, villages razed, populous cities reduced to rubble by the contending armies. In all, forty per cent of the total acreage in the collective farms of the USSR given over to the raising of wheat were devastated, herds and flocks had vanished, and virtually all the farm machinery, tractors, and combine-harvesters upon which the villagers were utterly dependent, had been destroyed. As another sign of the catastrophic consequences of the invasion, the Soviet output of steel dropped in 1943 to approximately half the pre-war production. Shortages of everyday necessities, acute enough before the war, grew progressively worse.

As the invader was expelled, the enormous task of reconstruction was set in motion. From the remote interior, even from Siberia, peasant families trekked back to their birth-villages. In many places rehabilitation had to begin at the beginning, for what once were homes were merely mounds of debris and wood. Without machinery, the peasants worked the soil with the most primitive tools and some livestock was shipped into the liberated areas from the rest of the Union. A few coal mines, after water was pumped out, and a few factories were put in operation.

For all the hardships it was apparent that the tide of Russian patriotism was flowing strong and more considerate treatment of the Church by the Soviet government brought comfort to many a bereaved and disconsolate mooshik. Orthodox clergymen, out of gratitude, offered up prayers for the victory of the Red army and solicited funds to pay for tanks and planes.

Undoubtedly the moderate attitude of the Kremlin in matters of religion was partly motivated by a desire to lessen animosity toward the Communist regime in the Christian world. And similar in intent was the dissolution in May, 1943, of the Third International (or Comintern) on the declared score that the organization had outlived its usefulness; and, instead of the stirring Marxist *International,* a new patriotic Russian anthem was introduced. Occasional Soviet press articles, shying away from doctrinaire Marxist dogma, now interpreted the Bolshevik Revolution as the redemption of Mother Russia from tsarist obscurantism and foreign domination rather than as the first episode in a world-wide and Messianic struggle against bourgeois capitalism. Yet there was no official sign that the ideal of international revolution had been repudiated.

Russia and the West

As the Red armies stormed westward questions were raised in the outer world as to whether the massive Soviet power would be used for imperial conquests or perhaps for attaining "strategic frontiers" against possible invasion in the future. Field Marshal Jan C. Smuts set diplomatic and journalistic chords vibrating by his characterization of the Soviet Union as "a colossus bestriding the continent." It was entirely natural for Nazi propagandists, with defeat staring at them, to play upon the theme of impending Bolshevik domination of Europe; in that manner they might sow distrust within the Grand Alliance, awaken old prejudices, latent dreads and suspicions, and, mayhap, smooth the way for a conclusion of hostilities, short of unconditional surrender.

The USSR emphatically asserted claims to permanent retention of the Baltic Republics, Bessarabia, the Bukovina, and eastern Poland, all of which had been occupied during the Soviet-Nazi collaboration. There was, however, another side of the story, for Russia as a member of the Grand Alliance had signed binding engagements to eschew aggression, territorial aggrandizement, and boundary changes at variance with the principle of self-determination. By endorsing the Atlantic Charter, the USSR promised political freedoms to nations "forcibly deprived of them."

Poland was the principal storm center of inter-Allied tension and politics. In the first terrible months of the German war, the men in the Kremlin had officially agreed with the exiled Polish government in London that boundary questions should be resolved at a conference after the war. But the Russo-Polish honeymoon became a memory when the Nazi invader was thrust to the west and Russia indicated her intention to annex eastern Poland, holding that the Atlantic Charter was inapplicable, since Russia had occupied the district before the Charter was framed.

On the other hand, the London Poles intransigently and noisily demanded that the national border of 1939 must be the frontier of the New Poland. The accidental death in 1943 of General Wladyslaw Sikorski, foremost leader of the London Poles, who combined a high order of statesmanship and generalship, removed the one man who might conceivably have been able to work out a Polish-Russian accommodation. Old distrusts between Pole and Russian surged up afresh and Nazi propaganda shrewdly embittered feelings with every device that came to hand.

Russo-Polish antagonism grew in fact so strained in 1943 that the Kremlin cut off diplomatic relations with the London Poles and promoted the organization of a group of Polish Communists, domiciled in the Soviet Union, in frank opposition to the London group. (The Sovietophile Polish group came to be known as the Lublin government). Even so, Stalin stated over and over again that the USSR desired "a strong and independent Poland," and that assurance of purpose was accepted by Prime Minister Churchill as satisfactory. It was proposed that Poland should have territorial compensation for the loss of the eastern provinces at the expense of the Third Reich. Unappeased by that prospect Polish politicians abroad, or at least the army leaders, kept up a running criticism of Soviet "imperialism," while the Soviet press in turn brusquely pilloried the Polish "Fascists."

Planning for Victory and Peace

Tangled problems connected with the coordination of Allied efforts to defeat the enemy and with the drafting of the blueprint of a constructive and durable global peace engaged the energies of Allied policymakers while the pendulum of battle was swinging to their side. Notable progress was registered at a succession of epochal inter-Allied conferences.

For ten days in January, 1943, President Roosevelt, Prime Minister Churchill and the best military brains of their two nations conferred at Casablanca in French Morocco on plans for the heavy tasks that lay ahead. Complete understanding was attained and it was proclaimed that the only terms upon which the western nations would make an armistice with the Axis were unconditional surrender, the famous formula which Grant had propounded for Lee at Appomattox.

That pronouncement ruled out of course any settlement with the enemy through the channels of diplomatic negotiation. Critics, at the time, and indeed at intervals until almost the close of the war, wondered whether a phrase such as "honorable capitulation," which would have amounted to the same thing as unconditional surrender, but which had a softer sound to professional military ears, might not have encouraged Nazi commanders to break off the fighting long before they did. Marshal Stalin, who was invited to the Casablanca parley, begged off on the score that home conditions required his constant presence in Moscow, but he endorsed the unconditional surrender formula and on several later occasions the Big Three nations reaffirmed their allegiance to it. The Casablanca communiqué bestowed glowing praise upon the Red military effort and assured the world that Stalin was being kept fully informed on the military intentions of the western Allies.[3]

Everywhere it was appreciated that after the fighting ceased the world would be faced by gigantic problems of reconstruction. To prepare against that day a conference of Allied specialists on food and agriculture was convoked at Hot Springs, Virginia, in May, 1943. The result of the deliberations was a vague understanding—subsequently somewhat clarified—to work for better dietary standards for the peoples of the United Nations and to raise the economic level of farmers and peasants. For instance, a corps of agricultural experts would be created to furnish advice to any member state on problems related to food production. Representatives of forty four nations, the Soviet Union for one, shared in the Hot Springs consultations and accords.

More urgent, however, than long range projects for agricultural improvement were the formidable tasks of providing basic necessities of existence for millions upon millions as soon as the bombs stopped falling. The need for food, clothing, medical care, seeds, tools, cattle, and the like would be staggering, and, as one angle of rehabilitation, it would be necessary to look after displaced persons in Europe— refugees, men and women who had been dragooned into German farms and factories—very conservatively estimated at 12,000,000. It was the part of wisdom as well as primitive humanitarism to make ready to meet those post-war conditions.

Against that background, at a meeting in Atlantic City in November, 1943, the United Nations Relief and Rehabilitation Administration (spoken of as UNRRA) was born. Special committees were set

[3] Toward the end of the conference Roosevelt and Churchill strove to effect a reconciliation between General Charles de Gaulle, petulant leader of the Fighting French, and General Henri Giraud, the veteran soldier whom the Allies had placed in authority in French North Africa. These generals had been wrangling over which should be the head man of the French forces abroad.

to work on shipping, food, public health, and similar questions. Direction over the entire administration was placed in the competent hands of Herbert H. Lehman, man of affairs and former governor of New York.

To finance the activities of UNRRA, each member of the United Nations whose soil had not been invaded bound itself to contribute one per cent of its national income, which would yield an annual revenue of about $2,000,000,000. Countries which had been invaded would be expected to do what they could out of their resources to sustain their own populations. Originally it was decided that no assistance should be given to ex-enemies, except as required to prevent epidemics, but later limited aid was promised to Italy, which had become a co-belligerent.

It was definitely understood that the paramount aim of UNRRA would be to help liberated peoples to help themselves and that agents of the administration would enter a country only after being specifically invited in by the government. In no case should UNRRA representatives meddle in the home politics of the country they were serving.

Other gatherings of vital importance for Allied solidarity in war and in peace had, meantime, been held. At Quebec, in August, Roosevelt and Churchill and their military counselors had refined plans for the prosecution of the fighting against Japan and for the invasion of western Europe. Once more Stalin was conspicuously absent, technically at least because the Soviet Union was not at war with Japan. Undoubtedly, relations with the USSR consumed a large part of the time at Quebec and at subsequent Roosevelt-Churchill conversations in the White House. It was broadly intimated that a parley of top representatives of the "Big Three" was in the offing.

That intimation became reality with a meeting of Secretary of State Cordell Hull, British Foreign Secretary Anthony Eden, and Soviet Commissar for Foreign Affairs Vyacheslav Molotov. Convened in Moscow, the first time a Russian capital had ever been host to so distinguished an array of diplomatists, and in October when the Red armies had the Nazis on the run, the sessions lasted for twelve days and produced a sheaf of agreements and understandings.

The principal achievement of the Moscow Conference was a mutual pledge to perpetuate the Grand Alliance after the war for purposes of international peace and security. Specifically, it was stated that a world authority to keep the peace would be set up and that all peace-loving nations would be eligible for membership on the basis of sovereign equality. This was the seed of the United Nations in the world after the war. Since the Chinese ambassador in Moscow attached his signature to the pact, the foundations of the future peace structure had the official blessings of all four of the major Allies.

It was further declared that the United Nations would confer with the object of reaching an accord to regulate armaments after hostilities were over. The statesmen reaffirmed, moreover, the pledge to prosecute hostilities until the enemy surrendered unconditionally, and to the Russians were vouchsafed the military plans of the western Allies.

Vexing questions of frontiers and the economic terms of the settlements to be made with the Axis were reviewed though left unresolved. But a European Advisory Council of the Big Three would carry forward the discussions initiated in Moscow and study European problems as the war proceeded.

On three points of common concern, Italy, Austria, and war criminals, the Allied statesmen at Moscow published declarations. Fascism would be utterly destroyed in Italy and a democratic regime which assured the ordinary civil liberties would be established. To advise on Italian affairs a council would be set up containing representatives of the Big Three, of General de Gaulle, Greece, and Yugoslavia. So far as Austria was concerned, that country would be separated from Germany and restored to the list of free and independent states; and the Austrians were counseled to do all in their power to facilitate their liberation from German dominance. Austria was singled out for special treatment because its independence would weaken Germany and assure the freedom of neighboring states.

At Moscow it was agreed, too, that run-of-the-mill German war criminals would be tried on "the scene of their crimes and judged on the spot by the peoples whom they have outraged." The major Nazi criminals would, however, "be punished by the joint decision" of the Allied governments.

Remarkable alike for accomplishments and omissions, the Moscow Conference inaugurated another chapter in the history of the Grand Alliance. In an atmosphere of genial comradeship, mutual suspicions tended to be dissipated, new warmth and feelings of confidence were manifest. The vaunted Nazi allegation that differences among the Big Three were irreconcilable was spiked, and whatever likelihood there may have been that the USSR would quit the war before the Hitlerite armies had been completely smashed was dispelled. A brave start, too, had been made in the formation of a world authority to maintain the peace, but much remained to be done.

Hard on the heels of the Moscow talks, Roosevelt and Churchill conferred at Cairo with the Chinese Generalissimo, Chiang Kai-shek, on the war and the peace in the Orient. While military aides discussed strategy and campaigns to compel the unconditional surrender of Japan, the politicians laid the Japanese Empire on the operating table. Nippon, it was agreed, would be stripped of all the territories that had been brought under Japanese domination since 1894.

China would recover Manchuria and Formosa, and Korea "in due course" would regain her freedom and independence. Presumably, it was understood that the Kurile island chain and the southern half of Saghalen would pass to the USSR, while the Japanese mandated archipelagoes in the central Pacific would pass to the United States.

It was gratifying to war-weary China to be recognized at Cairo as one of the Great Allies and to be promised that the reward for the prolonged ordeal would be the recovery of lost provinces. A British reaffirmation of intention to keep fighting Japan after Germany had been defeated comforted "doubting Thomases" in the United States, who imagined that as soon as Germany had been beaten the British would pull out of the Great Pacific War.

Climax of the inter-Allied gatherings was a conference in December at Teheran, Persia, of Marshal Stalin with Roosevelt and Churchill, attended by their top military strategists and prominent diplomatic advisers. Little that was new was added to the understandings that had been come to at Moscow. Yet the long-standing desire of the Anglo-American chiefs to talk face to face with the all-powerful Soviet leader was at last gratified. Allied solidarity was attested on the highest possible level, and military and peace plans canvassed at Moscow were advanced another stage. Once again it was asserted that Allied soldiers who were stationed in Persia (Iran) would be evacuated after the war, and that the independence of that ally would not be infringed upon.

Great good fellowship prevailed at Teheran among the Big Three policymakers. At a birthday party for Churchill the guests in high spirits drank no fewer than fifty toasts. One proposed by Stalin, "Without American production the United Nations could never have won the war," created a happy impression in circles of the transatlantic Republic which doubted whether the USSR was properly appreciative of the Lend-Lease assistance that had been flowing in such lavish abundance.

"We came here with hope and determination," read the closing paragraph of the Teheran communiqué. "We leave here, friends in fact, in spirit, and in purpose." That indeed was a fitting apostrophe on the outcome of the arduous labors to weld the Grand Alliance into a more perfect union.

CHAPTER XXIV

The Allied Triumph

THE broad outlines of the Allied march to victory over the Axis and Japan had become apparent in the crucial years of 1942-1943. That pattern had four paramount pieces: the irresistible, time-consuming pressure of American forces across the Pacific vastness to the portals of the Japanese homeland; the convergence of Allied might upon Nazi Germany, the Russians rolling on from the east, the forces of the western Allies hammering their way in from the west through France and plodding up the rough terrain of Italy from the south; the ceaseless pounding of Axis Europe from the air, while seapower kept open the routes of transport and enforced the blockade; and, lastly, Allied planning for reconstruction and peace once hostilities had ceased.

The present chapter follows the course of developments in 1944 and 1945, in an episodic manner. It is hoped that this approach will evoke for the reader something of the atmosphere and something of the emotions of those who watched events unfold with all the grandeur and all the misery of Greek drama.

Up the Pacific Ladder

The higher Allied strategy dictated that the weight of military resources should be concentrated on the European war theaters. But the Pacific and Japan were in no sense neglected. Huge expansion of the American fleet—in August, 1944, there were nearly 100 aircraft carriers alone, fourteen of them large—and the transfer of British naval units to the Pacific after the elimination of Italian seapower afforded the Allies immense superiority on the water. Those resources, under the direction of the American Admiral Chester W. Nimitz, together with experience picked up in earlier "leap-frog" operations, made possible stupendous advances up the Pacific ladder.

From footholds established on the Gilberts at the end of 1943, the Japanese archipelago of the Marshalls was subjected to heavy aerial punishment. Then, striking in force at the naval base of Kwajalein, in the heart of the Marshalls, American forces carried the island by assault in February of 1944—the first parcel of Japanese-owned territory conquered by the Allies. Japanese strongpoints in the Marianas, Saipan, Tinian, and Guam were the next major Pacific objectives and all were taken in the early summer of 1944, though not without stubborn fighting and large casualty lists.

While operations against Saipan were in progress a Japanese fleet appeared on the horizon. It declined to risk a decision with the immensely superior forces of the United States. From Saipan in November, new and exciting Superfortresses (B 29's), which packed twice the destructive power of the Flying Fortress, started to bomb the teeming industrial cities of Japan.

Already, late in October, the campaign to regain the Philippine Islands had commenced. Surprise American landings were effected on the Gulf of Leyte, lying between Mindanao and Luzon. General Douglas MacArthur, wading ashore with the vanguard of the invaders, fulfilled his three-year old pledge to return to the Philippines. Hoping to upset these operations, a Japanese battle fleet in three squadrons moved upon Leyte Gulf, where one of the largest naval engagements of the entire war was fought (October 23-26). Never before had the Japanese command ventured so large a proportion of its seapower on a single encounter and never before had the sailors of Japan suffered so thorough a drubbing. All three enemy task forces were beaten piecemeal, some sixty nine ships were destroyed, and the shattered Nipponese remnants limped away to safer waters.

That smashing blow left the Philippines open to relatively easy invasion. American landings were effected on Luzon with Manila as the appointed goal and, by the invasion of Mindoro, the Philippine archipelago was cut in two. Filipino guerilla resistance forces, who had bedeviled the Japanese throughout the dark years of the subjugation, fought valiantly and well alongside MacArthur's men. But Japanese ground forces in the archipelago were large and they were steadily augmented by reinforcements. Tough fighting lay ahead, yet it was gratifying that in the course of 1944 the battlefront had been pushed 2,500 miles closer to Tokyo.

At other points in the Oriental theater the Japs were obliged to relinquish part of the gains won in the first phase of the Great Pacific War. True, for a time early in 1944, Nipponese arms hacked their way from Burma into the Indian state of Manipur, but British troops threw them back and, in combination with American and Chinese armies, assumed the offensive and cleared northern Burma of the invader before monsoons stopped the fighting. Also, for most practical purposes, New Guinea and the Solomons were conquered. In mid-February Admiral Raymond Spruance's carrier task force, catching the Japanese off guard, knocked the naval station of Truk out of the war. Truk had been spoken of as the "Nipponese Gibraltar" in the Carolines.

Only in the fighting with China did the Japanese have cause for jubilation. There the enemy captured air bases and strategic points which gave them a land corridor from Malaya, by way of Korea, to the home islands themselves. Transportation over that thoroughfare offered an alternative to the ever more hazardous travel by sea. By August, 1944, American submarines claimed the sinking of 700 Japanese ships. Moreover, B 29's winged their course to Nipponese industrial targets from Chinese stations, showing the way in fact to their fellows on Saipan.

The Liberation of Western Europe

Prodigious though the progress was in the Pacific area in 1944, it was eclipsed by the epochal developments in European theaters. Yet popular Allied expectations that history would record the dying gasps of Hitlerism in 1944 were unfulfilled.[1] In fact, in December the Nazis launched a terrifying assault in the Ardennes and for ten days rolled the Allies back with disconcerting speed.

The supreme event of the year was the Anglo-American amphibious landings on the Norman beaches of France—one of the most wonderful adventures in military history. Known in its final form as the "Overlord Project," the invasion, which American military strategists wanted to undertake in the summer of 1943—but could not secure the assent of their more cautious and perhaps more far-sighted British colleagues—was planned to the minutest detail.

Against the day of the mass assault men and supplies had been transported from the United States to Britain in such volume that the island kingdom fairly groaned. On D-Day (June 6) the armed forces of the United States in Britain totalled 1,533,000. Techniques of amphibious operations which had worked well in North Africa, in Sicily, and in the Pacific war, were scrupulously studied and refined. Novel and wondrous contrivances were prepared to facilitate the occupation. Two huge pre-fabricated harbors, to be towed across the English Channel close to the landing beaches, were most ingenious. If the

---

[1] Such hopes were quickened by General Eisenhower's statement at the end of 1943 that "the only thing needed for us to win the European war in 1944 is for every man and woman all the way from the front line to the remotest hamlet . . . to do his or her full duty."

enemy should resort to gas warfare to repel the invaders, the Allies were ready to retaliate a dozen times over.

Beginning in February, Allied bombers struck savagely at enemy industrial targets, plane factories, and synthetic oil plants, smashed railway and sea transportation facilities, and harried the already badly battered Luftwaffe. From April until the invasion actually started, the coast of France from Dunkirk to Cherbourg was pummeled incessantly, save as adverse weather conditions forbade it. That sustained program of aerial "softening up" paid rich dividends; the output of German oil, for example, was cut to five per cent of former production.

While the German commanders felt that an attack upon France impended, they could not tell where it would fall. Apparently the area picked by Eisenhower and his aides, the coast of Normandy, midway between Le Havre and Cherbourg, was not the region the German strategists thought most likely. Yet there, as along other strategic stretches, mines had been sown, formidable underwater obstructions had been built, barbed-wire fences were strung out. On land the much vaunted Atlantic Wall, made up of pillboxes, machine-gun nests, and heavy artillery, had been much extended in 1943-1944, under the direction of Rommel, who quarreled furiously with von Runstedt, the top commander in the west, over plans to deal with the invaders.

At 6:30 on the morning of June 6—D-Day—the first Allied assault wave crowded onto the Norman beaches.[2] A vast armada of nearly 4,000 vessels, accompanied by 702 men-of-war, carried their precious burdens from southern England. Mines were swept up in a remarkable manner by twenty four flotillas of sweepers, enemy coastal batteries were hammered by the big guns of the Allied battleships, and destroyers "drenched" the beaches with their guns, prior to the shoreward dash of the landing craft. Skies were alive with some 11,000 planes, which in the course of twenty four hours unloaded over 15,000 tons of bombs on enemy positions; gliders and paratroopers admirably performed their appointed tasks.

By the end of D-Day 250,000 soldiers, half Americans, half Britishers, had disembarked at four points on the soil of France. Terrible fighting occurred at Omaha and Utah beaches, but once footholds had been established, the forward movement proceeded methodically, thanks to the advance guard of airborne troops. And by D-Day plus five, the beachheads had been merged along a front of sixty miles.

Nazi submarines and swift motorboats, which had been held in port throughout much of May waiting for the invasion, caused little

[2] Weather hazards had caused the delay of the attack for a day, and a northwester almost postponed the invasion indefinitely.

trouble for the invading hosts. Indeed, in any analysis of the factors that made the landings on the continent possible, prominence must be given to the Allied success in combating U-boats, months before the assault was delivered. So thoroughly had Allied airmen executed their pre-invasion assignments that the Luftwaffe was capable only of sporadic and not particularly effective support for the German ground forces. It was not until the third day of the attack that Rommel was able to mass his resources for a counterblow and that turned out to be too late.

From the beginning and throughout the Battle of France, French underground bands (the *Maquis*) rendered invaluable aid to the liberators. They intensified their work of sabotage, derailed German troops, cut communication lines, wrecked bridges, and made themselves generally useful.

The initial stage of the Allied onslaught into France proved less difficult and less costly in lives than the Allied High Command had reckoned on. Nor was the enemy able to undertake a large-scale counterattack because of the superiority which the Allies enjoyed in air and on sea and because the pressure of Soviet arms on the eastern front required the presence of large German forces out there.

Normandy, the fairest region of France no doubt, was the scene of some of the hardest and most desperate fighting of the entire war and a heavy toll was taken of the beautiful architecture of the province. Fighting to the west of the landing beaches, American troops slashed into the port of Cherbourg on June 27. Although the Germans had severely wrecked the harbor facilities, they were speedily repaired. Through Cherbourg more and more troops were funneled to the Continent. Britishers, long since, had firmly entrenched themselves at Bayeux, ten miles inland, seaborne troops linking up with airborne.

During most of July savage fighting took place in Norman towns and hedgerows. Casualties were huge and on certain days the Allied gains were measured in rods. Until the Cherbourg harbor was put into commission, the difficulties of supplying the invading forces were immense. On schedule, the artificial harbors were floated into place. One of them was wrecked by the angry sea lashed by a great gale, and rough weather for a fortnight cost the Allies four times as many ships as enemy action (118-27).

Matters shifted decisively toward the end of July when American divisions cracked enemy formations at St. Lô and Avranches. That laid central France open to rapid conquest. In less than a month armored columns, commanded by General George S. Patton, most picturesque of American soldiers, galloped into Paris and on September 7 they crossed the Moselle, having advanced 750 miles in the space of thirty five days. Five days more and American forces crashed across the border of Germany. Weather permitting, aerial attacks were waged round the clock, causing immense destruction to German military resources, airdromes especially.

Simultaneously, another American army (General Patch's Seventh) was put ashore on the French Riviera from Italy and North Africa. That invasion, though it had little bearing on the course of the Battle of France to the north, laid the foundation for a drive up the Rhone valley and contact with the Patton army.

In the meantime Britishers and Canadians, after slugging it out in their sector of Normandy with Germans, broke through enemy lines early in August. Spearheads raced northward at a furious rate pressing over the Seine near Rouen on August 26 and reaching the Belgian frontier, 150 miles beyond, in less than a week more. Brussels and Antwerp quickly capitulated and the British tide poured on into Holland. Many a French seaport, such as Brest, Calais, and Dunkirk were invested by the Allies and by-passed.

By expelling the Germans from the coastline of western Europe, the British armies captured launching ramps from which the enemy had been assailing the island kingdom with merciless flying bombs. These pilotless, jet-propelled aircraft traveled at a speed in excess of 350 miles an hour, carrying a ton of explosives, and were called V-1, *Vergeltungswaffe* — weapon of vengeance. While most of the bombs were intercepted by plane or gun or balloon barrage, better than one out of four reached their destination in Britain. In some sections of London this novel scientific robot, which, in September of 1944 was supplemented by the long-range, giant rocket bomb (V-2), wrought quite as destructively as the aerial blitz of 1940, damaging well over 1,000,000 dwellings and causing 8,000 deaths in the British capital alone.[3]

Rapidly though the Nazi defences in France had disintegrated, the German armies were pulled back without envelopment to the soil of the Fatherland at many points. Behind the West Wall and in front

[3] Allied secret agents and air reconnaissance disclosed that an experimental station for the flying bomb was located at Peenemünde on an island high up on the Baltic. R. A. F. raiders in August, 1943, put a crimp in the Peenemünde base and later blasted to bits the original launching sites that were strung along the French coast from Calais to Cherbourg. The substitute ramps which the Germans constructed were less efficient than the first ones, and the work of Allied airmen delayed the use of the flying bomb for almost a year, until D-Day plus six.

of the Rhine the harassed troops were drawn up for a desperate stand.[4] To blaze the trail for an irresistible and swift thrust into northern Germany, an Anglo-American airborne contingent of some 3,000 men was dropped, in mid-September, near Arnhem, in the midst of enemy forces. That daring operation won a few towns but the Germans fought back desperately and only about a third of the Allied paratroopers escaped uninjured. The Arnhem setback further dimmed Allied expectations that an early ending of hostilities would be attained. Even the War Department of the United States had picked October as the month of armistice.

At the middle of November the Allied winter offensive got underway with a slow drive across the plains lying before Cologne and the Rhine. It was hard, tough going, for the enemy, now that the Fatherland itself was in peril, fought with tenacity and technical efficiency, and the relaxation of Soviet pressure to the east made feasible the transfer of German reinforcements to the western front.

Before the Allied authorities suspected what was afoot, Field Marshal von Rundstedt, who had returned to supreme command in the west, counterattacked furiously against the Americans in the Ardennes region of Belgium. The battle attained crisis proportions from December 18 to 21. The Allied world, or at least the civilians, had fears of an enemy drive to the Channel ports.

Employing flocks of heavy tanks, the heaviest armored spearhead of history, the Germans actually pushed to within easy distance of the Meuse river, carving out a salient fifty miles in depth and as broad at the base. But Rundstedt's tanks, unsuited for the exploitation of the strategic surprise, fell far short of Liége and Namur, their primary objectives. Field Marshal Montgomery was put in command of the whole Allied northern front, American resistance quickly stiffened, and a beneficient shift in the weather enabled Allied airmen to administer tremendous blows on columns of enemy armored vehicles, as well as on supply and assembly bases to the rear.

At year's end the melodramatic German gamble in the Ardennes had not only been stopped, the Americans had begun to recover the ground from which they had been expelled. Yet the main Allied offensive in the north was delayed for about six weeks by the Ardennes nightmare. A large part of the German reserves, however, had been

---

[4] Just before the Allied break-through in Normandy, Rundstedt was replaced by another professional Prussian soldier, Field Marshal Guenther von Kluge. He in turn, was superseded by Field Marshal Walter Model, whose capable handling of the difficult withdrawal from France enhanced his reputation. Model was not of the traditional officers corps, in that sense resembling Rommel, who died in the autumn of 1944 by his own hand after conspiring against Hitler, it may be.

used up, nullifying the chance of carrying on a prolonged defense of Nazidom itself.

The Italian Front

Stalemate on the Italian front followed the initial Allied attempt late in 1943 to pierce the winter line of the enemy. It was all too evident that the Allied code-name for the invasion of Italy, "Avalanche," was ill-chosen. Conditions of terrain and weather reminded military historians of the circumstances under which Italian soldiers had fought against the Central Powers in World War I. Yet Allied aerial offensives upon enemy airfields, transportation and industrial centers, and railway lines were waged almost without interruption.

Over on Italy's west coast, Allied forces, protected by an umbrella of planes, made a spectacular leap-frog jump to the beaches near Anzio (January 22), not more than thirty miles from Rome. Violent and repeated German onslaughts obliged the invaders to yield ground but fell short of the objective of hurling them into the sea.

In the rugged mountainous district south of Cassino and in that town itself, fighting was heavy, the Germans doggedly contesting every yard, and the Allied progress was painfully slow. On a single day a single square mile of Cassino was showered with 2,500 tons of Allied bombs, but even that made possible only artillery duels and patrol activities. To stop the use of the famous Benedictine monastery on Monte Cassino as an enemy military base, Allied bombers pounded it to rubble.

Not until the middle of May was Cassino captured and a general Allied forward movement undertaken, Americans with French support striking up the western flank of the peninsula while Britishers and Poles advanced on the east. German positions in the vicinity of Rome were pulverized and on June 5, the Fifth American army of General Mark Clark entered Rome amidst scenes of tempestuous mass enthusiasm—a triumph largely overshadowed by the simultaneous Allied landings in Normandy. Every precaution had been taken to safeguard the historical and architectural monuments in the ancient capital of Caesars and Popes.

Weeks of tough fighting carried Allied banners across the famous hill towns and cultural centers of central Italy, up to the mountains on the edge of the Po valley. The diversion of Allied troops from Italy to the war in southern France somewhat hampered the pace of military operations. On the other hand, the sabotage activities of the anti-Fascist underground in the industrial North were an asset of no mean value to the Allied cause.

The Soviet Advance

1944 was a year of military glory and thrilling triumphs for the Red armies no less than for the western Allies. Fighting almost the entire twelvemonth, the Russians recovered area after area of their own country and pressed far beyond the Soviet frontiers of 1939. At some points, in fact, the Russian front line was pushed forward as much as 700 miles. Ceremonial cannon in Moscow, which fired salvoes on the news of important victories, were constantly busy. In the face of the uninterrupted retreat, Nazi communiqués spoke of "heavy defensive fighting against numerically superior enemy forces." As the Germans fell back they destroyed property ruthlessly—anything likely to be of service in sustaining human or animal life. Casualties on both sides of the fighting fronts, as in the initial phases of the war, were enormous.

Although the Russians themselves reported offensives on seven different fronts, the fury of battle flowed in three main currents: north, center, and south. Striking from the Leningrad district, the Red forces hurled the Germans into the former Baltic Republics and then hammered the enemy almost completely out of those areas. In June Red detachments inflicted severe blows upon the Finns, rolled into their country and by September the Finns were so thoroughly whipped that they begged for an armistice. In the main the territorial terms of the armistice fixed the boundary at the limit set at the end of the first Finnish war in 1940, except that the USSR acquired the Petsamo district, containing small nickel mines. Finland undertook to indemnify the Russians in the amount of $300,000,000.

On the central sector the Russian armies thrust forward rapidly across White Russia in June and July and over the 1939 Polish frontier, the tempo slackening only when the waters of the Vistula were reached. Late in the year the eastern fringes of East Prussia, German soil, were crossed by Russian troops.

The approach of the Red armies upon Warsaw set off a desperate uprising of the Polish Home Army in the Polish capital. Confident that a Russian offensive upon Warsaw was imminent, Polish underground forces started to fight in the open on August 1 and sustained the struggle for sixty three heroic days; neither the Russians nor the western Allies rendered the insurgents much effective assistance. To put down the insurrection the Germans freely employed heavy siege artillery and heavy tanks, killing a quarter of a million Poles and obliterating large sections of Warsaw. Failure of the Soviets to cooperate with the rebels further embittered Polish-Soviet relations.[5]

Off to the south the Russian gains were, if anything, even more breath-taking. Commencing in February mass Red assaults compelled the enemy to withdraw from the Ukraine and the Crimea; Sevastopol was taken by storm after three days of most intense and bloody fighting. By July the Reds had captured Lvov in Galicia and were driving hard upon ancient Cracow. As early as April, Soviet advance guards had penetrated into the Balkan Kingdom of Rumania, and in August the offensive was stepped up to a terrific pitch of intensity. A major battle fought near Kishinev cost the Germans over twelve divisions and Rumania lost practically all its organized army. As a result, Rumania, in September, signed an armistice and quit the war. In exchange for cessions of territory to Russia—Bessarabia and the Bukovina—and a pledge to fight the Axis, Rumania was promised the restoration of the part of Transylvania which Hungary had taken. Reparations of about $300,000,000 would be paid by Rumania in the course of six years.

The elimination of Rumania opened a path into Bulgaria and Hungary. Upon the former the Soviets declared war and compelled surrender in a few days. Armistice terms broadly resembled those that had been granted to Rumania. Bulgarian territory, which with the blessing of the Axis had been snatched away from Yugoslavia and Greece would be returned, and restitution would be made to both those states for the Bulgarian wartime extortions and depredations. Deep into Hungary the Russian arms moved, encircling the capital, Budapest, by the end of 1944. It surrendered after a terrific pummeling that lasted almost fifty days. That cleared the way for a Russian offensive up the Danube toward Austria.

In the meantime Yugoslav partisans, under the direction of Marshal Tito, had been conducting effective guerilla warfare, eating away the enemy's resources, destroying men and supplies as conditions provided opportunity. They pushed northward to join hands with Russian columns coming in from the east and on October 20, Belgrade, Yugoslav capital, was recovered. Farther to the west, Allied units, cooperating with native partisans, were ousting the enemy from Albania.

To round out the portrait of Balkan liberation, Greece, which had

[5] A Polish version of the tragic Warsaw episode has been written by the Commander-in-Chief of the Polish Home Army, General T. Bor-Komorowski, *The Unconquerables* (New York, 1946).

lain under the Axis heel for three years, was liberated by British forces ably abetted by irregular Greek soldiers. British paratroopers landed late in September, 1944, and in two months almost all of the Greek state had been cleared of the enemy. Barely was Greece freed before rival factions fell to fighting one another, with the British occupation troops in the very vortex.

Inside Germany

Except for blindly fanatical or congenitally obtuse Germans, the Allied convergence upon the Third Reich, from the west, from the south, from the east, from the air, spelled only one conclusion: total defeat. As the loss of the Balkans and the Ukraine had cut away sources of food, natural oil, and other industrial rawstuffs, so the retreat in western Europe had deprived Germany of other sorely needed supplies. Sweden, too, now interposed objections to furnishing iron ore to the Nazis. Allied aerial warfare, furious and relentless, smashed down factories, railway lines, homes and rendered existence for the German urban millions little short of intolerable. Yet Nazi propaganda services circulated the standard stories about German invincibility and Hitler and his closest followers clung stubbornly to their conviction that Nazidom should be smashed to smithereens rather than surrender.

Professional German soldiers, or some of them, felt otherwise. They resented the growing ascendancy of upstart Nazi generals and party leaders in their peculiar province of war. Certain officers joined with German civilians in a conspiracy against Nazi dominance, plotted to remove Hitler and then, presumably, to sue for peace. There is some evidence that this conspiracy had its start in the first winter of the war at least and possibly the anti-Nazi underground reached back to the very beginning of the Hitlerian dictatorship. At any rate, varied German elements were drawn in, trade unionists, Social Democrats, churchmen, and industrialists as well as disgruntled military leaders and members of the Prussian and Bavarian aristocracy. Overtures to secure British blessings on the anti-Hitlerian conspiracy came to naught because Foreign Secretary Eden thought that traffic with the plotters, who had intense anti-Soviet leanings, would excite suspicions and mistrust in the Kremlin.

Allied victories in June and July, 1944, appear to have convinced the conspirators that the time for an attempt at a coup d'état had arrived. On July 20, at a meeting in German staff headquarters in East Prussia behind the Eastern Front, with Hitler present, a time-bomb exploded. Four were killed and thirteen injured, though the Führer miraculously escaped with slight wounds, partial paralysis, and a temporary concussion.

It is doubtful whether the Führer ever recovered from the effects, both psychological and physical, of that attempt on his life. Dosages of medical injections with which his energies had been sustained during the war had to be enlarged. Thenceforth Hitler was as fearful as any Turkish sultan of an act of treachery and his ranting denunciations of the generals for their inability to produce victory grew more and more hysterical. Conspirators in Berlin tried to occupy the War Office and enlist the garrison of the capital in a general anti-Nazi insurrection. But they were frustrated, as were resistance leaders elsewhere.

Charging that "a very small clique of ambitious, unconscientious, and at the same time criminally foolish officers" was responsible for the plot, Hitler struck at suspects in characteristic fashion. In that, he had the cooperation of Heinrich Himmler, ruthless chief of the ruthless Gestapo, who was now elevated to the supreme role in German affairs. Even Hitler appears to have taken second-place, while Goering was crowded out of the limelight.

Himmler, in panic, ordered the shooting of many Germans, some of whom were not even remotely connected with the assassination plot. The corpses of Field Marshal Erwin von Witzleben and a dozen other officers were gruesomely exposed to public inspection in the streets of Berlin. Among the civilians executed was Dr. Karl Goerdeler, sometime mayor of Leipzig and a respected manufacturer, who was believed to have been the Chancellor-designate of the projected anti-Nazi Republic. In all, probably 20,000 Germans were killed or killed themselves, or were herded into concentration camps. It may be that Field Marshal Rommel was implicated in the plot and committed suicide when the plans failed. The conspiracy, which came near to succeeding, was extinguished in blood.[6]

In their desperate suicidalism the Nazi chieftains mustered the last resources of the Reich to fight to the bitter end, in a way that recalls the herculean French effort of 1793 or, better perhaps, Napoleon's futile stand in France in 1814. Men, hitherto exempt from bearing arms because of physical deficiencies, were now enrolled. An October decree made every male from sixteen to sixty liable for service in the new *Volksturm*, which would somehow save the Fatherland from large-scale invasion. German women and children were drawn into the war effort as never before. Food and clothing rations were

[6] See Alexander B. Maley, "The Epic of the German Underground," *Human Events*, III (February 27, 1946).

further reduced and public services were slashed to release manpower and goods for military purposes. To buoy up popular courage and hope, the Nazi propaganda barrage promised that decisive "secret weapons" would presently be unveiled.

For years the Nazis had called upon their countrymen to perform the extraordinary. Now they were summoned to achieve the impossible. There could be but one answer.

More Inter-Allied Conferences

Amid the relentless fury of battles Allied statesmen and experts conferred from time to time on the paths to victory and the manner of insuring international security and peace once the enemies were vanquished. At the rambling summer hotel in Bretton Woods, New Hampshire, in the spring of 1944, economic and financial experts of forty four United Nations worked out two provisional understandings to restore international financial health and to facilitate post-war reconstruction.

One Bretton Woods accord called for an International Monetary Fund of $8,800,000,000 which would be manipulated, under the supervision of the United Nations, to hold national currencies on a stable basis so that importers and exporters could buy and sell without fear of losses through sudden fluctuations in exchange rates. Thus world trade would be promoted. Members would contribute to the fund as their economic resources permitted, the United States bearing about a third of the burden. A second agreement set up a World Bank, which would make loans for reconstruction purposes that, for one reason or another, were not attractive to private banking interests, or would guarantee loans advanced by private lenders. Loans would be extended for long periods at low interest rates on reconstruction projects, whose desirability was adequately demonstrated. Here, too, the funds to be allocated would be paid in by the various states in accordance with their financial power. Thus the United States would make available approximately a third of the lending fund of $9,100,000,000 and the Soviet Union about a seventh. Together the World Bank and Fund represented the financial section of the emerging United Nations structure. They were designed, above all, to forestall economic warfare between the nations in the guise of competitive currency depreciation and financial penetration.

The Bretton Woods delegates submitted their proposals to the various governments for approval and, in March, 1946, when the first meetings of the governing boards of Bank and Fund were convened, thirty five nations had ratified the Bretton Woods agreements. The USSR, Australia, New Zealand, and six others had not signed. For failure to ratify, the Russians offered the explanation that more time was needed for a study of the plan, though in other quarters it was thought that Russia was unwilling to disclose her gold holdings, as the Bretton Woods agreements required, or that she intended to make ratification contingent upon a special reconstruction loan from the United States.

At Quebec in September, 1944, another parley was held by Roosevelt and Churchill and their most respected military and political advisers. The official Quebec communiqué spoke only of the final decisions to finish the war in Europe and to destroy "the barbarians in the Pacific." Subsequently it was disclosed that discussions had ranged over a wide variety of European topics such as the drastic de-industrialization of Germany after the war and measures to be taken to avert a civil war in Greece. Churchill promptly took off for Moscow, there to exchange views with Stalin, apparently on problems of eastern Europe, and to set the stage for another gathering of the Big Three.

The historic Dumbarton Oaks mansion near Washington was the setting for seven weeks of complicated negotiation between representatives of the United States, Britain, the Soviet Union, and China on the nature of the joint security organization which had been decided upon in principle at Moscow in 1943. Out of these deliberations emerged the Dumbarton Oaks Proposals, which specified plans for the prevention of war in the future and for the promotion of world economic and social stability and progress.

By the sponsoring governments these proposals were submitted to all the United Nations for scrutiny in anticipation of a general meeting to draw up a definitive charter for international peace and security. That conference, convened at San Francisco in the spring of 1945, brought forth the Charter of the United Nations, whose content is summarized elsewhere (Chap. XXV).

Allied Lunge from the West

Once the Ardennes offensive had been defeated, the Allied forces in the west were in a position to proceed with the march to Berlin. With the Russian troops to the east of the Hitlerian Reich, Allied armies, 10,000,000 strong, were available for the grand climax. Red troops started moving in force in mid-January of 1945, obliging the Germans to shunt soldiers to the east to meet the threat.

Throughout 1945 until the surrender of the enemy, Allied air operations were conducted on a prodigious and relentless scale, flyers launching their blows not alone from the west but from aerodromes in Italy as well. Allied attacking armadas of a thousand bombers were almost a commonplace and they dropped improved bombs weighing as much as six tons. Strategic targets and railway centers in a score of famous German cities were subjected to pounding that left them in ruins. As in the previous year, manufacturing communities in the Ruhr valley and Berlin received particular attention. Seldom did the Luftwaffe offer anything more than token retaliation and the efficiency of German anti-aircraft weapons grew progressively worse.

In preliminary probings early in February, American and British spearheads on the ground pierced the West Wall, which Germans had been taught to regard as impregnable. On February 23 the mighty Allied "victory" offensive commenced rolling across the plains before the historic cathedral city of Cologne on the Rhine. Cologne was seized on March 6 while, north and south, Allied armies cracked enemy defenses and rapidly broke through to the Rhine.

By rare good fortune an American armored division speeding up the Rhine found the Ludendorff railway bridge at Remagen standing, and on March 7 crossed over. With only slight opposition a foothold was gained on the east bank. That notable achievement, which occurred precisely nine years after the German soldiers had reoccupied the Rhineland in defiance of the Versailles and Locarno treaties, saved many Allied lives and shortened the war. At the same time Zhukov's Russians were crossing the Oder river, 335 miles to the east.

Mighty Allied armies, seven of them in all—British, Canadian, French, and four American—pressed over the Rhine at several points within a few days. American engineers performed herculean labors in constructing railway bridges to speed along the pursuit of the demoralized enemy. A month after the Remagen crossing the Battle for the Rhineland had been fought and won with surprising ease and tens of thousands of prisoners had been captured.

To the north, British and American troops surrounded and destroyed some 350,000 Germans in the Ruhr district, which Allied aircraft had battered to a shambles. The conquest of the Ruhr inaugurated in fact the last stage of the struggle in the west and from that point on the chief characteristic of the western campaign was its fluidity. Britishers and Canadians thrust the enemy into pockets along the North Sea and virtually liberated Holland. American armored columns raced almost at will through the collapsing Reich, reaching the Elbe near Magdeburg on April 11, probing southward into Bavaria, and

ALLIED CONVERGENCE
ON GERMANY
APRIL, 1945

Miles

0   20   40   60   80   100

NETHER-
LANDS

Emden

Wilhelmshaven

Kiel

Lubeck

Hamburg

Bremen

Weser R.

Aller R.

Hannover

Brunswick

Magdeburg

BERLIN

Stettin

Oder R.

Frankfurt

AMERICAN
BRITISH
CANADIAN
DRIVES

Halle

Leipzig

Elbe R.

Cottbus

Chemnitz

Dresden

Nürnberg

CZECHO-

Pilsen

PRAGUE

SLOVAKIA

RUSSIAN
DRIVES

Augsburg

Danube R.

Munich

Linz

G E R M A N Y

Innsbruck

Berchtesgaden

VIENNA

ITALY

AUSTRIA

Graz

HUNGARY

Tschirky

smashing over the frontier of Czechoslovakia. On April 25 an American patrol linked up with the Soviet vanguard at the village of Torgau on the Elbe, cutting Germany in two.

The Soviet Avalanche

Off to the east the massive Soviet jaw of the Allied vise had been clamping down upon the doomed Reich. Opening a winter offensive in mid-January from the Baltic to the Carpathians, the Soviets cracked the Vistula river rampart and deployed their tanks in a hurricane onslaught up to the Oder river. Three weeks after the great drive began the Wehrmacht, greatly outnumbered and outpowered, had reeled back 300 miles, and the Russians had won half a dozen bridgeheads on the Oder, the last substantial defense bastion in the German east. There the vast Russian forces paused to prepare for the final stage in the drive upon Berlin. Small wonder that the Nazi radio announced that "what is happening on the east will determine the fate of the German people and the Continent."

Other Soviet armies crowded hard upon the Baltic, fighting their way against fierce though dwindling resistance across East Prussia. When Danzig capitulated (March 30) and Königsberg surrendered, warfare in the Baltic theater resolved itself into mopping up operations. Refugees from these districts of Germany and from the conquered lands east of the Oder swarmed into the abridged Reich in droves, multiplying the problems of the military and civilian authorities and further depressing mass morale.

On March 24 Soviet troops started a big new offensive, broke over the Oder on a broad front and surged headlong to the west. Less than a month later nine Russian armies were reported to be converging upon Berlin whose suburbs had already been entered. The junction with the Americans at Torgau in central Germany completed a decisive chapter in the war.

In southeastern Europe, too, the Soviet tide rolled irresistibly onward. After the capitulation of Budapest (p. 603), the Russians carved out deep salients in northern and western Hungary, and then, crossing the Austrian frontier, they fought into Vienna. On April 13, that ancient Danubian metropolis surrendered.

Yet another Soviet army—Malinovsky's "wild men"—charged over Slovakia as though engaged in a springtime excursion. Inspired by Allied gains on every sector, Czechs in the city of Prague struck against their Nazi oppressors and drowned the six year overlordship in blood. On May 10, Russian troops marched into the Czech capital; and shortly before, the soldiers of Marshal Stalin had clasped hands in

Belgrade with Marshal Tito, whose Yugoslav partisans had battled up from Sarajevo. Presently, Yugoslav contingents occupied Italian Fiume of inglorious memory and pressed rapidly upon Trieste, claiming for Yugoslavia territory partly peopled by Italians. In western capitals, there were uneasy feelings that Tito might copy D'Annunzio's coup at Fiume after World War I, only in reverse and with a broader sweep, and thus set a disastrous precedent for many another dispute over frontiers.

Collapse in Italy

So static was the warfare in the muddy valleys and ice-covered peaks of Italy that the Italian theater was frequently called the "forgotten front." Yet from airfields in the peninsula Allied bombers administered deadly blows to north Italian cities, and to the railway line over the Brenner Pass, as well as to targets in the Balkans and in central Europe.

For ground operations a remarkable collection of Allied contingents were assembled—American units, white, colored, and Nisei, Brazilians, British, Indian, Anzac and South African divisions, Poles, French, a Jewish Brigade, and soldiers of free Italy. After preliminary maneuvres, a big Allied push was launched on April 10 and in three weeks the German armies were done for. The Allied flood raced to the Alps there to link up with troops that rolled down through Austria. French soldiers meantime marched into Italy's northwest. The German commanders in Italy, on May 2, signed terms of unconditional surrender.

In this final stage on the Italian front the Allies received noteworthy assistance from Italian guerilla fighters who, redoubling their activities, cut enemy lines of communication and organized successful risings in Milan and other industrial cities. Into the hands of the partisans fell Mussolini and his Fascist Republican cabinet as they attempted to escape to Switzerland. With scant ceremony, the partisans cold-bloodedly shot the whole group in a village on jewel-like Lake Como. The bodies of il Duce, his mistress, and his colleagues were hung on display in Milan.

"Twilight of the Gods"

Germany's western and eastern fronts had caved in. It was nothing short of fantasy, incredible senseless fantasy for the Nazis to keep on fighting. Yet Hitler could assert on January 30, "Almightly God will not abandon the man who throughout his life wanted nothing but to preserve his people from a fate they did not deserve. . . ." Although the German armament and food supply potential had already suffered fatally and the nation had been forced on to a vegetarian diet the Nazi chief of state showed no sign of halting the bloodshed.

A Swedish nobleman, Count Folke Bernadotte, who called in Berlin in February, reported that the Nazi leaders still believed that total disaster could be averted by splitting the Allies diplomatically. But party counsels were divided on precisely how to reach that objective. While one faction subscribed to an approach to the Russians, another urged dickering with the western Allies. Hitler was mum.

Presently, men, women, boys, and girls, called "werewolves," were organized to expel the Allied invaders from western Germany, in itself an invitation to universal destruction. Never did Goebbels cease talking about "new weapons," which would confound the enemy; never did he cease assuring his bewildered countrymen that "I know for certain that the Führer will find a way out."

Nazi radio and press harped upon the grave political dissensions between the United States and Great Britain, on the one side, and the Soviet Union on the other. For example, the insurmountable differences over the Polish Question, they stated, would one day crack the Grand Alliance asunder and thus spare Germany from defeat. Alternately warnings were intensified of the fate that awaited the Germans should they surrender. Millions would be condemned to slavery in the reconstruction of Soviet Russia and the reparations that would be exacted would make the Versailles prescriptions seem like a summer idyl.

The invading Russians, meanwhile, had slackened neither in speed nor aggressiveness. Having driven to the outskirts of Berlin they went on to strike at Unter den Linden, the very heart of the capital. Ferocious fighting, in which building after building was taken by storm, marked the progress through the city, and on April 30 Red soldiers occupied government offices. That day, Hitler charged Admiral Karl Doenitz with the responsibilities of government and shortly thereafter committed suicide. Dutifully his henchman, Martin Bormann, obeyed the Führer's orders to cremate the body. Just before his death Hitler went through a symbolic wedding ceremony with his enigmatic companion, Eva Braun, who perished with him.

Amidst the resounding downfall of a nation whose suicide he himself had ordained, Hitler—who at his zenith dominated an empire broader than Napoleon's and broader by far than Charlemagne's—the erstwhile master of Norway, Denmark, Holland, Belgium, France, Poland, Czechoslovakia, Austria, Yugoslavia, Greece, and the Soviet Union up to the threshold of Moscow, that man sought the easiest way out of an agonized and shattered world. Total in all things, the Führer and his Nazis brought destruction to their country about as complete as the human brain can conceive.

Berlin formally capitulated on May 2. Caught between Allied bombers and desperate ground fighting, Berlin had been pounded into a city of ghosts. Ruined factories, dwellings, and public buildings had been blasted to empty shells, as though like ancient Pompeii, the city had been the victim of some gigantic cataclysm of nature. And befouling the atmosphere was the unescapable stench of the dying—men and beasts.

Whatever hope German commanders may have cherished of making a final stand in the "southern redoubt" of Bavaria and Austria was foiled by the swiftness with which American armored columns cut through and into Bohemia and down to the Brenner Pass. Upsetting the calculations of high Allied officers, who thought the war would rage on into the summer, German troops surrendered en masse here, there, and everywhere. First, Nazi generals and leaders tried to give up to the western Allies alone. When those overtures were rejected, they bowed to a general surrender which was as abject as any in the history or war.

Count Schwerin von Krosigk, sometime Rhodes scholar and never active in the Nazi Party, whom Doenitz had named Foreign Minister, announced on the seventh of May, "The High Command has today . . . declared the unconditional surrender of all fighting German troops." That very day Nazi emissaries signed a formal armistice document in a dismal schoolhouse in the French city of Rheims; on May 8 surrender was made to the Soviets in Berlin. Marshal Keitel, chief of the High Command, signed for the German army, Admiral Friedeburg, commander-in-chief of the navy for the fleet, and General Stumpf, commander-in-chief of the Luftwaffe for the air arm.

Since the Nazi invasion of Poland, the clock of time had ticked off five years, eight months, and seven days.

Imitating Hitler, prominent Nazi personalities, including Himmler, Goebbels, and Henlein among others, died by their own hands. More than a score of other top military and civilian authorities were apprehended by the Allies and held for trial as war criminals.

The Surrender of Japan

Inescapably the collapse of the Third Reich, which implied among other things that Allied military resources engaged in Europe could now be deployed to the Pacific, caused violent reverberations in Tokyo. For the Japanese, moreover, the Pacific conflict had been going badly, month upon month. Very largely the campaign against Nippon was an

American assignment, but valiant cooperation was rendered by British, Chinese, Dutch, and French forces and also by resistance bands in the countries that had been overrun.

The task of expelling the Japanese from Burma, a tedious and difficult job indeed, was undertaken mainly by British and Chinese armies. They advanced steadily during the early months of 1945 and in May occupied Rangoon, Burmese capital. After that, the work of liberation in Burma took on the appearance of a mopping-up process, which was finished in the early summer. French units, meantime, were performing yeoman service in Indo-China and Allied airmen delivered telling blows on cities under enemy occupation. Resurgent armies of Nationalist China, equipped with American weapons, gave a good account of themselves in fighting along the Chinese coast and Chinese guerilla warriors, who throughout the years of alien domination had fought on unceasingly, plucked up fresh courage.

Supreme alike at sea and in the air, the United States forces pressed forward with the reconquest of the Philippines, landing troops on many beaches in the archipelago almost at will. On the Lingayen Gulf of Luzon, for example, a thousand ships put 100,000 men safely ashore on a single January day. In the bitter fighting on Luzon that followed, the Americans marched triumphantly upon Manila, and after destructive house-to-house fighting and several false alarms the Nipponese surrendered in late February. Other places that had become American household words—Corregidor and Bataan—were rapidly taken from the foe. Much costly campaigning was needed, however, to break enemy resistance in outlying sections of the Philippines.

Farther north, the United States marines fought for and won the volcanic isle of Iwo Jima which had been softened up by prolonged pounding by battleship and aircraft. It required almost a month of the toughest fighting in marine history to subdue the island, a base for intensified aerial attack upon the homeland, some 750 miles away.

After Iwo Jima came Okinawa, one of the Ryukyu Islands, less than 325 miles from Japan, and needed as a base for the final amphibious assaults upon the Japanese home islands. Troops were put ashore (April 1) in the largest amphibious operation of the western Pacific war and at first penetration was not especially difficult. Then the Japanese resistance stiffened. Attacks and determined counterattacks raged week after week with heavy casualties for both invader and defender.

Into the struggle the Japanese flung suicide planes—*Kamikaze*—whose fliers deliberately sacrificed their lives as they hurled their craft against the great American naval armada offshore. On some

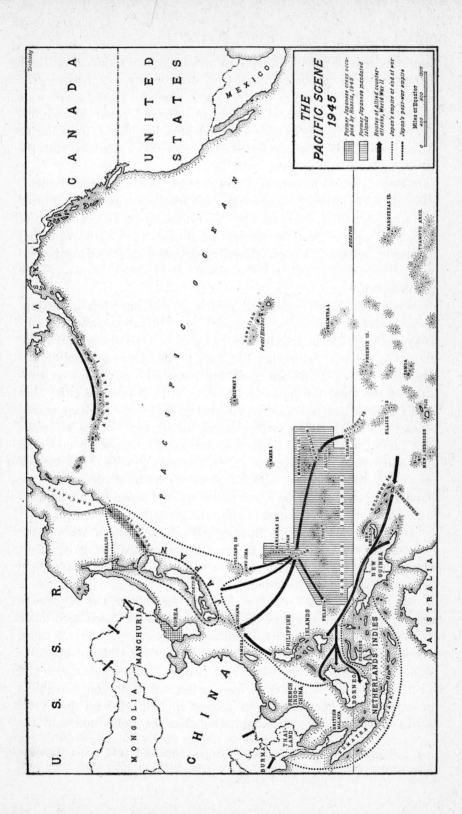

days hundreds of suicide attacks were delivered resulting in no small damage to American men-of-war. Only after eighty two days of grim battle were the Americans masters of Okinawa. Wrecked ships were piled high on the shores and the debris of planes littered the countryside. Altogether in this engagement—the bloodiest of the Great Pacific War—the United States suffered almost 80,000 casualties and the enemy at least half as many more.

Okinawa revealed as well as will ever be known the magnitude of the undertaking if the Japanese home islands were ever to be captured by storm. Actually, Okinawa was the last major ground campaign of the war. At about the time the fighting stopped there, Tokyo put out feelers for peace in Moscow. American and British scientists speeded up the experimentation on the deadliest of lethal weapons—the atomic bomb.

While high drama was being written on outlying islands, the Japanese homeland was being subjected to obliteration from the air. Tokyo, Nagoya, Kobe trembled as had Berlin, Magdeburg, and Hamburg before them. Something like half of the Japanese capital was leveled by B 29's. In all, the aerial bombardment destroyed over two-fifths of the industrial areas of the sixty eight Nipponese cities that were attacked. The toll of dead or homeless Nipponese civilians soared beyond 8,000,000. Bold airmen battered the remnants of the Mikado's once proud fleet in the Inland Sea; submarines, operating under an improved version of "wolf-pack" tactics, carried on with the sinking of enemy commerce carriers, and the noose of the blockade around the "land of the cherry blossom" was pulled tighter. Japan in sum appears to have been well-nigh whipped before the first atomic bomb exploded.[7]

Before the unleashing of the atomic bomb the western Allies in the Potsdam declaration of July 26 presented the Japanese government with the unpalatable alternative of unconditional surrender or complete destruction. Tokyo deliberated.

On August 6, 1945—a day that will far outlive the Nipponese assault upon Pearl Harbor—an American plane unloosed an atomic bomb upon the populous city of Hiroshima. That was, in literal truth, a bomb heard round the world. Behind the act lay years of intensive Anglo-American scientific research carried on in secret laboratories in the United States. A matter of days before the attack on Hiroshima an experimental bomb had been successfully exploded on the desert wastes of New Mexico. It would seem that the stubbornness of the

[7] During the war United States submarines torpedoed 1944 major Japanese ships, among them 194 men-of-war. Fifty two American submarines were lost, seven at least due to operational accidents.

Japanese soldiers on Okinawa, foreshadowing the kind of war that would be met in conquering the homeland, tipped the scale in favor of applying the murderous bomb. The object was to break the Japanese will to fight, without invasion. After the bomb was hurled, the psychological warfare was redoubled, the Japanese being invited to surrender or face "utter devastation of the Japanese homeland."

On the character of the destruction caused by the atomic bombing of Hiroshima, an eye witness, the German Jesuit father, John A. Siemes, has written, ". . . As a result of the explosion, almost the entire city was destroyed at a single blow. The small Japanese houses in a diameter of five kilometers collapsed or were blown away, those in the houses were buried in the ruins, those in the open sustained burns. Fires spread rapidly, the heat which rose from the ground created a whirlwind which spread the fire throughout the whole city. As much as six kilometers from the center of the explosion, all houses were damaged, and many collapsed and caught fire. . . . Since the whole city had been knocked out at a blow, everything that had been prepared for emergency work was lost." [8] Small wonder that the Allied world shuddered as men contemplated the consequences if the enemy had perfected the atomic energy explosive first.

The Soviet Union, still neutral in the Great Pacific War, though it had cancelled the Soviet-Japanese Non-aggression Treaty of 1941, intended it seems to go to war with Nippon on August 15. But two days after the epochal bombing of Hiroshima, Red armies started to march rapidly into Manchuria, Korea, and other Japanese holdings in the Far East. Lest it be assumed that the United States possessed only a solitary atomic bomb, a second was dropped upon Nagasaki.

Whereat Japan begged for peace on condition that Emperor Hirohito might retain his throne. Allied military operations slackened while diplomatic exchanges proceeded, resulting (August 14) in the unconditional surrender of Japan on the understanding that Hirohito would continue to reign, subject to the Supreme Allied Commander. Early in September, American occupation of Japan having already begun, Japanese representatives signed a formal document of surrender aboard the battleship *Missouri* in Tokyo Bay. [9]

[8] John A. Siemes, "From Hiroshima: A Report and a Question," *Time*, XLVII (Feb. 11, 1946), pp. 26-27. It was officially announced that the dead in Hiroshima totalled 78,150; missing 13,983; seriously injured 9,428; slightly injured 27,997. According to two German Nobel Prize winners, Otto Hahn and Werner Heisenberg, Germany know the secret of harnessing atomic energy in 1941, but could not "apply it because of shortages of manpower and material."

[9] Plans for the subjugation of Japan that had been drawn up called for amphibious operations upon Kyushu in the autumn of 1945, to be followed in four months by a full-scale assault upon the Tokyo area.

It was three years, eight months and twenty five days since Japanese airmen had winged their treacherous way to Pearl Harbor.

High though spirits ran in Allied countries because of the global triumph, the fine rapture was soberly tempered by the awful implications of atomic energy. It was evident that the problem of controlling the atomic bomb, together with the tremendous task of rebuilding a shattered Eurasian continent and conversion from war to peace, would be not less exacting than the arduous process of defeating the enemy.

The shining goal of military victory toward which the United Nations had been struggling so long, and at such unprecedented cost, had at last been attained. The dangers and horrors of the prolonged orgy of violence were at an end, and, as in 1918, the victors were faced with the ancient riddle of arranging a constructive and durable peace. Two devastating atomic explosions not only made tranquillity between the nations more desirable than ever. They made peace in fact the price of civilized existence.

New Ways of War

Tools of war evolved at a dazzling pace during World War II, relegating the fighting equipment of World War I to museums. By reason of the improved weapons and techniques, the older concept of warfare as limited essentially to enemy fighting services was discarded, to a far greater degree than in World War I, in favor of extermination of civilian populations. Bombardment of cities from the air, brutalities visited upon conquered nations, upon men wounded in combat and prisoners, and wholesale looting shattered accepted standards for the conduct of war. There was in fact a reversion to the inhumanities and devastation that had attended the wars of early modern Europe and the medieval epoch, but which had gone out of style in the 18th century.

Certain of the jealously-guarded military secrets were revealed after the armistices, but it was known that other weapons were still in the laboratory stage. As never before, in World War II, the accent was on the machine and on scientific ingenuity applied to the art of war.

Although the pre-war prophesies of ardent airpower enthusiasts that the air-arm would bring a quick decision fell short of realization, their speculations might have come true had either belligerent possessed overwhelming superiority and the right kind of airpower for strategic employment. The evolution of the military plane, fighter and bomber alike, is one of the outstanding phenomena of World War II: for the fighter, greater speed, faster climbing ability, and an ever-higher ceiling; for the bomber, increased carrying capacity and endurance, with due concern for speed. The demand for bombers capable of flying the immense distances to Japan was met by the gigantic B-29, one of whose features was centralized fire-control. As the Luftwaffe was responsible for the installation of cannon on fighting-planes, so the Allies took credit for the progressive increase in the weight of bombs: 250 pounds in 1939, 8,000 pounds in 1943, and toward the end of the war, a bomb of 12,000 pounds, capable of blasting an area of sixteen acres.

It was abundantly shown during World War II that ground forces could not go forward unless given protection in the air against dive-bombing and that battleships without air cover were inviting targets for enemy planes. And for reconnaissance and the protection of convoys aircraft was indispensable.

Among the important novelties of three-dimensional warfare were the German-devised V-1 and V-2 weapons, which caused such havoc in the British Isles. It was asserted in Germany after the armistice that if the struggle had lasted six months longer American cities along the Atlantic Coast would have been smashed by super-V-2 rockets. But experts cast doubts on the immediate practicality of transatlantic rockets, because of the very high cost, the dangers connected with launching, and the inaccuracy of the V-2.

Another innovation was the extensive use of airborne transport and paratroopers. Developed first by the Russians, the paratroop technique was effectively employed by the Germans, as in the conquest of Crete, and carried to a high state of excellence by British and American forces. German military research also created the crewless bomber, loaded with explosives, and carrying a fighter plane on its back. At the proper moment, the fighter pilot detached his aircraft and by radio directed the bomber to its target.

Means of defense against air attack underwent constant improvement. In that department an ingenious development of the utmost importance was radio-location or radar. A British invention, on which work started secretly as early as 1935, the original purpose of radar was to give warning information of the approach of hostile aircraft. By the outbreak of the war radar was competent to guard practically the whole eastern approach to the island kingdom. Its value was famously demonstrated during the aerial Battle of Britain in 1940 and before long radar was applied to offensive as well as defensive fighting. Installed on night fighters in 1941, radar proved an instant success. Supplied to coastal batteries, radar made possible the destruction of vessels which the gunners never saw. On ships radar devices were useful in tracking down U-boats, bombarding unseen targets, and spotting land even on the darkest night or through impenetrable fog. The range of effective detection advanced from fifty miles to five times that distance by the close of the struggle.[10]

For sea warfare an epochal development in World War II was the advancement in aircraft and, as so vividly demonstrated in the great Pacific contest, the serviceability of the swift, hard-striking carrier task force. It seemed to some students of naval strategy that the aircraft carrier had rendered the conventional battleship obsolete; in any event, the aircraft carrier had superseded the battleship as the spearhead of the navy.

Throughout the war the design, engineering, equipment, and tactics of the submarine were constantly modified. New devices made the torpedo more remorselessly efficient. An electrical drive, for instance, eliminated the tell-tale bubble streak of older torpedoes and an acoustic contrivance was invented that enabled a torpedo to follow the evasive maneuverings of an enemy ship and hunt it down "by ear." Moreover, the torpedo was so perfected that it would explode even if it hit a ship at an acute angle.

To beat off air attacks German U-boats were equipped with multiple twenty mm. anti-aircraft cannon and machine guns. About the last invention for the U-boat was the "Schnorkel apparatus," or breathing pipe, which permitted the submarine to remain submerged for weeks with safety; one German submarine so equipped is known to have stayed underwater for seventy days. The "Schnorkel" paralleled the periscope, protruding only a few feet out of the water and leaving only a thin wake, so that detection by radar or plane was extremely difficult.

Japanese naval architects built at least three submarine aircraft carriers, whose value appeared to be dubious. However, a small Nipponese reconnaissance plane, catapulted from a submarine, caused a scare at Pearl Harbor late in 1943.

Mention has already been made of the Nazi "wolf-pack" tactics, which the Allies copied and improved, and of Allied perfection of depth charges and instruments of detection for the war upon the U-boat. Antidotes, too, were found by the Allies for magnetic and acoustic mines which German science invented.

In the course of the fighting the technique of amphibious operations, requiring the closest coordination of sea, air, and land services, was carried to a high degree of perfection. One innovation in this

[10] With benefit of radar, scientists in January, 1946, reached for the moon.

connection was ocean-going vessels which opened huge jaws and emitted men and machines upon landing beaches. Another was waterproofed vehicles which, under their own power, moved from landing craft to shore and then rolled across reef or swamp. Repeatedly it was demonstrated that possession of port facilities was not indispensable for successful landings on enemy territory.

So also the development of the floating naval base, with mobile drydocks, repair shops, and facilities to supply combat ships, showed that permanent naval stations were no longer absolutely necessary. On one occasion, at least, a floating drydock picked up a damaged destroyer in the open Pacific and made repairs while proceeding to a harbor.

Weapons of warfare on land were steadily improved throughout World War II reaching a climax with the atomic bomb. Machine guns, for example, were manufactured which had no recoil and were light enough for soldiers to carry and fire from the shoulder or on tripod mounts. Land mines of non-metallic stuffs were so made as to defeat detecting devices. Moreover, the tank underwent successive changes. It grew bigger and was equipped with special guns to fight planes or enemy tanks. Perhaps the German "Royal Tiger" was the most powerful tank that the war brought forth. Armored warfare which figured so conspicuously in ground operations and made for a war of movement, maneuver, and bold strategy, in contrast to World War I, which was fought in trenches except for the first and last few weeks, was, comparatively speaking, an innovation. So was the self-propelled anti-tank gun. German armament-makers are said to have produced a cannon capable of hitting a target 100 miles away.[11]

Engineering feats during World War II verged almost on the miraculous. Airfields were laid out in jungle fastnesses in a matter of hours with mammoth bulldozers. Harbors were built or reconstructed at incredible speed. British Bailey bridges were used to span gaps of any kind quickly. Pipelines under the English Channel (Pluto) were surreptitiously laid by the British fleet in a couple of hours, through which flowed 1,000,000 gallons of gasoline daily to meet the fuel requirements of the armies of invasion. The construction of the Alaskan highway across western Canada and of the Ledo or Stillwell road to the north of Burma were outstanding accomplishments of human ingenuity and dauntless fortitude.

These newer ways of war were somewhat overshadowed by the advance in explosives. TNT of World War I was surpassed by RDX,

---

[11] Out of fear of ruinous counter-attacks, presumably, the Axis and Japan refrained from invoking gas warfare.

henonite, and torpex. All were cast into the shade by the atomic explosive, reported to be 2,000 times more destructive than any of its predecessors. That crowning demonstration of Allied technical, scientific, and material superiority was a triumph of coordinated British and American research and ingenuity and resourcefulness.

When World War II started atomic physicists of all countries knew many of the basic principles of nuclear fission and were aware of the possibility of releasing atomic energy, though huge and complicated problems still awaited solution. Physicists in Allied and in enemy nations set to work to unravel those problems. Before the United States had become a belligerent, arrangements were completed for the "full interchange of ideas" on atomic research between British and American scientists; on the proposal of President Roosevelt British specialists moved to the United States so as to facilitate investigations.

So far had atomic studies progressed by the summer of 1942 that it was decided to construct colossal mass-production plants. They were erected—three of them—in the United States, inasmuch as British industrial resources were concentrated on war goods and because factories in the United States would be immune from enemy attack.

At the peak, as many as 125,000 workers were involved in making the A-bomb, and the immediate reward of that $2,000,000,000 gamble, almost all of which was borne by the United States, was the speedy capitulation of Japan. Whether the most stupendous scientific achievement of the 20th century, perhaps of any century, would usher in an era of mutual annihilation or a golden age of plenty and prosperity, beyond the imaginings of all but the most Utopian speculators, the future would have to determine.[12]

To the superficial eye, contemplating the wartime advances in weapons, in electron tubes, penicillin, sulfa drugs, and the like, it might appear that science had richly prospered. But, while the products of the laboratory moved forth to battle in an endless stream, the fundamentals of science stagnated. Perhaps as a by-product of atomic research, however, physics, chemistry, and biology would profit in the long run.

Many wartime discoveries would of course serve the ends of peacetime living. In the field of medicine DDT was used wholesale in combatting typhus, remarkable work was accomplished in controlling tropical diseases, dramatic progress was made in surgery, and new

[12] For a short, learned discussion of the atomic bomb by a distinguished galaxy of men of science and others, consult Dexter Masters and Katherine Way (Eds.), *One World or None: A Report to the Public on the Full Meaning of the Atomic Bomb* (New York, 1946.)

techniques were applied in psychiatry and neurosurgery. The developments in aeronautics, too, were easily adaptable to civilian needs: huge factories to manufacture planes, a wealth of trained flying personnel, and airdromes scattered strategically all over the globe.

Another Shared Victory

Such is the nature of man that he is tempted to claim for his own country, or if a military technician, for his particular branch of the service, highest credit for the ultimate defeat of the enemy. So far as the war in Europe was concerned there is scope for debate. But in the great Pacific conflict the role of the United States in every department of war so far transcended that of the other Allied nations as to preclude argument as to the brow on which the laurel must be placed.

Britain's share in the eventual downfall of the Axis may long be a source of national pride and colonial inspiration. The python-like embrace of the British blockade of Axis Europe; the tireless naval struggle against U-boat, mine, surface raider, and enemy battle fleet units; the protection of shipping lanes; the dogged heroism of the merchant navy on the seven seas—these added fresh luster to the traditions of Nelson. So, also, the valor of the RAF in the Battles of Britain and in operations in the Mediterranean and Near East, together with the record of the British land forces in Africa, in the initial and final campaigns in western Europe, and in the tough warfare in the Italian peninsula and Burma were indispensable assets of Allied victory.

Behind the fighting men drawn from the United Kingdom, from the Dominions and the Empire, stood the whirring factories and forges and farms of the British realm. These turned out the sinews of survival in spite of bombing, blackout, and grinding fatigue. Not the least of Britain's contributions was the inspiration which her courageous example in the dark months of 1940 gave to freedom-loving men the globe around.

Marshal Stalin, it is reported, once observed that for the Allied victory the Russians gave blood, the British contributed time, and the Americans supplied goods. Distorted though that summary was, it points up the tremendous human sacrifices that the Soviet Union suffered while falling back before the enemy, then holding him, and in the end expelling him from the homeland and hoisting the Hammer and the Sickle over Berlin's Brandenburg Gate. Almost all of the Balkan region, too, was wrested from the Axis by Soviet arms. Russian spokesmen reported that the war cost the lives of 7,000,000 Soviet soldiers and double that many civilians. It must also be remembered that Soviet forces in eastern Siberia kept substantial Japanese military resources pinned down and delivered telling blows against Nippon in the last days of the Oriental conflict.

Not soon will the world forget the steadfastness of Russian morale and the amazing resourcefulness of the Soviet nation in producing military supplies despite enormous handicaps after the enemy had conquered the western and southern sections of European Russia. Nor may the influence of the Socialist Commonwealth upon Communist resistance movements in Axis-occupied countries be overlooked in any full reckoning of the causes of the ultimate Allied triumph.

The part of the United States in the defeat of the Axis followed closely, though on a vastly more prodigious scale, the share it took in World War I. The fabulous expansion of the seapower of the United States, the even more stupendous growth of the airforces, the raising, training, and equipping of an army of some 12,000,000, none of them to be sure exclusively for the European theaters, exceeded anything in the history of war.

By reinforcing Britain's might on the blue waters of Europe, by carrying the aerial assault upon the enemy to an unprecedented blaze, and by the tenacity and resilience of the ground forces in North Africa, Italy, France, and Germany the United States surprised itself and astonished friend and foe alike. On battlefield after battlefield the reputedly "soft" Americans showed that they could not only take hard knocks but could learn and profit from adversity and move forward to success. In all, American armies fought thirty five major campaigns and battles from Guadalcanal to Pilsen in Czechoslovakia.

At the signing of the armistices the American air armadas were the largest of all.[13] The American navy packed more power than all other fleets combined, almost all of it created since 1940, and distinguished by the preponderance of aircraft carriers. Merchant tonnage, too, exceeded that of the rest of the world. If the American army stood below the Russians in sheer numbers, the overall equipment, particularly transport, was distinctly better. And the moral effect of American participation upon peoples in other lands, Allied and enemy alike, could not be measured but was none the less real.

An impressive aspect of the American contribution to victory was the effective teamwork with the British. Scientists and economic administrators of the two nations worked together in a spirit of comradely collaboration. Military and naval staffs were intertwined and

[13] From 1942 through 1944 American industry and workmen manufactured 230,000 planes, or probably more than the output of the next two highest countries, the Soviet Union and Germany.

the mutual confidence that developed between American and British commanders, despite occasional lapses, has seldom been duplicated in the case of sovereign allies. It was General Dwight D. Eisenhower's responsibility and proud achievement to reconcile radically different British and American concepts of strategy and to weld the disparate Allied elements into the homogeneous team which broke the veteran German armies in the west. Not a brilliant strategist, Eisenhower nonetheless possessed high administrative gifts, talent as a leader of men, and ability to reach vital decisions rapidly.

Then, too, the industrial resources of the United States—the amazing record written by mass-production techniques—laid solid foundations for victory in Europe and in the Great Pacific War. In the quantity of matériel of war, though not on all points in quality, the United States far outpowered the enemy nations. Through the medium of Lend-Lease, moreover, the United States supplied the Allies with commodities and services in the amount of nearly $51,000,000,000, while on reverse Lend-Lease the United States benefited to the tune of approximately $7,300,000,000.

In every phase of war production, from food to fighter planes, the United States reached colossal heights, despite the high level that was maintained in civilian consumption. The final accounting by the War Production Board revealed that the United States turned out $186,000,000,000 worth of war goods.

The other members of the Grand Alliance each played a commendable part in the shared victory. For example, soldiers of France, of Poland, of China, of Brazil, and the rest fought valiantly in bringing to pass the final denouement of the common enemy. The patriotic resistance movements in occupied countries, from France to the Philippines, each made a dent in the armor of the foe and facilitated the common triumph.

It was emphatically the combination of nations and the combination of resources, the collective and consolidated efforts of all the United Nations, which brought the war to a close at the time it ended. Looking on the other side of the battleline, it must be said, that the absence of an overall plan of strategy on the part of the German High Command, the absence of intimate strategic coordination between the Axis and Japan, and, not least, the follies, bunglings, and miscalculations in Hitler's personal and impetuous direction of the splendid German armies were of high value to the Allied cause.

As the well-known British military historian, B. H. Liddell Hart reads the record, "The German generals of this war were the best finished product of their profession—anywhere. They could have been better if their outlook had been wider and their understanding deeper. But if they had become philosophers they would have ceased to be soldiers." [14] So far as fighting qualities were concerned the soldiers of Germany were not surpassed, either in hardihood, or—until their resources were depleted—in technical efficiency, or in fanatical devotion to the national objectives. Overtaxed and exhausted by the extravagant political ambitions of the Führer and his henchmen, the German armies nevertheless preserved their reputation for disciplined obedience to the very end.

Just as no one of the Allied nations may justly claim priority in the pattern of victory in Europe, so no one arm of the fighting services can reasonably be credited with top importance. Airpower, the ships of the navy, the hard-slugging ground troops, and the dozen and more specialized services, each performed its essential assignment in the success of the team. The contribution of women in uniform—a radical innovation of World War II—who released men for combat duty must not be overlooked.

Beyond that, in this total war, as in World War I, the energies of virtually every man, woman, and child were enlisted in one capacity or another. It was the uniform that most vividly distinguished the warrior hosts from the workers in shipyard, on farm, in factory, in office, or in the scores of wartime services at the home-front, from the civilian spotters of enemy aircraft to the multifarious activities of the Red Cross.

[14] B. H. Liddell Hart, "The German Generals," *Harper's Magazine,* CXCII (1946), 192.

CHAPTER XXV

In Search of Peace

After the Battles

EXACT computation of World War II casualties will probably never be possible. For the struggle in Europe, the war department of the United States tentatively estimated the soldier dead at 14,000,000; permanently incapacitated, 5,500,000; wounded and returned to duty, 30,300,000; and prisoners, 10,200,000. These totals did not of course include civilian losses. Official figures for the entire British realm as of February 28, 1945, stood at 1,126,000 casualties, of which 376,000 were either killed or missing; 422,000 wounded; the rest, presumably, captured. British civilian deaths resulting from the German aerial assault were just over 60,000 and the seriously injured, 85,000. For the United States, the toll of combat dead passed 400,000; wounded, missing, or prisoners fully 750,000.

Measured in terms of lives lost and maimed, the cost of World War II was grim enough. But there was another side of the story: the cost to those who remained. It would require the pen of a Dante, or rather of several Dantes, to do justice to the terrors, the sufferings, the agonies of heart, mind, and spirit of the war-years and their aftermath. Only through exercise of the imagination can Americans in general appreciate the experiences that Europe underwent. Cold statistics only dimly suggest the misery and distress which history's most terrible war entailed, and the hardships by no means ceased when the fighting stopped, neither in the victorious, nor in the liberated, nor in the vanquished nations.

It is not too much to speak of Europe after the war as the new "Dark Continent." To begin with, over broad sections of the continent, the economic mechanism, which under Nazi regimentation had been more or less skillfully integrated, was profoundly dislocated, and channels of distribution were incredibly disrupted. Warring armies and aerial bombing had smashed means of transportation, factories, and homes, especially in Germany, in Poland, in Yugoslavia, and in western Russia. It was estimated that the physical destruction in the Soviet Union, for instance, amounted to a quarter of the fixed capital

627

of the nation, or something like $50,000,000,000. Vast expanses, once dotted with villages, lacked so much as a single habitable dwelling, and Foreign Commissar Molotov reported that 25,000,000 of his countrymen were homeless at the end of the fighting.

Large tracts of European farmlands were unusable due to "scorched earth" tactics, blasting by shell or bomb, and "strategic" flooding. Productivity of the soil was further reduced by inadequate fertilization in the war years, by the unskilled cultivation of inexperienced workmen, and by the scarcity of farm implements and draft animals. Flocks and herds, moreover, were decimated and a world-wide drought in 1945 cut harvests generally. Finally, the ravages of currency inflation ate into the weakened economic fabric of the liberated nations, furnishing an added incentive for more thorough state direction of economic activities.

Two of the dread horsemen of the Apocalypse, Conquest and Slaughter, had been reined in, but the other two, Famine and Death, galloped hard across Europe and Asia. Appalling deficiencies in the basic necessities of existence—food, clothing, fuel, housing, medical supplies—after six years of death, destruction, and privation made discontent and restlessness well-nigh universal. Minds and bodies of tens of millions were frayed almost beyond endurance.

Human conditions to be sure were not uniformly bad. Many a peasant family, for example, had the fundamentals it required, had the know-how to get food and fuel, and profited from years of practice in the art of hoarding and concealment; and urban dwellers who were well-off patronized black-markets which flourished luxuriantly. But the industrial workmen, many of them without employment, experienced acute suffering, existing somehow on a skimpy starvation diet of bread and potatoes.

Aggravating the tragedy of Europe were the millions of displaced persons: Axis prisoners of war, or men and women from conquered countries who had been hauled into Germany to work, refugees who had fled before invading armies, or Germans who after the collapse of Nazidom were expelled from their ancestral homes in eastern Germany and the Czech Sudetenland. The mystery is not that there was wholesale tragedy on a scale perhaps unprecedented in Europe's history, certainly not approached since the Thirty Years' War of the 17th century, but that mass famine of gigantic dimensions was averted.

Impossible of estimation were the immediate, disintegrating effects of World War II upon the moral fabric of entire nations. War knocked the props from under the orderly pattern of living and destroyed familiar securities upon which everyday existence so heavily rested. Years of indoctrination with ideas of hate and paganism, years of naked terror, morale-corroding noise, the emotional torment of air-raids, the separation of children from their families, malnutrition, the gaunt specter of famine—these could not fail to upset accepted standards of right and wrong. Small wonder that as a by-product of the war, thievery, sexual promiscuity, and crime in general rose prodigiously.

Then, too, ideological tensions and social antagonisms within nations were sharpened by the long, grueling struggle. Except in Soviet Russia, where voters in 1946 cast ninety nine and eight tenths per cent for Communists, sweeping changes came over the government of every European belligerent, accented by a powerful current of leftward sympathies. The achievements of Russian arms deeply impressed Europe, enhanced the prestige of Moscow, and fostered the growth of the Communist outlook.

Up to a line from Stettin to Trieste, Communist-dominated regimes were set up, save in Austria and Hungary where free elections installed comparatively conservative governments in power. Communism, moreover, emerged as the strongest political faith of France, with democratic Socialism only slightly weaker, while the British version of democratic Socialism, the Labour Party, triumphed at the polls in July, 1945, and its leaders assumed the administration of British public affairs.

So far as the Axis nations were concerned, Germany was partitioned for the time being into four zones of Allied military occupation, fully a quarter of her territory was taken away and her economic structure was drastically overhauled (p. 641). Italy, though it suffered no immediate territorial impairment and had a government of Italians, was subjected to far-reaching control by the Allies. Italians debated on whether they should perpetuate the discredited monarchy or introduce a republican form of government and in the end decided for the latter; debated, too, the degree of state authority over productive facilities and impatiently awaited the verdict of the victors on the terms of peace.

American armies of occupation assumed control of the Japanese homeland. General Douglas MacArthur, Supreme Allied Commander, published a stream of directives ordering the arrest of Nipponese war criminals, total demilitarization, dissolution of huge financial and industrial combinations, disestablishment of Shintoism as the official religion, and other measures calculated to bring about a radical transformation in most aspects of the life of Japan.

Across the Asiatic world the cessation of battle allowed nascent or developed nationalist movements to come into the open and challenge the authority of alien rulers. In Korea, for example, Japan's erstwhile colony, which was partitioned into a northern, Soviet zone of administration, and a southern, American one, competing schools of nationalism clamored for full and immediate independence. A bitter feud between Communists and Nationalists disturbed the political waters of China, and British and French troops, which undertook the occupation of liberated areas in southeastern Asia, had to contend with serious nationalist insurrections.

Cries for independence for India were mixed with fresh evidence of the deep-rooted Hindu-Moslem feud, while a billowing tide of social and political unrest raced over the countries of the Arabs and Mohammedans. As never before in history, World War II had opened the Pandora's box of Asiatic nationalisms.

Reasonably representative of the after-war ferment in the Arab world was the situation in Egypt. Nationalist sentiments had grown more volatile during the war, due to British interference in domestic affairs, to the feeling that British influence was a barrier to educational and broadly social progress, and to economic dislocations partly caused by the presence of Allied troops. Egged on by the educated middle class and restive university students, Egyptian Nationalists indulged in anti-British press polemics and physical violence, which British and native soldiers sternly repressed.

Formally the Egyptian government demanded revision in the Anglo-Egyptian Treaty of 1936 (p. 216), withdrawal of British troops, and unqualified Egyptian control over the Sudan. While the London government, in 1946 expressed willingness to discuss revisions in the treaty, it was doubtful whether it was ready to entrust the security of the vital Suez Canal area to Egyptian arms alone.

Many of the grosser ills of war-torn Europe (outside of Germany) and to a lesser degree in the straitened Orient were tempered by the energetic operations of UNRRA, which, despite formidable handicaps, wrought near-miracles with goods furnished chiefly by the Americas and Australia. Surveying the work of this organization to March, 1946, Director-General Herbert H. Lehman reported that upwards of 6,000,000 tons of supplies had saved millions from starvation, immeasurably useful humanitarian work had been done in health, agricultural, and industrial rehabilitation, and several millions of homeless had been looked after. Not the least meritorious by-product of UNRRA was the faith and the hope for the future it encouraged among the beneficiaries of its assistance.

The return of peace and the healing influence of time would no doubt gradually lighten the woes and sorrows of men, for technological progress, which applied to war destroyed quickly, could speedily restore as after World War I. A case in point was one aspect of French reconstruction. When France was liberated 2,603 railway bridges, 534 overbridges, and seventy tunnels were either damaged or in ruins, yet by the beginning of 1946 only fifty seven bridges were unrepaired.

As the tidal wave of war receded, nations, it was expected, would grow calmer and more reasonable. But could the three principal members of the victorious Grand Alliance, upon whom the future depended, establish and then maintain durable peace and international security?

Yalta and the Charter of the United Nations

The designing of machinery to prevent a recurrence of war and to cure or mitigate the known sources from which international strife has arisen was the work of many minds, operating through the years of World War II and instructed by the experience of the League of Nations. As with the earlier League of Nations, the new security institution was in a peculiar sense the product of American diplomatic talent and popular American aspirations for peace.

Along the road to the actual adoption of the Charter of the world security organization at San Francisco in June, 1945, a series of inter-Allied conferences and deliberations stood like milestones: the Atlantic meeting of 1941; meetings at Moscow (October, 1943), Cairo, and Teheran; the actual drafting of a tentative constitution by delegates of the Big Four at Dumbarton Oaks just outside Washington in October, 1944; and the smoothing out of controverted points at the Crimean or Yalta conference of the Big Three chiefs of state in February, 1945.

But the Yalta parley of the Big Three ranged over many topics other than the prospective world security organization. It yielded military decisions and accords on political questions, some of them of the utmost delicacy.

It was reaffirmed, for instance, that the defeat of Germany was the primary, immediate concern of the Grand Alliance and military plans to attain that objective were mapped out. Once Nazi armed might had been broken, Germany, it was agreed, should be divided into four zones of military occupation; measures should be applied to uproot Nazi institutions and militarism, and exorcise the Nazi mentality. And Germany should make partial restitution in the form of goods for damage to the Allied nations.

On the delicate subject of the Poland of tomorrow—the chief political obstacle to concord among the major Allies—it was decided at Yalta that a provisional government should be formed out of the "Lublin" Polish group, which the Soviet Union sponsored, plus democratically minded Poles abroad. After the Polish government had been formed "free and unfettered elections on the basis of universal suffrage and [the] secret ballot" would be conducted. In the matter of territory, the frontier of Poland bordering on Russia would conform to the Curzon Line, extended southward to the pre-war border of Czechoslovakia, and "substantial accessions" of territory would be allowed to Poland on the north and west at the expense of Germany.

Similarly the government of Yugoslavia would be reorganized and the Allies would assist other liberated nations or former Axis satellite states in setting up political regimes by democratic processes.

Far Eastern affairs evidently were subjected to general review at Yalta, and the active support of the Soviet Union in the war against Japan was purchased by concessions, not at once divulged. To Russia was promised special railway and harbor rights in Manchuria, corresponding to privileges which Imperial Russia had held before the war with Japan, forty years earlier, and set forth in detail in a Sino-Soviet Treaty of August, 1945. From Japan, Russia would likewise obtain the southern half of Saghalen island and the Kurile string lying between Japan and Kamchatka.[1]

So as to facilitate diplomatic cooperation of the Big Three nations and to attend to specific problems of common interest as they arose, it was arranged that the foreign ministers of the three countries should consult periodically, quarterly or more frequently. Finally, at Yalta, certain problems connected with the evolving international institution to keep the peace, such as voting procedure and the admission of the Soviet Ukraine and White Russia, were resolved. It was agreed that a general conference of the United Nations should meet in April at San Francisco to prepare the charter of the security organization along the lines of the Dumbarton Oaks proposals. Only states belonging to the United Nations would be eligible to attend the San Francisco deliberations, a pointed invitation to laggard nations to clamber aboard the Allied band-wagon, as nine of them proceeded to do.

Taken all in all, the Yalta arrangements, covering so many points that might have upset the Grand Alliance, smoothed out tensions (or by-passed them). They represented an impressive stride in the direc-

---

[1] In another secret Yalta understanding, the United States and Britain promised to release to Russia all citizens of Soviet territory who had fought as soldiers in Axis armies and had been taken prisoner.

tion of the reordering of Europe as soon as the enemy had been over-come.

While the plans for the San Francisco Conference were maturing, the Allied world suffered an incalculable loss in the sudden death (April 12) at Warm Springs, Georgia, of President Roosevelt. The passing of the main architect of the United Nations for war and peace plunged the United States and the United Nations into deep grief and mourning. Revered in his own country as no man since Lincoln, a reverence that transcended sectional bounds, Roosevelt, for his assurance, his resourcefulness, and his confidence in the future, was respected and admired in foreign countries as no other character in American life. Millions who never saw him felt they had lost a valuable friend.

Roosevelt's leadership in the momentous decisions to support Britain and to assist the Soviet Union before the active entrance of the United States into the war, and his success in cementing the United Nations, subsequently, had prepared the stage for the United Nations meeting at the Golden Gate. At the final meeting of the important steering committee of the San Francisco Conference, it was humbly resolved that, "Now that we have finished our work, let us stand in a minute of silent thought for the man who not only conceived the idea of a United Nations, but gave his life for it—Franklin Delano Roosevelt."

Cosmopolitan, friendly, hospitable San Francisco provided an ideal setting for the lengthy discussions and final approval by delegates of fifty states of the Charter of the United Nations.[2] Press and radio representatives in the number of 2,636 deluged the world with as much of the transactions as rules of secrecy permitted. They focused the glare of publicity upon the principal delegates: the Soviet Foreign Commissar, Molotov, described as "a blue-eyed affable bull in a navy-blue suit," tenacious and combative; the suave and eloquent Foreign Secretary of Great Britain, Anthony Eden; his American counterpart, Edward R. Stettinius, Jr., Secretary of State, newly come to the perplexities of world diplomacy; and the tall, smiling spokesman of China, T. V. Soong.

Of the lesser delegates, Australia's Foreign Minister, Herbert V. Evatt, stood out from the crowd by reason of his belligerent championship of the interests and aspirations of the middle-sized and small

---

[2] For a compact analysis of conference methods, consult G. Kirk and L. H. Chamberlain, "The Organization of the San Francisco Conference," *Political Science Quarterly*, LX (1945), 321-342.

nations. Commander Harold E. Stassen, a delegate of the United States, earned acclaim for the unusual lucidity with which he explained technicalities in the work being done and his yeoman toil in committee rooms. Nine weeks in all were needed to fashion the United Nations Charter, to placate exponents of divergent views on the content of the document. While the deliberations started from the Dumbarton Oaks proposals, men with ideas had propounded a host of revisions or expansions, so that a mere listing of recommended changes or additions in Dumbarton Oaks filled seventy two pages.

Having said that, it must be added that the Dumbarton Oaks scheme in its fundamentals was incorporated in the final charter, and that alterations made at San Francisco conformed to the wishes or the whims of the Big Three. Twice the length of the League Covenant, the United Nations Charter contained 111 articles under nineteen chapter titles and the statute of the International Court of Justice. The preamble, beginning "We the peoples of the United Nations," was largely the product of the patriarchal Field Marshal Jan Smuts, who had shared in the composition of the League of Nations Covenant. It enumerated eight far-ranging expressions of the aims of the United Nations, which the text of the Charter refined by definition. Central in the entire pattern was the intention to perpetuate the wartime coalition of the Big Three—or, by courtesy, the Big Five—for the maintenance of security and an orderly world. Central in the obligations undertaken by each signatory were pledges to abstain from war or the threat of war and to combine to repress violation of the peace by military action if necessary.

Organization and Functions of the United Nations

Any peace-loving nation is eligible to membership in the United Nations. There are six main agencies: the General Assembly, the Security Council, the Economic and Social Council, the Trusteeship Council, the International Court, and the Secretariat.

Sometimes spoken of as a "world town-meeting," or "the chief forum of world opinion," the Assembly contains representatives of every member country, each state having one vote. It is convoked once a year but may be called in special sessions. Delegates may discuss anything under the sun that has bearing on peace, even a specific international dispute, provided the dispute is not at the time under scrutiny by the Security Council, and may pass recommendations for the consideration of the Council. Then, too, the Assembly elects the six non-permanent members of the Security Council and all the members of the Economic and Social Council and the International Court;

it also has jurisdiction in United Nations budgetary matters, admits new members to the United Nations and suspends or expels members on recommendation of the Security Council. The most important acts of the Assembly require a two thirds majority.

The primary organ for handling international quarrels is the Security Council of eleven members; that is, the Big Five, the United States, the USSR, Great Britain, France, and China which have permanent seats, and six others selected for a term of two years by the Assembly. It is prescribed that "the Council shall be so organized as to be able to function continuously." Decisions on questions pertaining to *procedure* require the concurrence of any seven Council members, but on other matters there must be seven affirmative votes, including the votes of all of the permanent members; in other words, each of the Big Five nations possesses the right to veto almost any action by the Council.

If the Council is *investigating* a dispute in which a Big Five state is involved, that state must abstain from voting. But the veto may be invoked by any one of the Big Five to prevent the Council from undertaking *enforcement* action against a wrongdoer, whether or not the Big Five nation is a party to the quarrel. Stated otherwise—and flatly— if any one of the Big Five should choose the road of aggression the United Nations is impotent to restrain it. The preferential status in voting allotted to the Big Five evoked doubts and sharp criticism in some quarters, but it was defended on grounds of practical expediency and because the nations which had the heaviest responsibilities, the possessors of the main reservoirs of power, should have special voting privileges.

It is the supreme duty of the Security Council to discuss and to investigate international disputes and to take action to prevent threats to the peace or to combat acts of aggression. When a controversy arises the Council is authorized to seek a settlement by means of ordinary diplomatic negotiation or arbitration or mediation, or other peaceful means. If that fails to lead to adjustment, then the Council may order partial or complete economic sanctions against the party in the wrong; as a last resort, the Council may unloose military forces—planes, troops, warships—against a Charter-breaker.

Member-states promise to place certain military forces at the disposal of the Council, the quantity to be fixed in special treaties, and to hold on call contingents of airpower to be directed against the Charter-violater, if the Council deems that such action is wise. To advise on all the military affairs of the Council, there is a Military Staff Committee composed of the chiefs of staff of the Big Five or their

THE UNITED NATIONS: ITS

GENERAL ASSEMBLY

Up to five delegates from each of fifty-one member nations, but only one vote for each nation. Its duties are to discuss any questions within the scope of the Charter, and submit recommendations to the Security Council.

SECURITY COUNCIL

Eleven members — the Big Five permanent, the other six elected for two-year terms by the Assembly. Investigates international disputes; takes action against aggressors if necessary.

TRUSTEESHIP COUNCIL

Composed of any members administering trust territories; plus those of Big Five not administering such trusts; plus as many others as are needed to ensure equal representation of members who do and do not administer trusts.

SECRETARIAT

Headed by a Secretary General, it includes administrative and research staffs serving the entire United Nations.

ATOMIC ENERGY COMMISSION

Eleven members of the Security Council plus Canada. Will "consider problems arising from the discovery of atomic energy".

MILITARY STAFF COMMITTEE

Composed of Chiefs of Staff of U.S., Britain, U.S.S.R., China and France. Decides composition and directs forces against aggressors under the Security Council.

INTERNATIONAL ARMED FORCES

To be composed of a quota of forces readily available from all members for putting down threats to peace. (Not yet organized. To be decided by Military Staff Committee.)

Special text — revised for the Board of Education, City of New York

ORGANIZATION AND FUNCTIONS

ECONOMIC-SOCIAL COUNCIL

Eighteen members elected for three-year terms by the Assembly. Will coordinate the work of specialized agencies to eliminate economic and social roots of war.

INTERNATIONAL COURT

Fifteen members, chosen for 9-year terms, by Assembly and Council, from candidates nominated by national groups in Permanent Court of Arbitration. Will meet in permanent session to decide legal disputes between nations.

INTERNATIONAL BANK

Part of the Bretton Woods plan, ratified by thirty-five nations. Will provide funds for reconstruction and develop resources not fully employed.

INTERNATIONAL MONETARY FUND

Also part of the Bretton Woods plan. Will be employed by member nations to help stabilize currencies.

FOOD & AGRICULTURE ORGANIZATION

A research and study organization to help ensure freedom from want, increased food production, improved agricultural methods and higher food and nutrition standards throughout the world.

CIVIL AVIATION ORGANIZATION

Organized in 1944 to deal with complex economic and legal problems in commercial air transport operations, and inspect travelers and cargo to prevent spread of disease.

UNITED NATIONS EDUCATIONAL, SCIENTIFIC AND CULTURAL ORGANIZATION

Drafted at London 1945, to develop international cultural understanding and to help make the world's accumulated knowledge available to all.

deputies. Inasmuch as the veto power held by each of the Big Five implies that the military resources of the Security Council will not be applied against a formidable foe, the armed forces which each member would contribute to the United Nations pool would presumably not be large. Not provided for in the San Francisco Charter is an Atomic Energy Commission created by the Assembly in January, 1946, and containing the eleven members of the Security Council and Canada, to "consider problems arising from the discovery of atomic energy."

It is prescribed in the Charter that "regional organizations," such as the Inter-American Union, should be encouraged to adjust minor local quarrels and so reduce the burdens on the Security Council. But these bodies might not order economic or military sanctions without the approval of the Security Council.

Next of the principal organs of the United Nations is the Economic and Social Council of eighteen members chosen by the Assembly. It is the high responsibility of this group to study and make recommendations on world social and economic conditions that are conducive to international discord and strife. In other words, whereas the Security Council handles immediate international disputes as they arise, the Economic and Social Council seeks to prevent such disputes from arising. It is responsible for working out reasonable settlements on such questions as rivalries over oil-lands, tariff barriers, and other basic causes of economic and social antagonism, as well as the promotion of higher standards of living and better educational and cultural opportunities all over the globe.

With this Council are affiliated several bodies charged with looking after special areas of international affairs: the World Bank, the International Monetary Fund, the Food and Agriculture Organization, the Civil Aviation Organization (established in 1944 to deal with problems connected with commercial air transportation) and the Educational, Scientific, and Cultural Commission (UNESCO), to foster understanding between the peoples of the world. As an instrument to facilitate international cooperation and to promote prosperity and preserve peace, the Economic and Social Council ranks with the Security Council—potentially, in fact, above it.

To supervise the administration of colonial territories that may be assigned to the United Nations, a Trusteeship Council is authorized. Seats on this council are restricted to the Big Five and any other countries administering "backward nations." Based upon the mandate system instituted after World War I, the Trusteeship Council is obligated to further the welfare of the inhabitants in any areas that may be placed under its jurisdiction. It was assumed that the first territories to be placed under United Nations trusteeship would be the League mandated areas. It is also prescribed that parts of trustee territory may be set aside as strategic zones under the supervision of the Security Council.

The principal judicial organ of the United Nations is the International Court of Justice, the lineal descendant of the World Court organized after World War I and meeting like it at the Hague in Holland. Made up of fifteen jurists of the highest competence, elected by the Assembly, the Court will be in permanent session for the settlement of quarrels between nations that are "justiciable," such as interpretation of treaties and points in international law.

As the coordinating agency of the whole United Nations institution, a Secretariat is provided for, another heirloom of the League of Nations. Its duties involve research for and administration of the United Nations project; it is responsible to the Assembly and the Security Council, both of which share in the selection of the Secretary-General, the key administrative official. He may bring to the attention of the Security Council any matter that he thinks may threaten peace. And he is provided with authority to appoint the staff members of the Secretariat. Much of the success of the United Nations will depend upon the competence and devotion of these international civil servants.

Amendments to the Charter require that a proposal must first be approved by two thirds of the Assembly and then ratified by two thirds of the member governments, including all of the Big Five. Provision is made to encourage the calling of a conference in ten years or earlier "to review the present Charter" and presumably to make revisions in the light of actual experience.

Charter and Covenant

In several particulars, it is worth noting, the Charter of the United Nations diverges from the ill-starred Covenant of the League.[3] One striking difference is the provision of an armed force to be applied against an international trouble-maker (other than one of the Big Five) by the Security Council, if normal diplomatic or international economic pressures are incapable of bringing the erring nation to terms. Members, second, are not committed to a hard and fast territorial guarantee as in the Covenant (Article X).

Moreover, whereas decisions on matters of consequence required unanimous consent under the Covenant, in the Charter actions of

[3] The physical assets of the League and its records were in April, 1946, transferred to the United Nations.

similar gravity are validated by seven votes in the Security Council
—including all of the Big Five; by two thirds in the Assembly, and a
simple majority in the Economic and Social Council. It may well be
that the largest distinction between Charter and Covenant is the
special rights of veto accorded to the Big Five and therewith their
special responsibilities for keeping the peace. Again, the Economic
and Social Council possesses greater potentialities than corresponding
bodies of the League. And, lastly, the International Court is an integral part of the security organization, and the Charter is entirely
separated from the treaties of settlement with the ex-enemy nations.

From the standpoint of membership the paramount difference between the League and the United Nations is the inclusion of the
United States and Soviet Russia, both immensely more powerful in
1946 than when the League project was launched. For the first time,
in other words, the recognized Great Powers are pledged to cooperate
to maintain peace and to promote human welfare.

Such in skeleton is the content of the constitution for durable
world peace brought forth by World War II. So warm a partisan of
the document as Commander Harold Stassen likened it in a fine phrase
to a "beachhead" for peace, properly implying that only a start had
been made. Addressing the last plenary session at San Francisco,
President Truman remarked, "This Charter, like our own Constitution,
will be expanded and improved as time goes on. No one claims that it
is now a final or a perfect instrument . . . Changing world conditions will require readjustments. . . ."

Whether the slight limitations imposed upon sovereign states
would be adequate to the task of keeping the peace, whether peoples
would gradually learn to work together, whether, above all else, the
Big Three would be able to find accommodations on issues where their
interests and aims diverged and would exercise their veto right with
restraint, all these considerations would go far to determine the future
of the latest adventure in global relationships.

Perhaps the crux of the matter was expressed by Lord Halifax,
who described the United Nations as "an instrument by which, if men
are serious in wanting peace and are ready to make sacrifices for it,
they may find means to win it." Machinery alone surely is not enough.

Approved by all the nations represented at San Francisco, the
Charter was forwarded to the several governments for acceptance and
ratifications were promptly forthcoming. In January, 1946, the United
Nations became a reality, a going concern after organizational sessions
in London.

The Potsdam Declaration

Early in the summer of 1945 the chiefs of state of the Big Three, their principal advisers, and technical experts conferred for more than two weeks in Potsdam. Negotiations were interrupted by British parliamentary elections, in which the victory of the Labour Party caused the replacement of Churchill, as Prime Minister, by Clement R. Attlee, a veteran of the war Cabinet. Marshal Stalin spoke for the Soviet Union and for the United States, the new President, Harry S. Truman.

Out of the Potsdam deliberations emerged a detailed blue-print for the future of Germany. Previous inter-Allied understandings concerning demilitarization, denazification, and trial of the principal German war criminals would be put into force at once. Germany was carved into four administrative zones—Russian in the east and center, American in the south, French in the southwest, and British in the northwest—though it was provided that during the occupation Germany should be treated as a single economic whole. The industrial power of Germany would be sharply curtailed, leaving it primarily an agricultural nation stripped of the greater part of its heavy industry and other manufacturing facilities that were capable of producing matériel of war. In no case would German standards of living be allowed to rise above "average European standards."

So far as reparations were concerned the Potsdam Declaration prescribed that the Soviet Union might obtain reparations in the form of goods and industrial equipment in the Russian zone of occupation and as well, a fourth part of the plant and machinery in the British and American zones, not required for Germany's peacetime economy. For sixty per cent of the latter equipment Russia would reimburse Germany with raw materials of various kinds. Britain and the United States were authorized to expropriate manufacturing equipment in their zones as reparations.

In each of the zones of occupation a distinctive pattern of administration was applied, military rule being gradually replaced in all zones by a mainly local civil administration under foreign military authorities.[4] Here was a wholly unprecedented attempt by four powers of differing philosophies and methods to rule, reorganize, and re-educate in their own separate fashion a highly integrated nation. The French

[4] It was estimated that 20,000,000 Germans lived in the Russian zone, 17,000,000 in the American, 6,400,000 in the French, and 22,000,000 in the British. These figures were raised by the influx of Germans expelled from Czechoslovakia and other countries. Soldiers of the four occupying nations garrisoned sections of Berlin.

stubbornly blocked the formation of the central administration for
Germany stipulated in the Potsdam pact.

In the matter of German territory the Soviet Union was "tentatively" allotted the northern portion of East Prussia, including the
great port of Königsberg. Poland was given the rest of East Prussia,
along with Danzig, and the district of eastern Germany running from
the Baltic along the line of the Oder and Neisse rivers to the Czech
frontier, pending final delimitation in a peace conference. With the
object of mitigating the lot of Germans in this area who were being
roughly driven out by the Poles, the statesmen at Potsdam called for
"orderly transfers" and applied the same formula to Germans who
were leaving Czechoslovakia and Hungary. As a result of these decisions, Germany lost a quarter of her territory as of 1937, and was no
larger than New England, New York, and Pennsylvania, containing a
population of some 65,000,000, which would reach about 72,000,000
when transfers of Germans from neighboring countries were completed.
Population density in "Rump Germany" would rise to 518 per square
mile as against 364 in 1937.

It was also agreed at Potsdam that preparations should be initiated
to draw up treaty settlements with Italy and the satellites of the Axis.
For that purpose a Council of the Foreign Ministers of the Big Five
was authorized and that body would also deal with other problems of
general Allied concern, until, presumably, the United Nations was in
working order.

Parleys at London and Moscow: 1945

Accordingly, Foreign Commissar Molotov, Secretary of State
James Byrnes, who in the interval had replaced Stettinius, and Ernest
Bevin, the Labour head of British diplomacy, met in London in
September, 1945. At London differences between the Big Three which
hitherto had been overlooked or by-passed crowded into the open
with vengeance. It is the common experience of history that once
victory has been won, military coalitions are split by cleavages and
controversies.

The diplomatists clashed over several specific questions: the political complexion of the small states of eastern Europe; the reparations
to be taken from Italy; the future of the Italian colonies, the Russians
entering a bid for Libya, which encroached upon the British "lifeline"
over the Mediterranean, and Soviet claims to dominance in the Turkish Straits. Opinions differed, too, as to whether the treaties with Italy
and the satellite nations should be drawn up by the Big Three as
Russia preferred, or whether France and China should also have a
hand in peacemaking.

On these issues the London Conference became deadlocked and then dissolved without reaching decisions. The outstanding phenomenon of the parley was the obduracy and assertiveness of the Soviet Foreign Commissar. Behind that attitude were no doubt irritation in the Kremlin because of the unwillingness of the western Allies to extend rehabilitation loans, and resentment and suspicion due to the Anglo-American monopoly on atomic bomb secrets. It is, however, fair to point out that the Russians had denied western military men the privilege of observing Soviet military methods or innovations in weapons while the fighting was on.

Furthermore, American policies in Japan and the Far East generally, and the Anglo-American attempts to take a hand in eastern Europe, which the Russians regarded as their own preserve, had bearing on the intransigence and aggressive tone of Soviet diplomacy. The old Russian phobia of "capitalist encirclement" of the Communist commonwealth cropped up anew.

As a way of solving the atomic energy problem the United States, Britain, and Canada, soon after the London meeting, proposed international control, with proper safeguards to prevent the misuse of the atomic weapon.

Happily the grave deterioration in the relations of the Big Three resulting from the London gathering was checked and gathering international gloom was somewhat lifted at a second meeting of the Big Three Foreign Ministers in Moscow at the end of 1945. Certain of the issues which had caused antagonism at London appear not to have been reviewed in Moscow, but it was arranged that an Allied Council consisting of representatives of the United States, Russia, China, and the British realm would be formed, to advise the American occupation authorities in Japan and with authority to block fundamental governmental changes there.

It was decided, too, that other Allied nations than the Big Three would have a share in making treaty settlements with the late enemies. France, for instance, having signed the armistice with Italy, might participate in making the treaty of peace with Italy. It was agreed, moreover, at Moscow that draft treaties would be drawn up for Italy and the satellite nations for submission to a general peace conference in May, 1946.

Launching the United Nations

Since the San Francisco Charter had been duly ratified by fifty one states, the first session of the United Nations was convened in London in January, 1946, much sooner after the conclusion of hostilities than the League of Nations had met. While this meeting was intended primarily to set the wheels of United Nations' machinery revolving, the statesmen had to grapple with urgent problems of food and refugees, and with several highly inflammable political disputes.

Indeed, dramatic, heated clashes developed in the Security Council between the chief Soviet and British spokesmen, Vice-Commissar Vishinsky and Foreign Minister Bevin, respectively. Russian military pressure into Iran (Persia), alleged British threats to peace in Indonesia, Greece, Syria and Lebanon supplied plenty of fireworks, of precisely the character the United Nations was organized to handle. In one way or another the controversies were either sidetracked or smoothed over.

On the other side, the principal organs and bodies of the United Nations were set up, officers were chosen, commissions were appointed, and modes of procedure were roughed out. All started to perform their assigned responsibilities, except the Trusteeship Council, whose composition was adjourned to the second part of the Assembly meeting in the fall of 1946.

It was decided at London that the permanent home of the United Nations should be located in the United States. A site not far from New York City was tentatively chosen, with New York itself the interim headquarters. Thus was tacitly acknowledged for the first time in western history that the largest single power potential lay outside the continent of Europe.

The choice for the crucial office of Secretary-General fell upon the Norwegian Foreign Minister, Trygve Lie. A huge hulk of a man, endowed with immense energy, Lie had made his way out of his peasant environment by becoming a lawyer and rising through Norwegian Social Democratic politics. His distinguishing traits were shrewdness, a strong-will, simplicity in speech, and friendliness. Entering the Norwegian Ministry in 1935, Lie had been assigned the portfolio of Foreign Affairs in the Ministry-in-exile five years later. Immediately upon his selection as Secretary-General Lie set about recruiting the staff to assist him in his ticklish job of "world watchman." The United Nations had become a going concern.

The Case of Iran

An old arena of Anglo-Russian rivalry, politically backward Iran or Persia, important for its oil resources and strategic location, provided a real and very serious test of the United Nations in its infancy. During World War II, Soviet, British, and American troops, as has been elsewhere explained (p. 538) entered Iran, primarily to ensure the safe passage of Lend-Lease supplies to the Soviet Union. On more occasions than one the occupying powers pledged to pull their soldiers out after the war was over, and to maintain "the independence, sovereignty and territorial integrity of Iran."

In conformity with those commitments British and United States troops were withdrawn before March 2, 1946, the specified day, but Red soldiers lingered on in the northern provinces. Aggravating the problem was an uprising in Azerbaijan province, which may or may not have been engineered by Soviet agents, and the establishment of a separate regime there. Iran protested that the Soviet Union was in fact interfering in her affairs, and the controversy was aired at the first or London meeting of the Security Council. It was decided that the two disputants should try to work out an accommodation, the Security Council retaining, however, the right to seek information on the course of the negotiations.

When no settlement was reached by the two directly interested parties, Iran made complaint to the Security Council again—this time at the March sessions of the Council in its temporary quarters in New York City. Adamantly opposed to consideration of the controversy, the Russians, nevertheless, promised to evacuate all troops from Iran by early May, 1946. Nonetheless the Council voted to hear the case, whereat the Soviet spokesman, Andrei Gromyko, stalked dramatically from the chamber. A tense situation developed, yet the Council proceeded with the discussion. And in the end it was voted to postpone further consideration of the case of Iran until the May date set by Russia for the complete withdrawal of its armed forces.

Seemingly in this first test of strength the United Nations had emerged with somewhat heightened prestige, for it had acted against the desires of a Big Three nation and stood forth as the champion of a small and weak power. On the other hand, it had not compelled the acquiescence of the Soviet Union, and presently the world was apprized that a Soviet-Iranian agreement had been signed regarding the evacuation of Red troops, Soviet oil concessions, and "arrangements" pertaining to Azerbaijan. It looked very much as though Iran under Soviet pressure had become a Russian client akin to the states of eastern Europe. In spite of reports that Russian soldiers had quit Iran by the appointed day, the Security Council, not entirely convinced, chose to keep the case on the docket.

Another Paris Conference

Inasmuch as the deputies of the foreign ministers of the Big Three states were unable to reach accords on draft treaties with Italy

and the Axis puppets, Secretary of State Byrnes proposed another
meeting of the diplomatic principals to discuss and presumably to
work out solutions of controversial issues. That conference of Foreign
Ministers, the fifth in eight months, assembled in the spring of 1945
in the famed Luxembourg Palace at Paris.

Since the last parley of the chief policymakers, international affairs
had taken a turn for the worse. Suspicion, irritation, mistrust, and disunity were openly manifested, for instance, in the turbulent debates
over Iran in the Security Council. There was much talk in press and
radio of an open breach between Britain and the Soviet Union, or even
that a war between them impended. On many counts the absence of
treaty settlements with the late enemies was detrimental to the restoration of some kind of economic and political stability. More, the dark
menace of famine was haunting Europe; the food, security, and welfare of tens of millions were tragically affected by the progress (or
lack of it) in the making of peace treaties.

In make-up this Paris Conference resembled its predecessors
though the Soviet delegation was rather larger than customarily. The
American contingent included Senators Connally and Vandenberg,
the one a Democrat, the other a Republican, serving as advisers to
Byrnes and giving United States policy a character above party concerns. France, for the first time, was admitted to the councils of the
victors on a footing of equality.

The course of the discussions on the tangled and discordant issues
followed a familiar pattern. At first, matters of small moment were
amicably adjusted, giving rise to a feeling of optimism; then business
slowed to a standstill and disenchantment set in. In the main, British
and American diplomacy ran parallel on the larger questions, the
United States displaying greater firmness and more initiative than
had been its wont. Though here and there the Russians modified positions they had previously taken, the Soviet mood was more intransigent than conciliatory. The Foreign Minister of France, Georges
Bidault, oscillated uneasily between West and East, bent on avoiding
too close identity with either.

While the main business at Paris was to prepare settlements with
Italy and the Hitlerian satellite nations, several other European items
were insinuated into the discussions. For example, the boundary between Italy and Yugoslavia, involving the future of the commercial
center of Trieste and the adjacent district of Venezia Giulia and
Istria, came under scrutiny several times. Experts of the Big Four
presented four different proposals for the new frontier, and Byrnes
urged that a plebiscite should be conducted in the contested areas,

but no agreement was reached. It was, however, decided that the South Tyrol, another hardy perennial of international politics, to which Austria entered claims, should remain under the flag of Italy.

In a surprise move Foreign Commissar Molotov spoke out in support of a French-sponsored plan to place the Italian colony of Libya under United Nations trusteeship with Rome as the exclusive administrator. The Russians appeared to favor the award of the Dodecanese archipelago to Greece, on ethnic grounds. So also, the Russians drastically scaled down the amount which Italy would be summoned to pay on reparations.

None of these issues passed beyond the discussion stage at Paris, all were definitely tentative. But the Italian armistice of 1943 was formally revised allowing Italians full jurisdiction in internal affairs, except the military. That understanding had, however, little practical significance, for much of the original armistice had been nullified in reality.

At this Paris Conference, the treaty settlement with Finland was virtually completed and the terms closely paralleled the armistice that had been signed with the Soviet Union when Finland dropped out of the war. Rumanian sovereignty over northern Transylvania, which Hitler had bestowed upon Hungary, was recognized and the cession of Bessarabia and the northern Bukovina to Russia was formally approved.

Byrnes insistently pressed for drastic reduction of the occupying armies in Austria but Molotov adamantly opposed that. So far back as September, 1945 the United States had confidentially proposed that the Big Four should make a twenty five year treaty to keep Germany permanently disarmed, and at Paris this plan in detail was unveiled publicly.[5] Intended to diminish if not to remove Soviet—and French —fears of a German war of revenge, and to consolidate and maintain peace, this unprecedented American overture evoked little enthusiasm, was not even discussed by the policymakers at Paris.

On the other hand, a four-power commission was created to study German disarmament in the four zones of occupation. That was done after Russians charged that the war potential of Germany was not being eliminated in the western zones, an accusation which Britain and the United States hotly denied. Russia, moreover, vetoed, as premature, American recommendations for a general allied peace conference on Germany and a similar conference for the other late European enemies.

[5] It was also recommended that a comparable treaty should be made to keep Japan militarily impotent.

After a thorough re-examination of a wide variety of outstanding differences, the Council of Foreign Ministers recessed for a month, without accomplishing much that was concrete. In the interval deputies would once more try to fit into place some of the pieces in the European jig-saw puzzle and proposals on peacemaking would of course proceed through normal channels of diplomacy.

Undisguisedly disappointed by the trials and failures in the Paris deliberations, and guardedly critical of Soviet policies, Byrnes declared that unless the next Foreign Ministers' parley agreed to hold a peace conference in the summer of 1946, the United States would recommend that settlements be arranged through the agency of the General Assembly of the United Nations.

Unfinished Tasks

In his report to the nation on the Paris parley Secretary of State Byrnes admonished his countrymen against expecting too much too quickly in the sphere of peacemaking. Said he sagely, "A people's peace cannot be won by flashing diplomatic triumphs. It requires patience and firmness, tolerance and understanding."

Hardly had the Byrnes' pronouncement been delivered than Foreign Commissar Molotov offered his version of the Big Three malaise. After stridently criticizing American and British aims and actions he flatly charged those nations with striving to coerce the Soviet Union to their will and to establish English-speaking dominion over the globe; thereby they were gravely endangering the outlook for peace. That broadside was scarcely conducive to active trust and friendly cooperation between nations upon whom the burden of peacemaking rested.

What, then, were the larger problems of Europe, or rather of the defeated nations, that awaited ironing out in the summer of 1946? So far as Italy was concerned, the main dispute was over the destiny of Trieste, through which the nations of south-central Europe were accustomed to trade with the outer world, and whose inhabitants were predominantly Italian in national sentiment. It was generally agreed that the community should be internationalized, in spite of the melancholy Danzig experiment in the epoch between World Wars.

But should sovereignty and administration reside with Italy or Yugoslavia? While the powers of the West backed the Italian case, the Soviet Union stood solidly by Yugoslavia, a nation devoted to Russia as the symbol of the common Slav heritage and of resistance to the late enemies. For those observers who conceived of Yugoslavia as the pliant puppet of the Kremlin, to transfer Trieste to her would be

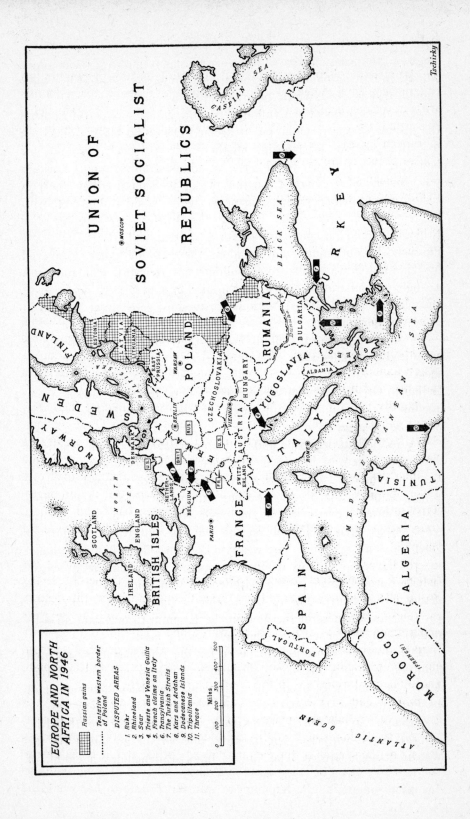

EUROPE AND NORTH
AFRICA IN 1946

Russian gains

.... Tentative western border
of Poland

DISPUTED AREAS

1. Ruhr
2. Rhineland
3. Saar
4. Trieste and Venezia Giulia
5. French claims on Italy
6. Transylvania
7. The Turkish Straits
8. Kars and Ardahan
9. Dodecanese Islands
10. Tripolitania
11. Thrace

Miles
0 100 200 300 400 500

UNION OF

SOVIET SOCIALIST

REPUBLICS

● MOSCOW

CASPIAN SEA

BLACK SEA

TURKEY

FINLAND

SWEDEN

NORWAY

ESTONIA
LATVIA
LITHUANIA

BALTIC SEA

POLAND
WARSAW ●
EAST PRUSSIA

NORTH SEA

SCOTLAND
ENGLAND
IRELAND

BRITISH ISLES

DENMARK

GERMANY
● BERLIN

RUS

BRIT

U.S.

FR.

NETHER-LANDS

BELGIUM

PARIS ●

FRANCE

CZECHOSLOVAKIA

AUSTRIA
VIENNA

SWITZ-ERLAND

HUNGARY

RUMANIA

YUGOSLAVIA

BULGARIA

ALBANIA

ITALY

ROME ●

SPAIN

PORTUGAL

MEDITERRANEAN SEA

AEGEAN SEA

ALGERIA

TUNISIA

MOROCCO (FRENCH)

ATLANTIC OCEAN

Tschirky

to extend the Russian zone of influence too far to the west for comfort. Marshal Tito intemperately threatened to seize Trieste by force should the city not lawfully be assigned to his country.

The disposition of the Italian African colonies also stood high on the agenda of the peace-to-be. It seemed clear that they would pass to United Nations trusteeship and there were persuasive grounds for believing that Italians would serve as administrators, though Britain felt constrained to honor a wartime pledge to Senussi tribal chiefs in eastern Cyrenaica promising that never again should Italian authority be restored in any guise. Equally the British were urging that Ethiopia should be compensated for evil treatment at the hands of Fascismo by obtaining a harbor along the coast of Eritrea. Favored by Britain, too, was a plan to consolidate the African Somalilands into a single administrative entity, add a slice of southern Ethiopia to it, and place it under United Nations trusteeship, with Great Britain in charge of government.

It was the American contention that the Italian colonies should be permitted to manage their own affairs after a period of tutelage under the United Nations. That the Dodecanese would be transferred from Italian to Greek sovereignty appeared certain, and there was a strong likelihood that minor rectifications in the Franco-Italian frontier would be effected.

In the Balkan peninsula and in the lower Danube region, wholly in the Soviet sphere of influence, the West and Moscow were radically at odds. Whereas Russia desired the institution of planned economy extended into these areas, the West, more particularly the United States, wanted the principle of the "open door" applied. Similarly the West desired free navigation on the Danube, but Russia would not concur in that. Seemingly the western Foreign Offices had abandoned hope of having acceptably democratic regimes in the nations of southeastern Europe which were garrisoned by Red soldiers. In fact, one of the matters that postponed the making of Balkan peace settlements was the unwillingness of the men in the Kremlin to evacuate an estimated 2,000,000 troops from Europe's Middle East.

The economic conditions of peace for the Balkan nations awaited definition, but some decisions had been reached on questions of frontiers. The boundaries of the new Rumania had been determined at the Paris meeting. Hungary presented no territorial problem. On the other hand, Greece raised claims to a section of southern Bulgaria, and the latter, with Russian backing, pressed for an outlet on the Aegean through Greece. The Greeks likewise demanded a chunk of

Albania, basing the claim, as in the case of southern Bulgaria, upon strategic and ethnic arguments.

Except for possible acquiescence in a Czech demand for a parcel of land along the Danube above Bratislava, the territory of the Austrian Republic seemed unlikely to be altered. As has been stated above, the Austrian ambition to regain the South Tyrol was denied at Paris by the Big Four.

From a long range viewpoint the most complicated and most important task of European peacemaking was of course Germany. Should, for example, the western part of Germany be lopped off as eastern districts had been taken away in the Potsdam settlement? As in 1919, sentiment in France, except among the Socialists, warmly demanded that the Rhineland—the vital Ruhr valley and of course the Saar Basin included—should be politically and permanently detached from Germany; only thus, the French logic ran, could the security of France and of Europe be safeguarded.

Great Britain, whose troops were in control of the greater area of the Rhineland, was impaled on the horns of a dilemma. While Britain eagerly desired the friendship of France and wanted to prevent German aggression in the future, British thinking steadfastly opposed the French separation formula. It was the British conviction that an independent Rhineland, inhabited by some 16,000,000 intelligent and energetic Germans, would surely try to merge with the rest of Germany unless held down by Allied bayonets. Yet another reason for resisting separation had considerable acceptance in Britain; namely, that the Ruhr valley as an integral part of the German nation was indispensable for European political and economic convalescence and stability.

Britain officially recommended that some kind of international regime should be charged with the administration of Ruhr resources and that they should be harnessed first to pay reparations and later used for the material benefit of all of Europe. The United States Department of State was inclined to side with the British on the Rhineland problem. The attitude of the Kremlin was not clear. For Russia to favor separation of the Rhineland would antagonize German Communists; to deny separation would embitter the Communists of France.

Unless and until an accommodation was worked out on the Rhine valley, the French would not hear of a unified administrative system for the German nation nor of a co-ordinated economy. Equally with the French, the Soviets were opposed to merging the several zones of occupation. The United States and Britain, failing to obtain French and Russian sanction for German unification, approved plans in September, 1946, for the union of their own zones.

Human conditions in Germany, especially shortages of food in the west, were appalling. Production of goods fell progressively lower. To maintain the population Britain and the United States were spending at the rate of half a billion dollars a year, quite apart from the expense of the army of occupation. The merger of the British and American zones, which contained the larger part of the German people and the bulk of the German industry, would produce, the exponents of the plan contended, somewhat more tolerable living standards in the areas affected and perhaps prepare the way for full reunion of Germany, since the door was left open for France and Russia to come in. On the other hand, it was possible that the Anglo-American move would intensify the ill-will with the Soviets.

Paris Peace Conference

On July 29, 1946, another international conference convened in Paris. It would consider treaties of peace with Italy and four Axis confederates, Hungary, Rumania, Bulgaria, and Finland. The groundwork for the meeting had been laid by the Council of Foreign Ministers which had prepared skeleton settlements, indicating points on which there was agreement as well as problems on which the Big Four were at odds. Present at Paris were the diplomatic chiefs of the Big Four, wearied by almost a year of vexatious and grueling diplomacy, and representatives of seventeen of the smaller victor countries. Spokesmen of the ex-enemy nations would be granted an opportunity to present their claims before the world.

Unlike the Peace Conference of 1919, that of 1946 would not deal with the principal vanquished power, Germany, on whose future the major victors were far, very far, from unity. As one commentator aptly remarked, "to hold a peace conference without disposing of the remains of Nazi Germany is to play 'Hamlet' without the Prince of Darkness." Settlements with Japan and Austria were likewise excluded from the agenda of the Paris Conference. Yet Allied diplomatists were on the alert lest precedents should be set in the negotiations over the treaties with the secondary states that might prove undesirable or embarrassing when the time arrived to deal with Germany and Japan.

While the deliberations at Paris proceeded, the international scene was gravely troubled by tumult and ferment at several points on the globe. Palestine, Egypt, and India were in an uproar. Skirmishing went on between native fighters and British troops in the Dutch East Indies, and in China factional divergences had expression in actual armed combat. Relations between the United States and Yugoslavia became dangerously strained when Yugoslav airmen shot down unprotected American transport aircraft, killing some of the crews and detaining the remainder. After a sharply phrased demand from Washington, the Yugoslav government released the surviving American flyers and promised to make due reparation for their dead companions. At the same time disturbing verbal fireworks punctuated the sessions of the Security Council, the Atomic Energy Commission, and other agencies of the United Nations.

At Paris the work of peacemaking was entrusted to large commissions. An acrimonious battle over procedure and voting consumed almost two weeks of time. In that befuddled debate the Soviet-Slav bloc of Russia, Poland, Yugoslavia, and Czechoslovakia was pitted, as a rule, against the other delegates, except the French who essayed the role of balancer.

One novelty, a dubious one, of this Paris parley was the lavish publicity. Pressmen were even admitted to the discussions of the commissions. Given that audience, speakers were prone to dramatize and dogmatize so as to impress their publics at home. So the pace of the conference was slowed up and controversies were aggravated to a degree that would not have prevailed had the debates been conducted less openly. Another innovation in peacemaking was the decision to take votes on specific questions, which would permit each nation to register its point of view.

Small nations offered a great many amendments to the draft treaties prepared by the Foreign Ministers of the Big Four. As had been true more than once in the diplomacy of Europe during the last century, the Balkan peninsula was the focal point of dissension and disharmony. Acrimonious charges and counter-charges and shrill polemics reflected the underlying fear and distrust between the Soviet group and the West.

Once the treaties had been drawn by the Paris negotiators, they would be transmitted to the Council of Foreign Ministers, which would write the definitive settlements. Even when settlements with the smaller enemy nations had been completed, the work of peacemaking would still be at its beginning. Treaties with Germany, and Japan would have to be prepared.

Into Tomorrow

It was plain in 1947, as indeed it had been in 1919, that the search for peace would be a long, wearisome process, interrupted by grave disappointments, if not worse. It was plain that workable compromises, odious to passionate natures because they looked like surrenders, would have to be discovered. It was plain too that policymakers were gripped by a time-lag in their thinking when dealing with frontiers and "disarmament," as though ignorant of the fast-flying plane, the rocket bomb, and the atomic bomb which required radical revisions in conventional conceptions of strategy.

It was not at all surprising that the most gigantic of wars in the most intricate of societies should have bequeathed a vast complex of political, social, and economic instabilities. Wide divergencies in national ideology and interest among the Big Three sowed dragon's teeth of distrust and rendered harmonious solution of problems exceedingly difficult. Men who under the exaltation of wartime fervor indulged in roseate anticipations of a wholly new temper in international relationships, men who had pinned their faith on the aspirations of the Atlantic Charter or on the immediate attainment of the Four Freedoms, experienced chilling exasperation.

There was much talk, a year after the cessation of hostilities, of the inadequacy of the United Nations and even of another war, before the grass had hardly had time to grow on the graves of World War II. The lamentations of certain Jeremiahs were loud and long, but Jeremiahs have been belied as frequently as the painfully naive, who are unwilling to face disagreeable facts. Heads in the clouds command no more sympathetic consideration than heads in the sand.

For all the misgivings about the future, the fact stood out in bold relief that the greater states, in spite of deep ideological cleavages, had closely and fruitfully collaborated in World War II. And it was to their common advantage to work unitedly in avoiding a renewal of strife. The only feasible means to that end was the United Nations, which was dedicated to the most colossal revolution in the drama of the planet: to victory over war itself. But the maintenance of an orderly and secure world rested not upon any parchment, not upon any machinery, but rather upon what was in the minds and hearts of men.

Wise men, whether professedly realists or idealists, or those in whom these strands were variously blended, kept reminding themselves of the stark fact that the atomic age of history had dawned and of the grim alternative of one world or none. They gazed into the future less in a spirit of shallow optimism than in a mood of cautious hope and dedicated resolution.

Bibliography

SELECTED BOOKS FOR FURTHER STUDY

For more extensive bibliographies consult Allison, W. H. et al., eds., *A Guide to Historical Literature* (1931), general; Langer, W. L., and Armstrong, H. F., eds., *Foreign Affairs Bibliography* (1933), contains some seven thousand items on the 1920's with terse comments; Woolbert, R. G., ed., *Foreign Affairs Bibliography* (1945), the sequel to the foregoing with ten thousand titles into 1942; Ragatz, L. J., *A Bibliography for the Study of European History, 1815 to 1939* and *Supplements* (1942, 1943), restricted to works of real merit.

Fundamental documents illustrating various aspects of the history of the period are available in Cook, A. N., *Readings in Modern and Contemporary History* (1937); Cooke, W. H., and Stickney, E. P., *Readings in International Relations since 1879* (1931); Langsam, W. C., *Documents and Readings in the History of Europe since 1918* (1939); and for the years after 1928 the annual *Documents on International Affairs,* edited by J. W. Wheeler-Bennett.

For the broad sweep of Europe's past, which reached culmination in the epoch under review, no work quite equals in grandeur of narrative and depth of penetration Fisher, H. A. L., *A History of Europe* (3 vols., 1935–1936), which commences with neolithic beginnings and closes with Stalin and Hitler. Textbooks dealing with the period include Benns, F. L., *Europe since 1914 in Its World Setting* (new ed., 1945); Chambers, F. P., et al., *This Age of Conflict* (1943); Hall, W. P., *World Wars and Revolutions* (1943); Langsam, W. C., *The World since 1914* (new ed., 1943); Lipson, E., *Europe, 1914–1939* (1943), stresses the interaction of economic and political forces.

CHAPTER I

THE ECONOMIC ENVIRONMENT: Blanchard, W. O., and Vischer, S. S., *Economic Geography of Europe* (1931), useful; Bogardus, J. F., *Europe: A Geographical Survey* (1934); Clapham, J. H., *The Economic Development of France and Germany* (new ed., 1928), standard; Clapham, J. H., *An Economic History of Modern Britain* (3 vols., 1930–1938), a massive work, the third volume has special value; Dawson, W. H., *Social Insurance in Germany* (1912), standard; Day, C., *Economic Development in Europe* (1942), general; Fay, C. R., *Cooperation at Home and Abroad* (1920), on the movements for economic cooperation; Fay, C. R., *Life and Labour in the Nineteenth Century* (1920), valuable;

Feis, H., *Europe the World's Banker* (1930), an extremely important and scholarly study; Gompers, S., *Labor in Europe and America* (1910), by an American labor leader; Hindus, M. G., *The Russian Peasant and the Revolution* (1921), brilliant description of rural Russia; Hobson, J. A., *The Evolution of Modern Capitalism* (new ed., 1926), a much-prized work; Irvine, H. D., *The Making of Rural Europe* (1923), excellent; Knowles, L. C. A., *Economic Development in the Nineteenth Century* (1932), a clear outline; Mavor, J. M., *Economic History of Russia* (2 vols., 1914), good; Nussbaum, F. L., *A History of the Economic Institutions of Modern Europe* (1933), thoughtful, analytical; Orth, S. P., *Socialism and Democracy in Europe* (1913), clear treatment; Riesser, J., *The Great German Banks and Their Concentration* (1911), informing; Veblen, T., *Imperial Germany and the Industrial Revlution* (1915), thoughtful; Weber, A. F., *The Growth of Cities in the Nineteenth Century* (1899), standard.

INTELLECTUAL CURRENTS: Barzun, J., *Darwin, Marx, Wagner, Critique of a Heritage* (1941), valuable insights into intellectual trends; Hayes, C. J. H., *A Generation of Materialism, 1871–1900* (1941), splendid survey; Merz, J. T., *A History of European Thought in the Nineteenth Century* (4 vols., 1912–1923), a monumental study; Randall, J. H. Jr., *The Making of the Modern Mind* (new ed., 1940), excellent, general; Ruggiero, G., *A History of European Liberalism* (1927), stimulating.

NEW SOCIAL PHILOSOPHIES: Beer, M., *Fifty Years of International Socialism* (1935), excellent description; Bober, M. M., *Karl Marx's Interpretation of History* (1927), standard analysis; Carr, E. H., *Michael Bakunin* (1937), on the most feared revolutionary anarchist of the age; Fainsod, M., *International Socialism and the World War* (1935); Flint, R., *Socialism* (new ed., 1908), a classic critique of the Socialist ideology; Gray, A., *The Socialist Tradition* (1946), an appraisal of the leading Socialist philosophers; Harley, J. H., *Syndicalism* (1912), short, lucid analysis; Mayer, G., *Friedrich Engels* (1934), on Marx's friend and collaborator; Mehring, F., *Karl Marx* (1935), reliable; Miller, A., *The Christian Significance of Karl Marx* (1946), closely reasoned; Price, J., *The International Labour Movement* (1945); Sprigge, C. J. S., *Karl Marx* (1938), short, excellent; Strachey, J., *The Coming Struggle for Power* (1934), excellent on Marxist economics; Wagner, D. O., *Social Reformers* (1934), selections from their writings.

THE POLITICAL FRAMEWORK: Fisher, H. A. L., *The Republican Tradition in Europe* (1911), standard; Lowell, A. L., *The Governments of France, Italy and Germany* (1914), excellent survey; Lowell, A. L., *Greater European Governments* (1918), brief, authoritative; Ogg, F. A., *The Governments of Europe* (1913 edition), clear and compact.

NATIONALISM AND INTERNATIONALISM: Bentwich, N., *The Religious Foundations of Internationalism* (1933); Carr, E. H., *Nationalism and After* (1945), stylistically attractive, thoughtful but brief; Chadwick, H. M., *The Nationalities of Europe and the Growth of National Ideology* (1945), a work of thorough learning; Cobban, A., *National Self-Determination* (1945), broad and analytical study; Dominian, L., *Frontiers of Language and Nationality in Europe* (1917), a useful survey; Hayes, C. J. H., *Essays on Nationalism* (1926), illuminating studies; Hayes, C. J. H., *Historical Evolution of Modern Nationalism* (1931), very good; Hertz, F., *Nationality in History and Politics* (1944), clear exposition of nationalism in its diverse manifestations; Hull, W. I., *The Two Hague Conferences* (1908), still serviceable; Kohn, H., *Prophets and Peoples* (1946), candid, scholarly portraits of nineteenth century exponents of nationalism; Oakesmith, J., *Race and Nationality* (1919), accent on Britain; Perla, L., *What Is National Honor?* (1918), a searching inquiry; Reisner, E. H., *Nationalism and Education since 1789* (1921); Royal Institute of International Affairs, *Nationalism* (1939), a calm, detached study, important; Rundle, S., *Language as a Social and Political Factor in Europe* (1946), by an eminent philologist; Zimmern, A. E., *Nationality and Government* (new ed., 1919).

IMPERIALISM AND COLONIALISM: Bakeless, J., *Economic Causes of Modern War* (1921), provocative; Brailsford, H. N., *After the Peace* (1922), an angry castigation of imperialism by a British publicist; Clark, G., *The Balance Sheets of Imperialism* (1936), a first-rate investigation; Hallberg, C. W., *The Suez Canal: Its History and Diplomatic Importance* (1931); Hobson, J. A., *Imperialism* (new ed., 1938), important arraignment of imperialism which was widely influential among intellectuals, Marxists especially;

Hoskins, H. L., *European Imperialism in Africa* (1930), clear, incisive survey; Latourette, K. S., *History of Christian Missions in China* (1929); MacDonald, A. J., *Trade, Politics and Christianity in Africa and the East* (1916), points up difficulties between evangelists and natives; Moon, P. T., *Imperialism and World Politics* (1926), historical and interpretative; Power, T. F., Jr., *Jules Ferry and the Renaissance of French Imperialism* (1943), a thoroughly documented reappraisal; Raphael, L. A. C., *The Cape to Cairo Dream* (1936), an able, detailed study; Rudin, H. R., *Germans in the Cameroons* (1938), excellent case-history; Townsend, M. E., *European Colonial Expansionism since 1871* (1941), careful outline by a leading authority; Townsend, M. E., *The Rise and Fall of Germany's Colonial Empire* (1930), informing and thorough; Viallate, A., *Economic Imperialism and International Relations* (1923), short, balanced account; Williams, B., *Cecil Rhodes* (1921), somewhat out of date.

MILITARISM AND PACIFISM: Angell, N., *The Great Illusion* (new ed., 1933), a famous book proving that the economic gains of war are fanciful; Beales, A. C. F., *The History of Peace* (1931), short, pointed summary of the ideas of pacifism; von Bernhardi, F., *Germany and the Next War* (1912), a typical specimen of the outpourings of the military cultists; Coulton, C. G., *The Main Illusions of Pacifism* (1916), lively; Enoch, A. G., *The Problem of Armaments* (1923), mathematical demonstration of the relationship between armaments and war; Henderson, E. F., *Germany's Fighting Machine* (1914); Marder, A. J., *The Anatomy of British Sea Power* (1940), much original material and interpretation; Nasmyth, G., *Social Progress and the Darwinian Theory* (1916), able criticism of the doctrine that "man is war"; Pauli, H. E., *Alfred Nobel* (1942), on the paradoxical munitions king; Tate, M., *The Disarmament Illusion* (1942), good; Vagts, A., *The History of Militarism* (1937), invaluable, though faulty in organization.

DIPLOMATIC METHOD AND THE PRESS: Cambon, J., *The Diplomatist* (1931), by a distinguished French practitioner; Carroll, E. M., *French Public Opinion and Foreign Affairs* (1931), able survey; Carroll, E. M., *Germany and the Great Powers* (1938), companion volume to the foregoing, excellent; Gaselee, S., *The Language of Diplomacy* (1939), interesting British treatise; Hale, O. J., *Publicity and Diplomacy* (1940), mainly on the British press, thorough; Nicolson, H., *Diplomacy* (1939), the best outline in English; Satow, E. M., *A Guide to Diplomatic Practice* (new ed., 1932), standard on the practical and legal aspects of intergovernmental negotiation.

GENERAL INTERNATIONAL HISTORY: Anrich, E., *Europas Diplomatie am Vorabend des Weltkrieges* (1937); Barlow, I. C., *The Agadir Crisis* (1940), definitive; Barnes, H. E., *Genesis of the World War* (new ed., 1928), expounds the thesis that France and Russia were mainly responsible for the coming of the war; Brandenburg, E., *From Bismarck to the World War* (1927), a scrupulously honest study by a German scholar; Dickinson. G. L., *The International Anarchy* (1926), once extremely popular; Fay, S. B., *The Origins of the World War* (new ed., 1930), a masterpiece that should be compared with another learned treatment, Schmitt, B. E., *The Coming of the War* (2 vols., 1930); Gooch, G. P., *Before the War* (2 vols., 1936–1938), impartial, ripe scholarship; Gooch, G. P., *Franco-German Relations, 1871–1914* (1923), short, judicial; Gooch, G. P., *Recent Revelations of European Diplomacy* (new ed., 1940), a masterly appraisal of the printed literature; Hoffman, R. J. S., *Great Britain and the German Trade Rivalry, 1875–1914* (1933), able study from the British literature; Kantorowicz, H., *The Spirit of British Policy* (1931), by an Anglophile German; Korff, S. A., *Russia's Foreign Relations during the Last Half Century* (1922), sketchy and antiquated; Langer, W. L., *The Diplomacy of Imperialism, 1890–1902* (2 vols., 1935), brilliant and exhaustive account; Langer, W. L., *The Franco-Russian Alliance* (1929), detailed, definitive; Nicolson, H., *Portrait of a Diplomatist* (1930), in the nature of a biography of the writer's father, lucidly written.

Pribram, A. F., *England and the International Policy of the European Great Powers* (1931), admirable outline by a Viennese scholar; Schmitt, B. E., *Triple Alliance and Triple Entente* (1934), concise and clear; Seymour, C. S., *Diplomatic Background of the War* (1916), interesting as a contemporary treatment by an American historian; Sforza, C., *Makers of Modern Europe* (1930), entertaining portraits by an Italian statesman; Sontag, R. J., *European Diplomatic History, 1871–1932* (1933), splendid account; Sontag, R. J., *Germany and England* (1938), indispensable; Woodward, E. L., *Great Britain and the Germany Navy* (1935), broad summary.

SPECIAL STUDIES IN DIPLOMACY: Anderson, E. N., *The First Moroccan Crisis, 1904–1906* (1930), outstanding treatise; Askew, W. C., *Europe and Italy's Acquisition of Libya* (1942), definitive; Churchill, R. P., *The Anglo-Russian Convention of 1907* (1939), thorough; Helmreich, E. C., *The Diplomacy of the Balkan Wars, 1912–1913* (1938), standard; Lutz, H., *Lord Grey and the World War* (1928), a judicial German examination; Porter, C. W., *The Career of Théophile Delcassé* (1936), scholarly; Schmitt, B. E., *The Annexation of Bosnia* (1937), first-class; Sumner, B. H., *Tsardom and Imperialism in the Far East and the Middle East, 1880–1914* (1943), a brilliant essay; Tyler, J. E., *The British Army and the Continent, 1904–1914* (1938); Wedel, O. H., *Austro-German Diplomatic Relations, 1908–1914* (1932), meticulous and enlightening analysis; Wolf, J. B., *Diplomatic History of the Bagdad Railway* (1936), definitive.

CHAPTER II

SARAJEVO AND THE SEQUEL: The studies by S. B. Fay and B. E. Schmitt, cited above, contain extensive treatments of Sarajevo and its aftermath; Durham, M. E., *The Serajevo Crime* (1925), should be read along with Seton-Watson, R. W., *Sarajevo* (1926), detailed studies; Renouvin, P., *The Immediate Origins of the War* (1926), by a learned French authority; Sosnosky, T., *Franz Ferdinand* (1929), the best study; Wegerer, A., *Refutation of the Versailles War Guilt Thesis* (1930), a militant German discussion.

THE WAR IN GENERAL: Aston, G. G., *The Great War of 1914–1918* (1930), short and general; Churchill, W., *The World Crisis* (4 vols., 1923–1927), spirited exposition; Cruttwell, C. R. M. F., *A History of the Great War* (1934), best one volume summary; Liddell-Hart, B. H., *A History of the World War* (1935), good.

MILITARY AND NAVAL OPERATIONS: Chatterton, E. K., *The Dardanelles Dilemma* (1935); Churchill, W., *The Unknown War: The Eastern Front* (1931), a classic; Corbett, J. S., *History of the Great War: Naval Operations* (5 vols., 1920–1931), official; Emin, A., *Turkey in the World War* (1930); Frost, H. H., *The Battle of Jutland* (1936); Germains, V. W., *The Kitchener Armies* (1930); Gibson, R. H., and Prendergast, M., *The German Submarine War* (1931), detailed and rather unselective; Golovine, N. N., *The Russian Army in the World War* (1931), by a Tsarist general; Guichard, L., *The Naval Blockade* (1930), valuable; Jellicoe, J. R. L., *The Submarine Peril* (1934); Knox, A., *With the Russian Army* (2 vols., 1921), valuable diary by British military attaché; Larcher, M., *La Grande Guerre dans les Balkans* (1930), thorough treatment; Lawrence, T. E., *Revolt in the Desert* (1927), epic account of the Arabs; McEntee, G. L., *Italy's Part in Winning the World War* (1934), slim and somewhat exaggerated; Moberly, F. J., *Mesopotamian Campaign* (1923), official history; Newbolt, H., *A Naval History of the War* (1920), preliminary account of Britain at sea; Raleigh, W., *The War in the Air* (6 vols., 1922–1937), official British treatment; Scheer, R., *Germany's High Sea Fleet in the World War* (1920), by the successor of Tirpitz as head of the German Admiralty; Schubert, P., and Gibson, L., *Death of a Fleet, 1917–1919* (1932), on the fate of Tirpitz's folly.

WARTIME LEADERS: Aston, G., *Marshal Foch* (1929), official and not very critical; Bacon, R. H., *The Life of Lord Jellicoe* (1936), generally balanced portrait; Baldini, A., *Diaz* (1935), Italian military chief; Brusilov, A. A., *A Soldier's Notebook* (1930), by the best of the Tsarist generals; Duff-Cooper, A., *Haig* (2 vols., 1935), authoritative; Falkenhayn, E., *General Headquarters, 1914–1916* (1919), intimate account from the German side; Foch, F., *Memoirs* (1931), interesting; Hindenburg, P. von, *Out of My Life* (2 vols., 1921), interesting; Jellicoe, J. R. L., *The Grand Fleet* (1919), a large part in the form of a diary by the British commander; Liddell-Hart, B. H., *Foch, the Man of Orleans* (1932), sympathetic portrait; Liddell-Hart, B. H., *Reputations Ten Years After* (1928), critical estimates of the commanders; Lloyd-George, D., *War Memoirs* (6 vols., 1933–1936), richly documented and highly personal narrative of British war leader; Ludendorff, E., *Ludendorff's Own Story* (2 vols., 1920), intimate, revealing narrative; Madelin, L., *Foch* (1929), good; Recouly, R., *Joffre* (1931), uncritical; Salandra, A., *Italy and the Great War* (1932), personal narrative by Italian premier; Tschuppik, K., *Ludendorff: The Tragedy of a Specialist* (1932); Wavell, A., *Allenby, Soldier and States-*

man (1946), revision of an authoritative work; Wheeler-Bennett, J. W., *Wooden Titan* (1936), critical, sound life of Hindenburg.

OTHER ASPECTS: Chambers, F. P., *The War behind the War* (1939), accent on civilian activities; Fradkin, E., *Chemical Warfare* (1929), enlightening; Fuller, J. F. C., *Tanks in the Great War* (1920), interesting; Juenger, E., *The Storm of Steel* (1929), specimen of the literature by a German participant; Read, J. M., *Atrocity Propaganda, 1914–1919* (1941), detailed revelations; Sumner, B. H., *War and History* (1945), a philosophical exposition; Swinton, E. D., *Eyewitness* (1932), the development of the tank; Witkop, P., ed., *German Students' War Letters* (1929).

CHAPTER III

GENERAL: Bruntz, G. C., *Allied Propaganda and the Collapse of the German Empire in 1918* (1938); Doob, L. W., *Propaganda, Its Psychology and Technique* (1935), valuable; Lasswell, H. D., *Propaganda Technique in the World War* (1927), a singularly fine survey; Lutz, R. H., *The Fall of the German Empire* (2 vols., 1932), a sourcebook of immense interest; Peterson, H. C., *Propaganda for War* (1939), one of the most reliable books on an elusive subject; Stuart, C., *Secrets of Crewe House* (1920), British publicity activities in final stage of the war.

AMERICAN INTERVENTION AND ROLE: Baker, N. D., *Why We Went to War* (1936), a spirited criticism of the economic interpretation; Baker, R. S., *Woodrow Wilson: Life and Letters V–VIII* (1935–1939), monumental authorized biography; Bane, S. L., and Lutz, R. H., *Organization of American Relief in Europe, 1918–1919* (1943), documents; Bernstorff, J. H. A., *My Three Years in America* (1920), by the German Ambassador; Clark, J. M., *The Costs of the World War to the American People* (1931), standard; Clarkson, G. B., *Industrial America in the World War* (1923); Dumba, K., *Memories of a Diplomat* (1932), by the Hapsburg envoy to the United States; Frothingham, T., *The American Reinforcement in the World War* (1927); Grattan, C. H., *Why We Fought* (1929); Harbord, J. G., *The American Army in France* (1936); Lansing, R., *War Memoirs* (1935), much on the submarine controversy with Germany; Millis, W., *The Road to War* (1935), written with verve, persuasive, and distorted; Mock, J. R., and Larson, C., *Words That Won the War* (1939), enlightening on official publicity activities; Morrissey, A. M., *The American Defense of Neutral Rights, 1914–1917* (1939), a scholarly dissertation.

Paxson, F. L., *American Democracy and the World War* (2 vols., 1936, 1939), full summary; Pershing, J. J., *My Experiences in the World War* (1931), interesting; Robinson, E. E., and West, V. J., *The Foreign Policy of Woodrow Wilson, 1913–1917* (1917), an interesting contemporary appraisal; Seymour, C. S., *American Neutrality, 1914–1917* (1936), a vigorous reply to Millis; Seymour, C. S., *American Diplomacy during the World War* (1934), thoughtful and balanced summary; Seymour, C. S., ed., *The Intimate Papers of Colonel House* (4 vols., 1926–1928), an indispensable work; Sims, W. S., *The American Navy in the War* (1920); Slosson, P. W., *The Great Crusade and After: 1914–1928* (1930), excellent; Squires, J. D., *British Propaganda at Home and in the United States* (1935), detailed; Surface, F. M., and Bland, R. L., *American Food in the World War and Reconstruction* (1932); Tansill, C. C., *America Goes to War* (1938), thoroughly documented study; Viereck, G. S., *Spreading Germs of Hate* (1930), the doings of German publicity agents in the United States.

EFFORTS AT PEACE NEGOTIATION: Forster, K., *The Failures of Peace* (1941), a study of the search for a negotiated settlement; Johnson, H., *Vatican Diplomacy in the World War* (1933), short account; Manteyer, G., *Austria's Peace Offer, 1916–1917* (1921); Slice, A. V., *International Labor, Diplomacy, and War, 1914–1919* (1941).

CHAPTER IV

GENERAL ASPECTS: Berber, F., *Das Diktat von Versailles* (1939), an official Nazi selection of documents; Birdsall, P., *Versailles, Twenty Years After* (1941), a model treatise whose conclusions are friendly to Wilsonian diplomacy; Bonsal, S., *Unfinished Business* (1944), straightforward account by an eyewitness; Bonsal, S., *Suitors and Suppliants* (1946), a sequel to the previous citation; Brunn, G., *Clemenceau* (1943), the best study; Churchill, W., *The Aftermath* (1929), engaging narrative, critical of R. S. Baker's treatment; Clemenceau, G., *Grandeur and Misery of Victory* (1930), a spirited apologia; Donald, R., *The Tragedy of Trianon* (1928), eloquent plea for revision; Gathorne-Hardy, G. M., *The Fourteen Points and the Treaty of Versailles* (1939), short, provocative; Huddleston, S., *Peacemaking at Paris* (1919), useful account by a pressman; Jessop, T. E., *The Treaty of Versailles: Was It Just?* (1942), a masterly analysis; Lloyd-George, D., *Memoirs of the Peace Conference* (2 vols., 1939), frank, polemical, documented exposition of his course; Molony, W. O., *Nationality and the Peace Treaties* (1934).

Nicolson, H., *Peacemaking, 1918–1919* (new ed., 1945), captiously critical of Wilson's role, valuable diary; Noble, G. B., *Policies and Opinions at Paris* (1935), an able appraisal of French attitudes; Nowak, K. F., *Versailles* (1929), a German version; Riddell, G. A., *The Treaty of Versailles and After* (1935), interesting; Shotwell, J. T., *At the Paris Peace Conference* (1937), an interpretation and personal record; Tardieu, A., *The Truth about the Treaty* (1921), an important French interpretation; Temperley, H. W. V., ed., *A History of the Peace Conference of Paris* (6 vols., 1920–1924), the work of many hands, dispassionate, detailed; Ziegler, W., *Versailles* (new ed., 1933), straightforward, colorless summary.

SPECIFIC PHASES: Albrecht-Carrié, R., *Italy at the Paris Peace Conference* (1938), definitive; Almond, N., and Lutz, R. H., eds., *The Treaty of St. Germain* (1934), documentary; Beer, G. L., *African Questions at the Peace Conference* (1923), thorough and comprehensive; Burnett, P. M., *Reparations at the Paris Peace Conference* (2 vols., 1940), authoritative and detailed; Deák, F., *Hungary at the Paris Peace Conference* (1942), useful; Genov, G. P., *Bulgaria and the Treaty of Neuilly* (1935); Haskins, C. H., and Lord, R. H., *Some Problems of the Peace Conference* (1920), rather objective studies of certain territorial settlements by American experts; Keynes, J. M., *The Economic Consequences of the Peace* (1920), a famous and caustic indictment of reparations; Keynes, J. M., *A Revision of the Treaty* (1922); Luckau, A., *The German Delegation at the Paris Peace Conference* (1941), documentary history with interpretative prologue; Macartney, C. A., *Hungary and Her Successors* (1937), a monumental piece of scholarship; Miller, D. H., *The Drafting of the Covenant* (2 vols., 1928), solid and indispensable; Morrow, I. F. D., *The Peace Settlement in the German-Polish Borderlands* (1936), voluminous, very useful; Rudin, H. R., *Armistice, 1918* (1944), standard; Wambaugh, S., *Plebiscites since the World War* (2 vols., 1933), standard; Woodhouse, E. J., and Woodhouse, C., *Italy and the Jugoslavs* (1920), still useful.

THE UNITED STATES AND THE PEACE: Bailey, T. A., *Woodrow Wilson and the Lost Peace* (1944), a comprehensive interpretation; Bailey, T. A., *Woodrow Wilson and the Great Betrayal* (1945), vigorous and thoughtful; Baker, R. S., *Woodrow Wilson and World Settlement* (3 vols., 1922–1923), classic apologia on the President's policies; Dickinson, T. H., *The United States and the League* (1923), condemnatory of the foes of ratification; Fleming, D. F., *The United States and the League of Nations* (1932), detailed, definitive; Lansing, R., *The Peace Negotiations, a Personal Narrative* (1921); Lodge, H. C., *The Senate and the League of Nations* (1925), as seen by a Republican leader; Marburg, T., *The Development of the League of Nations Idea* (2 vols., 1932), standard.

CHAPTER V

GENERAL TREATMENTS: Berdyaev, N. A., *The Origin of Russian Communism* (1937), philosophical; Buxton, D. F., *The Challenge of Bolshevism* (1928), stimulating, philosophical essay; Chamberlin, W. H., *The Russian Enigma* (1943), by a leading student and interpreter; Chamberlin, W. H., *Russia's Iron Age* (1934), Citrine, W. M., *I Search for Truth in Russia* (1937), diary of a British trade union leader; Cressey, G. B., *The Basis of Soviet Strength* (1945), detailed work by a scientific geographer; Dallin, D. J., *The Real Soviet Russia* (1944), a critical analysis by an émigré; Duranty, W., *I Write as I Please* (1935), sketchy, revealing, balanced; Duranty, W., *U. S. S. R.* (1944), popular; Florinsky, M., *Toward an Understanding of the U. S. S. R.* (1939), solid;

Fülop-Miller, R., *The Mind and Face of Bolshevism* (1928), a wide-ranging psychological exploration; Gide, A., *Return from the U. S. S. R.* (1937), by a disillusioned yet hopeful Frenchman; Gregory, J. S., and Shave, W. R., *The U. S. S. R.* (1944), a thorough geographical survey; Karlgren, A., *Bolshevist Russia* (1927), good on peasant land seizures; Koestler, A., *The Yogi and the Commissar* (1945), shrill arraignment of Stalin's ways.

Kravchenko, V., *I Chose Freedom* (1946), autobiographical piece by a disenchanted ex-official; Lauterbach, R. E., *These Are the Russians* (1944), a friendly report in war-time, to be read together with White, W. L., *Report on the Russians* (1945); Maisky, I. M., *Before the Storm* (1944), analysis of conditions before the Revolutions; Pares, B., *Russia* (1943), important; Pares, B., *Russia Admits a Critic* (1936), who found much that was admirable; Rosenberg, A., *A History of Bolshevism* (1934), analytical, useful; Sloan, P., *Russia without Illusions* (1938), a reply to the disillusioned; Strauss, E., *Soviet Russia* (1941), illuminating on the economic side; Sumner, B. H., *A Short History of Russia* (1943), curiously organized but learned; Timasheff, N. S., *The Great Retreat* (1946), important; Webb, S., and Webb, B., *Soviet Communism: A New Civilization* (2 vols., new ed., 1941), comprehensive, sympathetic contribution; Wheeler-Bennett, J. W., *The Forgotten Peace: Brest-Litovsk* (1938), standard; Williams, A. R., *The Soviets* (1937), the question and answer technique on Russian affairs.

REVOLUTIONS, GOVERNMENT AND POLITICS: Barbusse, H., *Stalin* (1935), a flattering, uncritical portrait; Borkenau, F., *World Communism* (1939), unsympathetic, illuminating; Bunyan, J., and Fisher, H. H., *The Bolshevik Revolution, 1917–1918* (1934), documentary; Bunyan, J., *Intervention, Civil War, and Communism in Russia* (1936), original materials; Callcott, M. S., *Russian Justice* (1935), standard; Chamberlin, W. H., *The Russian Revolution* (2 vols., 1935), full and dispassionate; Chernov, V. M., *The Great Russian Revolution* (1936), authoritative on March upheaval; Cole, D. M., *Josef Stalin, Man of Steel* (1942), brief, laudatory; Davies, J. E., *Mission to Moscow* (1941), an interesting treatise by the sometime Ambassador of the United States at the Kremlin; Duranty, W., *The Kremlin and the People* (1941), much on Moscow treason trials; Fedotoff White, D., *Growth of the Red Army* (1944), a social treatise; Harper, S. N., *The Government of the Soviet Union* (1938), an objective summary; Harper, S. N., *Making Bolsheviks* (1931), authoritative; Hill, E., and Mudie, D., eds., *The Letters of Lenin* (1937).

Kerensky, A. F., *The Crucifixion of Liberty* (1934), an explanation and a condemnation; Kerr, W., *The Russian Army* (1944); Lasswell, H. D., *World Revolutionary Propaganda* (1939), scholarly; Lockhart, B. H., *Memoirs of a British Agent* (1932), fascinating record of revolutionary days; Marcu, V., *Lenin* (1928), a balanced picture; Mavor, J. M., *The Russian Revolution* (1928), Popov, N., *Outline History of the Communist Party of the Soviet Union* (2 vols., 1935), official Bolshevik account; Schuman, F. L., *Soviet Politics at Home and Abroad* (1946), a sympathetic interpretation; Simon, E. D., et. al., *Moscow in the Making* (1937), on urban construction; Souvarine, B., *Stalin* (1939), by a renegade Communist, hostile to the dictator; Stalin, J., *Leninism* (new ed., 1941), lectures; Stewart, G., *The White Armies of Russia* (1933), not satisfactory but as good as anything on the subject; Trotsky, L., *The History of the Russian Revolution* (3 vols., 1932–1933), indispensable interpretation, flattering to the author; Trotsky, L., *Stalin* (1946), chapters by Trotsky are bitterly critical; Vernadsky, G., *Lenin, the Red Dictator* (1931), by a critically minded émigré; Yaroslavsky, K. E., *Landmarks in the Life of Stalin* (1942), a sketch by a Communist official.

ECONOMIC TRENDS AND RECORD: Antsiferov, A. N., et al., *Russian Agriculture during the War* (1930), a mine of data; Arnold, A. Z., *Banks, Credit, and Money in Soviet Russia* (1937); Baykov, A., *The Development of the Soviet Economic System* (1946), exhaustive, dry scholarship; Bazili, N. de, *Russia under Soviet Rule* (1938), unsympathetic account with the accent on economic matters; Bergson, A., *The Structure of Soviet Wages* (1944), very useful; Bienstock, G., et al., *Management in Russian Industry and Agriculture* (1944); Brutskus, B. D., *Economic Planning in Soviet Russia* (1935); Dobb, M., *How Soviet Trade Unions Work* (1941), short and excellent; Dobb, M., *Soviet Economy and the War* (1941), concise handbook; Dobb, M., *Soviet Planning and Labour in Peace and War* (1942), learned essays; Dunn, R. W., *Soviet Trade Unions* (1928), short; Eastman, M., *The End of Socialism in Russia* (1937), sharp arraignment of Stalinist economics.

Fisher, H. H., *The Famine in Soviet Russia, 1919–1923* (1927), authoritative; Francis, P., *I Worked in a Soviet Factory* (1939), experiences of a British artisan; Freeman, J.,

The Soviet Worker (1931), conditions in 1920's; Gordon, M., *Workers before and after Lenin* (1944), argues that standards of living have fallen; Hindus, M., *The Great Offensive* (1933), colorful narrative by an American journalist, one of several useful books on the Soviet Union by the same author; Hoover, C. B., *The Economic Life of Soviet Russia* (1931), sound; Hubbard, L. E., *The Economics of Soviet Agriculture* (1939), important; Hubbard, L. E., *Soviet Labor and Industry* (1943), comprehensive to mid-thirties; Liberman, S., *Building Lenin's Russia* (1945), interesting sidelights; Maynard, J., *The Russian Peasant and Other Studies* (1942), a fresh interpretation; Molotov, V., *The Success of the Five Year Plan* (1931); Normano, J. F., *The Spirit of Russian Economics* (1944); Scott, J., pseud., *Behind the Urals* (1942), what a young American experienced and thought; Yugow, A., *Russia's Economic Front for War and Peace* (1942), admirable.

Social and Religious Affairs: Ammende, E., *Human Life in Russia* (1936), much on the famine of the thirties and Ukrainians; Anderson, P. B., *People, Church, and State in Modern Russia* (1944), friendly to Soviet policies; Casey, R. P., *Religion in Russia* (1946), a well-informed study; Emhardt, W. C., *Religion in Soviet Russia* (1929); Fisher, M., *My Lives in Russia* (1944), factual and informing on domestic life; Halle, F. W., *Woman in Soviet Russia* (1935), comprehensive and reliable; Heller, A., *Die Lage der Juden in Russland* (1935), informing; King, B., *Changing Man: the Soviet Educational System* (1936), valuable; Koerber, L., *Soviet Russia Fights Crime* (1935); Lamont, C., *The Peoples of the Soviet Union* (1946), lucid sketches of nationalities and their customs; Serebrennikov, G. N., *The Position of Women in the U. S. S. R.* (1937), by a Russian investigator; Sigerist, H. L., *Socialized Medicine in the Soviet Union* (1937), standard; White, W. C., *These Russians* (1931), interesting character sketches of ordinary folk; Yarmolinsky, A., *The Jews and Other Minor Nationalities under the Soviets* (1929), short, useful.

CHAPTER VI

General Works: Ashmead-Bartlett, E., *The Tragedy of Central Europe* (1923), colorful, mainly on Hungary; Basch, A., *The Danube Basin and the German Economic Sphere* (1943), excellent; Gedye, G. E. R., *Heirs to the Hapsburgs* (1932), by a competent newsman; Graham, M. W., *The New Governments of Central Europe* (1927), standard; Gross, F., *Crossroads of Two Continents* (1935), contains the important plans for union; Hartmann, J., *Versuch einer Politischen Organisation im Donauraum von der Pariser Frieden bis zum Anschluss* (1940); Jordan, P., *Central Union of Europe* (1944); Lehmann, J., *Down River: A Danubian Study* (1939), advocates a confederation on a Communist foundation; Pasvolsky, L., *Economic Nationalism of the Danubian States* (1929), good; Schlesinger, R., *Federalism in Central and Eastern Europe* (1945), thorough discussion from a variety of approaches; Seton-Watson, H., *Eastern Europe between the Wars* (1945), wealth of information; Tiltman, H. H., *Peasant Europe* (1934), informing and well-written.

Austrian Republic: Bauer, O., *The Austrian Revolution* (1925), sound; Borkenau, F., *Austria and After* (1938), interesting analytical studies; Bullock, M., *Austria, 1918–1938* (1939), careful survey; Dutch, O., pseud., *Thus Died Austria* (1938), on the doings of the Nazis; Fodor, M. W., *Plot and Counterplot* (1937), a moving narrative by a journalist; Germains, V. W., *Austria Today* (1932), very good; Gregory, J. D., *Dollfuss and His Times* (1935), useful; Hardy, C. O., and Kuczinski, R. R., *The Housing Program of the City of Vienna* (1934); Macartney, C. A., *The Social Revolution in Austria* (1926), an admirable account; Schuschnigg, K., *My Austria* (1938), autobiographical and defense of his administration; Starhemberg, E. R. von, *Between Hitler and Mussolini* (1942), as seen by a "playboy"; Strong, D. F., *Austria: Transition from Empire to Republic* (1939), detailed and scholarly.

Hungary: Jászi, O., *Revolution and Counter-Revolution in Hungary* (1924), reliable, by a minister of state; Macartney, C. A., *Hungary* (1934), a charming summary; Macartney, C. A., *Hungary and Her Successors* (1937), a mine of valuable information; Mende, T., *Hungary* (1944), brief summary; Perényi, E., *More Was Lost* (1946), glimpses of the aristocracy by the American wife of a lesser noble; Rutter, O., *Regent of Hungary, Horthy* (1939), by a friendly critic.

CZECHOSLOVAKIA: Bloss, E., *Labor Legislation in Czechoslovakia* (1938); Cisar, J., and Pokorny, F., *The Czechoslovak Republic* (1922), useful; Crabitès, P., *Beneš, Statesman of Central Europe* (1934); Grant-Duff, S., *German and Czech* (1937), excellent; Kerner, R. J., ed., *Czechoslovakia: Twenty-years of Independence* (1940), a solid, permanently useful set of essays; Lias, G., *Beneš of Czechoslovakia* (1940), a skilful tribute and character sketch; Martel, R., *La Ruthénie Subcarpathique* (1935), standard; Masaryk, T. G., *The Making of a State* (1927), the faith and work of a great leader; Seton-Watson, R. W., ed., *Slovakia, Then and Now* (1931), short essays by Slovaks; Textor, L. E., *Land Reform in Czechoslovakia* (1923), standard; Thomson, S. H., *Czechoslovakia in European History* (1943), a general work of fine scholarship; Wiskemann, E., *Czechs and Germans* (1938), a splendid, remarkably detached treatment.

POLAND: Buell, R. L., *Poland: Key to Europe* (new ed., 1940), masterly analysis; Bujak, F., *Poland's Economic Development* (1926), a general sketch; Cohen, I., *Vilna* (1944), enlightening on the Jewish community; Dyboski, R., *Poland* (1933), largely on internal rehabilitation; Felinski, M., *The Ukrainians in Poland* (1931), from the Polish angle; Goodhart, A. L., *Poland and the Minority Races* (1922), based on first-hand observations; Górecki, R., *Poland and Her Economic Development* (1935); Kónopko, J., *Dust of Our Brother's Blood* (1941), portraits of Polish types; Landau, R., *Ignace Paderewski* (1934), tends toward the romantic; Lennicki, W., *Life and Culture of Poland* (1944); Machray, R., *The Poland of Pilsudski* (1936), full survey except on minorities; Murray, M., ed., *Poland's Progress, 1919–1939* (1944), a symposium on achievements; Reddaway, W. F., *Marshal Pilsudski* (1939), vivid, sympathetic sketch; Rose, W. J., *Poland* (1939), should be read in conjunction with the Buell volume cited above; Schmitt, B., ed., *Poland* (1945), very useful; Segal, Simon, *New Poland and the Jews* (1938); Slomka, J., *From Serfdom to Self-Government* (1941), an engaging peasant's tale; Wellisz, L., *Foreign Capital in Poland* (1938), thin; Zweig, F., *Poland between Two Wars* (1944), on social and economic affairs.

DANZIG FREE STATE: Leonhardt, H. L., *Nazi Conquest of Danzig* (1942), detailed documentary record; Mason, J. B., *The Danzig Dilemma* (1946), thorough, scholarly.

BALTIC REPUBLICS AND FINLAND: Atchley, T. W., *Finland* (1931); Bilmanis, A., *The Baltic States and the Baltic Sea* (1943), by the Latvian Minister to the United States; Harrison, E. J., ed., *Lithuania* (1928), essays by native experts; Jackson, J. H., *Estonia* (1941), popular but reliable; Jackson, J. H., *Finland* (1940), comprehensive; Pick, F. W., *The Baltic States* (1945), standard; Reddaway, W. F., *Problems of the Baltic* (1940), short, suggestive; Royal Institute of International Affairs, *The Baltic States: A Survey of the Political and Economic Structure and Foreign Relations* (1938), detailed and authoritative; Simutis, A., *The Economic Reconstruction of Lithuania after 1918* (1942), a preliminary survey; Urch, R. O., *Latvia* (1938), by a journalist; Wuorinen, J. H., *Nationalism in Modern Finland* (1931), careful and scholarly.

CHAPTER VII

GENERAL WORKS: Ashton, E. B., *The Fascist: His State and His Mind* (1937); Chakotin, S., *The Rape of the Masses* (1940), brilliant philosophical analysis and criticism; Ebenstein, W., *Fascist Italy* (1939), scholarly, comprehensive; Finer, H., *Mussolini's Italy* (1935), important; Gay, H. N., *Strenuous Italy* (1927), sympathetic; King, B., *Fascism in Italy* (1931), slender; Mathews, H., *The Fruits of Fascism* (1943), report by an American journalist; Nathan, P., *The Psychology of Fascism* (1943), incisive analysis; Pellizzi, C., *Italy* (1939), by Mussolini's apologist in the English-reading world; Villari, L., *Italy* (1929), a reasoned defense of the Fascist system; Volpe, G., *History of the Fascist Movement* (1934), revealing.

GOVERNMENT AND POLITICS: Beals, C., *Rome or Death* (1923), racy account of the "March on Rome"; Bonomi, I., *From Socialism to Fascism* (1924); Megaro, G., *Mussolini in the Making* (1938), model study of il Duce's early career; Mussolini, B., *My Autobiography* (1928), what the writer desired the reader to believe; Reut-Nicolussi, E., *Tyrol under the Axe of Italian Fascism* (1930); Rossi, A., *The Rise of Italian Fascism* (1938), important; Salvemini, G., *The Fascist Dictatorship in Italy* (1927), a sharp arraignment by an exiled scholar; Salvemini, G., *Under the Axe of Fascism* (1936), an account of workers' hardships; Schneider, H. W., *The Fascist Government of Italy* (1936), balanced and detailed; Schneider, H. W., and Clough, S. B., *Making Fascists* (1929), a careful study; Spencer, H. R., *Government and Politics of Italy* (1932), clear, critical; Sturzo, D. L., *Italy and Fascismo* (1927), indictment by leader of Catholic Party.

ECONOMIC AND SOCIAL AFFAIRS: Einzig, P., *The Economic Foundation of Fascism* (1933), by a journalistic economist; Marraro, H. R., *The New Education in Italy* (1936); McGuire, C. E., *Italy's International Economic Position* (1926), very good; Meenan, J., *The Italian Corporative System* (1944), thorough, standard; Rawlins, C. D., and Carpenter, H. C., *Economic Conditions in Italy* (1930); Schmidt, C. T., *The Corporate State in Action* (1939), very enlightening; Welk, W. G., *Fascist Economic Policy* (1938), sound in places.

CHAPTER VIII

GENERAL WORKS: Anastasoff, C., *The Tragic Peninsula . . . the Macedonian Movement since 1878* (1938); Armstrong, H. F., *The New Balkans* (1926), excellent for early twenties; Bonné, A., *The Economic Development of the Middle East* (1945); Boveri, M., *Minaret and Pipeline* (1939), a fascinating volume; Driault, E., *La Question d'Orient, 1918–1937* (1938), by a distinguished expert; Geshkoff, T. I., *Balkan Union: A Road to Peace in Southeastern Europe* (1940), useful; Hocking, W. E., *The Spirit of World Politics* (1932), a philosopher's interpretation of the Near East; Ireland, P. W., ed., *The Near East: Problems and Prospects* (1942); Mitrany, D., *The Effect of the War in Southeastern Europe* (1936), general; Mitrany, D., ed., *Economic Problems of Southeastern Europe* (1945), thoughtful; Newman, B., *Balkan Background* (1945), popular and reliable; Ross, F. A., *The Near East in American Philanthropy* (1929), enlightening; Roucek, J. S., *The Politics of the Balkans* (1939), thorough; Toynbee, A. J., *The Western Question in Greece and Turkey* (1922), stimulating.

ALBANIA: Mousset, A., *L'Albanie devant L'Europe* (1930); Robinson, V., *Albania's Road to Freedom* (1941); Swire, J., *Albania, the Rise of a Kingdom* (1929), raw material of history; Swire, J., *King Zog's Albania* (1937), a continuation of the foregoing.

YUGOSLAVIA: Baerlein, H. P., *The Birth of Yugoslavia* (2 vols., 1922), discursive; Beard, C. A., and Radin, G., *The Balkan Pivot* (1929), interesting survey; Graham, S., *Alexander of Jugoslavia* (1939), popular sketch; Lodge, O., *Peasant Life in Jugoslavia* (1942), colorful; West, R., *Black Lamb and Grey Falcon* (2 vols., 1942); brilliant literature, faulty history; Yanochevitch, M., *La Yougoslavie dans les Balkans* (1936).

RUMANIA: Bolitho, H., *Roumania under King Carol* (1940), an uncritical estimate; Cabot, J. M., *Racial Conflict in Transylvania* (1926), a judicial survey; Clark, C. U., *Greater Roumania* (1922); Clark, C. U., *Racial Aspects of Roumania's Case* (1941); Clark, C. U., *United Roumania* (1932), good; Evans, I. L., *Agrarian Revolution in Roumania* (1924), standard; Kormos, C., *Rumania* (1944), brief; Mitrany, D., *The Land and the Peasant in Rumania* (1930), scholarly; Nistor, I., *Bessarabia and Bukowina* (1939); Roucek, J. S., *Contemporary Roumania and Her Problems* (1932), substantial; Seton-Watson, R. W., *Transylvania: A Key Problem* (1943), by a leading British authority.

BULGARIA: Desbons, G., *La Bulgarie après le Traité de Neuilly* (1930), excellent; Logio, G. C., *Bulgaria, Past and Present* (1936), useful; Pasvolsky, L., *Bulgaria's Economic Position* (1930), very good; Pipinelis, M. P., *Caitiff Bulgaria* (1944), a publicist's survey.

GREECE: Alastos, D., *Venizelos: Patriot, Statesman, Revolutionary* (1942), interesting; Eddy, C. B., *Greece and the Greek Refugees* (1931), an eye-witness account; Forster, E. S., *A Short History of Modern Greece* (1942), informing on the thirties; Gomme, A. W., *Greece* (1945), reliable; Mears, E. G., *Greece Today* (1929); Miller, W., *Greece* (1928), broad, by an expert.

TURKEY: Allen, H. E., *The Turkish Transformation* (1935), short, largely on social reforms; Armstrong, H. C., *Grey Wolf, an Intimate Study of a Dictator* (1932), sympathetic portrait of Mustapha Kemal; Edib, H., *Turkey Faces West* (1930), valuable account by a native feminist; Howard, H. N., *The Partition of Turkey* (1931), standard; Jaeckh, E., *The Rising Crescent* (1944), by a German student; Lengyel, E., *Turkey* (1941), journalistic; Ostroróg, L., *The Angora Reform* (1928); Parker, John, and Smith, C., *Modern Turkey* (1940), useful on the changing scene; Tobin, C. M., *Turkey* (1944); Toynbee, A., and Kirkwood, K. P., *Turkey* (1926), clear and friendly to Kemal; Ward, B., *Turkey* (1942); Wortham, H. E., *Mustapha Kemal of Turkey* (1931), a laudatory portrait.

THE FREE ARAB STATES: Armstrong, H. C., *Lord of Arabia* (1934), interesting; Bey, Y., *Independent Egypt* (1940); Byng, E. J., *The World of the Arabs* (1944), general guide; Gaury, G., *Arabia Phœnix* (1946), illuminating travelogue; Harris, M., *Egypt under the Egyptians* (1925), useful; Newman, E. W. P., *Great Britain in Egypt* (1928), good; Philby, H. St.J., *Arabia* (1930), general; Stark, F., *East Is West* (1945), admirable description of Arab lands in general; Symons, M. T., *Britain and Egypt: The Rise of Egyptian Nationalism* (1925), able; Williams, K., *Ibn Sa'ud* (1933); Young, G., *Egypt* (1927), general, very readable.

THE ARAB MOVEMENT: Antonius, G., *The Arab Awakening* (new ed., 1946), standard; Faris, N. A., ed., *The Arab Heritage* (1944), useful, poorly written; Katibah, H. I., *The New Spirit in Arab Lands* (1940), interesting.

CHAPTER IX

GENERAL WORKS: Bernanos, G., *A Diary of My Times* (1938); Brogan, D. W., *France under the Republic* (1940), standard, emphasis on politics; Brogan, D. W., *French Problems and Personalities* (1946), thoughtful; Claydon, C., *The Struggle for French Democracy* (1945), a Marxist interpretation; Curtius, E. R., *The Civilization of France* (1932); Daniels, H. G., *The Framework of France* (1937), illuminating survey; Hale, R. W., *Democratic France* (1941), thin; Maillaud, P., *France* (1942), short and delightful; Munro, K., *France Yesterday and Today* (1945), lucid, comprehensive; Siegfried, A., *France: A Study in Nationality* (1930), piquant, full of dubious generalization; Thomson, D., *The Democratic Ideal in England and France* (1940), small, penetrating; Vaucher, P., *Post-War France* (1934), clearly written.

GOVERNMENT AND POLITICS: Adam, G., *The Tiger, Georges Clemenceau* (1930), good; Blum, L., *A l'Échelle Humaine* (1945), the Socialist leader's analysis of events; Bois, E. J., *Le Malheur de la France* (1942), very valuable, by a journalist; Bruun, G., *Clemenceau* (1943), the best study; Clemenceau, G., *Grandeur and Misery of Victory* (1930), an apologia; Daladier, E., *In Defense of France* (1939), brief biography and speeches; Dumensil, R., *Raymond Poincaré* (1934); Gaulle, C. de, *France and Her Army* (1945); Geraud, A., *The Gravediggers of France* (1944), violent arraignment of politicians; Hayes, C. J. H., *France: A Nation of Patriots* (1930), illuminating and very readable; Huddleston, S., *France* (1927), a broad treatment; Huddleston, S., *Poincaré: A Biographical Portrait* (1924), thin.

Lazareff, P., *Deadlines: The Last Decade in France* (1942), enlightening on the French press; Levy, L., *The Truth about France* (1941), a democratic Socialist's version; Micaud, C. A., *The French Right and Nazi Germany* (1943), very revealing; Middleton, W. L., *The French Political System* (1932), standard; Pickles, D. M., *The French Political Scene* (1939), brief; Simon, Y., *The Road to Vichy* (1942); Soltau, R. H., *French Parties and Politics* (1930), useful; Stokes, R. L., *Léon Blum* (1937), a preliminary portrait; Thomson, V., *Briand: Man of Peace* (1930), a contemporary sketch; Thorez, M., *Son of the People* (1938), by the Communist leader; Torrès, H., *Pierre Laval* (1941), extremely hostile exposition; Werth, A., *France in Ferment* (1935), on the years of the depression; Werth, A., *Which Way France?* (1937), by a British journalist.

ECONOMIC AFFAIRS: Clough, S. B., *France: A History of National Economics* (1939), valuable; Einzig, P., *France's Crisis* (1935), high-grade journalism; Gide, C., *Effects of the War upon French Economic Life* (1923), standard; Haig, R. M., *The Public Finances of Post-War France* (1929), thorough; Haight, F. A., *A History of French Commercial*

Policies (1941), partly on interwar epoch; MacDonald, W., *Reconstruction in France* (1922), informing; Ogburn, W. F., and Jaffé, W., *The Economic Development of Post-War France* (1929); Peel, G., *The Economic Policy of France* (1937), thoughtful on Blum administration; Rogers, R. H., *The Process of Inflation in France* (1929), excellent.

CHAPTER X

SPAIN, GENERAL WORKS: Blasco Ibáñez, V., *Alfonso XIII Unmasked* (1924), a fiery indictment; Brenan, G., *The Spanish Labyrinth* (1943), a remarkable study; Castillejo, J., *Wars of Ideas in Spain* (1937), valuable; Madariaga, S., *Reality and Myth in Modern Spain* (1943), controversial, thoughtful; Peers, E. A., *Catalonia Infelix* (1937), standard; Peers, E. A., *Spain, the Church and the Orders* (1939), a conservative approach; Smith, R. M., *The Day of the Liberals in Spain* (1938), valuable; Trend, J. B., *The Civilization of Spain* (1944), an admirable little book; Young, G., *The New Spain* (1933), contains much informing data.

SPAIN, CIVIL WAR: Barea, A., *The Clash* (1946), a Socialist's account of the civil war; Borkenau, F., *The Spanish Cockpit* (1937), very good; Buckley, H. W., *Life and Death of the Spanish Republic* (1940), sympathetic to Loyalists; Crabitès, P., *Unhappy Spain* (1937), friendly to Franco; Gannes, H., and Repard, T., *Spain in Revolt* (new ed., 1937), Leftist viewpoint; Godden, G. M., *Conflict in Spain* (1937); Hamilton, T., *Appeasement's Child* (1943), journalistic; Last, J., *The Spanish Tragedy* (1939); Loveday, A. F., *World War in Spain* (1939), an apologia for the Nationalists; Mendizabal, A., *The Martyrdom of Spain* (1938), dispassionate; Ortega y Gasset, J., *Invertebrate Spain* (1937), a philosopher's analysis; Palencia, I., *Smouldering Freedom* (1945), interesting; Peers, E. A., *Spain in Eclipse* (1943), a running account; Sencourt, R., pseud., *Spain's Ordeal* (1940), sees Communism as the enemy; Vayo, del, J. A., *Freedom's Battle* (1940), by the Foreign Minister of the Loyalist regime.

PORTUGAL: Bragança-Cunha, V. de, *Revolutionary Portugal* (1938), thin; Derrick, M., *The Portugal of Salazar* (1939), brief, sympathetic; Egerton, F. C., *Salazar* (1943); Gallop, R., *Portugal* (1936), general.

SWITZERLAND: Brooks, R. C., *Government and Politics of Switzerland* (1920), standard; Rappard, W. E., *The Government of Switzerland* (1936), substantial; Rougemont, D. de and Muret C., *The Heart of Europe* (1941), excellent.

BELGIUM AND HOLLAND: Barnouw, A. J., *The Dutch* (1940), able; Cammaerts, E., *Albert, King of Belgium* (1935), full-length portrait; Eppstein, J., ed., *Belgium* (1945), succinct survey; Goris, J. A., *Belgium* (1945); Landheer, B., ed., *The Netherlands* (1943), has considerable merit; Vlekke, B. H. M., *Evolution of the Dutch Nation* (1945), adequate.

THE SCANDINAVIAN COUNTRIES: Birch, J. H. S., *Denmark in History* (1938), general; Childs, M., *Sweden, the Middle Way* (1936), valuable; Cole, M., and Smith, E. C., eds., *Democratic Sweden* (1939); Gathorne-Hardy, G., *Norway* (1925), very good; Hamilton, C., *Modern Sweden* (1939), rather light; Howe, F. C., *Denmark, the Cooperative Way* (1936), useful; Keilhau, W., *Norway in World History* (1944), a learned treatment; Simon, E. D., *The Smaller Democracies* (1939), excellent.

CHAPTER XI

GENERAL: Brebner, J. B., and Nevins, A., *The Making of Modern Britain* (1943), stimulating summary; Brogan, D. W., *English People* (1943), delightful sketch; Dibelius, W., *England* (1930), contemplative, comprehensive study by a German; Graves, R., and Hodge, A., *The Long Week-End* (1940), chatty social survey; Inge, W. R., *England* (1926), by an ecclesiastical Cassandra; Masterman, C. F. G., *England after the War* (1922), a far-ranging estimate; Somervell, D. C., *Modern Britain, 1870–1939* (1941), good; Wingfield-Stratford, E., *Before the Lamps Went Out* (1945), thoughtful.

BRITISH GOVERNMENT AND POLITICS: Brand, C. F., *British Labor's Rise to Power* (1941), scholarly essays; Cohen, E. W., *The Growth of the British Civil Service* (1941); Fyfe, H., *British Liberal Party* (1928); Germains, V. W., *The Tragedy of Winston Churchill* (1931), an ill-tempered indictment; Gore, J., *King George V* (1941), popular; Guedella, P., *Mr. Churchill* (1942), sprightly portrait; Iconoclast, *James Ramsay MacDonald* (1931); Jennings, W. I., *The British Constitution* (1941), standard; Kiernan, R. H., *Lloyd George* (1940); McHenry, D. E., *His Majesty's Opposition* (1940), detailed treatise on the Labour party in the thirties; Tracy, H., ed., *The Book of the Labour Party* (1925), interpretative essays; Steed, H. W., *The Real Stanley Baldwin* (1930), by an admirer.

ECONOMIC DEVELOPMENT: Abel, D., *A History of British Tariffs, 1923–1942* (1946), excellent; Abrams, M., *The Condition of the British People* (1945), sociological; Batten, E., *National Economics for Britain's Day of Need* (1926), how to solve unemployment; Cadbury Brothers, *Industrial Record, 1919–1939* (1945), enlightening case-history; Cole, G. D. H., *Labour in the Coal Mining Industry* (1923); Dearle, N. B., *The Labor Cost of the World War to Great Britain* (1940), informing; Hamilton, M. A., *Sidney and Beatrice Webb* (1933), full-length study of Fabian leaders; Heaton, H., *The British Way to Recovery* (1934), excellent; Hill, A. C. C., Jr., and Lubin, I., *The British Attack on Unemployment* (1934), very enlightening; Lawrence, F. W. P., *The Gold Crisis* (1931), technical; Peel. G., *The Economic War* (1930), mainly on Britain; Priestley, J. B., *An English Journey* (1934), a novelist's impressions of the depressed districts; Siegfried, A., *England's Crisis* (1931), superficial.

CHAPTER XII

COMMONWEALTH AND EMPIRE: Amery, L. C., *The Empire in the New Era* (1928), addresses by a prominent Conservative; Baker, P. J. N., *The Present Judicial Status of the British Dominions in International Law* (1929), excellent; Barker, E., *The Ideas and Ideals of the British Empire* (1941), excellent; Cook, A. N., *British Enterprise in Nigeria* (1943), original, judicial; Elliott, W. Y., *The New British Empire* (1932), important; Hall, W. P., *Empire to Commonwealth* (1928), still useful; Keith, A. P., *Dominion Autonomy in Practice* (1930), short; Knaplund, P., *The British Empire, 1815–1939* (1941), standard; Mair, L. P., *Welfare in the British Colonies* (1945), short, enlightening; Newton, A. P., *A Hundred Years of the British Empire* (1940), comprehensive, standard; Schuyler, R. L., *Parliament and the British Empire* (1929); Zimmern, A. E., *From the British Empire to the British Commonwealth* (1941), by a learned Britisher.

IRELAND: Beasley, P., *Michael Collins: Soldier and Statesman* (new ed., 1941); Curtis, E., *History of Ireland* (new ed., 1942), scholarly, general; Figgis, D., *Recollections of the Irish War* (1927), good; Gwynn, D. R., *DeValera* (1933), a fair portrait; Gwynn, D. R., *The Irish Free State* (1928); Gwynn, S., *Ireland* (1924), a broad survey; Harrison H., *Ulster and the British Empire* (1939); Mansergh, N., *The Irish Free State, Its Government and Politics* (1934), substantial; McManus, M. J., *Eamon DeValera* (1946), a highly flattering portrait; Phillips, W. A., *The Revolution in Ireland* (1926), detailed, hostile to insurgents.

INDIA: Amery, L. C., *India and Freedom* (1943), able presentation of British imperial viewpoint; Andrews, C. F., *Mahatma Gandhi's Ideas* (1930), in the prophet's own words; Anstey, V., *The Economic Development of India* (1931); Beauchamp, J., *British Imperialism in India* (1934), intemperately critical; Brailsford, H. N., *Subject India* (1943), by a Labour Party publicist; Coupland, R., *Britain and India* (1941), well-written historical survey; Coupland, R., *India: A Restatement* (1946), very valuable; Duffett, W. E., et al., *India Today: The Background of Indian Nationalism* (1942); Dutcher, G. M., *The Political Awakening of the East* (1925), on Asiatic developments generally; Mayo, K., *Mother India* (1927), vivacious, distorted; Mitchell, K. L., *India without Fable* (1942), a journalistic antidote to the Mayo book; Nehru, J., *Toward Freedom* (1941), self-portrait by a leading Hindu Nationalist; O'Malley, L. S. S., *Modern India and the West* (1941); Read, M., *The Indian Peasant Uprooted* (1931), scholarly; Thompson, E., *Reconstructing India* (1930), balanced; Thompson, E., and Garratt, G. T., *Rise and Fulfillment of British Rule in India* (1934), good.

CHAPTER XIII

GENERAL WORKS: Anrich, E., *Deutsche Geschichte, 1918–1939* (1940), a Nazi version; Bane, S. L., and Lutz, R. H., *The Blockade of Germany after the Armistice* (1942), documents; Benoist-Méchin, J., *History of the Germany Army since the Armistice* (1939); Diesel, E., *Germany and the Germans* (1931), good; Gooch, G. P., *Germany* (1925), permanently useful; Haffner, S., *Germany: Jekyll and Hyde* (1940), important; Knight-Patterson, W. M., *Germany from Defeat to Conquest* (1946), thin; Lowenthal, M., *The Jews of Germany* (1936), good; Lutz, R. H., *The Fall of the German Empire* (1932), valuable documentary history; Marcus, J. R., *The Rise and Destiny of the German Jew* (1934), refutes Nazi calumnies; Marquand, H. A., ed., *Organized Labour in Four Continents* (1939); Mühlen, N., *Schacht: The Magician* (1938), useful for interwar economic policies; Rosinski, H., *The German Army* (1940), excellent; Shotwell, J. T., *What Germany Forgot* (1940), shows how World War I had ruinous consequences for Germany; Wheeler-Bennett, J. M., *Wooden Titan* (1936), a splendid portrait of Hindenburg.

WEIMAR GOVERNMENT AND POLITICS: Brecht, A., *Prelude to Silence. The End of the German Republic* (1945), careful exposition of parties; Brunet, R., *The New German Constitution* (1922), standard analysis of the Weimar document; Bryant, A., *Unfinished Victory* (1940), brilliant interpretation of the twenties; Clark, R. T., *The Fall of the German Republic* (1935), very good; D'Abernon, H., *Red Cross and Berlin Embassy, 1915–1926* (1946), excerpts from diaries; D'Abernon, Lord, *Diary of an Ambassador* (3 vols., 1929–1930), by the British representative in Berlin; Daniels, H. G., *The Rise of the German Republic* (1928), useful; Francke, K., *German After-War Problems* (1927), interesting; Froelich, P., *Rosa Luxembourg* (1940), a study of the Communist leader; Gedye, G. E. R., *The Revolver Republic* (1930), a journalist's treatment of French maneuvers in the Rhineland; Grzesinki, A. C., *Inside Germany* (1939), valuable on the Weimar epoch; Halperin, S. W., *Germany Tried Democracy* (1946), detailed political history; Hoetzsch, O., *Germany's Domestic and Foreign Policies* (1929), polemical; Kessler, H., *Walter Rathenau* (1930); Lethbridge, A., *Germany as It Is Today* (1921), sympathetic to Weimar Germany; Lutz, R. H., *The German Revolution* (1922), thorough and contains much original data; Scheele, G., *The Weimar Republic* (1946); Scheidemann, P., *The Making of New Germany* (2 vols., 1929), by a Socialist leader; Sender, T., *The Autobiography of a German Rebel* (1940), by an eloquent Socialist; Spiecker, K., *Germany from Defeat to Defeat* (1935), a Centrist account of the Weimar regime; Young G., *The New Germany* (1920).

WEIMAR ECONOMIC HISTORY: Angell, J. W., *The Recovery of Germany* (new ed., 1932), excellent on late twenties; Brady, R. A., *The Rationalization Movement in German Industry* (1933), learned; Bresciani-Turroni, C., *The Economics of Inflation: A Study of Currency Depreciation in Post-War Germany* (1937), exhaustive; Dawson, P., *Germany's Industrial Revival* (1926), thorough; Holt, J. B., *German Agricultural Policy, 1918–1934* (1936), original; McPherson, W. H., *Works Councils under the German Republic* (1939), valuable; Reich, N., *Labour Relations in Republican Germany* (1938).

NAZI GOVERNMENT AND POLITICS: Abel, T., *Why Hitler Came into Power* (1938), a study in biographies; Armstrong, H. F., *Hitler's Reich: The First Phase* (1933), penetrating analysis; Bartlett, V., *Nazi Germany Explained* (1933), by a thoughtful British journalist; Baynes, N. H., *The Speeches of Adolf Hitler* (2 vols., 1942), topically arranged; Blood-Ryan, H. W., *Goering, the Iron Man of Germany* (1938); Brady, R. A., *The Spirit and Structure of German Fascism* (1927), a shrill Leftist critique; Coole, W. W., pseud., and Potter, M. F., *Thus Speaks Germany* (1941), an informing compilation; Dutch, O., *The Errant Diplomat: A Biography of Franz von Papen* (1940), hostile; Ebenstein, W., *The German Record* (1945), valuable; Gangulee, N., *The Mind and Face of Nazi Germany* (1943), passages from the writings and speeches of Nazi chieftains; Goebbels, J., *My Part in Germany's Fight* (1940), the diary of a militant Nazi; Greenwood, H. P., *The German Revolution* (1934), a pro-Nazi interpretation; Heiden, K., *History of National Socialism* (1935), very good; Heiden, K., *Der Fuehrer: Hitler's Rise to Power* (1944), best portrait of the man.

Hitler, A., *Mein Kampf* (1939), unexpurgated edition; Kandel, I. L., *Making of Nazis*

(1935); Lichtenberger, H., *The Third Reich* (1937), a remarkable study by a French scholar; Marx, F. M., *Government in the Third Reich* (1936), provocative; Murphy, R. E., et al., *National Socialism* (1943), an official American exposé; Olden, R., *Hitler* (1936), interesting; Pollock, J. K., *The Government of Greater Germany* (1938), standard; Prange, G. W., ed., *Hitler's Words* (1944), important compilation; Rauschning, H., *The Voice of Destruction* (1940), revealing chats with Hitler; Reed, D., *Nemesis? The Story of Otto Strasser* (1940), on internal friction in the Nazi Party; Roberts, S. H., *The House that Hitler Built* (1937), good on domestic affairs; Santoro, C., *Hitler Germany as Seen by a Foreigner* (1938), sympathetic with Nazism; Schumann, F. L., *The Nazi Dictatorship* (1935), fully documented; Stutterheim, K., *The Two Germanys* (1939), a spirited defense of Hitlerism; Thyssen, F., *I Paid Hitler* (1941), on the linkage of "Big Business" with National Socialism.

Nazi Economic and Social Policies: Bischoff, R. F., *Nazi Conquest through German Culture* (1942); Einzig, P., *Germany's Default* (1934), on the èconomics of Hitlerism; Guillebaud, C. W., *The Economic Recovery of Germany, 1933–1938* (1939), excellent; Guillebaud, C. W., *The Social Policy of Nazi Germany* (1941), enlightening; Hartshorne, E. Y., Jr., *The German Universities and National Socialism* (1937), careful scholarship; Herman, S. W., Jr., *It's Your Souls We Want* (1943), on religious matters; Kneller, G. F., *The Educational Philosophy of National Socialism* (1941), indispensable; Mac-Kenzie, V., *Here Lies Goebbels* (1940), on the Nazi propaganda machine; Mason, J. B., *Hitler's First Foes* (1936), on the religious resistance to Nazism; Micklem, N., *National Socialism and the Roman Catholic Church* (1939), very good; Nathan, O., *The Nazi Economic System* (1943); Niemoeller, M., *The Gestapo Defied* (1941), a selection of sermons; Pick, F. W., *The Art of Dr. Goebbels* (1942), useful on Nazi journalism; Poole, K. E., *German Financial Policies, 1932–1939* (1939), informing; Ullstein, H., *The Rise and Fall of the House of Ullstein* (1943), much on Hitlerism and press control; Wolf, A., *Higher Education in Nazi Germany* (1944), a careful study.

CHAPTER XIV

Education: Alexander, T., and Parker, B., *The New Education in the German Republic* (1929), important; Dottrens, P., *The New Education in Austria* (1930), interesting, badly organized; Flexner, A., *Universities, American, English, German* (new ed., 1930), important, though little on interwar epoch; Kotschnig, W. M., *Slaves Need No Leaders: An Answer to the Fascist Challenge to Education* (1943), a searching examination, eloquent; Moller, J. C., and Watson, K., *Education in Democracy, Folk High Schools* (1944), excellent; Pinkevitch, A. P., *The New Education in the Soviet Republic* (1929), valuable description by a prominent Russian schoolman; Robertson, C. G., *The British Universities* (1930); Roman, F. W., *The New Education in Europe* (new ed., 1930), a useful survey on comparative education.

Feminism: Prickett, H. M., *Germany's Women Go Forward* (1930), enlightening on the twenties; Rachel, C., *The Cause* (1928), short description of the women's movement in Britain; Schirmacher, K., *Modern Women's Rights Movements* (1912), somewhat antiquated but presents material on the growth of feminism; Smith, J., *Women in Soviet Russia* (1928); Woodsmall, R. F., *Moslem Women Enter a New World* (1937), optimistic.

Science: General: Bernal, J. D., *The Social Function of Science* (1939), an important, though somewhat confusing work by a British physicist; Dampier, W. C. D., *The History of Science and Its Relations with Philosophy and Religion* (new ed., 1943), a distinguished survey dealing in the last section with the interwar years; Marvin, F. S., ed., *Science and Civilization* (1923), thoughtful; Randall, J. H., Jr., *The Making of the Modern Mind* (new ed., 1940), Chaps. XVIII–XXI; Stokley, J., *Science Remakes Our World* (1942), lucid, broad summary; Taylor, F. S., *The World of Science* (1937); Taylor, F. S., *The March of Mind* (1939), short survey of science; Westaway, F. N., *The Endless Quest* (new ed., 1936), a magnificent summary, Chaps. XXXVI–LV; Whitehead, A. N., *Science and the Modern World* (1926), brilliant, by a philosopher.

Science: Special Aspects: Clarke, B. L., *The Marvels of Modern Chemistry* (1932), clear outline; Congress of American-Soviet Friendship, *Science in Soviet Russia* (1944), essays by American specialists; Crowther, J. G., *Soviet Science* (1936), enlightening; Gregory, R., *Science in Chains* (1941), on the Nazi debasement of science; Jeans, J., *The Mysterious Universe* (1930), excellent; Keith, A., *New Discoveries Relating to the Antiquity of Man* (1931); Lichtenstein, P. M., and Small, S. M., *Handbook of Psychiatry* (1944), general survey; Needham, J., ed., *Science in Soviet Russia* (1942), brief.

CHAPTER XV

RELIGION: GENERAL: Keller, A., *Church and State on the European Continent* (1936), by a leading authority; Keller, A., *Christian Europe Today* (1942), comprehensive, much doubtful interpretation; Latourette, K. S., *Advance Through Storm* (1945), part of a monumental study of the Christian movement.

ROMAN CATHOLICISM: Agar, W. M., *Catholicism and the Progress of Science* (1940), valuable; Bernhart, J., *The Vatican as a World Power* (1939), brilliant essay; Binchy, D. A., *Church and State in Fascist Italy* (1942), massive, well-documented study by an Irish scholar; Dinneen, J., *Pius XII, Pope of Peace* (1939); Eckhardt, C. C., *The Papacy in World Affairs* (1937), section on the very modern papacy; Fontenelle, R., *His Holiness, Pope Pius XI* (1938), a contemporary portrait; Guilday, P., ed., *The Catholic Church in Contemporary Europe* (1933), useful essays; Gwynn, D. R., *The Catholic Reaction in France* (1924); Hughes, P., ed., *The Pope's New Order* (1944), convenient summary of papal encyclicals; Maritain, R., *Adventures in Grace* (1945), semi-autobiographical, enlightening on the Catholic intellectual revival in France; Marshall, C. C., *The Roman Catholic Church in the Modern World* (1931), as understood by a critically minded American lawyer; Petre, M. D., *Alfred Loisy* (1944), a brief study by an admiring friend of the leader in the Catholic "modernist" cause; Rope, H. E. G., *Benedict XV: The Pope of Peace* (1941); Teeling, W., *Pope Pius XI and World Affairs* (1937); Windle, B. C. A., *The Catholic Church and Its Reactions to Science* (1929).

PROTESTANTISM: Curtis, W. R., *The Lambeth Conferences: the Solution for Pan-Anglican Organization* (1942); Horton, W. M., *Contemporary Continental Theology* (1938), a clear survey; Keller, A., and Stewart, G., *Protestant Europe* (1927), very good; Oldham, J. H., *The Oxford Conference* (1937), official report; Pauck, W., *Karl Barth, Prophet of a New Christianity?* (1931).

ORTHODOX EASTERN CHURCH: Bulgakov, S. N., *The Orthodox Church* (1935); Latourette, K. S., et al., *Church and Community* (1938); Zankov, S., *The Eastern Orthodox Church* (1929), slight; Zernov, N., *Church of the Eastern Christians* (1944).

JUDAISM: Agus, J. B., *Modern Philosophies of Judaism* (1942), good survey of the intellectual ferment within Jewry; Isserman, F. M., *This Is Judaism* (1945), an interpretation by an American rabbi of the reformist school; Jung, L., ed., *Judaism in the Changing World* (1939), useful.

ISLAM: Arberry, A. J., and Landau, R., eds., *Islam Today* (1943), comprehensive symposium; Gibb, H. A. R., ed., *Whither Islam? A Survey of Modern Movements in the Moslem World* (1932); O'Leary, L. E., *Islam at the Crossroads* (1923), superficial.

CHAPTER XVI

LITERATURE, GENERAL: Buck, P. M., *Directions in Contemporary Literature* (1942), an appraisal of the ideas of thirteen writers, Europeans mainly; Hansen, A. C.., *Twentieth Century Forces in European Fiction* (1934); Hoffman, F. J., *Freudianism and the Literary Mind* (1945), scholarly contribution; Loehrke, E. W., *Armaggedon: The World War in Literature* (1930); Mann, K., and Kesten, H., eds., *Heart of Europe* (1943), an anthology of representative selections from writings of men of letters, except those "in whose ideology fascist elements predominate."

NATIONAL LITERATURES: Routh, H. V., *English Literature and Ideas in the Twentieth Century* (1946), brilliant contribution to the subject; Brodin, P., *Les Écrivains Français de l'Entre-Deux Guerres* (1942), short, sprightly analyses of outstanding authors; Michaud, R., *Modern Thought and Literature in France* (1934); Stansbury, M. H., *French Novelists of Today* (1935); Northrup, G. T., *Introduction to Spanish Literature* (new ed., 1936), general; Vittorini, D., *The Modern Italian Novel* (1930); Bertaux, F., *A Panorama of German Literature* (1935); Hoyland, J. D., *History as Direction* (1930), an interpretation of Spenglerism; Pfeiler, W. K., *War and the German Mind* (1941), how novelists conceived of World War I; Stirk, S. D., *The Prussian Spirit: A Survey of German Literature and Politics, 1914–1940* (1942), illuminating; Fen, E., *Soviet Stories of the Last Decade* (1945), throws light on Russian domestic manners; Reavey, G., and Slonim, M., *Soviet Literature* (1933); Struve, G., *Twenty-five Years of Soviet Russian Literature* (1944), a guide and critical appraisal; Harris, E. H., *Literature in Estonia* (1945); Nosek, V., *The Spirit of Bohemia* (1926), has sections on Czechoslovak culture.

ARCHITECTURE: Gropius, W. A. G., *The New Architecture and the Bauhaus* (1937); Pevsner, N., *Pioneers of the Modern Movement . . . to Walter Gropius* (1937), on the innovators in architecture; Richards, J. M., *An Introduction to Modern Architecture* (1940).

PAINTING AND SCULPTURE: Epstein, J., *Let There Be Sculpture* (1940), autobiographical; Frost, R., *Contemporary Art* (1942), a survey with a wealth of reproductions; London, K., *The Seven Soviet Arts* (1938); Orpen, W., *The Outline of Art* (2 vols., 1923–1927); Robb, D. M., and Garrison, J. J., *Art in the Western World* (1935), general; Wilenski, R. H., *Modern French Painters* (1940).

MUSIC: Copland, A., *Our New Music* (1941), on the leading composers; Ewen, D., *Twentieth Century Composers* (1938), brief popular portraits; Goffin, R., *Jazz: From the Congo to the Metropolitan* (1944); Gray, C., *A Survey of Contemporary Music* (1927); MacLeod, J., *The New Soviet Theatre* (1943); Nestyev, I., *Sergei Prokofiev* (1946); Stravinsky, I., *An Autobiography* (1936).

MOVIES, RADIO, TELEVISION: Bardèche, M., *The History of Motion Pictures* (1938); Bryher, W., *Film Problems of Soviet Russia* (1929); Carter, H., *The New Spirit in the Cinema* (1930), a British view; Dunlap, O. E., *Radio's 100 Men of Science* (1944), history in terse biographical sketches; Hubbell, R., *Four Thousand Years of Television* (1946), popular; Rotha, P., *Celluloid, the Film Today* (1931); Rotha, P., *The Film till Now* (1930), sketchy.

CHAPTER XVII

GENERAL INTERNATIONAL HISTORY: Boveri, M., *Mediterranean Cross-Currents* (1938), very interesting; Butler, H., *The Lost Peace* (1941), an interpretation by the director of the International Labor Office; Carr, E. H., *The Twenty Years' Crisis* (1939), invaluable treatise; Chamberlin, W. H., *The World's Iron Age* (1941), suggestive interpretation of the period; Coates, W. P. and Z. K., *A History of Anglo-Soviet Relations* (1944), a Leftist treatment; Currey, M., *Italian Foreign Policy* (1932), from the war to 1932, pro-Fascist; Day, J. P., *World Economic History since the Great War* (1939), short survey by a Canadian scholar; Fischer, L., *The Soviets in World Affairs* (2 vols., 1930), sympathetic to Kremlin, most detailed survey for the twenties available; Ford, G. S., ed., *Dictatorship in the Modern World* (1939), a calm, penetrating set of essays; Gathorne-Hardy, G. M., *Short History of International Affairs* (new ed., 1938), excellent summary by a Britisher; Haines, C. G., and Hoffman, R. J. S., *The Origins and Background of the Second World War* (1943), good general account; Jordan, W. M., *Great Britain, France and the German Problem* (1943), indispensable; Laserson, M. M., *The Development of Soviet Foreign Policy in Europe* (1942), a general survey; Lee, D. E., *Ten Years* (1942), a careful record of the 1930's; Macartney, M. H. H., and Cremona, P., *Italy's Foreign and Colonial Policy* (1938), useful on Fascist regime.

Maddox, W. P., *Foreign Relations in British Labour Policies* (1934); Medlicott, W. N., *British Foreign Policy since Versailles* (1940), clear, compact narrative; Newman, E. W. P., *Britain and the Baltic* (1930), excellent; Petrie, C., *Twenty Years Armistice and After* (1940), a British summary; Pink, G. P., *The Conference of Ambassadors, Paris, 1920–1931*

(1942), standard; Rappard, W. E., *The Quest for Peace* (1940), an able survey by a Swiss savant; Robbins, L. C., *The Economic Causes of the War* (1939), thoughtful; Schmitt, B. E., *From Versailles to Munich* (1938), a brilliant essay; Shotwell, J. T., and Laserson, M. M., *Poland and Russia, 1919–1945* (1945), brief survey; Simpson, J. H., *The Refugee Problem* (1939), wide-ranging report; Soward, F. H., *Twenty-five Troubled Years* (1944), good wartime account of the interwar period; Taracouzio, T. A., *War and Peace in Soviet Diplomacy* (1940), of mixed value; Toynbee, A. J., ed., *Survey of International Affairs,* issued annually from 1924 on, sometimes in more than one volume, thorough and indispensable; Vondracek, F. J., *The Foreign Policy of Czechoslovakia, 1918–1935* (1937), a solid piece of work; Wolfers, A., *Britain and France between Two Wars* (1940), a work of great learning.

POST-WAR FERMENT: Crane, John O., *The Little Entente* (1931), valuable; Cumming, H. H., *Franco-British Rivalry in the Post-War Near East* (1938), short, good; D'Abernon, Lord, *The Eighteenth Decisive Battle of the World: Warsaw, 1920* (1921), by a British observer; Dawson, W. H., *Germany under the Treaty* (1933), important; Kaeckenbeeck, G. S., *The International Experiment of Upper Silesia* (1942), excellent; Keynes, J. M., *The Economic Consequences of the Peace* (London, 1920), a very influential tract for the times; Ladas, S. P., *The Exchange of Minorities* (1932), standard account of Greek, Turkish, and Bulgarian transfers; Machray, R., *The Little Entente* (1939), good; Machray, R., *The Problem of Upper Silesia* (1945), useful, hostile to Germany; Nicolson, H., *Curzon* (1934), clear exposition of British post-war policies; Nitti, F., *The Decadence of Europe* (1923), an angry appraisal of the times; Pallis, S. A., *Greece's Anatolian Venture and After* (1937), valuable study of the Greek defeat; Rose, W. J., *The Drama of Upper Silesia* (1935), detailed, by a friend of Poland; Selsam, J. P., *The Attempts to Form an Anglo-French Alliance* (1936), thorough; Smorgorzewski, C., *About the Curzon Line and Other Lines* (1944), a Polish view; Stamp, J., *The Financial Aftermath of the War* (1932), excellent; Woodhouse, E. J., and Woodhouse, C. G., *Italy and the Jugoslavs* (1920); Zimmern, A. E., *Europe in Convalescence* (1922).

WASHINGTON CONFERENCE: Buell, R. L., *The Washington Conference* (1922), detailed, contemporary analysis; Ichihashi, Y., *The Washington Conference and After* (1928), a useful survey by a Japanese.

REPARATIONS, WAR DEBTS AND RHINELAND: Allen, H. T., *The Rhineland Occupation* (1927), the role of the United States; Antonucci, A., *Le Bilan des Réparations* (1935), very good; Bergmann, K., *History of Reparations* (1927), authoritative, by a German expert; Dexter, P., and Sedgwick, J. H., *The War Debts* (1928); Fraenkel, E., *Military Occupation and the Rule of Law* (1944), legalistic study of the Allies in Rhineland; Frasure, C. M., *British Policy on War Debts* (1941), scholarly treatment; Lichtenberger, H., *The Ruhr Conflict* (1923), by a French scholar; Stegemann, H., *The Struggle for the Rhine* (1927), as seen by a German; Williams, B. H., *Economic Foreign Policy of the United States* (1929), section on war debts.

DAWES PLAN, LOCARNO AND AFTER: Auld, G. P., *The Dawes Plan and the New Economics* (1927), useful; Berber, F. J., ed., *Locarno* (1936), a Nazi selection of documents; Chamberlain, A., *Peace in Our Time* (1928), speeches by the British Foreign Secretary; Fabre-Luce, A., *Locarno* (1928), somewhat critical of the agreements; Moulton, H. G., *The Reparation Plan* (1924), learned study of the Dawes Plan; Petrie, C., *The Life and Letters of Austen Chamberlain* (2 vols., 1939–1940), useful on Locarno; Stern-Rubarth, E., *Three Men Tried* (1939), accent on Stresemann and Locarno; Sutton, E., ed., *Stresemann: Diaries, Papers and Letters* (3 vols., 1935–1940), indispensable, the editor believed Stresemann to be a man of good will, but later wholly changed his mind; Vallentin, A., *Frustration: Stresemann's Race with Death* (1931), flattering study by his private secretary.

THE LEAGUE AT WORK: Bentwich, N., *The Mandates System* (1930), excellent; Davis, H. E., ed., *Pioneers in World Order* (1945), essays on achievements and failures of the League; Dell, R., *The Geneva Racket* (1941), vigorous criticism of the League and the statesmen; Fachiri, A. P., *The Permanent Court of International Justice* (new ed., 1932), a lawyer's account; Hambro, C. J., ed., *World Organization* (1943), an analysis of League work by twenty experts; Hudson, M., *The World Court* (1938), standard; Knudson, J. I.,

A History of the League of Nations (1938), sympathetic, factual; Rappard, W., *The Geneva Experiment* (1932), short, serviceable; Russell, F. M., *The International Government of the Saar* (1927), standard; Shotwell, J. T., *The Origins of the International Labor Organization* (2 vols., 1934), standard; Webster, C. K., *The League of Nations in Theory and Practice* (1933), the doings of the League in its first decade; Zimmern, A. E., *The League of Nations and the Rule of Law* (1936), very useful.

PALESTINE AND THE ARAB MANDATES: See items under Arabs, Chapter VIII; Abcarius, M. F., *Palestine* (1946), a vigorous statement of the Arab case; Bentwich, N., *Judea Lives Again* (1944), good study; Byng, E. J., *The World of the Arabs* (1944), general guide by a friend of the Arabs; Cohen, I., *The Zionist Movement* (1945), excellent brief summary; Foster, H. H., *The Making of Modern Iraq* (1935), a clear account; Friederick, C. J., *American Policy toward Palestine* (1944), standard; Goodman, P., ed., *The Jewish National Home* (1943), a full treatment by a score of pens; Hanna, P. L., *British Policy in Palestine* (1942); Hourani, A. H., *Syria and Lebanon* (1946), accurate, balanced; Infield, H., *Cooperative Living in Palestine* (1946), by a participant; Ireland, P. W., *Iraq* (1938); Jeffries, J. M. M., *Palestine: The Reality* (1939), friendly to the Arabs, critical of British policy; Lowdermilk, W. C., *Palestine, Land of Promise* (1944), revealing on economic potentialities; McCallum, E. P., *The Nationalist Crusade in Syria* (1928), able treatment; Ruppin, A., *The Jewish Fate and Future* (1940), indispensable on all phases of Jewry; Sidebotham, H., *Great Britain and Palestine* (1937); Van Ess, J., *Meet the Arab* (1943).

SEARCHING FOR PEACE: Baker, P. J. N., *Disarmament* (1926), a thoroughgoing examination of the problem; Herriot, E., *The United States of Europe* (1930), a plea by a French statesman; Madariaga, S., *Disarmament* (1929), very useful; Miller, D. H., *The Peace Pact of Paris* (1928), authoritative; Morgan, J. H., *Assize of Arms* (1945), how Germany evaded the military restrictions of Versailles; Shotwell, J. T., *War as an Instrument of National Policy and Its Renunciation in the Pact of Paris* (1939), sound, thoughtful; Stuart, G. H., *The International City of Tangier* (1931).

CHAPTER XVIII

THE GREAT DEPRESSION AND AFTER: Allen, F. L., *Only Yesterday* (1931), an engaging summary of the twenties in the United States; Allen, F. L., *Since Yesterday* (1940), a sequel to the foregoing; Beard, C. A., and Beard, M. R., *America in Mid-Passage* (1939), model contemporary history; Berle, A. A., Jr., and Means, G. C., *The Modern Corporation and Private Property* (1933); Brookings Institution, *The Recovery Problem in the United States* (1936), scholarly; Douglas, P. H., *Social Security in the United States* (new ed., 1939), valuable; Einzig, P., *The World Economic Crisis* (1932), written with a facile pen; Gordon, M. S., *Barriers to World Trade* (1941), valuable analysis of commercial policies; Hacker, L. M., *American Problems of Today* (1938); Hodson, H. V., *Slump and Recovery* (1938), a distinguished summary; Lindley, L. K., *Half-Way with Roosevelt* (1936); Malin, J. C., *The United States after the World War* (1930), general; Moulton, H. G., and Pasvolsky, L., *War Debts and World Prosperity* (1932), highly useful; Patterson, E. M., *The World's Economic Dilemma* (1930), by a distinguished American economist; Robbins, L. C., *The Great Depression* (1936), valuable account; Salter, J. A., *Political Aspects of the World Depression* (1932), able analysis; Salter, J. A., *Recovery, the Second Effort* (1932), excellent; Seldes, G. V., *The Years of the Locust* (1933), the United States in the grip of the depression; Stolberg, B., and Vinton, W. J., *The Economic Consequences of the New Deal* (1935), thoughtful; Varga, E., *The Great Crisis and Its Political Consequences* (1935), valuable summary.

REPARATIONS AGAIN: McFadyean, A., *Reparation Reviewed* (1930), authoritative; Schacht, H. G., *The End of Reparations* (1931), German expert criticism of the Young Plan; Wheeler-Bennett, J. W., *The Wreck of Reparations* (1933), a careful study.

DISARMAMENT AND REARMAMENT: Baldwin, H. W., *The Caissons Roll* (1938), on the rearmament of the nations; Chaput, R. A., *Disarmament in British Foreign Policy* (1935), good; Engely, G., *The Politics of Naval Disarmament* (1932); Liddell-Hart, B. H., *Europe in Arms* (1937), descriptive; Maginot, M. J., *He Might Have Saved France* (1941), eulogistic biography of the builder of the Maginot Line; Myers, D. P., *World Disarmament* (1932), good; Sloutzki, N. M., *The World Armaments Race* (1941), careful study of the interwar epoch; Talbot-Booth, E. C., ed., *All the World's Fighting Fleets* (1937), contemporary estimates; Temperley, A. C., *The Whispering Gallery of Europe* (1938), by the leading British military expert at the Geneva Arms Conference; Wheeler-Bennett, J. W., *The Pipe Dream of Peace* (1935), excellently informed history of "disarmament" efforts; Williams, B. H., *The United States and Disarmament* (1931), useful.

FAR EAST, GENERAL: Allen, G., *Japan, the Hungry Guest* (1938), on social and economic developments and problems; Buss, C. A., *War and Diplomacy in Eastern Asia* (1941), solid and balanced; Condliffe, J. B., *China Today* (1932), deals with basic economic problems; Friedman, I. S., *British Relations with China* (1940), accurate summary of the 1930's; Griswold, A. W., *The Far Eastern Policy of the United States* (1938), factual, interpretative, an engrossing chronicle since 1898; Hindmarsh, A. E., *The Basis of Japanese Foreign Policy* (1936), valuable; Hisida, S. G., *Japan Among the Great Powers* (1940), a sort of official version of Nipponese diplomacy; Hudson, G. F., *The Far East in World Politics* (1937), admirable summary; Kent, P. H. B., *The Twentieth Century in the Far East* (1937), the author lived in China for two generations; Lyall, L. A., *China* (1934), broad survey; Moore, H. L., *Soviet Far Eastern Policy* (1945), splendid summary from 1931 to 1945; Nitobe, I., *Japan* (1936), companion volume to Lyall; Tawney, R. H., *Land and Labour in China* (1932), top-notch scholarship.

MANCHURIA: Lattimore, O., *Manchuria, Cradle of Conflict* (new ed., 1935), authoritative· Stimson, H. L., *The Far Eastern Crisis* (1936), by the American Secretary of State at the time; Wang, Ching Ch'un, *Japan's Continental Adventure* (1941), bitter arraignment of Japan, a collection of essays; Willoughy, W. W., *The Sino-Japanese Controversy and the League of Nations* (1935), contains pertinent documents; Young, C. W., *The International Relations of Manchuria* (1929), good for background.

NATIONAL SOCIALISM AND THE WORLD: Amery, L. S., *The German Colonial Claim* (1939), cleverly reasoned by British imperialist; Florinsky, M. T., *The Saar Struggle* (1934), excellent; Goblet, Y. M., *The Twilight of Treaties* (1936), the "liquidation" of Versailles, by a French journalist; Johannsen, G. K., and Kraft, H. H., *Germany's Colonial Problems* (1937), what Germany wanted; Reynolds, B. T., *The Saar and the Franco-German Problem* (1934), interesting; Schacher, G., *Germany Pushes Southeast* (1938), revealing; Schwarz, P., *This Man Ribbentrop* (1943), unsympathetic sketch of Hitler's lieutenant in foreign affairs; Stephens, W. E., *Revisions of the Treaty of Versailles* (1939), good; Wambaugh, S., *The Saar Plebiscite* (1940), thorough, definitive.

BALKAN UNION: Geshkoff, T. L., *Balkan Union* (1940), able, interpretative; Kerner, R. J., and Howard, H. N., *The Balkan Conferences and the Balkan Entente* (1936), full and clear.

THE SOVIETS' NEW COURSE: Davis, K. W., *The Soviets at Geneva* (1934); Dulles, F. R., *The Road to Teheran* (1944), has section on Soviet-American relations; Litvinov, M. M., *Against Aggression* (1939), speeches by the Russian Foreign Commissar; Pope, A. U., *Maxim Litvinoff* (1943), a sympathetic portrait.

CHAPTER XIX

ETHIOPIA: Badoglio, P., *The War in Abyssinia* (1937), by the second Italian commander; Baskerville, E., *What Next, O Duce?* (1937), lucid critique of Fascist operations; Bono, E. de, *Anno XII* (1937), by Italian commander at the beginning of the conquest; Garratt, G. T., *Mussolini's Roman Empire* (1938); Highley, A. E., *The First Sanctions Experiment* (1938); Martelli, G., *Italy against the World* (1938), lively; Sandford, C., *Ethiopia under Haile Selassie* (1946), valuable, based upon long residence in the country; Work, E., *Ethiopia, a Pawn in European Diplomacy* (1936).

SPAIN AND THE STRAITS: See items under Spain in Chapter X; Padelford, N. J., *Inter-*

national Law and Diplomacy in the Spanish Civil War (1939), standard; Salter, C., *Tryout in Spain* (1943), racy; Shotwell, J. T., and Deák, F., *Turkey at the Straits* (1940), broad, concise survey.

THE UNITED STATES AND WORLD AFFAIRS: Alsop, J., and Kintner, R., *American White Paper* (7th ed., 1940), running commentary; Bailey, T. A., *Diplomatic History of the American People* (new ed., 1943), general; Beard, C. A., *Giddy Minds and Foreign Quarrels* (1939), brief plea for aloofness; Eliot, G. F., *The Ramparts We Watch* (1938), an examination of defense requirements of the United States; Hinton, H. B., *Cordell Hull* (1942), sketch of the American Secretary of State; Nevins, A., and Hacker, L. M., eds., *The United States and Its Place in World Affairs* (1943), valuable, covers 1918 to 1943; Perkins, D., *America and Two Wars* (1944), scholarly survey; Tasca, J. H., *The Reciprocal Trade Policy of the United States* (1938), thorough.

BRITISH AND FRENCH POLICIES: Angell, N., *The Defence of the Empire* (1937), shrill arraignment of British "appeasement"; Churchill, W., *While England Slept* (1938), stirring appeals for rearmament; Daladier, E., *In Defence of France* (1939), addresses; Einzig, P., *Appeasement: Before, During, and After the War* (1942), sharply critical of British economic foreign policy; Henderson, N., *Failure of a Mission* (1940), by the last British Ambassador to Berlin, on the years 1937–1939; Hogg, Q., *The Left Was Never Right* (1945), a Tory treatment of British policy; Johnson, A. C., *Anthony Eden* (1939), useful sketch; Johnson, A. C., *Viscount Halifax* (1941), interesting; Kennedy, A. L., *Britain Faces Germany* (1937), argues for reconciliation with Germany; Leeds, S. B., *These Rule France* (1940), on French public leaders; Londonderry, Marquis, *Wings of Destiny* (1943), much on history of the Royal Air Force; Scarfoglio, C., *England and the Continent* (1939), shrill castigation of British diplomacy; Spender, A., *Between Two Wars* (1943), by an advocate of "appeasement"; Walker-Smith, C., *Neville Chamberlain* (1940).

CHAPTER XX

AUSTRIA: Ball, M. M., *Post-War German-Austrian Relations* (1937), standard; Gedye, G. E. R., *Betrayal in Central Europe* (1939), a journalist's narrative of Austria and Czechoslovakia; Machray, R., *The Struggle for the Danube and the Little Entente* (1938).

THE DOOM OF CZECHOSLOVAKIA: See items under Czechoslovakia in Chapter VI; Armstrong, H. F., *When There Is No Peace* (1939), valuable estimate of Sudeten crisis, critical of western policy; Fabre-Luce, A., *Histoire Secrète de la Conciliation de Munich* (1938), important; Hadley, W. W., *Munich: Before and After* (1944), a defense of the Chamberlain policy; Hutton, G., *Survey after Munich* (1939), broad analysis, valuable; Maugham, Viscount, *The Truth about the Munich Crisis* (1944), special pleading on behalf of Chamberlain; Ripka, H., *The Fall of Czechoslovakia* (1939), from the pen of a Czech observer; Schuman, F. L., *Europe on the Eve* (1939), critical account of the years 1933–1939; Seton-Watson, R. W., *From Munich to Danzig* (1939), fervent condemnation of "appeasement"; Werth, A., *France and Munich* (1939), valuable, many documents; Wiskemann, E., *Prologue to War* (1940), balanced review of Europe after Munich.

POLAND AND GERMANY: Harley, J. H., *Colonel Beck* (1939), character sketch and speeches of the Polish Foreign Minister; Heiss, F., *Deutschland und der Korridor* (1939), a Nazi study; Machray, R., *Polish-German Problems* (1941), brief, by a friend of Poland; Mackiewicz, S., *Colonel Beck and His Policy* (1945); Martel, E., *The Eastern Frontiers of Germany* (1930), good on "Polish Corridor"; Wegerer, A. von, *The Origins of World War II* (1941), a German interpretation.

ADDRESSES AND DOCUMENTS: Chamberlain, N., *In Search of Peace* (1939), addresses by the British Prime Minister; *Documents Concerning German-Polish Relations and the Outbreak of Hostilities between Great Britain and Germany* (1939), British official literature on the eve of the conflict; *Documents on Events Preceding the Outbreak of War* (1940), a sheaf of German papers; *The French Yellow Book* (1940), a selection of French documents; *The German White Paper* (1940), German publication of Polish diplomatic records; Halifax, E. F. L., *Speeches on Foreign Policy* (1940), important; *Official Documents*

Concerning Polish-German and Polish-Soviet Relations, 1938–1939 (1940), documents from the Polish Foreign Office.

CHAPTER XXI

GENERAL WORKS: Angell, N., *For What Do We Fight?* (1940), by a distinguished British thinker; Bilainkin, G., *Diary of a Diplomatic Correspondent* (1942), valuable on personalities in London; Britain, *Build the Ships* (1946), short official account of British shipyards at war; Brodsky, G. D., *Design for Power: The Struggle for the World* (1942); Cianfarra, C. M., *The Vatican and the War* (1944), by an American journalist in Rome from 1935 to 1941; Dorpalen, A., *The World of General Haushofer* (1942), the visions of the German geopoliticians; Fisher, H. A. L., ed., *The Background and Issues of the War* (1940), learned British essays; Greenwood, A., *Why We Fight* (1940), the viewpoint of a British Labour leader; Harrison, H., *The Neutrality of Ireland* (1942); Henrey, R., *Village in Piccadilly* (1942); Henrey, R., *The Incredible City* (1944); Henrey, R., *The Siege of London* (1946), a trilogy on London in wartime.

Korson, G. G., *At His Side* (1945), the work of the American Red Cross overseas; Prittie, T. C. F., and Edwards, W. E., *South to Freedom* (1946), tales of escapes from German war prisons; Root, W., *The Secret History of the War* (2 vols., 1945), much on political and economic affairs, not well proportioned; Schuman, F. L., *Night over Europe* (1940), useful account of diplomacy, 1939–1940; Taylor, E., *The Strategy of Terror* (1940); Tolischus, O. D., *They Wanted War* (1940), forthright exposition of Nazi ambitions by an American journalist; Vansittart, R., *Black Record: Germany's Past and Present* (1941), develops the theme that Germans are incorrigibly wicked; Whittlesey, D., et al., *German Strategy of World Conquest* (1942), on Nazi geopolitics; Young, G., *Outposts of Peace* (1945), neutral Sweden in wartime; Zink, H., and Cole, T., *Government in Wartime Europe* (1941).

MILITARY AND NAVAL AFFAIRS: Butcher, H. S., *My Three Years with Eisenhower* (1946), excerpts from diary of naval aide, of mixed value; Commager, H. S., ed., *Story of the Second World War* (1945), largely military, by many writers; DeWeerd, H. A., *Great Soldiers of World War II* (1945), tentative portraits of eleven headliners; Edwards, K., *Seven Sailors* (1945), portraits of British naval chiefs; Graves, P. P., ed., *The War by Quarters* (22 vols., 1940–1946), valuable contemporary estimate of the war by many writers, comprehensive, balanced; Grey, C. G., *The Luftwaffe* (1944), useful; Hall, W. P., *Iron out of Calvary* (1946), an interpretative narrative of the war and its background; Hart, W. E., *Hitler's Generals* (1944), intimate, thin; Hatch, A., *General Ike, a Biography of Dwight Eisenhower* (1946), popular; Hermann, H., *Rise and Fall of the Luftwaffe* (1944); Karig, W., et al., *Battle Report: The Atlantic War* (1946), from original sources, somewhat disappointing; Lee, A., *The German Air Force* (1946); Low, A. M., *The Submarine at War* (1942); McInnis, E., *The War* (5 vols., 1940–1945), a broad annual summary by a Canadian historian; Marshall, G., *Biennial Report of the Chief of Staff of the United States Army* (1945), comprehensive account from the middle of 1943 to mid–1945, indispensable; Martel, G. L., *Our Armoured Forces* (1945), by a leading British commander, important; Spaight, J. M., *Bombing Vindicated* (1944), by an attaché of the British Air Ministry; Strategicus, *To Stalingrad and Alamein* (1943) and *The Tide Turns* (1944).

POLAND AND THE BALTIC STATES: *Black Book of Polish Jewry* (1944), a documented treatment of Nazi destruction of Polish Jews; Finland, *The Development of Finnish-Soviet Relations* (1940), government documents; *Finland Reveals Her Secret Documents on Soviet Policy* (1941), official; Karski, J., pseud., *The Story of a Secret State* (1944), by a participant in the Polish underground; Keeton, G. W., and Schlesinger, R., *Russia and Her Western Neighbors* (1942), small, favorable to Soviet interests; Lemkin, R., *Axis Rule in Occupied Europe* (1944), very revealing; *The Polish White Book* (1942), documentary testimony on German occupation; Pusta, K., *The Soviet Union and the Baltic States* (1942).

AXIS CONQUEST AND RULE OF WESTERN EUROPE: Armstrong, H. F., *Chronology of Failure: The Last Days of the French Republic* (1940); Barlone, D., *A French Officer's Diary* (1942), frank and revealing; Belgium, *The Official Account of What Happened*

(1941), critical of France; Divine, A. D., *Dunkirk* (1945), a first-hand account; Hambro, C. J., *I Saw It Happen in Norway* (1940), a moving report; Marchal, L., *Vichy* (1942), critical, by a well-informed man; Masefield, J., *The Nine Days Wonder* (1941), graphic description of Dunkirk evacuation; Pickles, D. M., *France between the Republics* (1945), a record of the years 1940–1945; Somerhausen, A., *Written in Darkness* (1946), a diary on life in Belgium under German rule; Tissier, P., *The Riom Trial* (1942), trial of French political and military chiefs; Werth, A., *The Last Days of Paris* (1940), mainly a diary by an astute British journalist.

ITALY ENTERS: Gibson, H., ed., *The Ciano Diaries* (1946), very interesting; Macartney, M. H. H., *One Man Alone* (1943), on Mussolini and the Axis by a British journalist.

BRITAIN FIGHTS ON: Churchill, W., *Blood, Sweat and Tears* (1941), principal addresses, 1938–1940; Reynolds, Q., *London Diary* (1941), by an American journalist; Spaight, J. M., *The Battle of Britain* (1941), very enlightening.

THE BALKANS AND THE MIDDLE EAST: Casson, S., *Greece against the Axis* (1943); Greece, *The Greek White Book* (1942), documents on Italian war upon Greece; Guedalla, P., *Middle East* (1945), engaging account of British airpower; Kerr, C., *Tanks in the East* (1945), operations in Syria; Sayre, J., *The Persian Gulf Command* (1945).

CHAPTER XXII

SOVIET RUSSIA AND THE WAR: Bilainkin, G., *Maisky* (1944), affectionate sketch of the Soviet Ambassador to London; Dallin, D. J., *Russia's Foreign Policy* (1942), comprehensive analysis; Gafencu, G., *Prelude to the Russian Campaign* (1946), by the Rumanian Ambassador to Moscow; Murphy, J. T., *Russia on the March* (1941), popular, by a British admirer; Pritt, D. N., ed., *Soviet Peace Policy* (1941), addresses by Foreign Commissar Molotov; Sayers, M., and Kahn, A. E., *The Great Conspiracy. The Secret War against Soviet Russia* (1946), an example of how contemporary history should not be written; Scott, J., pseud., *Duel for Europe: Stalin versus Hitler* (1942), a valuable record; Stalin, J., *The Great Patriotic War* (1945), collected addresses, 1941–1945.

THE UNITED STATES AND WORLD WAR II: Baxter, J. P., 3rd, *Scientists against Time* (1946), official history of the contributions of American scientists to victory; Beard, C. A., *A Foreign Policy for America* (1940), should be read together with Buell, R. L., *Isolated America* (1940), the first presents the case for non-intervention, the second for intervention; Bisson, T. A., *America's Far Eastern Policy* (1945), mainly after 1937, calm and reliable; Borchard, E., and Lage, W. P., *Neutrality for the United States* (new ed., 1940), argues for non-intervention; Craigie, R., *Behind the Japanese Mask* (1946), slight reminiscences by the last British Ambassador in Tokyo; Davis, F., and Lindley, E. K., *How War Came to America* (1942), a good account of the subject; Finney, B., *Arsenal of Democracy* (1942), the role of industry; Fraser, C. E., and Teele, S. F., *Industry Goes to War* (1941); Grattan, C. H., *The Deadly Parallel* (1939), a statement of the case against American involvement in the war; Grew, J. C., *Ten Years in Japan* (1944), by the American Ambassador, supplements *Papers Relating to the Foreign Relations of the United States: Japan, 1931–1941* (2 vols., 1943); Holmes, H. N., *Strategic Materials and National Strength* (1942).

Johnson, W., *The Battle against Isolation* (1944), factual, informing; Johnstone, W. C., *The United States and Japan's New Order* (1941), indispensable summary; Lippmann, W., *United States Foreign Policy* (1943), by an able commentator; Morton, H. V., *Atlantic Meeting* (new ed., 1945), valuable record on the Atlantic Charter Conference; Nelson, D. M., *Arsenal of Democracy* (1946), on American war production by the man in supreme charge; Perkins, D., *America and Two Wars* (1944), vigorously written, thoughtful; Puleston, W. D., *Armed Forces in the Pacific* (1941), interesting data and forecasts; Sorokin, P. A., *Russia and the United States* (1944), stresses similarities between the two nations, helpful to mutual understanding; Spykman, N. J., *America's Strategy in World Politics* (1942), by a leading geopolitician; Stettinius, E. R., Jr., *Lend-Lease: Weapon for Victory* (1944), a preliminary accounting; Stone, W. T., *America Rearms* (1941).

CHAPTERS XXIII AND XXIV

PLANNING FOR VICTORY AND PEACE: Arne, S., *United Nations Primer* (1945), running commentary and official texts of the various Allied agreements; Churchill, W., *Onwards to Victory* (1944), the Prime Minister's addresses in 1943; Churchill, W., *Dawn of Liberation* (1945), war speeches for 1944; Dean, V. M., *The Four Cornerstones of Peace* (1946), very useful summary of interallied meetings, with documents: Dolivet, L., *United Nations* (1946), an elementary analysis; Holborn, L., ed., *War and Peace Aims of the United Nations* (1943), the documents to the end of 1942; Schnapper, M. B., ed., *United Nations Agreements* (1944), a documentary compilation.

NORTH AFRICA AND ITALY: Buckley, C., *The Road to Rome* (1945), instructive, vivid; Clifford, A. G., *The Conquest of North Africa* (1943); Divine, A. D., *Road to Tunis* (1944), a very readable description of the war in North Africa by a British correspondent; Majdalany, F., *The Monastery* (1945), fighting around Monte Cassino; Massock, R. G., *Italy from Within* (1943), careful journalist's report; Mauldin, B., *Up Front* (1944), the real thing from the soldier's side, with choice cartoons; Middleton, D., *Our Share of the Night* (1946), by an American reporter, excellent on the African campaign; Pendar, K., *Adventure in Diplomacy* (1946), on North African politics and Franco-American diplomacy; Pyle, E., *Brave Men* (1944), graphic descriptions of men and events by the "Boswell of the G. I."; Tregaskis, R. W., *Invasion Diary* (1943), realistic report on the thrust into Italy.

RUSSIA AND THE BALKANS: Bor-Komorowski, T., *The Unconquerables* (1946), Polish account of Warsaw rising of 1944; Byford-Jones, W., *Greek Trilogy* (1946), thrilling record of Greek liberation; Cardwell, A. S., pseud., *Poland and Russia* (1944), sympathetic to traditional Poland; Dallin, D. J., *Russia and Postwar Europe* (1943), interesting, not optimistic; Fadeyev, A., *Leningrad in the Days of the Blockade* (1945), vivid; Halpern, A., *Liberation—Russian Style* (1945); Jacob, A., *A Window in Moscow* (1946), loose journalism on wartime Russia; Joesten, J., *What Russia Wants* (1944), to be compared with Dallin, cited above; Kirkien, L., *Russia, Poland, and the Curzon Line* (new ed., 1945); Kolarz, W., *Myths and Realities in Eastern Europe* (1946), an ideological survey; Krieger, E., *From Moscow to the Prussian Frontier* (1945), by a competent Soviet war correspondent; Rootham, J., *Miss Fire* (1946), readable report of a British agent with Mihailovitch; Vóyetekhov, B., *The Last Days of Sevastopol* (1943); Werth, A., *Leningrad* (1944), partly an eye-witness account of the siege; Werth, A., *The Year of Stalingrad* (1946), a moving and appreciative study; White, L., *The Long Balkan Night* (1944), important, journalist's report; Winterton, P., *Report on Russia* (1946), British correspondent in Moscow, 1942–1945, factual, critical.

CONQUEST OF WESTERN EUROPE: Arbib, R. S., Jr., *Here We Are Together* (1946), by an American soldier in Britain; Dawson, J. D. A., *European Victory* (1946), exciting narrative by a Britisher; Edwards, K., *Operation Neptune* (1946), enlightening on naval aspects of the invasion; Eisenhower, D. D., *Eisenhower's Own Story of the War* (1946), report by Supreme Commander from Normandy to German capitulation; Ingersoll, R., *Top Secret* (1946), an appraisal of military strategy, of mixed value; Leigh, R., *48,000,000 Tons to Eisenhower* (1945), graphic portrayal of shipment of American supplies to Europe; Maillaud, P., *Over to France* (1946), eye-witness record of French liberation; Melville, A., *First Tide* (1945), fascinating narrative on the invasion of Normandy; Millis, W., *The Last Phase* (1946), short, popular account of the last year of the fighting.

WARTIME GERMANY: Bernadotte, F., *The Fall of the Curtain* (1945), observations in Germany early in 1945; Knauth, P., *Germany in Defeat* (1946), an excellent piece of journalism; Kris, E., and Spier, H., *German Radio Propaganda* (1944), an appraisal of material broadcast for domestic consumption; Padover, S. K., *Experiment in Germany* (1946), on German attitudes after the defeat, by an American intelligence officer; Schultz, W., *The German Home Front* (1943), valuable insights into conditions; Seydewitz, M., *Civil Life in Wartime Germany* (1945), by a German Socialist living in Sweden; Shirer, W., *Berlin Diary* (1941), graphic portrayal of Germany at war and before; Smith, H. K., *Last Train from Berlin* (1942), enlightening.

THE GREAT PACIFIC WAR: Cant, G., *America's Navy in World War II* (1943); Cant, G., *The Great Pacific Victory* (1946), good account from Guadalcanal to Tokyo; Coast, J., *Railroad of Death* (1946), autobiography of Britisher taken captive by Japan; Considine, R., *General Wainwright's Own Story* (1946), moving account of American defeat in the Philippines; Eldridge, F., *Wrath in Burma* (1946), of mixed value, on the manner of reconquest; Hailey, F. B., *Pacific Battleline* (1944), comprehensive record of the first two years of war; Hunt, F., *MacArthur and the War against Japan* (1944); Karig, W., et al., *Battle Report* (1944), preliminary account of the first phases of the war in the Pacific, based on original sources; Miller, E. H., *Strategy at Singapore* (1942); Pratt, F., *Fleet against Japan* (1946), uncritical summary of last part of the fighting; Rosinger, L. K., *China's Wartime Politics* (1944), enlightening, reliable; Tregaskis, R. W., *Guadalcanal Diary* (1943), dramatic; Wagg, A., *A Million Died* (1943), a survey of the fighting in Burma; White, O., *Green Armour* (1945), a New Zealand journalist in New Guinea, vivid.

TOOLS OF WAR: Brodie, B., ed., *The Absolute Weapon* (1946), essays on atomic power; Burton, E., *By Sea and by Land: The Story of Our Amphibious Forces* (1944), a compact, well-written account; Liddell-Hart, B. H., *The Revolution in Warfare* (1946), by a leading British student of war; Masters, D., and Way, K., eds., *One World or None* (1946), discussions on the atomic bomb by experts; Schnapper, E., ed., *United States Aviation in Wartime* (1944), reliable summary of developments; Smyth, H. D., *Atomic Energy for Military Purposes* (1945), official American account; Wimperis, H. E., *World Power and Atomic Energy* (1946), on military and peacetime potentialities.

CHAPTER XXV

AFTER THE BATTLES: Bourne, G. H., *Starvation in Europe* (1943), a preliminary forecast; Jackson, R. H., *The Case against Nazi War Criminals* (1946), the ringing indictment of the American prosecutor at the Nuremberg trial; Kulischer, E. M., *The Displacement of Population in Europe* (1943), praiseworthy survey.

THE WORLD OF TOMORROW: Becker, C., *How New Will the Better World Be?* (1944), thoughtful essays by a distinguished American historian; Carr, E. H., *Conditions of Peace* (1942), a searching analysis by a Britisher; Dallin, D. J., *The Big Three* (1946), an important prospectus of the future; Feis, H., *The Sinews of Peace* (1944), by an American economist; Gelber, L., *Peace by Power* (1942); Hambro, C. J., *How to Win the Peace* (1942), by a Norwegian statesman; Hamzavi, A. H., *Persia and the Powers* (1946), documented summary of Iranian diplomacy 1941 to 1946; Heywood, V., ed., *Rebuilding Europe* (1942), a symposium by Allied statesmen residing in Britain; Hoover, H., and Gibson, H., *Problems of Lasting Peace* (1942), the views of the former President of the United States; Kohn, H., *World War in Historical Perspective* (1942), an excellent statement; Laski, H. J., *Reflections on the Revolution of Our Times* (1943), provocative speculations; Lippmann, W., *United States War Aims* (1944), controversial proposals on world settlement; Lorwin, L. L., *Economic Consequences of the Second World War* (1942).

Macartney, M. H. H., *The Rebuilding of Italy* (1945), slight; MacCurdy, J. T., *Germany, Russia and the Future* (1945); Meade, J. E., *The Economic Basis of a Durable Peace* (1940), rather thin; Moulton, H. G., and Marlio, L., *The Control of Germany and Japan* (1944); Newman, B., *The New Europe* (1942), much valuable material with proposals for dealing with minority problems; Reves, E., *The Anatomy of Peace* (1945), vigorous argument for world government; Salvemini, G., and La Piana, G., *What to Do with Italy* (1943), by distinguished Italian refugees in the United States; Sturmthal, A., *A Survey of the Literature on Post-War Reconstruction* (1943); Welles, S., ed., *Intelligent American's Guide to the Peace* (1945), encyclopedic data on the nations, their interests, and resources; Welles, S., *Time for Decision* (1944), by the former Undersecretary of State of the United States; White, T. H., and Jacoby, A., *Thunder out of China* (1946), an informed exposition of problems and prospects; Willkie, W., *One World* (1943), an eloquent tract for the times; Wriston, H. M., *The Strategy of Peace* (1944), thoughtful contribution by the president of Brown University.

Index

Äaland Islands, 176, 416
Abbéville, 527
Abdullah, Emir, 438
Abyssinia, *see* Ethiopia
Acción Popular, 244
Action Française, 223
Aden, Gulf of, 563
Admiral Scheer, 543
Adriatic Sea, 28, 103
Aduwa, 475
Aegean Sea, 104, 207, 208, 583
Africa, 3, 8, 47, 99, 236, 249, 280, 285-286, 349, 362, 532. *See* also colonies
Afrika Corps, 576
Agadir, 27
Agriculture, in Europe (1914), 4; in France, 220, 232, 233, 234; in Nazi Germany, 320; in Great Britain, 266; in Hungary, 157-158; in India, 293; in Italy, 191-192; in the Near East, 199, 203, 208-209, 212; in Poland, 171; in Russia, 139-140, 344; after World War II, 628. *See* also Peasantry
Airplane, 7; in World War I, 77-78, 84; between the wars, 345, 348, 351, 493, 496; in World War II, 522, 524, 527, 536-537, 541, 543, 552, 562, 568, 570, 574, 575, 576, 579, 580, 581, 584-585, 586, 587, 594-596, 597-601, 604, 608, 611, 614, 616, 618, 623, 624 n.
Aisne River, 42
Alaska, 570, 621
Albania (Albanians), 17, 23, 28, 50, 51, 198, 200, 373, 432-433, 443, 507; and World War II, 539, 603; after World War II, 651
Alcock, Captain, 345
Aldington, Richard, 378
Aleutian Islands, 570, 581
Alexander I, of Yugoslavia, 201, 202, 470
Alexander, General Harold, 576
Alexandria, 216, 576
Algeciras Conference (1906), 26
Algeria, 236

Allied Military Control Commission, 424
All-Union Congress of Soviets, 127, 131
Alphonso XIII, of Spain, 240, 243
Alsace-Lorraine, in 1914, 20, 29; and World War I, 40, 74, 75, 88, 95, 96; as part of France, 220, 227, 430, 531
Alto-Adige, *see* South Tyrol
Altmark, 525
American University in Cairo, 200
Amiens, 80, 527
Amritsar, 290
Amundsen, Roald, 348
Anatolia, 106, 212
Anarchism, defined, 16-17; in Spain, 242, 247, 385
Anarcho-Syndicalists, 244, 247
Anglo-American Shipping Allocation Board, 579
Anglo-Catholic movement, 360
Anglo-Egyptian Treaty (1936), 216, 630
Anglo-French Alliance (1938), 495-496
Anglo-French Entente (1904), 25
Anglo-German naval treaty (1935), 465-466, 468 n., 472, 512
Anglo-Japanese Alliance (1902), 25, 418
Anglo-Polish Treaty (1939), 509
Anglo-Russian Alliance (1942), 566
Anglo-Russian Entente (1907), 25-26
Angola, 249
Ankara, 212
Anschluss, 154, 155, 497, 498. *See* also Austro-German Customs Treaty
Antarctica, 348
Anthropology, 349-350
Anti-Comintern Pact, 484, 488, 507
Anti-Semitism, *see* Jews
Antwerp, 40, 599
Anzacs, 46, 537, 611
Anzio, 601
Appeasement, meaning of, 494
Aquitania, 7
Arabs, 23, 198, 349, 374, 435-438; and World War I, 51, 73, 81, 93; after World War II, 630

Archaeology, 350
Archangel, 45, 125, 575
Archipenko, A., 400, 401
Architecture, 176, 397-399
Ardennes, Battle of the, 596, 600, 607
Argentina, 565
Aristocracy, in Europe (1914), 8-10
Armament Limitation, 417-418, 420, 439-442, 454-457
Armenia (Armenians), 23, 50-51, 106, 127
Armistice, German (1918), 82, 87-88, 101 n.; French (1940), 530-534; Italian (1943), 582-583, 647; Bulgarian (1944), 603; Finnish (1944), 602, 647; Rumanian (1944), 603; German (1945), 613
Arnhem, 600
Asch, Sholem, 395
Asia, 3, 8, 215; after World War II, 630
Asquith, Herbert H., 34
Astronomy, 346-347
Athens, 208, 540
Atlantic Charter, 368, 561-562, 566, 581, 588, 589, 631, 654
Atlantic Wall, 574, 597
Atomic bomb, 343-344, 564, 616, 617, 618, 621, 622, 643
Atomic Energy Commission, 643, 653
Attlee, Clement, 526, 641
Australia, 280 and n., 281, 287, 349; in World War II, 567, 568, 570
Austria-Hungary, 5, 6, 8, 9, 10, 17, 18, 19, 22, 23, 25, 26, 27, 28, 29, 30; in World War I, 33-36, 43-44, 46-49, 51-53, 61, 68, 72-75, 81-82, 151, 159, 160, 162, 180, 189, 200, 201, 203
Austria, Republic of, 98-99; and Treaty of St. Germain, 102-105, 152, 156; political parties in, 152-153; government of, 153; municipal Socialism in, 153-154; Dollfuss period, 154-156; chancellorship of Schuschnigg, 156; customs union of, with Germany, 307, 452-453; annexation of, by Germany, 497-499; and World War II, 592, 603, 611, 613; after World War II, 647, 651, 652
Austro-German Customs Treaty, 307, 452-453
Aviation, *see* Airplane
Avranches, 598
Axis (German-Italian), 158, 190, 202, 208, 210, 211, 238, 248, 479, 482, 498, 506-508, 511, 513, 535, 539, 548, 556, 557, 566, 574, 580, 581, 582, 591, 594, 603
Azaña, Manuel, 243, 244, 245

Azerbaijan, 645
Azores, 249, 584

Babel, Isaak, 393
Badoglio, Marshal Pietro, 582, 583
Bagdad, 50, 73, 438
Bagdad Railway, 7, 29
Baikal, Lake, 137
Baird, John L., 407
Baku, 125
Bakunin, Michael, 16
Baldwin, Stanley, 263-264, 265, 268, 269, 272, 274, 493, 494
Balearic Islands, 239
Balfour Declaration, 435, 437
Balkan League (1912), 27-28
Balkans, 6, 7, 23, 27-28, 29, 30, 33-36, 45, 49-50, 198-199, 214, 319-320; and World War II, 534, 539-542, 548, 583, 604, 611, 623; after World War II, 650-651, 653. *See* also individual countries
Balkan Union (1934), 198, 205, 207, 210, 470
Balkan Wars (1912-1913), 28
Baltic Republics, 175-178, 416, 467 n., 512, 548, 602
Baltic Sea, 3
Balts, 177
Bank of France, 228, 234
Barbusse, Henri, 383
Barcelona, 242, 243, 247, 248, 397, 505
Baroja, Pío, 385
Barrie, J. M., 379
Barth, Karl, 371-372
Barthou, Louis, 470
Bartók, B., 404
Basques, 242, 246, 248
Bata Company, 165
Bataan, 567, 614
Battle of the Atlantic, 542-543, 579, 584
Battle of Britain, 536-537
Battle of France (1940), 528; (1944), 597-599
Baum, Vicki, 389
Bavaria, 311, 312, 326, 608, 613
Bayeux, 598
Bedny, D., 394
Beirut, 218
Belgium, 4, 6, 17, 23 n.; and World War I, 37-38, 40, 54, 64, 83, 98, 99, 102; between World Wars, 250-251, 252, 362, 412, 426, 430, 468, 469, 482, 495; and World War II, 524, 525-526, 550, 599, 600
Belgrade, 603, 611
Beli, Andrei, 393
Belloc, Hilaire, 379
Benedict XV, Pope, 61, 74

Beneš, Edward, 160, 166
Bengal, Bay of, 568
Bengazi, 195, 537, 538
Berchtesgaden, 314
Berchtold, Count Leopold von, 34
Berg, Alban, 403
Bergson, Henri, 360
Berlin, 39, 299, 321, 585, 608, 610, 612, 613, 623
Bernadotte, Count Folke, 612
Bessarabia, 22, 52, 124 n., 203, 204, 523, 539, 603, 647
Bethmann-Hollweg, Theobald von, 74
Bevin, Ernest, 526, 644
Bidault, Georges, 646
Biology, 349, 350-352
Bismarck, 543, 544, 584
Bismarck, Prince Otto von, 17, 64, 92, 96, 219, 502
Bizerte, 237
Black Sea, 203, 211
Blasco Ibañez, V., 385
Blockade, in World War I, 44, 54, 58; in World War II, 524, 533, 543, 567, 585
Blok, Alexander, 394
Blum, Léon, 233-234, 235, 485, 496
Bock, Field Marshal Fedor von, 551 and n.
Boer War, 478, 481
Bohemia, 4, 5, 7, 104, 105, 159, 160, 162, 163, 165, 166, 502, 613. *See* also Czechoslovakia
Bojer, Johan, 396, 397
Bolsheviki, 15 n.; and World War I, 72, 75, 81, 83, 86, 104; and November Revolution, 118-119; and the world, 121-122. *See* also Communist Party in Russia, Russia, Soviet
Bordeaux, 528
Borgese, G. A., 386-387
Boris III, of Bulgaria, 206, 207
Bormann, Martin, 612
Bosnia-Herzegovina, 23, 27, 33
Botany, 350-351
Bougainville, 580
Bourdet, Edouard, 384
Bratianu, Jon, 204
Brauchitsch, General W. von, 552
Braun, Eva, 612
Brazil, 71, 237, 249, 560, 565, 625
Bremen, 307
Bremen, 580
Brenner Pass, 47, 103, 156, 611, 613
Brest, 579, 599
Brest-Litovsk, Treaty of, 72, 86, 120-121
Bretton Woods Conference (1944), 606-607

Briand, Aristide, 74, 222, 226, 301, 358, 430-432, 443 n., 452 n.
Briand-Kellogg Pact, *see* Paris Peace Pact (1928)
Bridges, Robert, 379
Briey, 80
British Commonwealth of Nations, nature of, 279-280; between the wars, 280-285
British Empire, 17; nature of 279-280; between the wars, 285-295. *See* also British Commonwealth of Nations
British guarantee policy, 509-510, 539
British Imperial Conference (1926), 280
Brock, W. L., 7
Brown, Lieutenant, 345
Brüning, Heinrich, 306-308, 452, 453, 456
Brusilov, General, 51-52
Brussels, 599
Buchenwald, 317, 532 n.
Buchman, Frank, 369-370
Budapest, 603, 610
Buerckel, Joseph, 467
Bukovina, 52, 523, 539, 603, 647
Bulgaria (Bulgars), 7, 23, 25, 27, 28, 198, 201, 205; and World War I, 48-49, 53, 81; and Treaty of Neuilly (1919), 105, 205, 208; between World Wars, 205-208, 433, 443; and World War II, 539, 540, 541, 548, 550, 603; after World War II, 650, 652
Bunin, Ivan, 392
Burma (Burmese), 568, 581, 595, 614, 623
Burma Road, 489, 555, 568
Bury, J. B., 12-13
Byrnes, James F., 642, 646, 647, 648

Caillaux, Joseph, 74
Cairo Conference (1943), 592-593, 631
Calais, 599
Cambon, Jules, 429
Cambrai, 71
Cameroon, 236
Cammorra, 189
Camranh Bay, 237
Canada, 237, 263, 280, 281, 491; in World War II, 556, 574-575, 599, 608, 621
Canary Islands, 246
Čapek, Karel, 395
Capitalism, 6
Capitalistic Production, by Karl Marx, 13
Caporetto, 72, 75, 180
Carelians, 176

Carmona, Antonio, 249
Carnegie, Andrew, 24
Carnegie Endowment for International Peace, 84
Carol II, of Rumania, 204, 205, 539
Carolines, 596
Carossa, Hans, 389, 391
Carpathian Mountains, 4, 53, 610
Carpatho-Ukraine, 506. *See also* Ruthenia
Cartels, 6
Casablanca Conference (1943), 589-590
Caspian Sea, 575
Cassino, 601
Casualties, in World War I, 84, 220, 261; in World War II, 574, 585, 602, 623, 627
Catalonia (Catalans), 242, 243, 244, 245, 246, 248
Caucasus Mountains, 4, 125, 551, 571, 572
Center party, of Germany, 297, 299, 301, 306, 308, 310 and n., 362
Ceylon, 285, 568
Chamber of Fasci, 187
Chamberlain, Austen, 430-431
Chamberlain, Joseph, 271
Chamberlain, Neville, 271, 274, 275, 494-495, 500-505, 511, 516, 526
Charles I, Emperor-King, 73, 81-82, 157, 416
Chateaubriant, Alphonse, 384
Cheka, 119, 128
Chemistry, 345-346
Cherbourg, 597, 598
Chervonetz, 135
Chesterton, C. K., 360 and n., 379
Chetniks, 540
Chiang Kai-shek, Generalissimo, 445, 487-488, 489; and World War II, 555, 564, 592-593
China, and World War I, 38, 44, 71, 93, 99; and Germany, 305; and Washington Conference (1921-1922), 417, 418, 420; nationalist movement in, 445, 487-488; Communism in, 445, 487; and Japan, 457-460, 487-490, 563-564, 566; in World War II, 591-593, 595, 596, 614, 625; after World War II, 630, 652-653
Chinese Eastern Railway, 462
Christian Science, 358
Christian Socialists, 16, 152, 153, 154, 362
Chungking, 489
Church of England, 361, 367, 368, 369, 373
Churchill, Winston, 45, 265-266, 273, 282, 292, 295, 493, 495; and World War II, 526, 530, 533, 534, 537, 545,

547, 550, 559, 561, 568, 575, 578, 579, 589, 591, 592, 593, 607, 641
Ciano, Count, 533
Clark, General Mark, 601
Claudel, Paul, 384
Clemenceau, Georges, 71, 74; and Paris Peace Conference (1919), 88, 91-93, 94, 96, 98, 103, 480; rejected for Presidency, 226
Collectivism, *see* Communism, Socialism
Cologne, 580, 608
Colonies, 17, 45, 53, 95, 99; Belgian, 252; British, 279-280, 285-295, 488, 568-570; Danish, 252; Dutch, 252-253, 488, 555, 568, 644; French, 220, 236-238, 442, 488, 532, 614; German, 434, 468-469, 481, 524; Italian, 180, 186, 195-196, 642, 647, 650; Portuguese, 249; Spanish, 240
Columbus, 525
Comintern, 121, 129, 142, 143, 184, 209, 224, 257, 265, 588
Communism (Communists), defined, 14; in Russia, 118, 120, 133, 146; in Austria, 152; in Hungary, 156, 157; in Czechoslovakia, 163; in Italy, 181, 182, 184, 185; in the Near East, 203-204, 207, 209, 210; in France, 224, 225, 233, 234, 235, 495, 503, 629, 651; in Spain, 242, 245, 247; in Great Britain, 259 n., 265, 268; in India, 288; in Germany, 296-297, 307, 308, 309, 310 and n., 315, 319, 651; and the Vatican, 365-366; in China, 445, 630; in Yugoslavia, 540; in Poland, 589; after World War II, 629
Communist Manifesto, by Karl Marx, 13
Communist Party in Russia, 128-129, 132, 146, 147, 149. *See also* Bolsheviki
Como, Lake, 611
Compiègne, armistice at (1940), 530
Confederación Nacional del Trabajo, 242
Confédération Générale du Travail, 231
Confédération Générale du Travail Unitaire, 232
Congo, French, 27, 236
Connally, Tom, 646
Conrad, Joseph, 378
Constantine I, of Greece, 53, 209
Constantinople, 28, 30, 31, 38-39, 45-46, 81, 105-106, 211, 212. *See also* Turkish Straits
Conte di Savoia, 193
Convoys, in World War I, 76-77; in World War II, 525, 579, 584
Cooperatives, in Europe (1914), 6; in Europe's Middle East, 151; in Czech-

oslovakia, 164; in Poland, 171; in the Near East, 199; in France, 233; in Great Britain, 277
Coral Sea, Battle of the, 570
Corfu, 50, 210, 433
Corporazione, 187, 191-192
Corregidor, 567, 614
Corsica, 442, 506, 533, 583
Cossacks, 587
Council of *Corporazione*, 187, 191
Council of Foreign Ministers (1945-), 642, 645-646, 652-653
Council of People's Commissars, 119, 128, 132, 135
Council of Ten, 94
Council of Three (Big Three), 94
Courageous, 525
Coventry, 536
Coward, Noel, 379
Cracow, 603
Craigie, Sir Robert, 558 n.
Crete, 541, 543, 619
Crimea, 571, 603
Cripps, Sir Stafford, 547, 568-569
Croatia (Croats), 23, 201-202. *See also* Yugoslavia
Croix de Feu, 230-231, 234
Cromwell, Oliver, 169
Crusades, 3, 73
Cunard Company, 7
Curtin, John, 580
Curzon Line, 414, 632
Cyprus, 39, 209
Czechoslovakia (Czechoslovaks), 22, 44, 102, 104, 105, 106, 122; establishment of, 159-160; minorities in, 160-162, 165-166; Constitution of, 162-163; political parties of, 163; social progress of, 163-164; agriculture in, 164; industry in, 164-165; and the Sudeten problem, 165-166; foreign policy of, 166-167; religion in, 362; literature in, 376, 395; and Britain, 499-506; and France, 423, 430-431, 469, 499-506; and Germany, 430, 499-506; and Russia, 471, 500, 504, 505; and World War II, 610; after World War II, 642, 651, 653
Czech-Soviet Pact of Mutual Assistance (1935), 471

Dachau, 317
Dakar, 237, 535
Daladier, Édouard, 235, 500
Dalmatia, 47, 103, 189
Damascus, 439
D'Annunzio, Gabriele, 180, 182, 386, 416, 611
Danton, 480

Danube, 4, 151, 157, 164, 203, 603, 650, 651
Danube Monarchy, *see* Austria-Hungary
Danubian confederation, idea of, 151
Danzig, 98, 172, 174-175, 434, 465, 508-509, 512, 610, 642, 648
Dardanelles, 45-46, 53, 81, 525. *See also* Straits, Turkish
Darlan, Admiral Jean-François, 578
Darwin, Charles, 12, 340, 342, 349, 358
Daudet, Léon, 223
Dawes, C. G., 427
Dawes Plan, 226, 264, 301, 302, 303, 427-428, 444, 454
D'Azeglio, Massimo, 180
D-Day, 596, 597
Decline of the West, The, by Oswald Spengler, 391-392
Dedeagach, 207 n.
de Gaulle, General Charles, 496, 532, 535, 576, 590 n., 592
Denmark (Danes), 17, 20, 54, 98, 250, 251 n., 252, 468, 525
Depression, The Great, 177, 366, 374, 422, 447-453; and Austria, 153, 154, 155; and Czechoslovakia, 165-166; and Poland, 173; and Italy, 193, 194, 475; and the Near East, 199; and France, 228, 231; and Spain, 241; and Great Britain, 269-271; and the United States, 447-450; and Germany, 303, 305-310, 314-315, 319, 322 n., 451-453; and Japan, 458
Detroit, 7
DeValera, Eamon, 283, 284
Dieppe, raid on, 574-575
Disraeli, Benjamin, 265
Ditzen, Rudolph, 389
Djibouti, 237
Dnepropetrovsk Dam, 137
Dobrudja, 539
Dodecanese Islands, 27, 195, 209, 210, 414, 583, 647, 650
Doenitz, Admiral Karl, 583-584, 612, 613
Dollfuss, Engelbert, 154, 155
Dominions, British, 42, 262, 268, 269, 271, 280-285, 418, 422; and World War II, 515, 534, 538, 567, 568, 570, 623
Don River, 571
Donath, 352
Donaumont, 57
Donetz Basin, 4
Doolittle raid, 570
Doumergue, Gaston, 229, 230
Dublin Uprising, 283
Duhamel, George, 383
Dumbarton Oaks Conference (1944), 607, 631, 632, 633

Dunkirk, evacuation of, 527, 541; assault on, 597; investment of, 599
Durazzo, 200
Duryea, H. B., 24
Dutch East Indies, 286, 488 n.; in World War II, 555, 568, 652. See also Indonesia
Dzhugashvili, J. V., see Stalin, J.

East Prussia, 40, 43, 98, 415, 508, 602, 610, 642
"Eastern Locarno", 470
Ebert, Friedrich, 296, 299, 304
Eden, Anthony, 478, 495, 507, 591, 604, 633
Education, in Europe (1914), 11-12; in Czechoslovakia, 163; in Estonia and Latvia, 177; in Europe, between wars, 334, 335-336; in Finland, 176; in the French empire, 237; in Nazi Germany, 323-324, 336; in Great Britain, 276, 278, 335, 336; in India, 293-294; in Italy, 189; in the Near East, 199, 212-214, 335; in Palestine, 436; and Roman Catholicism, 363-364; in Russia, 145-146, 149, 335, 336
Edward VIII, of Britain, 273-274
Egypt, 30, 39, 215-217, 218, 437, 507; and World War II, 537, 538, 541, 563, 576; after World War II, 630, 652
Ehrenburg, Ilya G., 393
Einstein, Albert, 340, 342, 398
Einthoven, 341
Eire, see Irish Free State
Eisenhower, General Dwight D., 576, 586, 596 n., 597, 625
El Alamein, 576
Elbe, 164, 608
Elgar, E., 405
Eliot, T. S., 379
Emerson, Ralph W., 356
Emigration, 11, 194, 199, 209 n., 232, 249
Engels, Friederich, 13, 85
England, see Great Britain
Epp, General von, 469
Epstein, Jacob, 400, 401
Eritrea, 195, 217, 537, 650
Erzberger, Matthias, 299
Erzerum, 50
Essen, 580
Essenine, Sergei, 394
Estonia (Esths), 22, 162, 177, 178, 370, 396, 523. See also Baltic Republics
Ethiopia, 194, 195, 230, 472; conquest of, by Italy, 273, 474-480, 481, 507, 534; and World War II, 537; after World War II, 650
Eugenics, 354.

Evatt, Herbert V., 633-634
Everest, Mount, 349
Ewing, Sir Alfred, 343

Fabian Society, 260
Fadayev, A., 393
Falange Party, 248
Falkenhayn, Field Marshal, 52
Falkland Islands, 44
Faruq I, of Egypt, 217
Fascism, meaning of, 186, 196-197; in France, 230-231, in Spain, 240; in Belgium, 251. See also Italy
Fascist Grand Council, 188-189, 582
Fascist Republic, 582, 611
Fatherland Front, 156
Faulhauber, Cardinal Michael von, 326
Feisal, King of Iraq, 438
Feminism, see Women
Ferdinand I, of Bulgaria, 49, 81, 206
Ferdinand I, of Rumania, 204
Feuchtwanger, Lion, 389
Fibiger, 341
"Fighting French", 532, 578
Finland (Finns), 22; between World Wars, 162, 176-177, 370, 396, 454, 512; wars of, with Russia, 148, 523, 546, 549, 550, 551, 555, 602; after World War II, 647, 652
Finlandia, 176
Fiume, 104, 180, 201, 416-417, 611
Five Year Plans, of Russia, 135-139
Flanders, 527
Fleming, Alexander, 341, 353
Foch, Marshal Ferdinand, 40, 79, 96, 527
Formosa, 593
Forster, E. M., 378
Four Freedoms, The, 559, 581, 654
Four Power Pacific Pact (1922), 418
Four Power Pact (1933), 472 n.
Fourteen Points, of Wilson, 75-76, 87, 88, 94, 98, 101 n., 298, 325, 561
France, 4, 6, 7, 10, 17, 18, 19, 25, 26, 29; in World War I, 36-37, 40-42, 56-58, 71-74, 79-81, 83, 86, 220; and Paris Peace Conference, 88, 91-93, 96-98, 99; government of, 221-222; political parties in, 223-225; politics in 1920s, 225-227; the Alsatian problem, 227; the Great Depression in, 227-229; politics in early 1930s, 229-231; economic record of, 231-233; politics in late 1930s, 233-236; the empire of, 236-238; religion in, 361-362; literature in 380-384; music in, 404; and Belgium, 469; and Czechoslovakia, 167, 423, 430-431, 469, 499-506; and Weimar Germany, 225-228, 300, 415, 424-428, 430, 441, 456-457;

and Nazi Germany, 463, 468, 481-483, 498, 516-517; and Great Britain, 235, 422-424, 426, 427, 430-431, 457, 466, 468, 472, 476, 481-482, 494-496, 530, 535; and Greece, 210, 413, 509; and Italy, 236, 430, 441-443, 454-455, 471-472, 476, 478, 506, 507; and Little Entente, 416, 444; and Poland, 414, 423, 430-431, 444, 465, 469; and Rumania, 205, 443, 469, 509; and Soviet Russia, 470, 471, 505, 523; and Spain, 235, 485, 486; and United States, 219, 220, 228, 231, 427, 532; and Yugoslavia, 202, 443, 469; and rearmament, 495-496; in World War II, 524, 525-533, 550, 597-599, 611, 614, 625; after World War II, 629, 631, 641-642, 646, 651, 653

Francis Ferdinand, Archduke, 33-34

Francis Joseph, Emperor-King, 61

Franco, General Francisco, 244, 245, 246, 247, 248, 484, 486, 535

Franco-Russian Alliance (1893), 25, 471

Franco-Soviet Pact of Mutual Assistance (1935), 471, 480, 505

French Indo-China, *see,* Indo-China, French

French Revolution (1789), 150, 221, 223, 224, 241

Friedeburg, Admiral, 613

Front of National Rebirth, 205

Front Populaire, 233-234, 235

Frunze Academy, 147

Galicia, 5, 22, 43-44, 48, 51, 102, 104, 603

Gallipoli, 46

Galsworthy, John, 378

Gamelin, General M. G., 524

Gandhi, Mahatma, 288, 289, 382

Gas warfare, 56, 597

Gay Pay O (O.G.P.U.), 128

Geneva Arms Conference (1932), 456-457

Geneva Naval Conference (1927), 441-442, 454, 455

Geneva Protocol (1924), 429-430

Genoa Conference (1922), 421

Genocide, meaning of, 522

Geology, 347-348

George V, of Britain, 273

George VI, of Britain, 274, 361, 496

George II, of Greece, 210

George, Stefan, 390-391

German Colonial League, 468, 469

German Constitutional Assembly (1919), 297

German Empire, 4, 5, 6, 7, 8, 9, 10, 12,
17, 18, 19, 25, 27, 28, 29, 30, 31, 32; in World War I, 34-38, 40-44, 48-49, 51-53, 56-62, 65-70, 72-75, 77-82, 296; revolution in, 296-297

German Evangelical Church Federation, 370

German-Italian Alliance (1939), 507-508. *See also* Axis

German Republic, National Socialist, 132, 145, 199; emergence of, 306-307, 309-310, 314, 451-453; nature of, 311-314; reasons for victory of, 314-316; government of, 316-318; economy of, 318-323, 346; cultural uniformity in, 323-325, 400; and the churches, 325-327, 368, 369, 370-372; paganism in, 326-327; persecution of Jews in, 327-328, 436; literature in, 388-392; music in, 403-404; and Austria, 155, 466, 468, 497-499; and the Balkans, 319-320, 499; and Bulgaria, 208; and Czechoslovakia, 499-506; and France, 314, 463, 468, 481-483, 498, 515-516; and Great Britain, 314, 463, 465-466, 468, 481, 483, 498, 506, 510-511, 513, 515; and Greece, 210-211; and Italy, 314, 463, 488, 498, 506-508; and Japan, 23, 472, 488, 547, 558; and Latin America, 320, 556; and League of Nations, 457, 464, 481; and Poland, 464-465, 508-509, 512-513, 516; and Rumania, 205; and Russia, 314, 463, 465, 498, 505, 511, 513-514, 545-549; and Spain, 484-486; and Turkey, 214, 542; and the United States, 314, 463, 482, 557, 560, 565; rearmament of, 464, 467-468; occupies the Rhineland, 479, 480-483; in World War II, 521-523, 524-531, 535-543, 549-554, 571-580, 582, 584-586, 587, 597-606, 607-613, 625-626.

German Republic, Weimar, and Paris Peace Conference (1919), 95-102, 110, 298; Constitution of, 297-298; politics in, 298-300, 304-310; economic conditions in, 299-300, 301-304, 309-310, 318, 428; fall of, 309-310; and Czechoslovakia, 430; and France, 300, 415, 424-428, 430, 441, 456-457; and Great Britain, 415, 423-424; and the League of Nations, 431; and Lithuania, 416; and Poland, 415, 430; and Russia, 123, 305, 421, 444. *See also* Reparations, Versailles, Treaty of

Germany, after World War II, 627, 629, 631, 641-642, 647, 651-652, 653

Gestapo, 316, 322, 326, 328, 532, 605

Ghenghis Khan, 568

Gibraltar, 54, 195, 240, 535
Gide, André, 381
Gilbert Islands, 581, 594
Giolitti, Giovanni, 47-48, 184
Gione, Jean, 384
Giraud, General Henri, 578, 590 n.
Giraudoux, Jean, 382
Glanville, Joseph, 407
Gneisenau, 579
Goebbels, Paul, 324-325, 612, 613
Goerdeler, Karl, 605
Goering, Field Marshal Hermann, 316, 318 n., 584, 605
Goetal, F., 395
Gomel, 586
Gorki, Maxim, 392-393
Gosplan, 135, 136
Graf Spee, 525
Gran Chaco war, 475 n.
Great Britain, 4, 5, 7, 8, 10, 11, 17, 18, 19, 25, 26, 28, 29, 31, 32; in World War I, 36-38, 40-42, 50-51, 58-61, 68, 71-74, 78-81, 83; and Paris Peace Conference, 90-91, 96, 98, 99, 100, 101, 103; government of, 254-255; political parties in, 256-260; economic conditions in, 260, 262, 266-268, 269-270, 272-278; politics in 1920s, 260-261, 263-267, 269; politics in 1930s, 270-275; tariffs in, 271-272, 450; social welfare policies in, 275-278; religion in, 360-361, 367, 369, 370-371; literature in, 377-380; music in, 404, 405; rearmament of, 493-494; new diplomatic course of, 508-513; and the Arabs, 218, 435-438; and Czechoslovakia, 499-506; and Egypt, 216-217, 630; and France, 235, 422-424, 426, 427, 430-431, 457, 466, 468, 472, 476, 481-482, 494-496, 530, 535; and Weimar Germany, 415, 423-424, 430; and Nazi Germany, 273, 275, 463, 465-466, 468, 481, 483, 498, 506, 510-511, 513, 516; and Greece, 210, 263, 413, 509, 604; and Italy, 273, 275, 443, 468, 472, 476-478, 480, 507, 533-534; and Japan, 487, 488, 565, 592-593; and Poland, 414, 509, 511; and Rumania, 205, 509; and Soviet Russia, 263, 265, 268, 269, 445, 486, 498, 505, 511-512, 523, 547, 550, 552, 566, 591-592, 593, 604, 631-633, 641-653; and Spain, 485, 486, 535; and Turkey, 214, 413, 438, 484, 509, 541-542; and the United States, 268, 274, 283, 284, 417-418, 441-442, 444, 454, 455, 487 n., 491, 543, 554-555, 558-563, 589-590, 592-593, 607, 631-633, 641-653; in World War II, 524, 525-528,

534-544, 567-569, 574-575, 576-580, 582, 584-586, 595, 596-601, 603, 607-610, 611, 613-617, 623-625, 627; and settlements after World War II, 629, 641-653. *See also* British Commonwealth of Nations, British Empire, India, Irish Free State, Mandates
Great Pacific War (1941-1945), 99 n., 420, 567-570, 580-581, 594-596, 613-618
"Great Purge", 132-133, 138, 494
Greco-Turkish War, 413
Greece (Greeks), 8, 17, 23, 27, 28, 200, and World War I, 46, 50, 53, 106; between World Wars, 208-211, 373, 413, 432-433, 507, 509; and World War II, 210, 211, 539, 540-541, 548, 583, 592, 603-604, 607; after World War II, 644, 647, 650-651
Greek Orthodox Church, *see* Orthodox Eastern Church
"Green International", 206-207
Greenland, 252, 563 and n.
Greer, 560
Grew, Joseph, 488
Grey, Sir Edward, 36, 58, **517**
Gromyko, Andrei, 645
Gropius, Walter, 398
Grosz, George, 399
Grozny, 571
Guadalcanal, 570, 576, **623**
Guam, 567, 595
Gulflight, 59
Gydnia, 172, 174

Haakon VII, of Norway, 525
Hague Court of Arbitration, 24, 36
Hahn, Otto, 617 n.
Haifa, 436
Haig, Sir Douglas, 57, **71**
Haile Selassie, 476, 537
Hainisch, Michael, 153
Halifax, Lord, 513, 536, 640
Hamburg, 164, 585
Hamburg-America Company, 7
Hamsun, Knut, 396
Hapsburg Monarchy, *see* Austria-Hungary
Harris, Sir Arthur, 580 n.
Hašek, J., 395
Hatvany, L., 396
Haushofer, Karl, 549
Hawley-Smoot Act, 450
Hayes, C. J. H., 246
Heisenberg, Werner, 617 **n.**
Hejaz, 217
Heligoland, 43
Helsinki, 176
Henlein, Konrad, 166, 499, 613
Herriot, Édouard, 226, 427

Hertzog, General, 281
Himmler, Heinrich, 605, 613
Hindemith, P., 403-404
Hindenburg, Field Marshal Paul von, 43, 52, 82, 84, 125, 304, 306, 307, 308, 309, 316, 431, 451, 551
Hindenburg Line, 71, 80
Hindu Nationalism, 273, 288-290, 294, 295, 568-569, 630
Hinsley, Cardinal, 360-361
Hirohito, 565, 617
Hiroshima, 564, 616-617
Hitler, Adolf, 90, 141, 155, 182, 186, 300, 306-307, 308, 309, 312, 313-314, 316, 317, 323, 327, 328, 329, 467, 468, 469, 480, 482, 492, 497, 500-506, 513-514; and World War II, 516, 524, 552, 565 n., 572, 575, 578, 582, 604-605, 611, 612, 625; death of, 612-613
Hitler Jugend, 324, 326
Hoare-Laval Plan, 478
Hoare, Sir Samuel, 476, 478
Hoffmann, Colonel, 43
Holland, 4, 7, 17, 54, 250, 296, 495; and World War II, 524, 526, 599, 608, 614. *See* also Dutch East Indies
Honegger, A., 404
Hong Kong, 280, 555, 567
Hood, 543
Hoover, Herbert, 308, 453
Horthy, Nicolas, 157
Hot Springs Conference (1943), 590
House, Edward M., 32, 61
Hull, Cordell, 491, 558, 591
Hungary, 4, 5, 6, 10, 18, 23; and Treaty of Trianon (1920), 105, 155, 416; minorities in, 156-157; government of, 157; agriculture in, 158; industry in, 158; foreign policy of, 158; irredentism in, 158, 506; literature in, 396; and World War II, 539, 540, 548, 549, 603, 610; after World War II, 642, 650, 652. *See* also Austria-Hungary
Hussein, 51
Huxley, Aldous, 378

Ibn Saud, 217, 218, 273
Iceland, 252; and World War II, 525, 560, 563
Imperator, 7
Imperialism, 8, 17; as a cause of war, 30-31; British, and the United States, 64. *See* also Colonies
India, 26-30, 211, 249, 280, 286-295, 437; and World War II, 538, 549, 568-569, 611; after World War II, 630, 652

Indian Government Act (1919), 290-291
Indian Government Act (1935), 273, 292
Indo-China, French, 236, 237, 238, 489; and World War II, 555, 564
Indonesia, 252-253, 644
Industry, in Europe (1914), 3, 6-7; in Soviet Russia, 133-139, 147-148; in Europe's Middle East, 151-152; in Hungary, 158; in Czechoslovakia, 164-165; in Poland, 170, 171; in Italy, 193; in the Near East, 199, 203, 204, 206, 211, 212, 217; in France, 220, 231; in Great Britain, 266-268; in India, 294; in Weimar Germany, 302-303; in Nazi Germany, 311, 318-319, 320-321, 322, 346
Inönü, Ismet, 214
Inter-Allied Reparations Commission, 101
International, 588
International Court of Justice (1945), 639
International Labor Office, 439, 491
International Macedonian Revolutionary Organization, 207
International Monetary Fund, 606, 638
Internationalism, in 1914, 23-24
Iran, 211 n., 218; and World War II, 538-539, 575, 593; dispute over, 644-645
Iraq, 211 n., 434, 436, 438-439; and World War II, 538
Ireland (Irish), 20, 64, 112, 162, 361, 380
Irish Free State, 263, 273, 274, 280, 281-285; and World War II, 516, 543
Iron Guard, 204, 205
Isonzo, 48
Istanbul, *see* Constantinople
Istrian Peninsula, 47, 646
Italo-Turkish War (1911-1912), 77
Italy (Italians), 4, 6, 8, 17, 18, 22, 24, 25, 26, 27, 30; in World War I, 36-37, 46-48, 64, 71-72, 74, 81-82, 83, 86, 180; and Paris Peace Conference (1919), 93, 102-104; democracy in, 181; situation in after World War I, 181-184; rise of Fascism in, 182-186; Fascist government of, 186-189; minorities in, 189-190; economic theory in, 190-192; economic history of, 192-194; empire of, 195-196; the Church and, 364-365; literature in, 386-387; and Albania, 200, 443, 507; and Bulgaria, 208; 443; conquest of Ethiopia, 194, 474-480; and France, 236, 430, 441-443, 454-455, 471-472, 476, 478,

505, 507; and Nazi Germany, 463, 488, 498, 506-508; and Great Britain, 273, 443, 468, 472, 476-478, 480, 507, 533-534; and Greece, 210-211, 413, 433, 507; and Soviet Russia, 546, 549; and Spain, 245, 247, 248, 484-486; and Turkey, 413; and the United States, 193, 533, 560, 565; and Yugoslavia, 201, 202, 416, 507; in World War II, 517, 528, 533-534, 537-540, 575, 578, 581-583, 591, 592, 601, 611; after World War II, 629, 642, 645, 646, 648, 650, 652. *See* also Axis, Mussolini
Iwo Jima, 614
Izvestia, 129

Jansen, 352
Japan, 25, 122-123; in World War I, 38, 44, 45, 67, 76-77, 93, 99, 108; and the Washington Conference (1921-1922), 417-420; and China, 422, 457-460, 487-490, 563-564, 566; and Geneva Naval Conference (1927), 441; and London Naval Conference (1930), 454, 455; and Russia, 445, 460-462, 489-490, 511, 547, 581, 632; and Nazi Germany, 472, 488, 547, 558; and the United States, 417-420, 422, 455, 460, 487, 490, 555, 558, 563-565; and Great Britain, 487, 488, 565; and World War II, 238, 252-253, 295, 534, 556; in World War II, 567-570, 580-581, 584, 594-596, 613-618, 622; after World War II, 629, 643, 652, 653
Jauregg, Julius Wagner von, 355
Jeannert, Charles E., 398, 399
Jellicoe, Admiral John, 60
Jerusalem, 73
Jewish Brigade, 611
Jews, in Russia (1914), 22; and World War I, 64, 106; in Austria, 155; in Hungary, 156-157; in Poland, 168, 173, 374; in Italy, 189, 190, 365; in Near East, 204; in France, 231; in Germany, 299, 301 n., 307, 311, 312, 313, 315, 317, 323, 327-328, 367, 374, 392, 398, 436; in Soviet Russia, 374; religion of, 359, 373-374; literature of, 395; and Palestine, 435-438; in World War II, 522
Jinnah, Mohammed Ali, 293
Joad, C.E.M., 340
Joffre, Marshal J.J.C., 40 n.
Johnson Act (1934), 492
Johst, Hanns, 392
Joyce, James, 380, 387
Judaism, 143, 373-374
Jugoslavia, *see* Yugoslavia

Junkers, 5, 9, 158, 315, 319
Jutland, 60-61

Kafka, Franz, 390
Kai-shek, *see* Chiang Kai-shek
Kallas, Aino, 396
Kamikaze, 614, 616
Kanolt, A., 399
Kasserine Pass, 578
Kataev, Valentin P., 393
Katanga, 252
Kavalla, 207 n.
Keitel, Marshal, 613
Kellogg-Briand Pact, 443 n. *See* also Paris Peace Pact (1928)
Kemal, Mustapha, 211, 212, 214, 373
Kerensky, Alexander, 118, 119
Kesselring, General Albert, 582
Keynes, J. M., 413
Kharkov, 551, 586
Kiaochau, *see* Shantung
Kiel, 296, 466
Kiev, 414, 551, 586
Kingdom of Serbs, Croats, and Slovenes, *see* Yugoslavia
Kishinev, 603
Kitchener, Lord Herbert, 39
Klaipéda, *see* Memel
Kluck, General von, 40
Kluge, Field Marshal G. von, 600 n.
Koenigsberg, 43, 642
Kolkhoz, 139, 140
Koran, 214
Korea, 458, 593, 596, 617, 630
Kornilov, General, 119
Kredit Anstalt, 307
Kremlin, 120, 124
Krleza, M., 396
Krosigk, Count S. von, 613
Kuibishev, 552
Kulaks, 139
Kurdistan (Kurds), 51, 211 n., 438-439
Kuriles, 564, 581, 593, 632
Kut-el-Amara, 50
Kutuzov, General, 586
Kwajalein, 594

Labour Party, of Great Britain, 224, 629
La Guardia, F., 492
Lake Ladoga, 176
Lansdowne, Lord, 74
László, P. A. de, 400
Lateran Treaty (1929), 364
Latin America, 8, 66, 71, 239, 320, 491; and World War II, 556, 557, 563, 565
Latvia (Letts), 22, 177, 178, 523. *See* also Baltic Republics
Lausanne Reparations Agreement, 453

Lausanne, Treaty of (1923), 215, 413-414, 483
Laval, Pierre, 230 and n., 235, 478, 531
Law, Bonar, 263
Lawrence, D. H., 378
Lawrence, Colonel T. E., 73
League of Nations, 94, 95, 98, 99, 100 n., 165, 207, 216, 247, 250, 338, 358, 371, 398, 429, 432-439; and minorities, 106-107; formation of, 107-108; content of the Covenant of, 108-109; rejection of by the United States, 112-114, 432; aid to Austria, 153; and Danzig, 174; and Germany, 301, 431, 457, 467, 481; and Upper Silesia, 415; and the Corfu affair, 432-433; and the Greco-Bulgar crisis, 433; and the Saar Basin, 434, 466-467; and mandated territories, 434-439; miscellaneous activities of, 439-440; and "disarmament," 439, 456-457; and Mosul quarrel, 438; and Manchurian "incident," 459-460; and Russia, 470-471, 523; and conquest of Ethiopia, 474, 476-479; and Sino-Japanese war, 489; and Munich crisis, 505; end of, 639 n.
League of the Godless, 144
Lebanon, see Syria
Ledo Road, 621
Leeb, General von, 551
Le Havre, 597
Lehman, Herbert H., 591, 630
Lend-Lease, 454, 559-561, 563, 575, 581, 593, 625, 645
Lenin, Nicholas, 85; return to Russia, 119, 550; career of, 123-124; and new economic policy, 134; and religion, 143
Leningrad, 124 n., 176, 523; and World War II, 551, 585, 602. See also Petrograd, St. Petersburg
Leo XIII, Pope, 16, 366
Leonov, L., 393
Leopold II, of Belgium, 527
Leroy Beaulieu, Pierre P., 30
Leyte, Gulf of, 595
Liberalism, defined, 14
Libya, 27, 195, 217, 507, 537, 576, 578, 642, 647
Liddell Hart, B. H., 625-626
Lie, Trygve, 644
Liebknecht, Karl, 296-297
Liége, 40, 43, 600
Lindbergh, Charles, 345
Lingayen Gulf, 614
Literature, 337, 376-397; in Germany, 324, 388-392; in Czechoslovakia, 376; in Great Britain, 377-380; in Ireland, 380; in France, 380-384; in

Spain, 384-386; in Italy, 386-387; in Russia, 392-394; Jewish, 395; in Poland, 395-396; in Finland, 396; in Estonia, 396; in Yugoslavia, 396; in Hungary, 396; in Norway, 396-397
Lithuania, 98, 168, 172, 177-178, 415-416, 465, 506, 523. See also Baltic Republics
Little Entente, 157, 202, 205, 416
Lloyd George, David, 160; and World War I, 60, 75, 76; and Paris Peace Conference (1919), 88, 90-91, 96, 98, 100, 101, 103, 262; as Liberal Party leader, 258, 261, 263, 283
Locarno Treaties (1925), 227, 257, 268, 301, 429-431, 444, 468, 480, 481 n.
Lodz, 43, 170, 395
Loisy, Abbé, 358-359
Lombardy, 187, 192
London Conference (1945), 642-643
London Monetary and Economic Conference (1933), 462-463
London Naval Conference (1930), 454-455, 487
London, Treaty of (1915), 47, 102-103
Lorraine, 4. See also Alsace-Lorraine
Louis XIV, 219
Low Countries, see Belgium, Holland
Lublin government, 589, 632
Ludendorff, Field Marshal Eric, 43, 52, 67, 74, 79, 82, 87, 300, 313, 550
Ludwig, Emil, 377
Luftwaffe, 493, 496, 505, 522, 528, 536, 552, 575, 597, 598, 608, 619
Lusitania, 59-60, 64
Luther, Martin, 68
Lutheran Church, 174, 176, 325, 368, 369, 370
Luxembourg, 17 n., 37, 98, 467 n., 526
Luxemburg, Rosa, 296-297
Luzon, 595, 614
Lvov, 603
Lyons, 231
Lytton Commission, 459

MacArthur, General Douglas, 567, 595, 629
MacDonald, Ramsay, 264, 269, 270, 271, 272, 441
Macedonia, 28, 202, 207, 541
Machek, Vlasko, 202
Mackensen, Marshal August von, 50
McPherson, Aimee S., 369
Madagascar, 568
Madeiras, 249
Madrid, 243, 248, 505
Maffia, 189
Magdeburg, 608
Maginot Line, 229, 444, 469, 481, 496, 500, 524, 526

Magyars, 10, 49, 52, 105, 106, 156, 157, 160, 162, 165, 166, 204. *See* also Hungary
Maikop, 571
Maillol, A., 400, 401
Malaya, 567, 596
Malinovsky, General, 610
Malraux, André, 383
Malta, 195, 542
Manchukuo, 459, 460, 581, 617
Manchuria, Japan seizure of, 273, 456, 457-462, 563; return of, to China, 593; after World War II, 632. *See* also Manchukuo
Mandates, 99, 236, 280, 433-439
Mandates Commission, 434-435, 437
Manila, 614
Manipur, 595
Maniu, Julius, 204
Mann, Thomas, 389
Maquis, 598
Marianas, 595
Marcks, Erich, 32
Maritain, Jacques, 361
Marne River, 40, 52, 79-80, 528
Marseilles, 231, 470
Marshall Islands, 594, 595
Martin du Gard, Roger, 383
Marx, Karl, (Marxism), defined, 13-15; 118, 120, 121, 123-124, 131, 143, 149, 189, 224, 231, 242, 259, 297, 311, 313, 329, 392, 545, 588
Masaryk, Thomas G., 159-160
Masefield, John, 379
Maspero, H., 532 n.
Matapan, Battle of, 540, 542
Matisse, H., 399
Matteotti, Giacomo, 187
Mauriac, François, 381
Maurois, André, 377
Mayakowski, V., 394
Mecca, 217
Medicine, 352-354, 622-623
Mein Kampf, by Adolf Hitler, 178, 313-314, 327, 463-464, 468, 514, 549, 563
Memel, 98, 178, 416, 506
Mendelsohn, Erich, 398
Mercier, Cardinal, 360
Mesopotamia, 7, 73, 81
Messersmith, G. S., 464
Messina, 582
Méstrovič, I., 400, 401
Metaxas, General Yanni, 210
Methodist Church, 369, 370
Meuse River, 56, 80, 600
Mexico, 67, 130, 565
Michael I, of Rumania, 539
Middle class, in Europe (1914), 10

Middle East, World War II in, 537-538, 551
Midway Island, Battle of, 570
Miës van Rohe, Ludwig, 398
Mikhailovitch, General D., 540
Miklas, Wilhelm, 153
Milan, 182, 183, 185, 611
Mindanao, 595
Mindoro, 595
Minerals, in Europe, 4
Minorities, in Europe (1914), 20-23; and the Paris Peace Conference (1919), 90, 98, 106-107; in Soviet Russia, 127, 149; in Austria, 155; in Hungary, 156-157; in Czechoslovakia, 160-162, 165-166; in Poland, 167-168, 172-174; in Italy, 189-190; in the Near East, 200, 204, 205, 207; in Spain, 242; in Belgium, 251
Mkwawa, Sultan, 102
Model, Field Marshal Walter, 600 n.
Mohammedanism (Moslems), 51, 143, 145, 200, 205, 214, 215, 216 n., 217, 218, 285, 286, 287, 290, 291, 292, 359, 374-375, 435, 437, 438, 568
Molnár, F., 396
Molotov, V. M., 514, 523, 545-546, 547-548, 591, 628, 633, 642, 647, 648
Moltke, General H. von, 52
Monkhouse, Allan, 379
Montenegro, 17, 27, 28, 38, 50, 201, 202
Montgomery, General Bernard L., 576, 578, 600
Montherlant, Henri de, 381
Montreux Convention (1936), 214, 483-484
Morand, Paul, 382
Moretti, Marino, 387
Morocco, 26, 27, 29, 99, 236, 240, 241, 244, 246
Moscow, 120, 122, 137, 143; and World War II, 551, 552, 571, 601
Moscow Conference (1943), 591-592, 631; (1945), 643
Moselle River, 599
Moslems, *see* Mohammedanism
Mosse, Irene F., 389
Mosul, 438
Movies, 406-407
Mozambique, 249
Munich, 311, 312, 313, 314, 321
Munich crisis (1938), 500-505
Murmansk, 125, 575
Muscat-Oman, 218
Music, 402-405
Mussolini, Benito, 47, 180, 182, 433; early career of, 182-184; his version

of Fascism, 184-186; master of Italy, 186-197; and Austria, 154, 155, 156; and Hungary, 158; and France, 442-443; and Munich crisis, 500; and World War II, 528, 533-534, 581-582; death of, 611. *See* also Axis
Mustapha Kemal, *see* Kemal, Mustapha

Nagasaki, 617
Nagoya, 616
Namur, 600
Naples, 583
Napola, 323-324
Napoleon I, 29, 125, 183, 313, 411, 528, 537, 545, 551, 572, 574
Napoleon III, 219
Narvik, 525
Nationalism, meaning of, 19-20; in 1914, 28-30; in Soviet Russia, 142; in Italy, 186, 195, 416; in Near East, 198, 200, 204, 212, 214, 215, 435; in the French empire, 237; in the British Dominions, 280, 281, 282, 284; in India, 287-290, 291, 294, 295, 568-569, 630; in Nazi Germany, 315
National Socialism, 142, 228; and Austria, 153, 154, 156; and Hungary, 156, 158; and Czechoslovakia, 159, 164, 166; and Poland, 170, 173-174; and Danzig, 174-175; and Spain, 247; and Great Britain, 273; rise of, in Germany, 306-307, 308, 309-310, 314; nature of, 311-314. *See* also German Republic, National Socialist
Naval warfare, in World War I, 44-46, 58-61, 70; in World War II, 525, 535, 539-540, 542-544, 567-570, 575, 576, 578-582, 583-584, 594-596, 620-621
Navicerts, 543, 554-555
Nazis, *see* German Republic, National Socialist, Hitler, Adolf
Nazi-Soviet Accords (1939), 225, 514, 545, 560
Nehru, Jawaharal, 287-288
Neisse River, 642
Nejd, 217
Neo-Mercantilism, 450
Netherlands, *see* Holland
Neuilly, Treaty of (1919), 105, 205, 207, 208
Neutrality Acts (1935-1937), 492-493; revision of, 554, 563
Neuve Chapelle, 56
New Deal, 234, 462, 463, 490
Newfoundland, 280
New Georgia, 580
New Guinea, 280 n., 349; in World War II, 570, 580, 581, 596

New Mexico, 616
New Zealand, 280, 281
Nice, 442, 533
Nicoll, Allardyce, 406
Niemöller, Martin, 326
Nigeria, 280, 285
Nile, 215, 216, 217, 537, 538
Nimitz, Admiral C. W., 594
Nine Power Treaty on China (1922), 418-420, 459, 489, 564
Nisei, 611
Nivelle, General Robert, 71
N.K.V.D., of Soviet Russia, 128
Nobel, Alfred, 24, 355, 383, 389, 390, 396
Normandy, 596-599, 601
North Africa, World War II in, 537-538, 542, 570, 575-578
Northern Ireland, *see* Ulster
Norway, 8, 17, 54, 68, 70, 250, 252 n.; literature in, 396-397; and World War II, 525-526
Noyes, Alfred, 379
Nurmi, Paavo, 176

O'Casey, Sean, 380
Oder River, 608, 610, 642
Odessa, 551
Office of Production Management, 562
Ogynov, N., 394
Okinawa, 614, 616, 617
Old Catholics, 370
Omaha Beach, 597
Oran, 535
Orient Express Railway, 205
Orkney Islands, 70
Orlando, V. E., 93, 94, 104
Orpen, Sir W., 400 and n.
Ortega y Gasset, José, 384-385
Orthodox Eastern Church, 367, 370, 371, 372-373; in Russia, 143, 144, 372-373, 587-588; in Poland, 172; in the Balkans, 201, 372, 373
Ossorgin, M., 393
Ottawa Conference (1932), 271-272, 282
Ottoman Empire, *see* Turkey
Overlord Project, 596
Oviedo, 245
Oxford Conference (1937), 370-371
"Oxford Group" movement, 369-370

Pacific Area, 8, 44-45, 93, 99, 215, 285, 348, 418, 420, 434, 487. *See* also Great Pacific War
Pacifism, 24, 74-75, 259, 476, 493, 530-531
Painting, 399-400

Pakistan, 293, 569

Palestine, 51, 81, 218, 374, 435-438, 652

Pan-American Conference (1940), 555-556

Pan-Arabism, 217, 218

Panay affair, 490

Pan-Germanism, 29, 66, 153, 314, 464

Pantelleria, 195 n., 578

Papen, Franz von, 308, 309

Papini, Giovanni, 387

Papua, 280 n.

Paris, 39, 40, 528-529, 599

Paris Peace Conference (1919), 87-114

Paris Peace Conferences (1945), 645-648, 652-653

Paris Peace Pact (1928), 443, 460, 489

Pasteur Institute, 341

Patch, General, 599

Patton, General G. S., 598

Paul, Prince, of Yugoslavia, 202, 540

Peace Proposals, during World War I, 61-62, 73-76; during World War II, 524, 535

Pearl Harbor, attack on, 564-565, 616, 618, 620

Peasantry, 6, 422, 590; in Soviet Russia, 133, 139-140, 141; in Hungary, 157-158; in Czechoslovakia, 163, 164; in Poland, 171; in Finland, 176; in Estonia and Latvia, 177; in Lithuania, 178; in Italy, 192-193; in the Near East, 199, 203, 204, 205-206, 208-209, 212, 215-216; in France, 232, 233, 234; in Spain, 240-241, 242, 243; in India, 293; in Nazi Germany, 311, 320; after World War II, 628. *See also* Agriculture

Peenemünde, 599 n.

Penicillin, 353, 622

Permanent Court of International Justice, 109, 440, 452-453, 639

Pershing, General John J., 70

Persia, *see* Iran

Persian Gulf, 7, 50, 438, 575

Pétain, Marshal Henri Philippe, 57, 71, 223; and World War II, 530, 531

Peter II, of Yugoslavia, 202, 540

Peter the Great, 130, 149

Petrograd, 118, 119. *See also* Leningrad, St. Petersburg

Petsamo, 602

Philippines, 460; in World War II, 567, 595, 614, 625

Phillimore, Lord Richard, 107

Physics, 343-345

Piave River, 72, 81, 180

Picasso, 399

Pilnyak, Boris, 393

Pilsen, 624

Pilsudski, Marshal Josef, 168-169, 170

Pirandello, Luigi, 387

Pius XI, Pope, 326, 365-367

Pius XII, Pope, 326, 360 n., 367-368, 516

Plebiscites, 95, 415, 467 and n., 498, 502, 508 n., 523

Po Valley, 192, 601

Poincaré, Raymond, 226, 229, 426, 427

Poland (Poles), 22, 362; and World War I, 43-44, 48-49, 64, 75, 88, 412; boundaries after World War I, 95, 98, 102, 104, 106; war with Russia (1920), 122, 169, 170, 171, 414-415; establishment of, 167; minorities in, 167-168, 172-174; government of, 168-170; industry in, 170, 171, 267; agriculture in, 171; literature in, 396-397; and Rumania, 205, 465; and Germany, 170, 415, 430, 464-465, 508-509, 512-513, 516; and Lithuania, 416; and France, 414, 423, 430-431, 465, 469; and Russia, 464-465, 512, 522-523, 588-589, 602-603, 631-632; and Britain, 509, 511; in World War II, 521-523, 601, 602, 611, 612, 625; after World War II, 627, 631-632, 642, 653

Polish Corridor, 98, 465, 508, 512

Politburo, of Russia, 128, 131, 546

Pomorze, *see* Polish Corridor

Pons, Lily, 219

Pontine Marshes, 193

Popolo d'Italia, 183

Population, 333-334

Popular Front, 143, 496

Port Said, 216

Portugal, 17, 18, 25, 53, 248-250, 535, 584

Potocki, Count Joseph, 9

Potsdam Declaration (1945), 616, 641-642

Prague, 159, 165, 207, 610

Pravda, 19, 129, 546

Press, The, in 1914, 31; in Nazi Germany, 315; between World Wars, 336-337

Prince of Wales, 567

Princip, Gavrilo, 33

Prinz Eugen, 543, 544, 579

Pripet Marshes, 49

Prokofieff, S., 403

Protestantism, 16, 20, 368-372; in Ireland, 283-284; in Germany, 325-326, 370, 371, 372; in Italy, 365; in Great Britain, 361, 367, 368, 369, 370-371; missions, 370, 371

Proust, Marcel, 379-380

Prussia, 308-309. *See also* East Prussia

Psychiatry, 355, 623

Psychoanalysis, 355, 358, 376, 387
Psychology, 354-355
Punch, 112
Pushkin, Alexander, 142
Pyrenees, 10

Quebec Conference (1943), 591;
(1944), 607
Queen Elizabeth, 542
Querschnitt, 337
Quisling, V., 525-526

Rabaul, 581
Radar, 619-620
Radical Socialist Party, of France, 224,
225, 226, 230, 233, 235
Radich, Stefan, 202
Radio, 267, 316, 348, 407
Ramsay, Admiral Bertram, 527-528, 586
Rangoon, 614
Rapallo, Treaty of (1922), 421, 444
Rashid Ali, of Iraq, 538
Rathenau, Walther, 299
Ravel, M. J., 404
Raynal, Paul, 384
Red Cross, 56, 625
Red Sea, 215
Regia Aeronautica, 527
Reichswehr, 299, 300, 304, 305, 317
Remagen, 608
Remarque, E. M., 388
Renn, Ludwig, 388
Reparations, and World War I, 75-76;
and Paris Peace Conference (1919),
100-101, 104; France, and, 225, 226,
227, 300, 424-428; Great Britain,
and, 264, 269, 424-428; Germany,
and, 300, 302, 303, 306, 307-308, 310,
325, 413, 420-421, 424-428, 451-454;
German, after World War II, 631,
642
Republicanism, in Europe (1914), 18
Repulse, 567
Respighi, O., 404
Rex, 193
Rheims, armistice of (1945), 613
Rhineland, 88, 96, 97, 100, 220, 305,
306, 310, 322, 326, 430, 431, 452,
480, 608, 651
Rhineland Security Pact (1925), 430,
444. *See* also Locarno Treaties
Rhine River, 10, 80, 494, 600
Rhone valley, 599
Richelieu, 535
Riga, 177
Riga, Treaty of (1921), 414
Rilke, Rainer M., 390
Rivera, General Primo de, 240, 241, 242

Riviera, 599
Riza Shah Pahlevi, of Iran, 538
Robin Moor, 560
Robles, Gil, 244
Rockefeller Foundation, 341 n.
Rocque, F. de la, 231
Rodimtsev, General Alexander, 586
Roehm, Ernst, 317
Rogers, Will, 222
Rolland, Romain, 382
Romagna, 182
Romains, Jules, 382-383
Roman Catholic Church, 160, 167, 178,
359-368; in Poland, 167, 172; in
Italy, 189, 364-365; in the Balkans,
201; in France, 223, 224, 361-362;
in Spain, 243, 244, 363; in Nazi
Germany, 326; in England, 360-361;
in Czechoslovakia, 362, 363; in Rus-
sia, 363; and secular affairs, 365-368.
See also Pope Benedict XV, Pope
Pius XI, Pope Pius XII
Rome, 185, 192; in World War II, 583,
601
Rommel, General Erwin, 538, 541, 575-
576, 582, 597, 598, 600 n., 605
Roosevelt, Franklin D., on Stalin, 131;
sends envoy to Vatican, 365; and
London Monetary Conference (1933),
462; "quarantine" speech, of, 490;
and Munich crisis, 500; on Finland,
523; and World War II, 515, 554,
555, 558, 559, 560, 561, 565, 589,
591, 592, 593, 607, 622; and the
United Nations, 566, 633; death of,
633
Roosevelt, Theodore, 24, 26 n.
Rostov-on-Don, 551, 571
Rotterdam, 193, 397, 526
Rouen, 599
Rowntree, B. S., 277-278
Royal Air Force, 493, 527, 534, 536,
537, 539, 541, 585, 599 n., 623
Royal Oak, 525
"Royal Tiger", 621
Rudelsystem, 579, 583, 616, 620
Ruhr, 4, 8, 193, 225, 226, 250, 267,
299, 300, 314, 315, 424-428, 433, 608,
651
Rumania, (Rumanians), 4, 17, 22, 23,
25, 28; and World War I, 37, 46,
51-53, 72, 86, 102, 105, 106, 203;
economic affairs in, 203-204, 205;
government of, 204; politics in, 204-
205; foreign relations of, 166, 205,
443, 469, 509; and World War II,
523, 539, 548, 549, 550, 603; after
World War II, 647, 650, 652
Rundstedt, General Gerd von, 551, 552,
597, 600 and n.

Russell, G. W. (AE), 380
Russia, Imperial, 3, 4, 5, 7, 9, 10, 11, 17, 18, 19, 25, 27, 28, 29, 30; in World War I, 36-38 43-46, 48-49, 68, 71-72, 83; downfall of, 117-118
Russia, Soviet, November Revolution, 118-119; and Treaty of Brest-Litovsk, 72, 86, 120-121; and the world, 121; Allied intervention in, 122-124; civil war in, 122-123; geography and resources of, 124-126, 348; peoples of, 126-127; government of, 127-131; Constitution (1936) of, 131-132; Great Purge in, 132-133; war communism in, 133-134; new economic policy of, 134-135; planned industrial progress of, 135-139; agricultural record of, 139-140; Stalinism in, 141-143; religion in, 143-145, 150, 359, 363, 365, 587-588; education in, 145-146, 149, 335, 336; military forces of, 147-148; in 1939, 148-150; literature in, 392-394; music in, 402-403; expansion of (1940), 523, 539, 547, 588-589; and Bulgaria, 208, 603; and China, 445, 489; and Czechoslovakia, 167, 471, 500, 504, 505; and Finland, 148, 523, 546, 549-551; and France, 470, 471, 486, 505, 523; and Weimar Germany, 305, 421, 444; and Nazi Germany, 463, 465, 498, 505, 511, 513-514, 545-549; and Great Britain, 263, 265, 268, 269, 445, 486, 498, 505, 511-512, 523, 547, 550, 552, 566, 591-592, 631-633, 641-653; and Italy, 546; and Japan, 445, 460-462, 489-490, 511, 547, 581, 617, 632; and League of Nations, 432, 470-471, 523; and Poland, 414-415, 464-465, 512, 522-523, 588-589, 602-603; and Rumania, 205, 523, 603; and Spain, 246, 247, 484-486; and Turkey, 212, 214, 483-484, 541-542, 548-549; and the United States, 123, 471, 547, 552, 560-561, 591-593, 631-633, 641-653; and World War II, 517, 545-549, 561; in World War II, 549-554, 566, 571-574, 585-589, 600, 602-603, 607, 612-613, 617, 623-624, 627-628, 629; and settlements after World War II, 641-653. *See* also Comintern, Communist Party of Russia
Russia, Tsarist, *see* Russia, Imperial
Rust, Bernhard, 323
Ruthenia, 160. *See* also Carpatho-Ukraine
Rutherford, Lord, 340, 344
Rydz-Smgly, General Edward, 170
Ryukyu Islands, 614

Saar Basin, 95, 97, 220, 392, 434; recovered by Germany, 466-467; after World War II, 651
Safeguarding of Industries Act, 263
Saghalen, 593, 632
St. Germain, Treaty of (1919), 102-104, 156
St. Lô, 598
St. Mihiel, 80
St. Petersburg, 39. *See* also Leningrad Petrograd
Saionji, Marquis, 93
Saipan, 595, 596
Salandra, Antonio, 46-48
Salazar, Oliveria, 249
Salerno, 583
Salisbury, Lord, 19
Salonika, 46, 53, 81, 208, 540
Salvemini, Gaetano, 196
San Francisco Conference (1945), 607, 631, 632, 633-634
Sarajevo, 33-35, 96, 611
Sardinia, 540, 583
Sargent, J. S., 400
Saseno, 200 n.
Saudi Arabia, 217-218
Saxony, 4
Scandinavia, 4, 11
Schacht, Hjalmar, 318 n.
Scharnhorst, 579, 584
Schleicher, General Kurt von, 309
Schleswig, 54
Schools, *see* Education
Schnorkel apparatus, 620
Schönberg, A., 403
Schuschnigg, Kurt von, 156, 497-498
Schutzstaffel, 312, 316
Science, 12, 84; between the wars, 340-356; physical, 343-347; "earth", 347-349; biological, 349, 350-352; anthropological, 349-350; archeological, 350; medical, 352-354; psychological, 354-355; in World War II, 618-623
Scott, Walter, 42
Sculpture, 400-402
Second Front, 574, 575
Second International, 15
Security, meaning of, 429
Sedan, 527
Seeckt, General Hans von, 304-305
Seeley, Sir John, 279
Seine River, 599
Seipel, Ignaz, 362
Sender, Ramón J., 386
Senegalese, 236
Senussi, 650
Serbia (Serbs), 17, 23, 25, 27, 28, 29, 30; and World War I, 34-35, 44, 47, 49-50, 83, 201. *See* also Yugoslavia
Sevastopol, 571, 603

Sèvres, Treaty of (1920), 105-106, 413
Seym, 168, 169, 170, 171, 172
Shakespeare, William, 69
Shantung, 38, 45, 93, 99, **112, 420**
Shaw, G. B., 260, 377-378
Sheriff, R. C., 379
Shintoism, 629
Sholokov, M., 393
Shostakovitch, D., 403
Siam, 99, 564, 567
Sibelius, Jan, 176, 405
Siberia, 7, 45, 73, 124, **125**, 130, **137**, 169, 348, 393, 461, 462, 514 n., 550, 581, 587, 624
Sicily, 192, 578, 582
Siegfried Line, 322, 482, 499, 599, 608
Siemes, John A., 617
Sikorski, General Wladyslaw, 589
Silesia, 4
Sillanpää, F. E., 396
Silone, Ignazio, 387
Simeon II, of Bulgaria, 206 n.
Sindacato, 191
Singapore, 257, 354, 418, 494; in World War II, 567-568, 579
Singer, I. J., 395
Sinn Fein, 283
Sino-Soviet Treaty (1945), 632
Sixtus, Prince, 73-74
Skoda, 165
Slav (Slavs), 30, 36, 49, 83, 103, 159, 189, 208
Slovakia (Slovaks), 23, 160, 162, 165, 362, 363, 506, 539, 549, 610. *See* also Czechoslovakia
Slovenes, 23, 201-202. *See* also Yugoslavia
Smith, Alfred E., 449
Smolensk, 551, 586
Smuts, Jan C., 101, 111, 281-282, 502, 588, 633
Smyrna, 413
Social and Economic History of the World War, 84
Social Democrats, *see* Socialism
Socialism, (Socialists), 11; in Austria, 152-154; in Hungary, 157; in Italy, 181-182, 187; in the Near East, 210; in France, 223, 225, 227, 233, 234, 235, 495, 629, 651; in Spain, 242, 243, 245; in Great Britain, 259; in Germany, 296, 297, 301, 305, 307, 308, 309, 310 and n., 316, and religion, 358. *See* also Marx, Karl
Social Revolutionary Party, of Russia, 119
Soderblom, Nathan, 370 n.
Sofia, 207
Solomons, 570, 580, 581, 596. *See* also Guadalcanal

Somalilands, 195, 237, 537, 650
Somme River, 57, 528, 585
Sonnino, Baron Sidney, 47
Soong, T. V., 633
South Africa, *see* Union of South Africa
South Slavs, *see* Yugoslavia
South Tyrol, 47, 104, 190, 442, 508 and n., 647, 651
Soviet-Japanese Pact (1941), 547, 550, 560, 617
Soviet Union, *see* Russia, Soviet
Spain, 5, 9, 12, 17, 23 n., 26, 54; importance of, 239; military dictatorship in, 240-241; political groups in, 241-243; republican democracy of, 243-244; Fascism in, 248; civil war in, 235, 239, 245-248, 484-487, 505, 586; religion in, 363; literature in, 384-386; and World War II, 517, 535, 550
Spartacists, 296-297. *See* also Communism, Germany
Spee, Admiral von, 44
Spencer, Herbert, 12
Spengler, Oswald, 384, 391-392
Spitteler, C. F. G., 390
"Stakhonovites", 138
Stalin, Joseph, 118, 127, 129; rise to power, 130-131; Constitution of, 131-132; and the Great Purge, 132-133; on income, 138; shifts in policy, 141-143, 144-145, 146; and World War II, 545 and n., 546, 548, 574, 575, 586, 589, 590, 591, 593, 607, 623; at Potsdam Conference, 641
Stalingrad, Battle of, 571-572, 576, 586
Stambulisky, Alexander S., 206-207
Stassen, Harold E., 634, 640
Statute of Westminster (1931), 281
Stavisky, Alexander, 229
Stettin, 629
Stettinius, Edward R., Jr., 633
Stockholm Conference (1935), 370 n.
Strachey, G. L., 377
Straits, Turkish, 31, 38-39, 45-46, 75, 105, 126, 211, 214, 414, 483-484, 548, 642. *See* also Constantinople, Dardanelles
Strauss, Richard, 404-405
Stravinsky, Igor, 402-403
"Strength Through Joy", 321
Stresa Front, 468, 472, 507
Stresemann, Gustav, 301, 430-431, 451
Stumpf, Admiral, 613
Stürmer, Der, 327-328
Sturzo, Don Luigi, 182
Submarine warfare, in World War I, 45, 54, 58-60, 66, 67-68, 76-77; limitations on, 455; in World War II, 524-525, 542-543, 560, 563, 566, 579-

580, 583-584, 596, 597-598, 616 n., 619

Sudan, 215, 216 and n., 217, 280, 537; after World War II, 630

Sudermann, H., 390

Sudetenland (Sudetens), 162, 163, 165, 166, 499-504, 628. *See* also Czechoslovakia

Suez Canal, 195, 215, 216, 437, 478, 538, 541, 549, 576, 629

Suttner, Bertha von, 24

Suvorov, General, 142, 586

Svevo, Italo, 387

Swaraj, 288, 291

Sweden, 4, 17, 18, 54-55, 176, 193, 250, 251, 368, 370, 416; and World War II, 526, 585, 604

Switzerland, 17, 18, 106, 250, 495

Sykes-Picot Pact (1916), 51

Syria, 51, 236, 435, 439, 538, 541, 644

Tallinn, 177

Tanganyika, 280

Tangier, 443, 472, 535

Tanks, in World War I, 57, 71, 82; in World War II, 522, 528, 538, 540, 552, 562, 572, 576, 587, 600, 610, 621

Tannenberg, Battle of, 43

Taranto, Battle of, 539, 542

Tarawa, 581

Tartu, 177

Tata Company, 294

Taylor, Myron C., 555

Tedder, Sir Arthur, 586

Teheran, Conference at (1943), 539, 593, 631

Tel Aviv, 436

Television, 407

Temesvar, Banat of, 52

Temperley, H. W. V., 504 n.

Temple, Archbishop, 258

Teschen, 502

Teutonic Knights, 177

Thailand, *see* Siam

Third International, *see* Comintern

Third Reich, *see* German Republic, National Socialist, Hitler, Adolf

Tigris River, 50

Times, The London, 524

Tinian, 595

Tirpitz, Admiral von, 60

Tito, Marshal J., 540, 603, 611, 650

Togoland, 236

Tokyo, 570, 595, 616

Toller, Ernst, 390

Tolstoi, Alexei, 393

Tolstoi, Count Leo, 16, 382

Tomlinson, H. M., 378

Torgau, 610

Toulon, 535, 578

Trade unions, in Europe (1914), 10; in Soviet Russia, 137; in Italy, 182, 191; in France, 231-232; in Spain, 242; in Nazi Germany, 320; in Great Britain, 258-259, 260, 267

Transcaucasia, 128

Trans-Jordan, 435, 438

Transylvania, 52, 53, 203, 539, 603, 647

Treaties, *see* individual treaties by name

Trebizond, 50

Trench warfare, 42

Trianon, Treaty of (1920), 105, 155, 158, 416

Trieste, 47, 48, 104, 164, 189, 201, 611; after World War II, 629, 646-647, 648

Triple Alliance (1882), 25, 26, 27, 37

Triple Alliance (1940), 547, 558, 564, 565

Triple Entente, 25, 26, 27, 35, 37

Tripolitania, *see* Libya

Trotsky, Leon, 119, 129-130, 147, 241, 550

Truk, 596

Truman, Harry S., 640, 641

Tula, 4

Tunisia, 236, 237, 442, 472, 506; in World War II, 576, 578

Turkestan, Russian, 137

Turkey (Turks), 17, 23, 25, 27, 28, 30, 31, 198; in World War I, 38-39, 47, 49-51, 73, 75, 81, 211, 215, 217; and Treaty of Sèvres (1920), 105-106, 413; between World Wars, 211-215, 373, 374-375; and France, 484, 509; and Germany, 214, 542; and Great Britain, 438, 484, 509, 541-542; and Greece, 208, 211, 214-215, 413; and Soviet Russia, 212, 214, 483-484, 541-542, 548-549. *See* also Straits, Turkish

Tuscany, 192

Tutankhamen, 350

Tyrol, *see* South Tyrol

Ual Ual, 476

Ukraine (Ukrainians), 4, 8, 22, 72, 81, 104, 119, 122, 125, 126-127, 128, 137, 139, 140, 160, 165, 168, 172, 204, 362 n., 414, 504 n., 513, 514 n.; and World War II, 547, 550, 551, 603, 604, 632. *See* also Russia, Soviet

Ulster, 162, 283-284, 293

Unamuno, Miguel de, 384, 385

Undset, Sigrid, 360, 396-397

Uniate Catholics, 172, 362 n.